ARMENIA

The Survival of a Nation

Revised Second Edition

CHRISTOPHER J. WALKER

Routledge, 11 New Fetter Lane,
London EC4P 4EE

First published in England in 1980
Revised edition first published in England in 1990
Reprinted 1991

Printed and bound in Great Britain by
Mackays of Chatham PLC, Chatham, Kent

British Library Cataloguing in Publication Data
Walker, Christopher J, *1942–*
    Armenia: the survival of a nation. — Rev. 2nd ed
    I. Armenia, history
    I. Title
    956.62
    ISBN 0-415-04684-X

Auden material on page 121 courtesy of Faber & Faber Ltd.

Contents

Maps

Although we are small and very limited
in numbers, not a powerful people, and
many times have been subjugated by
foreign kingdoms, yet too, many deeds of
bravery have been performed in our land
which are worthy of record, but which
no one has troubled to write down.

Movses Khorenatsi,
History of the Armenians, I, 3
(*c*. AD 480)

Introduction

Today, on a map of the world, the only region shown as Armenia is the Soviet republic of Armenia – 29,000 square kilometres, smaller than Belgium, about the same size as Albania. This is a fraction, which Armenians themselves put at one-tenth, of the historic land of Armenia, and of the region shown as 'Armenia' on maps of sixty or more years ago. Even Mount Ararat, closely identified with Armenia throughout her history, towering today over the Armenian capital of Yerevan and represented on the Soviet insignia of the republic, now stands in Turkey.

About three million Armenians live in Soviet Armenia, half their world-wide number. Approximately a million live in other parts of the USSR, especially in the neighbouring republics of Georgia and Azerbaijan. Upwards of half a million live not in other Asiatic countries, where snow-capped peaks surmount harsh plateaux, but in North America, especially in Massachusetts and California. Another quarter of a million live in Syria and Lebanon. A somewhat smaller number live in Iran. Other Armenian communities, from Buenos Aires to Shanghai, make up the total picture.

The Armenian dispersion, or *ëspiurk*, is an ancient phenomenon. Enterprising Armenians have for centuries sought their fortunes in lands other than their own – although they have seldom lost their connections with and affection for their mother country. However, the majority of dispersed Armenians did not leave their land voluntarily. From the time of Armenia's loss of sovereignty over her lands, many centuries ago, until the present borders were fixed in 1921, the country has been characterised by misrule, by invasion, by imperial rivalry and in more recent times by outright and deliberate massacre. The refrain of a well known Armenian song, addressed by an Armenian far from home to a crane flying overhead, goes: 'Do you bring good news from our land?', but it is expressed with such doleful melancholy that the singer knows the answer as he puts the question. Misrule, deportation and massacre swelled the communities in North America and Syria–Lebanon to their present large numbers.

Soviet Armenia is the inheritor of what was known, before the first world war, as Eastern, or Russian, Armenia. What of Western, or Turkish, Armenia? For Armenians the land today – known simply as eastern Turkey – is a terrible, scalding emptiness, where, apart from a tiny handful of their compatriots, living in remote and isolated communities, only ruined churches and heavily overgrown villages testify to the former presence of the native population of this once fruitful and flourishing land. Deportation and massacre have all but denuded the region of its Armenian inhabitants. To be a Western Armenian is, with few exceptions, either to be dead or in exile. Nevertheless the spirit, and to a remarkable extent the cultural tradition, of the Western Armenians live on, whether in Lebanon (with increasing precariousness), or in Paris, Boston and Los Angeles. Even though Western Armenians live in intensely cosmopolitan cities, many of them – but not all – have the knack of keeping alive their historical traditions and their devotion to their homeland, now lost to them. These things are to them, in the words of the poet Hovhannes Tumanian, their sea of treasure, which, despite the many attempts to drain it from them, has always survived intact.

Non-Armenians, if they think of Armenians at all, think of them as entrepreneurs and businessmen; but throughout Armenia the largest class was, until the catastrophes earlier this century, the peasantry. Until then this class constituted probably 70 per cent of the entire Armenian population. Few European travellers bothered to search them out in their villages; so the notion grew up, fostered by the superficial, snobbish impressions of men such as Sir Mark Sykes, who carried with them their imperial and racist prejudices to all corners of the globe, of the Armenian only as an entrepreneur, with all the middleman's vices. Those travellers (such as H. F. B. Lynch) who actually bothered to visit the people in their villages gained an entirely different picture. But the myth of the eternal middleman has proved strong.

One cannot deny that Armenians make good businessmen; and this in turn has led to another myth – that of the Armenian Jew. Several non-Armenian writers, of varying degrees of literacy, have written of this semi-mythical creature; a recent popular book on the 1920s ascribed this identity to Michael Arlen senior (*né* Kuyumdjian), author of the best-selling novel *The Green Hat*. In fact the number of Jews in Armenia, in the past and present, is very small indeed, and a number of those are of the Karaite sect, considered to be outside the mainstream of Judaism.

Almost without exception, Armenians are Christians, although often in a sociological rather than a religious sense. Their devotion to their ancient Church as the main embodiment of their traditions, and as the one institution which remained alive when their country was enshrouded in the night of alien empires, is immensely strong. During the centuries when Armenia was divided between theocratic despotisms, the Church became the only mouthpiece for the people. Today, too, the Church has more than a theological significance. It is also an important point of reference for an individual's personal identity. Many Armenians hold that, in a profound way, their children are not fully Armenians until they are baptised by their Church. Even party officials in Soviet Armenia have been known to ask for the baptism of their children.

If Christianity holds a somewhat paradoxical position in the world-wide community of Armenians today, so does Soviet Communism. Expatriate Armenians of all political hues have expressed pride in Soviet Armenia, and many of the most capitalistic of them would be appalled by the thought of the collapse of the Soviet regime in Armenia. In this way expatriate Armenians differ radically from expatriate Russians, Ukrainians or Georgians. Armenians see Armenia, protected by Soviet power, as a small part of their ancient, continuously inhabited country which has survived against incredible odds. If the alternative to obliteration is the Soviet regime, then long may it live. Westerners, living in secure, stable countries with well defined borders may find this acceptance of Soviet rule rather shocking; if so, they will have to make a gigantic imaginative leap into a world where *nothing* was secure: not life, livelihood, sex or property; a world too where the defenceless civilian population was frequently subjected to brutal inhumanities by representatives of its own government, and where armies ignorant of any rules of warfare swept through the land, bringing fire, wreckage and death. In these circumstances the survival of Soviet Armenia appears as a miracle. In the context of Armenia's history, Stalin's purges are historical memories which, although tragic, were transient. The Armenian culture and language have survived in Soviet Armenia, and are even flourishing there (despite attempts by the bureaucrats to enforce Russian as the language of government). When this is set against the ruin and desolation of Western Armenia, and against the pitiless manner in which it was carried out, the average Armenian's pride in Soviet Armenia becomes understandable.

The central and most critical issue, the activating principle which unites almost all Armenians – a people not given to unity – whatever their political affiliation, whether living in America, Europe or Asia, is that a great crime was committed against them by Ottoman Turkey in the early part of this century, which has gone unrecognised and unpunished. In the first world war and its aftermath they lost perhaps one-third of their world-wide population through deportation, deliberate starvation and outright massacre. The size of this catastrophe, and the calculated manner in which it was carried out, have given the memory of the events a stabbing, unresolved quality to the average aware Armenian. Other historical events can perhaps be passed over, but 1915 is an unhealed wound – the year that the Armenian people were cut down and uprooted from their native land. Earlier decades had foreshadowed this event, and it has coloured all Turko–Armenian perceptions thereafter. It remains unexorcised.

From 1828 until the first world war Armenia was divided between two opposing empires, those of Russia and Turkey. It became usual to speak of 'Russian Armenia' and 'Turkish Armenia' – although at the popular level there was a common outlook among both peoples, based on their adherence to their Church. This division of Armenia between the domains of tsar and sultan has dictated the structure of this book. After an opening chapter, establishing the ancient and medieval background, there follow two chapters showing the development of Russian Armenia to 1914 and giving a brief glance at the military campaigns in the Armenian highlands. Turkish Armenia, and the

Armenian question as an international issue, take up the next four chapters. (There is a little overlap with the Russian chapters, but this is, I think, out-weighed by the gain in clarity.) All strands are unified for the period of the Republic of Armenia, and the final working out of the Armenian question, including the French occupation of Cilicia. The year 1921, which fixed the present frontiers and which froze the Armenian question into immobility, is in an important sense the year in which the door was slammed shut on Armenians; so my last chapter, on Soviet Armenia and the dispersion since then, is only an epilogue.

This book developed from a general interest in the later Ottoman empire, and from a realisation that there was very little on Armenians in modern times. It was really quite hard to find out in any detail what actually happened. Since the subject of modern Armenia seemed to be covered by such a cloak of obscurity – whether from our universities, where the subject cannot be taught since it falls outside the strait-jacket of the syllabuses, or from the press – it took only a little persuading for me to embark on the subject.

'The author bespeaks the reader's patience with the *hard names* which he will encounter in perusing this work' (Eli Smith, *Missionary Researches in Armenia*, 1834). Armenian proper names pose certain problems. Some are difficult to pronounce, since they place a number of consonants together without an intervening vowel. And there is no single accepted manner of pronouncing the language: the western dialect (traditionally of Constantinople and Turkish Armenia) differs from the eastern (which is spoken in Soviet Armenia today, and by the Armenian communities of Iran and India). For example, a famous Armenian medieval dynasty is known as the 'Bagratuni' to easterners, and as the 'Pakraduni' to westerners. Authors who strive for precise and scholarly consistency transliterate into the eastern form; but in my opinion this loses the flavour of many western names, and makes them unrecognisable. So I have adopted my own formula: where possible (and where the original is known to me) I have transcribed proper names from Eastern Armenia accord-ing to the eastern pronunciation, and Western according to the western. Names of individuals whose activities take them to both east and west appear in the eastern form; and ancient and medieval names are also given in the eastern form. Accepted English forms, such as 'Echmiadzin', are exceptions to this rule. It goes without saying that I have avoided systems of transliteration, spell-ing words instead so that the reader will approximate to their sounds by pronouncing them as if they were ordinary English. Thus *ch* is pronounced as in 'church'. Slight problems are posed by *kh* and *gh*, which respectively sound like the *ch* in Scots 'Ben Vorlich' and like the *r* in the northern French pronunciation of 'Paris'. Armenian has an indeterminate vowel, which sounds like the *e* in 'laurel'; this appears as *ë*. *G* is always hard, as in 'gear'.

Place names pose certain other problems. In works in English, Armenia's present-day capital was known as 'Erivan' until comparatively recently; yet to

Armenians it has always been 'Yerevan', which is the form I prefer. Perhaps, by such reasoning, Georgia's capital should appear as 'Tbilisi', but since Armenians, Russians and English all knew it as 'Tiflis', that is the form I have preferred. I hope that thereby I have not offended against Georgian national pride.

I would like to thank all who have assisted me in this work, principally the Winston Churchill Memorial Trust, which awarded me a travelling fellowship to embark on my research. Individuals to whom I am greatly indebted for help and advice include Garbis Armen; the late Revd. Harold Buxton, of the Armenian (Lord Mayor's) Relief Fund; Garbis Essayan; E. V. Gulbekian, who supplied me with many references, and corrected my translation of Vratsian's account of the fall of Kars; Asatur Guzelian, whose library contains many out-of-the-way items; Jacques Kayaloff, who reminisced to me about the battle of Sardarabad; Professor D. M. Lang, whose understanding of the Caucasus has given me many insights; Zaven Messerlian, who has tirelessly answered my letters, and compiled the facts for the biographical notes (pp. 379–428), for which I have done little more than act as editor; David MacDowall, whose spirited knowledge of both Ottoman and military matters has been uniquely valuable; Brian Pearce, who has located Soviet and other Russian sources for me; Zohrab Shamlian; and Hayastan Vartanian. I must also add my parents, who have been unfailing in their support. Thanks too to Sara Harper for typing the manuscript. To Tim Harvey, who has painstakingly drawn the maps and designed the jacket, any expression of gratitude will always fall short. To all these, and friends and acquaintances who have been generous in comments, ideas and criticisms, I am most grateful, but should add that responsibility for everything in the book is mine alone.

I would like also to thank the librarian and staff of the London Library; and the keeper of Public Records for permission to reproduce extracts from documents in the Public Record Office which are Crown Copyright.

Prologue

1   Theatre of Perpetual War

From the earliest period to the present hour, Armenia has been the
theatre of perpetual war – Edward Gibbon, *The Decline and Fall of
the Roman Empire*, Ch. 47.

Millennia ago, as the earth was cooling, parts of its crust had hardened while the
rest was still contracting inwards. The regions created by this primal solidifica-
tion include the vast plains of European Russia and Siberia. The force exerted
by the pressure of these immense tracts of unyielding material upon the rest of
the shrinking surface threw out the Asiatic mountain chains, as layer was
folded upon layer. In two areas, the Hindu Kush and Armenia, the folding was
particularly intense. Here the outward thrust from the north was met by a
degree of resistance from the south; the mountain ranges were most con-
stricted, and vividly articulated.

The distinctive nature of Armenia's landscape developed from this massive
folding of the earth's crust. Her most characteristic physical aspect is of
volcanic tablelands, broken up by soaring mountain systems topped by peaks
of which Ararat is the highest. Many of the tablelands are over 1,500 metres
above sea level; and the soil itself is rich, black laval earth. The folding of the
crust too gave Armenia the specific direction of her mountain chains, for since
they reared up as a result of pressure from the north meeting resistance from
the south, they are spread out in a direction from west to east; so that, although
her mountains give the impression of a fortress, it is a fortress exposed on those
two sides. Throughout Armenia's history the most serious invasions and the
heaviest disruption have almost always come from east or west.

If the conqueror was tempted to invade, the climate did not encourage him
to linger. Long, bitterly cold winters result from the extreme elevation of the
plateaux, with snow lying for as long as eight months. On several occasions the
Armenian winter has trapped rash generals: Lucullus was caught in 68 BC, an
Ottoman Turkish army was forced to desist from trying to seize Yerevan from
the Persians in 1616, and, most notably, the Turkish war minister, Enver
Pasha, taking personal command, was defeated at Sarikamish in 1914–15 less
by the Russian army than by the cruel weather of the Armenian highlands. The
intense cold has passed into legend, too. The Turkish traveller Evliya Chelebi
relates how a dervish, asked whether there was any summer in Erzerum,
replied:

By God, I remained there eleven months and nine and twenty days, the
people said that summer was coming, but I did not see it. It happened,
however, that a cat, which ran over the roofs of the houses, became froze
there while in the act of running, and remained so for the space of nine
months, when the spring arriving, the cat began to thaw, cried 'Miau!' and
fell down.[1]

19

When winter eventually cracks and slides, a beautiful landscape unfolds in many parts of Armenia. Macdonald Kinneir, writing in a Theocritan vein, described the country thus in 1813:

> The country is mountainous, diversified with extensive plains and beauti-
> ful vallies, and the inhabitants are blessed not only with the necessaries but
> even the luxuries of life. Almost every kind of grain is cultivated with
> success, and the gardens, with which the towns and villages are surrounded,
> yield abundance of the most delicious fruits, such as grapes, olives, oranges,
> peaches, apricots, nectarines, mulberries, plumbs, apples, pears, walnuts and
> melons. Wax and honey are procured from the mountains and raw-silk,
> hemp and cotton are exported to Constantinople and Russia. The mineral
> productions are silver, copper, loadstone, saltpetre and bitumen. The
> country is intersected by innumerable streams of water, the majority of
> which contribute towards the formation of three great rivers, the Tigris,
> Euphrates and Araxes.[2]

This remarkable land has been continuously inhabited by settled, civilised men since before the fourteenth century BC, when the Hittite annals refer to small kingdoms there. It was not, however, until the ninth century BC that the first unitary state emerged there. This was the kingdom of Urartu, whose first king, Aramé or Aramu, established his capital at 'Arzasku', a site that has not been established. His successor moved his capital to Van, where a royal inscription in cuneiform script can be seen today. By the following century the state was extensive and prosperous; and in 782 BC its king, Argishti, built the palace of Erebuni, just outside modern Yerevan, from which, indeed, the capital of the Armenian SSR derives its name.

An invasion by Sargon II of Assyria in 714 BC brought to an end the expansive and wealthy period of Urartu. The kingdom was, however, able to continue until the end of the seventh century BC. In 612 the Medes (of northern Persia), hitherto tributaries of Assyria, overthrew their imperial masters and seized the reins of empire for themselves; two or three years later they sacked the Urartu capital, and incorporated the state into their own.

The same imperial fate greeted the Medes as they had inflicted on Assyria: in 550 BC their empire collapsed, overthrown by its subject Persians, led by the renowned monarch, Cyrus I.

It is at about this time that we first hear of the Armenians in the highlands, amid the people of Urartu. Who they were, where they came from and how they established their power there are questions still open to speculation. Herodotus says that they settled there from Phrygia (western Asia Minor). Other theories hold that they originated further east – that they were indeed a native people who perhaps extended their power locally. Their language shows that they were an Indo–European people, kinsmen of most of the Europeans, and of the Persians. By 520 the Urartu people and the Armenians were – according to one interpretation of a passage of Herodotus – both paying tribute to the Persians as members of different *satrapies*, or autonomous regions. It is possible that the Armenians, like the Persians and before them the Medes, were a subject people who had staged a *coup* against their former masters.

Besides their mysterious origin, the name which they call themselves poses a problem. To this day an Armenian calls himself a 'Hai'; Armenia is 'Haiastan'. Hai is traditionally derived from Haik, the heroic patriarch of Armenia, a great archer, who slew the titan Bel in an epic battle beside lake Van. Less colourfully, the word might come from Khayasha, the eastern region of the Hittite empire (pre-1200 BC). Even more uncertain is the origin of our word 'Armenia', for which no one has produced more than tentative clues.

When Darius the Great became ruler of Persia in 522 BC, he recorded a series of victories on the rock of Behistun (modern Bisitun, in north-west Iran). One of the *satrapies* of his empire mentioned there is called 'Armina'. From that time until Persia's destruction by Alexander the Great two centuries later, Armenia was part of the Achaemenid Persian empire, and as such flourished and prospered. There is a lively account of Achaemenid Armenia in Xenophon's *Anabasis*; Xenophon, who passed through the country in 401–400 BC, describes the plenty that he found in the villages (and the local barley wine, which the villagers used to drink through a straw). A few years after Xenophon had led his Ten Thousand through Armenia, the local ruler Orontes was able to set himself up as virtually independent of the Persian empire, and to establish himself as the founder of a dynasty. Nevertheless neither he nor his successors really threw off the empires that surrounded them; a pattern began to emerge, of an Armenia with a wide measure of autonomy within the orbit of whichever great power happened to be in the ascendant.

Alexander the Great's victory over Persia (331 BC) meant an influx of Greek civilisation into Armenia, which had hitherto drawn its culture from the east. This process continued after the death of Alexander (323), an event which signalled the division of his empire among his generals. Armenia became part of the Seleucid empire, an empire suffused with the glow of late Hellenism but whose authority was so shaky that the dynasty which Orontes had founded was able to elevate itself into a royal family.

Monarchy in Armenia had certain features characteristic to it which help explain problems which habitually threatened Armenian political stability. There was no concept of absolute monarchy, or of 'divine right' in Armenia. The monarch emerged from the specific social and geographical conditions of the country. Since Urartian times Armenia's characteristic ruling elite had been the class of dynastic princes; in the words of Professor Cyril Toumanoff, they

were older than kingship, which derived from them. Their principalities were self-sufficient and self-determined, being territorialized tribes and clans of old. And their rights over these states were fully sovereign, including execu-

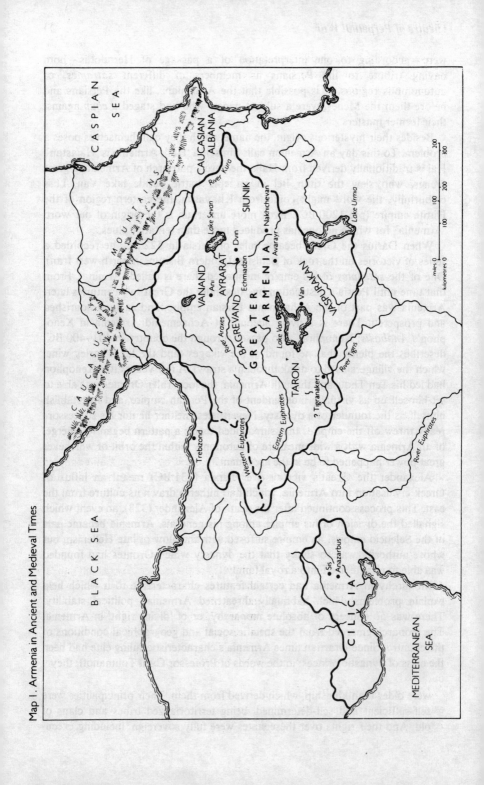

Map 1. Armenia in Ancient and Medieval Times

tive, judiciary, legislative and fiscal independence, control of their own armed forces, and, from the princes' point of view at least, the right to negotiate with foreign powers.[3]

Thus the Armenian king should never be seen as more than the first among equals.

Seleucid power was undermined by the raw, martial values of Rome after the battle of Magnesia, 190 BC. At about the same time the Armenian Orontid royal dynasty was overthrown by a local ruler named Artaxias (Artashes). His new power was confirmed by the Romans, and he instigated a vigorous period of Armenian history.

Within Persia herself a new power had emerged less than a century after the empire of Darius had been brought to its knees by Alexander. This was Parthia, destined to become the great rival of Rome. Armenia, linked by treaty with Rome but geographically closer to Parthia, was forced to exercise diplomatic skill – a skill which became necessary to her if she was to maintain her autonomy, but which did not stop her seizing the initiative when the moment was opportune in the first century BC.

Parthia at this time was weak. Rome was troubled by internal instability, and with an uncertain foreign policy; she was also unpopular as an imperial power in Asia. The Armenian king, Tigran II (95–55 BC), forged an alliance with Mithradates, the king of Pontus, on the southern shore of the Black Sea.

After a series of victories against Rome, Parthia and the Seleucids, Tigran united all the territories inhabited by Armenians, and added northern Syria and Mesopotamia, as well as Cilicia and Phoenicia to his domains; by 70 BC he had an empire stretching from the Caspian to the Mediterranean. He built himself a new capital, Tigranakert (Armenian: 'built by Tigran'), and adopted the Parthian title of 'King of kings'. The site of Tigranakert cannot be determined with accuracy, but it is probably the modern town of Silvan, to the north-east of Diyarbekir.

But to Rome the massive, if haphazard, empire of Tigran posed a threat; and in the autumn of 69 BC a Roman army, under the command of Lucullus, laid siege to Tigranakert and captured it. (In the following year his forces pursued Tigran, who had fled with his ally Mithradates to the Eastern Armenian capital of Artashat, or Artaxata; but when the winter supervened the Roman legions were forced to withdraw amid frost and sickness.)

In 66 BC Tigran surrendered to Pompey. The brief Armenian experiment in empire-building was over. Armenia reverted to her position as a semi-autonomous state between an eastern and a western empire – in this case, Rome and Parthia. Within Armenia the Artaxiad dynasty spluttered and died out in AD 1.

During a period of Parthian dominance, a new and important dynasty was established in Armenia – one whose name lingers to this day in the memory of Armenians. This was the Arshakuni (or Arsacid) dynasty, AD 53–428. Its first representative, King Tiridates (Trdat) I, was the brother of the Parthian monarch. On his gaining the Armenian throne, Rome sensed that Parthia was gaining too great an ascendancy in Armenia, and an army was despatched under Corbulo, whose varying fortunes are vividly described by Tacitus. Eventually the parties compromised; a negotiated settlement was reached and in AD 66 Tiridates was crowned in Rome by Nero.

The balance achieved at this time was destroyed by the emperor Trajan, who, eager to display his military prowess and yearning for victories, attacked Parthia in AD 113 and killed the king of her ally, Armenia. The vigour with which Trajan and his successors conducted their campaigns against Parthia was their own undoing, for it led to the decline of Parthia and its overthrow in AD 226 by the militant and nationalist Sasanid dynasty.

Sasanid Persia was to prove a serious and implacable foe to Armenia, and to lead her to revitalise her association with Rome. The bases of Sasanid ideology were the re-establishment of the borders of the Achaemenids and the enforcement of the Zoroastrian religion. Armenia and Rome grew close again as a result of Sasanid attempts to bring Armenia wholly within the Persian sphere of influence, and to supplant the deeply held Armenian paganism (which was quite similar to the Greco–Roman type) with Zoroastrian reverence for the 'sacred elements', earth, air, fire and water.

For over 150 years, with the exception of a forty-year period of respite, Armenia was a 'theatre of perpetual war'. The great powers appeared to have lost any ability to compromise. Ultimately, Armenia suffered the pernicious expediency of unyielding superpowers: partition. In AD 387 the country was divided between Rome and Persia, along a line extending roughly from – to give their modern names – Erzerum to Moush. Sasanid Persia received the lion's share. But in the meantime an event of far greater and longer-term significance had occurred in Armenia: the conversion of the country to Christianity.

Christianity had reached Armenia quite early on; tradition relates that Bartholomew (from the Twelve Apostles) and Thaddeus were the first to preach the gospel in Armenia. Their preaching would appear to have taken root, since there were martyrs during the persecutions of the second and third centuries. The Armenian Church can thus be said to be of Apostolic origin, and to have grown up independently of the Greek Church, an important point in the conflicts of succeeding centuries. The date of Armenia's actual conversion to Christianity is usually put at 301; estimates vary between 286 and 314. The actual tale of the conversion, according to Armenian Church tradition, is interesting.

Tiridates III was restored to his throne by the Roman emperor in 287; he thereupon learnt that his father, King Khosrov I, had been assassinated by a member of a Parthian noble family. In the turmoil of the subsequent blood feud Gregory, a young member of this family, was taken to Cappadocia, where he grew up among Christians. Gregory later returned to Armenia, and began preaching the gospel. The king learnt of his return and also found out that he

was related to the murderer of his father. He ordered Gregory to be tortured
and cast into a dungeon. There the Parthian nobleman remained for fifteen years.

One day, the Armenian king spied a young girl who awoke his lust; on her
rejecting his advances, he killed her and her companions, 39 in number. Then,
according to the chronicler Agathangelos:

> losing all contact with humanity, the king took on the appearance of a wild
> boar, and dwelt among the beasts. He went to a place covered in reeds,
> where he munched the grass like a wild animal, and rolled in the fields
> entirely naked.[4]

In other words, like Ferdinand in Webster's *The Duchess of Malfi*, he was
afflicted with lycanthropy (albeit of a porcine variety).

Tiridates' sister told him that she believed that none but Gregory could cure
him. The prisoner was released from his dungeon, whereupon he healed the
king, and converted him. The conversion of the Armenian nobility followed,
and Christianity was proclaimed the state religion.

In the long run, the adoption of Christianity had the effect of making
Armenia look westward and northward rather than eastward; but at the time it
was not a sign of political identification with any power bloc. Rome was at the
time still pagan. Christianity had reached Armenia as an Asiatic, Palestinian
religion, not as the teachings of missionaries from Europe.

One of the immediate effects of the official adoption of Christianity was to
create political division within the country. Tiridates himself was killed while
out hunting and the weakness of his successors led to an increase of dissension
among the nobility.

As if in defiance of the great-power partition of Armenia in AD 387, and of
the feuding nobility, within two decades there had occurred an event which was
to unite the Armenians at a profound level. This was the invention in 404 of the
Armenian alphabet by the scribe Mesrop-Mashtots. His alphabet precisely
reflected the sounds of the Armenian language; it was written from left to right,
initially with 36 letters. Armenian rapidly progressed from being a market-
place vernacular – for Greek and Syriac were the languages of scholarship and
of the liturgy – to the status of a literary tongue. The alphabet is still in use
today, and has unquestionably assisted the survival of the Armenians as a
people.

Despite the inner strength that possession of an alphabet gave them, divided
Armenia was without clear political direction. The policy of the Byzantine
empire – as the dominions of Rome are known from about this time – was to
weaken its portion of Armenia, and it enacted a number of measures to that
end. In Persian Armenia the damage was self-inflicted, for in 428 the turbulent
nobility petitioned the Persian king of kings to abolish their own
monarchy – an 'act of political suicide', in the words of Sir Percy Sykes.[5]
Eastern Armenia was thenceforth a province of the Sasanid empire.

Within a few years the Persians took advantage of Armenia's inner weakness, and launched a campaign to stamp out Christianity there and replace it by Zoroastrianism. Under this common threat the princes and nobility of Armenia rallied, and in 451 under the leadership of Vardan Mamikonian, the Armenians heroically faced the Persians at Avarayr in defence of their faith. Heavily outnumbered, they were defeated; Vardan was killed. But the Armenians stubbornly refused to take the verdict of the battlefield as final, and with the accession of a more conciliatory Persian monarch, an agreement was reached in 485 whereby Armenia was granted liberty of Christian worship.

During the fifth century, the entire Christian world was racked by a series of theological disputes. The point at issue was the nature of Christ: was he both fully God and fully man and, if so, how were the divinity and humanity intermixed?

Nowadays, these questions are usually dismissed by westerners (who seldom bother to think them out) as absurd trifles – 'How many angels can balance on the head of a pin?' But a moment's reflection will show that such disputes are fundamental. The conflict over the nature of Christ concerned the most central teaching of Christianity: the redemption of mankind by the crucifixion. To a profoundly Christian thinking society like that of the fifth century, the significance of this is obvious.

At that time a number of theologians – principally in Antioch – were stressing the practical, working aspects of Christ the man, and separating them from his divine nature. Christ was seen as a human temple in which God dwelt. Now, the danger to redemption posed by this doctrine (which gained the name of Nestorianism) is that it is a short journey thence to believing that it was not *really* God who died on the cross – it was only the man-part of Christ.

This doctrine was condemned at the council of Ephesus in 431. But then there was a rebound. Another school of theology grew prominent, holding that the divine and human natures of Christ were so close and intermixed that they virtually made up a *third* nature, neither fully human nor fully divine. This was known as monophysitism. Again, redemption was threatened, since the conditions for its efficacy are that Christ who died be both fully human and fully divine.

The council of Chalcedon was called in 451, to condemn this heresy. Political considerations – the rivalry between Constantinople and Alexandria – meant that the formula adopted swung back considerably towards the two-nature doctrine. The Armenians could not be present, since they were fighting at Avarayr for the very existence of their faith. When they heard of its conclusions they rejected them (as did the bishops of Alexandria), and a schism resulted which endures to this day. But at the same time they rejected the extreme monophysite formula – by which the two natures together become a third; their theology could perhaps be best described as mildly monophysite. The political importance of the schism was that on the one hand it prevented any moves towards the dissolution of Armenian identity within

Byzantium, but on the other it left the Armenians exposed in the east, at the edge of the civilised world.

Throughout the sixth century the ferocious duel of empires continued; almost the only thing that brought the great powers together was revolt in Armenia, in whose suppression both empires collaborated.[6] In the seventh century, the imperial struggle assumed apocalyptic proportions: the Persians advanced right through Asia Minor, as far as the eastern shore of the Bosphorus; in the south they captured Jerusalem, and carried away the most holy relic of the True Cross in triumph to Persia (614). But within a few years Byzantium had counter-attacked, and with immense effort hurled the Persians back: the relic of the True Cross was restored to Jerusalem in 629.

Yet hardly had the two imperial giants tended their wounds than a new conquering force emerged, which was to make their own vast struggles irrelevant. This was Islam. By the middle of the seventh century Islamic armies captured Palestine, Syria and Egypt from Byzantium, and in a series of battles as remarkable as those of Alexander they shattered the Persian empire. After four hundred years the empire of the magi was no more.

Islam, with which the Armenians were to be in contact for the next thirteen centuries, was already a political system by the time the armies swept out of Arabia against the exhausted frames of Rome and Persia. The basis of this system is the Koran, and the *Hadith* (traditions of the Prophet). Unlike the Bible, the Koran contains a number of political and quasi-political directives, concerning the organisation of a state, and the *Hadith* point and clarify them. One of the matters dealt with is the position of non-Muslims. This developed from the Prophet Muhammad's own relations with Jews and Christians. As is well known, Islam drew heavily upon Judaism and Christianity, and Muhammad held that these religions, in their purest form, *were* Islam ('submission', to the will of God), but had become corrupted by their turbulent adherents. The basis for future relations with Jews and Christians who refused to accept Muhammad's message were two treaties that he concluded, one with the Jews of Khaybar and the other with the Christians of Najran (both in Arabia). In essence they held that the communities could keep their faith and most of their possessions on payment of a tax.[7]

This policy paid off – in a literal sense – when the Islamic armies conquered Syria, Egypt and Mesopotamia, with their vast Christian populations. Non-Muslim monotheists became known as the 'protected peoples' (*ahl al-dhimma*, or *dhimmis*), and gained that status by payment of their taxes. They were exempt from military service, since only a Muslim could draw his sword in the defence of Islam. Their own civil and criminal courts they were permitted to keep; these were to be run by their spiritual leaders.[8] As the conquering armies advanced, the populations were in theory given the choice of embracing Islam, of paying the taxes and becoming protected people, or death.

But in practice the alternatives were a good deal cruder. Armies are seldom enlightened with new principles overnight, and the enthusiasm of the soldiery for destroying political structures often carried over into their behaviour towards the people themselves.

The Arabs appeared in Armenia first in 640. In 642 they captured the capital, Dvin, and many of the inhabitants were killed. Armenia's struggle was now to maintain her autonomy on the one hand from Byzantium and on the other from the Arab caliphate. It might be imagined that Armenia would automatically side with Christian Byzantium; but the 'Christianness' of Byzantium was largely irrelevant: to Armenia it was a bureaucratic empire which strove to impose its own doctrines on the people and destroy the Armenian feudal structure. The more flexible nature of the caliphate was recognised by many of the Armenian princes, and under the leadership of Theodore Rshtuni a peace was negotiated with Mu'awiya I in 653–4 which recognised Armenia as an autonomous tributary state.[9]

But Islamic rule exhibited a weather-cock inconsistency. Fifty years after the Armenians had concluded a tolerable peace with the Arabs, many of the Armenian nobility were lured to Nakhichevan and slaughtered. A large number of Armenian families fled to the domains of Byzantium as a result. Tragic as this was, it had the rather ironic benefit to the country of narrowing down the field of quarrelsome nobility within Armenia, so that when an opportunity arose, there were fewer families to dispute the leadership. Arab imperial oppression of Armenia was heavy, too, in the century following the Abbasid seizure of the caliphate (750); yet this too contained the possibility of revival. In the words of Professor Toumanoff:

> The Saracen insistence of collecting taxes and tribute in money, not in kind, led to an economic revival. The nobility and peasantry found themselves obliged to abandon their autarkic, rural economy and to produce a surplus of raw and manufactured products for sale. Thus commerce and urban economy, stifled during the upheavals of the Sassanid and Saracen domination, recovered; the middle class revived; new cities like Ani, Kars, Baʃesh (Bitlis), Artanuji, rose beside the old, such as Artaxata, Dvin, Theodosiopolis, Tiflis, Partav (Bardhaʿa). Caucasia once again became the nexus of trade-routes connecting Europe and Asia, and the prosperity of the medieval period was founded.[10]

This splendid medieval period, in which life was good, the economy flourishing and the arts prolific, can be said to begin in 861, when the caliph conferred the title of 'prince of princes' upon Ashot Bagratuni. The Bagratunis (or Bagratids) were among the most skilful diplomatists of medieval times; they understood imperial power, and perceived the constraints that it imposed on them. They held no illusions about Christian Byzantium; rather the reverse – many of them were scrupulously loyal to the caliph. In 885 the Armenian nobility, acting with unanimity forged by the Catholicos, the supreme head of the Church, petitioned the caliph to recognise Ashot as king. The caliph, al-Mu'tamid, sent him a royal crown, and fitting regalia. 'After that', says the historian John Catholicos.

> Ashot did many fine things: he reestablished order in all the country under his control; he rebuilt family palaces, towns, buildings, and market towns; he reestablished order in the mountainous districts, in the hot valleys, the pleasant plains, all over the countryside, amid fields and sheepfolds; he improved and adorned meadows, vines and gardens; and he neglected nothing that could be useful or necessary to his realm.[11]

But the deadly spectre of civil strife had not been laid low, and before the end of the century a rival family, the Artsruni, was intriguing with the Muslim emirs of Azerbaijan* against the Bagratunis. Iron determination and attentive diplomatic skill were needed to secure the continued existence of the kingdom, and it was 922 before the Bagratid king, Ashot II, was able to assume the title 'king of kings', asserting his paramountcy over the other Caucasian monarchs.

A glittering century followed, when life and love blossomed amid the fertile Armenian uplands, when art and poetry flowed like wine. Of the Bagratid capital, Ani, the historian Aristakes of Laztivert wrote:

> Princes with joyous countenances sat on the princely thrones; they were clad in brilliant colours and looked like spring gardens. One heard only gay words and songs. The sound of flutes, of cymbals, and of other instruments filled one's heart with the comfort of great joy.[12]

Even today Ani – so massively built, as its walls testify, yet now derelict, forlorn and utterly abandoned after the devastations of savage invasion and earthquake – is a monument to the architecture of the Bagratid period, which was its chief glory. Today, of the many churches, eight remain. Among them is the magnificent cathedral, which was built between 989 and 1001; technically its structure is far ahead of anything that was built in Europe at that date, but what most delights the traveller on visiting it are perhaps details such as the superbly harmonious blind arcading and the triangular niches.† Ani's other churches, too, as well as the Shepherd's Chapel, outside the city walls, bear witness to the vitality of the culture.

---

*Almost the only part of the Caucasus in which Muslim power had established itself in a durable way, together with a Muslim population, was Caucasian Albania (modern Soviet Azerbaijan). The Sajid emirs had built a durable state – which was far from being a compliant instrument of the caliphate; it seems to have valued a certain lawless independence above all else. The existence of this Muslim state from quite early on is one reason for Azerbaijan today being a Muslim region, whereas Armenia and Georgia are Christian.

†The architect, Tiridates, was held in such high esteem throughout the eastern Christian world that when the dome of Sancta Sophia in Constantinople was damaged by an earthquake, he was summoned to repair it.

One other architectural marvel, not at Ani and of a slightly earlier date, cannot pass unremarked. It too shows the Armenian genius in this field, and bears witness to the astonishing artistic fertility of the period. The church of the Holy Cross (915–21) on the island of Aghtamar, in lake Van, lies within the domain of the rival Artsrunis. The outstanding feature of this church is its exterior, which is entirely decorated with sculpted friezes and biblical scenes in relief. The combination of figures of great spiritual dignity and abundant, fruitful vines and lively beasts is uniquely Armenian. These sculptures are a landmark in the religious art – whether Christian or Muslim – in the Near East.

In the early eleventh century Byzantine policy towards Armenia became frankly expansionist and annexationist. The Armenian nobility were bribed to cede their domains to the empire and were rewarded with lands firmly within its borders (mostly in Cappadocia). Mass transfers of the Armenian population took place. Armenian rulers showed themselves to be divisive and eager for short-term gains. The stability achieved by the Bagratids of Ani in the preceding century was rapidly lost. At the same time Armenia was threatened from other directions: the Muslim dynasts from Azerbaijan invaded and – the edge of a shadow that was to lengthen over all Armenia – bands of Seljuk Turks appeared in the Van region.

But principally at this time it was Byzantine pressure that weakened the foundations of Armenia. One by one the smaller independent principalities were extinguished, and the Bagratid king found himself fighting – as had his forerunner five centuries earlier – against the combined forces of west and east, which on this occasion were those of Byzantium and the emir of Dvin, whom the Byzantine emperor had incited against the Armenians.

At this time Byzantium – in the uncertain hands of Constantine IX Monomachus – was almost devoid of any policy except military conquest and annexation. After a few years of flattery, persuasion and force the Bagratid king of Ani was lured into abdication, and his kingdom incorporated into the empire in 1045. The same fate awaited the king of Kars, and other Armenian kinglets. However, to quote Professor Toumanoff again:

> if the annexation was a crime, the government of Constantine IX now committed an error that was *plus qu'un crime*. Needing money, they replaced the feudal levy-in-mass obligations by heavy taxation. Armenia was not only leaderless, but also disarmed.[13]

The Seljuk Turks were rapidly able to overrun Armenia, now fatally weakened by Byzantium. In 1064 they attacked and destroyed Ani. (According to one account, the Turks had a dagger in either hand, and a third held between their teeth.) Too late, the Byzantine empire realised the folly of its policy of weakening vital frontier provinces and after a series of attempts to defeat the Turks the Byzantines themselves were catastrophically defeated at Manazkert in 1071. The emperor himself was taken prisoner. Thereafter all of

Armenia came under Seljuk Turkish control. Many Armenians fled, becoming pioneers of the world-wide dispersion of Armenians. With them they were careful to take their language, their alphabet and their faith.

In the centuries that followed, the history of Armenia is of almost uninterrupted woe and disaster. Her social organisation was wrecked, her people gradually rendered leaderless except for the clergy. Although northern Armenia revived somewhat during the expansion of Georgia in its golden age – especially under Queen Tamar (1184–1212) – the decline that followed was irreversible.

Perhaps the greatest disaster was the Mongol invasion (1236). Although individual Armenians were esteemed at the court of the Great Khan, the sheer destruction that the Mongol invasions had wrought left the country open to nomadic tribesmen, who flocked in when Mongol power waned.

The Mongol Ilkhanate became Muslim in 1302. Armenia came under the control of Ghazan Khan, ruling from Tabriz. Although this monarch reorganised his domains, and established a sound civil service, at the local level the adoption of Islam meant a deterioration of the position of Armenians *vis-à-vis* their Muslim neighbours. How low the Armenians sank in the following decades – deprived of their hereditary lands, heavily taxed, and subject to un-stable, capricious rule – can be gauged from the eloquent testimony given in colophons of the ecclesiastical manuscripts copied at the time. These colophons described the circumstances in which the manuscript was copied, and often included an account of the current political situation. A collection of these has been published[14] and the picture that they present is of a people struggling to maintain their very existence in their land. 'In bitter and grievous times' and 'in diminishing days and waning times' are phrases that run like *leitmotifs* throughout this collection. All the great feudal families, who had negotiated Armenia to its carefully balanced position between the great powers, had virtually disappeared, and the later ones (such as the Orbelians) were losing even the little authority that remained to them. Moreover, the quality of the imperial dynasties that surrounded her was vastly inferior to anything Armenia had ever been ruled by before. The Seljuks, Mongols and (especially) the Turkoman tribesmen who ruled Armenia in these dark centuries had nowhere near the level of culture or sophistication of any of the past empires, stretching right back to Achaemenid Persia. It was indeed tragic that as Europe was beginning her renaissance, Armenia was sunk beneath semi-barbarian conquest.

The most violent and destructive conqueror of Armenia was Timur-lenk (Tamerlane). His campaigns of 1386–8 in north Persia and the Caucasus brought devastation and death on a scale hitherto unknown. Yet neither Timur (who died in 1405) nor his successors could be said to have ruled Armenia or what remained of it; power lay rather with two rival Turkoman dynasties, the 'White Rams' (Ak-Koyunlu), based at Diyarbekir, and the 'Black Rams' (Kara-Koyunlu), based at Van. Both dynasties emerged as sovereign in 1378.

Their power was to a great extent circumscribed by their relations with their powerful eastern neighbour, the empire that Timur left; but as this empire declined into mediocrity, so local dynasts were able to strengthen their authority. Ultimately, too, their day was spent: the Black Rams were vanquished by Uzun ('Tall') Hasan of the White Rams in 1469, and the White Rams were themselves extinguished by the new, dynamic power of Safavid Persia, when they confronted Shah Ismail in battle at Sharur, Armenia, in 1502.

With the rise of Safavid Persia we reach the dawn of the modern era in Armenia. In the thickening darkness of the preceding centuries perhaps the only glimmer of light was the return of the Catholicos, the head of the Church, to Echmiadzin* in 1441 – and this was not to prove its benefit to the Armenian nation as a whole for several centuries. The colophons mentioned above are eloquent testimony to the utter collapse of Armenian social organisation as it had evolved over the preceding two millennia. All that remained was the clergy – often mercilessly harassed – and the people.

Within the medieval period Armenia – perhaps uniquely – shifted her sovereign power some six or seven hundred miles to the south-east. During the tenth century a large number of Armenians had been settled in Cilicia by the Byzantines, following the Byzantine victories over the Muslims. Others followed, as conditions worsened in Greater Armenia and as the Byzantine emperors encouraged them to move. The new arrivals in Cilicia were dominated by two families, Hetum and, later, Rupen. By 1080 Prince Rupen considered himself strong enough to declare his independence from the Byzantine empire. Cilician Armenia† was to last until 1375. Diplomatically, Cilician Armenia showed the same scepticism towards her two powerful neighbours, the Byzantine empire and the Muslim caliphate. Her leaders sought strange alliances with powers beyond her immediate neighbours, apparently not realising that great powers remain great powers even when not proximate, entertain the same coercive tendencies, and are subject to the same whimsical changes of policy. One such diplomatic infatuation was for the Mongol Court, by which Cilician Armenia hoped to outflank the caliphate. Even if we disregard the immense distance from Cilicia to the court of the Great Khan at Karakorum, this proved to be a political error when the Mongols adopted Islam in 1302. The other alliance that Cilicia struck up was with the Crusaders. Predating that with the Mongols, it had the same motive:

---

*Political circumstances had compelled the catholicosate to move with the moving fortunes of the Armenian people: thus although established at Echmiadzin (which means 'the Descent of the Only-Begotten') in 301, it had moved to Dvin in 485, to Aghtamar in 927, to Argina (near Ani) in 947, to Ani itself in 992. Thence the ecclesiastical office had moved to Cilicia.

†Sometimes called Lesser Armenia, a term which more usually denotes the area of Armenia north-west of the Euphrates, whose main town is Sebastia (Sivas). Confusingly, this latter territory is also known as Lower, or Upper, Armenia.

to outflank the neighbouring big power. Although this exploit certainly helped Cilician Armenia to establish itself in the late eleventh century, in the longer term it meant that the state was denied more than a brief period of existence. Moreover, the energetic courting of the Franks left a legacy of division within the Armenian community; for the Europeans were as Chalcedonianly 'orthodox' as the Byzantines (although they were less intelligent, and unable to understand the finer theological points), and hence were as keen as Byzantium on making Armenians apostasise from their Mother Church and accept the authority of Rome.

Nevertheless, throughout the twelfth century the Armenians steadily consolidated their position amid the craggy mountains and fertile plains of their new homeland, and in 1198 Prince Leo II was crowned king in the cathedral of Tarsus, receiving his crown, significantly, from Cardinal Conrad of Wittelsbach, archbishop of Mainz.

Yet already the fortunes of the Crusader states were waning. Islam had assumed a more militant garb with the establishment of the Zangid dynasty in Mosul in 1127, and the overthrow of the Fatimid dynasty in Egypt in 1171 by Saladin. From there this renowned Kurdish soldier turned his attention to Syria and Palestine, seizing the former in 1174 and going on to reduce the Frankish kingdoms in the Holy Land. Jerusalem was recaptured in 1187, and by Saladin's death in 1193 all that was left to the Franks in Palestine was a narrow coastal strip. Within about fifty years the Mamluks, Saladin's successors in Egypt, were pressing at the southern approaches of Cilicia. Temporarily checked by the Mongols, they were in control of Syria by 1260.

Much of the twelfth and early thirteenth century was, despite the darkening omens to the south of her, a period of stability and cultural development for Cilician Armenia: the epoch of Kings Leo (1186–1219) and Hetum I (1226–69) has been called Armenia's Silver Age. Economically Cilicia flourished as the main entrepôt for east–west trade, exporting spice, perfume and silk to Europe. Culturally, perhaps most notable was the religious poetry of Catholicos Nerses IV Shnorhali ('the Gracious'), the manuscript illuminations of Toros Roslin, and the medical advances of Mëkhitar Heratsi. But in the late thirteenth century, as repeated assaults were launched upon Cilician Armenia from the Seljuks in the north and the Mamluks to the south, the country's prosperity evaporated and political nightmares materialised into reality.

Cilicia itself was a prey to internal dissension during the fourteenth century: rival members of the ruling family struggled for the throne, and pro- and anti-Latin factions fought for supremacy. The fruits of Cilician Armenia's dependence on the Franks were harvested, with the papal insistence that the Armenian Church submit to the authority of Rome. Some of the leaders complied, giving us the origins of the Catholic Armenians today, but the mass of the people remained loyal to their own Apostolic Church.

In 1342 the strife intensified, when the Armenian throne passed, through the

female line, to Guy de Lusignan. Armenia was now a Frankish state. Two
years later, the populace, violently demonstrating their rejection of the Latin
connection and clamouring for a policy of peace with the Muslims, murdered
Guy and 300 Frankish knights.

But his successors were unable to create a new policy, and by 1373, when
the last king of Armenia, Leo V (VI), ascended the throne, Cilicia was little
more than the vicinity of Sis and Anazarbus. Sis itself was captured by the
Mamluks in April 1375; there appears to have been dissension to the last, with,
according to the historian Jean Dardel, the Catholicos and his supporters pre-
ferring the temporal domination of a Muslim to the spiritual supremacy of the
Pope[15] – which, in the context of the fourteenth century, was a perfectly
acceptable attitude and by no means 'traitorous', as later historians, bemused
by the seductive mythology of the nation-state, have branded it.

The end of Armenian political sovereignty in Cilicia did not, of course, mean
the end of the Armenian population there. Although, with the end of the
Crusader states, the Levantine Franks virtually disappeared from history, the
Armenians of Cilicia, a state which so resembled the Frankish states, demonstrated again their people's stubborn ability to survive. Many remained as
peasants and migrant workers in the Cilician plain until this century; a few
stuck firm to their mountain fastnesses, maintaining a turbulent and defiant
independence until the catastrophes during and after the first world war. Even
today, one or two Armenian villages remain, which could be said to be the
legacy of Cilician Armenia, notably Kessab, in northern Syria. In view of the
chasm of disaster between the medieval period and the present day, it is
astonishing that anything at all has endured.

Notes

1. Evliya Efendi, *Narrative of Travels* . . ., trans. J. von Hammer (London, 1850), vol. II,
p. 114.

2. J. M. Kinneir, *A Geographical Memoir of the Persian Empire* (London, 1813), pp. 319–20.

3. C. Toumanoff, 'Armenia and Georgia', *Cambridge Medieval History*, vol. IV (1966),
Part I, p. 596.

4. Agathangelos, in V. Langlois, *Collection des historiens anciens et modernes de l'Arménie*
. . . (Paris, 1867), vol. I, p. 150.

5. Sir Percy Sykes, *A History of Persia* (London, 1915 and reprints), vol. I, p. 468.

6. Toumanoff, 'Armenia and Georgia', p. 604.

7. M. Rodinson, *Mohammed* (London, 1971), pp. 254, 271.

8. Avedis Sanjian, *The Armenian Communities in Syria under Ottoman Dominion* (Cambridge, Mass., 1965), p. 5.

9. Toumanoff, 'Armenia and Georgia', p. 605.

10. Ibid., p. 606.

11. Jean VI (Catholicos), *Histoire d'Arménie* . . ., trans. M. J. St-Martin (Paris, 1841), p. 125.

12. Quoted in S. Der Nersessian, *Armenia and the Byzantine Empire* (Cambridge, Mass.,
1945), p. 10.

13. Toumanoff, 'Armenia and Georgia', p. 620.

14. Avedis Sanjian, *Colophons of Armenian Manuscripts, 1301–1480: a Source for Middle
Eastern History* (Cambridge, Mass., 1969).

15. Jean Dardel, 'Chronique d'Arménie', *Recueil des historiens des croisades* (Paris, 1906).

PART I

The Realm of the Tsars

2 Northern Light

The Frontier is Established

By 1502, when the Safavid shah of Persia, Ismail, conquered much of Armenia from the 'White Rams' Turcomans, all of Armenia's nobility and leading families had disappeared. Therefore when Armenia was again – as she had been so often in ancient and medieval times – a battlefield between opposing empires, she had no class who could uphold her own interests. Armenians were henceforth suppliants, a minority dependent on the goodwill of the ruling power, with almost no power to defend their own interests.

Throughout the sixteenth and early seventeenth centuries, the empires were those of the newly strong Persia and Ottoman Turkey. For almost 150 years these two fought numerous battles; and the frontier shifted accordingly. The Armenians themselves did not supply the motive for the bitter warfare upon their soil; the conflict derived from the fierce antipathy of 'orthodox' Sunni Muslim Turkey for Shi'a Muslim Persia.*

Thus the frontier which emerged in modern times dividing Eastern from Western Armenia, and which became accepted as natural, developed from the Turko–Persian conflict. The wars, with their changing fortunes – at one time Diyarbekir was in the hands of the Persians, at another the Turks held Tabriz – brought further chronic disruption for Armenians. In the interludes of peace Armenians found themselves more favoured by the Persian Safavis than by the Turkish Ottomans, because of the broader cultural outlook of the Persians, and the Shi'a tolerance of minorities, which contrasted with the Sunni Ottoman obsession with authority.

Shah Abbas and the Armenians

The bright adornment of the Safavi dynasty was Shah Abbas the Great (1587–1629), a ruler who combined military and administrative skill with a vigorous pursuit of the arts of peace. His attitude towards Armenians appears

*The division within Islam between Sunni and Shi'a dates from the seventh century, when Muhammad's son-in-law Ali failed in his bid to keep the caliphate in his own family in the face of opposition from the Umayyads of Damascus. With the subsequent tragic death of Ali's son Husain at the hand of the Umayyads, Shi'a Islam became elevated into an ideology of tragedy and mystical redemption. The basic distinction of theology is that Shi'a Islam holds that certain individuals are actually emanations of God himself – an idea abhorrent to Sunni thinking. Shi'ism, moreover, gives full rein to the intuitive, magical yearnings of the people, and to their religious fervour (described by puritanical Westerners as 'fanaticism'), whereas Sunni Islam takes a more practical and less imaginative view of the conduct and organisation of human affairs.

37

at first paradoxical: he is remembered for uprooting thousands of Armenians from Eastern Armenia and resettling them in 1605, after they had endured severe privations, in New Julfa, outside Isfahan;[1] yet once they were settled, he held them in great esteem. His harsh action had nothing to do with Armenians themselves: he merely intended to devastate Armenia for strategic reasons in his war with Ottoman Turkey.

To the Armenian community newly established outside his capital the shah granted a monopoly of the extremely valuable silk trade. Within a few years they had become, in the term used by the traveller Tavernier, 'exquisite' in the trade.[2] Shah Abbas moreover showed great interest in his Armenian subjects; on more than one occasion he was present at their Epiphany celebrations, held in the open air on the banks of the Zaindeh Rud, and questioned them on matters of Christian theology. New Julfa prospered, becoming one of the main entrepôts for trade between Persia and Europe, and remains to this day an Armenian district. The Armenians gained a reputation for skill at their trade, and for honesty and diligence in pursuing it.

Armenians Look for External Help

Not all Armenians were rich merchants, and among the peasantry within Armenia itself relations between Persian masters and subject Armenians were strained, both before and after the reign of Shah Abbas. The subject people conceived the idea of seeking assistance from abroad in throwing off the Persian yoke. They felt the overriding pull of a Christian power, and despatched embassies, initially to Europe and latterly to Russia. During the sixteenth century two missions were sent to Europe on orders from the Catholicos of Echmiadzin, requesting help; others followed during the next century. Best known, perhaps, of these suppliants was Israel Ori (who died in 1711). He was born in Karabagh, and was related to the leading Armenian families there. His name is almost certainly a pseudonym. In attempting to interest Europe in the liberation of Armenia, he offered the conversion of the country to Roman Catholicism, and the crown of the revived Armenia to Prince Johann-Wilhelm of the Palatinate. He also promised a native army of 200,000 infantry and 10,000 cavalry. But for various reasons – including the provision of the treaty of Carlowitz which prohibited European armies from crossing Ottoman territory – nothing came of his scheme. So he turned his attention to Muscovy, and in 1701 was received by Peter the Great in Moscow. Ori informed the tsar about the history and present condition of Armenia, and gave him a map of the country. To his request for an army to deliver it from its Persian overlords, Peter could give no more than indistinct assurances.[3] While in Moscow, Ori gathered a retinue of fifty men, and on his return to Persia, in a grand *coup de théâtre*, he descended upon the shah and his court at Isfahan, reducing them to panic. Rumour was spread about that his name was an anagram of *il sera roi*. He was ordered out of Persia, and by the time of his death he had gained no more than paper promises.

The North

Nevertheless the time was ripe for a serious approach from Russia to the Caucasus. Russians were not complete strangers to the region: almost eight centuries earlier, in 945, the ferocious people of the Rus had come by boat down the Kura river and, after defeating a local army, had occupied Partar (Bardha'a). Misfortune befell them in the shape of (we are told) an epidemic caused by their over-indulgence in fresh fruit; they departed soon afterwards.[4]

Contacts had been more fruitful (perhaps one should say less so) in the other direction: Armenians, travelling through the Byzantine empire, came into contact with Russians as early as the ninth and tenth centuries. In the following centuries Armenians acted as merchants and doctors in the Kiev kingdom. In Muscovy, they were reported to be selling luxury goods in the fourteenth century; Ivan the Terrible's expansion of his kingdom to Kazan (1552) and Astrakhan (1556) opened up great opportunities for Armenian enterprise.

Within a few years of Shah Abbas's grant to Armenians of a monopoly in the Persian silk trade, they had proved their skill at managing it. In 1667 an Armenian delegation from a trading company set up eight years earlier to promote trade between Persia and Muscovy visited Tsar Alexei Mikhailovich, and, in the course of their talks, presented him with an Armenian-made golden throne, studded with diamonds and amethysts; in return he granted the Armenians a monopoly of the sale of Persian goods (which mainly meant silk) within his realm. Another Armenian established a plantation of mulberry trees – food for silk-worms – on the banks of the Terek, leading to silk manufacture within Russia. By the early eighteenth century Armenians had entirely cornered the Russian market in cloths and textiles.

Peter the Great and the Caucasus

In 1715 Peter the Great appointed Artemius Volinsky envoy to the shah. Volinsky's principal task was to gather information about Persia; he was also to try to persuade the Armenian merchants to divert their trade with Europe from the land route through the Ottoman empire (that is, along the vale of Alashkert to Erzerum, and thence to the port of Trebizond) to the waterways of Russia, which would take their goods all the way to St Petersburg.[5] Peter was more interested in gaining the trade of Persia than seizing territory.

Despite reports from Volinsky that indicated that Persia was so weak that she would be unable to resist invasion, the tsar planned no campaign until the autumn of 1721, and then it was to crush tribal mountaineers who were disrupting trade between Persia and Russia. Within a few months his plans received fresh impetus from the news that Persia had collapsed under an invasion from the Afghans. The Afghans, like the Turks, were Sunni Muslims, and a potential Turko–Afghan union posed a grave threat to Russia.

With the intention of restoring the Persian throne to the shah in return for certain Caspian provinces (in which he would establish a grand trading city), Peter set out for Astrakhan in May 1722. He captured Derbend three months later without difficulty. Soon afterwards, however, he turned back, leaving the native Christian armies of the region – principally the Armenians – disappointed that he had not come to liberate their territories.[6] Peter did indeed plan to bring Armenia and Georgia under his protection,* but after his experience in the campaign of 1711 on the river Pruth, when he was let down by the native Christians, he was cautious in engaging local assistance.

Forces of both Armenians and Georgians had been armed and ready to give military assistance to the Russian tsar. The Armenians were commanded by a leading *melik*, or chief, of Karabagh, David Bek. David Bek represented the re-emergence of a warrior ruling class among Armenians after four or five centuries. As with other Christian warrior classes in the Islamic world it is noteworthy that it emerged in a mountainous region, virtually inaccessible both to emissaries of the central government and to the Muslim landlords of the plains.

Armenian overlordship of Karabagh, as represented by David Bek and his fellow meliks, lasted only until 1728, when David died and authority passed into the hands of ineffectual and quarrelsome successors. During his time he supported the claims of Shah Tahmasp (who had fled to the Armenian wilds around Mount Ararat) against those of the Afghan invaders. An alliance was drawn up, under which David recognised the suzerainty of Persia, but was himself supreme commander in the Caucasus, with the Muslim khans subject to his orders. The value of this treaty was proved during Turkish invasions of 1723–4 and 1727.

The Caucasus Reverts to Persia

After Peter the Great's Persian expedition, Russia found she could not keep her Caucasian spoils. Although Baku was taken in 1723, in the years that followed all captured districts were returned to Persia. The climate was too sultry and

---

*In his last memorandum on eastern affairs (1724) Peter the Great wrote to his special envoy in Constantinople:

If the Turks say anything about this [the permission he had granted to Armenians to settle in the Caspian provinces] reply that we have not invited the Armenians, but that they, on account of the unity of belief, had begged us to take them under our protection. For the sake of Christianity it is impossible for us to refuse this to the Armenians, who are Christians. As the vizier himself has often said, it is impossible to refuse protection to those of the same faith who ask it (Eugene Schuyler, *Peter the Great* (London, 1884), vol. II, pp. 603–4).

malarial for the Russians, and fresh melons had the same fatal effect that the Rus had discovered when they occupied Bardha'a many centuries before. Peter the Great died in 1725, and the dynamic from the north was lost. For almost half a century Russia took no further interest in the Caucasus. Persia, for her part, re-emerged as a great power under Nadir Shah (1736–49). In an important sense Russian intentions were achieved *by* the rise of Nadir Shah, since 'with Nadir on the throne, there was no danger of the Turks being allowed to approach the Caspian' (J. F. Baddeley).[7]

Catherine the Great

From 1762 Catherine the Great was sole ruler of Russia, and, dominated by the forceful figure of Prince G. A. Potemkin, she turned her attention to the Caucasus.

Catherine sought to establish a sound and unshakeable base for the Russian empire. In the Caucasus this entailed not so much direct expansion as pacification of the Muslim tribes. With Catherine the Great's reign the long period of the Russian struggle with 'the tribes' began, which was to last for almost a hundred years, until the capture of Shamil in 1859. The tribes were in revolt against Russia partly because of the deep-seated Muslim hostility to being subject to a Christian power – so profound that it is almost an article of faith – and partly because they were encouraged to revolt by generous subventions from Ottoman Turkish agents. Russia urgently sought to pacify them, fearing that Ottoman Turkey would gain a foothold in the Caucasus, and draw a chain across Russia's important outlet to Persia.

Catherine's activities against the tribes were judged hostile by Ottoman Turkey, and war broke out between the two in 1768. Six years later, with the victory of the Russian forces, the two sides signed a treaty on 10/21 July 1774*, at Kutchuk Kainardji on the banks of the Danube. This treaty was of great importance in the history of the Near East; it set the tone of relations between Russia and Turkey until 1914; it established the principle of foreign interference in Ottoman Turkey (see below, p. 90); and, with the capture by Russia of some of the coastline of the Black Sea (for until then the Black Sea had been an Ottoman Turkish lake) it led to Russia's concern with the problem of the Straits, which has lasted to the present day. A new era began after 1774. Driven by the necessities of imperial advance, Russia was compelled, step by step, to capture more and more of the Black Sea coastline – each further advance needed to 'protect' the last one. (Since, however, such gains were made at the expense of another empire which acquired these same territories in a rather more summary method a few centuries before, moralising about the wickedness of the process is pointless.)

---

*That is, 10 July according to the Julian calendar then in use in Russia; 21 July according to European reckoning.

Nine years after signing the treaty of Kutchuk Kainardji, the Russian movement southwards continued. In 1783 Russia both annexed the Crimea (following years of political turmoil there) and made the most important of the petty
Georgian kingdoms – that of Kartlo-Kakhetia – a Russian protectorate.[8]
Count Paul Potemkin, a cousin of Prince Grigory, led the latter expedition. In
the following year the fortress of Vladikavkaz – modern Orjonikidze – was
built, a forward post for the conquest of the Caucasus.

Agha Mohammed

In 1795 an event occurred which was strongly to influence the future of the
Caucasus. After a bitter struggle, the throne of Persia had been seized in 1794
by Agha Mohammed, of the Qajar tribe. He was the founder of the ruling
dynasty 'which persisted into our own century. He was also a eunuch – surely
one of the few examples in history of a eunuch founding a royal family. (The
line continued through his nephew.) A man of undoubted military ability, he
was – even by the standards of the time – ferociously cruel. Today we would
call him a psychopath. Some have alleged that his cruelty was in some way a
compensation for the loss of his masculinity. In a whirlwind campaign in 1795
he reduced Georgia, sacked Tiflis and massacred most of its inhabitants
(including the notable Armenian court poet, Sayat Nova). The following year
Russia intervened to save Georgia from obliteration.[9] She withdrew her troops
in 1797, as part of the general pull-back that followed the death of the Empress
Catherine in November 1796, and the abandonment of her forward policies;
but political chaos followed the death of the Georgian king Erekle (Heraclius)
II in 1798, and a number of Georgians appealed to Russia to protect them
from another devastating Qajar invasion. In 1801 the Russian tsar proclaimed
the annexation of eastern Georgia, and the abolition of the Bagratid monarchy
there.*

The 'Great' Powers

At about this time it is possible to discern the political current which was
arguably the single most debilitating and even destructive influence on the
Armenians in the years that followed: the great-power rivalry between Britain

*Georgians have latterly bemoaned their loss of independence; but at the time memories of
Agha Mohammed's cruelties were very fresh, and the fears of repetition real; so that if Russia
had not incorporated Georgia into her empire, there might be no Georgians left today to grumble
about the manner in which they lost their independence. Moreover, one is compelled to reflect
that if their own rulers had been less devoted to labyrinthine quarrelling, and more to ruling their
subjects, their kingdom might not have been reduced to such political infirmity. Similar factors
were to trouble the Transcaucasian republics over a hundred years later, and were to make the
notion of independence a luxury that ultimately they could not afford.

and Russia. The mildly schizophrenic Tsar Paul (1796–1801) conceived a vast plan for challenging British power in India, which was so megalomaniac that it could not be taken seriously;[10] but however flamboyantly expressed, it struck like an icicle of fear into the hearts of British policy-makers. Often the rivalry was concealed (as when both powers were ranged against Napoleon, or when they fought the Turks at Navarino) but it was always there. It led Britain to ally herself first with Persia, and when that power was knocked out of the Caucasian political equation, with Turkey: in each case Britain was directly opposing the interests of the Armenians, most of whom realised that, given their geographical position, their only real hope for the future lay under the shadow of the northern power.

At the time Britain's alignment was most clearly demonstrated by the series of British military missions to Persia of the period 1800–10, designed to strengthen Persia and to assure the paramountcy of British influence.[11] One British officer, Captain Lindsay, even became commander-in-chief of the Persian army. The most significant outcome of the missions was the Definitive Treaty of 1814, a bilateral agreement under which Persia was compelled to nullify treaties concluded with European powers hostile to Britain, and to forbid the entrance of armies of such powers into Persian territory. In return Britain granted Persia an annual subsidy of £150,000. The emerging pattern of diplomacy was that, out of fear of Russia, Britain was supporting those powers from which the Armenians were beginning to try to shake themselves free.

Prince Tsitsianov

For the five years following the annexation of Georgia, Caucasian affairs were dominated by the policies of one man: Prince Tsitsianov, Russian commander-in-chief in the Caucasus. A Russified Georgian who had already established for himself a fine military record, he soon showed a spirit in the Caucasus which was both aggressive and conciliatory. He was aggressive in his drive to expand Russian dominion in Transcaucasia,* but respectful of the existing social structures when he had obtained the rulers' submission. There was no large-scale settlement of Cossacks in the Caucasus, as there had been after Russian imperial expansion elsewhere.

If it is possible to call the imposition of imperial dominion on a population 'heroic', then the age of Tsitsianov was indeed heroic. His viceroyalty effectively marks the beginning of the period in which the Caucasus captured the imagination of Russian writers. Tsitsianov himself was a man of immense dash and bravado. On one occasion he wrote thus to Tsar Alexander I:[12]

---

*Having crossed the Caucasus mountains, the lands beyond constituted, from Russia's point of view, *Trans*caucasia. The term 'the Caucasus is', however, used almost interchangeably, if slightly inaccurately.

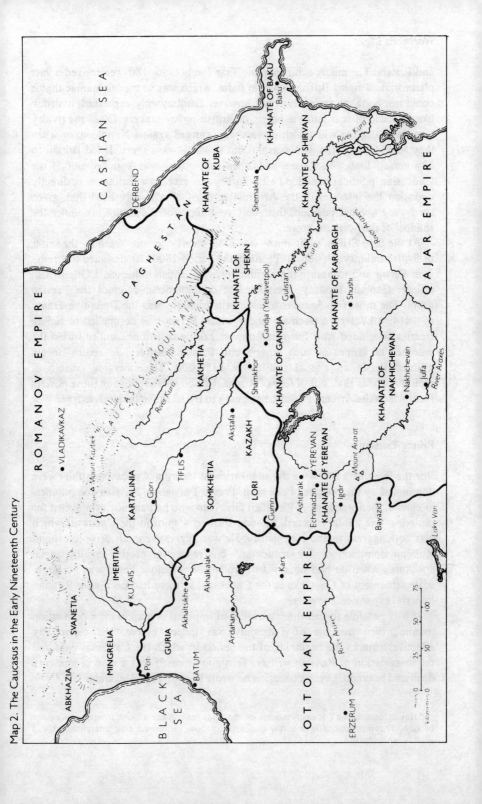

Map 2. The Caucasus in the Early Nineteenth Century

Fear and greed are the two mainsprings of everything that takes place here. These people's only policy is force, and their rulers' mainstay valour, together with the money requisite to hire Daghestanis. For this reason I adopt a system of rule contrary to that hitherto prevailing, and instead of paying, as it were, tribute in the shape of subsidies and gifts intended to mitigate mountain manners, I myself demand tribute of them.

Tsitsianov's main achievement was the unification of Georgia (divided for 400 years) under the Russian crown. First he persuaded the westernmost part (Mingelia, adjoining the Black Sea) to accept Russian protection; the remaining Georgian kingdom, Imeretia (with its capital Kutais) was thereby surrounded by Russian power, and it too submitted in 1804.

Tsitsianov next moved against the semi-independent Persian khanates. On the thinnest of pretexts he captured the Muslim town of Gandja, the seat of Islamic learning in the Caucasus, and renamed it Yelizavetpol, in honour of the tsarina. (Its present-day name is Kirovbad.) This was followed in the same year by an attack on another khanate, Yerevan, or Erivan; although Tsitsianov defeated the Persian troops, led by crown prince Abbas Mirza, at Echmiadzin, Yerevan itself – 'the strongest fortress in the country'[13] – held out against the Russians. His advance continued in 1805, with the submission of the khans of Karabagh and Shekeen (east of Gandja). Then, as part of his plan to secure Russian dominion from the Black to the Caspian Sea, he turned his attention to Baku. In February 1806, as, stricken with fever, he was riding out to negotiate with the khan of Baku, he was treacherously shot. His head and hands were carried off in triumph to Tehran. With his death the Caucasus was deprived of a man of undoubted ability, a servant of the Russian crown who tempered imperialism with deference to local traditions in marked contrast to Russian conquerors both before and after him.

The Russian movement southward continued after the death of Tsitsianov, albeit with less panache. Among the conquests of 1805 was the small village of Gumri, near the Turkish border, which was turned into a military settlement and renamed Alexandropol. The final capture by Russia of Derbend and Baku followed. War with Turkey herself resumed in 1806, and continued – inconclusively in the Caucasus – until 1812, when Russia, in grave peril from Napoleonic forces, signed a conciliatory treaty with Turkey at Bucharest (May 1812). Russia's treaty with Persia of the following year – the treaty of Gulistan – was altogether different, highlighting the political debility of Persia and the vanity of the crown prince: Russia held on to Karabagh, and almost all of the region which makes up the present-day Azerbaijani SSR; and Persia abandoned her claims to the Georgian provinces and Daghestan. (In return Russia agreed to support the claim of Abbas Mirza to the succession of the Persian throne.)

Yermolov

For ten years from 1816 the Caucasus was dominated by another Russian viceroy, more ferocious than Tsitsianov and without his civilised qualities: General A. P. Yermolov. Yermolov, who claimed descent from Chingiz Khan, said of himself:

> I desire that the terror of my name should guard our frontiers more potently than chains or fortresses, that my word should be for the natives a law more inevitable than death ... out of pure humanity I am inexorably severe.[14]

With ruthless efficiency Yermolov crushed native unrest. He abolished the semi-independence of the khanates, incorporating them wholesale into the Russian empire. Daghestan, hitherto inaccessible, was subjugated village by village. The peace that reigned in the Caucasus was most often the peace of the deserted village, destroyed as a reprisal for native insubordination.

During his viceroyalty Persia invaded Turkey (1821). The event was of no long-term consequence, but it pointed up some significant factors: the continuing instability of Persia, the overblown self-esteem of Abbas Mirza; and the plotting and counterplotting of the two rival powers, Russia and Britain. For Britain had conceived the plan of consolidating the two Muslim powers of Turkey and Persia – realising that every advance of Russia in the Caucasus had been due to conflict between Sunni and Shi'a. A Russian agent had, however, outwitted the British and negated their policy, by appealing to Abbas's pride, and encouraging him to invade. In the campaign that followed Persia briefly occupied Kars and Bayazid; but under pressure from Britain she withdrew.

Prince Paskievich

In December 1825 Tsar Alexander I died; the Decembrist rising followed, opposing the succession of Nicolas. Yermolov himself proclaimed to his troops Constantine, not Nicolas, as emperor; he was not, however, implicated in the rising. But the uncertainty in the Caucasus was too much for the over-ambitious Abbas Mirza, and in July 1826 he invaded Karabagh, which quickly fell to him.[15] Gandja (Yelizavetpol) opened its gates to him. Lenkoran was overrun. It looked as though the Russian conquests of the past 25 years might crumble to nothing. What of Yermolov, the lion of the Caucasus? He remained in Tiflis, giving orders to his commanders to hold out at all costs, but seemingly incapable of undertaking any action. Tsar Nicolas, deeply dissatisfied with Yermolov's conduct, appointed Prince I. F. Paskievich as commander-in-chief in the Caucasus, under direct instructions from himself. Within a fortnight of his arrival, Paskievich had routed the main Persian army – officered by Englishmen – at Akstafa, 30 kilometres west of Yelizavetpol.[16] Russian confidence was restored.

In the spring of the following year Paskievich took the offensive: Echmiadzin, the Armenian holy city, was occupied without resistance in April 1827. The siege of Yerevan was begun, under General Krasovsky. Paskievich himself rode south, and occupied Nakhichevan without opposition in June. But the summer was exceptionally hot and dry, and after two months Krasovsky was compelled to abandon the siege of Yerevan. Within six weeks Abbas Mirza, who never missed an opportunity, was beside Echmiadzin with a very large force. Echmiadzin itself was only defended by a small detachment of Armenian volunteer cavalry. The haphazard nature of the Russian campaign was again apparent, as it appeared that Russian forces were caught unprepared. But as a result of one of those stirring acts of bravery which adorn the pages of Caucasian warfare, the Russians saved the day. Krasovsky came to the rescue, in torrid heat and across harsh mountainous terrain, and defeated the Persians at Ashtarak in mid-July. This defeat was a severe blow to Persian morale. As a result Paskievich resolved to consolidate his gains, and to renew the siege of Yerevan. First he occupied the fortified village of Sardarabad, whose defence was commanded by the brother of the khan of Yerevan; then after a brief siege Yerevan finally fell to the Russians on 2/14 October 1827.[17]

The Treaty of Turkmen-chai

By the subsequent treaty of Turkmen-chai[18] (10/22 February 1828) Russia obtained possession of the khanates of Yerevan and Nakhichevan. (She also obtained the khanate of Talish, on the Caspian Sea.) In the south Russia's frontier with Persia was the river Araxes; upstream the frontier moved sharply west to include the district of Surmalu, whose chief town was the dusty village of Igdir, but whose main geographical feature was the towering Mount Ararat – of great historic and national significance for Armenians, who called it *Masis*.

However, the most important result of the treaty of Turkmen-chai was that it cut Persia out of the political affairs of the Caucasus. It was the severing of the link between Armenia and Persia which stretched back to the Achaemenids – an association which, despite religious difference, had been in the main a fruitful one. The artistic interplay between the two peoples (whether in carpet-making, painting or metalwork) is clearly apparent; and in the years of dark fanaticism, Persia had almost always treated Armenians with tolerance. Henceforward, in the cross-populated, disputed regions of Transcaucasia, the Armenians would look more and more towards Russia, especially as the condition of their fellow Armenians across the border in Ottoman Turkey deteriorated; while, with the growth of modern ideologies, the

Turkic-speaking Tatars, or Azeris (to give them their modern name) would be drawn more into alliance with Turkey – despite the fact that most of them were Shi'a Muslims, something which in the past had led them into profound conflict with the Sunni Muslim Turks.

The khanates of Yerevan and Nakhichevan soon became a 'quasi-Armenia' within the Russian empire. Together they even received the name *Armyanskaya oblast*, or Armenian province. Initially this quasi-Armenia was administered by an executive of three men: General Krasovsky, Lieutenant-Colonel Borodin and – riding on the first crest of Armenian nationalist achievement – Archbishop Nerses Ashtaraketsi, Armenian archbishop of Tiflis.

Living Conditions

The condition of the Armenian people living throughout historic Armenia was, with rare exceptions, backward and downtrodden. The vast majority of them lived in the villages of the plains such as Erzerum, Pasin and Moush. (Many of the Armenians of the plain of Ararat had been deported by Shah Abbas two centuries earlier.) Here they constituted an agricultural peasantry, most of whom seldom aspired to anything higher than mere survival. In the face of the harsh climate and instability of life, to exist was accomplishment enough. The descriptions of Armenian conditions that we have – whether in Turkish or formerly Persian Armenia – suggest a way of life that, despite the intermittent splendours of the medieval period, had remained fundamental and unchanging since Xenophon passed through with his Ten Thousand in 401 BC. Most strikingly similar are the houses of the Armenian villagers, of which Robert Curzon gives an account in his *Armenia* (1854). These were constructed like large underground burrows, centring round a stable, from which the rooms for members of the family led off. Rich and poor used to live thus, for, as Curzon tells us, 'The space of ground taken up by a rich man's house is prodigious, the turfed roof forming a small field.'[19] Light entered the rooms through a piece of oiled paper – or very rarely through glass – and was directed towards the centre of the room, opposite the fireplace, 'where a fire of *tezek*, or dried cow-dung and chopped straw, is constantly smouldering'. The chimneys resembled large toadstools, 'rising a little above the snow or the grass which grows upon the roof', and were covered with large flat stones. (Smoke escaped from apertures at the side.) According to Curzon,

> There are stories, perhaps founded on fact, of hungry thieves lifting the flat stone off the top of the chimney and fishing up the kettle in which the supper was stewing over the fire below, with a hooked stick – a feat which would not be at all difficult if the cook was thinking of something else, as sometimes will happen even in the best regulated families.[20]

By contrast, this is how Dr Humphry Sandwith, in his splendid *Narrative of the Siege of Kars* (1856) described an Armenian town house:

> The house-architecture of Asia Minor is peculiar, and, as I am writing at this moment in a large Armenian house in Erzerum, I cannot do better than describe it. The house externally has a most gloomy aspect, built as it is of dark-coloured stone, and having very small windows. You enter by a low door and find yourself in a stone passage. On your right is a door which opens into a stable; on your left are sundry odd-looking rooms, such as kitchens, pantries, &c, all excessively cold and damp. A stair on your left leads you into the upper rooms. Now all these apartments are built side by side, like so many small independent houses, and each has a roof of its own, so that when you step outside you find a separate roof for each room, the lower ones leading to the upper by stone steps. In the spring of the year the whole population of the city, chiefly women and children, bring out their cushions and matresses and sun themselves on these roofs; and a most gay and beautiful sight it is, from the brilliant costumes and bright colours in which the women delight. You can walk along the terraces from house to house over nearly the whole town, and if you are stopped by a street it would not require a very long leap to clear the chasm. The interior of the rooms is often very gaily decorated with painted roofs, which, though curious, are utterly wanting in artistic taste; they resemble very bad Persian painting. A native room possesses but little furniture – a carpet and a sofa are, strictly speaking, the whole of it; but the wealthier Christians and some of the Turks have latterly adopted much of European luxury, and it is not infrequent now to find chairs and tables.[21]

Towards Emancipation: the Mëkhitarists and the Indian Armenians

By the time of Paskievich's conquest of Yerevan, and even more so by the time of Curzon and Sandwith, a beginning had been made in the struggle to emancipate the Armenians, to return to them self-knowledge and self-consciousness, and to bring them out of the ignorance and servitude which was the lot of the overwhelming majority of them. In the Armenian colonies far from the land itself books were already being printed in the Armenian language disseminating new ideas. Armenian printing had begun as long ago as 1512, with the publication in Venice of the first Armenian book. Subsequently the community in Amsterdam established a press, which printed the Armenian Bible for the first time in 1666. At the same time, within Armenia itself, the Roman Catholic Church had developed its missionary endeavour. Although the direct influence of the missionaries was small, they were seen as rivals by the Armenian clergy and hence were instrumental in stimulating new ways of thought. The movement developed in the eighteenth century, with the foundation in 1701 of a Benedictine order by Mëkhitar (or Mkhitar) of Sebaste, or Sivas (1676–1749), in Constantinople. This order moved two years later to the Morea; and in 1715 it moved again, at the invitation of the Venetian Republic, to the island of San Lazzaro, Venice, where it remains to this day. (It was there that Byron submitted himself to the labour of learning classical Armenian in 1816 – perhaps as a contrast to the pleasures that he sought and found elsewhere in the city.) After Mëkhitar's death a branch of the order was set up in Trieste (1773), which moved to Vienna in 1811, where it too can be found today. The order was dedicated to scholarship and education, and its impact on widening the horizons of Armenians in Armenia was immense. Mëkhitar acted as a bridge between Europe and Armenia, using his printing press to convey the methods and approach of the west to the problems of a remote, scattered eastern people. Through the work of his order the Armenians began to move towards self-knowledge and emancipation.[22]

Equally significant in the Armenian emancipatory struggle was the contribution of the Armenians of India, specifically those of Madras. Armenians had been established in India since the time of the emperor Akbar (1542–1602).[23] By the eighteenth century there were a number of wealthy merchants in the community. One such was Grigor agha Chakikiants, who financed the first printing press in Armenia, at Echmiadzin (1771). Two Madras Armenians by the names of Shahrimanian and Gharamian provided the backing for the printing of various works, including Mikayel Chamchiants's *History of Armenia* (1784–6).

In 1772 a Madras Armenian, Shahamir Shahamirian, printed the first work of Armenian political philosophy. The author was Movses Baghramian, who had settled in Madras from Karabagh, and the work was called *Nor Tetrak, Vor Kochi Hordorak* ('A New Tract, Entitled Admonishment'). The aim of this book was 'to awaken the youth of the Armenians from their sleep and indolence which derived from a weakened condition resulting from their timidity and idleness'. From the standpoint of the present 'hopeless condition' of the Armenians, Baghramian surveys his people's history, and enquires how they lost their independence – and how they might regain it. He puts the blame on their passivity, their unwillingness to respond to non-Armenian and specifically European ideas, and their exile from their motherland. He notes that even if flight from Armenian soil gave his people physical freedom, it also made any future liberation of the country more difficult. Looking to the future, he envisaged Armenia as a constitutional republic; monarchy he saw as leading to absence of law, since what law there was depended solely on the whim of the monarch. Three constituents were essential for a future Armenia: political awareness, political freedom and the motherland. To regain the land, Baghramian suggested armed resistance – not to take away the rights of others, but to restore the lost Armenia. The leaders of the Armenian liberation he saw as Simeon, Catholicos (in Echmiadzin), King Heraclius of Georgia, and the *meliks* of Karabagh.[24]

Baghramian's interesting work was followed by a book by Hakob Shahamirian, with the curious title *Vorogait Parats* ('Trap of Glory'). It was published (also in Madras) with the date 1773, although some claim that its real date was nearer 1787. The author declared that his work was to be 'an obstacle to evil deeds arising from human self-glorification'. It is a manual for the constitution of a future Armenia, essentially democratic in spirit. Like Baghramian, Shahamirian concentrates on the concept of law, and comes to the conclusion that law should emerge from the will of the people, not from the whim of a monarch or the customs of past centuries. His book contained 521 articles, detailing in a somewhat haphazard manner how his idea of law should be implemented in practice in a future Armenia. The nucleus of the state was to be the members of the Armenian Apostolic Church; they alone would have full civil rights. They would elect the national assembly, who would grant power to the executive. Quite small matters of civil finance are proposed – such as that members of the assembly should be paid out of the local rates, and not from the central treasury;[25] but of awareness of the complexities of creating this country out of two mutually hostile Islamic empires, and of avoiding their ferocious retaliations, there is none. Nor was any real answer given to the problem of the large number of non-Armenian people now living in historic Armenia. Nevertheless, the works of Baghramian and Shahamirian were a serious attempt to grapple with the problems of Armenia using the terminology of the age of enlightenment. The authors sent copies of their books to the leaders of the people in Armenia; Catholicos Simeon, partly responding to the unreal, artificial quality, so greatly in contrast to his own, down-to-earth knowledge of his people and their circumstances, and partly because he saw a threat to the traditional position of the Church in the community, condemned Baghramian's work as *divashounch* – 'the breath of the devil'.[26]

In Madras the appearance of these two books was followed by the publication of a journal, *Azdarar* ('Monitor') in 1794. It was published by Harutiun Shmavonian, a man who originally hailed from Shiraz. Despite assistance (notably from Hovsep archbishop Arghoutian in Tiflis) it was forced to fold two years later, after eighteen issues, through lack of subscribers. (It had 28 subscribers in India, 10 in Turkish Armenia, and a handful in the Caucasus.) Shmavonian's press continued until 1809, and published in all twelve books.

Within the Russian empire three academic establishments had a great impact on the educational level of Armenians.[27] In 1815 the Lazarev (or Lazarian) Academy in Moscow was opened, founded by members of the wealthy family of that name. It served as an institute of higher education for Armenians. In 1827 its function was expanded and it became the Lazarev Armenian Institute of Oriental Languages; besides its educational role, it prepared orientalists for entrance into the Russian imperial service (rather like some English graduate establishments today). In Tiflis, the Nersisian academy was founded by Archbishop Nerses Ashtaraketsi, in 1816, an academy which educated many of Armenia's writers and thinkers of succeeding decades.

Somewhat later, in 1874, the Gevorgian seminary was founded at Echmiadzin, which acted partly as a seminary and partly as a teacher-training college. Among its students it was to number Anastas Mikoyan.

Strategic Considerations

Thus by 1827 Armenians were gaining the knowledge and self-awareness that are prerequisites of the members of modern nations. The groundwork had been laid for the emergence of a native educated elite. But, however able the educators of the Armenian people, their efforts were bound to be fiercely circumscribed unless the military and political circumstances of Armenia permitted peaceful development; and it is the misfortune of Armenia that from Paskievich's capture of Yerevan until the first world war two factors meant that she was denied peace: an imperial border traversed the middle of her territory, as alien to her as that of the Sunni and Shi'a empires of earlier centuries; and northern Armenia consisted of a series of forts of great strategic significance: Erzindjan, Erzerum, Kars and Alexandropol. Erzerum is so securely defended by its mountains that it requires a major strategist to take it. If it was the key to Anatolia for an army invading from the east, the possession of Kars enabled Turkey to threaten the whole of Transcaucasia. As Allen and Muratoff have written:[28]

> The importance of Kars lay in the fact that it covered the twin Turkish fortress at Akhaltzikhe and made possible a rapid Turkish advance both down the Kura gorges to Gori and along the affluents flowing to the middle valley of that river. Such line of advance at once turned the line of the Suram and threatened Tiflis. Tiflis covered all the middle and lower Kura and was the key to eastern Transcaucasia as far as the Caspian. Kars was the key to Tiflis and hence has been described as the 'key to Transcaucasia'.

The Russo–Turkish War of 1828–9

Within five months of signing the treaty of Turkmen-chai with Persia, General Paskievich had captured Kars from the Turks. The origins of the 1828–9 Russo–Turkish war are essentially European; in the Caucasus the prosecution of the war by the Russians had, according to instructions from the tsar to Paskievich, a double aim: to divert the Turks from the European theatre of the war, and to create a more defensible frontier in the Caucasus, by capturing forts which threatened recent Russian gains. First to be conquered by the Russians was Kars itself, which they captured with ease. However, Russian strategy was by no means infallible, as on one occasion during the war when a premature attack by an impetuous young lieutenant threatened to lead to disaster. At the moment when things looked grimmest for the Russians – to quote Baddeley:

> an incident, not without parallel in Russian warfare, before and since, changed the whole aspect of affairs. The pope or chaplain of the Armenian regiment, holding high the Cross, threw himself in front of the fleeing riflemen, shouting 'Stop, children! Is it possible that you will abandon here both me and the Cross of our Saviour? If, indeed, you are neither Russians nor Christians – run. I shall know how to die alone!' The flight was arrested, order restored, the Turks driven back, and Miklashevsky [the colonel of the relieving force] saved.[29]

Next, Paskievich moved against Akhalkalak, which succumbed after an assault late in July.[30] Thence, after a frightening, but rapidly staunched, outbreak of plague in his army, he besieged Akhaltsikhe, which he eventually stormed on 16 August 1828. To the south, General Chavchavadze was utilising the recently captured fortress of Yerevan as a base for attacks across the Ararat mountain chain, towards Bayazid, with the aim of cutting communications between Erzerum and Tabriz. Within a month he was in control of the *pashalik* (province) of Bayazid.[31] It looked as though the regions further south – perhaps as far as Lake Van – were ready to fall into the conqueror's hands; but with the approach of winter Paskievich decided to suspend operations.

In the winter of 1828–9 Paskievich proposed a bold new campaign to the tsar: the conquest of Erzerum, together with a seaborne attack on Trebizond, which would be followed by an assault on Sivas, considered by Paskievich to be the Ottoman centre of communications throughout its Asiatic provinces. Then he would proceed through Tokat to Samsun on the coast, and perhaps even threaten Scutari, across the straits from Constantinople.

However, before winter had lifted its mantle from the Caucasus, the Turks took the offensive, temporarily recapturing Akhaltsikhe and murdering the Armenian section of its population (5 March). As if a fly had settled on the bear's nose, the Russian army rapidly regained the initiative: Paskievich drove the Turks westwards, and was in possession of Erzerum by 25 June.* In the words of Allen and Muratoff, 'the seraskier's army thawed like snow in the spring'.[32] Monteith noted:

> Prince Paskievich was now in possession of the stronghold of Turkish power in Asia; the Ottoman forces were defeated and dispersed, and their commanders taken prisoners; the Russian communications were free, and a

---

*Among those who accompanied the victorious Russian army to Erzerum was, at Paskievich's express wish, Alexander Pushkin. He recorded his experiences in his *Putieshestvie v Arzrum* ('Journey to Erzerum').

sufficient quantity of provisions had been captured to supply the wants of the army. Nothing apparently could arrest their advance.[33]

Once in control of Erzerum, Paskievich instituted an administration which was in contrast both to those in Caucasian lands formerly occupied by the Russians and to the prevailing Ottoman system. Its basic qualities were its tolerance and impartiality. A Muslim of Circassian origin, Prince Bekovich, was appointed to liaise with the existing authorities, almost all of whom were maintained. Oppressive taxes were abolished; equality of Muslims and Christians proclaimed. Monteith (an eyewitness) comments that 'the population in general, but especially the Kurds and the Christians, would have been perfectly content to remain under the Russian government.'[34] (Throughout the campaign Paskievich had shown great skill in winning over the Kurds, and playing on their disaffection towards the Ottoman government.)

After Erzerum, Paskievich marshalled his forces for the planned attack on Sivas. Part of his army reached as far as Baiburt and Gumush-khana; but the weather indicated that the season was at an end, and so after a very successful campaign, Paskievich called a halt.

The war was terminated by the treaty of Adrianople, 14 September 1829.[35] Russian arms had been almost equally successful in the Balkan theatre of war (where Marshal Diebitch's leadership had matched that of Paskievich); but Russia forbore to make treaty gains comparable to her victories; she believed that the Ottoman empire was doomed to collapse, and for the moment was a useful protection for her own southern frontier.[36] Thus although she made some important gains in Asia – notably the harbours of Anapa and Poti on the Black Sea, and the final end of all Ottoman claims to suzerainty of Daghestan – the actual area of territory ceded was modest: the fortresses of Atskhur, Akhaltsikhe and Akhalkalak, together with a small strip of territory to the west ('at a distance which must be not less than two hours') of the latter two. The Ottoman empire retained the *pashaliks* of Bayazid, Kars and Erzerum; also the harbour of Batum. With the exception of the latter, and the district around the village of Igdir, the frontier of 1829 was almost identical to the Soviet–Turkish border of today.

The treaty was a great disappointment to Armenians. Nevertheless, even if the land of Armenia remained in Ottoman Turkish hands, the Armenian people themselves could be rescued from misrule and oppression. A number of Armenians, estimated variously between 60,000 and 90,000, fled with the withdrawing Russian army, under the auspices of an emigration committee. In doing so, they could be said to be going against the principles of Baghramian, who had claimed that Armenian emigration was one of the reasons for the weakness of the nation. Such emigration may have done long-term damage to the Armenian struggle to emancipate themselves in their own land; but it served one very clear advantage.

A Russian–Armenian Nucleus

One of the clauses of the treaty of Turkmen-chai of the previous year had laid down that inhabitants of Persian Azerbaijan – and the clear implication was that this referred to Armenians – would be accorded a period of a year 'in order to transport themselves freely with their families from Persian states into Russian states'.[37] Leading Armenian figures had requested the inclusion of this clause. The intention was to create a nucleus of Armenians in the newly conquered Russian Armenia, which at the time had a Tatar majority (due mainly to Shah Abbas's transfer of much of the Armenian population from the Ararat plain and surrounding region in 1605). This nucleus was created by emigration from Persia, and strengthened by a further influx from Ottoman Turkey; its value should be balanced against the loss of Armenians from their native lands. At the time it seemed a sound policy; the notion of political liberation of land was alien to a people who felt themselves to be a non-territorial religious community. It was also entirely secondary to the business of freeing the people, and creating for them an environment in which they could live and work without oppressive discrimination.

Armenians who went to Russia from Turkey or Persia travelled in time from static, medieval despotism to a country where progress was possible – which, indeed, since 1812 had become part of Europe and open to its technical and intellectual advancements. But despite the potential for advancement thus offered, the actual condition of Armenians in the new Russian province improved little. When Tsar Nicolas I visited the Ararat plain in 1838, the peasantry made visible their disappointment with Russian rule. Nevertheless, the groundwork was created for the development of the Armenian people as a modern nation; and this was symbolised by the struggle over the Armenian language that took place in Yerevan shortly after the Russian conquest.

Language Reform

A patriotic Armenian educator or thinker dedicated to the welfare of his people was confronted by a serious problem at this time: that there were two Armenian languages. One was the written language. It was the preserve of a small educated elite, and of the Church; no one was brought up to speak it, or to use it in his day-to-day dealings. It had to be learnt, and since it was very difficult to learn, progress in general literacy was bound to be extremely slow. The other language was the vernacular, which, although its roots can be found in ancient Armenian, was considered by the learned to be a mere language of the streets. Several schemes for elevating the spoken language into a written one, and for simplifying the ancient language, were devised at this time, both in Transcaucasia and Constantinople; but the one which became generally accepted was that pioneered by Khachatur Abovian. Abovian, born just outside Yerevan, received his early education from the Church, and, like any man with an aptitude for learning at the time, seemed destined to enter the Church. But in 1829 he acted as guide to the German scientist Dr Friedrich Parrot on his ascent of Ararat. His foreign guest invited him to study at his university, Dorpat, the modern Tartu, Estonia, where the bracing atmosphere of European thought led Abovian to view the condition of his people in a critical and objective manner. He saw that literacy was the key to advancement, and resolved to fight for the acceptance of the vernacular as the single Armenian language. He encountered stiff opposition to his proposals from the clergy and traditionalist circles, and the struggle may have cost him his life; but within a decade or so of his death, his views were generally accepted, and everyone both spoke and wrote the vernacular tongue.[38] The groundwork for a modern, widely spread, educated elite had been made. The ancient language remained, and remains, the preserve of Church ceremonial only.

Regulation of Church Affairs

In 1836 the Russian imperial authorities regulated the administration of the Armenian Church by a decree commonly known as *polozhenye* ('statutes'). Since the Church was the institution which controlled many aspects of the lives of ordinary people, the significance of *polozhenye* was more than ecclesiastical. It was a liberal, if somewhat two-faced, document: on the one hand it gave the Church a large measure of internal autonomy – certainly no attempt was made to force it to become part of the Russian Orthodox church – and laid down a precise – and democratic – procedure for the election of the Catholicos. (The ultimate choice for that office lay with the tsar, since two names had to be put forward, from which he chose one.) But on the other hand *polozhenye* gave extensive new powers to the synod, which had hitherto just advised the Catholicos. This body, consisting of eight priests, was now placed under the control of the tsar; its decrees were headed 'By order of the emperor of Russia'. It was almost impossible for the Catholicos to act independently of its decisions, and hence of those of the tsarist secret police. Nevertheless, in the context of the Russian autocracy, it was a liberal document; and moreover it worked in practice to the benefit of the Armenian people. Here again was some of their cherished autonomy.[39]

Mikayel Nalbandian

Almost all Armenian thinkers of this date saw that the imposition of tsarist rule was the first step towards emancipation; but for Mikayel Nalbandian (1829–66) the oppression of the Romanov yoke was too heavy a burden; he foresaw little change for the condition of Armenians until great changes took place within Russia herself. Nalbandian was born in the Armenian settlement of Nor (New) Nakhichevan, which had been established in 1778, during the reign of Catherine the Great, on the river Don. After teaching at the Lazarian institute in Moscow, he worked on an Armenian journal called *Hiusisapayl* ('Aurora borealis'). He became acquainted with Russian revolutionary thinkers, and the notion of liberty grew to be central to his political thought – whether of the people oppressed by an empire, or of the peasant ground down by his lord. He also enriched and deepened the eastern Armenian language, and clearly saw the significance of literature and literary criticism in the service of freeing the people. He was the author of the patriotic hymn *Mer Hairenik* ('Our Fatherland'), which became the national anthem of Armenia in 1918, and which is still sung at some Armenian meetings, as well as of a brave and fearless 'Song of Liberty' (*Yerg Azatutian*). Sent abroad by the Armenian community of Moscow in 1860, he met Herzen and Bakunin in exile; he also appears to have played some part in planning the rebellion in Zeitun of 1862 (see below, pp. 100–2) during a visit to Constantinople. On his return to Russia he was arrested by the secret police and thrown into jail, where he died in 1866. Despite his short life, his example and his writings remained a vivid inspiration to his people.[40]

Armenians in Transcaucasia

The years following the Russian conquest of Yerevan were filled with intellectual and political advancement for the Armenians; even though the tsar abolished the status of the *Armyanskaya oblast* in 1840, and reorganised the local boundaries in a manner unfavourable to Armenians,[41] the development and strengthening of the community that resulted from Russian tutelage boded well for Armenia's future. Yet even here there was a catch: for very few of Armenia's thinkers – and fewer of her wealthy capitalists – actually lived on the soil of Armenia. They preferred the sophistication of Tiflis, or the opportunities offered by the growing oil industry of Baku. Armenians have always been very profuse journalists; yet no really important Caucasian Armenian literary or political journals were published from either Yerevan or Alexandropol during the nineteenth century. Almost without exception they came from Tiflis.

Russian Armenia remained overwhelmingly an agricultural land, and within that context the benefits of Russian rule soon became apparent: thus, between 1830 and 1860 rice production increased two and a half times, wheat production three times and cotton production four times. In the same period the number of craftsmen doubled.[42] But despite this increase, and the prosperity it brought, the actual condition of the peasantry improved hardly at all as a result of the change from Persian to Russian rule. By a law of December 1846 the authorities recognised the traditional owners of the land as actual owners.[43]

This in turn led to risings against oppressive landowners, notably that at Bjni in March 1850 against the exactions of landowner Arsen Geghamov.

The Crimean War

During the Crimean war, the opposing armies fought in the Armenian highlands, as well as in the Romanian Principalities and in the Crimea itself. The battles around Kars, and the famous siege of the city itself, showed how hard it would be for Armenians to shake off the interests of foreign powers. Since the war of 1828–9 the citadel of Kars had been extensively fortified, and was now a fortress of international significance. It had been modernised by a British colonel, Fenwick Williams, RE, who along with other European officers had been training the Turkish army. The presence of Colonel Williams at Kars posed an acute question for Armenian nationalists, which was never really answered: Armenia could (it was held) only gain her freedom and enable her people and institutions to develop in an orderly, civilised manner, thus joining the community of nations, by adopting European institutions, which initially entailed exchanging Turkish for Russian rule, and to that end supporting Russia against Turkey; yet here, at Kars itself, Turkey was being supported and strengthened by those very European powers that had built their states on the institutions so admired by Armenians, and in comparison with which Russia was only a half-civilised autocracy. The relationship of the great powers to their own imperial interests seemed to be directly contradicting and negating the aspirations of the Armenians to emulate them.

Within Russia the Armenians supported their country's war effort as a matter of course, and one of the Russian generals, V. I. Bebutov, or Behbutian, was himself an Armenian.[44] Within Ottoman Turkey the situation was more complex, and the picture of the whole Armenian population working against their empire is an over-simplification. (Sandwith's diary informs us that during the siege of Kars an equal number of Muslim and Christian spies were executed.) Those Turkish Armenians who were less than dedicated to their country's war effort* adopted this stance from the immediate, day-to-day restrictions on their life, which put them actually outside the protection of the law (see below, pp. 87–9). Sandwith records the following; Colonel Williams was addressing the notables of Kars in March 1855:

> With regard to the Mussulmans, he knew they were men of courage, and ready to fight to the last. 'But', he added, turning to the Christians, 'we look to you also. The time has come when you may shake off your thraldom, and take your place as free citizens; for the sultan has granted you privileges,

---

*According to Sandwith, the men who hindered the progress of the war most were the Turkish pashas and merchants – and the generals themselves.

and declared all his subjects equal in the eye of the law. You will fight, then, for us; take your spades and come and dig with us at the batteries; we will welcome you as brothers.' On hearing these strange and soul-stirring words, the archbishop started up and exclaimed, 'Oh! English Pasha, we are your sacrifice. We will work, dig, fight, and die for you; since we are no longer dogs, no longer Ghiaours [infidels], but, though Christians, fellow-citizens and free men.' The next morning the Turks were astonished at the crowd of Christians assembled with spade and mattock, and still more at the good will with which they worked, and the endurance with which they continued their labours.[45]

The Crimean war again saw the Russians victorious in the Caucasus; the much-touted 'reforms' in the Turkish army proved as illusory as the political reforms that the foreign powers tried to impose upon Turkey throughout the nineteenth century. In the first few months of the war the Turks failed in their attempts to cross the frontier, culminating in their defeat at the battle of Bashgedikler (1 December 1853), which sent the whole Turkish army fleeing towards Kars. The day before the battle the Turkish fleet was sunk off Sinope, giving Britain and France the justification they sought to intervene against Russia.

The entry of the European powers was a shock to Russian morale in the Caucasus. The viceroy, Prince Vorontsov, became pathologically depressed and was forced to leave Tiflis; his interim successor, General Read (of Scottish descent), proposed abandoning vast areas of Transcaucasia, something that Tsar Nicolas would not countenance; he was therefore recalled.[46] Russian fears were based on an estimate of the potential strength of the joint forces of the Muslim rebels in Daghestan (led by the intrepid Shamyl) and the combined military strength of Turkey, Britain and France. But such men as Read underestimated the loyalty of the Christian populations of the Caucasus to Russia, in their determination to keep the Turks out, and also the inability of the Turkish army to put up even a modestly competent show, without which Shamyl would make no move. Despite – or rather because of – the appointment of a new Turkish field commander, Zarif Mustafa Pasha,* the Turkish army was soundly trounced at Kurukdere (5 August 1854); according to *The Times*'s reporter, 'downright cowardice alone gave the day to the Russians.'[47]

No military activity took place for several months after Kurukdere, apart from expeditions which, in Sandwith's words,

*'His antecedents were similar to those of many other Turkish pashas. He had been a handsome barber's boy originally, and by the favour of sundry pashas, more especially that of the minister of war, he had gradually crept up to the rank of pasha and governor of a province. His whole military experience had been acquired during the time he had served as *kiatib*, or writer, to a regiment in his young days, when he was on his preferment. He had, moreover, served in the commissariat, and had become rapidly rich. These great deeds were deemed sufficient to justify his being placed in command of an army in the presence of the enemy' (Dr Humphry Sandwith, *A Narrative of the Siege of Kars* ... (London, 1856), p. 97).

resembled Dyak head-hunts; the Pasha gave a baksheesh for each Ghiaour's head, and hordes of savage bashibozuks, as well as regular troops, fell upon the unoffending inhabitants of the [Armenian] villages, and reaped a rich harvest of heads. I was told that women and children, the old and infirm, were not exempt from these extraordinary forays.[48]

In Constantinople the fears of the complete collapse of the Asiatic army led to the despatch of reinforcements, and the appointment of Colonel Williams as British Commissioner and later as a pasha within the Turkish army. Williams arrived in Kars on 24 September, and immediately set about securing the fortifications of the town and victualling its defenders. He could do little else, since the condition of the Turkish army was so poor (he forbade any offensive); his plan was just to hold out in the hope that a relieving force would arrive. The Russians for their part, led by the new viceroy, General Muravyev, had almost total control of the region: in July 1855 Muravyev came within easy striking distance of Erzerum, which he could have occupied without difficulty; but he refrained from doing so for fear of provoking Britain and France into a large-scale Caucasian counter-offensive.

When, on 29 September, Muravyev attempted to storm Kars, his forces were beaten back with heavy losses; nevertheless, conditions within Kars became so terrible that Williams was forced to surrender on 25 November. He was magnanimously received by Muravyev, and the terms of the capitulation were generous.*

The behaviour of the Ottoman troops during the Crimean war strengthened the conviction among Armenians that the way forward for them lay with Russia. They also saw that within Turkey they themselves only received a fair deal if there was a representative of the Western powers present – a fact from which they were later to draw some dangerous conclusions, but which for the moment only emphasised the extreme disabilities under which they laboured in Turkey.

After the Treaty of Paris

Within Russia the Armenian community prospered in the decades following the Crimean war. But the separation of the bourgeoisie from the peasantry became more pronounced. The Armenian bourgeoisie developed and prospered outside the boundaries of present-day Armenia: they became the dominant

---

*Williams's surrender of Kars provoked the fierce 'Kars controversy' back in Britain, which exercised a large section of public opinion in 1855–6; did the town fall because it was impossible to relieve it, or did the fault lie with the dilatoriness of Lord Stratford in arranging relief to arrive? Or was it that, in Karl Marx's words, 'Lord Palmerston's cabinet has planned from the beginning, and systematically carried out to the end, the fall of Kars'? (Karl Marx, 'The Fall of Kars: I', *The Eastern Question* (London, 1897), p. 611).

commercial class in Tiflis, Baku and the other cities of Transcaucasia. By 1876 two-thirds of the merchants in Tiflis were Armenian, and four out of the six banks were controlled by Armenians; in Baku, by the last decade of the century, Armenians controlled more than half the oil wells.[49]

The economic condition of the peasantry was quite different. Figures show they were by far the largest class. In 1897, the Armenian population for the whole of Russian Transcaucasia (including the acquisitions of the 1876–7 war, Kars, Ardahan and Batum) was made up as shown in Table 1. When in 1846 the Russian viceroy decreed that the *de facto* landowners of Transcaucasia should be recognised as *de jure*, the majority of Armenian peasants reverted to their position as it had been under Persian sovereignty: the retainers of a largely Muslim landholding elite. (In the former Yerevan khanate, the land-owners numbered 1,778, of whom only 205 were Armenians, all the rest being Kurdish or Azeri khans, beys or aghas.[51]) The condition of the Armenian peasantry was not as bad as that of serfs in Russia itself – they were not treated as property to be bought and sold, in the manner of serfs. But prospects for the improvement of their lot were minimal, and throughout the second half of the century there was a gradual drift from the land to slums in the cities.

Tsar Alexander II liberated the serfs in February 1861. Soon afterwards, a cautious committee met in Tiflis to plan reforms in Transcaucasia. Changes were made in Georgia in 1864–5; Yerevan province had to wait until May 1870 for the decree freeing the peasantry.[52] Even then, very few of the peasants came within its terms; 80 per cent remained beholden to their feudal lords, and remained thus until 1912. Peasant rebellions continued in the 1870s: there was a resurgence of violence against Arsen agha Geghamov's property in Bjni, and similar outbreaks in 1875 near Yerevan (at the village of Novruzlu) and near Echmiadzin (Shahriar).

But despite the differing fortunes of bourgeoisie and peasantry, they were drawn together by the national spirit of the newly enriched commercial classes, which in many cases overrode purely class interests. It has been, and still is, a common feature of the Armenian business ethic to donate part of the wealth to educational institutions, or to the Church, and to make education possible for an ever-widening section of the Armenian community. A substantial amount of money was channelled in this way, to the benefit of the entire community.

The new intelligentsia, whose members came from the ranks of the

Table 1: Armenian Population in Russian Transcaucasia

	Per Cent
Landlords and clergy	0.8
Peasantry	70.0
Bourgeoisie	7.3
Workers	16.2
Artisans, craftsmen	5.7[50]

bourgeoisie, turned its attention to the condition of the peasantry. They saw that the peasant economy was stagnant, and that the peasant's very livelihood was threatened by the mass import of cheap Russian goods; so they proposed the encouragement of local trade and industries, and the improvement of the agricultural methods in the province of Yerevan.[53]

This class of thinkers and writers was influenced too by the waves of revolutionary and populist ideas that swept through Russia from the 1850s. But unlike adherents of these notions in Russia herself, who sought the over-throw of the tsarist autocracy, Armenian activists directed their attention across the frontier to Ottoman Turkish Armenia. Almost all Armenian political writers refrained from attacking Russia, aware of the much greater problem across the frontier. Probably the most influential political journalist was Grigor Ardsruni, editor of the outspoken *Mshak* ('Cultivator') of Tiflis from 1872 to 1884. His central theme was that Russia had been the main instrument that had brought Armenia to the threshold of nationhood. A much-quoted sentence from one of his editorials in 1872 summed up the feeling current among Russian Armenians at the time: 'Yesterday we were an ecclesiastical com-munity, today we are patriots, tomorrow we shall be a nation of workers and thinkers.'[54]

Notes

1. John Carswell, *New Julfa: the Armenian Churches and Other Buildings* (Oxford, 1968), pp. 3 ff.
2. Quoted in Carswell, *New Julfa*, p. 5; see also *Encyclopedia of Islam*, 2nd edn, supplementary volume (forthcoming), 'Dzhulfa'.
3. Eugene Schuyler, *Peter the Great* (London, 1884), vol. II, p. 228; Noel and Harold Buxton, *Travels and Politics in Armenia* (London, 1914), pp. 201–2; Louise Nalbandian, *The Armenian Revolutionary Movement* (Berkeley and Los Angeles, 1963), pp. 21–2.
4. W. Madelung, 'The Minor Dynasties of Northern Iran', *Cambridge History of Iran*, vol. IV (1975), p. 233.
5. Ian Grey, *Peter the Great* (London, 1962), p. 422; Sir Percy Sykes, *History of Persia* (London, 1915), vol. II, p. 214.
6. Grey, *Peter the Great*, p. 428.
7. J. F. Baddeley, *The Russian Conquest of the Caucasus* (London, 1908), p. 31.
8. Ibid., p. 45.
9. M. S. Anderson, *The Eastern Question, 1774–1923* (London, 1966), p. 31.
10. A. A. Lobanov-Rostovsky, *Russia and Asia* (New York, 1933), p. 101.
11. Sykes, *History of Persia*, vol. II, pp. 301–9.
12. Baddeley, *Russian Conquest of the Caucasus*, p. 65.
13. Sykes, *History of Persia*, vol. II, p. 238.
14. Baddeley, *Russian Conquest of the Caucasus*, p. 97.
15. Ibid., p. 154.
16. Ibid., p. 158; W. Monteith, *Kars and Erzeroum* (London, 1856), p. 128.
17. Baddeley, *Russian Conquest of the Caucasus*, p. 169.
18. Text in J. C. Hurewitz (ed.), *Diplomacy in the Near and Middle East* (Princeton, 1956), vol. I, pp. 96–102.
19. Robert Curzon, *Armenia . . .* (London, 1854), p. 46.
20. Ibid., p. 49.

21. Dr Humphry Sandwith, *A Narrative of the Siege of Kars* ... (London, 1856), pp. 66–7.
22. Nalbandian, *Armenian Revolutionary Movement*, pp. 32–4.
23. David Marshall Lang, *Armenia: Cradle of Civilization* (London, 1970), p. 211.
24. Artashes Ter-Khachaturian, 'Hntkahayots Npastë Hai Mshakoytin', *Spiurk* (Beirut), 31 December 1961, p. 24.
25. Ibid.
26. Ibid.
27. Vartan Gregorian, 'The Impact of Russia on the Armenians and Armenia' in Wayne S. Vucinich (ed.), *Russia and Asia* (Stanford, 1972), p. 199.
28. W. E. D. Allen and Paul Muratoff, *Caucasian Battlefields* (Cambridge, 1953), pp. 8–9.
29. Baddeley, *Russian Conquest of the Caucasus*, p. 187.
30. Monteith, *Kars and Erzeroum*, p. 177.
31. Ibid., p. 221.
32. Allen and Muratoff, *Caucasian Battlefields*, p. 38.
33. Monteith, *Kars and Erzeroum*, p. 275.
34. Ibid., p. 278.
35. Text in Sir Edward Hertslet, *The Map of Europe by Treaty* (1875), vol. II, pp. 813–23.
36. Anderson, *Eastern Question*, p. 71.
37. Hurewitz, *Diplomacy in the Near and Middle East*, pp. 99–100.
38. Nalbandian, *Armenian Revolutionary Movement*, pp. 38–40, 49.
39. H. F. B. Lynch, *Armenia: Travels and Studies* (London, 1901), vol. I, pp. 233 ff.; Gregorian, 'Impact of Russia', pp. 195–6.
40. Nalbandian, *Armenian Revolutionary Movement*, pp. 58–60.
41. Gregorian, 'Impact of Russia', p. 181.
42. V. A. Parsamian, *Hai Zhoghovrdi Patmutiun* (Yerevan, 1967), vol. III, p. 193.
43. Gregorian, 'Impact of Russia', p. 181.
44. Sandwith, *Narrative of the Siege of Kars*, p. 127.
45. Ibid., pp. 231–2.
46. Allen and Muratoff, *Caucasian Battlefields*, p. 66.
47. Quoted in Sandwith, *Narrative of the Siege of Kars*, p. 107.
48. Ibid., p. 129.
49. Gregorian, 'Impact of Russia', p. 187.
50. Ibid., p. 189.
51. Ibid., p. 181.
52. Ibid., p. 185.
53. Ibid., pp. 206–7.
54. Nalbandian, *Armenian Revolutionary Movement*, p. 48.

3 The Infirmities of Autocracy

The Russo—Turkish War of 1877–8

The war of 1877–8 differed from the Crimean war in originating less from the rivalries of the great powers than from the bid of subject peoples for freedom – in this case the people of eastern Europe under the heel of the Turks. The Ottoman empire was incapable of giving them the rudiments of a civilised administration, or, when they rose in revolt, of responding in any way other than massacre. Few acts of internal suppression have had such extensive repercussions as the 'Bulgarian atrocities' of April 1876 (see below, pp. 106–7). Such manifestations of Turkish policy increased the strength of the new ideology of *pan-Slavism* within Russia, creating a wave of feeling there which led to war, despite the fact that the tsar and his foreign minister were not men of a pan-Slavist outlook.

Pan-Slavism was a popular ideology, anti-Western, anti-Habsburg – it had emerged among the Czechs in the 1820s – and anti-Ottoman. Its devotees sought to unite the Slav peoples under Russian protection, and to control Constantinople and the Straits.[1] Its ideological ramifications could only be seen as insulting by the Asiatic non-Slav peoples of the Armenians and Georgians; but in the context of eastern Europe it constituted a genuine idealistic force, inspiring the people to throw off the alien yokes of Austria and Turkey. By extension it had the practical benefit of focusing attention on Turkey's unjust and cruel treatment of *all* her subject peoples (including the Armenians) at a curious and brief juncture in history when moral considerations were actually a factor to be taken into account. It is no accident that one of the most influential and able pan-Slav activists, the Russian ambassador at Constantinople, Count N. P. Ignatyev, was also a supporter of the Armenians.

Russia had made great economic and administrative advances in the two decades following the Crimean war, which were reflected in a confident foreign policy. In 1871 she took advantage of disarray among the other great powers to obtain their agreement for the nullification of the clauses in the treaty of Paris, which had concluded the Crimean war, which bound her not to build naval arsenals or dockyards in the Black Sea. Although there was no immediate aggressive intention in this action, Russia was thereby ready to seize any opportunity which was offered.[2]

The crisis which began with revolts in the Ottoman provinces of Bosnia and Herzegovina led to war between Russia and Turkey in April 1877. As in the Crimean war, the Asiatic theatre of the war was comparatively unimportant when set beside the struggle for eastern Europe. Exemplifying Armenian progress within Russia, and the alignment of the vast majority of Armenians in the imperial struggle fought in their land, six of the commanders of the Russian army in Asia were Armenians; in overall command of the Asiatic front was General M. T. Loris-Melikov (descended, as his name indicates, from the meliks of Lori, but 'at some remove'), who was later to become Alexander II's last chancellor.* Among those beside him were General Ter-Gukasov, in command of the Yerevan force, and Generals Lazarev and Shelkovnikov (né Ipekdjian).[3]

Loris-Melikov captured Ardahan on 17 May. But thereafter Russian progress was slow, chiefly due to the strong defence put up by the Turkish commander, Ahmed Mukhtar Pasha, whose ability was in complete contrast to that of the Turkish generals at the time of the Crimean war. The Russians were repulsed at Zivin (25 June) and on the Yahni hills (2 October), when Ahmed Mukhtar's stand earned him the title of *Ghazi*, but they broke through at the Aladja Dagh. On 18 November Russian forces, acting upon a plan drawn up by General Lazarev, took Kars by storm.[4]

Meanwhile on 4 November another Russian force, under the leadership of General Heimann (of Jewish extraction), a man with a taste for bold and spectacular exploits, had captured the vital, heavily defended Deve Boyun ('camel's neck.') pass, a feat of extraordinary bravery.[5] Four days later Heimann, impatient for action, made an attempt against Erzerum itself; but he was beaten back, and his soldiers paid dearly for it, for

> nearly every Russian found lying on the ground was decapitated, or otherwise mangled; and these dreadful crimes appear to have been perpetrated by women from the city, who, when it was seen that the Russians were defeated, issued forth with knives, hatchets, and other household weapons, to despatch the wounded who lay gasping on the ground.[6]

The Russians proceeded to lay siege to Erzerum. Weather conditions were extreme: streets were a mass of solid ice, and rivers froze to a depth of eighteen inches. Typhus raged in the Russian camps, claiming three Russian generals (including Heimann) as victims. The siege only ended with the Turkish capitulation in Europe on 31 January 1878. Under the terms of the armistice Russian forces entered the town eight days later.[7]

More than five months later the treaty of Berlin settled the affairs of the Near East to the satisfaction of the statesmen of Europe. The international footfalls that led to the convening of the Berlin congress and the conclusion of

---

*Loris-Melikov spoke Armenian as his first language, and remained a member of the Armenian Apostolic Church, thereby showing the high position that non-Orthodox could attain within the Russian empire (Capt. H. M. Hozier, *The Russo–Turkish War* (London, 1878?), p. 828).

the treaty belong more to the sphere of Ottoman Turkey, and are therefore discussed in the next chapter (pp. 111–16). But the outcome for the Asiatic boundary between Russia and Turkey was that, although Russia was compelled for the second time in the century to evacuate Erzerum, she kept Kars (captured for the third time), and gained Ardahan and Batum (which had remained unconquered by the time of the armistice).

Armenian Thought after 1878

With the addition of Kars to the Russian empire, a new confidence can be discerned among Armenian nationalists, writers and political thinkers. It was a confidence which led to impatience. The caution and steady advancement which most Armenians had pursued in the preceding half-century gave way to a fierce desire for change. But here their views mirrored those of earlier decades, since the change which they sought was not within Russian dominions, it was across the border, in Turkish Armenia. Most were still prepared to tolerate for the time being the restrictive bureaucracy of tsardom, which afforded them a secure base as they devoted their energies to amelioration of their fellow Armenians in the realm of the sultan.

Russian Armenians showed an increasing concern for their brethren in Ottoman domains: Armenian patriots considered Turkish Armenia as the *yerkir*, or the land, the real homeland of Armenians, of which Russian Armenia was just an outlying province. A movement came into being called *Depi Yerkir*, or 'Towards the Homeland', which directed the energies and attentions of Russian Armenians on conditions across the frontier. A number of Armenians from Transcaucasia went into Turkish Armenia to study and report on the conditions of their brethren there.[8]

Armenian writers of the time reflected this overriding concern with Turkish Armenia. The most important Armenian novelist of the period was Raffi (1835–88, the pen-name of Hakob Melik-Hakobian). Two of his works, *Jelaleddin* and *Khente* ('The Fool') were set in the period 1877–8 and depicted the sufferings of Armenians in Ottoman Turkey. He had travelled in Turkish Armenia as early as 1857. His novels had an overtly political content, even when they were historical romances. He advocated the use of arms for throwing off the Turkish yoke – a policy which had been so successful in the Balkans – but warned his fellow-countrymen not to expect assistance from Europe, since the great powers only used the Armenian question as a counter in their intrigues with one another.[9]

Another writer whose work encapsulates the new feeling after the war of 1877–8 was Rafael Patkanian, often known by his pen-name of Kamar Katiba. He spoke of a new life awaiting the Armenian people, and of the emancipation that would come to the Armenians as it had come to the Balkan peoples. The lesson was that they should awake, organise and arm themselves.[10]

Developments in education showed that the tendency towards emancipation was general. Paradoxically, the movement towards the secularisation of education came from the Church itself. When the Russian authorities had entrusted Armenian education to the Church (under the terms of the statutes of 1836) they believed that they had left it in the ineffectual hands of ignorant clerics. However, the Armenian Church again demonstrated its role as the bastion of the entire nation, for a number of the teachers in the parochial schools were men of a modern outlook, who had been educated in Europe or Russia. They taught their disciplines in a critical and scientific manner, and paid great attention to Armenian history and culture. The Armenian schools thereby became centres of opposition to Great-Russian assimilation.[11]

In Conflict with the Autocracy

It was the position of these schools which brought about a lengthy conflict between the Armenian people and the Russian government. Until the 1880s the tsarist authorities had in general favoured the Armenians, as they had favoured all eastern Christian peoples; and the Armenians had recognised the benefits of security and progress that Russian rule conferred. Many Armenians, while maintaining their allegiance to their Church, had since the Russian conquest been happy to speak Russian and to change the endings of their surnames from *-ian* and *-iantz* to *-ov*.[12]

Yet just at the moment when the Armenians in the Russian empire seemed to be gaining a new confidence, their political fortune changed. Tsar Alexander II, the 'Tsar-Liberator', was assassinated in 1881 by anarchists, and his successor, Alexander III, was an inflexible reactionary, dedicated to the extension of the Russian and Orthodox elements throughout the empire. The new tsar's mentor was a man of the narrowest outlook, K. P. Pobiedonostsev, procurator of the Holy Synod. His autocratic methods led to growing tension with Bulgaria, which since the Berlin congress had been a Russian satellite; Russo–Bulgarian disagreements culminated in a *coup* of 1885, when Bulgaria united with Eastern Rumelia, and ousted direct Russian influence from her affairs. Russia was thereafter very cautious about sponsoring nationalist movements among Ottoman Christian peoples. At the same time she needed to come to an understanding with Turkey over the Black Sea, where her ports were open to a possible British naval attack.

In the Caucasus, the viceroyalty was abolished in 1882 with the retirement of the Grand Duke Michael, and the post of the imperial functionary in Tiflis was downgraded to that of governor-general. The fairly relaxed political climate in Transcaucasia, where the nationalities had been granted a tolerable measure of autonomy, changed into one of discipline and suppression.[13]

In this atmosphere of non-interference abroad and hardening arteries at home the Russian government struck at the Armenian schools. In 1884 it ordered a general shift in the elementary curriculum, with Russian language, history and geography as compulsory subjects. It also tried to control the finances of the schools, so that the Armenian Church would no longer be able to found schools at will.[14]

The Armenian clergy rejected these demands; the government retaliated by closing all the schools. In 1886 the Armenian clergy acquiesced in the demands, and the elementary schools were reopened. For ten years the conflict smouldered, with the government demanding further Russification and the Armenians resisting it, but at the same time trying to keep the schools open.

While the conflict remained unresolved, developments occurred within the Armenian community which made the government yet more suspicious of Armenians. Revolutionary organisations began to make their appearance among them. The circumstances which gave birth to these societies derived without exception from the social and political condition of Armenians in the Ottoman empire; and the revolutionaries initially devoted all their attentions to their brethren across the border. But the presence of revolutionary organisations and their evident popularity among educated Armenians was sufficient for the whole Armenian population to be regarded with a suspicion and disfavour that would have been unimaginable even a decade earlier.

Since the origin and development of the Armenian political parties pertain to the course of events within the Ottoman empire, they will appear in that context (see below, pp. 125–31). But their impact within Russian domains was sufficient to merit a brief glance here. Moreover, the two main revolutionary organisations were founded by men from Russian Transcaucasia, and the imprint of Russian Populism[15] is strong on them – so strong indeed that it can be argued that they frequently misunderstood political relationships within the Ottoman empire.

The first Armenian political party, the Armenakan, was founded in 1885 on Ottoman soil, and its policies related directly to Ottoman conditions. Two years later a group of *émigrés* from Russian Transcaucasia founded the first Armenian revolutionary party, in Geneva. It became known as the Hunchakian party (or Hunchaks – properly Hnchaks – for short), *hnchak* being the Armenian for 'bell'. The party aimed at a liberated socialist Armenia as a beacon for world revolution, an idea of some promise in Russia, but irrelevant to the backward medievalism of Turkish Armenia.[16]

In 1890, a *dashnaktsutiun*, or federation, of the Armenian revolutionaries was formed, initially including the Hunchaks. But within a few years it had formed itself into a new, distinct organisation, Hai Heghapokhakan Dashnaktsutiun, or Armenian Revolutionary Federation. Its three intellectual fathers, Kristapor Mikayelian, Stepan Zorian and Simon Zavarian, had been educated at Russian universities, where they had been influenced by Populist ideas. Mikayelian was himself a member of the Narodnaya Volya.[17]

Within the first decade of their existence, the Hunchaks gained more supporters within Turkish Armenia and Anatolia, especially at the American missionary schools, but on Russian soil the Dashnaks (as members of Dashnaktsutiun became known) gained more support within the Russian Caucasus. The Dashnak party organ *Droshak* ('flag') was published in Tiflis, and soon they had cells in all the major cities in Transcaucasia. All their attentions were directed outside the Russian empire, towards Turkish Armenia; they were scrupulously careful not to attack the realm of the tsar in their early utterances.

The mid-1890s, far from seeing the progress of the Armenians towards constructive national goals, were a period of disaster for them. In Turkey the failure of the great powers (principally Britain) to persuade the sultan to undertake reforms was cynically demonstrated in a series of massacres instigated by Abdul Hamid himself. And at the time when Turkish Armenians most needed assistance and help, two appointments were made which minimised any aid which the 'supporting elm' of Russian Armenia might have given to alleviate the suffering across the border.

In January 1895 Russia's foreign minister, N. K. Giers, died. Giers's foreign policy, although formal and correct, was animated by a measure of concern. He was prepared to co-operate with the other great powers if events in the Ottoman empire became characterised by continuous massacre. This was not true of his successor, Prince A. B. Lobanov-Rostovsky. Prince Lobanov was a narrow reactionary, a stern upholder of the autocracy who refused to collaborate with the other powers in concerted action against the sultan. As Wilfrid Scawen Blunt, the brilliant and perceptive observer of the Near East, recorded in his diary:

I found out afterwards that on Giers' death the Russian policy towards Armenia underwent an entire change, though Philip Currie [British Ambassador at Constantinople] was not aware of it at the time. Instead of the old policy of protecting the Christian subjects of the Porte, Lobanov's policy was to encourage the sultan to exterminate the Armenians as allies of Russia's own Nihilists.[18]

Prince Lobanov only held office for a year, but the time was sufficiently critical for his policies to have permanent influence.

Prince Golitsyn

The other appointment had a more direct bearing on Armenians within the Russian empire. From 1896 until 1905 the governor-general of the Caucasus was Prince Grigory Golitsyn. Professor D. M. Lang has written of him:

Nicknamed 'Gri-Gri' in St Petersburg society, he was a man of the narrowest upbringing and outlook, owing his appointment to the personal patronage of a member of the imperial family. He had no understanding of the multiracial structure of Caucasian society, and of the flexible tactics needed to maintain peace and harmony. His one idea was to russify the Caucasus politically and culturally, not by persuasion and example, but by the crudest political methods.[19]

Golitsyn was just one arm of the ultra-reactionary bureaucracy that gripped the whole of the Russian empire at this time. Headed by Tsar Nicolas II, it included K. P. Pobiedonostsev, and the pogrom-fomenting V. K. von Plehve, minister of the interior. Golitsyn was von Plehve's creature in Transcaucasia.

Golitsyn did not take long finally to close the Armenian schools. Then most of the Armenians were removed from the civil service throughout Transcaucasia.[20] At the same time he encouraged the Russian colonisation of Armenia[21] – although this was never popular with Russians, since the land on the eastern fringe of the Armenian plateau was scrubby and poor.

His most spectacular assault on the Armenian community – one which irrevocably changed the relationship between the Armenians and the tsarist regime – occurred in 1903: a decree was issued on 12/25 June declaring that the state would henceforth manage the properties of the Church. Although the Church properties were not confiscated, since the Church still derived revenue from them, it henceforth had no control over the way in which it was spent. In the words of Luigi Villari, 'the Church was placed under tutelage, like an infant or a lunatic.'[22]

The Church was outraged, and refused to co-operate; Russian police reacted by occupying Echmiadzin. They demanded that the aged Catholicos – the great patriot Khrimian Hayrig – hand over the keys of the monastery's safe to Prince Nakashidze, vice-governor of Yerevan (and a whole-hearted supporter of Golitsyn's policies), so that he could obtain the title deeds: the Catholicos too refused, so they broke the safe open and seized the papers.[23]

Overnight, the entire Armenian nation in the Russian empire became converted to the cause of the revolutionaries. The revolutionaries, moreover, did not as previously direct their activities across the border, but against the functionaries of the tsar. They won over to their cause the two classes who had hitherto resisted them: the clergy and the bourgeoisie. Golitsyn's answer was police and Cossack terror; the Armenians retorted with bombing and shooting. An attempt was made on the governor-general's life in October 1903; although seriously wounded, he was able to continue for some months at his post. A number of other officials who had collaborated in the suppression of Armenians were assassinated.[24]

Although Golitsyn's policies had met with unexpected opposition, he was determined that his anti-Armenian campaign should continue. But there were problems: the Russo–Japanese war broke out in January 1904, so all available soldiers were despatched to the Far East. Of the peoples within Transcaucasia, both the Georgians and the Russian minority were brimming with revolutionary sentiments, and so could not be expected to be servants of the autocracy. However, there remained the Tatars.

Armenians and Tatars (Azeris)

The Tatars (or Azeris, as they have been known since the 1930s) were the least socially advanced of the three main national groups in Russian Transcaucasia. They had clung to their ancient loyalties to their feudal leaders, and remained obedient to the dictates of their mullahs. The Russian conquest had altered but little the traditional pattern of their life in the countryside, since the government had permitted their leaders, the khans, beys and aghas, to keep their lands. But in the towns the enterprise that the Armenians had shown far outstripped that of the Tatars – something that was most noticeable in Baku, the industrial centre of Transcaucasia.

Their predominant attitude to the Armenians was contempt; it would be wrong to say that there was a deep and bitter hatred towards them. There were indeed cases of extreme civility between the different nationalities – something that Baron von Haxthausen had found to be the general rule when he visited the country fifty years earlier.[25] But there was an entrenched feeling of superiority of Muslim over Christian, and now a jealousy at Armenian material progress; and among the educated classes the ideology of pan-Turkism was making advances, which gave 'intellectual' justification to anti-Armenian sentiments. (Pan-Turkism was a secular, anti-Shi'ite, pro-Turkish movement, which necessarily entailed a reduction of the Armenian element and a neutralisation of their political claims. It had made progress among educated Tatars since the launching of Ismail Gasprinsky's journal *Ekinchi* in 1875. See below, pp. 189–91).

The varying national antipathies were kept in check by the stern hand of tsarism; and for their part the authorities realised that, if their hold were to be relaxed, and if they were to support one faction against another, a wave of terror would be unleashed.

In July 1904 Golitsyn, who was said to have boasted 'In a short time there will be no Armenians left in the Caucasus, save a few specimens for the museum,'[26] left Tiflis for St Petersburg. His anti-Armenian policy was nevertheless pursued as vigorously as before; its main executant was Prince Nakashidze, now governor of Baku. Nakashidze paid a brief visit to Golitsyn in 1904.

Baku

Baku and the other industrial centres were at this time in a ferment of labour unrest. The labour movement in Baku had begun its work in 1898, and such was the exploitation of the work-force in the oil industry that it soon found a response. To a worker Baku must have seemed like a region of hell. There was no escape from the grime and grease; vegetation had fled from the peninsula decades ago. From time to time it rained oil. The oil magnates could impose the harshest and longest working days on their work-force in the certainty that nothing would stop them. At night the workers were herded into large rooms into which as many beds as possible had been crammed. ('Dormitory' would be a euphemism.) Almost the only solace was provided by vodka.[27]

But with the coming to Baku of the Social Democrats the workers soon gained the weapon of the strike. There was a series of strikes in 1903, culminating in a general strike in July, in which Armenians joined. The division of the Social Democrat movement in 1904 into Bolshevik and Menshevik factions did not slow down the labour agitation. In December 1904 there was another general strike in Baku, led by the brothers Lev and Ilya Shendrikov (sympathisers of the Menshevik faction), to which all radical groups gave their support.[28]

It has been said that this strike was one of the factors which precipitated the Russian revolution of 1905. Nevertheless, the 1905 revolution found Transcaucasia – and Baku in particular – in a turbulent and confused state. This was because there were two types of conflict in the region: the class conflict, between workers and capitalists, and the nationality struggle, between the various ethnic groups. Sometimes the conflicts merged into one another, when nationalist organisations (such as Dashnaktsutiun) assumed a vaguely socialist tinge. More often it led to a confusion of aim.

Prince Golitsyn was relieved of his office of governor-general of the Caucasus on 14/27 January 1905, just five days after Bloody Sunday. The tsar realised that the loyalty of the turbulent Caucasus was in doubt and that conciliatory measures had to be taken. The office of Viceroy of the Caucasus was restored, and Count I. I. Vorontsov-Dashkov appointed to it.[29]

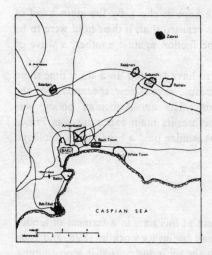

Map 3. Baku

Vorontsov-Dashkov did not reach Tiflis until May. In the meantime the officials of Golitsyn's era remained at their posts, notably Nakashidze in Baku.

The February Clashes

In early February 1905 bodies of murdered Armenians and Tatars were discovered in Baku. The atmosphere of wavering government authority had brought ethnic antipathies to the surface. The authorities for their part, by continually warning of the dangers of race conflict, could not fail to focus attention upon it. One day, a Tatar was arrested for offences against Armenians; as he was being taken away he tried to escape and was shot dead by an Armenian member of the police escort. His relatives thirsted for revenge, and a cousin named Babayev determined to do the deed. But Babayev was a poor shot, and in his attempt to get retribution he was himself shot by an Armenian. Baku seethed with racial hatred and fear.[30]

Babayev's funeral procession was a pretext for a political demonstration. But very quickly it developed further, as the Tatars saw the slain man's body. On 19 February/4 March they poured out of their quarter and slaughtered all the Armenians they could lay their hands on. The authorities remained impassive. Thousands of requests for help were sent to Nakashidze, and despite having 2,000 soldiers at his disposal, he replied that he had no troops. Observers saw him travelling around Baku giving encouragement to the Tatars. In one incident, seeing some soldiers disarming a Tatar, he ordered that the man's weapon be returned to him, which it was.[31] British consul Gough, who visited the city just after the outbreak, described the situation thus:

The Armenians were mostly taken by surprise, and were slaughtered in the most brutal manner in the streets. Shops were broken open and plundered, and men, women and children fled for their lives towards the Armenian quarter of the town. When the firing began, a few Cossacks were sent into the streets, and in many cases Armenians took refuge within their ranks, to be thrust out by the Cossacks and slaughtered by the Mussulmans. Fighting was going on in nearly every quarter of the town, and not a finger was raised by the authorities on either the Monday or Tuesday to put a stop to it.[32]

Many of the Armenians were slaughtered without mercy in the streets; but one – a wealthy oil magnate by the name of Adamov – defended himself and his family with great bravery. Adamov lived in one of the grand, showy palaces that were the characteristic dwellings of Baku capitalists. Very soon after the killing began his villa was surrounded by a horde of Tatars, bent on murder. However, Adamov was a crack shot, and in a siege that continued for several days he felled many of his would-be assailants with a bullet between the eyes.

Even when mortally wounded, and after the Tatars had set fire to the hallway of his palace, he continued to fire at his besiegers. When eventually he died his entire house was engulfed; but he had sold his life dearly.[33]

About 1,500 were killed in the fighting; the proportion of Armenians to Tatars was three to two.[34] Once the killing had ended the Tatar notables admitted, according to J. D. Henry, that they had been incited to violence by the authorities, who had armed many of them with rifles.

Peace was proclaimed by (as vice-consul Urquhart put it) 'the authorities calling "time" '.[35]

It was officially declared by a joint procession of the local Armenian bishop and the Chief Sayyid of the Shi'a Muslim community. The Sayyid later gave an address in the cathedral, and the bishop spoke in the mosque. The fires of hatred were damped down; nevertheless both sides continued to arm themselves.[36]

Two months later Vorontsov-Dashkov arrived in Tiflis. He was a humane and enlightened Russian nobleman, a complete contrast to Golitsyn, whose disastrous policies he set about undoing. He sought an end to enmities in the Caucasus, but some people feared he was not strong enough to bring this about.

Nakhicheven and Karabagh

Within a week of Vorontsov-Dashkov's arrival Nakashidze was assassinated by Armenians – members of Dashnaktsutiun, which at this time was virtually the only organisation which stood between the Armenian population and the tyranny and violence of the government and the Tatars. On the day following the assassination Vorontsov-Dashkov faced his first real political challenge: an outbreak of massacre in Nakhichevan. In the town of Nakhichevan there were 6,000 Tatars to 2,000 Armenians, and in the surrounding countryside the Tatars numbered 65,000 and the Armenians 33,000.[37] The landowners were all Tatar; the peasantry mixed Armenian and Tatar. Russian authority had never been powerfully exerted in Nakhichevan; most of the 'governing' was left to local Tatar feudal lords, whose policies amounted to little more than brigandage and extortion. Many Armenians had consequently abandoned the countryside; the large Armenian proletariat in Tiflis and Baku was drawn from the harassed peasantry of Nakhichevan.

An atmosphere of violence had built up in Nakhichevan since the Baku massacres. The Armenians had requested protection, but the district governor and his assistant (a Finn and a Georgian) were anti-Armenian and denied them protection. All the local officials were Tatars. Fear grew rapidly. On 20 May/2 June 1905 Armenian shopkeepers in Nakhichevan closed their shops, believing atrocities and looting imminent. Three days later officials tried to allay Armenian fears, and on the 24th/6th they were persuaded to open their shops on the following day.[38]

When they did so bands of Tatars at once converged on them, looting them and setting fire to them and killing their owners. Prior to the assault the Tatars had organised themselves into four groups: one to murder the Armenians, a second to plunder and burn the shops, the third to take away the loot in carts, and the fourth ready to tend the Tatar wounded.[39]

The Armenians were quite unprepared. Vile atrocities were perpetrated: Armenians were burnt alive in their shops. During the three hours of the attack about 50 Armenians were killed, and over a million roubles' worth of goods plundered.[40]

After the town, the countryside: in the following days the murder and destruction spread to the countryside around Nakhichevan. Over a dozen nearby villages suffered a similar fate, with the inevitable result that the countryside was further depopulated.[41]

Despite at first making the unsuitable choice of a Tatar general to conduct an enquiry, Vorontsov-Dashkov shortly afterwards appointed Prince Louis Napoleon, an officer with many years' service in the Russian army, as governor-general of Yerevan. (In Yerevan itself there had been a similar outbreak of massacre on 5–6/18–19 June.)

His position gave him authority over Nakhichevan and Zangezur too, and he travelled there in person. Napoleon was one of the best sort of imperial public servants: energetic, impartial and firm. His methods were entirely different from those intriguing tsarist officials of the Golitsyn type, who secretly encouraged the Tatars to attack Armenians, only to discover that their protégés had got out of hand. Napoleon managed to reassert a measure of order.[42]

At this time Russia itself was in revolution. Georgia too, especially after the massacre of her citizens at Tiflis town hall on 29 August/11 September, was in a state of total defiance of the regime. But within Armenia, and in the Armenian communities throughout Transcaucasia, there was almost no participation in the revolution: their struggle was with the Tatars, who had been permitted by the authorities to wage race war against Armenians. (Whether the Tatars themselves were acting purely out of localised hatred and greed, or whether their attacks amounted to a larger pan-Turkist campaign of reducing Armenians so as to pave the way for a greater Turkish state is open to question.) Armenian energies were almost entirely taken up in combating the Tatar movement. Only dedicated Social Democrats like Stepan Shahumian pitted themselves against the autocracy.

In late August further clashes occurred in Shushi (or Shusha), which is situated in the Karabagh district, and at this time was within the Yelizavetpol *guberniia* (province). The population of 35,000 was evenly divided between Armenians and Tatars, but the Armenians had the advantage of occupying the upper parts of the town. Armenians were also well organised at Shushi. The Tatars had been emboldened by the impunity of the Baku massacres, and adopted a truculent attitude towards them. The events on this occasion began with Tatars attacking and plundering a busload of Armenians; for a few weeks counsels of peace prevailed, but then the killing increased in intensity, until by 2/15 September about 300 lay dead, of whom two-thirds were Tatars.[43]

When the inhabitants of Baku heard of the Shushi outbreak, the city, fairly quiescent since February, grew tense. There had been a general strike in May, and three months later there was a tram strike. The workers were ordered back to work by the governor-general, and the trams were given armed escorts on 2/15 September. The strikers demonstrated and attacked one of the cars; shots were fired, and some Tatars were hit accidentally. At once firing became general throughout the city; soon several entire streets were alight. A strike had turned into a race riot.[44]

The Oilfields Ablaze

However, what made the September outbreak different from that of February was the effect that the news had on the population in the oilfields. Twelve miles to the north-east of Baku lies the triple oilfield of Balakhani-Sabunchi-Ramani. News of the outbreak in the city caused Armenians to close their shops, and flee to centres of safety. On 3/16 September, hourly telephone calls from Baku told of the ride of death; then the telephone failed. At 4.00 that afternoon shots were fired: a volley from the 'Black Hundreds' (the striking-force of reaction throughout Russia), who tried to incite the Tatars against Armenians. But the attack was delayed, and it was not until the following day that the killings began. During a night of terrible suspense the bell of the Armenian church at Balakhani tolled ominously; no one was ever able to ascertain by whom or why this was done.[45]

First target was some Armenian workmen who had taken refuge in a building of the Baku Oil Producers' Association; but the Tatars were driven off from here. They were driven off from a similar attack on workmen at the Va Wotan works. And, to their great surprise, they were themselves attacked and severely wounded by the Cossacks. A semblance of order returned. Later that day, however, encouragement came from Baku when the leaders of the Tatar community arrived at the oilfield. Then the inferno began. Oil wells and derricks were set ablaze; soon whole areas of Balakhani were engulfed in a great beard of flame. The speed and size of the blaze astonished all who saw it. Panic-stricken men rushed out of the blazing debris, only to be shot down by Tatars. Oil tanks exploded, heavy shooting continued in all directions, and over all hung a mantle of thick smoke. One of the works to be set ablaze was the Armenian Ter Akopov business; an Armenian caught fleeing from it was torn apart, and the pieces thrown back into the blaze. The Tatar mob went from one works to another, setting them alight. On 7/20 September it was the turn of the Mantashev company. Again there was an immense conflagration, and the Tatars claimed afterwards that every workman had either been burned to death or shot. In the Ramani section of the field the Melikov works were fired, and 70 Armenians were burned to death. Eleven derricks were even destroyed in the Vorontsov-Dashkov property, belonging to the Viceroy himself.[46] In the fields an estimated minimum of 1,500 men died.[47]

On the other side of Baku lies the Bibi-Eibat field, adjoining the Caspian Sea. When news of the killings came to Bibi-Eibat, most Armenians were able to escape to a hill overlooking the oilfield. It was a desperate flight, undertaken in a sandstorm, but it secured their safety. Burning and killing lasted for a week in Bibi-Eibat; three-quarters of the entire oilfield was destroyed. A sinister aspect of the Bibi-Eibat outbreak was that some vessels landed numbers of killers at the bay. One night a schooner without lights was seen to glide by, making its way to the landing-stage of the Tagiev works, owned by a Tatar millionaire from Baku. The next day hundreds of armed Tatars were discovered at the works, who ran off in all directions when the authorities tried to arrest them. The one man arrested said that they had thrown a cargo of rifles into the sea.

Close on 600 had been killed in a week – about three times as many Tatars as Armenians, for the latter had been prepared since the preceding February. This time the Tatars were denied the entire, overt complicity of the authorities, save for a few members of the Black Hundreds. During the week of conflagration, the monthly output of the five main fields was reduced from 735,036 tons to 296,218; out of 1,609 wells 1,026 had been destroyed.[48]

As a tailpiece, and as an indication of industrial relations in Baku in 1905, one story should be told. On 8/21 September, the day after the worst inferno, the workshops of one Balakhani company received an order for 'quick delivery of thirty troughs'. The ground was still littered with corpses – many not yet rigid – of men butchered or burnt to death, whose dependants would now be destitute. Such matters were, however, mere trifles to the employers, and on the morning of 9th/22nd the works whistle blew as on any other day. Unfortunately the prophet Ezekiel was not present, and the corpses remained dead.[49]

The 1905 Armeno–Tatar conflict, and the massive destructive violence of the September blaze in the oilfields, appear as a preposterous and gratuitous self-inflicted wound by the already weakened force of the tsar; but the situation has been duplicated elsewhere where 'subject races' have been controlled by a spiteful imperial functionary. Golitsyn's ill-educated, weak-kneed malevolence masquerading as strength has been echoed many times in other situations where the imperial power has been prepared to bring the country to the edge of ruin, and do serious damage to itself, rather than lose 'face' among the natives. This was the policy which Golitsyn and Nakashidze began. Once the policy had been initiated – once the Tatars had been incited to attack the disobedient Armenians – it proved very difficult to call a halt. The new conciliatory viceroy did not show himself strong enough to control the animosities; for if there is one thing that the low cunning of men of the Golitsyn type tells them it is that by playing with racial animosities they are playing with a very powerful poison indeed. The only antidote is an administrator of real authority and impartiality. It was not until 1912 that Vorontsov-Dashkov gained the confidence of the Armenians.

With the collapse of the revolutionary movement at the end of 1905, conditions returned to autocratic stability in Transcaucasia, as in the rest of Russia. One of the main lessons that the Armenians had learnt from the battles was that they could fight back perfectly well, and were not always 'suffering Armenians'; in view of the sultan's killings across the frontier ten years earlier, this was of importance.

After 1905

In 1907 the Dashnak party adopted socialism as its goal; it had grown more radical as a result of the 1905 events; at the same time the party was admitted to the Second Socialist International. Its primary aim was still the liberation of Turkish Armenia, and the creation of an Armenian autonomous (but not independent) region, to which end the party put forward a list of somewhat impractical demands, largely irrelevant to the harsh, backward conditions of Ottoman Turkey.[50]

Despite the autocracy's wish to consign Transcaucasia to slumber, revolutionary currents and nationalist activity continued. In one notorious incident, on 23 June/6 July 1907, a Bolshevik gang led by Kamo Ter-Petrosian raided the state bank at Tiflis, and netted a quarter of a million roubles for their party's funds.[51]

Dashnaktsutiun, for its part, having been the main defence of the Armenian people in 1905, was viewed with increasing suspicion by the authorities, especially the arch-reactionary P. A. Stolypin, president of the Russian Council of Ministers. In 1911 the autocracy undertook a mass trial of the party; advocates for the defence included Alexander Kerensky and Pavel Miliukov. The trial fizzled out in a shower of light sentences in early 1912, as the direction of Russian policy changed with the need for the government to receive the backing of all influential Armenian groups for her adventures in northern Persia. Russia revived the question of Turkish Armenia, dormant since 1878. A renewed sense of hope ran through Armenian patriots.[52]

On the Eve

Russian policy exhibited a complete change. In November 1912 representatives of all Russian Armenian bodies met in Tiflis to discuss the situation in Turkish Armenia, and to set up an information campaign about Armenians. All this was done with the full co-operation of Vorontsov-

Dashkov. Also with permission of the viceroy, the Catholicos of All Armenians established an 'Armenian Delegation' in Paris to co-ordinate pro-Armenian activities, and to publicise the Armenian case. In charge of the delegation was Boghos Nubar Pasha, wealthy son of Nubar Pasha, former prime minister of Egypt.[53]

The viceroy, too – in a remarkable gesture – admitted that mistakes had been made. In his report of 11/24 July 1913 Vorontsov-Dashkov declared that Russia herself had created the past friction with her Armenian subjects 'by careless interference with the religious and national ideals of the Armenians'. He acknowledged that Caucasian Armenians entertained no separatist tendencies, and that outbursts of nationalist feeling had resulted from the confiscation of Church property. He averred that he had tried to prevent the recent prosecution of Dashnaktsutiun (which had been set up 'to demonstrate the revolutionary tendency of the whole Armenian nation'); but the counsels of 'ill-informed persons' in St Petersburg had prevailed.[54]

There was in the air an almost palpable sense that Armenians were on the brink of a new political move, which would set to right the central, overriding concern of Armenians everywhere: the misrule of their people across the frontier at the hands of the Turks. The perceptive traveller, writer and Liberal member of Parliament Noel Buxton has given an unforgettable picture of Russian Armenia on the eve:

> One fine evening in September [1913] I took a drive from Erivan, the Russian town near Ararat, to see the Armenian villages in the Araxes valley. The plain, that would be arid waste without irrigation, has here come to look like the rich land one sees in Belgium from the Berlin express, small farms intersected with cypress-like Lombardy poplars, but here growing vines, rice and cotton. The presence of orchards – mulberry or peach – is denoted by high mud-walls along the road. As we moved farther the walls became continuous, and ripe apricots and quinces leaned over them. Water-courses lined our route on each side, feeding the roots of a double row of poplars. At intervals the wall was pierced by the windows of the farmer's house, flat-roofed, and at this season surmounted by stacks of corn. Old-fashioned mud-dwellings were yielding here and there to new fronts of stone, finely dressed. Big doorways at the side gave a glimpse of yards and verandahs, wellheads, great earthen jars, and farther on the orchard, with the raised wooden sleeping-platforms, used in the hot Araxes valley. In time the holdings become so thick as to give the effect of a continuous village, an unending community of picturesque market-gardeners – every man happy under his vine and his fig-tree.
>
> As we travelled southward, and the sun sank westward, Ararat, flanked with sunset colour, dominated the world below. Ararat is higher than Mont Blanc, and standing alone it towers uniquely. Yet there is something specially restful about its broad shoulders of perpetual snow. With the

soaring quality of Fuji it combines a sense of holding, up there, a place of repose:

> The high still dell
> Where the Muses dwell
> Fairest of all things fair.

In the shadow of the great mountain winnowers were using the last daylight on the green; a man was washing a horse after the burning day, standing shoulder-deep in the stream; buffaloes walked sedately home from their bath, shining like black velvet. The day's work was ending, and we now kept passing family groups sitting at the doorway. Here a boy was playing with a tame hawk; there a father, in most un-English fashion, held in his arms the baby.

The houses became continuous and shops appeared, wine-presses, forges, agricultural machines. Russian gendarmes gossiping outside the inn, wagon-builders and copper-pot makers. The slanting sun displayed a kaleidoscope of industry, not primitive and not capitalist – human economy at its most picturesque stage of development.

We halted to see the village priest, whose son was a student at St Petersburg University. As we sat in his balcony, the hum of village movement arose above the gathering stillness of nature, and we remarked on the prosperity of the priest's flock. He agreed; but there was a blot upon it – refugees from Turkey constantly arriving in rags, their property abandoned, driven out by violence and often by brutal violation, even of the very young. Russia was to them a godsend, though beggary was the price of escape from worse evil.

To the right of Ararat stretched the line of hills which forms the present Russo–Turkish frontier. Upon this horizon the sun set. It was a memorable combination – the eternal snow one associates with the north framed with the glowing brilliance of the southern sun. Byron was within the mark when he wrote of that sun:

> Not as in northern climes obscurely bright,
> But one unclouded blaze of living light.

There is something more than that. Those who have watched the white flames of a smelting furnace, and still more those who have climbed to its rim on a dark night, can picture something of the effulgence that streamed up from behind that blackening line of mountains – an effulgence quite correctly described as 'molten'. Hidden now from our view, it still bathed the hills from which these refugees had fled – that noble upland given over to misery and waste.

Why has the tide of civilisation paused at that particular line of hills? The frontiers of Turkey on the European side were easily held against the small Balkan states whose territories adjoined them, till those states became powerful by combination, but here the defence is obviously powerless. The fortifications of Erzerum itself have twice been in the hands of Turkey's great neighbour. Yet for thirty-five years the Russian armies have been as if paralysed. Forces even greater than they have said, 'Hands off that frontier, defenceless though it is.'

We are face to face with the Cyprus Convention and the Berlin treaty, which specify that this Turkish frontier is guaranteed by the powers, and by England in particular. Those documents, till you visit the spot, seem abstract and intangible embodiments of justice. Here they are concrete enough to the peasant escaping penniless through the hills; to the Armenian priest in Russia, trying to find him bread; to the Russian prefect, dealing with brigands who can always escape into a lawless country. These diplomatic instruments, usually cited as vague landmarks in past history, are here playing a tragically definite part.[55]

Buxton's account, written on the eve of the first world war, makes superbly clear the rich potential of Armenia, and sums up what Armenians had achieved in almost ninety years of Russian imperial rule. But the shadow across the hills is no less discernible, and it is now our task to discover why Turkish rule was so different for Armenians – why to describe it one employs an entirely new mode of discourse – and why, despite its cruelly inferior form of administration, the Turkish empire's frontier with Russia was 'guaranteed by the powers, and by England in particular'.

Notes

1. A. J. Grant and Harold Temperley, *Europe in the Nineteenth Century* (London, 1927), pp. 372–4.
2. M. S. Anderson, *The Eastern Question, 1774–1923* (London, 1966), pp. 172–3.
3. W. E. D. Allen and Paul Muratoff, *Caucasian Battlefields* (Cambridge, 1953), p. 216n.
4. Allen and Muratoff, *Caucasian Battlefields*, Chapters XII and XV.
5. Ibid., Chapter XIV.
6. *Cassell's Illustrated History of the Russo–Turkish War* (London, 1878?), p. 506.
7. Allen and Muratoff, *Caucasian Battlefields*, p. 212.
8. Louise Nalbandian, *The Armenian Revolutionary Movement* (Berkeley and Los Angeles, 1963), pp. 136–8.
9. Ibid., pp. 63–5.
10. Ibid., pp. 61–3.
11. Vartan Gregorian, 'The Impact of Russia on the Armenians and Armenia', in Wayne S. Vucinich (ed.), *Russia and Asia* (Stanford, 1972), p. 196.
12. Luigi Villari, *Fire and Sword in the Caucasus* (London, 1906), p. 148.
13. Ibid., p. 150.
14. Ibid., p. 153; Gregorian, 'The Impact of Russia', p. 197.
15. On Populism see Isaiah Berlin, *Russian Thinkers* (London, 1978), pp. 210–37.
16. Nalbandian, *Armenian Revolutionary Movement*, pp. 90–118.
17. Ibid., pp. 151 ff.
18. Wilfrid Scawen Blunt, *My Diaries* (New York, 1932), p. 192.
19. David Marshall Lang, *A Modern History of Georgia* (London, 1962), p. 119.
20. Villari, *Fire and Sword*, pp. 153, 155.
21. Gregorian, 'The Impact of Russia', p. 184.
22. Villari, *Fire and Sword*, p. 156.
23. Ibid., pp. 156–7.

24. Ibid., p. 157.
25. Baron von Haxthausen, *Transcaucasia* (London, 1854), p. 270n.
26. Villari, *Fire and Sword*, p. 157.
27. See Eva Broido, *Memoirs of a Revolutionary* (London, 1967), pp. 68–9.
28. Ronald Grigor Suny, *The Baku Commune, 1917–1918* (Princeton, 1972), pp. 28–35.
29. Villari, *Fire and Sword*, p. 127.
30. Ibid., pp. 193–4.
31. Ibid., p. 195.
32. Great Britain, Public Record Office, FO 881/8475, p. 71 (henceforward 'FO 881/8475', 'CAB 23/25', etc.).
33. J. D. Henry, *Baku: an Eventful History* (London, 1905), pp. 157–60.
34. FO 881/8475, p. 71.
35. FO 881/8560, p. 33.
36. Villari, *Fire and Sword*, pp. 195–6.
37. Ibid., p. 267.
38. Ibid., pp. 269–70.
39. Ibid., p. 271.
40. Ibid., p. 272.
41. Ibid., pp. 272–4.
42. Ibid., p. 276.
43. Ibid., p. 199; Henry, *Baku*, p. 172.
44. Henry, *Baku*, p. 174.
45. Ibid., pp. 181–2.
46. Ibid., pp. 183–5.
47. FO 881/8560, p. 35.
48. Henry, *Baku*, p. 215.
49. Ibid., p. 192.
50. Richard G. Hovannisian, *Armenia on the Road to Independence, 1918* (Berkeley and Los Angeles, 1967), p. 22.
51. David Shub, 'Kamo, the Legendary Old Bolshevik in the Caucasus', *The Russian Review*, vol. XIX, no. 3 (July 1960), pp. 227–47.
52. Hovannisian, *Armenia on the Road to Independence*, p. 22.
53. Ibid., p. 32.
54. *The Times Russian Supplement*, 20 October 1913, p. 5.
55. Noel and Harold Buxton, *Travels and Politics in Armenia* (London, 1914), pp. 140–4.

PART II

The Realm of the Sultans

4　Empires in the West, from the Ottomans to the British

The Ottomans and Armenia

If the homeland of an empire is where it puts down its deepest roots during its formative years, then the homeland of the Ottoman empire was western Anatolia and the Balkans. The first lands which the Ottomans were granted were near Angora; from there they expanded westwards to Nicomedia and Nicaea, and later to the Gallipoli peninsula. A large part of the Balkans was in their hands by 1362, and in 1368 Adrianople (Edirne) became the Ottoman capital. None of Armenia was yet conquered by them.[1]

It was not until 150 years later that the Ottomans pushed far enough east to capture part of Armenia. At the battle of Chaldiran (north-east of lake Van) in 1514 Sultan Selim the Grim defeated Shah Ismail, and conquered about half of the Armenian plateau. Twenty years later Suleiman I, 'the Magnificent' or 'the Lawgiver', conquered much of the rest.[2] Armenia thereafter remained on the periphery of the empire – a marchland, first on the border with Persia, and latterly with Russia. Notions that Armenia was a central province of the empire were nineteenth-century contrivances, based on the idea that the Ottomans maintained a racial link with their central Asian forbears, which was not true.[3]

When Armenia was conquered by the Ottoman Turks it was in a wretched state. The Mongols had wreaked devastation on it, destroying the settled society in order to create grazing land for their flocks and herds. The land had become more suitable for tribal communities than for civilised society. The Armenians themselves were either reduced to poverty, or had fled to new settlements in mountain fastnesses. In these circumstances, the Ottoman conquest was initially welcomed as bringing stability.

The Kurds

However, not long after Selim the Grim's conquest of Armenia there occurred an important and far-reaching shift of the population. Kurdish communities were settled in Armenia. The Kurds are an ancient people, Indo-European like the Armenians. They are mentioned by Xenophon. For many centuries they have been Muslim; probably since soon after the Muslim conquest of Syria and Mesopotamia. Most are Sunni Muslim, although religion has never been a matter which has troubled them deeply. Most too were until recently nomadic, although with the inevitable process of sedentarisation settled Kurdish communities were developing all the time. According to J. G. Taylor,[4] British consul in Erzerum, it was Selim the Grim's chief minister Idrisi who

divided the Kurdish provinces around Diyarbekir, recently acquired from the Persians, into eight sanjaks (districts), and forced a greater part of the nomad Kurds, who then as now preyed to a great extent upon the peaceable agricultural population and villages, to emigrate to the southern portions of the Georgian districts, about Erivan, Azerbaijan, and northern Armenia, which with other possessions fell to the Turks consequent upon Selim's victory.

To make full use of this forced emigration (ordered so as to weaken the political power of the Kurds) Idrisi at the same time assured the Kurds of perpetual immunity from taxation, if they would act as a militia to guard the extensive frontier with Persia on which they were now located. And later on,

sultan Murad still further strengthened the Kurdish element, by sending additional families from the south to these same districts; at the same time he fully guaranteed the privileges originally granted by Selim.[5]

With the settlement of the Kurds in their land, the prospect for the Armenians seriously dimmed.

The Armenian Patriarchate of Constantinople

In 1453 Sultan Mehmed II, installed in his new capital, had given the Greek Orthodox patriarch civil and ecclesiastical authority over all Orthodox Christians throughout the empire. Eight years later he summoned the Armenian archbishop of Brusa, Hovakim, to Constantinople, and with the title of 'patriarch' granted him similar authority over all the 'non-Orthodox' Christian peoples of the empire – who, of course, initially included many more than the Armenians. (Each community was eventually granted its own leader.[6])

The Armenian patriarchate of Constantinople was thus a creation of the Ottoman authorities, not of the Armenian Church. Its jurisdiction overrode that of the establishments created by the Church itself – the catholicosates of Sis and Aghtamar, and the patriarchate of Jerusalem. It was a political appointment; but since the Ottoman empire was a theocracy, it was expressed in ecclesiastical terms.

The Millets

Each community (*millet*) was to a large extent self-governing, and permitted to keep its institutions; internal, personal matters were controlled within the community itself, with no outside Turkish interference. Marriage, inheritance, the founding of schools and hospitals, and everything to assure the smooth running of the community's day-to-day affairs were dealt with internally. The community even had its own prison. The Ottoman Turkish ruling class in effect only required of them that they pay their taxes and create no disturbance.[7] No overt attempt was made to Turkise or Islamicise them, although social pressures were, as in any empire, exerted upon them for them to convert. The non-Muslim communities were known as *rayahs*, or flocks (derived from the Arabic *ra'ā*) not because they were 'human cattle', as some later commentators have held, but because they were the 'protected ones', as sheep by a shepherd, a fairly common image in the Middle East.[8] The protection that they received, however, was in practice closer to that of a racketeer than a biblical vision.

The *millet* system has been sometimes praised as a model of just administration for a conqueror, sometimes criticised for being opportunistic. Certainly, as a method of administration for conquered peoples, it was morally ahead of anything to come out of Europe at the time or for some time after: compare the Spanish conquest of South America, or the behaviour of the Portuguese conqueror D'Albuquerque who, during his expedition of 1507 along the shores of the Persian Gulf, mutilated Muslim prisoners of both sexes with the object of inspiring terror.[9] In terms of results, too, it was a cleverly contrived system, since the ruler soon drew the benefits that wary colonialists draw today by disturbing the *status quo* of their subjugated peoples as little as possible, while waiting for the districts to become profitable. But all such evaluations are out of place, since the principles on which the empire was based were absolute. These derived from two sources, the Muslim religion and the Ottoman dynasty; latter-day analyses in the context of an age of reason are irrelevant. Sultan Mehmed II, by making such provisions for non-Muslims, was acting in accordance with an Islamic tradition that went back to the Prophet Muhammad's early treaties.[10] The model was already there for a Muslim ruler to draw upon.

Ottoman Law and the Armenians

Even at the early stage there were flaws in the Ottoman system, which were later to make the position of Armenians quite intolerable. Most serious was that Muslim law was inapplicable to non-Muslims. Non-Muslims had their own courts and prisons; they could judge civil cases among themselves, and be assured of a fair hearing. But in conflict with a Muslim this was not the case, for the Muslim could always apply to have his case heard in the religious court (the *mehkémé*), where non-Muslim testimony was forbidden. Later, non-Muslims were allowed to testify in cases involving Muslims, but their testimony was almost always disregarded. As an example of how the system operated, here is an incident observed by the admirable Dr Humphry Sandwith, recounted in his *Narrative of the Siege of Kars* (1856):[11]

An Armenian tradesman, about to leave the town for another city, had been trying to change some paper-money into gold, the former not being current at the place of his destination. An officer, hearing of this, went and offered the Armenian gold for 5,000 piastres in paper (about £40), ten per cent agio being deducted. This offer the Armenian accepted, and gave the officer the paper-money, the latter promising to return immediately with the gold. Some time having elapsed, and the officer not having made his appearance, the Armenian went to look for him, and with much trouble succeeded in recovering, at various instalments, 4,060 piastres. The Armenian then applied to the Turk's commanding officer for the payment of the remainder, who recommended that the affair should be taken to the *mejlis* [civil court]. The Turk seeing that the proofs were rather strong against him, insisted on his right to be tried by the *mehkémé*, where he knew that the Koran would serve him in his need. Accordingly the Armenian and the Turk were confronted before this religious tribunal; and there the Turk, grown bold as a Mussulman, declared that, far from owing the Armenian anything, the latter wished to rob him; that he (the Turk) had placed the above-named sum in the hands of a third person to be changed into gold, and that the Armenian had taken it for that purpose, but that the gold was not forthcoming. 'Do you swear to this?' asked the president. 'I swear to it on the Koran,' answered the Turk. 'It is enough.' The Armenian had brought witnesses, but they were all Christians, their evidence was impossible; so the hapless Armenian was obliged to refund all the gold he had previously obtained, and found himself a ruined man.*

On this occasion justice was later done due to the presence of the two Englishmen; but the general rule was that, in disputes concerning members of his family, his land or his basic means of subsistence, justice did not exist for the Armenian.

Besides this enormous general disadvantage, Armenians suffered from certain specific discriminations. As Christians, they were not permitted to bear arms, which laid them open to their predatory neighbours. Their religion did give them the benefit of exemption from military service (although it also meant that no officer class could emerge among them), since only a Muslim might draw his sword in the defence of Islam. Nevertheless Christians were subjected to the *devshirme*, or boy-collection, whereby officials used to take children from the Christian communities, educate them as Muslims and put them into the Ottoman civil service. By the end of the sixteenth century *devshirme* was an established practice in certain Armenian localities. (It did, however, die out by the mid-eighteenth century.[12]) As regards taxation, all Christians were required

---

*Footnote to the original. This happened some months after the Firman accepting Christian evidence was issued.

to pay poll-tax and, where relevant, property tax. These taxes were not collected in an orderly manner; more often it was a question of officials just extorting as much as they could from the people, who had no redress.

One disability which the Armenians alone of the Christian peoples of the empire had to bear, and one that was resented most especially, was the obligation to provide free winter quarters (*kishlak*) to the nomadic Kurds and to their flocks, often for four to six months each year. Besides the disagreeable presence of squatters, they ran up large expenses in providing food and animal foodstuffs.[13] The system was a degrading humiliation.

All these factors led to the steady impoverishment of the Armenians. In every sphere they were reminded that they were inferior to Muslims, and were consequently reduced to frightened subservience.

The Capitulations

Rather more insidiously, the system of Capitulations which operated within the Ottoman empire served to endanger the position of Armenians. Capitulations were extra-territorial privileges granted by the Ottoman government to non-Ottoman subjects while they travelled or lived within Ottoman domains. The notion of them is an ancient one; its general features can be traced back to Roman law. In the Ottoman context the system dated from 1535, when Suleiman I granted a wide range of privileges to François I of France. Throughout the following centuries European nations made great use and abuse of the Capitulations that they were granted.[14]

The damaging effect of this system was twofold. In the first place it encouraged the European powers to get a paralysing hold on the political workings of the empire, reducing the overt masters of the empire, the Turks, to a bitter and vengeful xenophobia. It is ironic indeed that throughout the nineteenth century the powers tried to force Ottoman Turkey to reform, when, to the Ottoman ruling class, their own self-seeking interference had reduced the concept of law to something to abhor and avoid.

Secondly, since Ottoman law gave no assurance of security to Armenians, the wealthier and more astute ones among them sought the protection of the foreign powers under the Capitulations, as the only way of ensuring that they lived a reasonably unmolested life. As a result such people, *and* members of their communities who had not sought such protection, were viewed with suspicion by the Ottoman government, which saw them as agents of a foreign power. So more and more turned to the foreign powers for restitution of their serious grievances, rather than to their own government (although, considering the oppression and indifference of that government to them, it is hard to call it 'their own'); and they also believed, disastrously as it turned out, that foreign governments would intervene on their behalf if conditions became unbearable.

The Empire, the Powers and 'Reform'

Under the treaty of Kutchuk Kainardji (1774) Russia won the right to 'make, upon all occasions, representations, as well in favour of the new church in Constantinople ... as on behalf of its officiating ministers'.[15] From this text Catherine the Great assumed the right to protect all the Orthodox Christian members of the Ottoman empire. It was certainly a large assumption. Although Russia's protection appears to be blatant interference in the affairs of another state, the idea of extra-territorial privileges had already been sanctioned in the Capitulations. The Russian empress was merely extending, in a brilliantly opportunistic manner, a principle which already existed. Thereafter the other foreign powers, not to be outdone, extended their own privileges within Ottoman Turkey; while the Turks themselves, realising they were too weak to oppose the powers, retreated into a mood of sullen and obstinate reaction, which the activities of various reformist sultans did little to dispel. Stonewalling the demands of the foreign powers became the most typical Ottoman policy; one observer noted that '*how not to do it* is the perfection of Turkish diplomacy.'[16] At the same time the Sublime Porte* could always be sure that the powers would not turn their backs on Turkey for long, since she was so important to them for economic and strategic reasons. Economically, Ottoman Turkey was a mine of raw materials, and a vast market for the sale of surplus goods. Militarily, Turkey's geographical position assured her of the perpetual attentions of the powers, principally Austria and Russia, with their vast contiguous land masses, and Britain, with her fears for her Indian possessions.

Despite their perennial quarrels over the Ottoman empire, all the powers agreed (except for rare periods) that she had to be maintained, for should she collapse their rivalries would provoke a conflict of incalculable proportions. However, if she had to be maintained, she had to be kept *weak*; for a powerful empire might destroy the fabric of interests, commercial and otherwise, that the powers wove out of the decline of the Ottoman state. Hence they came to her aid when she was seriously threatened in 1839 by the more vigorous dynasty of Mehemed Ali of Egypt.

Of all the powers Britain was the most dedicated to the cause of Ottoman Turkey. Turkey prevented Russia from reaching the Mediterranean, and from gaining the headwaters of the Tigris and Euphrates, which would (so Britain believed) enable her to threaten the Persian Gulf. At the same time Britain became Turkey's best customer in the early nineteenth century, Turkey, for her part, becoming Britain's third-best customer by 1850.[17] So it is hardly surprising that the most ardent supporters of the Turks, and their most eager propagandists, came from the most conservative-minded members of the British political elite, who have never been able to resist a combination of

---

*The Sublime Porte (*Bab 'Āli*), or the Porte, was the usual way that foreigners referred to the Ottoman government from the eighteenth century.

imperial defence and commercial interest. Turkophiles seldom really cared for the Turks or Islam, except as a potential armed might to attack their imperial rival, Russia.

The Formalisation of Relations between the Ottoman Empire and Europe

As the treaty of Kutchuk Kainardji established the pattern of Russo-Turkish relations which persisted until 1914, so the treaty of Paris (30 March 1856) formalised relations between the Ottoman empire and the wider 'concert' of major European powers. Ottoman Turkey was, after 1856, on a par with the other powers; legally and diplomatically she entered a new category – something of greater importance than the clauses in the treaty about territorial sovereignty, demilitarisation and so forth. But since the nations of Europe were Christian, in the sense that the mass of their subjects adhered to a variety of the Christian creed, and since discrimination against Christians was an everyday fact of life in Ottoman Turkey (as Dr Humphry Sandwith and many others had observed), the European powers insisted that article 9 of the Paris treaty read, in the hypocritical terminology typical of diplomatic instruments:

His imperial majesty the sultan having, in his constant solicitude for the welfare of his subjects, issued a *firman* [decree], which while ameliorating their condition without distinction of religion or of race, records his generous intentions towards the Christian population of his empire, and wishing to give further proof of his sentiments in that respect, has resolved to communicate to the contracting powers the said *firman*, emanating spontaneously from his sovereign will.[18]

European governments realised that their subjects were apt to pay dangerously close attention to such matters as misgovernment, oppression and, in the case of some of them, lack of liberty, instead of concentrating on such matters as natural resources, market potential and strategic position, hence the need to persuade Ottoman Turkey to end her wide-ranging discrimination against non-Muslims. Ottoman Turkey for her part realised that she would lose the financial and military support of Britain and France if she continued to grind the faces of her non-Muslim subjects; so both parties agreed that reform, or words about reform, were necessary.

In the same manner, an earlier reform scheme had been proposed by the Ottoman foreign minister in 1839 in order to gain the support of Britain against Mehemed Ali. Neither this decree nor that of 1856 contained any measures for the enforcement of reform; and each time, after the foreigner's back was turned, almost all the measures were quietly dropped. In the provinces life continued as if they had never been.

Ottoman Finance

Nothing explains better why Britain and France were, in the second half of the nineteenth century, so harnessed to Ottoman Turkey, and why their attempts to make it reform were at best palliatives and at worst hypocrisy, than the nature of their financial involvement in the Ottoman empire. Until the Crimean war, Ottoman government 'if very bad, was also very cheap' (*The Times*).[19] Turkey possessed a 'barbarous state of finance' (*The Times* again).[20] If she had wanted to raise a loan, she had been able to do so internally, borrowing from the bankers (*sarrafs*) of Galata, most of whom were Armenians.* But by the 1850s larger loans were needed, specifically in 1854 to provide finance for the Crimean war. So a loan was floated on the European money markets for £3 million sterling, at 6 per cent. This was followed in the following year by another, for £5 million, at 4 per cent. The effective interest rate was often as high as 10 per cent,[21] and in the period 1863–73 12–13 per cent.[22] Thirteen more loans were raised until 1874, for the total of £191 million. Only 10 per cent of the total sum raised was used to increase the empire's economic strength; the rest was squandered.[23] To the mainly British and French investors the proposition was attractive: it offered (for the time) high rates of interest, and the investment was sanctioned by their governments. (The early loans were aimed at keeping the empire solvent during the Crimean war, and the later ones were in accordance with the governments' policy of upholding the empire.) Moreover the period was one of dynamic economic expansion for Europe, so that she was looking for outlets for her surplus capital; and it is possible, too, to see in the massive European investment in Turkey an intention to keep the Muslim empire backward and at the economic mercy of Europe. *The Times* commented on 20 February 1857:

> But our capitalists and men of enterprise have gone to Turkey because they see in it a country of great capability, where money and industry judiciously invested may bring large returns. ... The Turks have a fine territory and no money, energy or skill; we have all three, and they pour into Turkey as naturally as water finds its level.[24]

The Times understood the political .implications of what *prima facie* was a purely financial arrangement, pointing out that India was 'in the beginning conquered almost by private enterprise'.[25]

But money and industry were anything but judiciously invested. The Porte soon found it easier to negotiate new loans than to raise taxes. Confidence was shaken; so an 'Ottoman Bank' was founded in order to restore it, with a capital

---

*One should not overlook the point that the Armenian bankers in the capital were at this time devoid of any national spirit, and were themselves supporters of the extortions which the pashas used to inflict on the countryside.

almost entirely British and French. (The bank was about as Ottoman as a foreign embassy.) Still financial profligacy continued; Nassau Senior (1858) quotes a Constantinople banker saying, 'It is monstrous that the finances of a great empire should be ruined by the fantastic desires of a fool [Sultan Abdul Medjid] who, already having fifty palaces, wants fifty more.'[26]

In the same year *The Times*'s optimism had changed. On 15 September it wrote:

> We cannot but feel that the Turks have suddenly acquired a strange relish for this borrowing. But a few short years since they were as much strangers to the European money-market as the inhabitants of Timbuktoo. The faults of the Mussulman are apathy, sloth and self-indulgence and if there is one thing more than another likely to encourage these vices, it is the too easy grant of funds which other men are to repay.[27]

Of his own compatriots the anonymous writer added:

> As a people we are always building towers of Babel or washing blackamoors white in expectation of a dividend of 6 per cent. And the sight of the edifice in ruins, or the pack of savages as dusky and impudent as ever, does not prevent us from hailing the new prospectus with the same confidence as any of the old ones.[28]

The enthusiasm of the Porte for borrowing was only matched by that of Europe for lending; the financial profligacy of the one was only paced by the greed for quick profits of the other. By the mid-1860s the Porte was 'systematically living beyond its means, borrowing money everywhere to gratify its extravagances, and borrowing again to pay the interest of the loans already raised.'[29]

The crash came in the autumn of 1875: on 6 October Turkey defaulted on payment of interest. Immediately there were howls of anger in London and Paris (and at least some of the execration heaped upon Turkey in the following year over the Bulgarian atrocities can be traced to the sulky rage of thwarted investors). In its issue of January 1877 the *Edinburgh Review* pointed out that among the most clamorous

> there are those who are inflamed by the resentment of disappointed avarice, who lent their money by millions to support a government when it paid them 7 per cent, but who discover all its iniquities when the rate of interest is reduced to 3.[30]

The powers decided to seek settlement of the debt. They were held up by the Russo-Turkish war of 1877, and it was not until 20 October 1881 that the matter was resolved by the Decree of Muharram. (Muharram was the month in the Islamic calendar which corresponded to December in 1881.) The empire's indebtedness was reduced from £191 million to £106 million, and the Porte ceded 'absolutely and irrevocably . . . until the complete liquidation of the debt' certain revenues: the salt and tobacco monopolies; the stamp, spirits and fish taxes; the silk tithes in certain districts.[31] A 'Public Debt Administration' (PDA) was set up, with a board of seven men, six of whom were representatives of the European bondholders. Turkey was thereafter reduced to a state of economic vassalage; and when in 1905 the PDA came into conflict with the Porte, it only needed a naval demonstration to make the government acquiesce.

The Western powers' involvement in the finances of the Ottoman empire shows the hollowness of much of their rhetoric about 'reform'; for what was the Porte to make of powers which berated it for misbehaviour, and yet which baled out their own citizens when they had come unstuck in investing in it? Was not the whole point of reform not the condition of the subject peoples of the empire, but the rehabilitation of Turkish credit? It is noteworthy that in 1905, when the sultan's government was making meagre attempts to correct abuses in the tax-collecting system in Macedonia, it was opposed by the PDA, since the system proposed was less profitable.

Armenians in the Ottoman Empire

Before the emergence of the Armenian question as an international issue in 1878, the Armenian population of the empire was made up, broadly speaking, of four fairly distinct groups. There were the rich men in Constantinople or Smyrna, who sometimes had close ties with the Sublime Porte itself. This class was known as the *amiras*. At this stage they had little or no contact with their fellow nationals in Turkish Armenia, whom they described as *kavaragan*, or provincial. Secondly, there were the traders and artisans in the towns in the interior of the empire. It was this class that foreign travellers came into contact with most of all, and whom, with the haughty traveller's disdain for tradesmen, and admiration for warriors and horsemen, they were apt to despise, if not actively to detest. Sir Mark Sykes was the embodiment of such prejudices, according to the impressions that he has recorded in *The Caliphs' Last Heritage*, a source-book of pre-1914 snobbery in the Near East.[32] Thirdly, there were the villagers – the peasantry who made a precarious living out of the soil and from their flocks (and who had done so for at least two millennia past); these men were frequently heavily in debt to local Turks or Kurdish beys. The peasantry are seldom discussed by travellers (except perceptive ones like H. F. B. Lynch), but of all classes they were much the largest. There were many entirely Armenian villages on the plains of Erzerum and Moush; indeed, British consul Brant comments, in a report of one of his journeys (1 June 1839) that 'in the whole plain of Moush there are not any Mohammedan peasantry intermingled with the Armenians, a fact which would clearly point out this country as belonging to Armenia rather than to Kurdistan.'[33] Finally, there were the mountaineers – men who led a bold, semi-independent existence, untouched by the Ottoman empire and its tax-collectors. These included the inhabitants of Zeitun in Cilicia, and the inhabitants of the Sasun *caza*,* a confederation of about 40 Armenian villages. The mountaineers were a hardy breed, tough and independent of spirit. In Zeitun they were masters of their own affairs; the district has been described as a 'miniature Montenegro'. In Sasun, though paying tribute to local Kurdish beys (lords), they were able to live without the insidious humiliations of the plainsmen. In both places they were armed, manufacturing the weapons themselves. They were un-Ottomanised, and virtually untouched by the central government and its functionaries.[34]

By the nineteenth century, the Armenian population in Turkish Armenia had become heavily intermingled with Kurds and Turks. Even before Sultan Selim introduced the Kurds, and appointed them semi-autonomous dynasts, numbers of Turcoman tribes and settlers had appeared in Armenia – since indeed the Seljuk Turks had made their conquests in the eleventh century. Taking Turkish Armenia as a whole, the Armenians were outnumbered by the combined populations of Kurds and Turks; but it is unwise to put the latter two peoples together, since their outlooks and aspirations were often very different. (In 1849 the Porte crushed a serious Kurdish revolt led by Bedr Khan.) In some places, such as the province of Van, sources agree that the Armenians constituted a majority over the combined total of the other peoples.[35]

There were no reliable population statistics in the Ottoman empire, and so one has to rely on the estimates of travellers. M. A. Ubicini (1854) estimated the Armenian population throughout the Ottoman empire at 2,400,000 (almost certainly somewhat on the high side), and said that they constituted a majority in the Erzerum province (which included Kars, Bayazid and Childer), and in Kurdistan (which included Van, Moush, Hakkiari and Diyarbekir).[36] Even allowing for the emigration which continually went on into Russian Armenia, these estimates, especially of the majority in Kurdistan, are doubtful; though there were certainly some large areas with an Armenian majority. The Armenian patriarchate of Constantinople issued figures in 1882 which put the total Armenian population in the empire at 2,660,000, of whom 1,630,000 lived in the 'six *vilayets*' (provinces) of Turkish Armenia, that is, the provinces of Sivas, Mamuret el-Aziz, Erzerum, Diyarbekir, Bitlis and Van. Thirty years later the patriarchate produced further figures, which put the total Armenian

---

*Ottoman administrative divisions were as follows, with their approximate translations, beginning with the largest:

vilayet (province), governed by a *vali*
sanjak (district), governed by a *mutessarif*
caza (sub-district), governed by a *kaimakam*
nahiye (parish), governed by a *mudir*

population of the empire at 2,100,000, the reduction being due to massacre and the drift of the Armenians to Russian Armenia.[37] The 1912 figures also give statistics for Turks and Kurds in the same area: in percentage terms, these put the Turks at 25.5 per cent, the Kurds at 16.3 per cent, and the Armenians at 38.9 per cent.[38] (The remaining 19.3 per cent was made up of Assyrians, Greeks, Yezidis and so forth.) Even if these figures show partiality to Armenians, one can say with reasonable safety that for most of the nineteenth century the Armenians constituted about one-third of the total population of Turkish Armenia, and that in an area where all the peoples were minorities, they were the largest. (The adding together of the numbers for the Turks and the Kurds provides a phoney statistic, much used by Ismet Pasha at the Lausanne conference but of no significance beyond propaganda.)

Relations between Armenians and their Turkish and Kurdish Muslim neighbours differed in each locality, and there seems to have been no general pattern beyond the inferior position of Armenians. All the towns and many of the villages were mixed Muslim/Christian. Each community lived in its distinct quarter. The picture of life in and around Moush (to take one example) in the 1860s is of a Muslim ruling class and an Armenian merchant and entrepreneurial class. Armenians also, according to consul Taylor:

> form the principal portion of the industrious inhabitants in the plain and near the city, supplying all agricultural labour and trade, while the Muslims, mostly pastoral, living on the slopes of the hills bordering the plain, occupy themselves simply with their flocks.[39]

Muslims were found at the top and bottom places of the social scale, with Armenians precariously (because they were unarmed) in the middle. But merely because they were located in the middle, it would be wrong to see them as the economic masters of the land. Speaking of the Van district in the same report, consul Taylor points out that the *Kurds* were the monied class, 'the usurers of the country'.[40] They demanded an interest rate from their Christian debtors of between 3 and 4 per cent per month. Taylor comments, 'There is hardly one Christian not indebted to them for sums it will be impossible for him to pay without sacrificing his all.'[41]

National feeling, in the sense of an awareness of a unity of interest, barely existed among Armenians throughout the empire until the third quarter of the nineteenth century. Thus, the Armenians of Constantinople were involved in struggles from 1830 to 1860 which were in no way related to the oppression of the villagers in the eastern provinces. (The condition of the peasantry in the east was virtually forgotten in the capital until the election to the patriarchate in 1869 of Mëkërtich Khrimian, a leading educator and deep lover of his people; see below, pp. 102–4.) And when, in the 1890s, the sultan was organising massacres of Armenians in the east, and was being accused of doing so by the

European ambassadors, he could plead his friendship with leading Constantinople Armenians.

Despite the fact that government in imperial Turkey worked against Armenians, whether from the central policies of the sultan, the traditional oppressions of the pashas or the bully-boy extortions of the tax-gatherer, the Armenian people themselves made notable contributions to the public life of the empire.

In the provinces, Armenians filled significant if lowly positions in the administration. Typical posts held by them were those of inspector of forestry, municipal engineer, provincial translator, and assistant to the deputy governor. When the telegraph was introduced, one frequently found an Armenian managing it. With the spread of elementary health care, Armenians often appeared as doctors and pharmacists. They were present in almost any venture which brought progress and improvement.[42]

But it was in the imperial capital that Armenians of the *amira* class distinguished themselves in a wide variety of activities, some of considerable importance in the running of the empire. From 1757 to 1880, with the exception of a thirteen-year gap, the Armenian family of Duzian (or Duzoglu) held the position of superintendent of the Ottoman mint. They dominated the office so completely that the records were kept in Armenian. Most of their employees were Armenian, too. The few factories which were established in the Ottoman empire before the Crimean war were almost all funded by Armenian capital; and in many cases the factory managers were Armenian. The leading family in this sector was that of Dadian. In 1795 Arakel Dadian was appointed manager of the gunpowder factory at San Stefano; his son Hovhannes became director of the imperial paper mill in 1820, and later established the imperial silk mill at Hereke and an iron smelting foundry at San Stefano. He was also an innovator in small-arms manufacture. Further enterprise was shown by him in establishing a tannery and two broadcloth factories, to mention but a few; a list of all his interests would be lengthy. Another Armenian family, that of Kavafian, built and managed a shipyard in Constantinople.[43]

Armenians did not, however, only hold positions requiring capital and commercial enterprise. Many were organised into trade guilds, or *esnafs*. At this end of the scale, the stevedores (*hamals*), of whom there were scores in Constantinople, men who used to carry enormous quantities of goods on their backs, were until 1896 almost invariably Armenians.

In a quite different sphere, that of culture, Armenians were also prominent in the nineteenth-century Ottoman capital, and their activities showed the way Turko-Armenian relations might have developed had they not been strangled by despotism and ideology. Armenians shone in two fields, those of architecture and the theatre. As the Duzians dominated the mint and the Dadians factory management, so the Balian family dominated Ottoman architecture.[44] The father of this dynasty, and the most distinguished member of it, was Krikor Balian (1764–1831), who was accorded the title 'architect of the empire'. His most important building is probably the Nusretiye mosque – graceful, elegant and stylish. Situated in the Top-khana district of the capital, it was ordered by Sultan Mahmud II to celebrate the 'auspicious event' of the destruction of the Janissaries in 1826. Krikor's son Garabed (1800–86) built the immense and ornate palace at Dolmabahche (1853), as well as one of the factories managed by the Dadians. Other sons of Krikor, Nigoghos and Sarkis, built the Chiragan palace (1874, now destroyed), amongst other imperial and public edifices. Members of the family also built the smaller and lighter Beylerbey palace, on the Asiatic side of the Bosphorus. Their taste in the later decades may have been questionable – Mr Michael Levey describes the style of the Dolmabahche palace as 'Hollywood-Oriental'[45] – but of their loyalty and service both to the private whims of the sultan and to the expansion and development of the capital there can be no doubt.

The Turkish theatre was founded by an Armenian, one Hagop Vartovian, known to the Turks as 'Güllü Agop'.[46] His company, based at Gedikpasha, lasted from 1868 to 1882, critical years in the development of Ottoman political thought. Vartovian was a dedicated man of the theatre, inasmuch as he put on anything good that came his way; and it happened that, besides the adaptations of traditional romances and of light European novels that he put on, important and significant plays – landmarks in Turkish political awareness – figured among his productions. The most notable of these was Namik Kemal's *Vatan yahut Silistre* (Fatherland or Silistria; 1873), a historical play based on an episode in the Crimean war, imbued with Ottoman patriotism, and received with such enthusiasm that the government sent the author into provincial exile.[47]

Vartovian's theatre not only developed the political consciousness of the elite; from his activities there evolved the beginnings of a new Turkish language, at once popular and literary, which began to bridge the gap between the ornate official language and the vernacular of the man in the street. (Language reform is a matter which has concerned the Turks to this day, and Turkish scholars are beginning to evaluate the contribution of Vartovian's theatre.)

The Gedikpasha venture also quite naturally led to the creation of a theatre-going public, which included Muslim women, and to establishing a tradition of stage-craft. When under Abdul Hamid the political climate forced the theatre to close, and the atmosphere became stifling and repressive, a number of the company went to Transcaucasia; there they strengthened the Tiflis Armenian theatre, which survives to this day, now named after Stepan Shahumian.

Confronted by a resurgence of intractable Ottoman despotism, echoing round the cold stones of the Seven Towers, theatrical and other manifestations of the beginnings of cultural freedom, of creation and of diversity, withered like flowers in the desert wind. Armenians had competently and unselfconsciously contributed to the development of the empire, and especially of the Ottoman capital; as we shall see, they received their recompense in the days following 26 August 1896.

Internal Armenian Conflicts in Constantinople

In the brief period when political development seemed possible within the Ottoman empire, Armenians in the capital took the chance to organise their own internal affairs. The community passed through bitter strife until its conflicts were resolved. The issues related entirely to the community in the capital; there was nothing specifically Armenian about them, in the sense of pertaining to the land of Armenia.

The growing wealth and prestige of the *amira* families – the Duzians, Dadians and others – led to their acquiring almost dictatorial powers within the community, and, most significantly, being able to control the patriarchate. Against them a movement developed made up partly of young men educated abroad (especially in Paris or Venice), who had become imbued with democratic ideas, and partly of members of the trade guilds, or *esnafs*. The struggle centred around control of the Armenian college in Scutari, on the Asiatic side of the Bosphorus. From 1838, when the *esnafs* first tried to gain control of this institution, they sought to weaken the power of the *amira* oligarchy. Their opponents were very reluctant to relinquish their power, and used every ruse to maintain it.[48]

At the heart of the problem was the position of the patriarch himself: he was answerable to no one except the sultan; and whoever controlled the patriarch controlled the whole community. Hence the need came to be recognised for a written regulation of his election. Two drafts of such a document were drawn up in 1857 and 1859, but rejected by the *amiras* as too liberal. A third draft, considerably more restrictive, received the approval of all classes of Armenian society in the capital in 1860, and was ratified by the Porte three years later.[49]

The Armenian National Constitution is a liberal document. Its 99 articles are imbued with the principles of rights and duties. After its promulgation the internecine strife in Constantinople ceased. But it had absolutely no relevance to the condition of Armenians outside Constantinople; to this extent it was a very inward-looking document. To take one example: articles 57 to 62 provide for the establishment of the General Assembly of the community, its supreme legislature. It was composed of 140 members, made up as follows:

Ecclesiastics elected by the clergy of Constantinople	20
Lay members from the capital and its suburbs	80
Lay members from the provinces	40

But even if the Armenian National Constitution had paid more attention to the entire community, it is doubtful if it could have benefited the Armenians as a whole, and saved them from the disasters that were to come. For it took no account of the special conditions of the Ottoman empire – that the empire, being itself an autocracy without a comparable constitution, could lurch from an era of mild reformism to one of rigid reaction with the death of a sultan or his grand vizier. The Armenian National Constitution was based on the assumption that the era of Ottoman 'reform' (the *tanzimat*) would continue. When it ended in 1871 the bottom fell out of the Constitution; and against the new, profound and darkly sinister reaction and racism that the empire began to exhibit, the Constitution offered no protection at all. Thereafter it preserved the Armenian community in Constantinople from further disorder, but did nothing for the much more serious oppression of the Armenians in the provinces. Which, given its virtual ignoring of the *kavaragan* agricultural peasantry, is not in any way surprising.

Zeitun

In Constantinople the Armenians attempted to work out a political future for themselves within the Ottoman framework. But 500 kilometres away, in Cilicia, another relationship was emerging between government and subjects. Zeitun (which cannot be found on the map today) was a town hidden among high mountains, the chief of which, Astvadzashen ('established by God') is perpetually snow-capped.[50] The town could only be reached with difficulty along narrow defiles. The population of the town was almost exclusively Armenian and had been so for hundreds of years. A number of the surrounding villages were Armenian too; others were Turkish. It was seldom visited by foreigners – indeed, they were not welcome in this fortress town. But the French scholar Victor Langlois was able to visit it in 1862, and describes its setting thus:

> But when one pierces the mountainous region that girdles the plain of Tarsus and Adana like an impenetrable defensive wall, a rapid transformation takes place: the desert ends, grass grows, trees stretch forth their densely covered branches to the sky, and rocks disappear beneath a gracious mantle of turf and flowers. Nature, hitherto pale and wan, springs to life and decks herself out; the landscape appears all in magic splendour. A burning clear sky reddens the glaciers of the great peaks with blood-red streaks; torrents, rushing down, roar in the abysses, and from their spray silvery vapours escape, that dissolve at the breath of a breeze. Here and there one notices villages, and *yaila* or hamlets suspended like eagles' nests at the sides of the rocks, well-cultivated fields, vines bending beneath the weight of their grapes, goats and sheep wandering in their pastures, and mountaineers, at one and the same time shepherds and warriors, keeping an eye on harvest and herds. Such is the unexpected spectacle that unfolds before the eyes of a traveller.[51]

It is perhaps only fair to add that when British consul Chermside visited the town in 1879 he described it as 'the most unsuitable looking town I have seen in Turkey', commenting that at that time 'destitution, squalor and abject misery are its principal characteristics.'

Although foreigners knew little or nothing of Zeitun, Armenians never forgot it, and for many it was the symbol of something that had endured. Gifts used to be sent there, as to Echmiadzin or Jerusalem. The town itself was divided into four districts, each of which was ruled by a baron, whose main preoccupation seems to have been intriguing against the other three.

It is uncertain how the Zeituntzis arrived in their town. According to some, they fled there after the fall of the Bagratid monarchy in the eleventh century; others say they were the last of the Cilician Rupenids, who escaped there from the Mamluk onslaught in the late fourteenth century. Whatever its origins, Zeitun constituted a genuine survival of medieval Armenia. The people were proud, and independent of spirit; possession of arms meant that their spirit had never been crushed. They had used their arms to assist the Ottomans to assert their paramountcy over local Turkomen dynasts.[52] In return for a fixed annual tribute, the semi-independence of Zeitun had been assured by a decree of Sultan Murad IV dating back to 1618.[53] With the decline of Ottoman power, and the formalisation of tyranny, the spirit of the Zeitun mountaineers remained alert. The government launched a number of expeditions against the town, but these were unsuccessful. The warrior spirit of its armed inhabitants, and its fortress-like setting, made Zeitun a natural focus for the attention of a nationalist or revolutionary, who had seen the success of the revolts in Greece and Serbia. Perhaps a similar success could be gained in Cilicia.

An Armenian activist from Constantinople, Melikian Ardzruni Hovakim, visited Zeitun in 1853, and strengthened the town's defences. It is possible that he was preparing the town for some sort of uprising, especially in view of the fact that he was caught by the Ottoman authorities on his way to Russian Armenia the following year (during the Crimean war), and hanged as a spy at Erzerum.

In the succeeding years the people of Zeitun showed a militant spirit towards the government: they challenged it when it seized some of their lands to settle Tatars from Russia, and they refused to pay the higher taxes that were demanded. In 1860 the governor of nearby Marash despatched an armed force to demand the higher taxes; to his consternation, it was forced to beat an ignoble retreat. Turkish soldiery was no match for the braves of Zeitun.

In 1860–1 the Russian Armenian revolutionary thinker Mikayel Nalbandian was in Constantinople. His presence there was probably connected, in part, to preparing the groundwork for an insurrection in Zeitun.[54] While there he made contact with members of an organisation known as the Benevolent Union, which was, as its name implies, a charitable body, but also numbered revolutionary thinkers among its members. In early 1862 coded messages were exchanged between members of the Benevolent Union in Constantinople and Nalbandian in St Petersburg; one spoke of 'textbooks' to be delivered to a priest in Zeitun – perhaps a code-word for weapons and ammunition.[55]

In July 1862 there was a small incident – a local dispute – which served as a pretext for Aziz Pasha, governor of Marash, to send a punitive expedition against the Zeituntzis. In early August the army moved against Zeitun, beginning by surrounding the entire district; more than 10,000 men were moved up, and two cannon. One or two outlying villages submitted. But the actions of the Turkish forces followed an old pattern, and one often to be repeated: they looted and burnt houses and churches, and raped any attractive girls. The behaviour of the Turkish forces, which was always a more powerful stimulus to defiance than the words of activists, had the expected effect, and the Zeituntzis mobilised and took up defensive positions.

Battle was soon joined; and despite (or perhaps because of) the superior numbers of Aziz Pasha's forces, the confused Turkish soldiery soon fled in disarray. A second assault, from a nearby monastery which overlooked Zeitun, failed when the commander saw his shells fall short; he thereupon ordered a withdrawal to Marash.[56]

When news of the incident reached the capital, the Porte dismissed Aziz. Zeitun for its part sent out emissaries to state its case.[57] The four 'barons' and a priest went to Constantinople. Seeking foreign protection, a second delegation presented its case to Napoleon III in Paris.

It seems that in the subsequent discussion this delegation went somewhat beyond its mandate, offering union of the Armenian and Roman churches, in order to interest the prince-emperor in a form of protection for Cilicia similar to the autonomy which France had sponsored for Lebanon in 1861. But France was not really interested, and all that she did was to persuade Sultan Abdul Aziz to call the army away from Zeitun, and to issue a decree, which acknowledged certain freedoms for the Zeituntzis but limited others: law enforcement and justice would continue to be administered locally, and tax-collecting would be regularised. Thus there would be no more battles with the tax-collector – but with them would go some of Zeitun's prized sense of independence. Ottoman government was moving in. It was to move in more decisively in 1878, when a Turkish garrison was introduced into the town.

The pattern of the Zeitun rebellion was exceptional, because the inhabitants were conscious of their ancient privileges, which they were determined at all costs to uphold. They were exceptionally aware of Ottoman land theft and illegality; despite their internal feuds, their social cohesion was sufficient to make them defy the government, where others would have submitted. Their actions were to be increasingly copied. Government grew ever more corrupt and violent, and it needed only a few leaders to awaken a sense of defiance in the people; to persuade them to defend themselves, and not to submit to official assaults.

Van and Khrimian Hairik

At about the same time as the Zeitun battle there were small uprisings of Armenians in Van (in the spring of 1862) and in Moush (1863), but neither made as much impression as Zeitun. In the decade following, the new relationship of governed to government was developed. Societies were established dedicated to resisting the lawlessness and terror in the east, and to thwarting the 'birds of prey', as the Ottoman officials were known.[58] In March 1872 an organisation known as the Union of Salvation was formed at Van. In an introductory statement, one of its founders declared:

> Gone is our honour; our churches have been violated; they have kidnapped our brides and youth; they take away our rights and try to exterminate our nation ... let us try to find a way of salvation ... if not, we will lose everything.[59]

The ancient town of Van, set amid an incomparably beautiful landscape of lake, mountains and fertile plains, was the native city of a man who laboured more than anyone else to change the relationship – Khrimian Hairik. His achievements were twin: he broke down the barriers between the different classes of Armenians, especially that between the Constantinople Armenians and the men of the provinces; and with his unswerving devotion to his people he criticised the government relentlessly for its lethargy, corruption, injustice and violence. Mëkërtich Khrimian was born in 1820, of well-to-do parents. When he was 21 he visited Echmiadzin and Ararat; and four years later he married. But his wife died in childbirth, and his daughter a few years afterwards. He travelled to Constantinople and became a teacher, making further journeys to Palestine and Cilicia. He entered the priesthood in 1854, and the following year began publication (in the capital) of *Ardzvi Vaspurakan* (*Eagle of Vaspurakan*, that is, the province of Van), a pioneering journal which made a deep impact upon young Armenian writers. In 1858 the press moved to the monastery of Varak, near Van – an unprecendented move towards the people themselves. A sister journal, concerned with the region of Moush, was started up. Khrimian was elected patriarch of Constantinople in 1869, but was compelled by the government to resign four years later; it saw him awakening and strengthening the community, and was alarmed.[60]

While he was patriarch he started publishing details of the conditions of Armenians in the east (1871–6).[61] The evidence was collected by sending out a circular to Armenian bishops throughout the empire, in which they were asked to explain the problems of the people, and to suggest remedies. The oppressions of the people fell under four main headings: those caused by unjust and exorbitant taxation, by the actions of corrupt officials, by non-acceptance of Christian testimony in the *sharia* courts (the *mehkëmë*), and by the depradations of the nomadic Kurds.[62] Simple remedies were suggested: in the field of taxation, direct collection was proposed, since at the time barely 50 per cent of the taxes collected by the *multazims* (tax-farmers) reached the treasury. On local corruption, the committee of 1871 noted[63]

> The majority of officials being devoid of all knowledge of the laws and administrative science, themselves commit breaches of the law. .... They

profit by the ignorance of the inhabitants or connivance of the *chorbadjis* (Christian notables) to grind and oppress the people.

Thorough, cleansing reforms were needed. On the non-acceptance of Christian testimony there was a straightforward remedy:[64] 'Civil, commercial and criminal cases should come within the jurisdiction of the civil courts (*nizamiye*) instead of being tried by the *sharia* courts.'

Nevertheless, despite the efforts of Archbishop Khrimian, Armenian thinking in the Ottoman empire was still undeveloped by the time of the 'eastern crisis' of 1875–8. The groundwork for the establishment of political societies, and for resistance to the exactions of the Kurds and the government, had been made; yet with the exception of the Zeitun battle and the isolated instances in the east, there had been no armed encounters with the forces of the empire, as there had been in the Balkans. No nationalist spirit had developed throughout the Armenian community, to forge the people into a unity. The Armenians remained unwarlike; and so when the powers made their dispensation for the empire and its peoples, the pacific Armenians were almost completely overlooked, even though the treaty of Paris had referred without distinction to all Christian peoples of the empire. The powers were to confer liberty only on those in the Balkans, who raised the standard of armed revolt.

British Attitudes

Although no British army took to the field during the mid-1870s, Britain was without question one of the main contestants in the crisis. Her immense imperial power, and profound antagonism to Russia, meant that the conflicts were her conflicts too. This was especially true since the Conservatives governed; Disraeli had been returned to power in February 1874.

Three things made the Conservatives favour the Turks. All concerned prestige or money. The first and much the most important was imperial jealousy of Russia, and fear that she would either make a direct attack upon India, or impede Britain's communications with her possession. Secondly, there was the large British investment in Ottoman bonds, which, should Turkey be diminished or disappear, would go the same way too. Thirdly, there was the commercial value of the trade route which linked Trebizond with Tabriz via Erzerum and Bayazid. This route was the most important overland trade route to India; and it brought trade to Turkey (and hence to Britain) too. The journalist and pamphleteer Lucien Wolf gave the figure of £8,000,000 as the trade of Trebizond, £5,000,000 of which represented the imports, most of which went onwards through Erzerum.[65] (Wolf also quoted the figure of £2,000,000 as representing the proportion of British-made imports at Erzerum.) He describes the caravan routes as 'the only practicable road from the north into Central Asia which is not under Russian control'. This trade route, through the heartland of Armenia, was to figure in later negotiations.

With the Conservatives in power, the Ottoman government was assured of support by the one power whose Near Eastern policies were of supreme practical importance throughout this critical period for her – a period which also saw the emergence of the Armenian question as an international issue.

As Lord Stratford had been the most ardent supporter of the Turko–British alliance against Russia while he was British ambassador at Constantinople during the Crimean war, so, at this time, two British ambassadors articulated most clearly the reasons seen by the Conservatives for the continued British support of Turkey. Sir Henry Elliot wrote from Constantinople on 4 September 1876, in the turbulent period following the Ottoman government's proven implication in the Bulgarian atrocities:

To the accusation of being a blind partisan of the Turks, I will only answer that my conduct here has never been guided by any sentimental affection for them, but by a firm determination to uphold the interests of Great Britain to the utmost of my power; and that those interests are deeply engaged in preventing the disruption of the Turkish empire is a conviction which I share in common with the most eminent statesmen who have directed our foreign policy, but which now appears to be abandoned by shallow politicians or persons who have allowed their feelings of revolted humanity to make them forget the capital interests involved in the question. We may and we must feel indignant at the needless and monstrous severity with which the Bulgarian insurrection was put down, but the necessity which exists for England to prevent changes from occurring here which would be most detrimental to ourselves, is not affected by the question whether it was 10,000 or 20,000 persons who perished in the suppression. We have been upholding what we know to be a semi-civilised nation, liable under certain circumstances to be carried to fearful excesses: but the fact of this having just now been strikingly brought home to us all cannot be a sufficient reason for abandoning a policy which is the only one that can be followed with due regard to our own interests.[66]

Sixteen months later Sir Henry Layard wrote (2 January 1878):

It is the most monstrous piece of folly that we should be ready to sacrifice the most vital interests of our country, India, our position as a first-class power, the influence that we have hitherto exercised in the cause of human liberty and civilisation, rather than stand shoulder to shoulder with the Turks, because some bashibozuks [irregulars] have murdered some worthless and unfortunate Bulgarians.[67]

But the man whose policies and utterances showed the most cynical support for the Ottoman government – although he would never express himself with the vulgar forthrightness of Elliot or Layard – was Benjamin Disraeli, prime minister throughout the period of the crisis. Ottoman Turkey was for him a flight of steps to the garish triumphal arch which was his vision of imperial grandeur. Goaded by Queen Victoria, who translated her fears for her position in the east (she was created Empress of India in April 1876) into an unwavering devotion for the government in Constantinople, he brought Britain to the brink of war with Russia. He sought to re-impose the despotism of the sultan on the peoples of the Balkans when it had been cast off; and in Armenia his policies inspired the creation of a political structure from which we can trace the massacres of 1895–6, and the holocaust of 1915.

The Liberals who opposed the crude imperialism of the Conservatives spoke a different language. Led by Gladstone, they sought to make moral values the starting-point of policy – something that was incomprehensible to their opponents, and indeed to themselves, when they were returned to power in 1880. Gladstone specifically held that Britain had undertaken certain responsibilities for the nature of Ottoman rule by her close association with Ottoman reform at the end of the Crimean war, and that support for Turkey right or wrong was to negate those responsibilities. Needless to say, the idea of having to uphold any such responsibilities was laughable to the Conservatives.

The Eastern Crisis

In the summer of 1875 the Christian peasantry of Bosnia and Herzegovina rose in revolt against their Muslim landlords. The revolt dragged on until the winter; the Porte appeared unable to control it. On 30 December 1875 Count Andrássy, Austro-Hungarian minister of foreign affairs, proposed in a note a fair system of government for the rebellious provinces, whereby a just solution could be found for the peasants' grievances.[68] All the great powers agreed to align themselves behind Andrássy except Britain which demurred, and, although eventually agreeing to Andrássy's proposals, made no attempt to persuade the Ottoman government to accept them.[69]

The note, like many other reform schemes forced on Ottoman Turkey and accepted by the Porte, had no practical result. Indeed the situation grew worse; consequently Andrássy and his Russian opposite number, the elderly Prince Gorchakov, met in Berlin and devised a memorandum which was along the same lines as the Andrássy note, but stronger.[70] It was accepted at once by France and Italy, but this time entirely rejected by Britain. Disraeli, in a phrase of silly hysteria, complained that the northern powers of Russia, Austria and Germany were 'asking us to sanction them in putting a knife to the throat of Turkey, whether we like it or not'.[71]

The crisis intensified. There was a rising in Bulgaria in April 1876, which was cruelly put down by Ottoman irregulars, despatched on orders from Constantinople. Queen Victoria, apparently troubled by qualms of conscience, wrote of this incident:

Hearing as we *do* all the undercurrent, and knowing as we do that Russia *instigated* this insurrection which caused the cruelty of the Turks, it *ought* to be brought home to Russia, and the world *ought* to know that on *their* shoulders and *not* on *ours* rests the *blood* of the murdered Bulgarians![72]

In fact the rebellion had been organised by Bulgarian *émigrés*. In its suppression about sixty villages were destroyed and 12,000 to 15,000 massacred – men, women and children, old and young. In one notorious incident 1,200 people had gathered in a church for protection, and had been burnt alive there.[73]

Immense anti-Turkish agitation followed the publication of the facts of the atrocities (which Disraeli insisted on terming 'so-called atrocities'). The indignation would not die down, even though Disraeli tried to dismiss it as mere 'coffee-house babble'. Best remembered today of the expressions of revulsion for what the Turks had done in Bulgaria is Gladstone's pamphlet *The Bulgarian Horrors and the Question of the East*, which called for the Turkish government to carry itself off *bag and baggage*. It did not appear until September 1876, after the publication of a British Embassy report[74] had persuaded Gladstone that the allegations were true. The pamphlet sold 200,000 copies in a month.

The power of popular agitation over the Ottoman government's repression of the Bulgarian uprising was by the late summer of 1876 such as to persuade Disraeli that a conference was needed to discuss the ills of the Ottoman empire. These at this time were manifold: Serbia had declared war on Turkey in June, and Montenegro had joined her in early July.[75] Constantinople was in a state of political turmoil: earlier in the year the grand vizier and Sheikh ul-Islam (the supreme religious dignitary in the empire) had been driven from office; then Sultan Abdul Aziz himself was deposed (30 May). Two weeks later both the foreign and war ministers were murdered. At the end of August the new sultan, Murad, who had turned out to be feeble-minded, was deposed, and his half-brother, Abdul Hamid, was invested as sultan. 'Will he be a Solyman the Great?'[76] asked Disraeli of the man whose paranoia and cowardice were to be the main distinguishing feature of Near Eastern politics for the next thirty years.

So Disraeli decided 'there must be a conference, tho' I hate it', adding 'I am quite confident we cd. have managed without it, had it not been for this Bulgarian bogey.'[77] Lord Salisbury was to be British delegate. The conference eventually met in December 1876 in Constantinople. Its agenda was wholly concerned with the administration of European Turkey;[78] Armenia had not yet come under the scrutiny of the powers.

Then – the Turkish master-stroke: during the conference, on 23 December, the guns boomed out, and the Ottoman constitution was proclaimed, a liberal and democratic instrument.[79] The conference was now redundant, the presence of the powers superfluous: here was the easy way out that Disraeli and his ambassador, Elliot, had hoped for. The administrative reforms that the powers were seeking to impose on the Ottoman empire were now, apparently, being created by her own political institutions. The powers were disunited; even the British disagreed amongst themselves. Salisbury requested that the British fleet be sent to Constantinople to compel the sultan to introduce reforms; Disraeli refused.[80]

The conference broke up in disarray in late January 1877. Nothing had been achieved; and the Ottoman constitution, wheeled in at a critical moment, like a gigantic piece of stage scenery (depicting, perhaps, contented sunlit villages, fertile valleys) was wheeled out some months later, and the familiar Ottoman provincial backdrop was visible again, of local tyranny, extortion, oppression, wrecked homes, burnt fields, homeless refugees.

The lesson of the Constantinople conference (which none of the powers drew) was that the Ottoman empire was still a sovereign power. However much Europe, through her capitulations, her 'spheres of influence' and her financial involvement might think she controlled Turkey, the Ottoman government could still over-trump the powers with her own laws and 'assurances', especially if a power such as Britain were only to make a show of insistence. Whether or not Turkey's laws were sham was at this stage irrelevant; all she had to do was to convince the powers until they departed. Once the foreigners had gone, the laws could be quietly dropped. The powers were enormously reluctant to draw the conclusion before their eyes about Ottoman Turkey: that the only way to reform the administration of a Turkish territory was to detach it from the sovereignty of Turkey. They would not see this, since they needed a large Turkey to contain their own jealous rivalries, and to produce as large a return on their investments as possible. The method that they chose, of trying to impose schemes of reform, was the worst possible, since it achieved nothing, and only left the wretched subject peoples more resented and hated by both central and provincial Ottoman rulers.

Only one power was prepared to abandon vacuous diplomacy for action.

The Russo–Turkish War of 1877–8

Our faithful and beloved subjects know the lively interest which we have always devoted to the destinies of the oppressed Christian population of Turkey. ... We made it pre-eminently our object to attain the amelioration of the condition of the Christians in the east by means of peaceful negotiations and concerted action with the great European powers, our allies and friends. During two years we have made incessant efforts to induce the Porte to adopt such reforms as would protect the Christians of Bosnia, Herzegovina and Bulgaria from the arbitrary rule of the local authorities. The execution of these reforms followed, as a direct obligation, from the anterior engagements solemnly contracted by the Porte in the sight of all

Europe. Our efforts, although supported by the joint diplomatic representations of the other governments, have not attained the desired end. The Porte has remained immovable in its categorical refusal of every effectual guarantee for the security of its Christian subjects, and it rejected the demands of the conference of Constantinople. . . . Having exhausted our peaceful efforts, we are obliged by the haughty obstinacy of the Porte to proceed to more determined action. The sentiment of equity and that of our own dignity render it imperative. Turkey, by its refusal, places us under the necessity of having recourse to arms. . . . We expressed our intention of acting independently should we deem it necessary, and should the honour of Russia require it. Today, in invoking the blessing of God upon our valiant armies, we give them the order to cross the frontier of Turkey.[81]

With these words Alexander II, the tsar-liberator, declared war on the Ottoman empire on 24 April 1877. All the Slav peoples looked to Russia for deliverance from Turkey. But among the Armenians there was not the same unanimity. Some genuinely feared that if they were annexed by Russia they` would be swallowed by Orthodoxy, despite the statutes by which the Russians regulated the affairs of the Armenian Church. On the outbreak of the war, the Armenian patriarch Nerses Varzhabedian issued a pastoral letter calling on his flock to show loyalty to the Ottoman state, and to work and pray for an Ottoman victory.[82] However, there is little doubt that in the east, at peasant level, the vast majority of the Armenian villagers wanted an end of the corrupt tyranny which ruled them. Arminius Vambéry, no lover of the Armenians, made his first journey east in 1862; stopping at a village near Diadin (a few kilometres west of Bayazid) he saw how downtrodden the Armenians were. On asking them

why they did not ask assistance of the governor of Erzerum, [I] was told in reply, 'that the governor himself was at the head of the thieves. God alone, and his representative on earth, the Russian tsar, can help us'. And the poor people were certainly right in this.[83]

The war was disastrous for Turkey. In Europe Russian forces reached the outskirts of Constantinople, and in Asia they reached Erzerum. Many observers believed that the Ottoman empire was on the point of collapse. Liberals wondered whether Britain was again going to be forced to shore up an antiquated despotism for dubious strategic and financial returns. They sought co-operation with Russia in bringing about an eastern solution.

This, however, was the last thing that Disraeli and the Queen intended. Some of Disraeli's utterances bring to mind Trajan campaigning in Asia, driven by a mad passion for glory and prestige. 'The Empress of India should order her armies to clear Central Asia of the Muscovites, and drive them into the Caspian,' he wrote to his sovereign on 22 July 1877.[84] Three weeks later, at a

Cabinet meeting, he observed that a British force could be sent to Batum, 'march without difficulty through Armenia, and menace the Asiatic possessions of Russia'.[85] It was clear that he would envisage no solution with Russia other than one based on maximum confrontation.

He did, however, stop short of actually declaring war on Russia, thereby saving Britain from a fruitless replay of the Crimean war; though more than once he hinted to Turkey that there might be British help against Russia. Other than sending the fleet through the Dardanelles in January 1878 – and promptly having it ordered out again by the sultan, to the amusement of the statesmen of Europe – British support for Turkey was merely verbal and diplomatic.

The Armenians at the Close of the War

After the fall of Plevna (Bulgaria) on 11 December 1877, Russian troops advanced onward to the Ottoman capital; only an armistice, agreed on 27 January 1878 and signed on the 31st, halted them at Adrianople (Edirne). On the same day the 'preliminary bases of peace' between the parties were signed.[86] Bulgaria was to be autonomous, Montenegro, Romania and Serbia independent, and Bosnia and Herzegovina were to receive autonomous administrations. But there was no mention of Armenia, since the Armenians had not yet made any requests known.

The Armenian leadership resolved to change this. Although they had been loyal to the Porte at the start of the war – a position which had served their own interests – circumstances had changed this. The principal factor was the behaviour of the Kurdish irregular cavalry, which was in the pay of the Turkish regular forces commanded by Ahmed Mukhtar Pasha. C. B. Norman, special correspondent for *The Times*, wrote on 26 July 1877 that between his camp at Sabatan and Köprüköy (respectively 25 kilometres east and 40 kilometres west of Kars),

> I have not seen one Christian village which has not been abandoned in consequence of the cruelties committed on the inhabitants. All have been ransacked, many burnt, upwards of 5,000 Christians in the Van district have fled to Russian territory, and women and children are wandering about naked.[87]

In other words the Kurds, far from aiding the Ottoman war effort, had gone on the rampage, looting and murdering Armenian villagers. (The incidental consequence for the Ottoman army was near starvation, since many of the Armenians' flocks and herds, as well as their stores of grain, were pillaged.)

When these actions became known to the Armenian leaders in Constantinople – they were the subject of a debate in the Ottoman parliament just before it was disbanded by the sultan – attitudes shifted.[88] The Turkish government had permitted the destruction of numerous Armenian villages in the east; and the Turkish army was being defeated by the Russians. Hence the Armenian National Assembly authorised the patriarch to send a delegation to the Grand Duke Nicolas, at his headquarters in Adrianople. There, through the energetic mediation of Count Ignatyev, the leading pan-Slavist who was Russian ambassador to Constantinople, a clause was drawn up for inclusion in the forthcoming peace treaty, which read:

> For the purpose of preventing oppressions and atrocities that have taken place in Turkey's European and Asiatic provinces, the sultan guarantees, in agreement with the tsar, to grant administrative local self-government to the provinces inhabited by Armenians.[89]

San Stefano and its Aftermath

But Ottoman Turkey refused to countenance local self-government. Throughout February 1878 great-power tension was at its height, and the likelihood of an Anglo–Russian clash of arms most acute. Turkey, although defeated in the war, could afford to say what was or was not acceptable; and to the Russians the matter was not sufficiently important for them to push it at all costs. A visit by the Armenian patriarch himself failed to convince the Russians of the need to insist on local self-government. Ultimately, Russia and Turkey agreed on the wording of the article. In the peace treaty, signed at San Stefano (the modern Yeshilköy, site of Istanbul's international airport) on 3 March 1878, article 16 reads:

> As the evacuation by the Russian troops of the territory which they occupy in Armenia, and which is to be restored to Turkey, might give rise to conflicts and complications detrimental to the maintenance of good relations between the two countries, the Sublime Porte engages to carry into effect, without further delay, the improvements and reforms demanded by local requirements in the provinces inhabited by Armenians, and to guarantee their security from Kurds and Circassians.[90]

Russian territorial acquisitions in Asia were extensive; in the south, Bayazid and the vale of Alashkert, as far west as Khorasan; the fortress-town of Kars (captured by the Russians for the third time in 50 years), and Sarikamish (T.: 'yellow reed'); Olti, and in the north Artvin and the harbour town of Batum.[91]

As soon as the British Cabinet received a copy of the treaty (23 March), it opposed it vigorously, though the Cabinet was far from united on the issues. Disraeli himself proposed declaring an emergency, putting a force into the field, and sending an expedition to occupy Cyprus and Alexandretta (Iskenderun) – specifically with the intention of counterbalancing the alleged effect of the Russian conquests in Armenia. But the first systematic attack on the treaty of San Stefano was made by Lord Salisbury in his circular of 1 April 1878, the day after he assumed the office of foreign secretary.[92]

Salisbury attacked every proposal of the treaty, and demanded that the issues be settled by a European congress. His opposition to the Russian territorial gains in Armenia was twofold:

> The acquisition of the strongholds of Armenia will place the population of that province under the immediate influence of the Power which holds them; while the extensive European trade which now passes from Trebizond to Persia will, in consequence of the cessions in Kurdistan, be liable to be arrested at the pleasure of the Russian government by the prohibitory barriers of their commercial system.[93]

In reply to Salisbury's circular Prince Gorchakov, his Russian opposite number, said that the Russian acquisitions in Armenia possessed only defensive value.[94] (Strategically speaking, this is undoubtedly correct.) Gorchakov admitted himself perplexed by the British view on the caravan route through the vale of Alashkert, saying that it was in contradiction to former British government assertions that Russian possession of even Erzerum or Trebizond would not constitute a danger to British interests. To affirm that, with the vale of Alashkert, Russia would be in a position to wreck the trade of Europe was to carry distrust to an extreme.[95]

To resolve the differences of the great powers, it was decided to hold a congress. It would be at Berlin, with Prince Bismarck presiding as 'honest broker'. The lines of the Asiatic frontier between Russia and Turkey were, however, agreed beforehand: Russia would keep Kars, Ardahan and Batum, but Alashkert and Bayazid would revert to Turkey (so that Britain could keep her commercial route intact).[96]

Armenian leaders in Constantinople had felt their hopes for their people slipping with time. So an Armenian delegation, headed by ex-patriarch Khrimian, set out in March to acquaint European capitals with their proposals for Turkish Armenia. These were, as they had hoped at Adrianople, for some form of local self-government within the framework of the Ottoman empire, and for a strengthening of the forces of law and order.[97] But the leaders of Europe showed little interest in the cause of the Armenians – a people who had remained pacific, despite misgovernment. From April to June the Armenian leaders were in England, and met Lord Salisbury on 10 May; he gave them no more than platitudinous assurances.[98] British policy had more important things to deal with than humanitarian matters.

The Congress of Berlin and the Revelation of the Cyprus Convention

The Armenian delegates travelled on to Berlin, where the congress opened on 13 June. Their presence went unheeded, at this last occasion on which the great

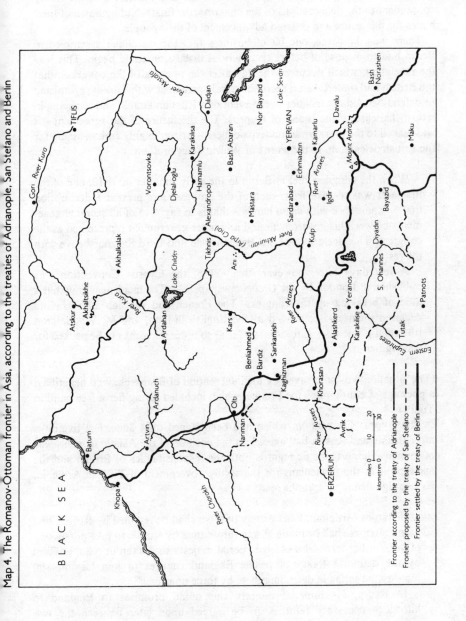

Map 4. The Romanov-Ottoman frontier in Asia, according to the treaties of Adrianople, San Stefano and Berlin

BLACK SEA

Khopa
Batum
Artvin
Ardanuch
River Chorokh
Nariman
Olti
Avnik
ERZERUM
River Aroxes
Khorasan
Kaghizman
Bardiz
Benliahmed
Sarikamish
Kars
Ardahan
Lake Childer
Ani
Tkhnis
Alexandropol
River Akhurian (Arpa Chai)
Atskur
Akhalsikhe
Akhalkalak
River Kura
Gori
River Kura
TIFLIS
Vorontsovka
Djelal-oglu
Hamamlu
Karakilisa
Dilidjan
River Aksidio
Lake Sevan
Bash Abaran
Nor Bayazid
Bash Norashen
Mastara
Sardarabad
Echmiadzn
YEREVAN
Kamarlu
Davalu
River Aroxes
Kulp
Igdir
Mount Ararat
Maku
River Aroxes
Yeranos
Alashkerd
Karakilise
S. Ohannes
Diyadin
Bayazid
Tutak
Patnots
Eastern Euphrates

miles 0   10   20
kilometres 0   30

Frontier according to the treaty of Adrianople
Frontier proposed by the treaty of San Stefano
Frontier settled by the treaty of Berlin

powers disposed of the affairs of the Near East without the presence of the people who actually lived there; and the Armenians witnessed, in the treaty consequent to the deliberations of the congress, the final whittling down of their hopes for the secure and ordered advancement of their people.

There was, however, one bit of business that the statesmen assembled in Berlin had to dispose of before their serious discussion could begin. This was the revelation, which occurred the day after the opening of the congress, that the British had undertaken a secret bilateral agreement with Turkey, promising to defend her Asiatic frontier in the event of a Russian attack, and receiving in return the lease of the island of Cyprus. The disclosure of the agreement – it was leaked to the press by an underpaid clerk – proved highly embarrassing for the British delegation. In the words of Wilfrid Scawen Blunt:

When the congress met in Berlin in the early summer of 1878, one of the first acts was to take from each of the ambassadors present a declaration that he came to it with clean hands – that is to say, free of all secret engagements between his government and any other government represented at the congress. This declaration Lord Beaconsfield and Lord Salisbury gave with the rest.

A few days after, however, the text of the Cyprus Convention was published in London by the *Globe* newspaper . . . The incident was within a little of breaking up the congress. The French and Russian ambassadors declared themselves outraged at the English ill-faith, and M. Waddington [the chief French delegate] went so far as to order his trunks to be packed for leaving Berlin.[99]

(The situation was only saved by the intervention of Bismarck, who negotiated a package of concessions for France, which included giving her a free hand in Tunis.)

The Cyprus Convention, which had been signed on 4 June, just five days after Britain and Russia had agreed on the position of the Asiatic frontier, was of immense importance as regards both the responsibilities of Britain and the aspirations of the Armenians for the secure government of Turkish Armenia. Its two significant paragraphs read:

If Batum, Ardahan, Kars or any of them shall be retained by Russia, and if any attempt shall be made at any future time by Russia to take possession of any further territories of his imperial majesty the sultan in Asia, as fixed by the definitive treaty of peace, England engages to join his imperial majesty the sultan in defending them by force of arms.[100]

In return, his imperial majesty the sultan promises to England to introduce necessary reforms, to be agreed upon later between the two powers, into the government, and for the protection of the Christian and other subjects of the Porte in these territories.

Britain undertook to defend Ottoman Turkey (as the cartoon from *Punch* shows); in return she obtained not only Cyprus – 'a place of arms in the Levant', in the words of Sir Stafford Northcote – but also a pledge from the sultan to 'introduce reforms'. Now, those who have studied former Ottoman reform schemes might view this new undertaking with scepticism. In comparison with the undertaking to Russia, as shown in article 16 of the San Stefano treaty, that to Britain was feeble, since in the former case there was an army in occupation, whereas there was no such British force to compel the sultan. And Britain had never shown much zeal in persuading Turkey to implement reforms.[101]

Despite the apparent manner in which Britain had eclipsed Russia as the guarantor of reforms in Asia, the congress found it necessary to include the matter in its deliberations. At the session of 4 July Lord Salisbury raised the question of revising the relevant article of the San Stefano treaty. He was happy about its second half (which laid down that the Ottoman government would introduce reforms without delay), but could not accept that the evacuation of Russian troops was to be conditional on the introduction of the reforms.[102] Russian troops, which to the Armenians of the provinces were the only guarantee against lawlessness, were to the British an object of obsessive imperial jealousy.

Two days later Salisbury indicated that he was planning to substitute for the guarantee of Russian military occupation one that said that Turkey would merely 'come to an agreement' with the great powers on the scope and execution of reforms. Nothing would be done to compel the Porte to act. Why Ottoman Turkey had to promise to reform *both* to Britain alone (in the Cyprus Convention) *and* to all six great powers together is puzzling; but to have only the former guarantee would make Britain's imperial concern embarrassingly plain; and moreover with the latter, when the reform scheme failed, the British prime minister could always point to the responsibility of all the powers, dismissing the Cyprus Convention with a remark such as 'We cannot say that we are the protectors of Turkey, or that the influence of a guardian over his ward is one that we can claim to exercise,' – as Lord Salisbury was to say on 28 June 1889.[103]

The text of the article on Armenian reforms, which was to become article 61 of the treaty of Berlin, was agreed on 8 July. It read:

> The Sublime Porte undertakes to carry out, without further delay, the improvements and reforms demanded by local requirements in the provinces inhabited by Armenians, and to guarantee their security against the Circassians and Kurds.
>
> It will periodically make known the steps taken to this effect to the powers, who will superintend their application.[104]

This article, together with the Cyprus Convention, brought the Armenians

PUNCH, OR THE LONDON CHARIVARI.—JULY 20, 1878.

"HUMPTY-DUMPTY"!

"HUMPTY-DUMPTY SAT ON A WALL;
HUMPTY-DUMPTY HAD A GREAT FALL:
DIZZY, WITH CYPRUS, AND ALL THE QUEEN'S MEN,
HOPES TO SET HUMPTY-DUMPTY UP AGAIN."

no security at all. The government of Turkish Armenia, if anything, deteriorated after their signature. In turn, Armenian self-defence groups and revolutionary societies grew up, provoking heavy retaliation. The most common British attitude was of studied ineffectualness; and Russia, partly for internal reasons and partly for the threats from Britain contained in the Cyprus Convention, refused to go to the aid of Turkish Armenians.

Expressing its deep disquiet at the text of article 61 of the treaty, the unheard Armenian delegation sent a protest note to all the plenipotentiaries, on 13 July, the day the treaty was signed:

> The Armenian delegation expresses its regrets that its legitimate demands, so moderate at the time, have not been agreed upon by the congress. We had not believed that a nation like ours, composed of several million souls, which has not so far been the instrument of any foreign power, which, although much more oppressed than the other Christian populations has caused no trouble to the Ottoman government (and, although our nation had no tie of religion or origin to any of the great powers, yet, being a Christian nation it had hoped to find in our century the same protection afforded to the other Christian nations) – we had not believed that such a nation, devoid of all political ambition, would have to acquire the right of living its life and of being governed on its ancestral land by Armenian officials.
>
> The Armenians have just realised that they have been deceived, that their rights have not been recognised, because they have been pacific; that the maintenance of the independence of their ancient church and nationality have advanced them nothing.
>
> The Armenian delegation is going to return to the east, taking this lesson with it. It declares nevertheless that the Armenian people will never cease from crying out until Europe gives its legitimate demands satisfaction.[105]

Disraeli, for his part, returned to England to tumultuous cheering crowds. He assured his adoring public that he had brought 'peace with honour' – a claim which, in view of the little trouble he had at the beginning of the congress, needed to be taken with a pinch of salt.

Archbishop Khrimian returned to Constantinople in deep despondency. Some weeks later he gave a sermon in the cathedral in which he painted a vivid picture of the Armenian claimants at Berlin. There, he said, the European diplomats had placed on the table a 'dish of liberty'. The Bulgarians, Serbs and Montenegrins had taken their portions of the tasty *harissa* with their iron spoons; but the Armenians had only a paper spoon, which collapsed when they tried to partake.[106]

Within a few years, as we shall see, Armenians had fashioned iron spoons for themselves; but the historic chance was past, and the dish of liberty, proferred to the Balkan people in 1878, was henceforward, like refreshment to Tantalus, held perpetually out of their reach.

Notes

1. Lord Kinross, *The Ottoman Centuries* (London, 1977), pp. 46–56.
2. Ibid., pp. 167, 229.
3. Eliot Grinnell Mears, *Modern Turkey* (New York, 1924), pp. 511–13.
4. Great Britain, Parliamentary Papers, Blue Book, Turkey no. 14 (1877), p. 28 (henceforward 'Turkey no. 14 (1877)', 'Treaty Series, no. 3 (1923)', etc.).
5. Ibid., p. 29.
6. Avedis K. Sanjian, *The Armenian Communities in Syria under Ottoman Dominion* (Cambridge, Mass., 1965), p. 5.
7. Ibid., p. 33.
8. Elie Kedourie, *The Chatham House Version and Other Essays* (London, 1970), pp. 362–3.
9. Sir Percy Sykes, *History of Persia* (London, 1915), p. 186.
10. Maxime Rodinson, *Mohammed* (London, 1971), pp. 254, 271.
11. Dr Humphry Sandwith, *A Narrative of the Siege of Kars* ... (London, 1856), pp. 168–70.
12. 'Devshirme', *Encyclopedia of Islam*, 2nd edn (Leiden, continuing).
13. Turkey no. 16 (1877), p. 18.
14. Sir Edwin Pears, *Turkey and its People* (London, 1911), p. 334.
15. J. C. Hurewitz (ed.), *Diplomacy in the Near and Middle East* (Princeton, 1956), vol. II, pp. 56–7.
16. George Washburn, *Fifty Years in Constantinople* (Boston, 1911), p. 11.
17. Hurewitz, *Diplomacy in the Near and Middle East*, vol. II, p. 110.
18. Sir Edward Hertslet, *The Map of Europe by Treaty* (1875), vol. II, p. 1255.
19. *The Times*, 8 October 1875, p. 7.
20. D. C. Blaisdell, *European Financial Control in the Ottoman Empire* (New York, 1929), p. 55.
21. Herbert Feis, *Europe: the World's Banker* (New Haven, 1930), p. 314.
22. Blaisdell, *European Financial Control*, p. 39.
23. Feis, *Europe*, p. 314.
24. *The Times*, 20 February 1857, p. 7.
25. Ibid.
26. Nassau Senior, *A Journal Kept in Turkey and Greece* ... (London, 1859), p. 108.
27. *The Times*, 15 September 1858, p. 6.
28. Ibid.
29. *The Times*, 9 October 1875, p. 7.
30. *Edinburgh Review*, no. 145 (January 1877), p. 265.
31. Blaisdell, *European Financial Control*, p. 90.
32. Sir Mark Sykes, *The Caliphs' Last Heritage* (London, 1915), especially pp. 414–18.
33. FO 195/112, p. 257.
34. Louise Nalbandian, *The Armenian Revolutionary Movement* (Berkeley and Los Angeles, 1963), p. 68.
35. H. F. B. Lynch, *Armenia: Travels and Studies* (London, 1901), vol. II, p. 424.
36. M. A. Ubicini, *Letters on Turkey* (London, 1856), vol. I, p. 19.
37. Richard G. Hovannisian, *Armenia on the Road to Independence, 1918* (Berkeley and Los Angeles, 1967), p. 36.
38. Ibid.
39. Turkey no. 16 (1877), p. 18.
40. Ibid., p. 26.
41. Ibid.
42. See Mesrob K. Krikorian, *Armenians in the Service of the Ottoman Empire 1860–1908* (London, 1977).
43. Hagop Barsoumian, 'Economic Role of the Armenian Amira Class in the Ottoman Empire', *Armenian Review*, vol. XXXI, (March 1979), pp. 312–13.
44. Godfrey Goodwin, *A History of Ottoman Architecture* (London, 1971), pp. 417–23.
45. Michael Levey, *The World of Ottoman Art* (London, 1975), p. 137.
46. See Metin And, *Osmanli Tiyatrosu* (Ankara, 1976); also its review by Margaret Bain-

bridge in *Bulletin of the School of Oriental and African Studies*, vol. XLI, no. 2 (1978), pp. 382–3.
47. Bernard Lewis, *The Emergence of Modern Turkey* (London, 1961), p. 154.
48. Sanjian, *The Armenian Communities in Syria*, pp. 35–9.
49. Text in Lynch, *Armenia*, vol. II, pp. 445–67.
50. See Nalbandian, *Armenian Revolutionary Movement*, pp. 67ff.
51. Victor Langlois, 'Les Arméniens de la Turquie', *Revue des deux mondes*, no. 43 (1863), p. 975.
52. Aghassi, *Zeitoun, depuis les origines jusqu'à l'insurrection de 1895* (Paris, 1897), p. 45.
53. Nalbandian, *Armenian Revolutionary Movement*, p. 68.
54. Ibid., p. 59.
55. Ibid., p. 72.
56. Ibid., pp. 70–1; also Aghassi, *Zeitoun*, pp. 122ff.
57. M. Voskerichian, *Zeitun Alpom* (Beirut, 1960), p. 21.
58. Nalbandian, *Armenian Revolutionary Movement*, p. 80.
59. Ibid.
60. Ibid., pp. 53–4.
61. G. Rolin-Jaequemyns, 'Armenia under the Treaty of Paris of 1856', *Armenia* (Boston, Mass.) vol. II, no. 7 (April 1906), pp. 21ff.
62. Ibid., p. 22.
63. Ibid., p. 23.
64. Ibid., p. 24.
65. Lucien Wolf, *The Russian Conspiracy* (London, 1877), p. 11. See also FO 881/3638.
66. Quoted in R. W. Seton-Watson, *Disraeli, Gladstone and the Eastern Question* (London, 1935), p. 63.
67. Ibid., p. 244.
68. Sir Edward Hertslet, *The Map of Europe by Treaty* (1891), vol. IV, pp. 2418–29.
69. Ibid., pp. 2430–40.
70. Ibid., pp. 2459–63.
71. W. E. Monypenny and George Earle Buckle, *The Life of Benjamin Disraeli* (London, 1910–20), vol. VI, p. 25.
72. G. E. Buckle (ed.), *The Letters of Queen Victoria* (London, 1926), vol. II, part 2, p. 480.
73. M. S. Anderson, *The Eastern Question, 1774–1923* (London, 1966), p. 184; also Sir Edwin Pears, *Forty Years in Constantinople* (London, 1916), pp. 12–25.
74. Monypenny and Buckle, *Life of Benjamin Disraeli*, vol. VI, p. 47.
75. Ibid., p. 36.
76. Ibid., p. 73.
77. Ibid., p. 54.
78. Hertslet, *Map of Europe*, pp. 2526–30.
79. Ibid., pp. 2531–40.
80. Anderson, *The Eastern Question*, p. 192.
81. Hertslet, *Map of Europe*, pp. 2598–9.
82. Turkey no. 25 (1877), p. 164.
83. A. Vambéry, *Arminius Vambéry: His Life and Adventures* (London, 1884 edn), p. 46.
84. Monypenny and Buckle, *Life of Benjamin Disraeli*, vol. VI, p. 155.
85. Ibid., p. 172.
86. Hertslet, *Map of Europe*, pp. 2658–60.
87. C. B. Norman, *Armenia and the Campaign of 1877* (London, 1878), p. 263.
88. A. O. Sarkissian, *History of the Armenian Question to 1885* (Urbana, Illinois, 1938), pp. 58–9.
89. Ibid., p. 64.
90. Hertslet, *Map of Europe*, p. 2686.
91. Ibid., pp. 2688–9.
92. Ibid., pp. 2696–706.
93. Ibid., p. 2704.
94. Ibid., p. 2713.
95. Ibid., p. 2714.
96. Anderson, *The Eastern Question*, p. 207.

97. Text in Krikorian, *Armenians in the Service of the Ottoman Empire*, pp. 111–12.

98. Sarkissian, *History of the Armenian Question*, pp. 78–9.

99. Wilfrid Scawen Blunt, 'Turkish Misgovernment', *Nineteenth Century*, no. 40 (November 1896), p. 839.

100. Hertslet, *Map of Europe*, vol. IV, pp. 2722–3.

101. G. D. C. Argyll (Duke of), *Our Responsibilities for Turkey* (London, 1896).

102. G. Rolin-Jaequemyns, 'Legal Position of Turkish Armenia', *Armenia* (Boston), vol. II, no. 8 (May 1906), p. 31.

103. *Hansard*, Lords, 3rd series, vol. 337, col. 988.

104. Hertslet, *Map of Europe*, vol. IV, p. 2796.

105. V. Aykouni (Kevork K. Baghdjian), '*Le problème Arménien*' (unpublished doctoral thesis, University of Montpellier, 1969), p. 88.

106. Nalbandian, *Armenian Revolutionary Movement*, pp. 28–9.

5   No Help Came

> The mass and majesty of this world, all
> That carries weight and always weighs the same
> Lay in the hands of others; they were small
> And could not hope for help and no help came . . .
> – W. H. Auden, *The Shield of Achilles*.

The Impotent Protectorate

Turkish Armenia appeared to have a special status after the Cyprus Convention. In view of Britain's responsibility, it could even be called a British protectorate. (A study of the area published in London in 1879 bears the title *Our New Protectorate*.[1]) But the region was never given the title officially, and those who wished to minimise British responsibility were able to claim that it was just a part of the Ottoman empire whose administration Britain was attempting to influence.

After the treaty of Berlin Britain despatched a series of special consuls to Asiatic Turkey. (She had had a regular consul in Erzerum since 1836.) Their ostensible purpose was to make the sultan keep the promise to introduce reforms which he had made in the Cyprus Convention. But their powers were very limited. Their chief, Col. C. W. Wilson, was based at Sivas and held the title 'military consul-general in Anatolia'. His instructions were to observe, to advise, to assist and if necessary to remonstrate.[2] His most extensive power was access to his ambassador.[3]

If one compares these powers with those which France exercised at almost the same time in her protectorate of Tunis – her part of the bargain struck at Berlin – through her resident-general and *contrôleurs civils*[4] (by which she soon got a firm control on the region), the difference is immediately striking, for France sought control of Tunis, whereas Britain, unimpressed by the colonial possibilities of Turkish Armenia and fearful of provoking the jealousy of the other powers, had no such ambitions. And with no such ambitions her actions were feeble, only adding up to an irritating intrusion, and in the process driving a deeper wedge between rulers and ruled.

The consuls, too, were not posted there solely to attend to the needs of the population. That indeed was a secondary job. Their principal task was that of gathering military intelligence. (All the consuls were initially army officers.) In the words of R. W. (later Sir Robert) Graves,[5] diplomat and uncle of the poet, they had been appointed, not so much in pursuance of the policy outlined in the Cyprus Convention as on account of the importance of maintaining posts of observation on the Russian and Persian frontiers, and this practice was continued, as far as Van was concerned, until the outbreak of the Great War in 1914.

Administrative Divisions

Soon after the treaty of Berlin, Sultan Abdul Hamid made extensive changes to the boundaries of the province of Turkish Armenia.[6] Hitherto, for ten years, the Armenian districts had been encompassed by the three provinces of Erzerum, Sivas and Diyarbekir. (Those provinces also included many areas which had never been Armenian, and where there were only a very few Armenians.) Of the three, that of Erzerum contained by far the largest share of Turkish Armenia, since it included the towns of Kars, Erzerum, Van, Bitlis and Moush. After the treaty, Kars was lost, and the other Armenian districts of the Erzerum province were divided to create three provinces: Erzerum, Van and Bitlis. These three, together with those of Sivas, Diyarbekir and Mamuret el-Aziz (or Kharput) became known as the 'six *vilayets* (provinces)' of Turkish Armenia. But in using the term, one should always remember that Armenians were far from an overall majority in the areas, although in many places, especially the fertile country regions, they constituted the largest group in an area in which, taken as a whole, none of the populations constituted more than 40 per cent.

Map 5 Administrative Divisions in Ottoman Armenia after 1878 .

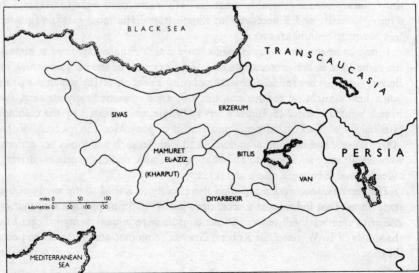

The Aftermath of the War of 1877–8

Conditions were very disturbed throughout Turkish Armenia after the war of 1877–8, so that there was scope for the British consuls to use any powers they had. Numbers of Circassians and Laz from the Russian empire had arrived in the Ottoman empire, and settled themselves at the expense of the local population. The Kurdish tribal leaders, who had fled during the war, reappeared, with apparently limitless licence to rob and kill. These men were truly the terrors of the countryside, not only to Armenians but to the settled, non-tribal Kurds as well. Major Trotter noted the following (which also gives an interesting picture of the coexistence of the settled communities), on 5 January 1879:

> I stopped a few minutes at the village [Madrak, in the Chabakchur district] and was at once surrounded by a crowd of Armenians, who, while loudly complaining of the misdeeds of the Kurds from the neighbouring country, professed to be on good terms with, and well treated by, the Kurds of their own village; and in truth the Kurdish priest or imam was standing by, and joining in all the assertions of the Armenian priest, who was the principal spokesman. There is no doubt that not only do both Christians and Kurds suffer terribly from bands of roving insurgent Kurds from the neighbouring mountains, but in many villages the Armenians also suffer terrible oppression at the hands of their own [Kurdish] beys and aghas, the old feudal lords of the soil. As far as I can make out, these beys, however oppressive themselves, are willing to protect their own subjects, as far as lies in their power, from external violence, but in the present disorganised state of the country they can defend neither their Christian serfs nor their own co-religionists.[7]

However, every attempt by the consuls to set up machinery to improve the administration of justice in the eastern provinces was met with calculated obstruction by the Ottoman government. But since they lacked all coercive power their only result was to produce a series of well researched reports, and nothing more. Even the arch-Turkophile Sir Henry Layard ultimately lost his temper with Sultan Abdul Hamid because the latter refused to make the reforms.[8]

The Liberals' Failure

When Gladstone returned to power in April 1880 one of his first actions was to recall Sir Henry Layard from Constantinople, and appoint George Goschen (MP for Ripon) to the post, with a special mission to see that the terms of the Berlin treaty were carried out. Goschen succeeded in compelling Turkey to hand over the port of Antivari on the Adriatic to Montenegro by means of a blatant threat of force.[9] But over Armenia Goschen attempted to act in concert with the other signatories of the Berlin treaty, instead of acting alone as Layard had done –and as he himself did over Antivari. The result was a series of identic notes and collective notes from all the powers addressed to the Porte, which brought no practical improvement at all to the situation.[10]

From 1880 to 1882 the powers deliberated, eventually agreeing in February 1882 to implement a plan of reforms. The possibility of action hovered in the air. But then there arose a new difficulty: Germany refused to act in concert with the other powers. In a despatch from Berlin on 16 May 1883 the British ambassador, Lord Ampthill, noted that Bismarck was basically prepared to act in concert with the other powers. Over one question, however, he could not follow Britain: the Armenian question.[11] Bismarck claimed that the constant pressure on the sultan humiliated him in the eyes of his subjects, and weakened him in the eyes of his enemies; besides, 'interference with the happiness of other sovereigns' subjects was philanthropy, and ... he hated philanthropy in politics.' He would decline to press the Armenian reforms on the sultan.[12] The concert of Europe was reduced to silence on this issue.

Nevertheless, Britain held certain individual responsibilities; and here it is *prima facie* puzzling that the British Liberal government, in power until 1885, did nothing about the condition of Armenia, despite much moralistic verbiage about the wickedness of the Turks in Armenia. Goschen left Constantinople as early as May 1881, to make room for a career diplomat, Lord Dufferin. Goschen had most lamentably failed to make the Porte implement article 61 of the Berlin treaty. There was no attempt at all to act alone, in accordance with the Cyprus Convention. Instead, as a result of Liberal policies elsewhere in the Near East, the autocracy of Abdul Hamid was made even more secure. The British occupation of Egypt of 1882, into which Gladstone and his fellow Liberals were swept by a tide of jingoism, had the effect of squashing constitutionalism throughout the Islamic world, and reinforcing despotism. So the total result of the Liberals' excursus into the affairs of the region was that the condition of the Armenians grew steadily worse. Wilfrid Scawen Blunt summed up the situation succinctly when he wrote (in 1896):

> Neither in 1880, when Mr Gladstone returned to office, nor at any subsequent period of Liberal ascendancy, has the smallest attempt been made to undo or repair the wrong. Mr Gladstone in office became undistinguishable in his treatment of the eastern question from Lord Beaconsfield.[13]

As evidence of the British government's embarrassment at its failure in Turkish Armenia, the Blue Books on the subject stopped appearing in 1881, and did not reappear publicly for eight years. Blue Books were collections of diplomatic documents edited from the Foreign Office's Confidential Print, which were made available to the general public, usually within a few months from the date of the last document in them. Their purpose was to keep Members of Parliament informed on current affairs. A confidential Blue Book was, however, 'laid but not distributed' – that is, made available to MPs only – in 1884.[14] The government was clearly too ashamed to give it wider currency.

Thus, vice-consul Eyres reported from Van on 15 September 1883 of the 'utter corruption and incapacity of the authorities'.[15] The governor of Van, Arif Pasha, was out collecting bribes most of the time, but when he returned, 'the nightly burglaries double in number and murders are of daily occurrence.'[16]

Eyres wrote from Van, 4 January 1884, that 'the courts of justice are a mere farce. They are neither more nor less than engines for extorting money from litigants for the benefit of officials.'[17] The *zaptiyes* (gendarmerie) were 'the scourge of the country ... they live on the people.' Many Armenians had emigrated, and Eyres added, 'I cannot understand how those who do remain still manage to exist.'[18]

The ambassador, Lord Dufferin, commented on a series of reports on four of the eastern provinces made in January and February 1884: 'These documents repeat the same tale of wrong, misery, corrupt and incapable administration.'[19] The condition of the country was declining steadily; poverty was increasing everywhere. Such were the blessings of the Liberals' foreign policy.

Political Stirrings

The situation for the Armenians was intolerable, and no people, even if they appear to have had fighting spirit knocked out of them by centuries of subservience, can endure such a situation for ever. The Armenians were in effect cornered by their own government. So they slowly moved towards defiance. In doing so, entire ideologies and self-images were called into question. In a people whose hope had hitherto been their religious faith alone, defence of the body became as assiduously cultivated as salvation of the soul.

Driven by Ottoman oppression, some of them began gradually to reject the theocratic system of the Ottoman empire, and to rethink their position in the world. From three directions ideas came to them, which chipped away at the Ottoman system. First, from across the alien, foreign-imposed border – that imperial convenience – which divided them from their fellow Armenians in Russian Transcaucasia. Radical, Populist political notions had been current there in recent decades. These ideas, or portions of them, were carried across the border, to Van, Erzerum and other Armenian centres. In the second place, since the 1820s American Protestant missionaries had established a network of congregations and schools throughout Anatolia and Turkish Armenia. They had gone there initially with the intention of converting the Muslims and Jews, but, making no headway, had taken it upon themselves to 'reform' the Christianity of the Armenians, which they considered to have become a very dark glass through which to see the teaching of the founder. By the end of the century the American Board of Commissioners for Foreign Missions had established there 127 Protestant congregations with 13,000 communicants, and 400 schools with 23,000 pupils.[20] The vast majority were Armenians; the others were Greeks, Assyrians and Syrian Jacobites. Colleges had been established by the missionaries at Marsovan, Aintab, Marash and Kharput. A new, quite un-Ottoman system of thinking developed among the Armenians; young Armenians rapidly assimilated European intellectual currents and moved from the fatalism of a subject minority in an age of faith to an attitude of energetic down-to-earth pragmatic realism. The third channel for new ideas was through Constantinople; many of the well established Armenian bankers sent their sons to Europe for their education.

Ottoman Armenians began to organise themselves politically. Rudimentary attempts at political organisation – secret societies, local groups and so forth – had existed since the early 1870s. In 1881 a new, more ambitious organisation, the 'Protectors of the Fatherland', was established in Erzerum.[21] It was dedicated, its historians tell us, to the defence of the Armenian population against the Kurds and Turks; but it was almost certainly a revolutionary organisation, since the words 'Liberty or Death' were found inscribed on an official document when members of the organisation were caught by Ottoman police in November 1882. After the arrest of these men, 76 were tried (twice, for there was a retrial) in 1883; 40 were found guilty.[22] The trial was a political confrontation, and it inspired the revolutionary song

Tsain më hnchets Erzrumi Haiots lerneren
Tount tount yelan Haiots srder zenki shachiunen. . .
A voice rang out from the Armenian mountains of Erzerum,
   Thrilled were the hearts of Armenians by the sounds of the weapons;
For centuries the Armenian villager had seen neither sword nor weapon –
   He left his field and, instead of spade, took sword and rifle.

Twelve years later this song was to be sung on the streets of Constantinople, as the Armenians staged a demonstration against Ottoman tyranny.

The Armenakan Party

The first recognisable Armenian political party – with a platform, a central body, and an official publication – was the Armenakan party, founded in Van in the autumn of 1885.[23] The guiding spirit behind its foundation was one Mëkërtich Portukalian, the son of an enlightened Constantinople banker. Portukalian was a distinguished Armenian figure; typically, a tireless educator. During the late 1860s he had been a teacher in Tokat; he had travelled extensively in western Anatolia and the Balkans in the mid-1870s, and had opened a school in Van in 1878. (Interestingly, it was open to Christian and Muslim alike; besides Armenians, Assyrians, Kurds and Turks could all enrol.)

Factional strife among the Armenians – a recurring impediment – forced it to close after less than a year; but in 1881 he was able to open another, the Central School (Kedronakan Varzharan). But this time it was the authorities that objected, and after four years of work the school was closed in March 1885. Portukalian left Van, to spend the rest of his life exiled in Marseilles.

It was as a direct result of his activity that the Armenakan party was founded in 1885; from Marseilles he himself kept in touch with its leaders, and published a journal of political and social enlightenment, *Armenia*. One of Portukalian's main points was that Armenians abroad should help those in their native land, both financially and by telling the world about their oppressed condition. Some expatriate Armenians took note: in December 1885 an Armenian Patriotic Society of Europe was founded; its headquarters were in Chesilton Road, Fulham – the private house of its leader, Garabed Hagopian. This society was to play an important part in disseminating news and arousing liberal opinion in Britain nine years later, when details of the Sasun massacre began to leak out.

Despite the absence of their leading spirit, the Armenians of Van worked out their political principles. In great secrecy – in a burrow used for pressing grapes, furnished with nothing but a straw mat – Portukalian's disciples met and hammered out their ideological platform. Their central aim, they decided, was to 'win for the Armenians the right to rule over themselves, through revolution'. The Armenakan concept of revolution was distinctly low-keyed, compared with that of succeeding organisations; terror, agitation and militant demonstrations were viewed with disfavour. The people were to be trained with arms, as guerrilla fighters, but essentially for defensive purposes, against the terrorism of the Ottoman empire. How would the land of Armenia be liberated from the Ottoman yoke – since self-defence and guerrilla warfare do not by themselves free a nation? Hope was placed in the great powers. Armenakans were to 'prepare the people for a general movement, especially when the external circumstances – the disposition of the foreign powers and neighbouring races – seem to favour the Armenian cause'.[24]

It is arguable that this belief – that the great powers would intervene in the Ottoman empire, and rescue the Armenian people and their revolutionary leaders from the clutches of Turkish misrule – was the greatest single error of the Armenian revolutionary parties throughout the period 1885–1908. With hindsight we can see that after 1881, when Tsar Alexander II with his unpredictable idealism was no more, and when Gladstone's Liberalism had become tarnished by experience and failure, it was futile to hope that the solid, bourgeois powers of Europe would intervene in favour of a revolutionary uprising. But Armenians placed enormous faith in those twin creations of British diplomacy: the Cyprus Convention and article 61 of the Berlin treaty. They believed that under the terms of these two instruments the powers, and especially Britain, were bound to intervene in their affairs when Ottoman rule manifested its true face.

The Armenakans soon had cells outside Van, in other towns in the province, as well as in Trebizond and Constantinople. Beyond the Ottoman empire the party developed in a small way in Russian Transcaucasia, in Persia and in the United States.

One of their exploits, although it failed, is of interest because of the testimony left behind by one of the participants. The incident was known as the 'Salmas affair'. Three Armenakans, Garabed Kulaksizian, Ohannes Akribesian and Vartan Koloshian, originally from Van, now living in Salmas (Persia), where two of them were schoolteachers, disguised themselves as Kurds and, armed, attempted to cross secretly from Iran to Turkey, probably to recruit adherents to their cause. They were caught by *zaptiyes* just inside the Turkish border; a dust-up ensued; one was killed, another seriously injured and later murdered, and the third got away (28 May 1889). A document was found on Kulaksizian headed 'My last decision', which, although not great literature, is remarkable for showing the mind of a man moving from passive acceptance to active challenge, and the painful readjustment necessary for a man belonging to a community which had eschewed violence for centuries. The following is part of his testimony:

I have come to the end of the last of those years in which I have begun to live. When I drifted into the current of life, I resembled a man whose eyes had been bandaged, who had been isolated from real life, and kept in an imaginary world for many years; at length this man is allowed to enter upon real life, the poor man opens his eyes which have been blindfolded for several years, he finds himself in a world totally different from the life which he has hitherto led; every obstacle that he meets causes him to stumble, he goes on foot, often he falls, but he takes courage and gets up again; he changes his path for another direction, hoping that this new way will lead him to a better road, although he is convinced that he will only discover a world more or less resembling that in which he has hitherto lived. . .

But he has not been taught how to set to work. He pauses a moment, looks around him; in every direction he sees misery, persecution, and baseness, and human corruption. Thinking of his childhood, he passes his hand across his forehead, and the fearful vision of the past presents itself before his eyes; he beholds the torture which his relatives have endured, he beholds his fellow-countrymen abandoned and despairing through the persecution of the cruel Turks.

Finally he calls to mind that he has sworn in his childhood to assist his compatriots when he grew up, and not to allow himself to be so mercilessly treated.[25]

However, resistance to robbery often degenerated into cold-blooded killing of Kurds; legitimate liberation and self-defence became short-sighted aping of the opponent's methods. Much of the enlightenment developed by Portukalian and his immediate successors was lost in sterile brutality. Agents of the government could not have thought up a more skilful scenario for delaying political development among the Kurds and Armenians, who, in revolt together, would have posed a serious threat to the empire. When Abdul Hamid armed the Kurds into Hamidiye battalions in 1891 he obtained the same result as those Armenians who indulged in vengeance: division of the two peoples from one another.

The Hunchaks

Against the background of a system of law which was the very denial of law, the first socialist and revolutionary Armenian party was founded. This society, whose doctrine was Marxist, was founded in Geneva in 1887.[26] Its members, all of whom were Russian Armenians, took the ideas of Portukalian and the Armenakans and gave them a clear imprint of Caucasian revolutionary thought. But the beam of their attention, along with that of other Russian Armenian groups, was directed upon Turkish Armenia, *yerkirë*, the homeland.

The aims of this party (which had no name yet) were drafted in 1886.[27] Broadly, they were for the achievement of socialism and the freedom of Turkish Armenia. A new, unified, socialist state was to be carved out of the existing imperial regimes; and this could only be brought about by revolution. The party would be a national one, in that it worked for the alleviation of the plight of the Armenian people, who were oppressed in eastern Turkey as a national group – that is, they suffered merely for being Armenians, not for being workers or peasants; but it would not be a nationalist party. The leaders saw the new, socialist Armenia as a beacon for the world socialist revolution. The draft of the party's principles contained a model of the Armenian state envisaged, and described how the revolution would occur; more extreme than the Armenakans, the party did not eschew agitation and terror. The instruments of the revolution were to be workers and peasants, whose activities were to be directed by a central committee.

In 1887 the party was actually formed, and the first issue of the party organ, *Hunchak* (properly *Hnchak* – 'bell'), produced. (It was probably thus named after Alexander Herzen's *Kolokol*.) Not until 1890 did the party adopt a name – the 'Hunchakian Revolutionary Party', or Hunchaks for short.

Leader of the Hunchaks was the young Avetis Nazarbekian (or Nazarbek; b.1866), a dedicated revolutionary and propagandist, but a man who seems to have enjoyed to excess the acclaim he received abroad for being a revolutionary. According to David Garnett, who met him and his future wife Maro when they were guests of Garnett's mother Constance, he was 'dark, slender, very handsome in an oriental style, and played the violin'.[28] In the early and mid-1890s he was frequently in European capitals, especially London; and in 1894 the Turkish government complained to Britain that she was harbouring a man who was a danger to the Ottoman state, and gave his address as 23 The Parade, Uxbridge Road, Acton.

The Hunchaks soon had agents in Ottoman Turkey, Europe and America, and in the Russian Caucasus. It was an international movement. Soon there emerged other organisations which stuck much more closely to the only practical centre for Armenian revolutionaries, the Caucasus, which, although ruled by the bureaucratic functionaries of the tsar, was nevertheless a place where Armenians could meet, collect funds and organise without too much secrecy.

The first native Caucasian-born organisation of any real significance was the Young Armenia Society, founded in 1889 by Kristapor Mikayelian.[29] It only lasted for a year, before developing into a greater and more comprehensive organisation. Although Mikayelian held genuine political principles, the Young Armenia Society's policy was crude. It largely consisted of making forays into Ottoman territory in order to 'punish' the Kurds for their oppression and violence towards Armenians. An important word in the Society's vocabulary was *vrezh* – revenge. The idea that Kurds too were victims, but less obvious ones, of the Ottoman system was not apparent. Moreover, the Society believed in foreign intervention; as Russia had intervened after the Bulgarian atrocities, so, it held, would one or more powers come to their aid. In this, its leaders failed to note the changed political circumstances of the late 1880s.

The oppression under which Ottoman Armenians lived, and the official manner in which it was sanctioned, were such as to make revolutionary terrorism an entirely natural consequence. The Ottoman system of law was a denial of law itself. It was symbolised at this time by the Kurdish brigand-chief Musa Bey, whose villainy and violence were so great that foreign representatives demanded his arrest. He was taken to the capital, and, after a trial that was a mockery of justice, set free. An outcry resulted in the European press, and the sultan thought it prudent to banish him to Arabia, whence he quietly returned to his former activities.[30]

Nevertheless Armenians were no longer suffering passively. They were raiding Ottoman territory, and, politically more significantly, the Hunchaks defied the government both in Constantinople and in Erzerum, 'the capital of Turkish Armenia'.[31] Social relationships throughout the empire were shifting as a result. George Washburn, principal of Robert College, Constantinople, noted of the years 1890–2 that 'the old friendly feeling between the Turks and Armenians, who had always been regarded with more favour than the other Christian nationalities,* and who seemed to understand each other better, had given place to distrust and fear.'[32] And in the Caucasus, also in 1890, a new word entered the vocabulary of the Armenian revolutionary societies – Dashnaktsutiun, or federation.

---

*Washburn is referring here to the position of the Armenians in the capital, and in a few other towns in the western part of the empire, not the poor, downtrodden agricultural class in the east.

Dashnaktsutiun

The Federation of Armenian Revolutionaries (Hai Heghapokhakanneri Dashnaktsutiun) emerged from the need for an umbrella organisation for all the groups. And initially they all belonged to it. Nazarbekian and Mikayelian planned jointly to edit *Hunchak* – the journal of the new Dashnaktsutiun – in Geneva. The main objective of the federation was to win freedom for Armenia by a people's war.

Details, however, were not worked out; perhaps because there were too many people pulling in different directions. Indeed, by the summer of 1891 the Hunchaks had split from the Dashnaktsutiun, less because of ideological differences than personal ones; and the following year the Federation's name was changed to Hai Heghapokhakan Dashnaktsutiun (Armenian Revolutionary Federation), the name it has today. Thereafter, Hunchaks and Dashnaks would almost always be rivals. Policy divergencies, in the early years, were often slight; but in succeeding years it became clear that the Hunchaks gave priority to socialism, while the Dashnaks, in general, pursued a more nationalist path. There were also differences in the internal structure of the two on the issue of centralisation. Both nevertheless believed that in the prevailing conditions armed struggle was essential, and were prepared to use terror and intimidation – which were, indeed, used all the time by both tsarist and Ottoman governments – in order to achieve their aims.[33]

Confrontation in Erzerum

The revolutionaries first showed their strength in 1890. No longer now were the men who were prepared to take action self-doubting, rather ineffectual intellectuals like Kulaksizian, but iron men, who were prepared to sink themselves, their wills and their consciences in the revolution. In June of that year there was a rumour that weapons were being stored in two Armenian establishments in Erzerum, the cathedral and the Sanasarian College, an educational institution founded by a Russian Armenian in 1880. The police searched them minutely on 18 June, and found nothing. Three days later the Armenian quarter was attacked by Turks and Kurds; there was some firing, and several on both sides were killed.[34]

Later that day 200 Armenians gathered in the cathedral churchyard to draw up a petition to the sultan. This was unprecedented in Ottoman Turkey; it was seen by the police as a hostile demonstration, and the Armenians were ordered to disperse. Initially they refused. This too was unprecedented. Finally, after a request by the Armenian bishop, an Ottoman battalion was despatched to Erzerum to keep order in the city. But revolutionary elements, Hunchaks – and this is the first time they made their presence known – would have none of it, and fired on the soldiers as they approached, killing two and wounding three.

The Armenian quarter was then attacked with ferocity; there was much looting and killing; 15 were killed, and 250 wounded.

A significant new division was emerging among the Armenians, between the old, clerical, Ottomanised leadership and the new revolutionary elite. Both strove to win the allegiance of the mass of the people, the clerical faction by means of their traditionally established power, the revolutionaries not hesitating to use terror and blackmail for their ends.

The Kum Kapu Affray

The following month this new division was brought dramatically into focus – in the capital itself, in the cathedral in Kum Kapu (T.: 'sand gate'), Stambul.

On Sunday morning, 27 July 1890, the Armenians of Constantinople were assembled in their cathedral for mass.[35] It was the feast of the Transfiguration. Suddenly a Hunchak from Van by the name of Harutiun Djangulian advanced towards the altar with a statement in his hand, which he evidently intended to read. The patriarch then indicated that this was not the time for reading such statements. Several members of the congregation thereupon shouted out, demanding that it be read. Among them were two men whose names would be renowned over the next five years – Mihran Damadian and Hampartsum Boyadjian. Djangulian then read the manifesto, which demanded Armenian reforms. Disorder then ensued, and as the patriarch was preparing to leave the cathedral, Djangulian drew a revolver and aimed it at him; but the patriarch escaped, assisted by his clergy. The disorder grew to a near-riot; a large number of Armenians from the eastern provinces of the empire entered the church, and started smashing windows. They accused the patriarch and his officials of neglecting the interests of the nation (*millet*), and of being indifferent to massacre. Their position was intolerable, they said.[36]

Outside the cathedral the demonstrators told – indeed ordered – the patriarch to go to the sultan with a petition, and after a heated argument he agreed to go. But just as his cab was preparing to leave, soldiers emerged from the neighbouring streets, surrounding patriarch and demonstrators. The patriarch melted into the background, and the confrontation developed into one between demonstrators and soldiers. In the ensuing fracas, shots were fired by demonstrators, and the police replied by bayoneting the crowd. Two soldiers were killed in the mêlée, and there were one or two deaths among the Armenians.

Of the Kum Kapu Affray – as it has become known – the British ambassador Sir William White wrote, with a colourful sense of history: 'The remarkable thing about it is, that this appears to be the first occasion since the conquest of Constantinople by the Turks on which Christians have dared resist soldiers in Stamboul.'[37] However, the real significance of the affray was the Hunchaks' challenge to their own traditional clerical leaders, whom they con-

sidered, *qua* leaders, as slothful and collaborationist, and their attempt to wrest
the leadership of the community from them. Implicitly it was a challenge to the
government; and it was a veiled threat too to the six powers, that they would
not be allowed to forget article 61 of the Berlin treaty and keep the Armenian
question entombed indefinitely, and that if necessary blood would be shed in
order to resurrect it.

The Gougounian Expedition

Two months later the revolutionaries struck in the Caucasus: a young man
named Sarkis Gougounian led an expedition planned to be a raid on Turkish
territory.[38] His plan had, in its early stages, been endorsed by Dashnaktsutiun
(at this time still the inclusive organisation), but they later disavowed it. Even
before Gougounian had crossed the Russo–Turkish border the expedition had
disintegrated; the partisans had lost their way, and grew short of supplies.
After three days' wandering they were captured by Russian Cossacks, put on
trial and jailed. Gougounian himself was given 20 years' hard labour in Siberia
(though he was pardoned in 1906). As an armed attack it had failed; but the
idea of the expedition struck a profound note among the people, and brought to
the surface their longing for liberation and their hatred for the irrelevant
empires that encompassed them. Henry Howard, of the British Embassy, St
Petersburg, wrote: 'The solidarity shown in this case between the Russian and
Turkish Armenians, as regards their patriotic aspirations, seems to me of
importance.'[39]

Pan-Islamism and the Formation of the Hamidiye Cavalry

At the same time there was an important and sinister development in Ottoman
policy. The sultan adopted a policy known as pan-Islamism. Despite its name,
pan-Islamism is essentially a political, and not a religious, programme: men
were able, after all, to be complete Muslims before the doctrine was invented.
Moreover, Sultan Abdul Hamid was by no means the faithful Muslim that he
has often been represented; like so many heads of state, he was an opportunist
as regards matters of religious faith. Wilfrid Scawen Blunt noted the following
after a conversation with Arminius Vambéry, who was the best-placed
European to understand the sultan at this time: 'He declares that, though
superstitious, the sultan is at heart a free thinker, his religion being with him a
matter of policy, and he related several anecdotes bearing on this point.'[40]
      Pan-Islamism is the attempt to unify the Islamic peoples against a non-
Muslim threat. As such, it can be used for either revolutionary or reactionary
ends. It was used as a revolutionary instrument by Jamal al-Din al-Afghani
(1837–97), who sought to kindle the fire of Islam among downtrodden Muslim

peoples, to enable them to withstand the corrupt and enslaving materialism of 'Christian' Europe; and it was used for reactionary purposes by Sultan Abdul Hamid II, who attempted, and to a large extent succeeded, in ironing out the difference between, say, Turk and Kurd, or Turk and Albanian, and uniting them against the alleged 'threat to Islam' posed by revolutionaries from the Christian communities – Balkan in the west, and Armenian in the east.

To this end, and to prevent a recurrence of Kurdish revolt – for the Kurds had been in revolt against the Porte in 1830, in the early 1840s, during the Crimean war, in the late 1870s and in 1880 under Sheikh Ubaydullah[41] – the sultan armed the Kurds, and enrolled them into cavalry regiments, which he named Hamidiye, after himself. The pattern was said to be that of the Russian Cossacks. British ambassador Sir William White wrote to Lord Salisbury on 24 February 1891:

> His majesty imagines that by organising the Kurds in a military fashion he will introduce discipline among them, and create a very efficient and loyal cavalry, thus strengthening the defence of the border provinces of the empire against a powerful military neighbour.[42]

However, he added: 'There is a great deal that might be *a priori* objected to the probable success of such a scheme.'

Four days later Consul Hampson, writing from Erzerum, pointed out that

> this measure of arming the Kurds is regarded with great anxiety here. This feeling is much increased by the conduct of the Kurds themselves, many of whom openly state that they have been appointed to suppress the Armenians, and that they have received assurances that they will not be called to answer before the tribunals for any acts of oppression committed against Christians.
>
> The Armenians in this town are very uneasy, and very many of those who are in a position to be able to do so have expressed their intention of leaving Erzerum as soon as the roads are open.[43]

The British military attaché reported on 15 December 1892 that to that date 33 regiments of 500 men each were in existence; 13 more were in the process of being formed. Their commanding officer was Zeki Pasha, a Circassian.[44] The following years showed that their military value as auxiliary frontier troops was practically nil; instead they only added to the lawless chaos of the region, looting and pillaging villages and travellers at will, and with complete impunity. They ruthlessly terrorised those whose land they shared. The creation of the Hamidiye cavalry was one of the cleverest and most effective pieces of divide-and-rule legislation ever devised by an imperial power.

The Yaftas: Revolutionary Strategy

The revolutionaries, for their part, extended the scope of their activities. Early in 1893 seditious placards (*yaftas*) appeared on the walls of several of the principal towns in western and central Anatolia. They were written in Turkish, and addressed exclusively to Muslims everywhere, even in India, and they bade them revolt against their oppressors.[45] Abdul Hamid was unworthy, incapable of ruling. He was only a Hamid *chavush* – 'Hamid the doorkeeper'. The Porte suspected, rightly, Armenian revolutionaries. Hunchak cells in Marsovan, Yozgat, Amasia, Chorum, Tokat, Angora and Diyarbekir had executed a plan which showed an internationalism which stood out in contrast to the pointless series of 'punitive' raids that some revolutionaries undertook in the east. But no Muslim revolt followed. Instead, on orders from the Palace, hundreds of Armenians were immediately rounded up and jailed throughout the length and breadth of Anatolia; typically, Ottoman Turkey over-reacted, and soon the allegations of arbitrary arrest, torture and punishment without trial reached the foreign embassies – especially the British, since many Armenians still vainly thought that Britain had some responsibility for their plight, in view of the Cyprus Convention. The British ambassador despatched his consul in Erzerum, R. W. Graves, to investigate. After a tour of the districts, Graves's conclusion was that it was 'more than probable' that Armenian revolutionaries were responsible for the *yaftas*, since this action was consonant with their overall strategy.[46] This, Graves figured, was to create 'a semblance of revolt' (by cutting telegraph wires, bombing the odd government building, etc.);[47] the sultan would then panic, and local authorities act in a stupid or over-zealous way. They would take excessively punitive measures and would arouse the Turkish and Kurdish masses with religious fanaticism, and a massacre would occur. The six powers would then be forced to intervene, in view of the relevant article of the Berlin treaty, and reforms would be imposed on the sultan (as indeed was to happen in Crete). Life would then be made at least tolerable for Armenians.

This plan, which was endorsed by some of the revolutionaries, was not the cold, vicious calculation that it has sometimes been represented to be, with the revolutionaries calmly accepting the possibility of thousands of deaths among their own people in order to gain narrow political objectives. In reality, the extreme measures to which they sought to provoke the Porte were only a speeded-up version of what was happening all the time to Armenians. There was little to choose between a thousand dying in a week and a thousand dying in a year. What the revolutionaries tried to do was to be catalysts – to show to the European powers (which had a certain, if ill-defined, responsibility for their government) the true nature of Ottoman rule, and to force them to do something about it. Assuredly Europe would do nothing if those thousand deaths were spread over a year; but there was hope that, if there was a sudden, frightful outbreak of bloodletting, the powers might intervene. Disraeli himself had acknowledged that British policy had been blown off course by the Bulgarian atrocities. Then (they reasoned) let there be atrocities, if this was the only way to stir Europe to honour its obligations. Morally, their case could be defended on utilitarian grounds. Moreover, the actual execution of such measures lay with the government, which was always more terrorist than any bunch of revolutionaries could ever hope to be. The revolutionaries' great error was one of tactics, believing they could force Europe to intervene – a perpetually false hope.

Sasun: the Preliminaries

South of Moush, between the mountain ranges of Kurtik (or Hachresh) and Andok, there lay, in 1894, three large Armenian villages – Semal, Shenik and Gelieguzan. One at least can be found on the map today. The scenery amidst which they are set is of breathtaking magnificence; a British vice-consul described the landscape in 1895 as 'alternate high ridges and deep valleys, many of them thickly wooded with walnuts, oaks, willows, mulberries, figs and vines, and abounding in streams'.[48] Travelling was very difficult, since there were none but the roughest footpaths.

Of the three villages, Semal was closest to Moush. A few miles east of Semal was Shenik; and closest to Mount Andok was Gelieguzan. At this time they were administered directly from Moush, though they were commonly said to belong to the sub-district of Sasun (or Sassoun – so named, allegedly, after Sannazar, one of the sons of Sennacherib). According to official figures – probably low estimates – there were 48 houses in Semal, 38 in Shenik and 82 in Gelieguzan (4 of which were Kurdish).[49] Their Armenian inhabitants, cut off from any urban life, lived in archaic, patriarchal style, with huge 'extended' families, numbering sometimes 40, 50 or even more in each house, but more usually about 10.[50] One contemporary British document describes them as 'a stalwart race of mountain shepherds'.[51]

The valley-land was rich and fertile – excellent cattle-rearing land. The streams which water it eventually gather themselves into the Talori Su, which flows south to join the Batman Su, and eventually broadens out to join the upper Tigris about 200 miles west of Jezirah. Amidst the twists and turns of the Talori Su, where the terrain is even more mountainous and impassable, there lay another cluster of Armenian dwellings, which together made up the *nahiye*, or parish, of Talori (or Talvorik). In the 13 wards of this district – for they were too small to be considered villages – there were approximately 450 houses.[52]

To the west of the entire district was a region known as Kurdish Sasun, inhabited by settled Kurdish farmers. Their society was dominated by powerful *aghas* (Lords), who often feuded amongst themselves. To the south, too, there were Kurdish villages.

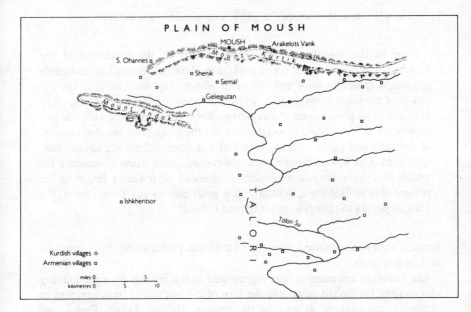

Map 6. Sasun

The third element in the population was the nomadic Kurds, who used to migrate from the Diyarbekir region in the summer through the district, in search of summer pasture, though in recent years they had been forbidden to do so, in view of the havoc they created. They were none too welcome to either settled population, bringing with them theft and lawlessness – although it was always possible to rob thieves as well as be robbed by them.

Armenians and Kurds got on with one another tolerably, but not particularly well. One Armenian woman described relations between her people and the nomadic Kurds as between 'brothers of earth and water',[53] and the phrase is apt for those between the two settled communities, too. Relations between the peoples only became impossible when the government supported one against another. However, the Armenians deeply resented the fact that the Kurdish *aghas* used to demand from them a kind of protection tax – an annual due of crops, cattle, silver, iron ore (for there were a few primitive mines in Sasun), agricultural implements or clothes. This unofficial tax was known as *hafir*.[54] And when an Armenian girl married, her parents were forced to press on to an agha half the sum which their son-in-law paid them as a dowry; this tax was called *hala*. With the half-hearted spread of government authority to the country areas – which always meant first and foremost government taxation – these local exactions had not disappeared, so in many places the Armenians were being forced to pay double taxes. As Col. Chermside put it to

Sir William White in the summer of 1889, after a tour of the district:

> Prior to the abolition of the feudal system by the enactment of the
> Tanzimat [reorganisation], the rayahs [non-Muslims] received considerable
> protection from the beys and aghas to whom they were subject. On the
> power of the latter being broken, and the substitution for it of a weak, often
> nominal, local government, the rayahs suffered much from the violence and
> oppression of their Kurdish neighbours. At the same time, the descendants
> of the beys and aghas in many localities still exacted from the rayahs con-
> tributions and forced labour, and maintained other ancient customs for
> which they gave no just equivalent. Remnants of feudality linger to the
> present day in Hakkiari, Bohtan and a great part of the Bitlis vilayet, the
> villages paying to the aghas taxes termed *kabal*.[55]

Sasun, Chermside continued, was one of the those places where the Armenians
paid double taxes.

The Ottoman government was represented in this district by a functionary
who, despite his limited powers in the face of the traditional structure, was as
villainous and corrupt as any in the empire. Hassan Tahsin Pasha, *vali*
(governor) of Bitlis, was described by the British vice-consul in Van, C. M.
Hallward, as 'continually trading on the "Armenian question", extorting
money by threats from Armenians in every part of the province'.[56] His method
was simple. He used to summon Armenians to appear before him, make his
illegal demands, and if they refused, jail them. Incarceration in the Bitlis jail
was sufficient to subjugate the hardiest spirits, and they would pay up.
However, the Sasuntzis outwitted Hassan Tahsin by an even simpler ruse: after
a summons to Bitlis, they failed to turn up at all.

Perhaps their disobedience was due to the presence in Sasun of two young
Hunchak revolutionaries, who had for some years past been laying the
groundwork of defiance there; though we should note that Sasun had been in a
state of limited rebellion in 1889, before the appearance of revolutionaries.[57]
Both had been at the Kum Kapu affray in June 1890. One was Mihran
Damadian, an Armenian Catholic from Constantinople. Born in 1863, he had
received his education in his native city and at the school of the Mékhitarist
Fathers, on the Isola San Lazzaro, Venice. In 1880 he became a teacher, and
from 1884 to 1888 was principal of an elementary school in Moush. It was this
experience, in which he saw the downtrodden aspect of his people, that made
him become a revolutionary, and join the Hunchaks. After the Kum Kapu
afíray he went to Athens, where he took part in an anti-Turkish demonstration
in July 1891.

In August 1891 he left Athens for Sasun, disguised as Melkon Khurshid, a
porter from Moush. Throughout the autumn and winter he was active in Sasun,
teaching, training and arming.

The following spring he was joined by another veteran of Kum Kapu, Hampartsum Boyadjian. He was a native of Hadjin, near Marash, and had studied medicine in Constantinople and Geneva. Travelling from Transcaucasia to Sasun, he had eluded the imperial spies by disguising himself as a Muslim sheikh with the name of Murad – a name which became his revolutionary name. With his medical skills and his message of defying the ever-present oppression and extortion, he soon gained the confidence of the villagers.

In the summer of 1892 Murad and Damadian together organised a seven-man guerrilla gang. Three years later, when Murad was being cross-examined about this period, it was put to him that he had instigated battles with the Kurds; he denied that this was so, saying that any blood shed among Armenians and Kurds was merely a function of the 'system of injustice', as he termed it, which the government upheld.[58] Nevertheless, there was at least one casualty in 1892 as a result of their activities. They spent the latter part of 1892 trying to calm things over, and reduce tension between the communities; but there were a few more incidents, and feeling ran high.

Early the following year Murad left for the Caucasus, to get funds. He said he would be back by May. Damadian continued to keep relations with the Kurds level. But while he was spreading revolutionary ideas among the villagers of the plain of Moush – west of the town – he was pursued by *zaptiyes* (mounted gendarmes) and arrested after suffering a leg injury from being kicked by a horse. He was taken to Bitlis and then to Constantinople, where he was granted a pardon. In summing up his activities in Sasun, vice-consul Hallward says, 'I do not believe that the agitation amounted to much, or had much effect on the villagers. One thing seems clear, that shortly after his capture the fate of the Sasun Armenians was sealed.'[59]

After the arrest of Damadian events moved fast in Sasun. In July the nomadic Kurds were for the first time for several years permitted to pass through Sasun and Moush. Their more lawless activities were patently supported by the government: they were co-ordinated by the *mutessarif* (local governor) of neighbouring Gendj, who also gave his backing to a notorious anti-Armenian fanatic, the sheikh of Zeilan. In a matter of weeks an unprovoked attack was launched by three to four thousand Kurds on the villages of the Talori parish. The Kurds attempted to lay siege to the Talori Armenians, but the latter withdrew into a stronghold they had prepared and successfully withstood their attacks. Several of their small villages were, however, sacked. The Kurds then gave up the attempt, to return to their winter quarters. But the Armenians were not left alone; shortly afterwards the *mutessarif* of Gendj arrived with soldiers, arrested some leading Armenians, sent them to Bitlis, and reported that the people were in revolt against the government.[60] Most of the Armenians were able to stay defiantly in their mountain fastnesses. With the onset of winter the troops withdrew, and the people came down.

The Battle

Next spring, as the frosts cracked, and the sun dazzled the beautiful valleys and streams back into life, the Sasuntzis must have known that they would confront the authorities again, in greater, and perhaps more terrible, form. In the empire of the Osmanlis no subject people could so challenge the government with impunity. However, Murad was among them – he had returned in the autumn, not in May as he had hoped – and it appears that the villagers placed enormous trust in him, and his presence gave them strength.

In June 1894 the *kaimakam* (sub-governor) of Kulp, a village to the west of Sasun, came to Ishkhentsor both to collect arrears of taxes from the Armenians of Talori and to arrest the notables who persisted in eluding the snares of the governor of Bitlis. He was accompanied by *zaptiyes*. The men of Talori said they were willing to pay government taxes if the government would put an end to unofficial Kurdish exactions. Then, according to R. W. Graves, British consul in Erzerum,[61] 'he proceeded to abuse and maltreat them. They then lost their temper, fell upon him, and, after administering a severe beating, drove him and his zaptiyes from the district.'

To the official this was armed rebellion, and he reported it as such, adding that a large force would be needed to put it down. About 300 soldiers and *zaptiyes* went to the spot; but the Armenians retired into their stronghold, and the Ottoman commander refrained from attacking. At about the same time a small Ottoman force went to Shenik and Semal, again to try to compel the notables to present themselves before the governor of Bitlis so that he could extract money from them. The troops arrested five Armenians – but were pursued by armed villagers, who managed to rescue four of the prisoners.[62]

In this tense situation the tribal Kurds appeared, on their seasonal migration, in very large numbers. Incidents occurred between them and the Armenians, often beginning in a trifling way – the stealing of a few sheep or oxen – but developing in a punitive, extremist manner. In at least one case the Armenians reacted harshly, killing several Kurds. These incidents aroused the Kurds, and the leaders of two of the main tribes, Bekiranli and Velikanli, met to discuss the situation. Another tribe, the Karikanli, were for attacking the Armenians at once, but were restrained by regular troops, stationed at Merghemuzan, half an hour from Shenik.[63]

Shortly afterwards, however, between 60 and 80 Bekiranli went to Merghemuzan, and conferred with the troops. The substance of their discussions became clear from the action which followed. On their return they fell upon Shenik and Semal. The villagers fled to the nearby heights of Chai and Köprü-sherif-khan, where fighting continued for two days. But there their position became impossible, and the women, children and flocks were moved to the greater safety of Mount Andok; the men were forced to retire to Gelieguzan.[64] Meanwhile Semal and Shenik had been gutted by fire. The troops, it was apparent, had changed from instruments of restraint to accomplices; not only had the Bekiranli attacked after conferring with them, but also, while the attack was continuing, the troops had made no effort to interpose themselves.

For 12 days (probably 14–25 August) a ferocious battle was fought at Gelieguzan between the tribal Kurds and Armenian defenders. Throughout that time the Armenians were able to hold the Kurds off. Three of the defenders managed to get a message[65] to Murad, probably on the 25th, in which they said:

> if you ask about us, we have nothing left, because for the last twelve days we have been fighting, and by the Lord's mercy we are conquerors; but yesterday morning the fighting began in all directions: we were attacked; he |their attackers| captured Husseindzik, and in the evening entered the village and laid all in ashes. Today, in the morning, he attacked us from all points on the Andok, and we only just escaped complete destruction.

On the back of the letter: 'At present we do not know what will happen; it may be that by the evening there will be a change, and that he will put us to the sword.' On the same day a detachment of Hamidiye cavalry had reached Gelieguzan, rushed there specially from Erzindjan. It succeeded in doing what the tribal Kurds had failed to do – dislodge the Armenians. However, when their position became hopeless most of the Armenians were able to escape to the heights of Mount Andok, where they took up protective positions below the women and children.

Massacre and Betrayal

But amidst the ravines and crags and soaring irregularities of Mount Andok, any attempt at an orderly defence was bound to break down. Soon the soldiers and Kurds broke through the rough defensive system, and then searched out and killed all they could lay their hands on, including many from the Talori district, by now likewise overrun and sacked by government forces 3,000 strong.[66] They killed entirely ruthlessly, the soldiers – a nightmare touch – dressed in black, the Kurds in white. Armenians, men, women and children, were 'the object of repeated pursuit on the part of the soldiers, Kurds and zaptiyes, who wounded or killed, without distinction of age or sex, all who fell in their hands.'[67] Children were dashed against the rocks, pregnant women barbarously mutilated.

In the words of H. S. Shipley, British delegate at the commission which followed these events,[68] for a period of some three weeks

> the Armenians were absolutely hunted like wild beasts, being killed wherever they were met, and if the slaughter was not greater, it was I believe solely owing to the vastness of the mountain ranges of that district, which

enabled the people to scatter, and so facilitated their escape. In fact, and speaking with a full sense of responsibility, I am compelled to say that the conviction has forced itself on me that it was not so much the capture of the agitator Murad, or the suppression of the pseudo-revolt, which was desired by the Turkish authorities, as the extermination, pure and simple, of the Gelieguzan and Talori districts.

Estimates of those killed vary between a very conservative 900[69] and 3,000.[70]

Some Armenians, however, in order to escape from this labyrinth of death, resolved to give themselves up. They were men and women of Semal, and their leader was their priest, Ohannes (one of the three who had signed the note to Murad, written just before the flight to Mount Andok).[71] The priest managed to make contact with the colonel, Tewfik Pasha, and he received assurances that they would be unharmed if they came down. With this promise the priest reassured his flock – the traditional leader taking the initiative and showing the authority that his people expected.

They reached Gelieguzan, only to be betrayed by the soldiers. On orders from the colonel, Ohannes was seized, his eyes gouged out, and amidst taunts from the soldiers, he was bayoneted to death. Of his followers, the men were separated from the women and children; and at night the women were mass-raped by the soldiers. The following night the men, in an adjoining field, were bayoneted to death like their priest.[72] The woman could hear the dreadful sounds of butchery. Trenches were dug for the corpses, which were thrown in, with only the thinnest covering of topsoil.

The Unravelling

For some days after that the pursuit over Andok Dagh continued; but by about the end of September the authorities felt themselves satisfied. Murad had been caught, the villagers taught a lesson. However, the row about Sasun, which would turn it into an incident with international repercussions, was only just beginning. It did not take long for the truth to leak out, and the more alert British consuls, noting the activity of the Kurds, had been expecting a conflict for some months. The two outstanding British consuls in the area were R. W. Graves in Erzerum and C. M. Hallward in Van. It would be difficult to praise the activities of these two men, their tenacity and their bravery, highly enough. In a sense, they complemented one another: Hallward was determined to get to the truth at all costs, to pierce the hide of Ottoman evasion, temporising and circumlocution, impelled, one feels, by the horror of Ottoman injustice he saw around him, and the powerless poverty to which it consigned so many Armenians; Graves, was less passionately committed (not, after all, what representatives of Her Majesty's Government are trained to be!), more of a sceptic, more accurate in his despatches, but sharing Hallward's contempt for

Ottoman misgovernment – his sense of justice more hidden behind a hearty, bluff exterior (he was keener on trout-fishing than rescuing Armenians). These two men, together with the British ambassador, Sir Philip Currie, made up a formidable, relentless trio of criticism to the Porte. Although it would be fair to argue that the events which had occurred in Sasun were due to the policies of their own government two decades earlier, none of the three was blinkered by the ass-like obstinacy of men such as Elliot or Layard, who had been unable to see outside their most immediate imperial interest.

On 2 September Currie sent a note to Said Pasha, the grand vizier, in which he said he had been informed that three 'Kurdish regiments of irregular cavalry', i.e. Hamidiye regiments, were being sent against the Armenians of Sasun. He reminded His Highness 'that it was the acts of irregular cavalry in Bulgaria which produced so painful an impression in Europe, and were the cause of so many misfortunes to Turkey', and urged him to do his utmost to prevent a repetition.[73] (Yet even now corpses littered Andok Dagh and filled the trenches at Gelieguzan, and the villages were charred ruins.) Not long afterwards he asked Hallward to visit Moush, to try to find out what had happened.[74] Hallward arrived on 30 September. He found the atmosphere thick with fear, suspicion, unwillingness to talk. The local Armenian bishop sent an urgent message to him begging him not to try to meet him. So Hallward tried to get the authorities' permission to visit the district in question, to see the three villages in question. No, he was told, you cannot proceed; the town of Moush is in quarantine after a cholera outbreak – there is still a battalion at Semal, and you must not infect them. This was a very feeble excuse for preventing him from going, since the soldiers had themselves brought the infection from their headquarters in Erzindjan. Hallward had to wait in Moush, and all the while he was chafing to reach the villages before winter supervened.[75] He managed, however, to collect enough material from second- and third-hand sources to send a devastating report to his ambassador on 9 October, much of which later proved to be true.[76]

The Porte not only obstructed in the east, it also sent a propaganda agent to Erzerum (where the more senior consuls resided) to process the news and make it palatable to the consuls. This man was a certain Ximenes, a Spaniard who received a regular salary from the Palace, now masquerading as a journalist and 'writer of distinction'. Graves soon realised what his real job was, perceiving that 'he was in constant communication by cypher telegram' with the Palace. Certainly, Ximenes told the consuls, massacres have taken place, but the Armenians were rebels, and the perpetrators of the massacres were Kurdish irregulars; the government's part was an honourable one, having attempted to restore order by calling in regular troops to restrain the Kurds.[77]

It should perhaps be noted that now and over the next 20 or 30 years, the Turkish government regularly ascribed the massacre of Armenians to the actions of wild, unsubdued Kurdish tribes, whereas in each case the 'thinning out' or straightforward extermination of Armenians was a matter of considered government policy. The 'Kurdish cover-up' is very frequently met, and only really ended when the Turkish government embarked on deporting and massacring the Kurds themselves, by which time there were, anyway, scarcely any Armenians left.

The Porte was agitated, and the sultan shaken by the bold plan and forthright action of a British vice-consul.[78] A claim was made in early November that Hallward was instigating the Armenians to hold meetings, to sign a paper against the government, even to rise against the imperial government. Currie retorted briskly to this serious allegation – a British vice-consul raising a rebellion – by declaring that he would immediately despatch his military attaché, Colonel Chermside, to the spot to investigate. The Porte, shuddering at the prospect of another foreign consular official at the scene of its atrocities, withdrew the allegation a few days later.[79]

Europe became apprised of the 'Armenian atrocities', as they were termed, at about this time. A letter in *The Times* of 17 November 1894 from G. Hagopian (writing from Fulham), in which he gave rather imprecise details of the massacre, marked the beginning of a campaign by liberal opinion in Europe to persuade their governments to act, and make the Porte implement article 61 of the Berlin treaty.[80]

The Porte was in a tricky position; Europe knew that a massacre had occurred in Sasun, and something had to be done to stop her nosy consuls, journalists and other intruders from making an on-the-spot investigation. Hence Said Pasha, the grand vizier, proposed to Currie that an Ottoman commission should be sent to Bitlis. Currie noted that the commissioners were a 'fairly good selection'. But shortly afterwards it was learnt that the terms of reference for the inquiry were to report on 'the criminal conduct of Armenian brigands'; there was no mention of allegations of massacre of Armenians.[81] Moreover, the sultan made it clear that 'if he was now sending one [a commission] it was only out of regard for the friendly representations of England, with whom he desired to maintain the good relations which existed'.[82] A sop to British liberals, in other words.

Then, apparently of his own accord, Currie thought it a good idea if the powers which had consuls at Erzerum – Britain, France and Russia – should send delegates to be present at the sittings of the commission, to survey its progress.[83] The three powers consented; and eventually M. Vilbert was delegated for France, M. Prjevalsky (Przhevalsky) for Russia, and H. S. Shipley for Britain. These men would not be actual members of the commission, but would be present to 'assist' it (giving it information if needed, suggesting questions to the commission's president, even themselves asking the witnesses questions, if necessary). They would see that the inquiry was conducted with impartiality, and ensure its sincerity.[84] The commissioners and delegates eventually assembled in late January 1895 in Moush, in the ice-bound heart of the Armenian winter.

Abdul Hamid, Arminius Vambéry and Armenians

In Constantinople the pressures from the ambassadors, and from liberal European opinion, had transformed what the Palace and the Porte hoped would be a trifling incident, soon forgotten, into a major issue. Abdul Hamid had for many years considered the Armenians a special kind of threat – those of the six *vilayets*, that is, not the wealthy, Ottomanised *amiras* of the big cities of the west, such as Smyrna and the capital, with whom on the whole he got on well. He feared the power of the peasant population of the east – that, since his own empire had reduced them to poverty unequalled since the Mongol irruptions, they were fair game for revolutionaries or foreign intervention.

One man who had discussed the Armenian question with the sultan was that part scholar, part clown, part spy-*manqué* figure Arminius Vambéry, at this time professor of oriental languages at the university of Budapest. A self-taught orientalist, in the 1860s he had travelled into Central Asia in disguise. Lately he had developed close links with the sultan – closer, perhaps, than any other foreigner. About twice a year, from the late 1880s, he used to go to the Palace, and have lengthy, detailed discussions with the sultan. The British foreign office paid for these trips, and in return Vambéry wrote them long reports of his conversations.[85] Clearly the sultan, who knew of the arrangement, liked Vambéry and talked freely to him. Vambéry's wide knowledge of Islam, Islamic peoples and the Turkish language made him a welcome guest in the otherwise plot-crazed labyrinth of the Star Palace. Another thing cemented the friendship of the two men: their bitter common hatred of Russia. Vambery was an extreme Russophobe-Turkophile, proudly sporting the cloak of a Disraeli or a Layard, in a curious, hyper-British manner, long after such fashions had been dropped in all but the crudest centres of British capitalism. Any bid made by a subject people of the Ottoman empire for the lessening of its oppression he regularly interpreted as the evil machinations of Russia, a power he detested with blind heartiness.

In the colourful reports which Vambéry sent to the foreign office, made pungent for its mandarins with more than a whiff of journalistic sensationalism, references to the Armenians occur from 1889 onwards. Vambéry's report of 22 October of that year is especially interesting.[86] He describes the nervous agitation which seemed to possess the sultan whenever the Armenian question was raised: he 'grew greatly excited while discussing it', and 'in his anger he lifted repeatedly his *fez*'. Disclaiming responsibility for the disorder in the east, Abdul Hamid put the blame for it on his pashas. (The possibility of dismissing them and appointing new ones does not appear to have been raised.) And the sultan is said to have added:

'Tell your English friends, and particularly Lord Salisbury, for whom I have a great consideration, that I am ready to cure the evils in Armenia, but I will sooner allow to severe [*sic*] this head from my body' (and here he grew very excited) 'than to permit the formation of a separate Armenia.'

Six years later he wrote – it is just possible recalling the 1889 discussion:

About two years ago he said to me whilst grasping nervously to his neck, 'They can severe [*again sic*] that head from my neck, but never Armenia from my empire . . . What is the Armenian question? One blow will suffice to stamp out the whole movement.'[87]

How much of this was Abdul Hamid, and how much the embellishment or the invention of the professor, we shall never know. Vambéry was prolix in his reports with his opinions, principally hatred of Russia, which he described as the *fons et origo mali*. He was so blinded by this hatred that the sufferings of the Armenians were completely excised from his mind. The potential freedom of Armenia was nothing more than the expansion of Russia, and he tried to insinuate such a viewpoint into the Foreign Office: 'From my English [point] of view I look upon every connivance shown to the creation of an Armenian province as upon a sinful attack against the vital interests of England.'[88]

The picture that emerges of Abdul Hamid, despite Vambéry's sympathy for him, is of a man at once tyrannical and craven, wearying himself with agitation that the Armenians, his subjects, had dared protest about their sufferings and oppression, and fawning for the aid of England, still playing that battered and torn trump card, the 'Russian danger', the northern menace.

Such was the man now confronted by the storm of the Sasun affair. Constantinople was in a state of turbulence, not least because the sultan's subordinates only reluctantly carried out the brutal orders of their imperial master. That they were the orders of Abdul Hamid there can be no doubt, in the light of a report of 25 December 1894 by Adam (later Sir Adam) Block, Chief Dragoman at the British embassy, which is marked Very Confidential and consequently not published in any of the Blue Books.[89] Block remarks that 'The sultan has from the first known that a massacre of some kind took place in consequence of his orders, and hence his aversion to any inquiry.' The memorandum also gives details of the consternation that had reigned in official Ottoman circles during the previous two months, and outlines the prospects of the Sasun commission. According to Block, Abdul Hamid was convinced that there was 'widespread sedition among his Armenian subjects'. On being informed by the governor of Bitlis that 'thousands of Armenians had assembled in open rebellion', the sultan, 'in a moment of panic or irritation, gave orders to stamp out the movement and destroy the villages'. Only reluctantly did the grand vizier pass the orders on to the marshal of the Fourth Army at Erzindjan, Zeki Pasha, who in turn sent a detachment of Hamidiye cavalry to Moush to do the killing, and later followed there himself to try to clear things up. Subsequently there was a furious scene between the sultan and his first secretary,

Sureyya Pasha, which concluded with the latter having a heart attack, collapsing and dying. Zeki himself – 'A very powerful man closely connected with the Palace' – stormed, 'I did not approve of the proceedings, but don't let them press me or make me speak out, for I still have the sultan's orders by me written by Sureyya.' Further disaffection was shown by the sultan's aide-de-camp, Abdallah Pasha, whom Block describes as 'a fairly straight man'; he was initially detailed by the Palace to be president of the Sasun commission, but 'received such instructions that he refused to go at first, and was kept a close prisoner at Yildiz until his departure'.

On the future of the commission, Block concludes that

> the ministers and Palace still hope that they will succeed in evading the presence and assistance of foreign delegates, and, in spite of them, will be able to hush up the affair, whitewash the culprits, and prevent the sultan's orders from becoming known. Every delay has been of assistance; at the very beginning the local authorities began to rebuild houses, to remove all traces of massacre, and to put out of reach all who could give information. I know that these orders have quite recently been repeated. The commission was in a hurry to get on the spot and get the job finished before our delegates arrived, and the snow and difficulty of moving about is hailed with delight by the Palace. The delegates will have to contend with all kinds of obstruction and chicanery, in which the Turkish official is a past master, and the climate and the preparations of the vali will render their efforts almost powerless. Hassan Tahsin has received his instructions, and no one will venture to speak out unless he is assured of protection after the commission leaves. I am informed that already the vali has informed the Porte that a new movement on the part of the Armenians is preparing, and that he has sent spies to investigate; this is impossible, with the winter season so far advanced, and can only be alleged with the object of either distracting attention from the Sasun incident, or of tightening his hold on the Armenians with the object of scaring them from coming forward to give evidence.

The Sasun Commission

Much of Block's gloomy prognosis proved true. The Sasun commission seemed intent on only attempting to prove the Porte's version of events. After the initial 12 sittings it had only attempted to investigate the allegations against the Armenians.[90] Important divergencies of evidence were not followed up; and only one hurried on-the-spot investigation was made – to visit the death-pit at Gelieguzan. Witnesses were tampered with by the authorities: as an afterword to the report of the proceedings for 14 March 1895, there is the following note:

> The delegates consider it their duty to point out that the three witnesses

heard at this sitting, illiterate peasants belonging to different villages, not only repeat the same facts, but make use of identical terms for an identical account, and seem to them to be repeating a lesson which they have learnt by heart.[91]

One man, an Armenian from Shenik, was told when he arrived in Moush that 'he must accuse the Kurds of all that happened, and not the soldiers'. A secret report from Prjevalsky gives further details of how the inquiry was stage-managed by the local authorities: 'Witnesses for the commission', he reported, 'are selected mainly, if not entirely, by the local police.'[92] Moreover the manner in which the inquiry was conducted was most irregular:

Depositions favourable to the Turks are not interrupted by the president, and are carefully written down by the secretary. But witnesses who speak against the authorities and the troops merely answer the questions put to them, and the interrogatory is conducted in the most confusing fashion in order to entrap them in contradiction of detail.[93]

Nevertheless a mass of grim and horrifying detail did emerge from the commission, so that it is possible to piece together what happened.

Despite strenuous attempts by the Ottoman government to impose a news blackout, two enterprising British special correspondents – E. J. Dillon of the *Daily Telegraph* and F. I. Scudamore of the *Daily News* – managed to reach Turkish Armenia, and to send long and graphic reports of the Sasun Commission to their papers.[94] The secret police were agitated by their presence. Dillon datelined his despatches from Moush, although he never got further than Erzerum; but since the news had travelled fast on the local grapevine, his reports were none the worse.[95]

Another 'Reform Scheme'

After the inquiry, action was needed; but the proponents of reform found themselves up against the perennial problems of Ottoman administrative change. It was immediately clear that it would be very difficult to get the six powers to act in concert. As regards Ottoman reform, three had virtually lost interest by 1895 – Germany, Austria and Italy. Russia's foreign policy was in the hands of Prince Lobanov, the inflexible aristocratic reactionary who had succeeded Giers. France would do nothing that would upset her intimate diplomatic relationship with Russia. Ironically, in view of her policy at Berlin, which had permitted this disastrous chain of misrule, insurrection and massacre to occur, Britain was now the only power prepared to take positive and realistic action.

A modest reform scheme for Turkish Armenia was drawn up after lengthy negotiations between the Constantinople ambassadors, and presented to the sultan on 11 May 1895, before the Sasun commission had finished its sittings. This programme,[96] prefaced as 'the minimum of the measures and reforms which it is necessary to apply in the provinces that have been disturbed by recent occurrences',[97] sought to establish just and reasonable governors at all levels from *vali* to *mudir*, who would be representative of the people they governed and – a major departure – not barred from office by religion. There would be police and gendarmes that protected, rather than attacked, the civilian population, and in which, again, Armenians could participate. The nomad Kurds would be controlled and there would be reforms in the administration of justice.

But this time Russia obstructed. Prince Lobanov was fearful that the alleviation of Armenian servitude would act as a dangerous precedent for similar moves in his own sovereign's empire. Typically, he justified his authoritarian decision by his fear of the 'Armenian committees', which, 'in London and elsewhere' – one notes his rigid distaste for the capital of free opinions – aimed at the creation in Asia Minor of a district in 'which the Armenians should enjoy exceptional privileges, and which would form the nucleus [*noyau*] of a future independent Armenian kingdom'.[98]

Thus Britain was left alone seeking effective action. But she could no longer act alone under the terms of the Cyprus Convention because such action would now be construed by the other powers as trying to seek an unfair advantage over them. So yet again the reform of affairs in Turkish Armenia was paralysed.

Lord Salisbury returned to power in July 1895. He lost no time in speaking 'very earnestly' to the Ottoman ambassador:

> The essential matter was that provision should be made for securing equitable government to the Armenians. I repudiated all ideas of autonomy as absurd, and I asked no privileges for them, but simple justice between man and man; that Kurds should not oppress Armenians, nor Armenians Kurds.[99]

On the 18th, probably in response to Salisbury's earnest speaking, the sultan's own reform plan was announced, putting into force 'reforms which are not contrary to laws and regulations already in existence'.[100] Taken aback, and somewhat sceptical, the powers waited. Their scepticism was well founded, for the linchpin of the scheme was to be Shakir Pasha, former Ottoman ambassador in St Petersburg. He had indeed already (28 June) been appointed 'inspector of certain localities in the provinces of Asiatic Turkey', and his position was confirmed by the sultan's new announcement. For an estimate of Shakir Pasha we need look no further than a letter from Arminius Vambéry; he described Shakir Pasha as 'not at all the man fit for that office', adding that he was 'the *diabolus rotae* of the whole disastrous policy of the sultan'.[101] It took only a few months to prove Vambéry right.

It was 20 October 1895 before the Grand Vizieral Order was finally issued, which detailed the reforms – in essence a thinner version of the May reforms.[102] One of the main proposals was that Muslim officials, whether *vali, mutessarif* or *kaimakam*, would have non-Muslim *muavins*, or assistants. This might seem sound; but the men appointed were in no sense representative of the people they controlled, and the Armenian population had no faith in them, believing they would soon inevitably become *evetjis*, yes-men. Adherence to the revolutionary parties grew apace.[103] The roving commission, of which Shakir Pasha was head, had moreover no executive power, so that even if the general inspector had not been the malevolent functionary that Vambéry describes, the commission could not have achieved anything.

Armenian Opinion after Sasun

In the east, many changes of opinion and attitude had taken place since the events in Sasun. The government-sponsored massacre had led to the destruction of what was left – admittedly little – of any sort of harmony and tolerance between the different communities. It is fashionable today to say that European nationalism destroyed what was good in the Ottoman empire, but in the eastern *vilayets* of Anatolia it was unquestionably the Ottoman government itself which brought fear, hostility, destruction and finally murder. Thus Hallward, writing from Van, 2 February 1895:

> On their Christmas it is the custom of the Armenians to exchange visits among themselves, and to receive visits from the Turks, but this year the Turks in general abstained from paying them any visits. There is really no special ill-feeling between the local Turks and Armenians, but the former take their cue from the government.[104]

A few sentences later he observes

> that all the local officials, high and low, are penetrated with the idea that any act of oppression or injustice towards Armenians will be overlooked, if not actually rewarded, by their superiors; an idea which has also taken root and borne fruit among the Kurds of the country districts.

In a long memorandum of 28 January 1895 Graves analyses the nature of the swing of opinion among Ottoman Armenians.[105] He divides the politically aware Armenians into three groups. First there were the conservative, or Turkophile, Armenians (officials in Ottoman employ, hangers-on, stewards, unofficial agents of leading Muslims), all of whom prospered under the old order. To these he adds the Armenian Catholics, who lived for the most part away from the turbulent regions where the Kurds roamed. They were able to pursue their educational activities without government interference, and would lose by a change such as Russian annexation, where they would be small fry lost in a shoal of adherents to the Armenian Apostolic church. The second group comprised those of moderate liberal views – businessmen, professional men, schoolteachers, and 'the best of the higher clergy'. The third group was the revolutionaries.

The conservatives and Catholics, Graves says, were deeply stirred by Sasun; many 'are already in secret sympathy and agreement with their former opponents'. Others too would join if changes were to be made in the empire, since, Graves points out, they 'are of the class which is always disposed to come over to the winning side'.

Most interesting is the change of opinion among the moderate liberals. Formerly they

were generally quite alive to the material impossibility of constituting an independent Armenia, as well as to the danger of ultimate denationalisation that perhaps awaited them in case of annexation by Russia; it was therefore their aim to avoid precipitating any violent solution of the Armenian question, and to maintain the Armenian element as such, by strengthening and developing the national church and schools, which enjoyed greater freedom under Ottoman than under Russian dominion; at the same time, they placed their hopes for the future in the ultimate introduction of those administrative reforms which have been so often promised by the Porte.

Now all that had changed. Development was useless, as was the hope of reforms, in view of what they believed to be 'the deliberate policy of the government for the weakening and ultimate extinction of the Armenian element in these provinces. What use, they ask, will there be for church or schools, if there is no Armenian population left to fill them?' Now, too, they had swung round to welcoming the prospect of Russian occupation – at least their lives and property (that is, what stood between them and starvation) would be secure, and their wives and daughters safe from rape. By comparison, Russian ecclesiastical and educational restrictions were trivial.

The revolutionaries, according to Graves, had sought to force the attention of the powers on the Armenian question, and they had succeeded. In this they had been 'ably seconded by the action of the Turkish authorities themselves in the provinces chiefly concerned'. Government policy, and the inevitable response it evoked, was destroying the tentative middle ground of opinion.

Autumn 1895

In the late summer of 1895, if the sultan seemed to be handing out reform and justice with his right hand, with his left he was dealing murder and atrocity on a scale hitherto unknown. In almost all of the impartial accounts there is mention of the complicity of soldiers, gendarmes and other officials.

These massacres, succeeding one another in rapid succession, were a drawn-out calculated brutality. The Bulgarian atrocities of 1876 and the Sasun massacre had been brief, and had soon passed. But this terror dragged on, as town after town was hit with death. For three months, and longer, there seemed no escape from blood and destruction.

Bab Ali

Immediately before the massacres in the east there was a large and violent Armenian demonstration in the capital. It may have provided the excuse for the authorities to begin killing Armenians in the east, but it cannot be said to have *caused* the massacres, since, however weak the Ottoman government had become, it was still a government, and as such it retained the freedom to kill or not to kill.

The organisers of the demonstration of 30 September 1895, which is known as the demonstration of Bab Ali (the Great Door, i.e. the Sublime Porte) were the Hunchakian Revolutionary Party. The events were carefully and lengthily planned. Finally, on the 28th, two days beforehand, the Hunchaks sent a letter to all the embassies, stating that the demonstration was to be held, and that the organisers intended that it should be peaceful; if there was a rough-up, it would be the police and military who would be responsible.[106]

This was, however, less than the whole truth. The Hunchak party was divided on the use of violence in the demonstration; a section of the executive committee favoured a demonstration that was not peaceful.[107] The fact that on the 30th many of the demonstrators were armed with pistols and knives of a

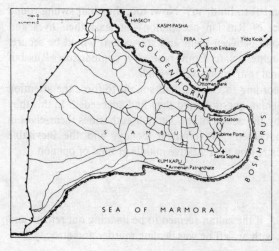

Map 7. Constantinople

uniform nature indicates that, to some extent, this section had its way; and the actual course the demonstration took shows that many of the rank and file supported them.[108]

On the day of the demonstration security measures were tight in the capital; police were out in strength, and the entire Sublime Porte was sealed off by cavalry and police. By noon there was a crowd of about 2,000 Armenians in the Kum Kapu district, by the patriarchate. The ostensible purposes of the demonstration was to present to the Sublime Porte a document which the Hunchaks termed their 'Protest-Demand'.[109] Copies of the document were also delivered to the embassies.

The Protest-Demand is a dignified and compelling document. It lists five individual protests: the first is

against the systematic persecution to which our people has been subjected, especially during the last few years, a persecution which the Sublime Porte has made a principle of government with the one object of causing Armenians to disappear from their own country.

Other protests were against the state of siege in the country, 'the source of all the arbitrary features of the administration' and of the poverty of Armenians; against the mass political arrests, and the brutal torture to which suspects were subjected; against the behaviour of the Kurds and Turkish regular troops, and against the iniquitous exactions of officials and tax-gatherers; against the Sasun massacre.

Peace and security, the document continues, were indispensable

to a nation which desires to reach by fair means a position of comparative prosperity, which it has certainly a right to aspire to, and to reach the level of progress and civilisation towards which other peoples are advancing.

The demands follow: for safety of property and persons, for freedom of conscience, of the press, and of public meeting, and for absolute equality of all before the law. Every arrest must be justified immediately before the courts, in view of the arbitrary arrests and excessively long provisional detention. Armenians must be permitted to bear arms, since it was impossible to disarm the Kurds.

Administrative reorganisation of the 'six *vilayets*' was demanded, since the current divisions were made without reference to geography or ethnography, and huge numbers of meaningless boundaries and divisions only meant a glut of rapacious officials. To administer the entire area the Hunchaks demanded a European governor-general, delegated by the powers in agreement with the Porte. The other main demands were for reforms of police and gendarmerie, economic and tax reforms, an end to migration of the nomadic Kurds, and finally a general amnesty of Armenians under detention or in exile.

A year had passed, the document concludes, since the Sasun massacre; nothing has been done; the harsh Armenian winter was approaching; immediate action was essential:

It is for this reason that we have decided to remind his imperial majesty the sultan and the powers in a decisive and demonstrative manner of the absolute necessity which exists for an immediate and favourable solution of the Armenian question.

This was the document which the crowd would take to the Sublime Porte. At Kum Kapu, where the big crowd had collected, a brief word was passed between some women demonstrators and the patriarch, Matteos Izmirlian, who advised patience, and told his people not to take any precipitate action. But one of the men of Sasun in the crowd shouted 'Liberty or death!'; the demonstrators took up the cry; and singing the revolutionary song *Tsain më hnchets Erzrumi Haiots lerneren*, they moved away from the cloistered councils of patience.[110]

But *en route* for the Porte the demonstrators were stopped by the police, under the control on this occasion of an allegedly able major, Server Bey. He first urged them to halt; when they refused and insisted on proceeding, he shouted 'Yasak!' – 'It's forbidden!' He then ordered his men to use the butt ends of their rifles to push the crowd back. An Armenian student then asked him on what authority he barred their way; they were, after all, just presenting a petition to the Sublime Porte. Server Bey had no time for this: he insulted him ('Damned infidel!') and struck him with his sword. The Armenian drew out a hidden revolver, and blew Server's brains out.[111]

Then the soldiers and police let loose hell on the demonstrators, beating and bludgeoning about 20 to death, and leaving 100 wounded. The rest fled. But the authorities had made plans to deal with them. A counter-demonstration had been arranged. As they fled, large numbers of *softas* (allegedly Muslim theological students, but often police agents in student dress)[112] appeared on the streets, clubs in hand, throughout the capital, and began beating the life out of any Armenians they could lay their hands on. In districts of the capital far from where the demonstration was taking place, Armenians were set on indiscriminately, and done to death. The attitude of the police and *zaptiyes* was one of almost entire collaboration with the killers – either they stood by and watched the bloody proceedings continue unhindered, or they took an active part in them: one *zaptiye* was observed by a German officer to be looking on while an Armenian was being held by a group of men and beaten on the head with sticks; when they had left him unconscious in the gutter the *zaptiye* finished him off with a couple of shots.[113]

Around the Armenian patriarchate the midday defiance of the demonstrators had turned to a deadly fear. Two hundred and seventy Armenians had gathered in the cathedral there – their plight seemed to them similar to that of their forefathers at Avarayr. Nazim Pasha, minister of police, sent a message to the Armenian patriarch, Matteos Izmirlian, asking him to send the men home. Izmirlian sent his secretary, Diran Kelekian, to the cathedral with the message, adding that the grand vizier had given assurances that they would not be molested. The refugees replied, 'We do not trust the promises of the massacrers of Sasun.' They spent the rest of the day, and the following night, in the cathedral.

Throughout the following day, 1 October, the massacres continued. The worst sufferers were the Armenians of the poorest class – porters, dockers and the like – probably because they were the most exposed. Fifty men were killed at Kasim Pasha, and a similar number of Armenian workers at Chukur Cheshme. Many of those who could escape the terror sought refuge in the capital's churches.[114]

On the 2nd, the fear continued: Armenians were still clustered in their churches, in Kum Kapu, Pera, Galata, Kasim Pasha, Hasköy and Scutari. Abdul Hamid sent a message to the patriarch to calm his flock. But the patriarch was ill from shock, and could receive no one. The foreign ambassadors, sick and revolted by what they had seen, sent a collective note to the Porte, calling the Porte's attention to the 'trustworthy intelligence' they had received: that prisoners, in the hands of the police, were struck down by private persons (that is, the '*softas*' and others hired for the occasion) without the police interfering; that absolutely inoffensive people were assaulted; and that wounded prisoners were killed in cold blood in the courtyards of police stations and in prisons. The government was urged to curb the disorders at once, since public security was at risk.[115]

Nothing, however, was done; and later the same day Currie was compelled to send a note to the grand vizier, pointing out that 'far from improving, the situation is getting worse'. Armenians were being massacred in the khans of the city, and terror reigned in Constantinople and its suburbs.[116]

On 3 October death continued in the city streets: at At-Meidan, Hampartsum Boyadjian himself, 'Murad', the activist of Sasun, since amnestied by the sultan, was injured. Near Dolmabahche 21 Armenian Catholic workmen were killed. The bodies of 106 Armenians, badly mutilated, were sent to the Yedi Kule hospital; some had about 40 wounds.[117]

But still, to the fury of the authorities, about 2,000 Armenians remained in their churches throughout the city, night and day. On 5 October the Palace sent an Armenian who was a high Ottoman official, Artin Pasha Dadian, to try to persuade them to leave, promising them that they would not be attacked. They replied, 'We trust you, but not your master. He has done nothing but deceive the Armenians since the days of patriarch Nerses [Varzhabedian]. Your sultan is only a liar.'[118] On 6 October police and troops laid siege to the churches. The refugees within were blockaded; no food was allowed in. The alternatives were starvation, or running the gauntlet of the '*softas*' and assorted terrorist irregulars hired by the Palace. Murders still continued in the streets, notably at Sirkedji (the capital's railway station). Again the powers protested with a strong collective note against arbitrary brutality by officials, and unchecked pillage and murder.[119]

It was 10 October when the Armenians were finally persuaded to emerge from their churches. Joint action and firm assurances by all six embassies convinced them that they would not be assaulted or murdered as they left. Any Armenian who requested was given a safe-conduct endorsed by the Russian ambassador, Nelidov, saying that the bearer was not to be arrested by the police. They were ordered to give up their arms. The total number of refugees, in six churches, was 2,414, of whom 12 per cent carried arms.[120]

What of the Bab Ali demonstration, which had initiated the reign of terror? Its organisers rated it a success. When the sultan signed the reform programme later that month, the Hunchaks believed their action had forced him to do so. They put out a statement which spoke of 'the party's great victory'.[121] Yet, even as they wrote, a rain of blood was falling in Turkish Armenia. Terror in the capital might be over, but in the east it was just beginning. The Hunchaks' statement was the premature boast of a *kusaktsakan*, a word which denoted a number of individuals of this period, meaning a man who is unable to see beyond his party, which is always right.

The Autumn Killings

The first outbreak occurred at Trebizond – the first of those massacres which were carried out with such smoothness and efficiency that many marvelled at the capacity of the Ottoman government for the destruction of its own subjects, as they had mourned its inability to create a viable political structure for the progress of these same citizens. The Trebizond Armenian community numbered some 7,000. Trouble began on 2 October 1895, when two unknown assailants shot and slightly wounded two officials: Bahri Pasha, a notorious ex-governor of Van, comparable in attitudes and methods to Hassan Tahsin of Bitlis, and the local *ferik* (commandant). Armenians were suspected. Shops were closed in the Armenian quarter by their owners. Two days later, armed Turks attacked the Armenian quarter on the pretext of searching for the two assailants. The Armenians repelled the attack, killing three and wounding eight.[122] The Turks, furious, threatened extermination of the Armenians. On 7 October the governor of Trebizond summoned a high-ranking Armenian cleric and bade him find the two fugitives 'to calm the Turkish populace'. Otherwise he could not guarantee the safety of the Armenians. The priest and members of the civil council replied that they did not know where the two were, and that it was absurd to hold the entire Armenian community of Trebizond responsible for the activities of two hotheads.[123]

On the 8th the Armenian shopkeepers cautiously opened their shops again.

About the middle of the morning a bugle sounded: instantly armed Turks, Laz brigands and soldiers poured into the Armenian quarter, killing any Armenian they could lay their hands on. Blood flowed fast. In reporting the outbreak, the British consul enclosed an account written by an unnamed resident of Trebizond:

> Unsuspecting people walking about the streets were shot ruthlessly down. Men standing or sitting quietly at their shop-doors were instantly dropped with a bullet through their heads or hearts. Their aim was deadly, and I have heard of no wounded men. Some were slashed with swords until life was extinct. They passed through quarters where only old men, women and children remained, killing the men and large boys, generally permitting the women and younger children to live. For five hours this horrid work of inhuman butchery went on, the cracking of the musketry, sometimes like the volley from a platoon of soldiers, but more often single shots from near and distant points, the crashing in of doors, and the thud, thud of sword blows sounded on our ears. Then the sound of musketry died away, and the work of looting began. Every shop of an Armenian in the market was gutted, and the victors in this cowardly and brutal war glutted themselves with the spoils. For hours bales of broad cloth, cotton goods, and every conceivable kind of merchandize passed along without molestation to the houses of the spoilers. The intention evidently was to impoverish, and as near as possible to blot out, the Armenians of this town. So far as appearances went, the police and soldiers distinctly aided in this savage work. They were mingled with armed men, and so far as we could see made not the least effort to check them.[124]

'The troops took a prominent part in the butchery,' reported one foreign consul. Another report tells how the governor, far from intervening, remained in the telegraph office all the while, keeping the capital in the picture on the progress of the massacre. The telegraph was a new and vital instrument for Abdul Hamid to control the pace of the massacre. Whole streets were desolated; but, remarkably, amid the tumult great care had been taken not to attack Armenians who were Catholics, or who were Russian subjects. To have attacked either would have been unnecessarily to incur the wrath of the powers. If there was one house left standing in a ruined street, the owner was certain to be a Catholic or a Russian.[125]

When the massacre had died down (a bugle signalled its end too), an estimated 920 lay dead;[126] and the rest of the Armenian community, impoverished, faced starvation in the following winter. Moreover – and this is a point often alluded to in the consular reports, but usually dismissed after a few lines – that figure did not include the Armenian villagers, who were mostly peasants, living in partly or wholly Armenian villages, which were in the neighbourhood of every town. Whenever any town was attacked, the massacre nearly always spread later to the villages; on occasion, the villagers were attacked first. It is very difficult to get any reliable estimate of those who died in the villages; but, remote and unprotected, living for the most part in wooden houses, the barely recorded deaths of these poor peasants must have been every bit as terrible as the urban slaughter. The village deaths of the Trebizond massacre probably amounted to 200.[127]

About a week later there was a massacre at Akhisar, near Ismid (over in the west). This was a relatively small affair – only 31 Armenians reported dead – but gruesome all the same, and there was again complicity of the officials.[128] There was no provocation. A contemporary report states that 'there were sixteen armed officials present . . . but their presence was evidently an encouragement to the killers.'[129]

It was the turn of Erzindjan on 21 October 1895: the outbreak here was provoked, according to the version of the authorities, by an Armenian assassinating a Turk; they failed to point out that between 15 and 20 Armenians had already been killed. It ended with about 260 Armenians dead, and about 850 villagers likewise.[130]

Friday, 25 October 1895 saw two major massacres. Friday was to be a common day for massacre.[131] The official explanation was that Armenians planned to massacre the Muslim population while it was at prayers in the mosque, or as it was leaving the mosque; but in the nick of time the plot became known, and the Muslims rushed out of the mosque and massacred all the Armenians. The only fault with this lively explanation is that there is no real evidence that Armenians on any occasion planned or carried out such an attack.

The massacres on the 25th were at Bitlis and Gumush-khana. An early consular estimate of the Bitlis deaths was 630, but later it was put at 800.[132] The villages suffered, too – but here not so much from outright massacre as from forced conversion to Islam. Forced conversion to Islam, like pan-Islamism, sounds like desperate religious fanaticism: it conjurs up lurid, Vathek-type images of wild-eyed zealots with huge curved swords. But just as Abdul Hamid was a diplomatic religious unbeliever, so his policy of forced conversion had a purely political purpose, removed from even the broadest interpretation of the Islamic faith. In order to curb the disaffection of the subjects of his empire, Abdul Hamid resorted to their extinction, and for this purpose conversion to Islam was an alternative – a less messy one – to plain murder. A man or woman who had repeated the formula for becoming a Muslim could not, on pain of death, abjure his new religion. And once a Muslim he ceased to be a member of the troublesome Christian minority. Conversion to Islam meant the death of his Armenian identity. Hence the forced conversions.

In Gumush-khana about 100 died in the outbreak – Armenians and a few Greeks, even though the Armenians had been carefully separated from the Greeks beforehand. Again, eleven surrounding Armenian villages suffered badly.[133]

It was the turn of Baiburt on 27 October. Here the massacre spread inwards from the outlying Armenian villages. When the townsmen heard of the village massacres, those in the market closed their shops. But troops arrived from Erzindjan, and compelled them to re-open. The massacre in the town followed, in which the populace was 'assisted by the soldiers' (consul Cumberbatch). Killing and pillaging continued for eight hours. Churches were despoiled. Several hundred men were killed, and a few women and children. For the survivors the prospect was destitution. Cumberbatch concludes:

> Nothing is said as to the attack having been provoked by the Armenians, as it is asserted by the authorities, but it is to be inferred from my informant's account that the disorders were the natural sequence of the attacks on the villages.[134]

There was a massacre at Urfa lasting two days, 27–28 October. Several hundreds died. Here the incident began in a small enough way – a quarrel between a Turk and an Armenian, the Turk kills the Armenian, friends of the Armenian kill the Turk, and the whole Turkish/Kurdish population lays into the Armenians. Two months later Urfa was to suffer a second, infinitely more frightful, massacre.[135]

Erzerum followed. Tension had been rising in the town for several days before the massacre (30 October). Armenian revolutionaries were active in the town, and the Turks and Kurds, led by the officials, were breathing fire. A single shot unleashed the massacre, an attempt by a Hunchak on the life of the chief of police. At once the Armenians closed their shops, and tried to flee in all directions from the bazaar 'only to be cut down, shot or clubbed by the mob and soldiery'.[136] The bazaar (1,000 shops) was completely wrecked, its contents looted.[137] Over 350 Armenians were slain; Cumberbatch witnessed the burial of 309 in one mass grave on the 31st.[138] Michael Herbert of the embassy in Constantinople cabled London on 2 November: 'The participation in excesses by soldiers has been established by personal visit to the pillaged houses and interrogation of surviving inmates.'[139]

There was a sizeable population of Greeks in Erzerum, but they escaped the massacre. (The only non-Armenian Christian killed was a Serb.) The Greeks had to run for it, though; but if they were caught, they escaped by declaring their national identity to be Greek.[140]

A sinister aspect of the Erzerum massacre is the presence there of two of the officers most responsible for the brutalities in Sasun the previous year: Colonels Ismail Bey and Tewfik Bey. In Cumberbatch's opinion, the presence of these men, who enjoyed an 'unenviable notoriety' might account for a great deal of the soldiers' 'unbridled licence'.[141]

Meanwhile, what of Shakir Pasha and his roving mission? Cumberbatch had earlier (18 October) written: 'No Armenian either dared or was allowed to approach him to set forth his grievances.'[142] The consul gave as a typical reply to the Pasha's meagre efforts the remarks of a Persian living in a town in the east:

'If you, one of the sultan's most powerful pashas, are unable to redress our wrongs, there is only his majesty left to do so, and he will never come here. After your departure our condition will be worse than it was, and will end disastrously. I warn you!'[143]

Graves was later to conclude that the alleged reforms 'were purely illusory and left the country in an even worse condition than that which they were supposed to remedy'.[144]

The Erzerum massacre, under the noses of the British, French and Russian consuls, led to yet another protest from the ambassadors to the Porte. A brief but firm identic note was delivered to the Porte on 5 November 1895.[145] The powers expressed anxiety about the state of the provinces 'where complete anarchy reigns', and added threateningly: 'The Porte must know from what happened in Syria in 1860 that this anarchy cannot continue with impunity.' The note said outright that the powers would act together if the sultan failed to 'adopt effectual measures immediately'.

The sultan's response to this note was to affect to be hurt. His reply ended with the appeal:

Why is it that England will not help me? I cannot understand it. Does Lord Salisbury not wish to help me? In spite of all my sincerest efforts [sic], I see that the English papers still abuse me. Can they not see that I am earnestly striving to put things straight? Cannot something be done to stop them? I expect England to give me great assistance.[146]

The sultan's desire to tamper with the British press was very droll. In this matter he received help from an unexpected quarter: from Theodor Herzl, the founder of Zionism, who believed that by discrediting Armenians in Europe he would gain the support of the sultan for his plans for the colonisation of Palestine. Herzl managed to influence journalistic opinion slightly in the sultan's favour.[147]

In his reply to the sultan, Lord Salisbury said that Britain was willing to help Ottoman Turkey, but that attacks on Christian peoples of the empire must stop. The sultan had attempted to show that the attacks were provoked by Armenians; however, Salisbury said, 'We are informed that on nearly every occasion this was not the case, and that in too many instances the Turkish authorities and troops have encouraged and even taken part in the outrages which have occurred.'[148]

During and after this exchange the massacres continued unabated. Three days of violence and murder gripped Diyarbekir, from 1 to 3 November.[149] About 1,000 Armenians were killed, and little care seems to have been made to protect the non-Armenian Christian peoples, for a number of Greeks and Assyrians died too. According to the French consul, the notorious sheikh of Zeilan, responsible for mass incitement at Sasun in 1894, had taken part in the plans for the massacre. During the onslaughts, about 500–700 Armenians and Assyrians took refuge in the French consulate which was 'practically besieged'.[150]

At about the same time Arabkir was plundered and set on fire.[151] 'The Turks and Kurds sacked the town,' reported the consul, and 2,800 Armenians were estimated to have died. Plundering and burning continued for ten days. Local villages were sacked; in one, only three out of probably over 100 were left alive.

Malatia fared even worse.[152] For six days (4–9 November) massacre and looting continued. Three thousand were estimated to have died, including many Catholic Armenians. (As the killings progressed, the authorities seem to have cared less and less whether they might invoke the displeasure of the powers.)

More than 500 died in Kharput on 10–11 November – an organised massacre, complete with bugle call;[153] and, over in the east, Sasun and Talori were again attacked on 10 November. Some villages were plundered, and Ishkhentsor sacked, and its inhabitants massacred.[154] Van, both town and province, was, though lawless, spared for a few months the ruthless massacre of other districts.

Sivas Armenians were massacred on 12 November; consular reports put the number of dead at 1,500.[155] Three days later it was the turn of Amasia (1,000), Aintab (also 1,000) and Marsovan (150); also of Gurun, where 'appalling barbarities' left only 500 of the 2,000 Armenian families alive.[156] Then on 30 November Kayseri; about 1,000 died. In Kayseri there was some rudimentary industry – a few Armenian small-scale factories. In one the owner and 21 workmen were killed, and in a shoemakers' craft centre 53 men were killed. Throughout the town there was looting, rape, fire and death – the pattern in Kayseri was the same as elsewhere, and was begun and ended with a bugle call.[157]

In one place, however, the pattern was not the same. In the craggy town of Zeitun the Armenians took the offensive, and actually managed, with the assistance of the powers, to force some concessions from the Ottoman government. Zeitun, remote and inaccessible, was a natural centre for revolutionaries. In recent years the district had been annually shredded by that voracious locust, the Ottoman tax-collector, and was thus well prepared for Hunchak revolutionary agents.[158] In July 1895 the Porte hoped to quieten the agitation by granting the town an amnesty for its seditious activity. But when reports started to reach Zeitun of the massacre of fellow Armenians, and when the Zeituntzis perceived that murderous agents were infiltrating into their regions, they themselves attacked some local Turks, raiding and killing. The ambassadors feared a massive Ottoman reprisal, but the Armenian patriarch intervened, and his mediation was successful. The government was taking no chances, and despatched troops in the direction of Zeitun, should trouble break out again. The Zeituntzis got wind of this, and a force of their fighting men intercepted and encircled the Turkish troops on the road between Zeitun and Marash. They came within an ace of occupying Marash itself. At the same time the insurgents occupied the citadel of Zeitun and put the Turkish garrison to flight, taking more than 400 Turkish prisoners. Donning Turkish uniforms, they proceeded to the neighbouring Turkish town of Andrin, and sacked and burnt it.[159] By mid-November they exercised a considerable, if undisciplined, control of the district around Zeitun; both Turks and Armenians held their respective positions through terrorism and brutality, rather than by any loftier ideals of liberation and justice. The entire Zeitun conflict, in fact, was fast deteriorating into a race war.[160]

In response to the Armenian challenge, the authorities prepared a huge army which would sit at all the roads from Zeitun, like an enormous cat, waiting for the surrender; and if there was no surrender, it would pounce. By 19 December, after considerable fighting on the hills around Zeitun, this army was in position, and the roads leading from Zeitun were blocked.[161]

Armenian community leaders in Constantinople appealed to the ambassadors to act as intermediaries. Currie was keen to send consul Barnham, who was stationed at Aleppo, to Zeitun.[162] He feared, as did the other ambassadors, that 'if the resistance of the latter [Armenians] is overcome, the whole population of the district will be exterminated.'

The fighting reached Zeitun itself on the 23rd: under a thick mist the troops tried to seize the barracks of Zeitun, whence a large part of the Armenian fire was coming. But the Armenians quitted it and set it on fire just in time. They also slaughtered all their prisoners, a grisly and gratuitous action. A heavy, but largely ineffectual, Ottoman bombardment of Zeitun followed.[163]

Attempts at mediation were stepped up after the atrocious second massacre at Urfa (see below). Currie told the Porte that unless he received a satisfactory answer on this issue by 2 January 1896, he would despatch his military attaché, Chermside, thither himself. On the 2nd the Porte accepted mediation, and four days later the Zeituntzis accepted too. The terms finally agreed on were simply that all (Armenians or Turks) living in the valley should surrender their arms (excluding sporting guns and so forth), and that a general amnesty should be granted.[164] Some Hunchaks were to be 'simply expelled from Ottoman territory'. Remission of tax arrears would be considered; and a Christian sub-governor would be appointed for the district. Another Zeitun rebellion was over, at considerable cost to the Porte, for, as Barnham reported to Currie on 27 December 1895,

the wildest reports are received from the Armenians in Aleppo of repeated disasters to the Turkish arms, and certainly these reports receive colour from tales told by deserters, and from the frequency with which reinforcements are sent to the front.[165]

In the meantime disaster had befallen Urfa.[166] The Armenian population of
that town (20,000 out of a total of 60,000) had been virtually besieged in their
quarter since the massacre of 28–9 October. No food had been allowed in, and
the water supply had been cut off. The government alleged that they had 1,800
Martini rifles, and demanded their surrender. The Armenians said they had
none, which was true. The authorities repeated their demands, and hinted that,
even if they had no arms, at least they had the money to buy them. By 6
December they had managed to deliver up 600 pieces – old guns, pistols,
daggers and so forth. The *mutessarif* and commander, however, again
demanded 1,800 Martini rifles.

The siege conditions soon made their situation desperate. Old wells were re-
opened; money, used for bribing their guards to let food in, was running short.
They tried to smuggle a message to Aleppo, but the messenger was caught.

A few days later (13 December) the commander feigned kindness: he let
some Armenians out to return to their businesses in other parts of the town
(mostly bakers). Instantly they were attacked and wounded, and fled back into
their starving quarter.

In the days following a whispering campaign that had been continuing since
the beginning of the siege grew to a crescendo: that their extermination had
been decided upon by the sultan and his ministers. (Thereby individual Turks
had attempted to extract cash from the Armenians as protection money.) A
great impending disaster was suggested.

At midday on the 28th, after the non-Armenian Christians, of whom there
were a number in Urfa, had been ordered to remain in their churches, a bugle
sounded, a few shots were fired; and the soldiers and Turkish crowd invaded
the besieged quarter, and the mass murder of the exhausted, starving, terrified
Armenians began. The doors were axed down, and the troops poured in, firing
on the occupants.

After the massacre, the plunder. Everything movable that could be taken
away was stolen. Then kerosene was poured on the rest, and on any residual
corn supplies, and they were burnt. Towards sunset the bugle sounded again,
and the killers retired.

The Armenians who had escaped, dazed with horror and misery, destitute,
sought refuge that night in their large cathedral, which could hold 8,000
worshippers. (Traditionally, under Islamic law, churches were respected as
places of refuge.) One thousand eight hundred sheltered there; a priest
administered the sacrament. By early Sunday morning their number had
reached 3,000.

But later that morning they were undeceived of their hope that they would be
granted asylum in their cathedral – that that at least was inviolate. Firing
began at the windows; then the iron door was broken down. Troops entered,
and began killing all that they could lay their hands on who were on the floor of
the building. The women and children were up in the gallery, terrified and
shrieking. To get a good aim at them, the Turks ran up to the raised sanctuary

of the cathedral by the altar, and began picking off those in the gallery with revolver shots. But they soon tired of this method. Amassing some bedding and church straw-matting, they poured 30 cans of kerosene on it and set fire to it. The conflagration was a vision of hell.

The gallery and wooden framework soon caught fire, whereupon, block-ing up the staircases leading to the gallery with similar inflammable material, they left the mass of struggling human beings to become the prey of the flames.

During several hours the sickening odour of roasting flesh pervaded the town, and even today, two months and a half after the massacre, the smell of putrescent and charred remains in the church is unbearable.[167]

Consul Fitzmaurice wrote that on 16 March 1896.

The massacres died down after the bestial cruelty of Urfa. The authorities only made sporadic further attempts against Armenians; and the latter were learning the technique of self-defence. They put up a memorable defence in Van in June 1896.[168] Ottoman forces had been mustering for several weeks in pre-paration of an attack, but when it was launched, the armed militias of all three Armenian political parties – Armenakan, Hunchak and Dashnak – joined together to defend the people. The success was, however, highly qualified, since the Armenian leaders were compelled to retreat into Persia; but there is little doubt that their action saved Van from suffering the fate of many other towns in Turkish Armenia.

The Ottoman Bank Incident

Although the systematic assaults on the population subsided in the provinces, Constantinople itself was battered by a storm of blood in August 1896, follow-ing the most sensational of all the exploits of Armenian revolutionaries.[169]

The Ottoman Bank lies in the heart of the Galata district of Constantinople, which had for decades been the banking quarter. The bank was Ottoman only in name; it was created during one of the crises about Ottoman credit-worthiness, and was the main instrument through which foreign capitalists did business with the Ottoman empire and asserted their financial dominance of it.

The building itself (still there) is imposing and fortress-like. At the time, offices surrounded an open central area, where the day-to-day business was conducted. There were two main cash counters, one for gold, the other for silver.

On Wednesday, 26 August 1896, at 1.15 in the afternoon, the bank was almost empty; clients and employees were at lunch, and only a residual staff was left. Two men, apparently businessmen, entered; one went to the gold counter, the other to the silver. They said that they wanted to change money.

The bank clerks agreed, and the men returned to the bank's entrance and signalled to their porters, who entered with silver sacks slung over their
shoulders.[170]

Suddenly there was a whistle, a rush from neighbouring streets, and the bank
was filled with 25 armed men, firing, it seemed, indiscriminately. The 'porters''
loads were revealed – not silver and gold, but bombs, dynamite and ammunition. The raiders declared that they were Armenians, members of
Dashnaktsutiun.

They set to work trying to close the main doors of the bank, but found that
they had enormous and unexpected difficulty in doing so. The quantities of
glass broken in the initial assault meant that it took them three hours to close
them; in the meantime they barricaded themselves in with sacks of silver
coin.[171] All the while a battle was raging between the Armenians and troops
and police positioned across the narrow street. Four Armenians were killed
while forcing the doors shut.

Meanwhile the bank's director, Sir Edgar Vincent (later Lord D'Abernon),
had rapidly sized up the situation, and escaped through a skylight to the
adjoining offices of the Tobacco Régie. The employees in the main exchange
area, however, were all held as hostages.

The battle continued for a couple of hours. Bombs were hurled at the troops
from within the bank; and the police fired at anything seen moving in it. Only
when the authorities realised that they could do nothing to dislodge the men
who occupied the bank, who were desperate men, ready to blow the bank and
themselves up rather than surrender, did the firing slacken off.

At about 3.00 p.m. it ceased. When the bank clerks, still very frightened,
began talking to the Dashnaks, they were told that this extreme act had been
undertaken to force the attention of the powers on the Armenians, and to
compel political changes to be made for their kinsmen in the east. The bank
would be held for 48 hours: if the demands were not met by then, the bank, its
employees and the group who had seized it would all be blown up.

Three letters from the Dashnaks spelled out their demands. The first
attacked the powers for conniving at the Porte's illegal removal of the
nationalist-minded patriarch Matteos Izmirlian and certain other high officials
in the community, and their replacement by a group of *evet effendis*. The
Armenian nation was (they implied) thus without a representative spokesman
at this critical time.

The second letter spelled out their political demands. After focusing on the
murderous policy of the sultan in the east, and the 100,000 dead (the powers
estimated 50,000),[172] they presented the demands. These, 12 in all, were for a
European high commissioner for the six *vilayets*; local officials to be appointed
by the high commissioner, and rubber-stamped by the sultan; a locally
recruited militia and police to be officered by Europeans; judicial reforms;
freedom of worship, education and press. They demanded three specific tax
reforms: first, that three-quarters of taxes drawn from the provinces should be

ploughed back locally into the public sector; tax arrears must be cancelled; and no further taxes to be levied on the population for five years. (This demand shows the extent of their impoverishment.) Usurped property should be returned; Armenians who had fled allowed to return; and an amnesty granted to Armenian political prisoners. Finally, a temporary commission set up by the powers should superintend the foregoing measures.[173]

The third letter stated their bargaining position: they would stay in the bank for two days, during which time the powers were to intervene in the country, and put their demands into practice. Nothing in the bank would be touched, and no money taken; but if their demands were not met, 'the money and all the business papers will be destroyed, and we, with the employees, will meet our death beneath the ruins of the bank'.[174]

Meanwhile in the bank the bargaining began. The Dashnaks agreed to let one of their hostages, M. Auboyneau, Sir Edgar Vincent's deputy, go free to explain the situation to him. Sir Edgar, after his escape through the skylight, had gone to the Porte for urgent consultations.

At the Porte it had been agreed that negotiations would be carried on through a representative of one of the ambassadors. Maximov, first dragoman of the Russian embassy, was there at the time, and he bravely volunteered to go and speak to the Dashnaks. First, though, he requested, from the sultan himself, a free pardon for the Dashnaks, and permission for them to leave the country. The sultan consented.

When Maximov reached the bank, late in the evening, he spoke eloquently to the Dashnaks for about three hours. Eventually, at 2.15 a.m., agreement was reached. The Armenians would leave the bank at once for Sir Edgar's yacht. They could keep their arms (but not the bombs), and the representatives of the powers would meet them in the morning.

As the Armenians trooped out of the bank, the foreign powers must have felt profoundly relieved that their determination had crumbled – that out of a proposed 48 hours, they were in the bank for barely 13, and from forceful and far-reaching demands (which were to be put into practice immediately) they meekly accepted assurances of 'talks'. It is not easy to pinpoint the reason for their collapse. It may have been due to plain hunger (they were said not to have eaten for a day or so before the capture of the bank); or they may have been disappointed at the escape of Sir Edgar, who would have been a prize hostage. Perhaps it was simply fear. They were not seasoned political adventurers, but young men (their leader, Babken Siuni, was only 17) whom some would call idealists, others reckless terrorists.

Four Armenians were killed and six wounded in the siege; casualties were the same among the bank employees. Left behind in the bank were 45 bombs and a large quantity of dynamite.

On board the yacht the 15 (one report gives 17) were interviewed by one of Sir Edgar's secretaries. It emerged that the Ottoman Bank incident was only one part of a concerted plan, worked out some three weeks earlier. Demonstrations had been planned in the centre of the city, and near the Armenian

Patriarchate; the Crédit Lyonnais was, like the Ottoman Bank, to be occupied. Bombs were to be thrown at a nearby police station to distract the police from the banks. In the diplomatic district of Pera (modern Beyoghlu), north of the Golden Horn, bomb attacks were to be made on another police station, and the Aya Triadha Greek church. But three days before the incident the authorities had got wind of the plan, and parts of it had to be abandoned. For seizing the Ottoman Bank they gave four reasons: all the powers would press the Turks to yield to the demands, since the bank's employees were of varied nationalities; secondly, the building was in practical terms not difficult to defend. Then, by seizing the bank, they would strike not only at the powers, but at capitalism itself; and finally, since the bank was such a prominent building in Constantinople, their daring seizure of it would dazzle fellow Armenians, and win their support.[175]

But those Dashnaks who escaped were the lucky ones. They were put on board the French steamer *Gironde* and set sail for France. Their fellow Armenians were left behind to expiate – many times over – the 'crime' of terrorising a terrorist society.

Almost as soon as the bank had been seized – indeed before the police reached the scene – bands of Turks appeared on the streets, partly of the most ignorant and easily roused sections of the populace, partly of religious extremists and fanatics – men wearing long robes and turbans. Almost certainly, following Blunt's observation, many of them were police agents. These men appeared throughout the city, and were most noticeable in the European and business quarters of the capital, where European dress was the norm. Some held clubs, surprisingly similar, carefully shaped. Others had iron bars. No troops or police were on hand to control or disarm these threatening crowds; none appeared until 6.00 p.m. and then their purpose was to encourage rather than to control.

When sufficient irregulars were on foot, there began an orgy of hacking, killing and looting. Any Armenian whom these *bashibozuks* met was butchered or clubbed to death; shops were looted in Galata. The great majority of those killed were not revolutionaries, nor, on the other hand, were they rich capitalists. They were mostly poor migrant workers (porters, dockers, caretakers), who had come to the capital, for the most part from Sivas province, as the countryside had become uninhabitable. The butchery was fiercest in the district of Kasim Pasha, and in the Jewish village of Hasköy, where the unfortunate Armenians of Kilidj Oglu, their quarter within Hasköy, were briskly despatched.[176] In those two districts the Armenian population was virtually annihilated. The mob, reported consul Herbert, were 'in high spirits, and laughing like children on holiday'. He added that 'the ostentatious efforts made by the police to disarm them were a simple farce'. George Washburn, of Robert College, recalled the day thus: 'It had been a beautiful day, and several of our lady friends had been in town and found it very difficult to get back through streets which were already running with blood.'[177]

Murder continued on the streets on the following day, Thursday 27 August.

Dragomans from the embassies went to the Porte at 2.00 p.m. to protest, in the name of the six powers, but the response was merely evasive; they were told that 'the council of ministers was sitting continuously in the Palace.' Only when news reached the Porte in the early evening that British marines had landed, 'to protect British lives', did the killing stop.

In the two days of killing, and the subsequent minor disturbances, between 5,000 and 6,000 were conservatively estimated to have died; in succeeding months the Armenian population of Constantinople was depleted by emigration by 75,000.[178]

There is no doubt that the murders were organised and directed by the authorities; this was the conclusion of all the powers, set forth in their collective notes of 27 August, 31 August and 15 September.[179] The evidence they cite is overwhelming and damning. The Porte placated them with promises of arresting those responsible; but that would have meant arresting themselves, a puzzling predicament. Instead, the authorities made a show of arresting some of the lower-class Turks, the poor and the unemployed whom they had press-ganged into service for them. The powers were not fooled, however; they knew the truth about the massacres, and soon ceased even to answer the bleating explanations for the bloodshed given them by the Porte.

The Constantinople massacre again roused liberal opinion in Europe against the sultan, and impassioned pleas were made for his dethronement; but the storm was less violent that it had been over Bulgaria in 1876. In Britain newspapers published the details of the massacres, and emphasised the official nature of the killings, but the public outcry was more restrained. Gladstone, now aged 87, spoke at Liverpool on 24 September, more thoughtfully than in earlier speeches on the eastern question. His speech showed that he had exorcised the crusading spirit that had enfeebled the moral power of his former attacks on the Ottoman empire; in this, his last great speech, he spoke in terms of universal principles. He implored Salisbury to disengage Britain from the concert of Europe, and act alone if need be.[180]

Salisbury was under popular pressure in the way that Disraeli had been in 1876; but unlike Disraeli, he was not a man who could abandon all concepts of right and wrong for the sake of his private vision of imperial grandeur; unlike Disraeli, massacre perpetrated by an ally was a matter of concern to him. He was in favour of forcing the Straits and deposing Abdul Hamid, but failed to obtain Russia's agreement on the future of the Straits. He summed up the immense problems of dealing with the Ottoman empire in his circular of 20 October 1896.[181]

In this document Salisbury surveyed, from the point of view of a British foreign secretary, the intractable problems of the Ottoman empire – the failed attempts at reform, the growing movements of discontent. 'In the interests of general peace' – that is, because of their profound mutual jealousies – the great powers were compelled to 'maintain the fabric of the Ottoman empire'; yet this creature reared on their collective mistrust and greed was a monster.

But despite the powerful, wide-ranging scepticism which informed Lord Salisbury's review of the past efforts of the powers to grapple with the Ottoman empire, his proposals were lame. Salisbury understood the vicious circle, that can be expressed diagrammatically thus:

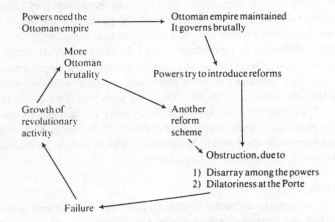

Yet Salisbury's recommendations were for another reform scheme, although he also proposed that prior agreement should be reached among the powers about enforcing it. But he did not specify how that agreement should be reached – especially with Russia, at heart deeply suspicious of acting in concert with Britain so long as the Cyprus Convention remained in force, since the Convention contained the threat of war.

Russia herself did briefly contemplate intervention against Turkey in late 1896.[182] The motive was to restore waning Russian influence in Ottoman affairs, and the plan was the drastic one of seizing the Bosphorus. If foreign warships should enter the Dardanelles in order to compel the implementation of reforms, Russia would act alone and occupy the Bosphorus. The sultan would be offered a guarantee of his own safety. There was little doubt that in any ensuing settlement the Armenian question – so great a risk to the stability of the Near East, and, since it was such a justified grievance, an enticement to an opportunistic power – would be settled to the advantage of Armenians. But this plan was scotched by France, Russia's close ally at the time. France would not countenance any moves leading towards the break-up of the empire, in view of her enormous investments in the country. (She held about 61 per cent of the Ottoman Public Debt.) So the Russian plan for a forcible solution came to nothing.

Nevertheless the Constantinople ambassadors of the six powers did meet towards the end of the year, and eventually decided upon a peaceful solution to the Armenian problem, which was embodied in yet another reform scheme (2 February 1897). Armenian revolutionaries had meanwhile threatened to blow up the Russian embassy if there were no effective results by the end of March.

But despite the agreement – and the threat – no effective measures ensued; the powers were distracted by war between Greece and Turkey, and thereafter in the Near East, until 1914, the Macedonian question was to be the heaviest incubus upon the great powers.

In the immediate aftermath of the Ottoman Bank incident there were sporadic official massacres, as if to remind the powers of the insidious and malevolent forces with which they had to contend: at Agn, or Eghin (modern Kemaliye), 2,000 died in three days (15–17 September 1896); 'many of the dead were left in the streets for days as food for the dogs, and large numbers were thrown into the Euphrates'; and, the report adds, 'all the testimony concurs in showing that the massacre was official . . . the work was done by citizens and soldiers.'[183] Six months later, at Tokat, 'after being encouraged to open their shops, the Armenians were mercilessly cut down';[184] 100 or so died. After vain attempts to persuade the Porte to bring those guilty to justice, Sir Philip Currie finally wrote to Lord Salisbury (3 August 1897):

> My Lord,
> I am compelled reluctantly to abandon all hope that the real perpetrators of the last two organised massacres in Asia Minor – namely those of Eghin and Tokat – will be brought to justice.[185]

Those implicated were too high in the local administration, and the rake-off that the lower officials got after the pillage was too great for them to incriminate their superiors.

With this double failure – on both the diplomatic and consular levels – the period of Armenian reforms came to an end. No more attempts were to be made to persuade the Porte to introduce Armenian reforms – except for one final, spectral effort, pushed through, with poignant timing, on the very eve of the first world war.

The Responsibility

Who was responsible for the slaughter of Armenians in the mid-1890s? For the Sasun massacre, Adam Block's memorandum of December 1895 could hardly be clearer: 'The sultan has from the first known that a massacre of some kind took place in consequence of his orders, and hence his aversion to any inquiry.' On the 1895 killings, C. M. Hallward notes (11 December 1895):

> Many Kurds have declared that they had distinct orders to plunder the Christian villages; and though their statements cannot be taken as proof of the fact, I do not think that those who know the Kurds of this province |Van| believe for a moment that they would be likely to start suddenly on such a general movement against the Christians entirely on their own initia-

tive. They habitually rob the Christian villages, but unless moved by special feelings of hostility or fanaticism, it is not generally their policy to plunder them to such an extent as has been done lately; in fact, they feel that it is contrary to their interests to ruin the Christians entirely, as by so doing they kill the goose that lays the golden eggs.[187]

The evidence of those on the spot, too, suggests overwhelmingly that the government was responsible: the planning and forethought (first the killers went in, then the looters followed, and the whole operation was started and ended by a bugle call), and the participation of troops in the killings – these things show that the government itself was guilty, and that the outbreaks were part of a premeditated Ottoman policy.

Two objections are possible to this thesis, but neither has much substance. The first is that 'really' the Armenian revolutionaries, or agitators as they are usually termed in this context, were responsible for the massacres: they sought reprisals, it is claimed, against the civilian population, in order to force European intervention which they anticipated under article 61 of the treaty of Berlin. Certainly, they did act provocatively, and in that sense did 'want' reprisals; but only in the sense of wanting to show to the world in one brief, dramatic flash the lingering inevitable horrors which they had to suffer more slowly, year in, year out. Quantitatively there was nothing to choose between a long-drawn-out massacre or a quick one. Armenians died whether the government pursued its usual course of malevolence and corruption, or whether it tightened its organisation and undertook a mass killing. Almost all of the massacres of the 1890s occurred without provocation; and to blame Armenian revolutionaries for the killings which occurred after the action of a revolutionary (such as at Erzerum) is to confuse provocation with executive decision, since it was and is the prerogative of a government to decide upon a policy, and to put that policy into action. A government is by its very nature responsible for the actions carried out by its servants acting upon its orders.

The second objection raised against blaming the Ottoman government for the killings is that the 'real' guilty ones were Western notions like nationalism and reform schemes, and Western technological hardware like 'railways, telegraphs, filing cabinets',[188] which made a hitherto inefficient tyranny an efficient one.

But this objection – which is like blaming vandalism on plate-glass windows – is just dust thrown in our eyes to deflect our attention from the intentions of the Ottoman government. Armenian nationalism grew naturally among Turkish Armenians as a result of several factors. In the first place, the Ottoman empire offered them nothing except misrule, theft of their land and livelihood, institutionalised discrimination and impoverishment. For decades they had seen the slow but steady improvement of the condition of their fellow-Armenians across the meaningless border which divided them, and no 'agitators' were needed to remind them of the difference between the two, or for them to feel drawn to their compatriots in Transcaucasia rather than to the barren institutions of Ottoman Turkey. Nor even did the draw of faith fix their attention on their patriarch in Constantinople, for the Catholicos in Echmiadzin had greater spiritual authority. These factors, rather than arid intellectual theories from Western Europe, led Armenians to reject the imperial system and develop national sentiment. Armenian nationalism was not a transplanted poisonous weed, but a natural organic growth from the circumstances of Ottoman Armenians.

The West's share of responsibility was not in exporting ideas or hardware: it was in weakening and humiliating the empire just enough to provoke its cruelty to an extreme level, without making any provision for those who suffered from that cruelty. The reason is not difficult to find: the enormous investment that Europe had sunk in the Ottoman empire, and fear that the dividends would suffer if part of the empire were removed, or if the entire structure were divided. The abuse made by the powers of the Capitulations and the institutionalised robbery of the Public Debt Administration debilitated the empire to a pathological level; when a break-up was the only way of restoring health to its peoples, a power such as France in 1896 objected, for fear of losing money.

Conclusion

There is nothing particularly mystifying or elusively strange about the massacres of the 1890s; there was no unfathomable 'eastern' characteristic in them. They follow an almost classic pattern: an empire rules part of its dominion by injustice, corruption and terror; the downtrodden people, emerging into political awareness, begin to ask for improvements. Nothing is done; political organisations spring up, and as nothing is still done, they become terrorist. The empire then reacts violently, believing that it can destroy the challenge by destroying the people themselves, or whittling them down until only a cowed remnant is left.

What was exceptional was the position of the 'six great powers'. They needed the Ottoman empire to continue, and the empire likewise needed them with their mutually suspicious alliances; but in order to appease their consciences the powers made certain imperfectly spelt-out guarantees for the good government of the subject peoples of the empire. With regard to the Armenians, nothing came of their undertakings, because they were too vague, and the powers themselves too irresolute and quarrelsome; so Europe was left giving support for an empire (which but for their support would have collapsed) as its misgovernment degenerated into organised massacre, in order to maintain its imperial necessities.

In this process the decision of some of the revolutionaries to provoke the government was essentially secondary; it presupposed a semi-savage government given to mass reprisals for civilian unrest. It was a very risky decision, and *prima facie* cruel; but it seemed less cruel to them than to see their fellow Armenians as the tortured playthings of Ottoman power. As a gamble it failed, because the circumstances of the Bulgarian insurrection and its aftermath could not be reproduced, and Britain was at first unwilling and later unable to act alone under the terms of the Cyprus Convention. Also Armenian revolutionaries believed, as did many Europeans, that the powers held the Ottoman empire as a quasi-colony, because of their extensive backing of it; whereas it was in fact a sovereign state, with the power to accept or reject the advice given by the powers, and to wriggle free from their coercion. They could not dictate policy to it, and the illusion that they could misled the Armenians.

It was also an illusion that deceived Western politicians and public; but with them it was a complaisant deception, since it permitted them to reap the interest from their investments in Turkey, with their consciences salved by the thought that their governments were putting things to rights – while all the time Armenians were being hacked to death on orders from the imperial capital.

Notes

1. J. C. McCoan, *Our New Protectorate: Turkey in Asia* . . . (2 vols., London, 1879).
2. Turkey no. 10 (1879), pp. 63–4.
3. Ibid., p. 76.
4. Peter Mansfield, *The Arabs* (London, 1976), p. 150.
5. Sir Robert W. Graves, *Storm Centres of the Near East* (London, 1933), p. 110.
6. Turkey no. 16 (1877), pp. 16–36; William J. J. Spry, *Life on the Bosphorus* (London, 1895), part 2, p. 316; A. de la Jonquière, *Histoire de l'empire ottoman* (Paris, 1881), pp. 13–14.
7. Turkey no. 10 (1879), p. 15.
8. Turkey no. 7 (1880), pp. 2–8.
9. Sir Edward Hertslet, *The Map of Europe by Treaty*, vol. IV, (1891), p. 3009.
10. Ibid., pp. 2958–61.
11. FO 881/5168, p. 3.
12. Ibid., pp. 3–4.
13. Wilfrid Scawen Blunt, 'Turkish Misgovernment', *Nineteenth Century*, no. 40 (November 1896), p. 840.
14. FO 881/5168.
15. Ibid., p. 17.
16. Ibid.
17. Ibid., p. 33.
18. Ibid.
19. Ibid., p. 23.
20. G. Warneck, *Outline of a History of Protestant Missions* (Edinburgh and London, 1901), p. 241.
21. Louise Nalbandian, *The Armenian Revolutionary Movement* (Berkeley and Los Angeles, 1963), p. 85.
22. *The Times*, 10 January 1883, p. 5; ibid., 8 June 1883, p. 5.
23. Nalbandian, *Armenian Revolutionary Movement*, pp. 90–103.
24. Ibid., pp. 97–8.
25. Turkey no. 1 (1890), pp. 11–12.
26. Nalbandian, *Armenian Revolutionary Movement*, p. 115.
27. Ibid., pp. 108–12.
28. David Garnett, *The Golden Echo* (London, 1954), pp. 39–40.
29. Nalbandian, *Armenian Revolutionary Movement*, pp. 145–7.

30. Turkey no. 1 (1890), pp. 31–130.
31. Nalbandian, *Armenian Revolutionary Movement*, p. 147.
32. George Washburn, *Fifty Years in Constantinople* (Boston, 1911), p. 219.
33. Nalbandian, *Armenian Revolutionary Movement*, pp. 151–5.
34. Turkey no. 1 (1890–1), pp. 54–6.
35. Ibid., pp. 62–4.
36. Ibid., p. 63.
37. Ibid., p. 62.
38. Nalbandian, *Armenian Revolutionary Movement*, pp. 155–60.
39. Turkey no. 3 (1896), p. 21.
40. Wilfrid Scawen Blunt, *My Diaries* (New York, 1932), p. 190.
41. W. E. D. Allen and Paul Muratoff, *Caucasian Battlefields* (Cambridge, 1953), pp. 536–7.
42. FO 424/169, p. 21.
43. Ibid., p. 30.
44. Turkey no. 3 (1896), p. 52.
45. Graves, *Storm Centres*, p. 132.
46. Ibid., p. 138.
47. Ibid., p. 139.
48. Turkey no. 1 (1895), part I, p. 200.
49. Ibid., p. 72; see also ibid., pp. 35–7, 175.
50. Ibid., p. 14
51. FO 881/6645, p. 3.
52. Turkey no. 1 (1895), part I, p. 200.
53. Ibid., part II, p. 282.
54. Ibid., part I, p. 262.
55. Turkey no. 1 (1890), p. 18
56. Turkey no. 1 (1895), part I, p. 38.
57. See *The Times*, 17 December 1889, p. 5.
58. Turkey no. 1 (1895), part II, p. 350.
59. Ibid., part I, p. 36.
60. Ibid., p. 70.
61. Ibid.
62. Ibid.
63. Ibid., p. 164.
64. Ibid.
65. Ibid., p. 182.
66. Ibid., p. 98.
67. Ibid., p. 171.
68. Ibid., p. 206.
69. Ibid., p. 204.
70. Graves, *Storm Centres*, p. 144.
71. Turkey no. 1 (1895), part I, p. 205.
72. Ibid., p. 114.
73. Ibid., p. 4.
74. Ibid., p. 13.
75. Ibid., p. 14.
76. Ibid., pp. 15–16.
77. Graves, *Storm Centres*, p. 144; also FO 424/178, p. 299.
78. Turkey no. 1 (1895), part I, p. 17.
79. Ibid., p. 28.
80. *The Times*, 17 November 1894, p. 5.
81. Turkey no. 1 (1895), part I, p. 27.
82. Ibid., p. 31.
83. Ibid., p. 32.
84. Ibid., p. 63.
85. FO 800/32–3.
86. FO 800/32, p. 58.
87. FO 800/33, p. 2.

88. FO 800/32, p. 322.
89. FO 424/178, pp. 388–9.
90. Turkey no. 1 (1895), part I, p. 76.
91. Ibid., part II, p. 262.
92. FO 881/6645, p. 28.
93. Ibid., p. 29.
94. Graves, *Storm Centres*, p. 146.
95. FO 881/6645, p. 12.
96. Turkey no. 1 (1896), p. 34; also Spry, *Life on the Bosphorus*, part II, pp. 316–30.
97. Turkey no. 1 (1896), p. 64.
98. Ibid., p. 81.
99. Ibid., p. 94.
100. Ibid., p. 95.
101. FO 800/33, p. 1.
102. Turkey no. 1 (1896), p. 160.
103. Graves, *Storm Centres*, p. 149.
104. Turkey no. 6 (1896), p. 238.
105. Ibid., pp. 222–4.
106. Turkey no. 2 (1896), p. 32.
107. Nalbandian, *Armenian Revolutionary Movement*, p. 123.
108. Turkey no. 2 (1896), p. 31.
109. Ibid., pp. 34–5.
110. |Anon.|, *La verité sur les massacres d'Arménie* (Paris, 1896), p. 28.
111. Ibid., p. 29.
112. Wilfrid Scawen Blunt, *My Diaries* (New York, 1932), p. 190.
113. Turkey no. 2 (1896), p. 31.
114. *La verité*, pp. 29–30.
115. Turkey no. 2 (1896), p. 36.
116. Ibid.
117. *La verité*, p. 30.
118. Ibid., p. 31.
119. Turkey no. 2 (1896), p. 41.
120. Ibid., pp. 50–3.
121. Ibid., p. 43.
122. Nalbandian, *Armenian Revolutionary Movement*, p. 126.
123. Turkey no. 2 (1896), pp. 48, 67, 68, 89, 266.
124. Ibid., p. 69.
125. Ibid., pp. 113, 89.
126. *La verité*, p. 34.
127. Turkey no. 2 (1896), pp. 89, 110.
128. Ibid., p. 54.
129. Ibid., p. 70.
130. Ibid., pp. 85–6, 152, 267; also Turkey no. 8 (1896), p. 8.
131. Turkey no. 5 (1896), p. 9.
132. Turkey no. 2 (1896), pp. 147–8.
133. Ibid., pp. 181, 319.
134. Ibid., p. 190.
135. Ibid., pp. 229–30.
136. Ibid., p. 150.
137. Ibid., p. 192.
138. Ibid., p. 150.
139. Ibid., p. 83.
140. Ibid., p. 192.
141. Ibid., p. 151.
142. Ibid., p. 100.
143. Ibid., p. 101.
144. Graves, *Storm Centres*, p. 162.
145. Turkey no. 2 (1896), p. 116.

146. Ibid., p. 127.
147. See Marwan R. Buheiry, 'Theodor Herzl and the Armenian Question', *Journal of Palestine Studies*, vol. VIII, no. 1 (Autumn 1978), pp. 75–97.
148. Turkey no. 2 (1896), p. 122.
149. Turkey no. 8 (1896), p. 126; also Turkey no. 2 (1896), p. 184.
150. Turkey no. 2 (1896), p. 85.
151. Ibid., pp. 211, 325.
152. Ibid., p. 257.
153. Ibid., pp. 257, 325.
154. ibid., pp. 124, 323.
155. Ibid., pp. 250, 328.
156. Ibid., pp. 142, 230, 238, 244, 330–1.
157. Ibid., p. 247.
158. Turkey no. 8 (1896), p. 213.
159. Ibid., p. 216; also Aghassi, *Zeitoun* . . . (Paris, 1897), pp. 227ff.
160. Turkey no. 8 (1896), p. 216.
161. Ibid., p. 218.
162. Turkey no. 2 (1896), p. 254.
163. Turkey no. 8 (1896), p. 218.
164. Aghassi, pp. 312–13.
165. Turkey no. 2 (1896), p. 294.
166. Turkey no. 5 (1895), pp. 7–14.
167. Ibid., p. 12.
168. Nalbandian, *Armenian Revolutionary Movement*, pp. 102–3.
169. Turkey no. 1 (1897).
170. Ibid., p. 11.
171. Oliver Baldwin, *The Questing Beast* (London, 1932), p. 186.
172. Turkey no. 2 (1896), p. 210.
173. Turkey no. 1 (1897), p. 14.
174. Ibid., pp. 15–16.
175. Ibid., pp. 16–17.
176. Ibid., p. 18; also Anon., 'The Constantinople Massacre', *Contemporary Review*, no. 70 (1896), pp. 457–65.
177. George Washburn, *Fifty Years in Constantinople* (Boston, 1911), p. 245.
178. Ibid., p. 249.
179. Turkey no. 1 (1897), pp. 21, 29, 52.
180. *The Times*, 25 September 1896, p. 5.
181. Turkey no. 2 (1897).
182. M. S. Anderson, *The Eastern Question, 1774–1923* (London, 1966), p. 258.
183. Turkey no. 3 (1897), p. 113.
184. Turkey no. 1 (1898), p. 252.
185. Ibid., p. 251.
186. FO 424/178, p. 388.
187. Turkey no. 2 (1896), p. 288.
188. E. Kedourie, 'Minorities', *The Chatham ouse Version and Other Essays* (London, 1970), p. 293.

6   The Rebirth of Oghuz

Still better known to my heart is Oghuz Khan, a dark and enigmatic figure in history. In me he still lives in all his fame and greatness – Zia Gökalp, quoted by Tekin Alp in *Türkismus und Pantürkismus*.[1]

The Twilight of the Red Sultan

Abdul Hamid's autocracy lasted longer than observers had anticipated. Through his obstinacy, his manipulation of the powers and the hordes of spies who kept him informed of even the most elementary plot against him, he was able to cling to his throne. His policies (if such they can be called) were of drift and inertia, deriving from his 'warped ideas and insane prejudices' (Adam Block).[2] As a result, by the beginning of this century the Ottoman empire had become (in the words of Dr Allan Cunningham) a clock which had stopped.[3]

Thousands of Armenians left their native soil after the events of the 1890s, and settled in Europe or America. The expansion of the community of Fresno, California, so vividly described by William Saroyan in *My Name is Aram*, dates from this period.

The villages which remained were in many cases impoverished, homes were wrecked, and the peasantry deprived of flocks of thousands of sheep, with which the Kurds enriched themselves.[4]

Prevailing conditions led to seething revolutionary activity in the mountains of Turkish Armenia. Chiefly concerned was Dashnaktsutiun, much the most prominent revolutionary body at this time. Dashnak *fedayis* operated throughout the land. (The term *fedayi* is an Islamic one, and signifies a man prepared to die for his faith; it was allegedly a designation given to the Armenian revolutionaries by the Turks and Kurds out of respect for their bravery.) Scores of expeditions and raids were mounted. But in political terms their influence was negligible. International speculation in the Near East centred almost exclusively on Macedonia; and Russia, at this time, was through the agency of Prince Golitsyn pursuing her vendetta against Armenians and in no mood for reactivating the Armenian question. The powers had developed a diplomatic strategy for avoiding the embarrassing consequences of their indifference. Only in 1903–4 did the *fedayis* come near to organising an uprising and shaking Ottoman power in Armenia. Even then it was unthinkable that the empire would lose any of her territory, since the idea of intervention was far from Russia.

Although matters remained deadlocked internationally for the Armenians, locally the *fedayis'* illicit arms were a guarantee of freedom from the government in some localities. The first outstanding leader in the mountains of Turkish Armenia was Serop 'pasha', whose Dashnak guerrilla bands neutralised the locust-like functionaries of the Ottoman government and established a degree of cherished autonomy for Armenians, instituting justice where before there had been none, and, by expelling the government, introducing those very institutions that we associate with government. Serop was killed by the ruse of a Kurd in 1900, and the leadership of the *fedayi* forces fell to Andranik, without question the most famous Armenian guerrilla fighter,[5] 'a very able man, and implicitly obeyed', in the words of British vice-consul Hampson.[6] Born in Shabin Karahisar in 1865, he had joined Dashnaktsutiun in 1892. During the killings of autumn 1895 he had defended the Sasun villages, and four years later had become the leader of the forces in Sasun. In November 1901 he effected a spectacular break-out from a besieged position at Arakelots Monastery, near Moush. His activities reached a climax in 1903–4, when much of the region of Van, Bitlis, Moush and Sasun was in a state of revolutionary turmoil.[7] In the spring of 1904 the Turkish army attempted to break the link forged between the villagers and the guerrillas by bombarding the Sasun villages for eight days in mid-April; but the villagers escaped, most to higher ground, and a few to the villages near Diyarbekir. Andranik and his forces were, however, compelled to retreat to Persia, via Aghtamar and Van; thence they moved to the Caucasus, leaving little more than a heroic memory. (Andranik himself resigned from the Dashnak party in 1907, because the party was entering into negotiations with *émigré* Turkish groups opposed to the sultan.)

The activity of Dashnak fighters in Turkish Armenia during this period did not stem from bravado and opportunism. It was based solidly on the needs of the people. Livelihood, land and possessions were slowly being stripped from the Armenians, with the connivance of the government.[8] British vice-consul Geary noted, in a despatch from Bitlis written on 18 September 1906:

> The creditors are almost without exception Turks or Kurds, who in many cases are gradually becoming proprietors of land formerly in Armenian hands. The system known locally as *selef* [literally 'predecessor'] contributes largely to this result. By this system money is borrowed on the security of future crops and repayment made in kind, the interest often amounting to 300 or 400 per cent. . . . Extortion and bribery appear to be the order of the day, and many tales of brutality were poured into my ears.[9]

On the notorious system of tax-farming, Geary adds: 'In this district the farmer of the tithes often acts in concert with the tax gatherer, and the latter compels the villager to borrow back at high interest the tithes which he has just paid to the former.'

Some Armenians plotted to assassinate the sultan, the corner-stone of the destitution, but no attempt was successful. One narrowly failed in Constantinople. In another incident, in 1905, the Dashnak party founder, Kristapor Mikayelian, was killed by the bomb he was handling in Bulgaria.[10]

Conflicting Aims

The forces that eventually succeeded in overthrowing Abdul Hamid were a combination of intellectual opposition in exile, mainly in Paris, and military force in Macedonia. A sizeable proportion of the exiles were from the empire's subject peoples, and of these perhaps the most active were the Armenian Dashnaks.

Some years earlier, both Hunchak and Dashnak groups had entered into a dialogue with Ottoman liberals in Paris. The presence among the Turks of Prince Sabaheddin, nephew of Abdul Hamid, gave genuine hope to them that they would receive autonomy, and not – once Abdul Hamid was overthrown – just a modernised tyranny. Sabaheddin, who had fled Constantinople in 1899, was a genuine believer in decentralisation. The Armenian groups took part in the First Congress of Ottoman Liberals, held in February 1902;[11] with them were Turkish, Arab, Greek, Kurdish, Albanian, Circassian and Jewish (not Zionist) representatives. The resolutions passed by the congress were humane and conciliatory, seeking equal rights for all, local self-administration, defence of the empire's borders and restoration of the Ottoman constitution of 1876, which had been suspended in 1878.

The Armenians initially held that only European intervention (of some sort) would be an effective guarantee of the reforms that they sought, and so they included it in their platform.[12] But in the years that followed they seem to have abandoned it, realising that it was seen by Turkish liberals as a negation of the empire's sovereignty. They became very close indeed to the Turks during the years of anti-Hamidian conspiracy; and indeed after the revolution had turned sour for other non-Turks, they were the last to be disillusioned. The Dashnaks really believed that constitutionalism could work in Ottoman Turkey, and while they held that belief they abandoned their hopes for foreign intervention in the empire. They ceased to look to article 61 of the treaty of Berlin, and instead trusted their own efforts, harnessed to those of their Turkish colleagues. It was a brave and historic attempt to break with centuries-old attitudes. For Turkish Armenia they sought not foreign intervention or independence, but only autonomy.

But not all of the Turks among the exiled conspirators were liberal, decentralist followers of the ideas of Prince Sabaheddin. Others believed that the entire empire should become a unitary, specifically Turkish state, whose dominant ideology should be Turkish nationalism. In the first place they realised that, with the onset of democracy, the Turks might easily lose their privileged position in the empire, since they constituted a minority far outnumbered by the combined total of other nationalities. And in the second place, with the disappearance of the former rigid Islamic loyalties, it was not only doctrines of liberty and equality that were taking their place. Sinister ideologies, with a hint of political fanaticism, were beginning to take shape. Deriving from European linguistic researches, the idea of a Turkish *race* as an incipient political unit was developing. (The European researchers included Arminius Vambéry, Leon Cahun, and Constantin Borzecki, who adopted the name Mustafa Jelalleddin Pasha, and tried to prove the 'Touro-Aryan' origin of the Ottoman Turks.)[13] Simultaneously, a number of Turks were becoming aware of the political aspirations of the Turko-Tatars of the Russian empire, especially those of Baku and the Crimea, and to a lesser extent of Kazan and Astrakhan; for their part, the Tatars from these regions approached Ottoman Turks with the idea of turning the tables on their Russian masters and unifying their forces to create a gigantic Turkish state. Numbered among them were Yusuf Akchurin (from Kazan), Ali Husseinzade (from Azerbaijan), Ahmed Agaev (also from Azerbaijan) and Ismail Gasprinsky (from the Crimea).[14]

In the ever more secular milieu of educated Ottoman Turks, these currents of thought made a deep impression. They made it possible for them to think in terms of pan-Turkism – the ambition to unite all the peoples who were linguistically related to the Turks, from the Balkans to Siberia.

Pan-Turkism (or pan-Turanianism, which is really just another name for it) is often confused with pan-Islamism, but a moment's reflection will show that the two are quite distinct. In the first place there were many non-Turkish Muslims, and a number of non-Muslim Turkish-speakers (such as the Yakuts of Siberia). Secondly, the racial ideology of pan-Turkism is not Islamic at all. A circular found on the body of a dead Turkish soldier at Medina during the first world war shows the essential antipathy between Islam and pan-Turkism.[15] (The soldier was a member of the pan-Turkist group *Turk Odjaghi*, founded by Yusuf Akchurin.)

> That monstrous fiction of the imagination, which is known as the community of Islam, and which has for long past stood in the way of present progress generally, and of the realisation of Touranian unity in particular, has now entered on a phase of decline and ruin. We need not apprehend from it any further danger to the execution of our hopes and principles.

However, pan-Turkist ideas had gained only a small currency before 1908; they had not yet gained mastery of the Young Turk exiles, as they plotted to seize power from the sultan. There seems only to have been a shadowy awareness of them. The most that the more nationalist among the Turkish members of the plotters held was that a Muslim was superior to a Christian (but by a smaller margin than hitherto), and that of Muslims the Turks deserved pride of place in the empire.

The 1908 Revolution

By early 1908 the centre of gravity for the revolution had shifted from the smoke-filled rooms of Parisian exiles to the barracks of discontented army officers in Macedonia; and on 23 July 1908 the revolution burst upon the capital. The 1876 constitution was restored. Freedoms were assured for the citizens of the empire. The happiness and relief were immense; the dark night of arbitrary violence seemed to be over. The manifestations of the citizens on the streets seemed to prove that the narrow divisive policies of Abdul Hamid had been swept away – that the Armeno-Turkish hostility had been a social phenomenon artificially engineered by the scheming sultan.

Mr. G. Barclay, British acting-consul in Constantinople,* wrote to the Foreign Office on 25 July, 'The crowd is animated with good humour, and it is remarkable to see the fraternisation of Muslims and Christians, especially Armenians.'[16]

Ten days later the newly arrived British ambassador, Sir Gerard Lowther, related (4 August):

An extraordinary event took place yesterday in the Armenian cemetery at Shishli, where the victims of the massacres in 1895 and 1896 were buried. A procession of Armenians and Turks numbering several thousand proceeded thither and prayers were offered by the priests of both religions over the dead.[17]

On 25 August he reported of the revolution that 'the Armenians fully approve, and are going into it heart and soul'.[18]

Who were the losers, among the euphoria? Barclay said on 26 July that 'practically the only victims have been spies'.[19]

But the euphoria, and the cries of 'Liberty, Equality and Fraternity', should not disguise the essential features of the men who made the revolution. They were plotters and conspirators; and even after the new day had dawned, their own politics remained in the shadows. The *Ittihad ve Terakke Jemieti*, or Committee of Union and Progress (CUP), as they called themselves, remained in the background, pulling the strings of power, and conspiring against their rivals. They remained in Salonika, guiding events from a distance. It was as though the light of freedom had penetrated everywhere except into the secret politics of the CUP itself. The CUP was keen at all costs to act through others; thus, they even kept Abdul Hamid on the throne, though they made sure he appointed officials only of their choosing. Only when there was fairly clear

---

*The Foreign Office had been caught napping by the *coup*. Not only was there no British ambassador in Constantinople, but at the very time of the revolution most of the embassy staff were out watching the lawn tennis finals of the Ottoman empire.

evidence of Abdul Hamid's complicity in the brief counter-revolution of April 1909, when for a fortnight it looked as though the old regime had returned, did they send him into exile in Salonika.

Nevertheless, the forms of parliamentary democracy were observed, and initially the debates in the chamber had real worth in airing grievances; the minorities, too, were able to come face to face with one another, and with Turks – who remained the 'ruling race', even though their numbers scarcely warranted it. (In the first parliament, out of a total of 288 deputies, there were 147 Turks, 60 Arabs, 27 Albanians, 26 Greeks, 14 Armenians, 10 Slavs and 4 Jews. In 1913 Armenian representation was increased marginally to 16.[20]) But the manner in which the Committee of Union and Progress managed its parliamentary business meant that very soon the chamber had almost no significance for the political development of the empire. Philip Graves, correspondent for *The Times*, noted:

I went frequently to the Chamber of Deputies, but I must confess that from 1909 onwards the parliamentary debates lost reality. The Parliamentary Committee [sc. of Union and Progress] Party, which could still count upon a large majority in spite of quarrels and secessions, was better organized and disciplined than the CUP itself. Its deliberations were held in secret and were often attended by ministers, summoned to defend their policies, or by leaders of the extra-parliamentary organization, who came to lay its counsels or commands before the deputies. Its members were said to be sworn to silence, and the reticence of those who had seceded from it was certainly impressive. Debates affecting the government as a whole followed a stereotyped procedure.

The opposition were allowed some liberty of criticism, while the Committee *bloc* listened in moody silence, broken by occasional protests, until its leaders rose, indicated the views of the majority in a few words, and moved the closure or a vote of confidence as the situation demanded. Then the party voted as one man, and all was over with the opposition until the next occasion when the same comedy would be played with the same *dénouement*.[21]

The situation in the provinces improved in the months following the 1908 revolution. British acting consul Safrastian reported from Bitlis on 1 September 1908 that there had been fraternisation in Moush, and that hundreds of Armenians were returning from Russia.[22] In succeeding despatches he stressed the security that prevailed in the eastern provinces, and the hopes for prosperity.

Adana

In the Cilician province of Adana conditions were, however, far from auspicious for the success of the constitution. The province was a rich and fertile region, where wheat, cotton and barley were cultivated. But on the proclamation of the constitution, Adana was appallingly governed; its governor, Bahri Pasha, was so corrupt that dishonesty and venality had become a way of life there. Notions of 'constitution' and 'justice' were fictions.

The revolution was ill-received here. During the months that followed, the Turks were angry that their dominance, unquestioned for centuries, was suddenly eroded. The Armenians, who constituted between a half and a third of the total population of the city of 40,000, and whom Major C. H. M. Doughty Wylie, the British vice-consul in Mersina, described as 'the most intelligent, the most educated, and by far the most talkative' section of the population,[23] imagined that the moment for demonstrating their superior ability had arrived, and that self-determination was virtually theirs for the asking; and they chattered about it, in the *khans* and coffee-shops, endlessly, and for men who knew the temper of the Turks, tactlessly.

Then in the second week of April 1909, at the same time that the forces were gathering for the counter-revolution in the capital, the atmosphere in Adana became charged: there were some murders, threats were made, and shops were hastily closed. The British dragoman, Athanasios Trypanis, reported this to Doughty Wylie on 13 April 1909 (the very day of the counter-revolution in Constantinople). Currently there were more than the normal number of Armenians in Adana and its surrounding villages, for this was the time of the seasonal migration of Armenian workers from Marash to gather in the barley harvest.[24]

When Doughty Wylie received Trypanis's letter on the following day, he resolved to go straight to Adana, and took the afternoon train. He saw no reason for exceptional precautions, and took his wife with him. From the train he began to suspect that things might be rather worse than he had anticipated: he saw the odd dead body near the track, and refugees running panic-stricken towards the train.

As they approached Adana more bodies were seen strewn beside the track. At Adana he went straight to Trypanis's house, quite near the station. There he changed into his uniform, secured an escort, and set off to the *konak* (government building). He found himself in the midst of a furious massacre; all around was screaming, killing, looting; firing in all directions.[25]

In the *konak* there was total disorder. The two men with authority, the provincial governor, Jevad Bey, and the commandant, Mustafa Remzi Pasha, behaved like cowards, and seemed to be in a state of hysterical panic. When Doughty Wylie demanded soldiers, with officers, he was unwillingly given a few soldiers, but no officers. Towards evening he crossed the town, and posted a guard beside the American mission. Heavy firing was continuing in the vicinity. Regardless, he returned to Trypanis's house; and thence again, through bullets and past blazing fires, to the *konak*. The governor and commandant had still done nothing to improve the situation; they sat in their offices, immobilised, it seemed, by fear. Doughty Wylie told them he would return in the morning, demanding 50 soldiers and an officer.

Early on the 15th Doughty Wylie again left for the *konak*.[26] On his way he caught sight of some soldiers taking part in the murders. At the *konak* he was given 50 men and the commandant of the gendarmerie.

In the city looting and murdering continued. Since no one else attempted to quell it, Doughty Wylie and his men set about doing the job themselves. They paraded up and down throughout the city, with bugles blowing: 'Wherever we went the fighting ceased. We cleared the streets sometimes by charging with the bayonet and sometimes by firing over the head of the crowd.'[27] Alternatively, Doughty Wylie had a crier order everyone to go home, warning them that he intended to fire down the street. But this proved only partially effective, since the city was large and impossible for one band of men to control all the time. Back near the station he was just in time to stop a large crowd of Turkish villagers from flocking into the town and joining the massacre.

By midday the town's main bazaar was on fire, and Turks and Armenians were engaged in house-to-house fighting, almost impossible to control. The poor quality of the soldiers aggravated the situation: in one place Doughty Wylie had posted a guard, but as soon as his back was turned the man joined in killing Armenians.

An urgent message came to him to go down to the Tobacco Régie factory, where there were many wounded. While there, he was shot by an Armenian at close range, and his arm was broken. Doughty Wylie comments: 'He was probably deceived by my military uniform into thinking I was a Turkish officer, or else too wild with terror or despair to know what he was doing.'[28] His injury did not prevent him from thinking fast: suppose the Turks learnt that the British vice-consul had been wounded by an Armenian? Would this not be a signal for a general storm on the Armenian quarter? He sent the commandant of the gendarmerie back to the *konak* with an urgent message to the two officials there that, even now, if they stopped the massacre, no indemnity or punishment would be demanded by Doughty Wylie. He backed up this request with a reminder to them that he had already telegraphed for a British warship, and that if the outbreak continued he would hold them responsible. As a practical solution he suggested that the Armenian quarter be sealed off with regular troops and good officers; no one should be allowed in or out; and the rest of the town should be patrolled, with people being driven indoors, shooting if necessary. Having despatched the commandant of the gendarmerie, he returned home to tend his wound.

The main authorities were acting like cowards; what of their subordinates, and those with lesser authority? Doughty Wylie relates that the reserves, called up by the commandant and roaming the streets, 'did an infinite amount of harm'.[29] The Muslim leaders were divided, some trying to quieten the crowd, others taking rifles and joining in the *mêlée*.

By the morning of the 16th the outbreak had died down, for the time being – not least because HMS *Swiftsure* and other foreign warships were cruising off the Cilician coastline. But the death, wreckage and homelessness resulting from 48 hours of uninterrupted massacre were vast. Doughty Wylie estimated 2,000 dead in Adana, and between 15,000 and 25,000 in the villages.[30] Such estimates were likely to be conservative. Homeless refugees, still frightened of further massacre, amounted to 15,000.[31]

During the period of the killings of 13–16 April the Young Turks had been ousted from power in Constantinople, and the reactionary regime had been reinstated. But on 24 April, as a result of the march on the capital by the 'Action Army' headed by Mahmud Shevket, the parties loyal to the constitution again seized power, and compelled Sultan Abdul Hamid (whom they suspected of complicity in the counter-revolution) to go into exile in Salonika.

One of the first actions of Mahmud Shevket was to order two regiments of Rumeliot troops – crack Young Turk soldiers – from Beirut and Damascus to Adana. But shortly after their arrival, at dusk on 25 April, further bloodshed and fire began in the city, perpetrated in a more thorough and brutal manner than before.[32] A Turkish version held that the initial firing of the second outbreak came from the Armenian quarter on the troops' encampment. But on inspection this was found to be physically impossible. An alternative explanation for the outbreak was that some Turks dressed up as Armenian revolutionaries, and, declaring that a revolution had begun, opened fire. What followed was that the Rumeliot troops opened fire on the Armenian quarter, and, in the words of H. Charles Woods (who visited Adana soon after these events), 'for a time at any rate took part in the looting of houses and the killing of innocents'.[33]

The most virulent Turkish fire was directed on the Mousheghian school, which contained many who had been wounded in the earlier massacre, and about 2,000 refugees. Firing was directed on the school from the house of a Turkish *bey* which was actually situated in the Armenian quarter; about 30 soldiers had collected there. The school was evacuated, but next to it was an Armenian church, where 600 people had sought refuge. As the situation of these people became critical, threatened by fire from the school, they were rescued by a Jesuit father and a Turkish officer.[34]

The worst feature of this second outbreak was the fires, which were much more extensive than during the first. In the old part of the city, where the houses were close-packed and back-to-back, fires spread rapidly. Doughty Wylie says that his impression while going around Adana at this time was of a great number of cartridges exploding in burning houses, and of wreckage falling across the street.[35] Woods was highly suspicious about the origin of these fires, when he went to investigate the disturbances in Adana. He felt that they had been started deliberately 'from the numerous blackened [kerosene] tins which for months told their tell-tale evidence wherever one turned throughout the ruins'.[36] Nearly all the houses which were burnt belonged to Armenians – 4,437 out of a total of 4,823.[37]

However, it was not only the city of Adana that suffered these outbreaks in April 1909. All across the Cilician plain villages were attacked and plundered – over 200 in all. Armenians were slaughtered, whether landowners, farmers, peasants or migrant workers assisting with the barley harvest. Many died amid organised brutality; thus, at Hamidiye, 40 kilometres east of Adana, virtually the entire Armenian population of 500 was wiped out after a siege of 22 days;[38] and those living in the nearby Armenian villages, a population of about 1,500, quite unprotected, were cudgelled to death.[39] Nor was it only on the Cilician plain that Armenians were killed – the whole of the coastline round the gulf of Alexandretta was hit. In Antioch 135 Armenian men were killed.[40]

Two towns, however – Hadjin and Dörtyol – resisted the onslaught. Hadjin, 110 kilometres north-east of Adana, is a remote mountain town inhabited exclusively by Armenians of the tough, defiant type, similar to the Zeituntzis. The Turks laid seige to it for about ten days, but failed to bend the stern Hadjintzis; then they tried to burn the town (much of which was constructed of wood), but fortunately the wind changed at the critical moment. Only 60 Armenians were killed or wounded, out of a total population of 20,000–30,000.[41]

In Dörtyol (T.: 'four ways') the 10,000 Armenians were besieged by 7,000 Turks, 400 of whom were armed with rifles. On the third day of the siege the Turks seized the water supply, turned it off and kept it off. Two days later the Armenians attempted unsuccessfully to force their way to the source. Negotiations took place three days later, and the Turks promised to turn it on again for a two days' truce. But they treacherously disregarded their promise, and continued their attack. A few days later a further attempt at a truce was made; this time one was arranged through the good offices of the British acting consul in Alexandretta: Turkish troops would re-occupy the barracks in the town, the water would be turned on, and the siege raised. But again, despite the undertaking, the besiegers made one last abortive attempt to capture the town, attacking from four directions simultaneously. It failed; and the siege was eventually raised on 26 April, with the loss of only ten Dörtyol Armenians.[42]

It appears, too, that attacks were planned throughout Asia Minor as well as Cilicia. At Kharput there were disturbances, but the firmness of the local governor prevented any trouble; at Kayseri a similar outbreak threatened, but again a local official took firm action; and at Van a late snowstorm put a blanket over the plans for killings.[43]

Responsibility for Adana

At a time when plots, hatred and rumours abounded, it is difficult to reach a clear verdict on the killings. The Ottoman government itself made a show of being keen to get to the truth of the matter. In early May it despatched a military tribunal to Adana, which did little except frame Armenians. This was followed by a special investigative commission, made up of two deputies from the recently re-assembled Parliament, Hagop Babikian and Yusuf Kemal; this in turn was followed by another commission, composed of two Turks and one Armenian. At all stages the attempts of the men to reach the truth were thwarted, apparently by orders from Constantinople. Babikian, the keenest investigator, died on 1 August, quite possibly from poisoning.

Sentences were carried out in the autumn and winter. Nine Turks and 6 Armenians were executed as a first group, and later on 25 more Turks:[44] the first time that Turks had been executed for massacring Armenians. But it was generally felt that the sentences were unsatisfactory, since the court itself adopted unusual procedures, examining witnesses in an unorthodox manner. Impartial observers considered that some of those sentenced (both Turks and Armenians) were wrongly convicted. By contrast the ex-governor was only sentenced to be debarred from holding office, and the former commandant got nothing more than three months in jail.

One man who put the blame on the CUP was Ihsan Fikri, the editor of the local paper of the Committee of Union and Progress, *Iktidal*, which had published inflammatory articles.[45] He was sentenced to two years' exile, and managed to escape to Cairo. There he implicated the CUP heavily in the massacres, alleging that the violent editorials published in his paper were in fact written by a local functionary of the Committee.[46]

In assessing blame there are three groups to consider: the Armenians themselves (who might have been staging an uprising, which could be said to be legitimately put down); the reactionaries, belonging to the group who staged the counter-revolution of 13 April, who were generally known as the Society for Muslim Unity, or *Ittihad-i Muhammediye Djemieti*; and the Young Turk progressives themselves.

The Armenians of Adana were not the innocent passive sufferers that they have sometimes been pictured. They were insufferably and tactlessly loquacious, and their archbishop, Moushegh, was a foolish firebrand who had urged his people to buy arms at any price during the months preceding the violence. (It later transpired that he had a commercial interest in the sale of arms.) The Turks claimed that he was seeking to force the foreign powers to intervene, with the ultimate end of declaring himself 'King of Cilicia'.[47]

Two objections, however, can be laid against this fanciful explanation. In the first place the powers had hardly any representatives in Cilicia; and secondly, direct occupation was not an idea that could be countenanced by Britain or France, the only possible occupying powers, in 1909, since belief was too strong in Turkey's own internal regeneration.

It was out of the question that any revolutionary would start an uprising on the Cilician plain. The fortress towns of Zeitun or Hadjin would be far more suitable. Furthermore, it was a most unfavourable time of year to choose for an uprising, since the town of Adana and its surrounding villages contained a large additional population of thousands of defenceless Armenian migrant workers, there to gather in the barley harvest. So any idea of Armenians fomenting the disturbances may be discounted.

There remain the Society for Muslim Unity and the Young Turks. It is clearly important to make a distinction between the first Adana massacre, which broke out on the day of the counter-revolution in the capital, and the second, which began the day after the Young Turks had regained power, and Mahmud Shevket had despatched the Rumeliot troops to Adana. There seems to be no evidence directly to implicate the Society for Muslim Unity in the first massacre; but circumstantially things are loaded heavily against them, since their agents might well try to re-assert the traditional position of Muslims against Christians, after nine months of disturbing notions of equality, on the very day that their colleagues seized power in the capital. (Some weeks after the events a certain Avnullah was arrested in Kirkuk, who was reported to have incited the Adana Muslims to attack the Armenians; he was said to be an agent for the Muslim Society.)

It is unlikely that the Young Turks would have fomented the first Adana massacre, on the very day that they were ousted from power; although it is possible, since political events moved more slowly in the provinces than in the capital. Evidence for the implication of the Young Turks is the attitude of the governor and the commandant – contrived cowardice, so that the killings could continue; but, on the other hand, it is quite possible they may have been ordered to adopt their attitudes by the reactionaries who were back in power.

But were the Young Turks behind the second outbreak – was this a grim foretaste of the killings which were to follow six years later? It is possible, but I think it credits even the able Rumeliot troops with too great an efficiency. They had just arrived in a strange city. Was it likely that they would be able to locate and deliberately attack the Armenian quarter in semi-darkness within a few hours of their arrival? Doughty Wylie, who was on the spot, does not think so. He points out that it was dusk when the killings began, and that troops, believing that they were being fired on, would fire back in the assumed direction of the attack, even if they were in error.[48] The extreme ferocity of their attack can be attributed to their training, not to the fact that they were firing into the Armenian quarter.

Whatever secret plots were afoot in Adana in April 1909, we must not overlook the local antagonisms. Without the local hatreds the explosion of violence would not have occurred. It needed very few terrorist emissaries to set the two communities at one another's throats; indeed, to keep the affair in proportion, it is probably fairest to say that local enmities caused the flare-up in Adana, and the part played by agents from one or another of the committees was marginal.

After Adana

After the events of April 1909 Armenians were more wary, but still prepared to co-operate with the Young Turks. The Dashnaks in particular held on to their hopes for an accord with the Young Turks, and on 6 September 1909 both bodies signed a five-point circular. They agreed to work unsparingly together to put the constitution into effect, and to consolidate progress in the country; to act with united resolution against any possible reactionary movement; to dissipate gossip in public opinion that Armenians aimed at independence; they also declared themselves in agreement on the subject of extending privileges in the provinces; and finally, warned by the counter-revolution and the 'regrettable disaster in Adana', to work hand in hand to bring into effect the foregoing points.[49]

The Dashnaks were criticised for signing this agreement by other Armenians, most of whom believed in CUP responsibility for the Adana massacre. Nevertheless, as the five points make clear, it was a positive gesture towards the Young Turks, and an attempt to salvage what was good in the Young Turk revolution: to try to slow down, or even halt, the slide into racist Turkish chauvinism, by demonstrating that at least one non-Turkish group in the empire was prepared to support them.

Zia Gökalp and Pan-Turkism

But the period of possible co-operation was rapidly vanishing, as the vestiges of liberalism disappeared from the Committee of Union and Progress. In 1910 the membership of its Central Committee changed radically, and it included men of a ferociously nationalist outlook: Eyub Sabri, Omer Nadji, Dr Nazim (a 'bleak fanatic' in the opinion of Philip Graves) and Zia Gökalp.[50] None of these held ideas remotely conciliatory towards non-Turks.

Zia was to become the chief theoretician of the CUP in succeeding years, and the political philosophy that he developed had grave implications for Armenians. He was the most articulate and persuasive proponent of pan-Turkism, and showed that, far from being a harmless movement for the unity of a dispersed people, it meant the ruthless suppression of the millions of non-Turkish people who lived in between the remote and haphazard concentrations of Turkic-speakers across the globe.

Zia adopted the second name of Gökalp – it was many years before the Turks had surnames – which already showed the line of his thinking: for *gök* is the Turkish for 'blue' or 'sky', with the further implication of 'eastern'; and *alp* means 'hero'. He was born in Diyarbekir (a Kurdish city) in the mid-1870s.[51] The political philosophy that he elaborated was more discriminatory and infinitely more sinister than that embodied in the corrupt *mehkémés* of the period of absolute autocracy. (Yet curiously Zia is hailed today by experts on Turkish history on both sides of the Atlantic as a 'progressive intellectual'.) According to his biographer, Zia believed that the 'Turkish nation' of the future would consist of Turkish-speaking Muslims only; Greeks, Armenians and Jews might be Turks in regard of citizenship, but not of nationality. Kurds, he hoped, would become assimilated.[52]

The profoundest of his ambitions was the great racist dream of pan-Turkism. He outlined three successive phases in its realisation. According to Serge Zenkovsky:[53]

> First, the Ottoman Turks had to consolidate their grip over their empire, and Turkize its minorities. In the second, 'pan-Turkic', phase, the closest relatives of the Ottoman Turks – the Azerbaijanis of Russia and Persia (the south-eastern group of Turkic peoples) – were to be taken into the Turkic state. The third step would be the uniting of all the Turanian people of Asia around the Turkish core.

Zia's biographer, Uriel Heyd, adds: 'In the succeeding years Gökalp, Halide Edib and their associates dreamt of a union of all the Turks under a single ruler who would renew the days of Attila, Jengiz Khan and Timur-leng.'

The implications for the Armenians of such racist-nationalist theorising were grave indeed. Zia's 'first step' would mean the forcible Turkisation of the Armenians – something which would not be accomplished easily, in view of the stubborn adherence of the Armenians throughout the centuries to their language and Church; but the Turks, longing to renew the days of 'Attila, Jengiz Khan and Timur-leng', would presumably not stop at employing the methods used by their illustrious predecessors. The second stage clearly involved, at the very least, expansion to Baku (something the Turks were indeed to achieve, briefly, in 1918), and north-west Persia. This would entail overrunning Russian Armenia (or, to be precise, the Kars district and Yerevan province); most of all, it meant annihilating Armenia in theory and practice, so that she would never again put forward political demands for independence or autonomy, both of which were anathema to the proponents of the establishment of an 'Oghuzistan', a Turkic state stretching from Anatolia to the shores (initially west and south) of the Caspian sea.[55] It entailed, too, ridding the region of the power of Russia, which alone in the area would protect Armenia. Another pan-Turkist, Tekin Alp (who, like Borzecki, was another renegade – he was born Moise Cohen, and his adopted name means 'unique hero'), explained the matter thus, in his book *Türkismus und Pantürkismus*, published in 1915:

> Ten centuries of history have brought about no change in the position of the Germans and Turks towards the Slavs. The two nations have always remained the common foe of Slav power, and must both protect themselves from the menace of the Muscovite empire. As long as the Russian colossus remains, Germanism [*Deutschtum*] is threatened with isolation, on account of her geographical position and ethnographical formation. In the same way pan-Turkism cannot come to its full development and realisation until the

Muscovite monster [*das moskowitische Ungeheuer*] is crushed, because the very districts which form the object of Turkish irredenta, such as Siberia, the Caucasus, the Crimea, Afghanistan, etc., are still directly or indirectly under Russian rule.[56]

These ideas permeated the Committee of Union and Progress in the years 1910–14, and made it impossible for nationalities such as the Armenians to work with them. Emphasising the importance of pan-Turkism in practice as well as in theory, a Tatar from Baku became a member of the Central Committee of the CUP in 1911: Ali Husseinzade. Here was a man not even born in the Ottoman empire, who was now a member of its supreme ruling body; a striking demonstration of how expansion, and specifically expansion eastwards, had become a dominant Ottoman obsession.[57] Ali Husseinzade lost his seat in the Central Committee in the following year; but among those appointed was, like Nazim, another coldly fanatical doctor, the Paris-educated Behaeddin Shakir, whose attentions too were above all focused on the east.

In public, Young Turk politics were dominated from about 1910 onwards by three men: Enver, Talaat and Djemal. Their precise relationship with the party's Central Committee need not concern us here;[58] but it should be noted that Enver belonged to it from 1908 to 1910, Talaat from 1908 to 1910 and 1911 to 1916. Djemal was a member before 1908. (He was the least important of the 'triumvirate'.) Talaat seems to have been the main channel through which the secret decisions of the Central Committee were translated into policy; whereas Enver was a man of action – or at least one who had an image of himself as a man of action – and had little time for committees. Enver nevertheless was dedicated to pan-Turkism as a political creed. His activities during the first world war demonstrate that. In the period before the war his dedication to this ideology took the form of patronage of the 'Turanian' youth movement, the *izji*, which appears to have been modelled on the British Boy Scout movement. The movement's banner showed a grey wolf (*boz kurt*) against a red background, symbolising the legendary belief that the Turks were led out of Central Asia by a grey wolf, and implying that their true destiny lay with racial origins, and not with the multiracial empire that they had built up around Constantinople (whose only racial quality had been the dynasty of the sultan himself).[59] The banner of the *izji* was a deliberate insult to Islam, an expression in terms of antique legend of narrow, exclusive racist intolerance – and a deeply sinister threat to those who lay outside the limits of the race as defined by its proponents.*

---

*A comparison of some aspects of the pan-Turkism and Nazism is striking and illuminating. Both ideologies despise conventional religion, and hark back to pagan mythologies in order to justify deeds that pagan man himself would have shuddered to accomplish. Both propound the notion of a master race, with the implication of legitimised terror towards those who do not belong to it. Yet it is a comparison that our professors seem reluctant to draw.

Turkism in Practice

By 1910 the Young Turks had overtly abandoned the idea of treating all the peoples of the empire as equals. This was demonstrated by their abandonment of the land question in Turkish Armenia. For decades before the 1908 revolution the Armenians had gradually been losing their lands to Kurds and Turks (and rapidly during the period of the 1894 –6 massacres), and as a result had become impoverished and been forced to quit their land. In the hey-day of co-operation after the revolution a scheme was devised which would lead to the restoration of some of the stolen lands to Armenians. In reporting that the CUP had abandoned the scheme, the British ambassador, Sir Gerard Lowther, commented in his annual report: 'The Committee prefer that there should be division between races.'[60] A few months earlier, Lowther had written (6 September 1910):

> That the Committee have given up any idea of Ottomanising all the non-Turkish elements by sympathetic and constitutional ways has long been manifest. To them 'Ottoman' obviously means 'Turk', and their present policy of 'Ottomanisation' is one of pounding the non-Turkish elements in a Turkish mortar. It was hoped that perhaps as they became more firmly seated in the saddle, and effective opposition had disappeared under the state of siege, the Committee would broaden rather than narrow their policy as regards internal administration, but Talaat Bey's utterances seem to make the fulfilment of such hopes more remote.[61]

In the same year the Armenian schools were subordinated to the Turkish Director of Public Instruction, an infringement of the guaranteed rights of the Armenian patriarchate.[62]

Towards Military Dictatorship

Until 1911 the Committee of Union and Progress dominated Ottoman politics almost unopposed. But then a split developed within its own ranks, with one faction of the CUP calling itself a 'New Party'. More seriously, a genuine opposition party, the Liberal Union, was formed in November. Within a month of its foundation it had won a by-election in Stambul. The Committee of Union and Progress was alerted to this threat to itself; it dissolved parliament, and in a massively corrupt general election in April 1912 procured an overwhelming majority for itself. Again a group of army officers took to the hills, determined this time to crush the CUP's illegal power. By a careful blend of threats and military manoeuvres in the wild hills of Albania these men, known as the 'Saviour Officers', secured their aim, and compelled the CUP to relinquish power in July 1912.[63]

But international developments were to forestall any hopes of a movement towards liberalism and democracy in Ottoman Turkey. Already in 1911 the Italians had invaded Libya, which they gained in the following year. Then in October 1912, only three months after the Saviour Officers had expelled the CUP from office, the hitherto quarrelling Balkan states of Bulgaria, Serbia, Greece and Montenegro united and drove the Turks out of Macedonia. Except for the small region of eastern Thrace, 'Turkey-in-Europe' was finished.*

Devoid of legitimate power the Committee used the pretext of national emergency – the government was thought to be about to hand over Edirne to Bulgaria – to stage a violent *coup d'état*. On 23 January 1913 Enver shot his way to power, by storming the Sublime Porte, killing the minister of war and compelling the grand vizier to resign. A military dictatorship was imposed, and tightened after the murder in June 1913 of the new grand vizier, Mahmud Shevket Pasha. The pattern was now in place for the outbreak of the war.

No Change for Turkish Armenia

In the face of the growth of the narrow and extreme nationalism of the CUP, Armenian disillusion was profound. Despite the Dashnaks' attempt to come to an agreement with the CUP after Adana, by 1912 they had quite broken with them. In the east, Armenians were, after a short spell of hope, suffering again as much from abuses as they had in the day of Abdul Hamid. Here the constitutional revolution was a sham. Two things were quite denied the Armenians: legitimate possession of their own lands and houses, and the impartial maintenance of the law. Denied these, existence, let alone progress, was almost impossible. In the course of his visit to Russian Armenia mentioned above (pp. 79–81), Noel Buxton also visited the Turkish part of the country, where he observed:

> We found many Kurd families [migrants from Russian-dominated northwest Persia] installed in an Armenian village, the ejected population being crowded into the remaining houses. Other peasants had been notified to give up their houses, by a fixed date, to Kurds still occupying their summer tents. This was not the usual phenomenon of robbery. It was systematically ordered and carried out by authority – vali, kaimakam, mudir and zaptiye – a far more scandalous matter. It proved to be in force in numbers of other villages.[64]

---

*Eight thousand Armenians (who of the Christians 'alone fought well') served loyally with the Ottoman armies – only to be opposed by Armenian volunteers fighting under Andranik with the Balkan armies (George Young, *Constantinople* (London, 1926), p. 269).

The Final Reform Scheme

Against this pattern of continuing oppression of Armenians the foreign powers moved towards the idea of another scheme of Armenian reforms for the Ottoman empire. The notion was at last agreeable to Russia, since she was keeping her options open for a decisive move into northern Persia. (Since the Anglo–Russian *entente* of 1907 Persia had been divided into a Russian 'sphere of influence' in the north and a British one in the south, with a neutral buffer zone in the middle. Armed with this legality, the Russians twice cynically assisted the crushing of the constitutional revolution, in 1905–6 and 1909; in alliance with the British they opposed the reforms of W. Morgan Shuster, and compelled the Parliament to close in 1911.) A quiet and co-operative Armenia – both Russian and Turkish – was essential to Russian designs.[65]

Reforms were discussed, in the classic nineteenth-century manner, at Constantinople, by the ambassadors of the six powers. The Triple Entente of Britain, France and Russia attempted to push them through, but they were obstructed by Germany and Austro-Hungary. Turkish nationalism, for its part, opposed intervention, but in April 1913 the CUP endorsed an idea that British officials might assist the administration of the eastern provinces, at a time when the proposal was seen as a means of arousing Russian suspicion of Britain and breaking the Entente.

Throughout the rest of 1913 the powers showed their endemic fears and jealousies of each other. Like paranoid hysterical lovers, each attempted to thwart and counter-thwart the others. They projected wild and contradictory guesses of the future: Germany, that a reform plan would partition the Ottoman empire; Russia, that a partition would occur if no reforms were introduced.[66]

Distractedly wandering through thicket and briar, like the unhappy lovers in *A Midsummer Night's Dream*, they sought a Puck who would squeeze Love-in-idleness upon the correct eyelids. The magic potion materialised as a reform programme, eventually signed – by representatives of the Russian and Ottoman empires only – on 8 February 1914.[67]

Here at last, it was felt, was a reform scheme which would work – which had teeth. Temporising and inaction would be things of the past. The six provinces of Turkish Armenia were to be divided into two administrative districts (thereby getting rid of the superfluity of corrupt and incompetent officials that had plagued the region since the accession of Abdul Hamid); each district would be administered by a European inspector-general, who would be appointed by the Turks but approved by the great powers. His job would be to supervise all aspects of administration. Bribery was to be prohibited, justice enforced. Interracial harmony was to be enforced, too. Tax-collecting was to be simplified. Nomadic populations would be settled.[68]

The two inspectors-general were appointed in April: they were Westenenk, a Dutch colonial administrator, and Major Hoff, of the Norwegian army. By the summer of 1914 Hoff had reached Van, and Westenenk was about to set off for Erzerum. But the hopes raised by the reform programme were blown apart by the outbreak of the first world war. The scheme was abandoned, and Hoff left for home.

It is interesting, but ultimately pointless, to speculate whether the reform scheme would have survived the militant pan-Turkism of the rulers of the empire if the war had not broken out. It was a gamble: on the face of it no more risky than the reform schemes of the period of Abdul Hamid. But the possibility of failure was more dangerous, for the Young Turks differed from Abdul Hamid in one vital respect – not that they were more patriotic or nationalistic, but that they were dedicated to an expansionist political philosophy. The sultan had been happy to stonewall, and to play off one self-appointed reformer against another. His 'pan-Islamic' policy beyond the borders of the empire had been merely a creaking contrivance. But the outward aspirations of the CUP were motivated by a militant racist determination, given strength by the secret councils of the politbureau of the CUP. Their provincial administration of the empire was as feeble and malevolent as that of the former times; but the resemblance ended there. The steely eye of the Young Turks was fixed on the land east of Armenia. With men of this chilling outlook the failure of a reform scheme was filled with foreboding.

Notes

1. Tekin Alp [Moise Cohen], *Türkismus und Pantürkismus* (Weimar, 1915), p. 16.
2. FO 424/198, p. 108.
3. Allan Cunningham, 'The Wrong Horse?: a Study of Anglo-Turkish Relations before the First World War' in A. Hourani (ed.), *Middle Eastern Affairs no. 4, St Antony's Papers no. 17* (London, 1965), p. 63.
4. FO 424/195, pp. 2–3.
5. Leon Trotsky, 'Andranik i ego otred', *Kievskaya Mysl*, no. 197 (19 July 1913); to be published soon in New York in a collection translated by Brian Pearce entitled *The War Correspondence of Leon Trotsky: The Balkan Wars*.
6. FO 424/205, p. 182.
7. Ibid., pp. 181–2.
8. See FO 424/203, pp. 147–8.
9. FO 424/210, p. 178; see also FO 424/197, p. 60.
10. Richard G. Hovannisian, 'The Armenian Question in the Ottoman Empire', *Armenian Studies* (Beirut) [no. 1] (1973), p. 14.
11. Ibid., p. 15.
12. Bernard Lewis, *The Emergence of Modern Turkey* (London, 1961), p. 138.
13. Ibid., pp. 339–42.
14. See V. Minorsky, 'Turan' in *Encyclopedia of Islam*, 1st edn; 'Gasprali', ibid., 2nd edn.
15. CAB 25/42, p. 23.
16. Turkey no. 1 (1909), p. 11.
17. Ibid., p. 44.
18. Great Britain, Foreign Office, *British Documents on the Origins of the War, 1898–1914*, eds. G. P. Gooch and Harold Temperley (London, 1928), vol. V, p. 267 (henceforward 'Britain, *Origins of the War*').
19. Turkey no. 1 (1909), p. 18.

20. Feroz Ahmad, *The Young Turks* (Oxford, 1969), p. 145.
21. Philip P. Graves, *Briton and Turk* (London, 1941), pp. 160–1.
22. Turkey no. 1 (1909), p. 89.
23. FO 424/220, p. 70.
24. FO 424/219, p. 80.
25. Ibid.
26. Ibid., p. 81.
27. Ibid.
28. Ibid.
29. Ibid., p. 82.
30. Ibid., p. 85.
31. Ibid., p. 84.
32. Ibid., pp. 92–3.
33. H. Charles Woods, *The Danger Zone of Europe* (London, 1911), p. 136.
34. Ibid.
35. FO 424/219, p. 93.
36. Woods, *Danger Zone*, p. 138.
37. G. F. Abbott, *Turkey in Transition* (London, 1909), p. 305.
38. Ibid., p. 304.
39. Woods, *Danger Zone*, pp. 155–7.
40. Ibid., p. 160.
41. Ibid., pp. 160–1.
42. FO 424/219, p. 199; Woods, *Danger Zone*, pp. 161–2.
43. Woods, *Danger Zone*, p. 165.
44. FO 424/219, p. 195.
45. Ibid., p. 107.
46. Woods, *Danger Zone*, pp. 186–7.
47. FO 424/220, p. 70n.
48. FO 424/219, p. 123.
49. Jean Mécérian, S. J., *Le génocide du peuple arménien* (Beirut), p. 39.
50. FO 371/1017.43063, p. 3.
51. Uriel Heyd, *Foundations of Turkish Nationalism* (London, 1950), pp. 19–21.
52. Ibid., p. 132.
53. Serge A. Zenkovsky, *Pan-Turkism and Islam in Russia* (Cambridge, Mass., 1960), p. 111.
54. Heyd, *Foundations of Turkish Nationalism*, p. 127.
55. See map in G. Lewis, trans., *The Book of Dede Korkut* (Harmondsworth, 1974), p. 8.
56. Alp, *Türkismus und Pantürkismus*, p. 47.
57. FO 371/1262.41648.
58. See Feroz Ahmad, book review in *Middle Eastern Studies*, vol. 6, no. 1 (January 1960), p. 102.
59. A. J. Toynbee, *Turkey: a Past and a Future* (London, 1917), p. 34; also Alp, *Türkismus und Pantürkismus*, p. 33.
60. FO 424/250, p. 39.
61. Quoted in Britain, *Origins of the War*, vol. IX, part I, p. 207.
62. FO 424/250, p. 39; see also FO 371/1017.46557.
63. Lewis, *Emergence of Modern Turkey*, pp. 217–19.
64. Noel and Harold Buxton, *Travels and Politics in Armenia* (London, 1914), p. 117; see also Britain, *Origins of the War*, vol. X, part I, p. 513.
65. Roderic H. Davison, 'The Armenian Crisis, 1912–1914', *American Historical Review*, vol. LIII, no. 3 (April 1948), pp. 481–5; see also Britain, *Origins of the War*, vol. X, part I.
66. Davison, 'The Armenian Crisis', p. 497.
67. Ibid., p. 504.
68. Richard G. Hovannisian, *Armenia on the Road to Independence, 1918,* (Berkeley and Los Angeles, 1967), p. 39; also FO 424/252, pp. 160–3.

7 The Death of Turkish Armenia

Turkey, Germany and the Outbreak of the War

Since the middle of Abdul Hamid's reign Turkey had been moving closer to Germany. A loan from the Deutsche Bank in 1888 financed the newly formed Anatolian Railway Company, and in the following decade two sections of the projected Berlin–Baghdad railway were completed. Germany, too, took an active interest in reorganising the Ottoman army – General (later Field-Marshal) von der Goltz had arrived in Constantinople as early as 1882, and his mission bore fruit in the Turkish defeat of the Greeks in Thessaly in 1897. The German reorganisation of the army was, however, only partial, since the sultan was concerned that his officers might become too successful or indeed too educated. Relations thereafter between the Germans and the revolutionary Young Turk officers were close and secret. After 1908 Enver himself went to Berlin to study military tactics and the German language. Nevertheless, the Ottoman army fared badly in 1911–13. A new and much larger German military mission arrived in Constantinople in 1913, headed by General Liman von Sanders. Forty-two German officers came with him. The Entente powers protested, to no avail; the battle-lines for the first world war were drawn.[1]

On 2 August 1914, two days before the outbreak of the war, Ottoman Turkey signed a secret agreement with the Central powers, which stipulated that if Russia, supporting Serbia, entered the war against Austria and Germany, Turkey would join the Central powers.[2] Enver, minister of war since January 1914, saw the chance of a war with Russia as a means toward the fulfilment of his pan-Turkist dream. His internal policy showed the same hankerings for conquest and glory, for on 5 August he ordered the setting up of a paramilitary 'Special Organisation' (*Teshkilat-i Makhsusiye*),[3] to be led by members of the Central Committee of the Committee of Union and Progress, who included Dr Nazim. Behaeddin Shakir was charged with the execution of its decisions. The purpose of this organisation was externally to prepare lands beyond the borders of the Ottoman empire (the Caucasus and Iran) for an Ottoman conquest; internally the Special Organisation controlled the administration of the empire. It was an instrument of the party which made sure that party decisions were carried out to the letter.

It was in this spirit that the CUP, before the actual formation of the *Teshkilat-i Mahksusiye*, attempted to intervene at the eighth general congress of Dashnaktsutiun, held in Erzerum in July 1914. The Ittihadist leaders present included Behaeddin Shakir. They pressed the Dashnaks to agree, in the event of the outbreak of war, to use their influence to encourage the Russian Armenians to rise against the tsar, thereby affording an easy passage for the Ottoman army in the Russian empire. In return the Ittihadists promised a semi-autonomous Armenia consisting of parts of Russian Transcaucasia and some *sanjaks* of Turkish Armenia. Dashnaktsutiun rejected the plan, and advised the Young Turk leaders to steer clear of an involvement in a European war; but should, the leaders added, a war break out in which the Ottoman empire was a participant, Armenian Ottoman citizens would enlist and fight as loyal nationals.[4]

Turkey Joins the War

The Ottoman empire entered the war on 30 October 1914. On the following day the Young Turk government issued a proclamation stating its war aims. Part of it read:

> Our participation in the world war represents the vindication of our national ideal. The ideal of our nation and people leads us towards the destruction of our Muscovite enemy, in order to obtain thereby a natural frontier to our empire, which should include and unite all branches of our race.[5]

Zia Gökalp, the CUP ideologist, issued a 'poem' reeking of blood and bones, containing the lines:

> The land of the enemy shall be devastated.
> Turkey shall be enlarged and become Turan.[6]

At the same time Armenians throughout the empire gave pledges of loyalty – which should not all be taken as bogus, when one remembers the fine showing that the Armenians had made in defence of the Ottoman empire just two years earlier in the Balkan war. Services were held in Armenian churches for an Ottoman victory; how many secretly prayed for the reverse cannot be known, but in the light of their treatment by imperial Turkey over the past 40 years, the number cannot have been small.

Some were openly defiant: the Hunchaks, at their party congress held in Constantza (Romania) shortly before the outbreak of the war, pledged determined opposition to the Ottoman empire. (As a result, 20 of their leaders were hanged in Constantinople in June 1915. Their leader, Paramaz, continued to declaim revolutionary utterances until the noose tightened around his neck.) One Armenian deputy in the Ottoman Parliament, Karekin Pastermadjian, known as Armen Karo, a Dashnak and a veteran of the Ottoman Bank incident of 1896, left to join up in one of the Armenian volunteer partisan units that were being formed in Russian Armenia.[7] The action was foolish and short-sighted, and shows that Pastermadjian cannot have appreciated the delicacy of the Armenian position. To the Ittihadist leaders his action must have cast a new light on Dashnaktsutiun's pledge of loyalty which had been given at the Erzerum congress.

Sarikamish

The first significant military activities in the Caucasian theatre of the war were astonishing and dramatic. Encouraged by Russian reverses in Europe, Enver took personal control of the Ottoman Third Army. His immensely ambitious plan was to advance on the Russian military base of Sarikamish, thence seize the fortress of Kars, and press eastwards to Baku, where he anticipated the first of the risings against the tsarist empire. In all seriousness, he told Liman von Sanders that he contemplated marching through Afghanistan to India.[8]

One factor, however, proved the nemesis of this Napoleonic ambition: the terrible Caucasian winter, the same winter that had checked Lucullus in 68 BC. Enver's offensive began on 25 December 1914; but within the next two weeks almost 80 per cent of the Ottoman Third Army (75,000 ill-equipped, poorly fed troops, out of a total of 95,000) had either been cut down by Russian guns or frozen to death amid crippling blizzards in the Turnagel woods overlooking Sarikamish.[9] Stories were told later of entire divisions killed by the frost *in situ*, discovered weeks later like the relics of some ice-bound Pompeii. For the Ottoman empire Sarikamish was a calamity.

Enver Pasha, totally defeated, returned to Constantinople, never to take personal command again. It is often held that the Sarikamish disaster was the decisive factor which precipitated the ensuing catastrophe for the Armenians; Enver is alleged to have used them as scapegoats for his folly, claiming that they acted as spies among the civilian population, and in the battle area. (A large number of Ottoman Armenians had, like Armen Karo, joined the Russian-sponsored volunteer regiments – perhaps an unwise move, but not surprising in view of the Ottoman empire's persistent rejection of them as its citizens.) Yet outwardly Enver was full of admiration for Armenians, as a message he sent in February 1915 to the Armenian bishop of Konya suggests:

> I am giving you my thanks and using this opportunity to tell you that the Armenian soldiers of the Ottoman army are executing their duty in the theatre of war scrupulously, as witness my own experience. I wish you to communicate to the Armenian nation, known for its complete devotion to the imperial Ottoman government, the expression of my satisfaction and gratitude.[10]

Enver also expressed, to the Armenian patriarch of Constantinople, 'special satisfaction as regards the conduct and bravery of the Armenians, who gave an excellent account of themselves'; however, he added ominously that in the event of 'the smallest occurrence' he would take 'most drastic measures'.

First Moves against Armenians

Even before the Sarikamish battle, measures were being taken against Armenians, according to articles in the Turkish newspaper *Kurun* in 1935, written by Aziz Samih, chief of the historical department of the Ottoman war ministry during the war. Samih showed that orders to attack Armenian villages were received in the east between 29 October and 5 November 1914. Some of the Armenian men were forced, in intolerable weather conditions, to act as pack animals until they dropped. At the same time Samih noted that Dr Behaeddin Shakir was at the headquarters of the Ottoman 34th Division at Moush, in early December 1914. The presence of the top party ideologue, a civilian, at army headquarters is puzzling until we realise that the Paris-educated doctor and intellectual was the chief organiser of the massacres.[11]

The actual decision to take measures against Armenians seems to have been taken by the Central Committee of the Committee of Union and Progress in mid-February 1915. From the actions which followed, which have been thoroughly documented, we can gather what the measures were: quite simply, the extermination of Ottoman Armenians in Armenia. Such a decision follows naturally from the development of meticulous Turkish racism since 1910. Turkish nationalism, plus the 'Turkey Faces East' ambitions of the pan-Turkists, meant that Armenia had to be emptied of Armenians. And what better chance than a world war, when there would be none of the foreigners present whom Abdul Hamid had to contend with, like Currie, Graves or Hallward? The war provided a thick black velvet arras, behind which the Young Turks could act with impunity.

In the last ten days of February 1915 Armenian government officials and employees were dismissed; and in the army Armenian soldiers were taken out of any combat positions and enrolled in labour battalions (*ameliye taburi*). Armenian officers were imprisoned. The American ambassador, Henry Morgenthau, puts it thus:

> Up to that time most of them had been combatants, but now they were all stripped of their arms and transformed into workmen. Instead of serving their countrymen as artillerymen and cavalrymen, these former soldiers now discovered that they had been transformed into road labourers and pack animals. Army supplies of all kinds were loaded on their backs, and, stumbling under the burdens and driven by the whips and bayonets of the Turks, they were forced to drag their weary bodies into the mountains of the Caucasus. Sometimes they would have to plough their way, burdened in this fashion,

almost waist-high through snow. They had to spend practically all their time
in the open, sleeping on the bare ground – whenever the ceaseless prodding
of their taskmasters gave them an occasional opportunity to sleep. They
were given only scraps of food; if they fell sick they were left where they had
dropped.[12]

At about the same time the civilian population was ruthlessly searched for
arms. Armenians had been permitted to bear arms for self-protection in the
years following the revolution of 1908, when the Young Turks realised that it
was impossible to disarm the Kurds. Now these same arms were held to be
evidence of plans for treason and insurrection. Violent and extreme methods
were employed against Armenians, isolated in the remote towns and villages of
the interior of Anatolia. Large numbers of Armenians were jailed, often as
many as 400–500 per town. No reason was given at first, but it was soon clear
that these men were to be used as hostages. Then each governor or other
official ordered the local Armenian community to deliver up as many arms as
he believed were in their possession. If they did not, it was intimated, severest
measures would be taken both against the hostages in prison and against the
Armenian community as a whole. Mass civilian reprisals, in other words, were
threatened. The people were unwilling to hand in their arms. They remembered
such things as the demand for the delivery of arms at Urfa in December 1895,
and sensed an imminent disaster of some sort. Reluctantly they handed them
in. Both clergy and political leaders persuaded them to do so, in the hope of
avoiding any pretext for measures to be taken against 'disloyal' Armenians.[13]
The total number of arms fixed in each case was arbitrary and quite in
excess of any reasonable estimate of the number of arms held by Armenians.
The arms searches became a pretext for brutal persecution: Armenians who
were searched were often beaten up, and to the hostages in jail the foulest
tortures were meted out, notably the time-honoured Turkish *falaka*, or
bastinado – beating the soles of the feet to a pulp while the victim is suspended upside down by a rope; also extraction of finger-nails, and other well-thought-
out brutalities.[14] Henry Morgenthau relates that the Constantinople chief of
police made no secret of the tortures formulated by the CUP at this time.[15] In
desperation, in order to fill their quotas, Armenians bought arms from their
Turkish neighbours. On several occasions the whole lot were then solemnly
photographed by the local authorities, and the pictures sent to Constantinople
as 'evidence of Armenian treachery'.[16]
Then, disarmed, the Armenians could be driven to their death. In the words
of Arnold Toynbee, writing in *The Times History of the War*, 'An atmosphere
of horror, which breathes through all the eye-witness accounts, had settled
down over the provinces of the empire.'[17]
That the killings were deliberate none but dedicated Turkists deny. The
horror of which Toynbee speaks was too similar in each locality for the killings
to have been spontaneous manifestations, or the actions of a few 'rogue cops'

exceeding their instructions.* The killings were deliberate, and government policy; this much is clear. (Talaat Pasha himself admitted it to Morgenthau.[18]) Were they also premeditated? In a sense any government policy is by its nature premeditated. The Armenian deportations and massacres were decided upon at least eight weeks before they were begun; but whether they represented the outcome of a well-prepared plot of perhaps months earlier is open to question. In view of the devotion of the Young Turks to pan-Turkism, and the necessary reduction of the Armenians that that ideology entailed, it would not be surprising. The evidence is not yet conclusive.

The System of Extermination

The pattern was this.[19] Initially all the able-bodied Armenian men of a certain town or village would be ordered, either by a public crier or by an official proclamation nailed to the walls, to present themselves at the *konak* (government building). The proclamation stated that the Armenian population would be deported, gave the official reasons for it, and assured them that the government was benevolent. Once at the *konak*, they would be jailed for a day or two. No reason was given. Then they would be led out of jail and marched out of town. At the first lonely halting place, they would be shot, or bayoneted to death. Some days later the old men, and the women and children, were summoned in the same way; they were often given a few days' grace, but then they had to leave. It was their misfortune not to be killed at the first desolate place. The government's reasoning appears to have been: the men might pose a threat – leaders might spring up among them, who would defy the order; but why waste valuable lead on women, old men and children? Instead they were

---

*Yet astonishingly this approximates to the view taken by Professor Stanford J. Shaw and Ezel Kural Shaw in their *History of the Ottoman Empire and Modern Turkey* (1977). They write (vol. II, p. 315):

> Specific instructions were issued for the army to protect the Armenians against nomadic attacks and to provide them with sufficient food and other supplies to meet their needs during the march and after they were settled. Warnings were sent to the Ottoman military commanders to make certain that neither the Kurds nor any other Muslims used the situation to gain vengeance for the long years of Armenian terrorism. The Armenians were to be protected and cared for until they returned to their homes after the war.

In support of these preposterous claims the authors quote Turkish official sources. One need do no more than remind them of Sir Charles Eliot's distinction between the real and the paper government of Turkey.

If one takes as a basis the laws, statistics and budgets as printed it is easy to prove that the Ottoman empire is in a state of unexampled prosperity. Life and property are secure; perfect liberty and toleration are enjoyed by all; taxation is light, balances large, trade flourishing. Those who have not an extensive personal acquaintance with Turkey may regard such accounts with suspicion and think them highly coloured, but they find it difficult to realize that all this official literature is absolute fiction, and for practical purposes unworthy of a moment's attention (*Turkey-in-Europe* (1908 and reprints), p. 130).

forced to walk, endlessly, along pre-arranged routes, until they died from thirst, hunger, exposure or exhaustion. Most were driven south to the burning Syrian desert; a few from Cilicia were initially sent in a north-westerly direction, towards the marshlands of Konya and the gloomy, empty landscape around the great salt lake. All suffered atrociously, as convoy after convoy, accompanied by gendarmes, was moved on. Very soon, under those conditions, when given food and water very erratically, if at all, life became unendurable. Like the first-person narrator in Samuel Beckett's *The Unnameable*, their life became 'You must go on, I can't go on, I'll go on' – for if they stopped, exhausted, they were mercilessly whipped by the Turkish soldiers (some regular, some irregular) until they continued. The soldiers who accompanied them, and the local populations who were encouraged to attack them *en route*, saw them as good for only two things: gold and rape. Once on the move, any money was liable to be stolen from them (the lucky ones were able to purchase water). Attractive girls were either raped then beheaded on the spot, or snatched away into a Turk's household. The Turkish soldiery in 1915, far from being the 'clean fighters' who figured among the legends of British Turkophiles, were worthy heirs of Attila and Jengiz Khan in their remorseless brutality.

Gradually the ranks of Armenians thinned – although remarkable survivals are recorded, such as a native of Hadjin, who survived a forced march all the way to Mosul; most died in these terrible convoys; the dead and dying, their throats parched, their lips cracked, their bodies racked with misery and pain, were left by the road, to be devoured, by day by the vultures, by night by the jackals.

Simultaneously, the government had arranged for their empty homes to be taken over by *muhajirs*, the 750,000 Turkish refugees mostly from western Thrace, who had either been driven out or left voluntarily from the lands conquered from the Ottoman empire during the Balkan wars. This policy was devised by Dr Nazim. Government resettlement of Turks, Kurds or Circassians was from this time onwards a central feature of the process of killing Armenians. Resettlement of refugees is too complicated a process to be conjured out of the air; the frequency with which it occurs in 1915 highlights again the deliberateness of government policy.

Zeitun

Zeitun, that miniature Armenian Montenegro, so troublesome to the rulers of the empire when they tried to curb its independence, was the first town to have its Armenian people departed. A Turkish general, Fakhri Pasha, went with two officers and 3,000 soldiers to Zeitun in late March 1915.[20] His mission can only have been to subdue Zeitun and expel its inhabitants, since Turkish *muhajirs* from Macedonia were waiting in the background, ready to move in at once and take over the homes of Armenians.[21] The Zeitun Armenians, for their part, were initially careful to avoid giving the Turks a pretext for action. But many of them expected the collapse of the Ottoman empire, and some, as revolutionaries, were working for that end. From February 1915 Armenians of Zeitun had been in touch with the Caucasian headquarters of the Russian army; they reached a rough agreement (nothing appears to have been formalised) that, given weapons, the Zeitun Armenians would facilitate the Russian advance through the Ottoman empire (in rather the same way that Enver had hoped that the *Teshkilat-i Makhsusiye* would ease *his* way to Russian Turkestan). But nothing came of the plan, nor of another similar, that Armenians in Cilicia might assist an Allied landing at Alexandretta, with the aim of breaking the Ottoman empire in half.[22]

No one from Zeitun had enlisted in the Ottoman army; an unwise move, but they had the legal right to claim exemption, on payment of a tax (£T44; £40 sterling, 1915 values). General Fakhri Pasha seized on this point, and demanded immediate enrolment of all fit men of Zeitun. The notables of Zeitun were in agreement, but the fighting men refused, and fled to the hills. Eventually 40 or 50 were persuaded to present themselves at the barracks. But they were not enrolled in the army – which was not surprising, in view of what had happened to Armenian soldiers elsewhere in the Ottoman army; instead, they were driven like cattle to Marash, and jailed.[23]

Then a band of about 25 young fighters came down from the hills, occupied the strategically placed monastery of the Mother of God, and took the offensive against the Turkish troops. The battle lasted for 24 hours; 300 Turkish soldiers were slain, and one of the officers, by the name of Suleiman. (Hence the name by which the Young Turks, and subsequently the Kemalists, have sought to rename Zeitun – Suleimanli.) The fighters withdrew to the mountains under cover of darkness. On capturing the monastery, the Turks burnt it to the ground.[24]

Then the deportations began: initially the families of the leading men, followed by more, and more, of the ancient indigenous inhabitants of Zeitun. In the succeeding days others followed. In the words of the Reverend Dikran Andreasian, Protestant pastor of Zeitun:

> In this way three or four hundred families at a time were sent off on foot, with no proper supply of food, by devious routes through the mountains, some north-west towards Konya, some south-east towards the hot and unhealthy plains of Mesopotamia.[25]

Recalling the sight of the last of his community streaming down the valley into banishment and parched, unutterable deprivation, he added, 'We had seen massacres, but we had never seen this before. A massacre at least ends quickly, but this prolonged anguish of soul is almost beyond endurance.'[26]

Initially some Zeituntzis were deported to Sultania, in the province of Konya. The Konya Armenians begged permission to help the deportees, most of whom by then were ragged and filthy skeletons; but they were forbidden.[27] However, a short while later an Albanian officer arrived in Sultania; he was disgusted by what he saw, and allowed relief to be given.[28] (He was one of the few Ottoman officers who showed compassion for Armenians, and, typically, he was not a Turk.) Some weeks afterwards these wretched people were sent back eastwards, to Aleppo, and on to Deir ez-Zor, which was to become a vast and horrific open-air concentration camp.

After Zeitun had been emptied other towns in Cilicia followed – Geben, Furnus and Albistan. Similar methods were used: first, the leaders of the community were isolated, and driven off in the first convoy (only later were the male deportees summarily despatched outside the town); lesser citizens followed. Some, not knowing the true purpose of the 'deportations' – for surely the term is too mild – paid to be taken by horse and cart; the driver of the cart would take them a short way out of the city, dump them and refuse to take them further, and turn back for more.

Van and Djevdet Bey

In the east, the Sarikamish disaster had not been the only Turkish failure of the early months of the war. To the south, Ottoman forces attacked Russian-occupied Persian Azerbaijan, and occupied its capital, Tabriz (January 1915). There was a large non-Muslim population in this district, consisting partly of Armenians, and partly of Assyrians – (Nestorian Christians, who call themselves Syrians). Many of these fled with the retreating Russian army, in a harrowing, destitute winter trek to the Russian border town of Julfa. Those that remained endured a grim period of looting and massacre; many villages were plundered and destroyed.

The Turks were thrown out of Tabriz on 30 January 1915, but remained in occupation of part of Persian Azerbaijan. A campaign to capture Khoi, 160 kilometres north-west of Tabriz, ensued, led by Djevdet Bey, brother-in-law of Enver. It was unsuccessful. Perhaps out of revenge, Djevdet ordered the cold-blooded killing of about 800 people – mostly old men, women and children – in the Salmas district (to the north-east of Lake Urmia) in early March.[29]

Djevdet had been governor of Van since February 1915. Van, and indeed the whole of the east, had been tense since the beginning of the war. In early 1915 there was a minor rebellion of Armenians at Koms, ten miles north of Moush, when they rose in self-defence against the brutal and threatening behaviour of some Turkish gendarmes. A commission of enquiry was appointed, consisting of two Turks and one Armenian, Vahan Papazian, Ottoman deputy for Bitlis, which found the gendarmes at fault, and for a short time there was peace.[30]

Several features meant that Van was especially tense. In the first place, both in the town and the province Armenians were in an actual majority over the combined Turkish and Kurdish population, and however much Armenians might protest their loyalty, both government and people could not ignore the fact of the pull of Russian Armenia.[31] (The Armenians of Van, too, were in dress and appearance like those of Tiflis – like, indeed, any urban population in Europe at the time.) As in Cilicia, the Armenian political leaders, the most important of whom were the Dashnaktsakans Vramyan, Aram (Manukian), Ishkhan and the Ramkavar Armenak Yekarian, told their followers to submit to anything rather than antagonise the government; for on past experience, they and all Armenians knew the propensity of any Turkish government to massacre Armenians. But the most critical feature of the situation in Van was the character of the governor, Djevdet Bey. He had replaced the cunning and plausible ostensibly philo-Armenian Hassan Tahsin Pasha, who had gone to Erzerum. Djevdet's extremism was more open, his streak of barbarity more pronounced. He was also, like Talaat, a man of dangerously unpredictable moods, friendly one moment, ferociously hostile the next, capable of treacherous brutality.

After his return from the abortive expedition in north-east Persia, Djevdet returned to Van and instigated a reign of terror in the outlying villages of the province on the pretext of searching for arms. But the Armenian leaders in the city did not protest. However, when Djevdet demanded 4,000 Armenians for the Ottoman army, the Armenian leaders demurred; they offered him 400, and the rest in exemption (which they were legally entitled to do). But Djevdet insisted on men, not money.[32] In mid-April – just a week or so after the deportation of Zeitun, of which, since all communication had been cut, the Vannetzis can have known nothing, there was trouble in the village of Shadakh, not far from Van: a schoolmaster had been arrested, and there had been a local demonstration in his favour. Djevdet asked four prominent Armenians to go there, together with four leading Turks, to mediate and conciliate. The commission set out, seen off by a Turkish guard of honour. Leader of the Armenians was Ishkhan. At the first village at which they stopped a feast was prepared for them; and it was there that the four Armenians were treacherously murdered.[33] It was Friday, 16 April 1915.

At the same time the arms searches were continuing. The gendarmes stopped at nothing in their treatment of Armenians; they liberally murdered those whose arms they were allegedly gathering. Partly in retaliation, and partly in self-defence, a patrol was attacked by Armenians in another village near Van. Djevdet's fury was extreme.[34]

By now the Armenians were thoroughly alarmed, and had almost decided to give up the 4,000 men for the army, but dared not do so, sure that they would all be killed immediately. They asked Dr Clarence Ussher, missionary and representative of the neutral United States, to mediate. Djevdet attempted to contravene the diplomatic immunity of Ussher's compound by trying to quarter 50 Turkish soldiers in it. It was clear to Ussher that any attempt at mediation would be futile.[35]

Monday, 19 April was a quiet day. Ussher says that Djevdet issued a general order throughout the province of Van, which read: 'The Armenians must be exterminated. If any Muslim protect a Christian, first, his house shall be burnt; then the Christian killed before his eyes, then his [the Muslim's] family and himself.'[36]

Before sunrise on the following day, shots were heard on the Varak plain, to the east of the city. It was a trivial incident: a group of Turks had seized a young girl, two Armenians had run up to rescue her, but they were then fired on and killed. This was the signal for a general fusillade on all sides.[37]

For over a week the Armenians had been carefully strengthening the defences of their quarters; leaders of all three political parties had been expecting a Turkish onslaught. Walls had been built within walls. There were two parts of the city to protect: the Armenian part of the old city of Van, consisting of old, tall, back-to-back houses, clustered together beneath the ancient citadel of Van along narrow, winding streets; and the new, prosperous garden suburb, known as Aikesdan (Armn: 'vineyard'), stretching eastwards from old Van, much of which consisted of villas built by prosperous Armenians from the mid-nineteenth century until the period of the Hamidian persecutions of the 1890s. Foreign vice-consulates were situated in the Aikesdan.

To defend their quarters, the Armenians had only 300 men armed with rifles, and 1,000 with pistols and antique weapons. The initial Turkish onslaught had been anticipated, and was thrown back. Firing continued all day, and by the evening Ussher counted ten houses in flames. In overall military command was Armenak Yekarian. The Armenians also coolly organised a provisional government of besieged Van, dealing with defence, provisions and administration – and foreign relations, to ensure that the neutrality of foreign property was respected. Judges, police and health officials were appointed.

Besides defending their own population of 30,000, Armenian strategy was to inflict as much damage on Turkish strongholds as they could, to try to hold off the Turks until the Russians could reach them, or to force Djevdet to see the folly of his murderous attack. In the first few days they tunnelled out and seized two barracks (one police and one military) and destroyed them with the aid of kerosene; likewise, too, the British consulate, which had become an important Turkish stronghold.[38] The Turks for their part hurled down grenades from the top of the rock of Van, also a kind of napalm (Ussher calls it Greek fire), and very large bombs. All this the Armenians took quite calmly; there was no panic among the besieged population, only a determination to cope with every hazard. Ussher himself noted incredible scenes of bravery among the Armenians, notably from Aram himself.

All Armenian villages throughout the province, that is all those under Djevdet's jurisdiction, had been attacked by Turkish soldiers on the 19th. The entire Armenian male population of Akantz (north-east of lake Van), about 2,500, had been murdered on that day. Three, feigning death, had escaped. Only inaccessible places, those heights that Armenians had come to know so well over the last thousand years, secured Armenians from attack – and also places under the protection of powerful Kurdish chiefs, who were friendly to Armenians and detested the government as much as they; Moks was one such place. Of these attacks on the villages Ussher says, 'We have absolute proof that 55,000 people were killed.'[39] The attack on the villages leads Ussher to conclude, quite plausibly, that 19 April was the date originally planned by Djevdet for a simultaneous attack on all Armenians throughout the province; but that the attack on the city was delayed for 24 hours because of Ussher's insistence on not accepting the 50 Turkish soldiers immediately.

While the Armenians of Van were battling to defend themselves, Djevdet worked out a scheme to force them to surrender: he allowed large numbers of refugees, women and children, to enter the besieged quarters. By the end of the month these numbered 15,000.[40] Of those still outside Ussher notes:

> Some of our patients had been protected and cared for by Kurds. One woman had fallen down the mountain and broken her thigh. A passing Kurd had taken her on his back, carried her up the mountain and laid her under the shelter of a haystack. Her children kept her supplied with snow, which was, with the exception of a few grass roots and flower bulbs, their only food for twenty days.[41]

Another patient, a young man, had been hidden by a Kurd in his house, disguised as a woman.

Food rapidly became low. It soon became urgent to get a messenger out, to tell the Russians of their plight. Twelve messengers were sent out in disguise, with messages sewn into the seams of their garments.

By the beginning of the fourth week of the siege, the outlook was grim. Djevdet was far superior in men and arms – although the Turkish fire, which was mostly shells, was fairly ineffectual against sun-dried brick.

Then on Friday evening, 14 May, Ussher saw a flotilla of ships sailing away from Van, westwards across the lake; and more followed the next day.[42] He realised that the Turks were evacuating their women and children. On Sunday there was a massive bombardment of 46 shells, and extra-territorial property was not spared. Ussher concluded, 'The Turks are saying goodbye.'[43] Through his field-glasses he descried some Turks hoisting the wheels of a mountain gun on to the back of a mule. Elsewhere, Turks were running away.

By Monday, 17 May 1915, Van was in the hands of the Armenians. The relief after five weeks of fighting was unimaginable. Soon the advance guard of the Russian army, consisting of Armenian volunteers, arrived. Russian regular soldiers followed. On his arrival, the keys of the city and citadel were handed to General Nikolayev;[44] a day or so later he confirmed the Armenian provisional government in office, with Aram as governor. But not for long; six weeks later the Russian forces were compelled to retire, and as many of the Armenians of

Van who could fled with them (Ussher too), a perilous and agonising flight into Transcaucasia.

It is important to get the events of Van in perspective, because Turkish writers and apologists have spoken of an Armenian 'revolutionary plot' to seize power and kill the Turks. Specifically, Dashnaktsutiun is blamed; but (as Professor Hovannisian points out), if there had been a plot, would the Dashnak party have allowed Ishkhan to leave for the peace mission on which he was so treacherously murdered?[45] In Van the attitude of the Armenians was initially cautious co-operation with the Turks, *yet* preparedness for everything that the last 40 years had taught an Armenian to expect from a Turkish government. Their five-week battle with the Turks was not a rebellion, but legitimate self-defence, a reaction to the terrorism of the government's representative, Djevdet, which he had directed against the entire Armenian community.

Events in Constantinople

During the siege of Van, as news of the armed confrontation between Armenians and Turks reached Constantinople, a calamity had overtaken Armenians throughout the empire: the government had begun to exterminate them. Only in March the Turkish leaders in Constantinople had been put under so great pressure by the British and French naval attack upon the Dardanelles that they had prepared to quit Constantinople and set up a temporary government in Eskishehir. Suddenly, on 18 March, the Allied naval attack was called off. In the interval between it and the Allied landings (25 April), the Turks regained their confidence. In their new mood, they struck at the Armenians. As darkness fell on 23 April 1915, throughout the night and into the morning of the 24th, the police arrested 235 leading Armenians – politicians, writers, educators, lawyers and so forth.[46] These men were held at the central police station for three days, before being exiled into the interior – half to Ayash, and half to Chankiri. Further arrests brought the figure to 600. Only a very few were ever allowed to return home; most, on being released in the wilds of Anatolia, were slaughtered. One of the few who were lucky enough to escape was Komitas, the composer and folk-song collector. But the sufferings of his fellow Armenians that he witnessed at this time and later, the butchery and torture, unhinged his mind, and he died in an asylum in Paris in 1935.

At the same time the Constantinople police arrested a much larger number – the figure is probably in the region of 5,000 – of Armenians of the poorest class – young men from the provinces, now working as labourers, doorkeepers or messengers.[47] These too were never seen again, but taken into the interior and murdered.

To the Armenians of the capital this action was totally unexpected. They considered themselves entirely loyal to the regime. Some were personal friends of Young Turk leaders: men like the parliamentary deputy for Rodosto, Krikor Zohrab, who had given shelter to Talaat during the counter-revolution of April 1909. Yet all such were dragged off to the interior, and bludgeoned to death with the others. (Zohrab and his fellow deputy Vartkes were exiled and killed a few weeks after 24 April.)

Today, Armenians all over the world hold 24 April as a day of mourning, the anniversary of the day on which the Turkish government began its systematic extermination of Turkish Armenians.

Talaat Pasha, minister of the interior, did not deny ordering the arrest of the Constantinople leaders on 23–4 April, or the mass killing of Armenians that followed it. To Henry Morgenthau he justified the action by saying that the government was acting in self-defence: Armenians had opposed the government at Van and Zeitun and were in communication with the Russians. Hence, he said, the deportations.[48]

'Deportation' was just a euphemism for mass murder. No provision was made for their journey or exile, and unless they could bribe their guards, they were forbidden in almost all cases food and water. Those who survived the journey landed up in appalling concentration camps beside the Euphrates, between Jerablus and Deir ez-Zor. Descriptions of those by visitors to them in 1915 and 1916 will show what the Turkish government intended by deportation. Moreover, no distinction was made between innocent, suspect or guilty – a point which prompted a query from a correspondent on the *Berliner Tageblatt*; any such distinction, Talaat replied, was 'utterly impossible', since 'those who were innocent today might be guilty tomorrow.'[49]

After 24 April, death shadowed every Armenian within the Ottoman empire. With the exception of the Armenian patriarch in Constantinople, Zaven, the people were leaderless. Even he was deported later on. The civilised, constitutional political world, based on the concept of law, that they had attempted to build in the Ottoman empire since 1908 had been smashed, and all that was left was their representative, whose office dated back to Mehmed II. All communication was cut between the capital and the provinces. The American ambassador himself complained that he was suddenly forbidden to communicate with his consuls in the interior by cypher.

Initially it seemed that only those Armenians in the security risk areas would be deported – those, that is, in Cilicia and in the eastern border region. But as 1915 wore on, it became apparent that Armenians far from the battle zone – in places like Kharput, Sivas, Mersifun, Angora – all were to be victims, too. With the typical thoroughness of the racist, the Turkish government was allowing none to escape.

By the second half of May Zeitun was empty of Armenians and full of Turks. Between 6,000 and 8,000 of its inhabitants were sent initially to the Konya district, and the survivors then continued to Deir ez-Zor.[50] Between 15,000 and 16,000 went directly to Deir ez-Zor.

Djevdet in Bitlis

Some of the earlier massacres were carried out directly by the embittered and vengeful Djevdet and his *kesab taburi* – 'butcher battalions', a name he gave them himself – after the failure to dislodge the Armenians of Van. Djevdet retreated south and west. Initially he attacked Sairt, and killed off a large part of its Armenian and Assyrian population. Then he moved on to Bitlis; and at about the same time reinforcements arrived from Erzerum, estimated at about 10,000 men. (The number of troops that the Turks used, while the war was on, to satisfy their own ideological fanaticism was quite remarkable.) At Bitlis Djevdet employed similar, but more ruthless, tactics to those at Van. After making certain demands, and hanging some of the leading citizens, he surrounded Bitlis with Turkish troops (25 June); nearly all the men were arrested and then shot. Women and children, as so often, were distributed like chattels among the Turkish/Kurdish population; and the rest – the 'useless ones' – were driven south to die with other deportees. Self-defence by an armed population, so successful at Van, was a lingering alternative to suicide in Bitlis. No Russian forces arrived; the defenders were quite cut off. An estimated 15,000 died in the siege, massacre and deportation of Bitlis.[51]

As in the days of Abdul Hamid, the Turks of 1915 took great care to kill off the Armenian peasantry, as well as the town-dwellers. The beautiful villages around Bitlis – one report specially mentions those of Rahva and Khultig – were systematically destroyed after the main town was silent.[52]

Moush and Sasun

Villages on the Moush plain, the next region to be attacked by security forces, appear to have been destroyed before the main town. They, and the villages in the Bulanik district (about 50 miles north-east of Moush) were attacked in late May. A big drive was made against nearby Sasun, too, using Kurdish irregulars. (Already the 15,000 inhabitants of Sasun had been joined by a further 15,000 Armenian villagers from the plain.) Sasun was under siege; but the Turks and Kurds again proved themselves to be no match for the Armenian defenders, and a truce was arranged at the end of May.[53]

For a few weeks there was peace, and an end to oppression throughout the district. But at the end of June a determined assault was made against the whole region – Bitlis, Moush and, of course, Sasun. Troops arrived from Erzerum with mountain guns, and severed all contact between Moush and Sasun. In Moush itself, in early July, the mood changed to one of the most dire oppression: further exactions were made, and demands for arms; moreover, leading Armenians of the towns and villages were subjected to frightful tortures – finger-nails pulled out, limbs twisted, teeth knocked out, noses beaten down; and wives and daughters were raped in public before their broken menfolk.[54]

From the villages – in all about 100 – around Moush the men were rounded up on 10 July; here, as elsewhere, the operation was conducted by the Teshkilat-i Makhsusiye, using Turkish prisoners who had been specially released from jail for the purpose. The villagers resisted as far as they could, but the special forces closed in on them, captured the men, herded them into concentration camps and bayoneted them all. In Moush itself the men resisted for four days from the stone-built houses and churches, before going down fighting. For the women and children of the town a grimmer death followed: they were driven out of the city into specially prepared large wooden sheds in the nearby Armenian villages; these were then set on fire, and amid scenes of horror, and the vilest, most sadistic brutality from the Turkish guards, the defenceless women and children were all burnt to death.[55]

Before the massacre of Moush 60,000 Armenians had been living in the town and surrounding villages of the plain; very few survived. Over the next few months occasional survivors escaped across the mountains and through the Russian lines to tell the story.

Having thus disposed of the Armenians of Moush, the Turkish forces moved against Sasun. Sasun, quiet since the pact made in late May, was invaded in July. Infantry and guns were brought from Moush; the Kurds, reorganised, invaded from south, west and north. Fighting was incessant in late July. The Armenians were prepared for another invasion; but the threat of starvation loomed large on this occasion, since thousands of plainsmen had been driven to seek refuge in the mountains. Soon they were living exclusively on unsalted roast mutton, since the rich harvest of fruit and honey, in which Sasun abounds, was rapidly finished. Ammunition, too, soon became low; and the defenders had the misfortune to lose all their leaders, with the exception of Ruben Ter-Minasian, by a single Turkish shell. Harder and harder the Turks pushed against the Sasuntzis, driving them up Mount Andok, so often their refuge in the past. When ammunition gave out, the defenders fought with knives, scythes and stones – anything they could find; and many boulders were rolled down the steep ravines against the enemy. By early August their position was hopeless, and on 5 August 1915 the Turks captured Andok. Very few Armenians survived. Sasun, to which Ottoman rule had bequeathed only corruption and murder, had received the ultimate imperial gifts – extermination, desolation and silence.[56]

Meanwhile, the frontier areas further north were being emptied of their Armenians, principally the province of Erzerum. Here the actual procedure of deportation was put into effect, which had been lacking in the attacks on the Armenians of Sairt, Bitlis, Moush and Sasun.

Erzindjan

The Armenians of Erzindjan knew of their forthcoming deportation in early June 1915. They would be transported to Mesopotamia (they were told), but there would be no massacre. Several days' grace was given to them to sell up their property, to get cash for the journey. They would be provided with food, and protected by a military escort.[57] The first convoy set off on 7 June. Rich people hired carts. (Again, one is amazed by their simple trust in Turkish words.) They were to go, in the first place, to Kharput, taking the lengthy, semi-circular route via the Kemakh gorge, a rough road full of twists and turns, some 300 kilometres to the south-west of Erzindjan.[58]

For four days convoys left Erzindjan. As they left Erzindjan, the process began: men were separated from the rest, and killed on the spot. Women and elderly men had to go on. (The authorities were initially lenient with regard to children, permitting them to be parcelled out among Muslim families, but after a few days insisted on their departure as well.) A terrible fate awaited all the exiles. Many were attacked in the early stages of the journey, and their clothes were taken from them. When they reached the Kemakh gorge – where the Euphrates flows between two sheer walls of rock – they were stopped, and their hands were tied behind their backs. The order was given to kill them by pushing them over, and they were cast into the ravine. Many were bayoneted to death, too; but the majority were despatched straight into the river, since this method proved speedier. For the numbers were large; probably 20,000 to 25,000 Armenians of Erzindjan were slaughtered, and of these about half at the Kemakh gorge.[59]

The Armenians of Baiburt, north-east of Erzindjan, were rounded up and deported at about the same time. Seventeen thousand Armenians lived in the town and surrounding villages.[60] They went in three main convoys, in the direction of Erzindjan and the Kemakh gorge. According to the account of one of the women on one of these convoys, who escaped, the Armenians, on asking the gendarmes whither they were being sent, were told 'To a safe place, away from the Turks, where the mob cannot massacre you. It is the duty of the government to protect its subjects. You will remain there until peace is re-established.'[61] All this the Armenians believed. Just outside the town, according to the same witness, the guards began to threaten, demanding first money, then girls, then more money, and more girls, until they had no money left to buy food, and all their prettiest young girls had been abducted. As they trudged onwards brigands would swoop down from the hills, and steal their clothing; and past Erzindjan they were physically attacked by more brigands. In desperation, worn out and weak though they were, they tried to run back to Erzindjan; but the gendarmes opened fire. Some lived to be driven onwards to Kemakh, where the atrocities recently visited upon the Erzindjantzis were visited upon them too.[62] Another report, from a member of one of the other convoys from Baiburt, tells how all the men were separated from the others and shot just outside the town; and how at the Euphrates the children were separated from their mothers, and thrown in: those who could swim to the sides were ruthlessly shot down by gendarmes.[63]

Hassan Tahsin and Erzerum

Erzerum and Baiburt were both at this time in the province of Erzerum. The governor was Hassan Tahsin, a plausible and ostensibly friendly and concerned man, but beneath this exterior a hardened Young Turk racist fanatic, dedicated like the others to riveting Ottoman Turkey to Russian Azerbaijan over the corpse of Armenia. He had been governor of Van before Djevdet's appointment there, at the time when the success of the February 1914 reform scheme seemed likely. The Young Turks had put him there knowing that his patina of civilisation would appeal to Europeans; while his mind was full of images of whitening skulls, typical of the other Young Turks of the period who sought to emulate Timur and Jengiz Khan.

In Erzerum in the spring Armenians had suffered the brutalities that accompanied arms searches elsewhere. On 18 April, at a public meeting, Armenians were branded as 'traitors' and enemies of the empire. Muslims were ordered on no account to shield Armenian friends; those who did so would suffer as Armenians.[64] Nevertheless, the German liaison officer General Posselt noted to a member of his embassy staff on 26 April that 'the Armenians will stay calm if they are not pressured or molested by the Turks,' and added, 'the behaviour of the Armenians has been perfect (*tadellos*)'.[65]

In late May, as the Russians advanced, Armenian refugees arrived from Melazkert and Pasin, driven by the Turks. Forbidden to enter Erzerum itself, half-starved and totally exhausted, they were kept outside the city, in the rain, for seven days.[66] Those that survived were then sent to the Kemakh gorge, and died there as so many others had.

On 4 June a convoy of peasant Armenians – mostly women and children – from the villages on the plain of Erzerum departed westwards. Their destination was to be Kemakh. Thither they trudged, through mud, along difficult, treacherous roads, slipping, falling and dying by the wayside. At nightfall the Turks took their usual levies – money and girls. In a few days they were robbed of almost everything – food, clothes and money. Then, as they approached Kemakh, a signal was given by a shot in the air, and merciless bands of irregulars shot or bayoneted to death the remnants of the convoy.[67]

Forty families from the city of Erzerum were deported on 16 June. They were to go to Diyarbekir, via Kighi and Palu. Between the latter two towns they were surrounded and nearly all killed. On the 19th about 10,000 Armenians left, initially to Baiburt. There the convoy was swelled to about 15,000 people. On they travelled, to Erzindjan. Tahsin, the governor, was there too, to 'check on their security'. From Erzindjan they had expected to go on the main road to Sivas, but they were led aside, as others had been before, to the deadly Kemakh gorge. There the men were separated from the women and children, and all killed. Women and children were forced to foot-slog to remote and burning areas of the empire: some were driven to Mosul in the east, to Raqqa in the south, and to Aleppo and Aintab in the west.[68]

The deportations of Erzerum continued until the end of July 1915. By the latter months of the year only those Armenians needed for essential services (such as building) were left in the town; this too was the pattern elsewhere. By February 1916, when the Russians entered the town, captured during their massive and successful spring offensive, there were only 80–100 Armenians left in the town,[69] out of a 1914 figure of 20,000. The total for the villages on the plain of Erzerum had been a further 45,000, the vast majority of whom had likewise been deported and killed.[70]

The Assyrians

Besides the Armenians, another Ottoman people was deported and killed by its own government in 1915. These were the Assyrians, who confusingly call themselves Syrians. As Armenians were divided by the Russo-Turkish border, so Assyrians were divided by the Perso-Turkish border. In the Ottoman district that they inhabited they constituted a minority, but a substantial one, interspersed with Kurds. They were politically less sophisticated than Armenians, but the education that they had been receiving had taught them to demand greater autonomy, less subservience, and security from their predatory neighbours.

Persian Assyrians had been looted, sacked and killed by Turkish forces during their occupation of north-west Persia in the early months of 1915.[71] This was only to be expected. But when the Turks were forced out of Persia by the Russians in May, the Turks turned on their *own* Assyrians. In mid-June (at the same time as the assaults on Bitlis and Moush) an attack was launched on the mountainous dwellings of the Assyrians, initially against Qodshanis (Kochannes) in the Hakkiari district, the seat of their spiritual leader, whose title is Mar Shimun. The mountains of Hakkiari, the homeland of this community, are more sheer and inaccessible than any of the mountains of Armenia. The attack was unprovoked. From within their church they defended themselves against Turkish regular soldiers for two days before their ammunition ran out, whereupon they escaped by night to Persia. At the same time a second attack was launched, against the Assyrian villagers of Tkhuma, Tiari and Baz. The villagers fought fiercely from their mountain strongholds for 40 days, before being compelled to take refuge near the top of a high mountain. The Turks tried to starve them out; but when the Russians had regained the initiative in the war, Mar Shimun (a good shot himself) was able to go with a band of men into the interior to bring relief to the besieged men. Astonishingly, he reached them, and after many encounters was able to lead them back across the mountains to Persia.[72] Fifteen thousand were saved. These episodes were only the beginning of the upheaval, dispersion and massacre that characterised the history of the Assyrians throughout the war and into the mid-1930s.

Shabin Karahisar

June 1915 was the peak month in the bleak story of Armenian deportations. But a significant exception to the tale of hopeless passive suffering took place at Shabin Karahisar, birthplace of Andranik, though it too was doomed, a brief flame of defiance soon extinguished in gloom and ashes. Shabin Karahisar is on the western fringe of 'historic' Armenia. It did not have a history of defiance of imperial Ottoman misgovernment, like Zeitun or Sasun. Nevertheless when its Armenian men guessed the intentions of the government, they took to the hills nearby, and withstood the Turkish forces. For four weeks they fought, from 2 to 30 June, and held off all attempts to force them into submission, until being overwhelmed and massacred to the last man.[73]

Trebizond

Also outside historic Armenia was Trebizond. The province had a total population of 1,000,000, only 53,000 of whom were Armenians; in the town itself the proportion of Armenians was somewhat higher. (The largest Christian population was the Greeks, and the largest Muslim grouping was Georgian-speaking Laz peasants. There were very few Turks.) Against the Armenian population threats, arbitrary arrests and arms searches had continued as elsewhere. The proclamation ordering the deportation of Armenians was posted on the streets at the end of June.[74] According to the Italian consul, Signor Gorrini:

> The official proclamation of internment came from Constantinople. It was the work of the central government and the 'Committee of Union and Progress'. The local authorities, and indeed the Muslim population in general, tried to resist, to mitigate it, to make omissions, to hush it up. But the orders of the central government were categorically confirmed, and all were compelled to resign themselves and obey.
>
> The consular body intervened, and attempted to save at least the women and children. We did, in fact, secure numerous exemptions, but these were not subsequently respected, owing to the interference of the local branch of the 'Union and Progress Committee' and to fresh orders from Constantinople.[75]

Trapezuntine Armenians, like those elsewhere, were forbidden to sell their property (or only to sell it very cheaply) so that they could have no money for the journey; and Muslims were forbidden to shield them.[76]

They were killed off by forced marches, by shooting and by bayoneting. Since, too, Trebizond is on the coastline, the CUP took full advantage of the fact and sent many out to sea before throwing them overboard. Indeed, on the very day of the decree 45 leading Armenians were put on a launch for

Kerasond (Giresun), and when a little way from the coast were capsized into the Black Sea. Deportations reached their peak in the last week of June and the first week of July; by the 7th the thousand Armenian houses of Trebizond were empty. All were expelled, including the old and sick – and the Catholic Armenians, too, who constituted a substantial proportion of the Armenian population of Trebizond.[77] Many were driven south, along the valley of Trebizond's river, the Deyirmeni, in the direction of Gumush-khana; but few got beyond the village of Djevizlik, six hours away. 'At the same time', reports the *kavass*, or caretaker, of the local branch of the Ottoman Bank, who was a Macedonian, 'The river Yel-Deyirmeni brought down every day to the sea a number of corpses, mutilated and absolutely naked, the women with their breasts cut off.[78]

Leon Surmelian, today a distinguished American-Armenian author and translator, is a native of Trebizond. He has recorded his boyhood experiences. Among other things, he notes the polished, civilised manners of the local leaders of the Committee of Union and Progress. Of the deportation he writes:

> They let us rest for a while on marshy ground. We were not allowed to go near the river and had to drink the water of stagnant pools swarming with tadpoles. I kept dipping my biscuit box in a slimy pond and passing it around to the women and girls.
>
> We had not gone far after this brief rest when I saw a woman's nude body in the river, which was rather shallow here. Her long hair floated down the current, her bloated white abdomen glistened in the sun. I noticed that one of her breasts was cut off. Further up I saw another body, this time a man's; then a human arm caught up in the roots of a tree. The corpses became a common sight, but after I had counted fourteen of them, Aunt Azniv scolded me and told me not to look at the river any more. I had never seen bodies of grown people in the nude and gazed at them with a morbid curiosity.
>
> When, some minutes later, I looked at the river again, I saw a long, long band of frothy blood clinging to its banks. It is impossible to describe the impression that ghastly scene made upon me, although I can see it now as if it were before my eyes. The exposed roots of trees and shrubs coiled around like blood-sucking, blood-loving red snakes. Now none of us spoke, we all tramped on silently, on our faces the solemnity of death.[79]

Consul Gorrini estimated that there were 17,000 Armenians in the town of Trebizond before the massacre; when he left, on 23 July 1915, there were hardly 100 left. During that appalling month, he says,

> I neither slept not ate; I was given over to nerves and nausea, so terrible was the torment of having to look on at the wholesale execution of these defenceless, innocent creatures.
>
> The passing of gangs of Armenian exiles beneath the windows and before

the door of the consulate; their prayers for help, when neither I nor any other could do anything to answer them; the city in a state of siege, guarded at every point by 15,000 troops in complete war equipment, by thousands of police agents, by bands of volunteers and by members of the 'Committee of Union and Progress'; the lamentations, the tears, the abandonments, the imprecations, the many suicides, the instantaneous deaths from sheer terror, the sudden unhingeing of men's reason, the conflagrations, the shooting of victims in the city, the ruthless searches through the houses and in the countryside; the hundreds of corpses found every day along the exile road; the young women converted by force to Islam or exiled like the rest; the children torn away from their families or from the Christian schools, and handed over by force to Muslim families, or else placed by hundreds on board ship in nothing but their shirts, and then capsized and drowned in the Black Sea and the river Deyirmen Dere – these are my last ineffaceable memories of Trebizond, memories which still, at a month's distance, torment my soul and almost drive me frantic.[80]

Kharput

Five hundred kilometres south of Trebizond, far inland, far from any border area, was Kharput, one of the intellectual centres for Ottoman Armenians; in the late nineteenth century American missionaries had established there a distinguished and progressive educational institution, Euphrates College. First there were the usual savage arms searches and arbitrary arrests, brutalisation in jail and photographing of arms (mostly bought from Turks) as 'evidence of revolution';[81] there followed the murder of 13,000 Armenian soldiers who had enrolled in the Ottoman army and who were stationed at Kharput.[82] Then the deportations began.

The first convoy left in late June. Little or no time was given to prepare for departure; all the local officials were hostile.

On the first convoy were four professors from Euphrates College. No better example can be given of the hostility of the Committee of Union and Progress towards learning and the intellectual development of the Ottoman Armenian people than to note the fates of these men, as recorded in the statement of 19 July 1915 made by the principal of the college, Professor Ernest W. Riggs, on the losses that the college had suffered:

Professors – Four gone, three left, as follows:–
Professor Tenekedjian. Served college 35 years; representative of the Americans with the government. Protestant *askabed* [community head], professor of Turkish and History. Besides previous trouble, arrested 1 May without charge; hair of head, moustache and beard pulled out, in vain attempt to secure damaging confessions; starved and hung by arms for a

day and a night, and severely beaten several times; taken out towards Diyarbekir about 20 June, and murdered in general massacre on the road.

Professor Nahigian. Served college 33 years, studied at Ann Arbor,
professor of Mathematics. Arrested about 5 June, and shared Prof. Tenekedjian's fate on the road.

Professor Vorperian. Taken to witness a man beaten almost to death;
became mentally deranged; started with his family about 5 July into exile
under guard, and murdered beyond Malatia. Principal of preparatory
department; studied at Princeton; served college 20 years.

Professor Boudjikanian. Served college 16 years, studied at Edinburgh;
professor of Mental and Moral Science. Arrested with Prof. Tenekedjian
and suffered same tortures; also had three finger nails pulled out by the
roots; killed in the same massacre.

Professor Soghigian. Served college 25 years. Arrested 1 May; not
tortured, but sick in prison; sent to Red Crescent Hospital, and after paying
large bribes is now free.

Professor Khatchadourian. Served college for over 15 years, studied in
Stuttgart and Berlin, professor of Music. Escaped arrest and torture and
thus far escaped exile and death, because of favour with the kaimakam
secured by personal services rendered.

Professor Luledjian. Served college about 15 years, studied at Cornell and
Yale (M.S.), professor of Biology. Arrested about 5 June, beaten about the
hands, body and head with a stick by the kaimakam himself, who, when
tired, called on all who loved religion and the nation to continue the beating;
after a period of insensibility in a dark closet, taken to the Red Crescent
Hospital with a broken finger and serious bruises. Now free.[83]

One of the grimmest and most vivid accounts of the expulsion of the
Kharput Armenians was sent by an American consul to ambassador
Morgenthau in Constantinople, using material gathered from a survivor of the
seventy-day foot-slog from Kharput to Ras ul-Ain, via Malatia, Kiakhta and
Viranshehir. It was a typical story – one that was repeated many times over in
the Ottoman empire during 1915 and 1916.

When this convoy left Kharput there were 3,000 people on it – including
women, girls and little children. They took with them what they could get
together in terms of food, belongings and money. Many hired carts to take
them as far as Malatia. Seventy gendarmes accompanied them. A Turkish
notable, Faiki Bey, came with them, saying that he would stay with them for
much of the journey. On the second day Faiki suggested he take £T400 from
them (£363 sterling, 1915 values), 'just to keep it safe', till they reached
Malatia. The same day he disappeared and was not seen again.[84]

By the third day the semi-civilised mountain tribes were swooping down and
carrying off the women (or simply robbing and killing them if they were plain),
being incited to do so all the while by the seventy 'protective' gendarmes.

On the following day they reached Malatia, where they stayed only very briefly, before setting off again for Ras ul-Ain. It was at Malatia that the gendarmes finally deserted them (not failing, however, to take a final £T200), leaving them to the mercy of a local Kurdish bey.

Two days later 150 men (aged between 15 and 90) were rounded up and murdered; at the same time the new 'protectors' carried out further robbery of the people. At that juncture, too, they met another convoy – an army of sufferers coming from Sivas; together they moved forward, in all 18,000 people.

On they went, a nightmarish spectacle of degraded humanity, subject to violence, robbery, girl-snatching and instant death for any stragglers.

Forty days from their day of departure they came to the Murad river (eastern Euphrates), where they saw the bodies of more than 200 men floating in the river. On the banks were bloodstained clothes. The headman of the village took £T1 from each man for the privilege of not being thrown in the river. Twelve days later, nearly demented with suffering, they arrived at another village,

and here the Kurds took from them everything they had, even their shirts and drawers, so that for five days the whole convoy marched completely naked under the scorching sun. For another five days they did not have a morsel of bread, nor even a drop of water. They were scorched to death by thirst. Hundreds upon hundreds fell dead on the way, their tongues were turned to charcoal, and when, at the end of the five days, they reached a fountain, the whole convoy naturally rushed towards it. But here a policeman barred the way and forbade them to take a single drop of water. Their purpose was to sell it at from £T1 to £T3 the cup, and sometimes they actually withheld the water after getting the money. At another place, where there were wells, some women threw themselves into them, as there was no rope nor pail to draw up the water. These women were drowned, and, in spite of that, the rest of the people drank from that well, the dead bodies still remaining there and stinking in the water. Sometimes, when the wells were shallow and the women could go down into them and come out again, the other women would rush to lick or suck their wet, dirty clothes, in the effort to quench their thirst.

When they passed an Arab village in their naked condition, the Arabs pitied them and gave them pieces of old clothes to cover themselves with. Some of the exiles who still had money bought some clothes; but some still remained who travelled thus naked all the way to the city of Aleppo. The poor women could hardly walk for shame; they walked all bent double.[85]

Twelve days later, at Viranshehir, only 300 remained out of the 18,000. Four days later, the sick women and children, and all the men, were collected together and burned to death. The rest were ordered to continue.

They reached Ras ul-Ain the next day. Here, for the first time, since they had started, the authorities gave them bread, and that was uneatable. The few wretched starved specimens of humanity that remained were here, after further bribes, able to get on a train for Aleppo. At Aleppo, ten days later, only 150 women and children remained from the two convoys.[86]

Sivas

Sivas was another of the towns where the Armenians took up arms against the brutal actions of the government. Persecution of Armenians began in the winter of 1914–15, partly due to general wartime suspicions against Armenians, partly due to allegations that they had poisoned the bread supplied to Turkish soldiers. Led by a Dashnaktsakan by the name of Murad, a band of Armenians made a brief stand of self-defence in the neighbourhood of Sivas; by their bravery and knowledge of the terrain, they were able to keep the Ottoman soldiers at bay until the autumn of 1915, when they were able to reach the Black Sea coast, and, with the aid of friendly Greeks, get a boat and escape to Batum safely.[87] But the villagers among whom they had moved in the Sivas district, and who had sheltered them, paid a heavy price in Turkish retribution – though perhaps no higher than the fate which would have befallen them in any case.

In Sivas itself the story was one of gloomy, silent familiarity. In April 1915 arms searches throughout the province were accompanied by violence against Armenians – extreme torture, often ending in death. At the end of June the expulsion and massacres began: the men separated from the women, and summarily despatched; the women and children driven off in a south-easterly direction, to become another wretched, parched, footsore and exhausted convoy. In this way the 25,000 Armenians of the town of Sivas were reduced to a shadow – a few hundred – consisting of the very old and the very young. Of the estimated 160,000 Armenians of Sivas province only 10,000 remained by the end of 1915.[88]

Angora

All other towns in central or eastern Anatolia with an Armenian population were subject to similar persecutions. In Angora (Ankara, Engürü), by far the largest section of the Armenian population was Catholic (15,000–20,000); it was polished, sophisticated and devoid of any Armenian nationalist aspirations. Turkish was its language. But they too were deported, a few weeks after the expulsion of those Armenians who were members of the Armenian Apostolic Church, always considered more defiant by the Turkish authorities. The Austrian ambassador in Constantinople, Count Pallavicini, managed to exert some pressure on their behalf, but only to the extent of commuting instant death to the slow, exhausted murder of deportation.[89] The political mania of the Committee of Union and Progress was such that no appeals or requests could temper it.

Marsovan

Marsovan (Mersifun) was an Armenian intellectual centre, dominated by Anatolia College, another American Protestant institution, which had 425 boy students, and an attached girls' school with 276 pupils. Over half the teaching staff were Armenian. In the town the Armenians numbered some 12,000 before the expulsions, just under half the total; after, a mere shadow of a hundred or so. According to the college's principal, Theodore Elmer, during the expulsions and the period of legitimised violence towards Armenians, the college itself, which was American property, held as many Armenians as possible within its precincts. The governor, who had expelled the mass of the people in late June and July, said he would deal with the rest as it suited him. The president of the college, fearful for their safety, sought assurances from the capital that those he protected would not be harmed. US ambassador Morgenthau was assured of their safety by Enver and Talaat, and conveyed his assurance back to the college. But the governor of Marsovan alleged that he had received contrary orders, and, with all the precise fanaticism and attention to detail that characterises an agent of systematic mass murder, sought out the few remaining Armenians within the American compound. Seventy-one men and boys were taken in early August, and 62 girls. They suffered the prescribed fate: death by expulsion into the desert wilderness.[90]

Diyarbekir

The great, grim city of Diyarbekir was an inferno of torture and murder at this time, since many Armenians were converging upon it, from all parts of Anatolia; and there was, throughout the province, a large Armenian population. Faiz al-Ghusain, a Muslim Arab, who was born a member of the Beduin tribe of the Sulut (in the Hawran, Syria), and who had become a *kaimakam* of Mamuret el-Aziz and later a practising lawyer in Damascus in partnership with the famous Arab nationalists (hanged by Djemal Pasha) Shukri al-Asli and Abdul Wahhab al Inglizi, was in jail in Diyarbekir in August 1915. While there he was visited by 'one of my Diyarbekir colleagues', and this man, who was close to those charged with carrying out the murders, told Faiz that the figure for all those killed to date – including those from other districts – in Diyarbekir province was the terrifying total of 570,000.[91]

Directions

All throughout the empire Armenians – disarmed, defenceless and terrorised – were being driven to their deaths, men mostly killed locally, women and children struggling over steep mountain paths to the parched deserts beyond, robbed of all they had, raped if attractive, and killed – thrown away like refuse, to be devoured by the scavengers of the desert. Those who survived were driven onwards in two directions – either towards Damascus, or along the Euphrates to Deir ez-Zor. The Damascus deportees escaped relatively lightly, many of them finding shelter in Arab villages between Aleppo and Homs; but an incomprehensibly frightful fate awaited those driven along the Euphrates, who were deposited in concentration camps which were little more than heaps of human wreckage. Only on a few occasions can the world have witnessed such a dense mass of suffering victims and such sadistic guards.

Musa Dagh

Across this darkened barren landscape of suffering there has only so far been one brief beacon of light – the rescue of the Van Armenians from the murderous siege of Djevdet in May. There was, however, in September 1915 another, more illustrious rescue – that of the tough mountaineers of Musa Dagh, or Jebel Musa – the mountain of Moses, situated in what is today the Turkish province of Hatay, the small finger of coastline territory that points southwards into Syria, seized from that country (then under French mandate) by the Kemalists in 1939.

The villages of Musa Dagh, six in number, together making up one *nahiye*, or parish, lay to the west of the mountain. The inhabitants of one of them, Yoghonoluk, are described by its Protestant pastor as simple, industrious folk:

> For years past their chief occupation has been the sawing and polishing by hand of combs from hard wood and bone. Many of our men are also expert wood-carvers. In the neighbouring villages the chief occupations are the culture of silk worms for producing raw silk, and the weaving of silk by hand looms into handkerchieves and scarves. Our people are very fond of their churches, and since the opening of schools by the American missionaries most of our children have learned to read. Every home is surrounded by mulberry trees, and many beautiful orchards cover the terraced slopes towards the south and west. Travellers who have been to southern Italy tell us that the villages near Naples very much resemble ours.[92]

On 13 July 1915 the order came: prepare yourselves for deportation eight days hence. What should they do? If they resisted, death would swiftly overtake them; yet the alternative was the parched, exhausted death in the desert, flogged by gendarmes, with vultures flying overhead. Some, too hopefully, thought that resistance was folly, and that death by forced march might after all – somehow, they knew not how – be modified into a more usual form of exile; they left, 60 families in all. None heard of them again.

The rest left their six villages in the foothills, and climbed up the mountain – their beautiful, sheltering mountain – taking with them their flocks, farm implements, and as much food as they could carry; and all the weapons they could lay their hands on – 120 modern rifles and shotguns, and about 350 old flintlocks and horse-pistols.

It took them a day to ascend the mountain, and they immediately began making barricades and building trenches. A committee of defence was elected to supervise the measures.[93]

The eight days' grace expired on 21 July. The Turks, who had realised what the villagers had decided, launched an assault on their positions with an advance guard of 200 regulars (*nizams*). Their commander allegedly boasted that he could clear the mountain in a day. But the early attacks were a failure, and after suffering several casualties, and being forced to abandon a mountain-gun, they were driven off.[94]

But only temporarily. All knew they were regrouping and massing their full strength, in order to squash the Armenians who dared defy the Turkish order for their sun-scorched death. Three thousand regulars were now gathered, and a huge crowd of local 'irregulars', ready to complete, in true Turkish fashion, the regulars' job of military victory with their own historic roles of looting and massacre.

Then one day the Armenians' scouts brought word that the enemy was all around – at every mountain pass. Small Armenian forces dispersed to oppose each of these concentrations; but all the Turkish moves were feints, except for one at a vital pass, where the Turks poured through in great strength. Soon they occupied the high ground, and threatened the Armenian camp; more and more kept pouring through, all equipped with sophisticated weapons. By the evening they were 400 yards from the Armenians, separated only by a deep ravine.[95]

A hasty, whispered congress of Armenians took place, in total darkness. Eventually a bold plan was hammered out: at the dead of that very night they would creep round behind the Turks and envelop their forces, surprise them and engage them in hand-to-hand fighting. Silently the men set out, and with their intimate knowledge of the mountain that had stood over them all their lives, they crept through the dense, dark woods and encircled the Turkish force. Suddenly they attacked. The Turks were thrown into total confusion, rushing, stumbling in the darkness, their officers shouting contradictory orders. Thousands of Armenians – so the Turks believed – had attacked; and soon the colonel gave the order to retreat.[96]

By dawn the woods were virtually clear of Turks; and the Armenians had augmented their precious store of weapons by seven Mauser rifles.

Shortly afterwards, however, an even larger Turkish force was assembled, with yet more 'irregulars'. Full siege conditions operated, as the Turks tried to starve the Armenians out. Soon bread, cheese and olives were exhausted, and they had to live on meat alone. Even that, by late August, was only sufficient for two more weeks.

Plans for an escape were made. A runner was despatched to Aleppo with a message for the American consul, but he failed to arrive; and a strong swimmer swam up to Alexandretta harbour, to the north, to see if an Allied warship was in her waters. But there was none. On 2 September, three swimmers were put on permanent alert, to be ready to dive in and swim out to any passing vessel. And two large flags were made, one with a large red cross in the middle of it, and the other with the legend (in black) writ large, in English: 'CHRISTIANS IN DISTRESS: RESCUE'. These were fastened to tall trees, and a dawn-to-dusk watch was kept. Hope was none too high, for in the coastal region it was the season of fogs and heavy rains.[97]

Days passed; the Turks attacked again, but more cautiously than before, and unsuccessfully; and nothing was seen. The sea was bleak and deserted. Then suddenly, on Sunday morning, 12 September 1915, the fifty-third day of the siege, a battleship was sighted, which had clearly seen the distress flags, since it was heading straight for them.

It was the French vessel *Guichen*. As she lowered her boats, a few of the Armenians raced to the shore. When they had told the captain of their plight, he telegraphed the admiral aboard the flag-ship *Ste Jeanne d'Arc*, in the vicinity, and the vessel speedily approached, along with others. An English cruiser, too, hove in sight. The French admiral, much moved by their story, gave orders for the entire community to be taken on board. Five vessels (four French, one English) finally transported the community to Port Said, where they arrived in the middle of September. One estimate gives the number of men, women and children saved as 4,200;[98] another 4,058.[99]

Urfa

Other than Musa Dagh and Van, 1915 was the year of total disaster for Armenians. While Musa Dagh was besieged, some towns in north Syria were attacked by the authorities. (Such towns were of second priority, and hence were cleared later than eastern Anatolia and Cilicia.) In Urfa 250 Armenians died on 19 August in an outbreak of killing, and on 23 September, after the death of a further 300, the community leaders decided on defiance rather than submissive death. Yet to Urfa – landlocked, and far from any relieving army – no relief came; the same death overtook its defenders as finally engulfed those endless convoys stretched out into the desert. By 23 October 1915 the silence of death reigned over the Armenian quarter of Urfa.[100]

The Measures Continue

By the autumn of 1915 most of the Armenians from Anatolia had been wiped out, and those few who remained were to be subjected to renewed fanaticism in

1916. Far from diminishing, with so many Armenians now dead, the chauvinism and brutality of the ministry of the interior and the Committee of Union and Progress increased. Liberal and tolerant governors (such as Ismail Kemal of Marash, and Djelal of Aleppo) were dismissed. Women and children who had been taken into Turkish homes or into the 'Turkish orphanages' – that is, institutions in which Armenian children would grow up as good Turks – were turned out. Talaat Pasha ordered Armenian orphans to be taken from these orphanages and killed; and he gave orders that Armenian women who had been forced to become wives of Turks should be put on the road to the desert. Later he ordered the seizure of Armenian children who had been adopted (and indeed Turkified) by Turkish families; they too were to be killed; and to the few remaining Armenian labour battalions extermination was ordered.

Many of the deportees remained obstinately alive; a number were fit enough to withstand the wide differences of climate, from the Mediterranean-type climate of Anatolia to the Arabian desert-type climate of north Syria, and the appalling privations of the journey. In the first place they were thinned out at Aleppo. Aleppo was a major staging-post for the deportations; nearly all deportees converged on Aleppo, as they left Anatolia and entered Arabia; thence the more fortunate ones were sent south towards Damascus (though many died on that journey, too); but the great majority were sent to a series of extermination camps along the Euphrates, especially Maskinah (Meskene), Rakka and Deir ez-Zor, and Ras ul-Ain, the furthest limit east at that time of the Baghdad railway – an isolated spot, but served by transport. But in late 1915 the problem confronting Talaat and the ministry of the interior was simply that there were too many Armenians at Aleppo; hence a series of directives demanding the death of Armenians there, in late 1915.[101]

At this time, and throughout 1916, attention was on the concentration camps; here the Armenians who had survived the murders, ambushes, unutterable privations and abductions were either killed outright, or taken a little way away and murdered in batches.

Ras ul-Ain

Ras ul-Ain was visited in early 1916 by two officers of the Ottoman army, who later deserted the Turks and went over to the Russians at Kermanshah in August 1916. They were Muslim Arabs, one from Damascus, the other from Acre. Sir Mark Sykes, who interviewed them soon after, records the following:

> The Armenians were dying of typhus and dysentery, and the roads were littered with their decomposing bodies. The empty desert cisterns were also filled with corpses. Both officers agree that this was the most appalling state of affairs, and that, unless it had been a matter of ocular demonstration, it

would be incredible. The Turkish officers of the battalion were horrified at the sights they saw, and the regimental chaplain [a Muslim divine], on coming across a number of bodies, dismounted his horse and publicly prayed that the divine punishment of these crimes should be averted from Muslims, and, by way of expiation, himself worked at digging graves for the dead bodies. When marching from Ras ul-Ain to er-Radi the soldiers of the battalion often put up their hands to avert the sight of the numerous bloated naked corpses of murdered women who lay by the roadside. Two sayings were common among the common soldiers: 'Ras ul-Ain is a shambles' and 'No man can ever think of a woman's body except as a matter of horror, instead of attraction, after Ras ul-Ain'. Ras ul-Ain was used as a place of concentration for Armenians, and 12,000 was the number usually there. The average number of the incoming parties and outgoing parties (viz., those going to be murdered) cannot be estimated accurately.[102]

Along the Euphrates

On the Euphrates camps, this testimony was given by Auguste Bernau, German representative of an American company in Aleppo:

It is impossible to give an impression of the terrible things I saw during my journey among the scattered camps along the Euphrates. I travelled on the right-hand bank of the river. One cannot really talk of 'camps'. The greater part of this miserable people, brutally expelled from their home and land, separated from their families, robbed of all they owned, either when they left or en route, and stripped of all they carried, are living in the open air, herded together like cattle, without any protection against heat or cold, almost without clothes, and given very irregular and entirely inadequate food. They are exposed to every change in the weather ... weakened by utmost deprivation and endless marches, treated appallingly and exposed to cruel torture and permanent fear of death, the few of them who have managed to keep some of their strength have dug holes by the bank of the river into which they crawl.

... Everywhere one only sees pale faces and haggard bodies, living skeletons which are suffering dreadful sickness and which will surely die of starvation...

The remainder of the Armenian nation, dispersed along the banks of the Euphrates, consists only of old men, women and children. Middle-aged men and younger people – those that have not been killed – are scattered over the roads of the empire, where they break stones or do other work for the army in the name of the state...

In the desert I met six refugees who were dying. They had escaped from

their guards; now they were surrounded by hungry dogs which were waiting
for their agony to end, in order to leap at them and devour them. . .

It would be easy for some stone or earth huts to be built for them – then
they might be able to work in the fields. But this hope too has been taken
away, and they are constantly being pushed from one place to another, in
order to give variety to their suffering. . .

Maskinah, located on the border between Syria and Mesopotamia, is an
ideal concentration-point for the transport of deported Armenians from the
Anatolian vilayets, whence they have been dispersed along the length of the
Euphrates river. Tens of thousands of them arrived here, but the larger part
of them died. The impression given by the great plain of Maskinah is
profoundly sorrowful and depressing. I can state clearly, from the information that I have been given, that nearly 60,000 Armenians are buried here,
victims of hunger, deprivation, dysentery and typhus. Wherever one looks
there are little hills, each of which contains 200–300 corpses. . .

At the moment there are still 4,400 Armenians herded between the town
of Maskinah and the Euphrates. They are no more than living ghosts. Their
overseers distribute a small piece of bread to them very irregularly and spar-
ingly. It often happens that they receive nothing for three or four days.

A terrible dysentery rages and demands appalling sacrifices from the
children. In their hunger these wretched little ones fall upon everything here
that they can find – they eat grass, earth, even excrements.

Under a tent measuring about five or six square metres I saw roughly four
hundred orphan children. They were starving. These wretched children are
meant to receive 150 grams [5½ oz.] of bread per day. It often happens that
they receive nothing for two or three days. The death rate is naturally
extremely high. As I saw myself, dysentery claimed seventy victims within
eight days.

Abu Herere is a small settlement north of Maskinah, on the banks of the
Euphrates. It is the most unhealthy place in the desert. On a hill, 200 yards
from the river, I found 240 Armenians; they were guarded by two gendarmes, who pitilessly let them die amid the terrible pangs of hunger. The
scenes that I have witnessed are beyond any possible conception of horror.
Near the place where my cart stopped I saw some women. Hardly had they
seen me when they prepared to pick the few undigested oat kernels out of
the horses' excrements, in order to eat them. I gave them bread. They threw
themselves at it, like starving dogs, and shredded it with their teeth, in nightmarish ravenousness, with violent shaking and epileptic convulsions; and as
soon as these 240 wretched people, or rather 240 hungry wolves (who had
had nothing to eat for seven days) had been told about my arrival, the entire
horde swarmed towards me, rushing down the side of the hill. They stretched
out their skeletal arms towards me, and with hoarse cries and sobs, begged
me for a piece of bread. Among them were only women and children,
and perhaps a dozen old men . . .

Hammam is a small village where 1,600 Armenians are imprisoned. Here too, the same spectacle of hunger and horror takes place every day. The men have been enrolled in labour battalions to work on the roads. As a reward for their labour they receive one piece of inedible and indigestible bread daily, quite insufficient to provide them with the strength needed for their hard work...

Zierrat lies to the north of Raqqa. Eighteen hundred Armenians camp there. There, they suffer more than anywhere else from hunger. Zierrat is nothing but desert. Groups of women and children roam along the river-bank in search of a few stalks of grass in order to still their hunger. Others collapse under the eyes of their indifferent, merciless guards. A barbaric order, barbaric in every sense, forbids anyone to leave the confines of the camp without special permission, on pain of bastinado...

Deir ez-Zor is the seat of the governor of the vilayet of the same name. A few months ago 30,000 Armenians were encamped in various camps outside the town under the protection of the governor, mutessarif Ali Suad Bey. I will not speak personally, but I must remember the name of this man, who has a heart, and to whom the deportees are grateful, since he tried to lighten their misery. He is to be thanked for the fact that some Armenians were allowed to earn something for themselves by hawking in the streets, and were thus able to make a little for themselves... The more favourable circumstances under which the Armenians of Deir ez-Zor lived led to the governor's denunciation to the central authorities in Constantinople. The 'guilty' Ali Suad Bey was sent to Baghdad, and replaced by Zeki Bey, who is well known for his cruelty and barbarity. I was told of frightful things that happen with the new governor in control. Imprisonments, horrific tortures, bastinado, hangings, were the order of the day. They were the daily bread of the deportees in this district. Young girls were raped and left to the Arab nomads. The children were thrown into the river. Ali Suad Bey, that rare Turkish official, had housed about 1,000 orphan children in a large house, and had fed them at the expense of the municipality. His successor, Zeki Bey, threw them on to the streets, where they died like dogs from hunger and appalling deprivation. And more. The 30,000 Armenians who were at Deir ez-Zor were despatched into the region along the Khabur river (a tributary of the Euphrates). This is the worst region of the desert, where it is impossible to find any means of livelihood. From the information that I have received a large number of the deportees are already dead. Those that are still alive will inevitably share the same fate.[103]

Another eyewitness of the concentration camp of Deir ez-Zor speaks of a great pit there, 'as though some immense body had fallen from the sky, making a deep hole in the ground'.[104] Into this pit, 150 feet deep, hundreds of Armenians were thrown; those at the bottom soon died, either crushed or smothered. while those at the top lived on for days *in extremis*. Guards prevented any from escaping.

The Completion of the Measures

By the end of 1916 the Turkish anti-Armenian measures were virtually complete. The figures produced by Lord Bryce during the war are similar to those of Dr Lepsius. published in his *Bericht* during the war, and confirmed in *Deutschland und Armenien, 1914–1918* (1919). The Armenians in the Ottoman empire before the war amounted to between 1,500,000 and 2,000,000; the Armenian Patriarchate gave the figure as 1,845,450. Of these about 250,000 managed to escape to Russia, either overland or (like Murad of Sivas) by sea. Of the remaining 1,600,000 about 1,000,000 were killed, half of whom were women and children.[105] Of the surviving 600,000 about 200,000 were forcibly Islamised; and the wretched remnant of 400,000 was found, starving and in rags, by the Allies (or those few representatives of them that bothered to penetrate into the interior of Turkey) at the end of the war.[106] A further figure of between 50,000 and 100,000 were killed off during the Turkish invasion of the Caucasus in May–September 1918; and probably another 250,000 or so during the years 1919–22, when surviving deported Armenians returned home to face further organised killings; treated by Britain and France 'with a callousness which would be deserving of condemnation in the case of a defeated enemy' (W. E. D. Allen[107]), they lived in a grim political vacuum, only filled with the establishment of the brave new world of Kemalist Turkey and Bolshevik Russia – and thousands of Armenians scraping a living in refugee camps in French-mandated Syria and Lebanon, and British-mandated Iraq. But this is to anticipate.

The Massacres and Foreign Opinion

Death on such a large scale in the interior of Ottoman Turkey could not escape the notice of the Allied nations, however stringent the wartime censorship imposed by Constantinople. The earliest news of the massacres came from refugees in the Russian Caucasus, and from those who had managed to escape from the western end of the empire into Europe. On 27 April 1915 the Catholicos. in Echmiadzin, petitioned the two neutral powers to intervene at the Porte. However they, and the Allies, saw that there was a dilemma: to make a complaint might only make things worse – increase the racist xenophobia of the Young Turks. Yet not to do anything might be taken to imply their tacit acceptance of the doctrine that wholesale extermination (genocide, in fact, except that the word had not yet been invented) was a legitimate wartime measure. The neutral powers pursued the matter through their own diplomatic channels, and the Allies issued a declaration on 23 May. It began: 'For about the last month Kurds and the Turkish population of Armenia have been engaged in massacring Armenians with the help and often the connivance of the Ottoman authorities.' It then named the areas where the massacres were known to have taken place, and concluded:

> In the face of these fresh crimes committed by Turkey the Allied governments announce publicly that they will hold all the members of the Ottoman government as well as such of their agents as are implicated personally responsible for such massacres.[108]

Articles on the terrible sufferings of the Armenians appeared in the American press, such as one in the *Christian Science Monitor* headed 'Atrocities in Turkey Called Worst in History'.[109] Such articles began a wave of intense pro-Armenian feeling throughout America, which was not surprising when Americans saw the labours of 80 years collapsing in ruins. Whether such sympathy, which lasted until 1920, was of any actual political benefit to the Armenians is open to doubt – not least because it engendered in Armenians themselves a trust in an alliance with America, which discouraged them from forging real links with their immediate neighbours; so that when American assistance finally proved itself an illusion, Armenians were left alone and deserted – save for one equivocal but securely placed power.

In Britain the first full parliamentary revelation of the massacres was given in a speech by Viscount Bryce in the Lords on 6 October 1915.[110] Bryce spoke of them as premeditated, not spontaneous outbursts of fanaticism. The orders, he said, came from Constantinople, and the penalty for disobeying them was dismissal (as had happened to Djelal Bey of Aleppo). The figure he gave for all those killed in this uniform and contrived manner was 'around 800,000'. A similar account, but more emotional, was given by Aneurin Williams, MP, to the Commons on 16 November.[111] In Paris, the grim details were given by M. Denys Cochin, a deputy well known for his pro-Armenian views. Soon the case of the Armenian massacres was taken up by the war propagandists: Germany's ally, they said, was committing the vilest atrocities. The fate of the Armenians was compared with that of the Belgians.

The Germans and the Killings

Were the Germans (or indeed the Austro-Hungarians) implicated in the Armenian massacres? Dr Lepsius was given full access to the files of the German foreign ministry after the war, and published many of the relevant documents in his volume *Deutschland und Armenien, 1914–1918*. In a review of that work,[112] J. Ellis Barker came to the conclusion that Germany was implicated; but using that and other material, Ulrich Trumpener has more recently come to the opposite conclusion in his book *Germany and the Ottoman Empire 1914–1918* (1968). The difference is basically a question of definition.

Baron von Wangenheim, German ambassador at Constantinople from before the outbreak of the war until his death in office in October 1915, was a man with a unique position to moderate the activities of the Turks – by pointing out, for instance, that the wholesale destruction of Armenians hindered the war effort, since it deprived the Central powers of a vital source of military supplies, and since it weakened the army – for the Turks were killing their own soldiers – and since it was spreading disease and death throughout northern Syria and Mesopotamia. But initially Wangenheim was concerned above all with not offending the Young Turk rulers, and 'getting on and winning the war'. He seems at this stage to have been barely aware that the Armenians were human beings. On 31 May 1915 he telegraphed Berlin:

> To limit Armenian espionage and to prevent extensive risings, Enver Pasha means to close a large number of Armenian schools, to suppress Armenian postal correspondence and Armenian newspapers, and to settle in Mesopotamia all Armenian families which are not entirely free from suspicion. He asks urgently that Germany should not interfere with him in this.
>
> Of course these Turkish measures will once more cause great excitement among all the powers hostile to Germany and will be exploited against us. These measures are certainly very harsh for the Armenians. However, I am of the opinion that we may only try to mitigate their form, but must not hinder them on principle.[113]

This was a puzzling despatch from Wangenheim, since his consuls in Erzerum and Aleppo had told him what was really going on. It seems almost certain that he was attempting to pull the wool over the eyes of his foreign ministry. However, Wangenheim's tone had changed by 17 June, when he wrote:

> It is obvious that the banishment of the Armenians is not due solely to military considerations. Talaat Bey, the minister of the interior, has quite frankly said to Dr Mordtmann (of the embassy) that the Porte intended to make use of the world war to deal thoroughly with its internal enemies, the Christians in Turkey, and that it meant not to be disturbed in this by diplomatic intervention from abroad.[114]

Little action seems to have resulted, although Wangenheim did arrange for Dr Johannes Lepsius, president of the German-Armenian Society, to visit Constantinople. He must have realised Lepsius would have been a gadfly to the supine body of German–Turkish diplomacy.

By the end of June Wangenheim and his Austro-Hungarian colleague, Count Johann Pallavicini, decided to act together. On 1 July Pallavicini told Talaat that the mass deportations 'seemed hardly justified', and on 4 July

Wangenheim sent a lengthy memorandum to the grand vizier.[115] This accepts the need for measures to be taken on military and security grounds, but continues:

> On the other hand, the German government cannot conceal the dangers created by these harsh measures and mass deportations, which include guilty and innocent without distinction, especially when these measures are accompanied by acts of violence, such as massacres and pillages.
>
> Unfortunately, according to information reaching the embassy, the local authorities have not been able to prevent incidents of this sort, which are regrettable according to all reports.[116]

The Entente powers would make war propaganda out of the situation, Wangenheim continued, which they would direct towards the United States. The German embassy, therefore, considered it urgent that 'peremptory orders be given to the provincial authorities so that they take effective measures to safeguard the life and property of banished Armenians, both during their deportation and in their new homes [sic]'. In his final paragraph Wangenheim reminded the Porte that their actions might be damaging German interests, both commercial and philanthropic, and requested that those who were to be deported be given a longer period of grace before they were actually deported.[117]

The Porte, however, typically for a government in the grip of a racist frenzy, did nothing to either Austrian or German requests. Pallavicini noted, 'Evidently there is a determination to render the Armenian element, which has become so suspect here, harmless once and for all.'[118]

On 12 July Wangenheim wrote to Talaat demanding that measures be taken against Reshid Bey, vali of Diyarbekir, who was organising massacres on a vast scale. Wangenheim quoted one instance:

> On the orders of Reshid Bey gendarmes from Diyarbekir proceeded to Mardin, and arrested there the Armenian bishop and a large number of Armenians and other Christians, in all 700 persons. This entire group was conducted by night to a spot outside the town and butchered like sheep.[119]

Again the Porte did nothing; and a few days later Wangenheim wrote to Chancellor Bethmann-Hollweg saying that no diplomatic pressure produced the slightest impact on the Porte, and that therefore Turkey must accept full responsibility for her actions.*[120] Wangenheim, very unwell with a heart condi-

---

*This contrasts strongly with the version given by Talaat Pasha himself to the extravagantly Turkophile British Tory MP, Aubrey Herbert. Herbert, keen to meet the war criminal and former enemy war minister and yearning to exculpate him, went to interview him in Hamm, Germany, in February 1921. Talaat declared to his devoted initiate that 'he himself had always been against the attempted extermination of the Armenians ... He had twice protested against the policy, but had been overruled, he said, by the Germans' (Aubrey Herbert, *Ben Kendim* (London, 1924), p. 309).

tion that was to kill him on 25 October, left for Berlin a few days later. (He returned to Constantinople on 2 October.)

His successor was Prince zu Hohenlohe-Langeburg. In a memorandum of 9 August he reiterated his government's criticism of Ottoman treatment of Armenians. He pointed out that massacre and pillage, instead of being stopped by the local authorities, 'regularly followed the expulsion of Armenians, so that the majority of them have perished before even arriving at the place of their destination'. The final paragraph begins: 'In the presence of these events the German embassy, by order of its government, is obliged to remonstrate once more against the acts of horror and to decline all responsibility for the consequences which may result from them.'[121]

Talaat and Khalil, in reply, pleaded the 'excesses of subordinates'.[122] Moreover, the German foreign ministry itself was either unwilling or unable to understand the full horror of the situation. Hohenlohe spoke with a voice very different from that of Zimmermann, under-secretary of state for foreign affairs, who wrote in a reply to Hohenlohe of the 'high sense of humaneness and culture which has characterised the Turkish conduct of the war'.[123]

Before he returned to Berlin, Wangenheim had arranged for Dr Lepsius to visit Constantinople. Lepsius arrived in late July, seeing Enver very soon after. (Wangenheim's action here is again hard to reconcile with the German stage-villain picture of him put forward by Morgenthau in his memoirs, and elsewhere; for the ambassador cannot have been ignorant of Lepsius's views, and the use to which the doctor would put the knowledge he gained while in Ottoman Turkey.) On Lepsius's return to Germany, his campaign began. Fifty pastors addressed a petition to the foreign ministry on 15 October, calling on Germany to do all she could to change Turkey's policy.[124] Three things in particular they demanded: that Armenians not yet deported (mostly in the west) should be left alone; that Armenians already deported should be treated as humanely as possible; and that aid should be sent from 'Christians of other countries' to the deportees. They also asked how Germany could have as an ally a power whose government pursued this kind of policy. In reply, Bethmann-Hollweg said he would instruct his *chargé* in Constantinople to continue with appeals to the Porte.[125] This intervention, however, does not absolve Bethmann-Hollweg from the very real charge of lack of concern during the early summer with what his ally was doing to its Armenian population.

The third wartime German ambassador at the Turkish capital was Count von Wolff-Metternich. He continued to press the Porte on the Armenian question, but met with obstinacy and inaction. On 7 December 1915 he reported that neither Enver nor Khalil would discuss the matter. Later that month he got a chance to discuss the matter with Talaat (whom he had described as 'the soul of the Armenian persecutions').[126] To his surprise Talaat seemed to agree with most of his points: the innocent had suffered; and (Talaat promised) henceforward everything would be done for them to alleviate their plight.

Talaat was, however, playing the wily game he was so adept at; and on 22

December his real response to the ambassador was delivered. It was a furious note.[127] It made two main points: that the measures taken against the Armenians were a matter of internal administration only (and therefore could not be a matter for a diplomatic approach); and, secondly, that the 'measures' taken were either dictated by military necessities or were legitimate self-defence against subversion. The Porte therefore rejected any representations that Germany might make.

The German foreign ministry seems to have concluded after that reply that it was not worth making such representations, since they achieved nothing for the Armenians, and only risked weakening the alliance with Ottoman Turkey. They realised that by raising the question of Armenian killings they were trespassing on the sacred precinct of Ittihadist fanaticism.

Most of the forced exilings were over by early 1916, although there were renewed outbreaks against the few unfortunate survivors, and the atrocities in the Euphrates camps had not yet reached their peak. The protests from Germany diminished too. The attitude of her foreign ministry became more passive and inert. But Wolff-Metternich continued to take a great interest in internal conditions, and to report what he learnt to Berlin. In a striking despatch of 30 June 1916 he explained how the Committee of Union and Progress was running the country, enforcing its ideological will at every level, and how its functionaries were enriching themselves by the annihilation of the Armenians.

No one any longer has the power to control the many-headed hydra of the Committee [sc. of Union and Progress], to control the chauvinism and the fanaticism. The Committee demands the annihilation of the last remnants of the Armenians, and the government must bow to its demands. The Committee does not only mean the organisation of the ruling party in the capital; it is spread all over the provinces. At the side of each provincial governor [vali], and on down to each kaimakam, a Committee member stands, with instructions either to support or supervise. The expulsion of Armenians has begun everywhere anew. But the hungry wolves of the Committee can no longer expect anything from these unhappy people except the satisfaction of their fanatic rage for persecution. Their goods have long since been confiscated, and their capital has been liquidated by a so-called commission, which means that if an Armenian owned a house valued at, say, £T100, a Turk – a friend or member of the Committee – could have it for around £T2.[128]

Not surprisingly the Porte demanded, and obtained, Wolff-Metternich's recall in September 1916.

In view of the steps taken by Wolff-Metternich and his predecessors, it is hardly possible to accuse the Germans of complicity in the Armenian massacres, let alone leading or directing them, as some Germanophobes have suggested. But a certain supineness can be detected in Berlin, an acceptance of

Turkey's actions, and above all a desire not to fracture the wartime alliance: something which almost any other power would have done in similar circumstances.

Lepsius's campaign, meanwhile, was continuing in Berlin. In the summer of 1916 he published his *Bericht über die Lage des Armenischen Volkes in der Türkei* (Report on the Position of the Armenian People in Turkey) – a political high explosive: it was a clear, documented report on the extermination of Ottoman Armenians, explaining plan, methods and procedure, and demanding to know who was responsible.[129]

The Ottoman ambassador in Berlin, Hakki, was furious. He demanded that the foreign ministry take steps against Lepsius and his fellow pro-Armenians. Tardily the ministry acted, and in late September issued an order forbidding Lepsius to travel; but by then he had taken up residence in Holland.[130]

In the German embassy in Constantinople hopes were again raised that persecution of Armenians might slacken after soothing words from Khalil to a member of the embassy staff; and further, when Talaat was appointed grand vizier on 4 February 1917, with a speech parroting phrases about equality and the rule of law – those that Ittihadist leaders had used so often before.[131] In reality nothing changed. The derelict Armenians were left to die in the desert, tormented by hunger and thirst, burnt by the sun by day, frozen by the wind at night, an easy prey to malignant humanity and indifferent nature.

When the German consulates at Aleppo, Damascus, Beirut and Mosul took stock of the situation in the spring and early summer of 1917, they found the situation much as it had been since 1915.[132] Talaat's silvery words had been calculated to deceive, to halt the criticism of their ally while the adepts of the Ittihad ve Terrake Jemieti pursued their fanatical aims. In a similar manner, but less ruthlessly and efficiently, Abdul Hamid had deceived successive British ambassadors in the years following the treaty of Berlin.

The Massacres of 1895 and 1915: a Comparison

When Abdul Hamid ordered the killing of Armenians in the mid-1890s his decision was part of a political campaign, and not the wild thrashings of a religious zealot. The massacres of the first world war, too, were clearly carried out by a deliberate decision of the Young Turks. So is there any difference between the two – besides the obvious point that far more people were killed by the Ittihadists, with much greater brutality?

The answer must be that there is, since in 1915–16 ideological fanaticism and extreme cruelty (untempered by any of the constraints of religion) in the service of an aggressive determination to expand characterised the killings. Abdul Hamid had attempted to hold his empire together in the simplest manner that he knew, and one that his predecessors had frequently employed. The Young Turks, by contrast, were imbued with a race consciousness which was essentially of the twentieth century in its ferocity, and in the fact that it excluded all other considerations. It is this that makes the use of the word 'genocide' perfectly applicable in the second case, even though it was not invented until 1944. The Young Turks made a calculated attempt to exterminate all Armenians in Turkish Armenia and central Anatolia. The despatch of June 1916 by Count von Wolff-Metternich quoted above (p. 235) is a clear description of the political fanaticism which is the concomitant of genocide. We recognise it as showing the chilling qualities of the politics of our own era. The 1915 genocide of Armenians was truly a twentieth-century phenomenon in its blend of racism and rationalism; its perpetrators had shuffled off the restraints which had historically shackled the darkest of man's political desires; laid bare was a remorseless and unalloyed desire to kill.

Omens for a Post-war Settlement

Military defeat of the Ottoman empire and the destruction of the Committee of Union and Progress within it saved the remnants of the Armenians of the empire; as General Allenby pressed north through Palestine and Syria in late 1917 and 1918, and Generals Sir Stanley Maude and Sir William Marshall moved on to Baghdad, the empire tottered and fell, and the Ittihadist leaders fled. For the Armenians new hopes arose out of the calamity that had overtaken them, that the Allies (who had made a number of statements in warm support and sympathy for the Armenian plight) would stand by them, and help them build a future for themselves. All ideas of any sort of co-operation with the Turks had been totally crushed by the massacres; Armenians could henceforth see Turks only through a curtain of blood. Ideas of autonomy for Armenians were finally seen as illusions; any future Armenia would have now to be separated from Turkey. This historic pattern of Armenia seeking autonomy from her neighbours – a pattern which stretched back to Rome and Parthia – had been finally smashed by the extermination of her people. The question which now sought an answer was: would the victorious Allies stand by their favourable utterances during the war, and enable Armenia to emerge from her shattered present to become a nation of the world and a member of the international community?

Notes

1. W. E. D. Allen, and Paul Muratoff, *Caucasian Battlefields* (Cambridge, 1953), pp. 228–9.
2. Richard G. Hovannisian, *Armenia on the Road to Independence, 1918* (Berkeley and Los Angeles, 1967), p. 40.
3. 'Enwer Pasha', *Encyclopedia of Islam*, 2nd edn (Leiden, continuing).
4. Hovannisian, *Armenia on the Road to Independence*, pp. 41–2.
5. A. J. Toynbee, *Turkey: a Past and a Future* (London, 1917), pp. 28–9.

6. Uriel Heyd, *Foundations of Turkish Nationalism* (London, 1950), p. 128.
7. Hovannisian, *Armenia on the Road to Independence*, p. 44.
8. Liman von Sanders, *Five Years in Turkey* (Annapolis, 1928), p. 39.
9. Ibid., pp. 39–40; see also Allen and Muratoff, *Caucasian Battlefields*, pp. 276–85.
10. *Osmanischer Lloyd*, 26 February 1915, quoted in Dr Johannes Lepsius, *Deutschland und Armenien, 1914–1918* (Potsdam, 1919), p. xvi.
11. See Haigazn Kazarian, 'The Turkish Genocide', *Armenian Review*, vol. XXX, no. 1–117 (Spring 1977), pp. 14–15.
12. Henry Morgenthau, *Secrets of the Bosphorus* (London, 1918), pp. 198–9.
13. Great Britain, Parliamentary Papers, Miscellaneous no. 31 (1916),pp. 638–9; edited by A. J. Toynbee, the volume was, also in 1916, published in London with the title *The Treatment of Armenians in the Ottoman Empire*. It was reprinted in Beirut in 1972 with a useful appendix giving the names of towns, villages and individuals which were coded in the original.
14. |A. J. Toynbee|, 'The Extermination of the Armenians', *The Times History of the War* (London, 1916), vol. VIII, pp. 363–4.
15. Morgenthau, *Secrets of the Bosphorus*, p. 202.
16. |Toynbee|, 'The Extermination of the Armenians', p. 363.
17. Ibid., p. 386.
18. Morgenthau, *Secrets of the Bosphorus*, pp. 221–3.
19. Miscellaneous no. 31 (1916), pp. 640–2.
20. Abraham H. Hartunian, *Neither to Laugh nor to Weep* (Boston, 1968), p. 54.
21. Miscellaneous no. 31 (1916), p. 488.
22. FO 371/2484.22083.
23. Miscellaneous no. 31 (1916), p. 480.
24. Ibid., pp. 480–1.
25. Ibid., p. 512.
26. Ibid., p. 513.
27. Ibid., p. 488.
28. Ibid., p. 490.
29. Ibid., p. 110.
30. Ibid., pp. 81–2.
31. FO 424/251, pp. 103–4.
32. Clarence D. Ussher, *An American Physician in Turkey* (Boston, 1917), pp. 235–6.
33. Ibid., pp. 236–7.
34. Ibid., pp. 237–8.
35. Ibid., p. 239.
36. Ibid., p. 244.
37. Ibid., p. 247.
38. Ibid., pp. 254–5.
39. Ibid., p. 265.
40. Ibid., p. 270.
41. Ibid., p. 267.
42. Ibid., p. 275.
43. Ibid., p. 280.
44. Ibid., p. 287.
45. Hovannisian, *Armenia on the Road to Independence*, p. 53.
46. Arshavir Shiragian, *The Legacy* (Boston, 1976), p. 10.
47. Ibid., pp. 11–12.
48. Morgenthau, *Secrets of the Bosphorus*, p. 221.
49. Ibid.
50. Miscellaneous no. 31 (1916), pp. 17, 472, 484–5.
51. Ibid., p. 84.
52. Ibid.
53. Ibid., p. 85.
54. Ibid.
55. Ibid., pp. 85–6.
56. Ibid., p. 87.
57. Ibid., p. 246.

58. Ibid., pp. 246–7.
59. Dr Johannes Lepsius, *Der Todesgang des Armenischen Volkes* (Potsdam, 1919), p. 47.
60. Ibid.
61. Miscellaneous no. 31 (1916), p. 234.
62. Ibid., pp. 234–5.
63. Ibid., p. 243.
64. Ibid., p. 231.
65. Lepsius, *Deutschland und Armenien*, p. 51.
66. Miscellaneous no. 31 (1916), p. 238.
67. Ibid.
68. Ibid., pp. 223–4.
69. Ibid., p. 231.
70. Ibid., p. 236.
71. Ibid., pp. 100–50.
72. Ibid., pp. 164–71.
73. Lepsius, *Der Todesgang*, pp. 63–4.
74. Miscellaneous no. 31 (1916), p. 286.
75. Ibid., p. 291.
76. Ibid., p. 286.
77. Ibid., p. 287.
78. Ibid., p. 293.
79. Leon Z. Surmelian, *I Ask You, Ladies and Gentlemen* (London, 1946), pp. 73–4.
80. Miscellaneous no. 31 (1916), pp. 291–2.
81. Ibid., p. 259.
82. Ibid., p. 286.
83. Ibid., pp. 278–9.
84. Ibid., p. 265.
85. Ibid., p. 266.
86. Ibid., p. 267.
87. Ibid., pp. 317–19.
88. Ibid., pp. 302–16, 320.
89. Ibid., pp. 382–4.
90. Ibid., pp. 336–46.
91. Faiz el-Ghusein, *Martyred Armenia* (London, 1917), p. 49.
92. Miscellaneous no. 31 (1916), p. 514.
93. Ibid., p. 515.
94. Ibid., p. 516.
95. Ibid.
96. Ibid., p. 517.
97. Ibid., pp. 518–19.
98. Ibid., p. 521.
99. Ibid., p. 520.
100. Ibid., pp. 530–2.
101. Aram Andonian (ed.), *The Memoirs of Naim Bey* (London, 1920), pp. 50–64.
102. FO 371/2781.201201, p. 7.
103. Lepsius, *Deutschland und Armenien*, pp. 486–93.
104. D. B. Eby, *At the Mercy of Turkish Brigands* (New Carlisle, Ohio, 1922), p. 34.
105. Lepsius, *Deutschland und Armenien*, p. lxv.
106. Ibid.
107. W. E. D. Allen, 'The Armenians: their Past and Future', *Quarterly Review*, no. 233 (January–April 1920), p. 241.
108. FO 371/2488.63095.
109. *Christian Science Monitor*, 15 September 1915.
110. *Hansard*, 5th series, Lords, vol. XIX, cols. 1000ff.
111. Ibid., Commons, vol. LXXV, cols. 1765ff.
112. J. Ellis Barker, 'Germany, Turkey and the Armenian Massacres', *Quarterly Review*, no. 233 (January–April 1920), pp. 385–400.
113. Lepsius, *Deutschland und Armenien*, p. 79.

114. Ibid., p. 84.
115. Ulrich Trumpener, *Germany and the Ottoman Empire, 1914–1918* (Princeton, 1968), p. 213.
116. Lepsius, *Deutschland und Armenien*, p. 96.
117. Ibid., p. 97.
118. Trumpener, *Germany and the Ottoman Empire*, p. 215.
119. Lepsius, *Deutschland und Armenien*, pp. 103–4.
120. Ibid., p. 103.
121. Ibid., p. 128.
122. Trumpener, *Germany and the Ottoman Empire*, p. 219.
123. Ibid.
124. Lepsius, *Deutschland und Armenien*, pp. 183–9.
125. Ibid., p. 191.
126. Trumpener, *Germany and the Ottoman Empire*, p. 231.
127. Lepsius, *Deutschland und Armenien*, pp. 210–11.
128. Ibid., p. 277.
129. Trumpener, *Germany and the Ottoman Empire*, p. 240.
130. Ibid., p. 242.
131. Ibid., p. 246.
132. Ibid., pp. 246–7.

8 Striving to Create a Republic

Transcaucasia and the March Revolution

The Russian–Armenian volunteer units which had been formed in 1914 were a focus of national feelings in that year and the early part of 1915, and of significant military benefit to the tsarist armies; but thereafter the Russian military leadership saw them as unwelcome centres of political aspirations, and ordered their disbandment in December 1915.[1] All Armenian soldiers henceforward had to serve as regulars in the Russian regiments. Discussion of Armenian political aims was suppressed too. The old Great-Russian steamroller, squashing the smaller nationalities, seemed to be in motion again.

The Russian armies scored a series of remarkable victories in the first six months of 1916: Erzerum was taken on 16 February, Trebizond on 18 April and Erzindjan on 25 July. In the south, the whole of Lake Van was in Russian hands by the early summer.[2] Earlier in the war such successes would have been an occasion for celebration by Armenian leaders in Tiflis; yet now the captured Armenian towns and villages were empty of Armenians. Only corpses and skeletons remained.

The tsarist army has been blamed for inefficiency and bureaucracy, but one cannot overlook the scale of these victories. The danger, however, lay in the manner in which they were achieved, since all Russian officers treated their men in an arrogant and bullying manner. They believed, blindly, that their social and military structure would last for ever; and when it fell apart, so too did the authority that they had unthinkingly wielded.

In March 1917 the edifice collapsed. The tsar abdicated, a liberal 'Provisional government' took power, and soviets (councils) of workers and soldiers were set up.

The March revolution was warmly welcomed in Transcaucasia. Despite tsarist censorship, ideologies which mixed socialism and nationalism in varying proportions were rife there. Among the Georgians, Menshevik socialism was strong; a number of educated Tatars of south-east Transcaucasia – later to become Azerbaijan – adhered to the Musavat or 'equality' party, basically a Muslim nationalist party, but one which was also coloured with a sinister, pan-Turkist hue, in view of its connections with the Ittihadists of Constantinople. Bolshevism had a small but dedicated following in Baku and Tiflis, but very little elsewhere.

Among the Armenians, the Dashnaks were especially popular throughout Transcaucasia, and with good reason: their arms had defended the people against the combined onslaughts of imperial Cossacks and Tatars in 1905. They had strong support from both peasantry and townsfolk. Some educated Armenians, however, were critical of Dashnak methods of secrecy and propaganda, and of their tendency to form close alliances with other political groups. This opposition was represented by the Populist, or Zhoghovrdakan, party, made up partly of liberal-minded teachers and doctors, and also of Armenian businessmen in Tiflis and Baku. The Populist party was the Caucasian equivalent of the Constitutional Democrat (Sahmanadir Ramkavar) party, which had been founded in Cairo in 1908, and which drew support from Armenians all around the Mediterranean. The Hunchaks were not strong in the Caucasus. Their only real strength had resided in Cilicia, and remained in cells in Europe and the United States. After a split in 1896, when the non-socialists left the party and founded the Verakazmial, or Reformed, Hunchaks, the party only occasionally emerged into the forefront of Armenian affairs.

Throughout Transcaucasia Georgians, Armenians and Tatars were strongly intermixed with one another. Tiflis and Baku had large Armenian populations, both of the merchant and the working class. (Tiflis was the Transcaucasian centre of Armenian political, cultural and intellectual life, and at the time its mayor, Alexander Khatisian, was an Armenian.) However, the mass of the Armenian peasantry lived in the Yerevan province; so that, although Yerevan was no more than a dusty provincial town, it held a definite primacy as the centre close to the mass of the people.

The three nationalities of Transcaucasia did not seriously consider the notion of the independence of their region. It was well integrated into the Russian empire. The tsarist authorities, for their part, had had no intention of granting it any autonomy. Indeed, after the anticipated capture of Turkish Armenia, they had planned to fill the land with Russian colonists; and to this end, by a secret Anglo–Russian agreement of May 1916, Russia had secured acceptance of the idea that most of Turkish Armenia should come under her administration in the event of an Allied victory.[3] But this agreement, together with tsarist rule itself, was swallowed up in the earthquake that shook Russia in 1917.

Soviets of workers, peasants and soldiers were set up throughout Transcaucasia. The Tiflis soviet was Menshevik-dominated; that in Baku inclined to the Bolsheviks, under the leadership of the popular and able exiled Bolshevik Stepan Shahumian.

The local soviets were one aspect of the political structures that emerged after the March revolution. The other derived from the central authority of the Provisional government. In Transcaucasia this led to the establishment of a Special Transcaucasian Committee (known as the Ozakom, an acronym of its Russian title), whose purpose was to administer Transcaucasia and the Ottoman areas that Russian forces were holding. For Turkish Armenia under Russian occupation a liberal administration was devised.[4] Armenians were put in positions of authority over the provinces of Van, Erzerum, Bitlis and

Trebizond. It seemed like a flowering of hope – Armenians with executive power in their own lands; a light after decades of Ottoman darkness. Would the front hold? This was the vital question. Soon after the March revolution the Russian army showed signs of demoralisation: soldiers flouted orders, and taunted their formerly arrogant superiors. 'Revolutionary unrest' has been blamed; but what agitation there was found fertile soil in the rigid structure of the tsarist army.

The recapture of Turkish Armenia was a desirable prize for the Turkish army; yet throughout 1917 little advantage was taken, and the frontier shifted only marginally. The Turkish Second Army did, however, recapture Moush and Bitlis. On this occasion it was commanded by Mustafa Kemal, with Kiazim Karabekir as his second-in-command.[5]

The loss of Moush was sufficiently worrying to the Armenians for them to appeal to Kerensky in Moscow to keep the Caucasus front firm. An Armenian delegation discussed the matter with the Provisional government, pointing out that the front could best be reinforced with Armenian soldiers, released from service on other fronts – men who had their homeland to fight for, rather than Russian soldiers, fighting what appeared to them as a pointless, imperial war. Several thousand Armenians did, as a result, head for the Caucasus, but many only got as far as Baku, denied further passage.[6]

The Provisional government was in deep trouble by the summer. It was seen to be incompetent in running both the war and the economy. In Transcaucasia, too, the government hardly deserved the name, and the Ozakom was criticised for being unrepresentative and ineffective. Two important conferences held in October 1917 showed how opinion on the ground was forming: the First Regional Congress of Caucasian Bolshevik Organisations, and the Russian Armenian National Congress. The Bolshevik congress demanded local self-determination – but not separation from Russia – and cultural autonomy, and claimed that only the Bolsheviks could solve the nationality problem.[7]

The Armenian National Congress met in Tiflis in October. It was a quasi-Parliament of all the Armenians in the Russian empire (estimated at 2 million). Two hundred delegates arrived, selected on a rough-and-ready but fairly representative basis. Politically it was dominated by Dashnaktsutiun, which held the allegiance of the greatest number of Russian Armenians. The congress proposed elections, and hoped for the emergence of a democratic spirit in Transcaucasia, especially in Armenia. This posed great difficulties, since for centuries Armenians had associated government *per se* with oppression and extortion, and unlike their neighbours (both Muslim and Christian) there was no native class which was accustomed to rule. The delegates also discussed possible boundaries for an autonomous Armenia, a very difficult problem in view of the intermixture of nationalities throughout Transcaucasia.

The Armenian National Congress also established two bodies later to be of importance when independence was thrust upon Armenia: a National Assembly, to act as a legislature for all Russian Armenians; and a National

Council, to act as an executive. The significance of the National Council was that, amid the growing political turbulence and uncertainty, it was a body to which almost all sections of Armenian opinion had given their assent, and which would take control when all else collapsed.[8]

The Bolshevik Revolution

Transcaucasia reacted to the Bolshevik revolution (7 November 1917) with extreme caution. Cat-like, it sat and observed. On the one hand, none except the Bolsheviks and far left groups wanted to throw in their lot with Bolshevik Russia, and they were a small minority. But on the other hand, none wanted to see Transcaucasia separated from Russia, for then it would be isolated and at the mercy of the Turks. Hence the shifting, pending, temporary nature of the councils that were set up at this time, tentative structures which outside events would solidify into hard political edifices.

With hindsight we see the vast implications of the Bolshevik revolution of 7 November; but at the time, and in Transcaucasia, it was seen by all except the local Bolsheviks as only another leftist feud. Local soviets remained loyal to the Provisional government after November – except for Baku, led by the Bolshevik Shahumian.

The Transcaucasian Commissariat

A further 'provisional' body, the Transcaucasian Commissariat, was formed in Tiflis in November 1917, to act as government of the Caucasus until, as was envisaged, the Constituent Assembly met in Petrograd. (At that moment elections were taking place for the Petrograd assembly.) The formation of the Commissariat was another interim measure, designed to fill the vacuum until outside events clarified themselves. Portfolios were handed out to members of all three major Transcaucasian parties. The president was a Georgian Menshevik, Yevgeny Gegechkori. Armenian Dashnaks acted as commissars for finance, public welfare and food.[9]

The commissariat was at once faced by the war. The Bolshevik revolution had further weakened relations between officers and men. A truce between Transcaucasia and Turkey was thus essential. Delegates from both sides met in Erzindjan on 15 December, and three days later a truce was signed, which permitted Trancaucasia to keep virtually all of the Russian conquests of 1916.[10]

The Turks understood well the dilemma of Transcaucasia, and saw their chance: to detach Transcaucasia finally from Russia (by, say, forcing diplomatic recognition on it); once it was independent, to betray the promises made to coax it to independence; then to overrun it – and pursue eastwards, to Turkestan, Bokhara and beyond. The pan-Turkist dream might come true, and

Enver himself might regain the prestige lost amid the snow-clad woods of Sarikamish.

The Turks Move

So in mid-January 1918 General Odishelidze, Caucasus Army Commander (based at Erzerum), received a note from Enver Pasha, communicated through his commander of the eastern front, Vehib Pasha. Enver wished to enquire about establishing relations with the independent government of Transcaucasia.[11] The Commissariat hedged and delayed, in the face of this attempt to force it out into the open by declaring the *de facto* situation *de jure*; a muffled reply was sent back to Vehib two weeks later, asking for three weeks' more grace.

Within those three weeks, however, the situation at the front had deteriorated. Atrocity and counter-atrocity by Turk and Armenian alike had brought the situation to flashpoint, particularly at Erzindjan. Wherever the truth about the atrocity stories lay (and it seems probable that the Armenians, seeking to avenge the genocide, were killing Turks without compunction), it was the Turkish forces that were poised to deliver an attack: the truce was broken in early February, and soon the Turkish forces, led by Kiazim Karabekir, had closed in and captured Erzindjan. By nightfall of the 13th the Armenians were compelled to evacuate the town. Most of them had been rehabilitated there since the deportations of 1915; of them, General G. Korganoff says:

> Their flight, in the middle of the night, on a road covered by a thick layer of snow, was extremely arduous, and was made more difficult by the necessity of repelling the attacks of the Kurds. All along the precipitous slopes the service wagons overturned into the Euphrates or plunged into the snow. Men were frozen. The retreat cost the lives of more than 100 refugees who perished on the way.[12]

Desperately Transcaucasia looked around for a foundation on which a more permanent peace could be built. An armistice was useless; what was needed was a treaty, to secure a lasting peace, and a legislature, to empower the Commissariat to sign a peace. Hence the Transcaucasian Seim (or 'Sejm'; Polish for 'assembly') came into existence. It was created by simply trebling the number of delegates elected the previous November to the abortive Constituent Assembly in Petrograd, making allowance for the minorities. President was to be the leading Menshevik Nikolay Chkheidze, veteran of the Petrograd soviet.

Peace was the Seim's first priority. But what boundaries would be accepted? Realistically, the Seim realised that the boundaries of 1914 would most likely be demanded by the Turks: Turkish Armenia, the focus of so much fiery hope and frozen despair, would be lost again. With this mandate, a peace delegation was to leave for Trebizond on 2 March 1918.

Brest-Litovsk

Then, on that very day they were leaving for Trebizond, an appalling telegram from the Bolshevik diplomat, Lev Karakhan, reached the Transcaucasian leaders: the Brest-Litovsk treaty, by which Bolshevik Russia pulled out of the war, would demand that the districts of Kars, Ardahan and Batum be handed over to Turkey.[13] Shock and disbelief swept through Transcaucasia – that these three districts, freed from Turkish rule since 1878, should be annexed by the Young Turks. Two questions exercised the minds of the leaders of Transcaucasia: what right had Soviet Russia, which held no authority in Transcaucasia, to sign away the three districts; and what right, too, had Germany to demand them?

In reality, such questions were arid legalities. The Brest-Litovsk treaty was imposed on Russia by Germany, and Russia accepted it in order to get out of the war at any cost, to get a breathing-space for the revolution: this was the intention of Lenin. No rights were recognised at Brest-Litovsk; these, the Bolsheviks believed, would be won later.

Bolshevism and Armenia

The Bolshevik attitude to Armenia was bound up with the Bolshevik view of the Russian empire that they supplanted. The nineteenth-century engulfing process of imperialism was hateful to Lenin. With the world-wide fostering of revolution the system of rival imperial advance and conquest would collapse.

In May 1917 Lenin had demanded that the Russian armies be withdrawn from Turkish Armenia. The principle on which this demand had been based was that of self-determination. However, reality diverged from theory. The immediate issue at stake was otherwise: to withdraw the Russian armies would be to permit the forces of Ottoman Turkey to re-enter the area, and to slaughter those Armenians who had been rehabilitated. Armenia wanted her freedom, but not yet. At that moment she needed a shield. Nevertheless, the Bolsheviks held that for a socialist party to adhere to the annexationist policies of the tsars, whatever the circumstances, would be hypocrisy. But Lenin's hope for the establishment of 'an independent Armenian republic', enunciated at the first All-Russian Congress of Soviets (22 June 1917) was illusory while such a hypothetical republic was menaced by a powerful non-revolutionary Turkish army. One observer wondered whether the Bolshevik decision was due to ignorance, *naïveté* or cynicism.[14]

Bolshevik policy towards Turkish Armenia after the November revolution was a development of the earlier views. A decree 'about Turkish Armenia' (drafted by Shahumian and the young poet Vahan Terian) was published in *Pravda* in January 1918: it called for the withdrawal of Russian troops, the establishment of a local Armenian militia, the return of refugees from wherever they had been forced to flee, and the setting up of a soviet.[15] But again, the underlying assumption seems to have been that the Imperial Ottoman army would somehow disappear.

In the same issue of *Pravda* in which the decree was published, the commissar for nationalities, Joseph Stalin, poured scorn on the historic interference of the powers in Armenia, and their endless self-interested diplomatic shuffles. He was of course correct to do so; but the alternative that he offered, liberation through the workers' revolution, was meaningless unless that revolution spread to Turkey too, and curbed the expansionism of the Turks. Could his statement have been motivated in part by the need to withdraw Russian troops from the Caucasus?

Anyway, Bolshevik policy with regard to Turkish Armenia was dissolved by the signature on the Brest-Litovsk treaty. Immediate necessity proved more powerful than theories.

Conference at Trebizond: the Fighting Continues

Despite the news of the Brest-Litovsk treaty, the Transcaucasian delegation set out for Trebizond on 2 March. When the talks began 12 days later, after absurd delays foisted on the delegates by the Turks, who tried to humiliate them as much as possible, it was clear that the two sides were irreconcilable. The point at issue was Brest-Litovsk: even before the start of any peace talks Enver had demanded, through Vehib, the evacuation of the districts of Kars, Ardahan and Batum. Transcaucasia refused to give them up.[16] So, before the talks began at Trebizond, Turkey launched an attack, aimed at clearing Anatolia of Caucasian troops. Since December 1917 the Caucasus front had been defended by local troops. A Georgian corps defended the approaches to Batum. Armenians held the front from Erzindjan to Van; total corps strength was 20,000. Two of the three divisions were made up of Russian Armenians, led by General Tovmas (Foma) Nazarbekian, with Dro as civilian commissar. The third was commanded by the intrepid guerrilla fighter Andranik. Further south, guarding north Persia, was a mixed corps comprising a Chaldaean brigade (under their spiritual leader, Agha Petros), a Nestorian brigade (commanded by the Mar Shimun) and an Armenian battalion. The task that the local forces had set themselves was almost impossible; but there is no doubt that they prevented the Turkish troops having a virtual walk-over, and made a small but significant contribution to the Allied war effort.[17]

Erzerum fell before the talks began: Kiazim Karabekir launched a great assault, and the city was captured on 12 March. For the Armenians of

Erzerum there was another panic-stricken, last-minute evacuation, and as they streamed eastwards, local irregulars harassed them mercilessly. One hundred and twenty Armenians, unable to flee the town in time, were slaughtered by the Turkish forces.

For the rest of March, and into April, Ottoman forces overran the temporary establishment of Armenian rule in Turkish Armenia, extinguishing the hope so recently raised.[18] This was a notable and tragic moment for Turkish Armenians, and for Armenian nationalists altogether: it was the liquidation of Armenian – or indeed non-Turkish – rule in Western Armenia. With the spring offensive of 1918 the homeland, *yerkirë*, was taken back by the Turks, and, despite the hopes raised at the Paris peace conference, has remained Turkish to this day. Korganoff remarks laconically, 'With the loss of Erzerum the struggle for Turkish Armenia ended, and the war crossed the frontier of Transcaucasia.[19]

Meanwhile the talks at Trebizond were making little progress. The Turks were meticulously trying to force Transcaucasia to define its status: if it was part of Russia, then the treaty of Brest-Litovsk definitely applied; if it was an independent state, then it must declare itself as such. For their part, they were happy to consider Transcaucasia as part of Russia for the purpose of imposing the terms of Brest-Litovsk on her, but preferred her to be independent when they desired to seize more than that treaty permitted. The Transcaucasian leaders hesitated and dithered, speaking in nebulous conundrums about the status of the land they represented. With the advance of Turkish forces actually beyond the 1914 boundaries and into Ardahan (19 March) the situation became farcical, as the diplomats laboured each theoretical point about the status of Transcaucasia, while the Turkish army moved in regardless.[20]

The Turkish delegates grew sick of talking. They knew that they could seize any part of Transcaucasia that the delegation refused to hand over. They issued an ultimatum: use the treaty of Brest-Litovsk as a basis for discussion, or war; and give your answer within 48 hours. After telegraphing Tiflis, Chkhenkeli answered that Brest-Litovsk would be used as a basis. But despite agreeing to this, so unstable was the situation that both sides found themselves at war.

The 'March Days' in Baku

Throughout Transcaucasia at this time the political and racial relations between the different peoples deteriorated. On the one hand, with every mile that the Ottoman forces advanced, further atrocities were committed. According to Firuz Kazemzadeh, 'Wherever the Turkish army advanced, Armenian massacres followed. The Soviet Russian government felt compelled to intercede with the Germans on behalf of the Armenian civilian population.'[21]

At the same time the Armenians showed that they were as capable of killing off large numbers of non-Armenians (in this case Azerbaijani Tatars) as the Turks were of killing them.

In Baku the political situation at the time was somewhat paradoxical. The soviet held full control in the city, which meant that the city was virtually in Bolshevik hands – the able, if impulsive, hands of one man, Stepan Shahumian. But the political allegiance of the majority of the people was for the petty bourgeois Musavat party, which was aligning itself more and more with the racist pan-Turkism of Enver and his colleagues, under the guise of being an authentically Muslim party. A Turkist army, too, had been formed, under the command of Enver's relative Nuri. Although both the Bolsheviks and the Musavatists had been prepared to work together to some extent immediately after the November revolution, in recognition of their complementary strengths, by March 1918 relations were very tense. The Bolsheviks derided the Musavatists in their publications. Then, on 9 March, the commander of the Tatar *Dikaia Diviziia* (Savage Division), just arrived in Baku, was arrested by the soviet. Suspicions ran high. Three weeks later a report was circulated that the Musavat-inclined crew of the vessel *Evelina* was armed, and ready to attack the soviet. The soviet disarmed the crew. A mass meeting was held in the courtyard of a Baku mosque: return the crew's arms to them.[22]

Then shooting started in the streets; civil war – known as the 'March days' – was soon raging in Baku. Allied with the Bolsheviks were all the other parties – Mensheviks, Dashnaks, Kadets, Social Revolutionaries. The Bolsheviks saw the Musavat defiance as counter-revolution; the Dashnaks in less ideological terms.

The shooting intensified in early April, and vast mobs ran riot, killing, burning, pillaging. The two sides that laid into one another with especial vigour were the Armenians and the Azerbaijani Tatars, the Armenians having the edge over the Tatars in ferocity. The bloodshed spread to the countryside, to the Yerevan province, throughout the land until the country seemed to be degenerating into atavistic anarchy; Kazemzadeh comments, 'The struggle which had begun as a political contest between the Musavat and the Soviet assumed the character of a gigantic race riot.'[23]

War between Transcaucasia and Turkey: Chkhenkeli Hands over Kars

In these circumstances the war had resumed. Batum rapidly fell to the Turks. The Georgians' defiant stand turned to an eager search for compromise and peace. But for the Armenians the situation was still threatening. Besides the harbour of Batum, the other important defensive position in Transcaucasia which the Turks demanded under the Brest-Litovsk treaty was the fortress city of Kars, a vital defence for Armenia. Armenian leaders met at Alexandropol on 20–21 April to decide on whether to hand it over to the Ottoman forces or to defend it. Military experts had inspected it on the 19th, and decided it could withstand an assault for several months. At Alexandropol they decided on defence.[24]

But other political currents were active in Transcaucasia which made a decision such as this appear as the busying of ants beneath a fall of rock. Transcaucasia was hurtling towards independence. The Azerbaijani members of the Seim had demanded the independence of Transcaucasia; if not, they would sign their own peace treaty with Turkey. The fighting spirit had been knocked out of the Georgians by the fall of Batum. The Armenians hesitated; but at the session of the Seim of 22 April a majority of them voted with the rest for the independence of Transcaucasia.

Akaki Chkhenkeli, the Georgian Menshevik who had led the delegation to Trebizond, a man who was a leading proponent of peace, was designated as prime minister. He believed that only acceptance of the terms of Brest-Litovsk would enable Transcaucasia to talk on equal terms with Ottoman Turkey.

Chkhenkeli acted fast. Before he was officially installed as prime minister he ordered the evacuation of Kars (23 April). Several days of confusion, astonishment and fury followed. The Armenians never forgave him for handing over Kars behind their backs. The population of Kars was given no time to evacuate in an orderly fashion, so impatient were the Turks. The exodus of civilians was more hasty and terrible even than those of Erzindjan or Erzerum: it was night, and several buildings were on fire, perhaps lit deliberately, or possibly fired accidentally in the confusion. In this flickering light the faces of the frightened refugees could be seen, terrified at the approach of the Turks, clutching what few belongings they could take with them, fleeing the approach of Kiazim Karabekir and his troops, eastwards to Alexandropol and an unknown future. In the evening of 25 April the Turks entered the city, which they found stacked with military supplies.

Transcaucasia Independent

Under the shadow of the loss of Kars, the first Transcaucasian Cabinet was formed. Chkhenkeli was prime minister, and his own foreign minister; Georgians also took the portfolios of war, the interior and agriculture. The Azerbaijanis held five ministries; their leader, Fat'h-Ali Khan Khoisky, became minister of justice. The Armenians held four; finance, welfare, food and labour, respectively Alexander Khatisian (Dashnak), Hovhannes Kachaznuni (Dashnak), Avetik Sahakian (Dashnak) and Aramayis Yerzinkian (Social Democrat). They were definitely the junior partners in the alliance.[26]

In his opening speech to the Seim as prime minister, Chkhenkeli made a number of points that seemed to signify that a new sense of realism had come to Transcaucasia. There could be no more indecisiveness. A constitution, agreed frontiers, ending the war, imposing the rule of law and land reform – these he promised. And, on the subject of frontiers, the leader of the Musavatists reminded the Seim that Baku was not yet part of the new state.

Realism in Tiflis; but a victory for Constantinople. The Turks could argue that their own force of arms had compelled Transcaucasia to declare its independence. If the Turks had not smashed through Erzindjan and Erzerum, if they had not exposed the absurdity of Transcaucasia's negotiating position at Trebizond and gone on to capture Batum, Transcaucasia would not have declared its independence.

Transcaucasia for its part, now an independent sovereign state, recognised by Ottoman Turkey, sought even more urgently than before a permanent peace with her western neighbour.

The Batum Conference

Turkey and Transcaucasia met at Batum for peace talks on 11 May. The Transcaucasian delegation consisted of between 45 and 50 self-styled diplomats, an absurdly large figure, made necessary by the mutual suspicions of the members of different nationalities and factions within Transcaucasia.[27]

Khalil Bey, minister of justice, led the Ottoman delegation. Vehib Pasha was beside him. Present too, at the request of their government, were three high-ranking Germans: General von Lossow, military attaché in Constantinople, the fashionable and elegant sportsman Count von Schulenberg, former German vice-consul in Tiflis, whose pre-war hunting trips in western Transcaucasia were widely held to have been reconnoitring expeditions; and Otto von Wesendonck, adviser on Caucasian affairs. Their presence was a small indication that German and Turkish interests might not be identical.

Soon after the start of the conference Khalil made it clear that the Turkish side would no longer accept the treaty of Brest-Litovsk as a basis for negotiation. Stunned, the Transcaucasians waited to see what he would demand instead. The most devastating aspects of his new draft treaty – for it was only to be a basis for discussion – were those that dealt with the new frontiers of Transcaucasia. The Armenian regions were all but wiped out. From the Yerevan province was taken the district of Surmalu (which contains the town of Igdir and the northern slopes of Mount Ararat) – a region which the Turks had only intermittently set foot in during past centuries – and all the territory up to and including the Kars–Julfa railway, including the city of Alexandropol. From the Tiflis province the districts of Akhalkalak and Akhaltsikhe, the majority of whose population was Armenian, were lost.

The Transcaucasians searched for a diplomatic formula which would halt the relentless emulation by the Young Turks of their imperial forbears. Chkhenkeli proposed mediation by the Central powers, hoping that Germany would curb Ottoman demands. Khalil rejected this: the treaty was a matter between Turkey and Transcaucasia only.

By 14 May no agreement had been reached on the new treaty, especially with regard to the railway. So late that night Khalil wrote to Chkhenkeli informing him that in view of the breakdown of the negotiations, the following morning he would begin troop movements in the direction of Julfa, along the Kars–Julfa railway. It was necessary for him (he said) to reach north Persia, to combat the British threat. But this was a smokescreen, since the British were still some way away. The real reason could be found in Enver's relentless pan-Turkish fixation with Baku and Central Asia.

No message reached the front in time; and as General Nazarbekian was informed of the Turkish advance, it was occurring; soon the Turks were at the outskirts of Alexandropol. After a morning's fierce fighting, enabling the civilians to evacuate, Nazarbekian gave the order to retreat. He moved his headquarters east yet again, to Karakilisa.*[28]

The Battle of Sardarabad

Only a small area of Armenian territory now remained unconquered by the Turks, and into that area hundreds of thousands of Armenian refugees had fled. It seemed only a matter of time before that too would be overrun.

By 22 May the Turks had captured Hamamlu (modern Spitak), half-way between Alexandropol and Karakilisa.[29] Communications between Tiflis and Yerevan were now cut. Then, from Alexandropol, Turkish forces began a three-pronged attack, in an attempt to seize all that remained of Armenia. In this encounter, usually known as the battle of Sardarabad, Armenian forces finally hurled back the Turkish army and saved the eastern heartland of Armenia from the Turks.[30]

The Turks attacked Nazarbekian at Karakilisa, and forced him back towards Dilidjan. But there he stood firm. Around Yerevan itself the Armenian forces were commanded by General Silikian (Silikov). Two prongs of the Turkish advance were aimed directly at Yerevan. To halt their approach from Hamamlu, Silikian formed a thousand-strong force of riflemen, under the command of the Dashnak partisan leader Dro. This force held the Turkish advance at the defile of Bash Abaran. Just a little way west of Echmiadzin, the Armenian holy city, the third section of the Turkish advance was held, at Sardarabad. Indeed, the Armenians not only held them, they managed to throw the Turks back, until by the evening of 24 May Silikian had forced them back 50 kilometres from Sardarabad, and a few days later Dro had driven them back towards Hamamlu.[31]

In this time of supreme crisis for the Armenians they had halted the Turkish advance for the first time since the dismal evacuation of Erzindjan, and succeeded in throwing it back. Had they failed, it is perfectly possible that the word Armenia would have henceforth denoted only an antique geographical

---

*Modern Kirovakan. Not to be confused with Karakilise in Turkish Armenia, modern Agri, the largest town in the Alashkert valley.

term (like Cappadocia). But despite being outnumbered by about two to one, and being deserted by their 'colleagues' in the Transcaucasian Federation (for the Georgians had obtained German protection, and the Tatars had no desire to hinder an advance of the Ottoman forces), they defeated the Turks in all three encounters.

Just as the Armenians had seized the initiative, and appeared able to force the Turks to retreat to Alexandropol and perhaps to Kars, Silikian received the order from Nazarbekian – 'Cease fire'. A truce had been concluded in Batum. Silikian and his men were amazed and angry, since the Turks were running like rabbits; he was advised to disregard the order, declare himself dictator and continue the counter-attack. But he obeyed the order, notwithstanding, for which there were in fact pressing reasons, since ammunition was extremely low, and it was doubtful whether the Armenians could have reached Alexandropol before Turkish reinforcements had been brought up.[32]

The Transcaucasian Federation Disintegrates

Despite this most significant victory for the Armenians, the political deterioration in Transcaucasia was so serious that there was no cause for rejoicing among Armenians.

At the Batum conference the Turks had seemed insatiable for territory. Khalil Bey's new treaty had been a blow to all the delegates, except the Tatars. The Georgians, as much as the Armenians, were having their country devoured by the Turks; and seizing on the point that German and Turkish imperial ambitions diverged over the Caucasus, Georgia had sought the protection of Germany. Germany had been cultivating influence in Georgia before the war, and willingly gave her protection. She had no wish to give assistance to the Young Turks' grandiose schemes for expansion to the east. Indeed, at this juncture, German generals were trying to persuade the Turks to send more troops south to the Arab provinces, threatened by the British advances.

On 24 May von Lossow failed in his attempt to mediate between Transcaucasia and Ottoman Turkey, and on that same day he reached a secret agreement with Georgia to grant her protection when she declared herself independent. Georgia's move was a skilful one. Turkey would hardly dare to attack another ally of her senior partner (although on one brief occasion, this did indeed happen!). The following day von Lossow sailed from Batum, with the documents necessary for the treaty, to arrive at Poti (another Georgian port) a day or so later, after Georgia had declared her independence.[33]

With that splendid paradox of which the Georgians are such masters, their Menshevik ideals of a universal socialist brotherhood had emerged in practice as a desire to maintain their place in the sun, a somnolent colony comfortably supported by imperial Germany and doing as little fighting as possible.[34]

Already, on 21 May, the Georgians had discussed independence and the future borders with the Azerbaijani Tatars, and neither party seriously thought that the Armenians had a chance against the Turks, so they were not even discussed. On the day following the Georgians privately decided on independence;[35] and on 26 May – at the moment that the Armenians were fighting with all their strength – Georgia declared her independence. With customary abuse against the other nations of Transcaucasia, Irakli Tsereteli dissolved the Seim, the Parliament of the state that had never really been. Georgian leaders then rushed to Poti, to meet von Lossow, and sign their first agreements with Germany.

The Azerbaijani Tatars followed suit on the 27th, establishing 'eastern and southern Transcaucasia' as the independent republic of Azerbaijan.[36]

The Armenians were dismayed by the Georgian proclamation. Their leaders were deeply divided on whether to declare independence, for many held the view that an independent Armenia would be at the mercy of Ottoman Turkey.* Yet peace was vital; and since Georgia had quit the Transcaucasian Federation, the delegation at Batum (there since 11 May) had disintegrated. There was now no mechanism with which to make peace.[37]

Armenia Declares its Independence

The Armenian National Council, the body set up in Tiflis in October 1917, was by now acting as a government for the Armenian people of Transcaucasia; and realising that there was now no hope for Eastern Armenians but as an independent state, and that no peace could be signed at Batum by any body except an independent Armenia now that the Transcaucasian Federation was defunct, it prepared a declaration. Armenian members of the delegation at Batum were told they could negotiate a peace on behalf of an entity that might call itself 'the Republic of Armenia'.

It was not until the evening of 29 May 1918 that a decision was finally made on the declaration of independence; only by then were the last doubters convinced. Armenia's declaration of independence (made on 30 May, but with effect from the 28th) must be one of the most defensive of such documents ever written. It read:

> In view of the dissolution of the political unity of Transcaucasia and the new situation created by the proclamation of the independence of Georgia and Azerbaijan, the Armenian National Council declares itself the supreme and only administration for the Armenian provinces. Due to certain grave circumstances, the National Council, deferring until the near future the formation of an Armenian national government, temporarily assumes all

---

*Andranik condemned the move to independence. He left the Caucasus shortly after the war, dying in Fresno, California, in 1928. He is buried in the Père Lachaise cemetery, Paris.

governmental functions, in order to pilot the political and administrative helm of the Armenian provinces.[38]

No brave words about freedom or rights, no 'cherished goal' rhetoric – not even the phrase 'Republic of Armenia'. Just a bare statement of the situation, from which one can sense the doubt, anguish and unwillingness that the Armenian leaders experienced. The Republic of Armenia, born amid the political collapse of Transcaucasia and taking its first breath of life on the battlefield of Sardarabad, could hardly be otherwise.

Independence had been thrust upon Armenia. Simon Vratsian had been an advocate of independence while others wavered; nevertheless in his history of the republic he likened Armenia's declaration to the birth of a sick child.[39] Certainly, in the circumstances of May 1918, the independence of Armenia was an occasion for sorrow rather than joy. Independence was declared because Transcaucasia had collapsed politically; as a ruined and desolate district of a once great city that has been bombed and cut off, local leaders assumed power in the dust-blown lots that survived. Yet that is only one way of looking at Armenia's situation. Increasing autonomy was an ideal that Armenian political thinkers had been striving towards for half a century, as they struggled to rid their people of the imperial bureaucracies that encompassed them. They wanted to put the destiny of the Armenian people into Armenian hands. Even at this moment, as Armenia was still in danger of being swept away by a strong Turkish current, Armenian leaders were assuming the power to determine their people's future. The compromises would have to be massive, but *theirs* would, henceforward, be the executive decision; and theirs too the responsibility. Armenia independent, even amid her war-broken misery and suffering, had entered a new category.

The Treaty of Batum

The first action of the infant republic was to make peace with Turkey; the treaty of Batum was signed on 4 June. The terms were humiliating for Armenia, but unavoidably so. As Germany had held the pen at Brest-Litovsk, so now Turkey held it as Armenia signed. Again, it was territory that the Ottomans seized above anything else. All that was left to Armenia was the district of Nor Bayazid (around Lake Sevan); parts of Sharur (to the south), of Yerevan and Echmiadzin, and of Alexandropol in the north. The Kars–Julfa railway and the town of Alexandropol were gone. The republic consisted of only 11,000 land-locked square kilometres – about the size of Lebanon. Turkey had taken all of Surmalu and Nakhichevan, as well as the predominantly Armenian districts Akhalkalak and Akhaltsikhe. The only railway left to Armenia was about 50 kilometres of track in the north, and 6 kilometres extending west from Yerevan.[40]

The Condition of the New Republic

The land was rocky and scrubby, lacking cultivation or industry. The fields of Kars had been seized by the Turks, as had the industrial centre of Alexandropol. On the land which remained to the republic there were 300,000 Armenians, and another 300,000 hungry, penniless refugees; and a further 100,000 Tatars. The circumstances of the birth of the Armenian republic – war, chaos and disaster – could not have been less propitious.

The Armenian National Council, which had declared the independence of Armenia, now chose the new state's first prime minister: Hovhannes Kachaznuni, a highly educated Dashnak thinker from Akhalkalak. This distinguished-looking figure was able, unlike others in his party, to compromise with non-Dashnaks. His cabinet – also at the behest of the National Council, itself echoing the wishes of Dashnaktsutiun – was to be a coalition.[41] Their main colleagues were to be the Populists; but the Populists, disliking what they saw as Dashnak adventurism, dictatorship and managed democracy, blamed Dashnaktsutiun for the state of affairs, and refused to join. (However, it is doubtful whether the Populists could have done any better; and it is also arguable that in a period of extreme crisis, such as a pan-Turanian offensive, a strongly motivated authoritarian regime is better able to cope than a group of open-minded liberals.)

It was the end of June – a month after the independence declaration – that Kachaznuni formed his five-man Cabinet; all Dashnaks, except for the non-partisan minister of war.*[42] Not until 19 July 1918 did the Cabinet reach Yerevan; only with difficulty, and regretfully, did Armenia's leaders relinquish non-territorial politics. They must have seen the irony of the situation in which there were more Armenians in Tiflis, now the capital of Georgia, than in the backward district called the Republic of Armenia. In the seven-week absence of the official government, Dashnaktsutiun had shown its strength at dealing with situations at grass-roots level. In January 1918 Dro and Aram had establishes a tough 'popular dictatorship' in the Yerevan province, which was able to keep control and stave off disaster in the isolated, friendless republic.[43]

A republic had to be constructed from virtually nothing. The tsarist autocracy had left almost nothing in Yerevan, no machinery of government that could be taken over and modified, as we are used to seeing in the new states of Africa and Asia today. All that the Armenian government inherited were a few government offices and police cells. The country itself presented a Bosch-like vision of limitless suffering. Starving, stricken refugees, homeless, ragged and verminous, lurked in every sheltering spot. For none of the popula-

---

*Prime minister: Hovhannes Kachaznuni
Foreign minister: Alexander Khatisian
Minister of the interior: Aram Manukian
Minister of finance: Khachatur Karjikian
Minister of war: Hovhannes Hakhverdian

tion was there anything but the smallest quantity of food; many dug for roots, and harvested the grasses of Yerevan. Death was the only constant in a world of many variables. If the republic was to survive, diplomatic approaches had to be made to Constantinople and Berlin. So, in these last months of the war, Hamazasp (Hamo) Ohandjanian left for Berlin, and Avetis Aharonian set up a mission in the Turkish capital.[44] Both went with begging bowls in hand; but their submission was short-lived, since the Central powers were disintegrating, and the war was drawing to a close.

Baku, Dunsterville and the Turkish Army

But before the end of the war there was one further disaster for the Armenians. It occurred at Baku. At the end of May 1918 Baku was 'a Bolshevik island in a non-Bolshevik sea' (Firuz Kazemzadeh).[45] After the battle of Sardarabad, the Turks pressed on eastwards across the Yerevan district, towards the Tatar oil city. They reached the welcoming city of Gandja,* Azerbaijan's temporary capital, in early June. Baku was well aware of the threat to itself. Moscow could offer little help at the time; however, the British, in the form of a 'hush-hush army', the schoolboy's-wheeze-come-true Dunsterforce, had reached Enzeli, on the southern shore of the Caspian Sea, on 27 June. The intentions of this force, and its commander, General L. C. Dunsterville, have been the subject of fierce debate. On the one hand, the official British version is that General Dunsterville's sole purpose was to keep the Caucasus, and specifically Baku, from the Central powers. But there are several puzzling features which do not quite fit in with such a simple explanation. In the first place, there is Dunsterville's avowed and deeply held hostility towards revolution, and Bolshevism in particular, which almost amounted to an article of religious faith. Since the defence of Baku would have meant co-operation with the Bolsheviks, Dunsterville seemed a curious choice. In the second place, Dunsterville received his orders to move from India to the Middle East only the day after an Anglo–French agreement of 23 December 1917, which awarded 'the Cossack territories, the territory of the Caucasus, Armenia, Georgia, Kurdistan' to Britain as 'zones of influence'.[46] Did the simple defence of Baku square with this award, which would certainly need to be secured? Thirdly, from June 1918 the British vice-consul in Baku, Ranald McDonell, was actively financing right-wing, anti-Bolshevik plots, according to his own memoirs.[47] And fourthly, there was the arrival in Baku of Captain Reginald Teague Jones, intelligence officer attached to General Malleson (who was then commanding a small force in Persia). Teague Jones made it clear to McDonell that Britain's new policy was to do all in her power to oust the Bolsheviks,

---

*Gandzak in Armenian. In tsarist times, Yelizavetpol; today, Kirovbad.

by rallying any forces in the outposts of the Russian empire opposed to Bolshevism.[48] British resolve about the defence of Baku is further brought into question by comments by Prime Minister Lloyd George at the Cabinet meeting of 24 June 1918. Part of the minutes for that session read:

> Mr Lloyd George expressed the opinion that it would be better for us for the Turks to hold Baku, as it was not probable they would ever be dangerous to our interests in the east, whilst, on the other hand, Russia, if in the future she became regenerated, might be so.[49]

It was appearing that the war with Germany was as good as over, and that the intervention against Russia had begun. The Turkish alliance with Germany was ceasing to matter, and the Turks were returning to the position that they held in the days of Disraeli, when confrontation with the Russians was an end in itself, and the Turks were a handy stick to beat them with.

The Baku soviet, for its part, was divided on the question of letting the British in. The Bolsheviks, led by Shahumian and Prokopii Japaridze, were opposed to it, echoing the sentiments of Lenin and Stalin. But Baku was in a state of siege by mid-July, as the Turks pressed forward. On 25 July the soviet voted by 259 to 236 to allow the British in.[50] This was a virtual vote of no confidence in Shahumian. A week later, with the Turks at the outskirts of Baku, the Bolsheviks resigned.

An uneasy coalition of right socialists succeeded, known as the Centro-Caspian Dictatorship. Within a few days the first British troops began arriving; and the Turks launched an attack on the centre of Baku, which was repulsed by mainly Armenian forces.[51] However, by 17 August, when the last British troops had disembarked, the defenders were dismayed to find that their reinforcements numbered only about 1,500.[52] Enver, meanwhile, was massing an army of 15,000.

The disagreements and misunderstandings between the Centro-Caspian Dictatorship and General Dunsterville were endless; the no-nonsense British general found Baku's new rulers as distasteful as the Bolsheviks; and the different factions in Baku had an infuriating tendency to discuss and pass resolutions rather than act, even with the Turks pressing close to the city. On 1 September Dunsterville wrote to the Dictatorship, saying bluntly that 'no power on earth can save Baku from the Turks,' and that he would be withdrawing his troops from the front line.[53] But the Turks were slow to break through, and it was 14 September before they were in a position to launch an attack on the heart of the city. That very same evening, under cover of darkness, Dunsterville and his troops sailed back to Enzeli. Baku, having lost the Bolsheviks in order to gain the British, had now lost them too.

A terrible panic in Baku ensued, as the Turks began to enter the city. As many Armenians as could crowded the harbour in a frantic effort to escape the fate that they knew always accompanied a Turkish conquest.

Regular Ottoman troops were not permitted to enter the city for two days, so that the local irregulars – *bashibozuks* – could perform their historic role of looting and pillaging. And the fury with which they turned on the Armenians knew no bounds. Khristofor Mikhailovich Evangulov, in charge of posts and telegraphs, one of those who negotiated the surrender of the city and vainly tried to prevent the worst excesses, noted:

Robberies, murders and rapes were at their height [at 4.00 p.m. on 15 September]. In the whole town massacres of the Armenian population and robberies of all non-Muslim peoples were going on. They broke the doors and windows, entered the living quarters, dragged out men, women and children and killed them in the street.

From all the houses the yells of the people who were being attacked were heard. ... In some spots there were mountains of dead bodies, and many had terrible wounds from dum-dum bullets. The most appalling picture was at the entrance to the Treasury Lane from Surukhanskoi Street. The whole street was covered with dead bodies of children not older than nine or ten years. About eighty bodies carried wounds inflicted by swords or bayonets, and many had their throats cut; it was obvious that the wretched ones had been slaughtered like lambs.

From Telephone Street we heard cries of women and children and we heard single shots. Rushing to their rescue I was obliged to drive the car over the bodies of dead children. The crushing of bones and strange noises of torn bodies followed. The horror of the wheels covered with the intestines of dead bodies could not be endured by the colonel and the *asker* (adjutant). They closed their eyes with their hands and lowered their heads. They were afraid to look at the terrible slaughter. Half mad from what he saw, the driver sought to leave the street, but was immediately confronted by another bloody hecatomb.[54]

Estimates for the number of Armenian dead are around 20,000; the figure may easily have been higher. In this way the government of Azerbaijan installed itself in Baku, backed by Ottoman Turkish forces.

And what of Shahumian and his comrades? They had twice attempted to quit Baku since their resignation; the second time they were arrested and imprisoned by the Dictatorship. But as the Turks approached on 14 September, they finally escaped in a small vessel, the *Turkmen*. From Baku Shahumian hoped to sail to the Bolshevik-held ports in the north of the Caspian. But the winds were unfavourable and the crew were unwilling to sail there. So the vessel sailed due east, to Krasnovodsk, where a right-wing government of Social Revolutionaries, with headquarters at Ashkhabad, held sway.[55] The Ashkhabad committee was, in turn, working very closely with General Malleson (who was based at Meshhed). When, on 17 September, Malleson heard of the arrival of the commissars in Krasnovodsk, he requested that they be transported to India; he considered that their presence in Transcaspia was undesirable. But the Ashkhabad committee made other plans. Meeting on the evening of the 17th, with British intelligence officer Captain Teague Jones present, they decided to shoot the commissars.[56] Despite this decision, Teague Jones made no reference to Malleson's declared request to have them taken to India.

Very early in the morning of 20 September the former commissars of Baku were woken up, and 26 of them were told to get ready for a journey to Ashkhabad. The young Anastas Mikoyan asked if he could go with Shahumian, but he was told to stay behind. The 26 were put on a train, and taken 210 kilometres east of Krasnovodsk. There they were bundled out, and immediately killed – some shot, others slain with hatchets and knives. They were buried unceremoniously where they lay. Of the 26, 22 were Bolsheviks, 2 were Left Social Revolutionaries, 1 was a Dashnak and 1 was a non-party Jew. The affair of the 'Twenty-Six Commissars' was one which was to have profound and lasting effects on Anglo–Soviet relations, centring on the fairly clear connivance, if not complicity, of Teague Jones in the murder of the commissars.[57]

The Mudros Armistice

By the Mudros armistice of 30 October 1918 Ottoman Turkey acknowledged her defeat. However, it let her off comparatively lightly. The complete demobilisation of the Ottoman armies was not demanded; a force was permitted to stand 'for surveillance of frontiers and the maintenance of internal order' (clause 5). The size and disposition of this force was to be decided jointly by the Allies and the Ottoman government; but anyone who knows the terrain and distances of Anatolia would know that this would be a virtually impossible task for the Allies. The phrase was a vague one, and left the door open for the formation of a new Turkish army in eastern Anatolia. In essence, the Allies were not concerned with the interior of Anatolia. Beside the Arab provinces, there were only three things that they wanted from the Ottoman empire: access through the Dardanelles, occupation of Baku and Batum and the railway that joined them (these two together would ensure that Baku's oil reached the British fleet in the Mediterranean), and access to the Taurus tunnel system of the Baghdad railway.[58] Turkey was not compelled to withdraw to the 1914 borders, and only 'in case of disorder in the Armenian vilayets' would the Allies occupy any part of them (clause 24). A supplementary clause did demand that the Turks evacuate the Kars district; but the occupiers were able to prevent its immediate implementation by means of delaying tactics. *The Times History of the War* made an accurate assessment of the armistice when it wrote:

The armistice made the military and naval situation of the Allies perfectly secure but they were less severe than the Turks had reason to expect. . . . The weakness of the armistice lay in that it did not bring home to the Turks in Anatolia the completeness of the defeat they had sustained and that no adequate provision was made for the security of the Armenians.[59]

Even as they were withdrawing, the Turks manifested bitter, defeated malignancy towards the unfortunate Armenians. A cable from the British General Officer Commanding, Mesopotamia, dated 21 December, relates the following:

An American officer name[d] Arrol who arrived from Yerevan saw on 4 and 5 December at Alexandropol Turkish regulars removing large quantities of household goods, railway engines and trucks, building material . . . cotton, foodstuffs which Turkish officers told him were going to Kars and into Turkey. On 2 and 3 December between Yerevan and Alexandropol there were wagonloads of grain and cotton at every station awaiting removal. Turkish officers state [?they] were dealing Armenians final blow and had taken from this district 7,000,000 poods [approximately 112,000 tons] of wheat, 200,000 poods [3,000 tons] of cotton, household goods, thousands of people and transport of all kinds. Where they were unable to remove wheat, the Turks let it rot. At every station there were large quantities being ruined by rain, and the people forbidden to touch it under penalty of death. During past few months Arrol has personally seen numbers of cases of raped children from 3 to 12 years old, numbers of Armenians who had been beaten until unable to stand, and once near Karakilisa over sixty corpses of women and children. He had also witnessed the perpetration of abominable tortures by Turkish troops.[60]

The Basis of Armenian Hopes

Few of the combatants in the first world war had greater hopes of the Allies than the Armenians. Enormous, verbose and rhetorical promises had been made throughout 1917 and 1918 to them for their restitution, at the very same time as the leaders of the Allied countries were giving the final revision and polish to their secret agreements for the division of the Ottoman spoils. In the House of Commons on 20 December 1917 Prime Minister Lloyd George described Armenia as a land 'soaked with the blood of innocents' and declared that it was one of the countries which would 'never be restored to the blasting tyranny of the Turk'. The following month, in a speech to the TUC, he affirmed that Armenia was one of the former Ottoman territories 'entitled to a recognition of their separate national condition'. In the summer of 1918 the same voluble premier proclaimed that Britain would 'not forget its responsibilities' to the Armenians.[61] (This was at about the same time as he was advocating the Turkish conquest of Baku.) French leaders made similar declarations.

Armenian assistance to the Allied war effort was frequently cited: the holding of the Caucasus front after the collapse of Russia, and the contribution of the mainly Armenian Légion d'Orient in Palestine as part of the Egyptian Expeditionary Force under General Allenby, notably at the battle of Arara, near Nablus, fought on 19 September 1918. On 8 November 1918 an Anglo–French joint declaration on Middle Eastern policy stated its aim to be

> the complete and final liberation of the peoples who have for so long been oppressed by the Turks, and the setting up of national governments and administrations that shall derive their authority from the free exercise of the initiative and choice of the indigenous populations.[62]

Italian Prime Minister Vittorio Orlando announced grandly in the same month, 'Say to the Armenians that I make their cause my cause.'[63] But perhaps the greatest sympathy for the Armenian people came from the United States. With the extermination of Turkish Armenians, Americans had seen the endeavours of 80 years collapse into nothing – endeavours which had been initially missionary, but which in the last few decades had taken on a more cultural and political hue. To most Americans their political concern was a natural development of their missionary interests. For them the issues at stake were an earthly representation of the cosmic struggle between good and evil. (Very few Americans knew of the conflicting elements of imperialism, nationalism and ideological religion that fuelled local hatreds.) American sympathy for Armenia was both practical and theoretical. An immense sum of money was contributed to the relief of suffering Armenians, although not all of it was distributed;* and a lobbying group was formed known as the American Committee for the Independence of Armenia (ACIA). President Wilson had a great personal sympathy for the Armenians, and the twelfth of his Fourteen Points had a direct relevance to Turkish Armenia:

> The Turkish portions of the present Ottoman empire should be assured a secure sovereignty, but the other nationalities which are now under Turkish rule should be assured an undoubted security of life and an absolutely unmolested opportunity of autonomous development.[64]

Armenia's hopes for the post-war settlement were pitched high, with some justification. Yet there were some points, of great importance, which were in the main overlooked. In the first place, in order to establish herself as a state, Armenia needed a protective power to act as mandatory. The most natural power for this purpose was Russia, but revolution and civil war had placed her, in the eyes of the Entente, in the position of a pariah nation. Looking at the

*The American Committee for Armenian and Syrian Relief (ACASR) was founded in November 1915. It changed its name to the American Committee for Relief in the Near East (ACRNE) in 1918, and to Near East Relief (NER) the following year.

map, it is very hard to see which other power could undertake the job. Besides the problem set by geography, Britain and France were both sick of war, and had no wish to take on onerous burdens with a questionable return. Italy declared her adherence to the principle of *sacro egoismo*, in which it is difficult to discern anything at all *sacro*. Finally, America was widely touted as a possible mandatory for Armenia. But there were formidable problems here: in the first place, the desire not to get involved in Europe's affairs ran wide and deep in American political life, and would quite possibly submerge the brief emotional burst of sympathy for suffering Armenia, and secondly, America had no experience in administering Eastern peoples.

The Paris Peace Conference

When the peace conference convened in Paris in January 1919, nearly all the participants foresaw that provision would be made for an independent Armenian state to be established within secure boundaries – at last the 'great powers' would be able to make amends for the murder and devastation that their policies had inflicted on Armenia for the past 40 years. But this was not to be; indeed, the suffering and wretchedness of Armenians – the pitiful, starving hopelessness – was worse in the years following the war than at any time except during the Ittihadist organised mass murder of 1915–16. Nothing that the statesmen said or did at Paris made any difference to Armenia; their weighty and wordy declarations appear, when one reads them, as utterances designed to give the speaker an aura of satisfied charitable well-being. For all the good they did Armenians they might as well have been random nonsense syllables. Hence the peace conference need not detain us for long.

Encouraged by Allied declarations and assurances, the Armenians staked out large claims at Paris. Already there (since 1912, see p. 79) was Boghos Nubar, as head of the Armenian national delegation. But in February 1919 a delegation arrived representing the Republic of Armenia, headed by the author and poet Avetis Aharonian. Nubar and Aharonian were widely dissimilar in background and outlook; Nubar with his origins in a wealthy Levantine minority, at ease among the statesmen of Paris, intensely conservative by nature; Aharonian, a man of ironical wit, as rugged as the Caucasian scenery that had given him birth; Nubar with unlimited faith in the 'civilised' west, Aharonian more sceptical, believing – as would anyone who had been close to the turmoil of the birth of independent Armenia – that the people's own strength on the ground is more valuable than the guarantee of a foreign statesman. Nevertheless the two agreed to merge their delegations into the 'All-Armenian Delegation' (Délégation de l'Arménie integrale), and to agree on all major issues.[65] They presented their joint memorandum to the peace conference in February 1919. Reviewing past Ottoman oppression, and the enormous losses that the Armenian people had sustained during the war (which gave them the right of the title of 'belligerent'), they now claimed their independence. Their state was to include the 'six *vilayets*' of Turkish Armenia (Van, Bitlis, Diyarbekir, Kharput, Sivas and Erzerum), excluding a few marginal non-Armenian districts; also the province of Trebizond, to give access to the sea. It should also include the Republic of Armenia as it was then constituted, plus Mountainous Karabagh to the east, Zangezur to the south, and to the north some Armenian-inhabited lands which it claimed from Georgia. But that was not all. Armenia also claimed the four districts of Cilician Armenia, on the Mediterranean coast, where there was quite a large Armenian population (both urban and agrarian) dating from the period of the medieval kingdom. Armenia would have been a gigantic country; yet the proposal differed only in some small particulars from the British and American proposals then current. (France opposed, since the Armenian claims for Cilicia and the land stretching north-east to Sivas, Kharput and Diyarbekir conflicted with France's share of the Ottoman carve-up as agreed by Sykes and Picot in 1915.) In this huge country Armenians would only be a small minority; but the Armenians insisted on including in their demographic estimates with some justification all those Armenians murdered as a result of the Turkish government's policies of 1915–16. Not to have done so would be to acquiesce in the Turks' government-sponsored genocide. This argument was also trenchantly put by Sir Eyre Crowe, a member of the British delegation in Paris. He wrote to a London colleague on 1 December 1919: 'To consider and decide the Armenian question purely on the basis of present numbers would surely amount to countenancing and encouraging the past Turkish method of dealing with the problem of their subject nationalities!'[66] Nevertheless, throughout 1919 and 1920 the Turks and their supporters naïvely laid claim to Armenian lands, on the grounds that there were no Armenians living in the areas, feigning ignorance of the policies of 1915–16. In their submission, the Armenians requested general protection for 20 years either from the Allies or the League of Nations, and the direct guidance of one specific mandatary.[67]

In response to this and every other request or appeal addressed to them the Allies did nothing. Despite their grandiose public statements, and despite the closeness at this date of Armenian bids to British and American policy outlines, nothing was done to secure a lasting Armenia out of the wreckage and disaster of the war. The Allies would not even recognise the Republic of Armenia, so keen were they to pursue their vendetta with the Bolsheviks, and so fearful of upsetting Russian 'democrats', who would demand the incorporation of Armenia into a reconstituted Russia. Their immobility in the face of continuous reports of Armenian wretchedness, starvation and death was as icy as their inaction during Abdul Hamid's persecutions. And here there was a further twist of fate. No decision was reached. At least the Berlin congress, for all its haughty imperialism, had been over in a month; but after 1918 it took, as we shall see, four and a half years for the wise statesmen to sort out a treaty that would stick. In the immediate aftermath of the war, the great powers were if anything more greedy, jealous and self-interested than formerly. The only action that they did sponsor was so foolish, short-sighted and ill-conceived that it proved, in its implications, disastrous to the non-Turkish peoples of east and west Anatolia, and to the designs of the powers themselves. That was the Greek occupation of Smyrna (Izmir), 15 May 1919.

Armenia Pitches into a New War

The Republic of Armenia was, in the meantime, appearing more like a normal state, not a mere patch of earth swarming with refugees, run by a dictatorship. The Populists (Zhoghovrdakans – eastern equivalent of the Ramkavars) agreed to take part in the government, and held four of the portfolios in Kachaznuni's new (4 November 1918) government.*[68]

However, no sooner was the Republic reasonably secure than it was involved in a tiresome and possibly avoidable war with Georgia. The origins of the conflict dated back to June 1918, when the Georgians, in order to forestall a Turkish advance on Tiflis, occupied (temporarily, allegedly) the region of northern Lori which was about 75 per cent Armenian. Towns in the area included Sanahin, Alaverdi and Uzunlar. After the Mudros armistice, when the Turks were withdrawing from Transcaucasia, the Georgians indicated that they desired to take their place. Iraklii Tsereteli maintained, with that self-denying altruism for which the Georgians are so renowned, that the Armenians would after all be safer from the Turk as Georgian citizens. The Armenians were suspicious, and rejected a Georgian proposal of a quadripartite conference to solve the conflict.[69] The participants were to have been the Mountaineer Republic of the North Caucasus (capital: Temir Khan Shura), Georgia, Armenia and Azerbaijan. In December the Georgians, who had imposed a tsarist-style military bureaucracy upon the Armenian peasantry of the district, were confronted by a rebellion, centring chiefly upon the town of Uzunlar. Within days hostilities began between the two republics. The Dashnaks seem to have been keen to prove that they could emulate the Georgians in their socialist imperialist aspirations, because the Armenian army, under Dro's command, pushed north far beyond the regions with an

---

*The complete Cabinet comprised:
   Prime minister: Hovhannes Kachaznuni (Dashnak)
   Foreign affairs: Sirakan Tigranian (D)
   Interior: Aram Manukian (D)
   War: Hovhannes Hakhverdian (non-party)
   Finance: Artashes Enfiajian (Populist)
   Justice: Samson Harutiunian (P)
   Public instruction: Mikayel Atabekian (P)
   Welfare: Khachatur Karjikian (D)
   Food: Levon Ghulian (P)

Armenian majority, and came to within 50 kilometres of Tiflis. Fighting continued for a fortnight; by the end of it the Georgian army, which had initially fared disastrously, began to stage a come-back. This pointless, damaging, Gilbert-and-Sullivan escapade came to a conclusion on 31 December with a cease-fire arranged by the Allies, who had been aghast at the petty squabble they had been witnessing.[70]

The war was inconclusive for both sides. But the real damage was that in the eyes of the world; here were two states, that had been born amid the fire and ice of the last four years, which had suffered deprivation and fearful onslaught, but which were now, while the rest of the world was healing its wounds and longing for peace, laying into one another like two hostile cats. Supporters of the Armenians, who had regarded the people they championed as a blameless, eternally suffering nation, received a rude shock. They appeared to be rather like everybody else.

Weather Conditions

The winter of 1918–19 was the most severe in memory in Armenia. For the republic, painfully constructing itself, this was a very serious setback.[71] Just under 20 per cent of the country's population was wiped out. Villages were desolated. The situation for the 300,000 Turkish Armenian refugees, lacking shelter or food, was catastrophic. Even the settled population of Armenia hovered on the edge of starvation, since the supplies which in former times would have reached Armenia from north of the Caucasus were now cut off by the Russian civil war. Appalled relief workers sent harrowing descriptions to Europe and the United States, and the phrase 'Starving Armenians' gained widespread and justified currency. It elicited genuine compassion from Europeans and especially Americans. Large shipments of food and clothing were sent to the suffering country.

For those Turkish Armenians who struggled to return home after the cruelties of the deportations the situation was ferociously bleak, and the utter lack of help that they received highlights again the distinction between the words and deeds of those powers with the power to be of assistance.

The Turks seemed not to consider that the war had ended, or that their government had signed an instrument of defeat. *The Times* (London) reported on 4 January 1919 that atrocities were continuing, homes were being wrecked and all available goods were being carried away by the Turks.[72] The same paper described on 16 January how the deported Armenians were struggling to return home: 'Few have any transport, and they are making long journeys on foot from the Mesopotamian deserts to the snow-bound districts in the north, barefooted, half-clad, hungry, sick, and exhausted.'[73] Within Ottoman Turkey itself, the Allied occupation extended no further east than Konya, and all Armenians were still terrified of further massacre.[74] *The Times* summed up the situation in a leading article of 2 May 1919:

> The Turkish soldiery, disbanded but not disarmed, is still wandering about the more inaccessible districts of Armenia. Famine has followed massacre, and with it, as so often, has come typhus and other diseases. Since the armistice the Armenians have been sustained by political hopes, soon destined, we hope, to be fulfilled; but a nation cannot live on politics alone, and the appeal now made is for the elementary needs of basic sustenance.[75]

The British in Transcaucasia

But instead of elementary sustenance, the Armenians found themselves occupied by the British, who, rather than show a humane, impartial and healing hand after the agony of the past four years, seemed keener to play at politics, in a disconcertingly parade-ground manner. British policy in the Caucasus was never clearly formulated. Its ostensible bases were to enforce the armistice terms, to secure communications between Baku and Batum, and to maintain law and order. In practice, two strands can be discerned. The first was to keep Bolshevism out of the area; and the second was to extract and appropriate as much of Baku's oil as possible.[76]

The first of these objectives involved them in a contradiction before even setting forth in the country. For in the first place they were committed to support General Anton I. Denikin, commander of the Volunteer Army, and in the second place their strategy demanded that they support, as far as possible, the existing regimes in the Transcaucasian republics, thereby implicitly recognising the independence of Georgia, Armenia and Azerbaijan. However, Denikin was determined to crush the republics; he was an old-fashioned Great-Russian chauvinist, who believed that the empire of the tsars should be re-established in all its majestic tyranny.[77] Hence international recognition was withheld from Armenia throughout 1919, when it would have benefited her enormously, for fear of upsetting Russian 'democrats'.

Very large quantities of oil were taken from Baku: almost half a million metric tons by August 1919, and another quarter-million by the end of the year. Altogether this amounted to just under 45 per cent of the annual production.[78] As the occupation continued, it was becoming clear that Azerbaijan was being considerably favoured by the occupying power at the expense of Armenia, and suspicion was expressed that the oil was determining policy, and that wartime promises and assurances were being disregarded.

Britain was in the Caucasus to smooth the way for the implementation of the decisions of the peace conference. But since the peace conference made no difference to conditions in Transcaucasia, the decisions of the British officers in the region had surprisingly long-term effects.

The British and the Disputed Territories

Thus it was the decisions of the senior British officer in Baku, General W. M. Thomson, and of his successor, Colonel D. I. Shuttleworth, that determined the fate of Karabagh and Nakhichevan (which Armenia disputed with Azerbaijan), and of Kars, whose Turko–Tatar leaders, having killed or expelled all the Armenians, had declared it a self-governing 'state'.

The consequences in Karabagh for the majority of its inhabitants were tragic, and persist to this day. In November 1918 General Andranik had been poised to capture Shushi, the capital of Mountainous Karabagh (whose population was 85 per cent mountaineer Armenian). But General Thomson told him to cease his advance, since all further matters would be solved at the peace conference; Andranik, trusting the British, complied.[79]

Soon afterwards Thomson appointed Dr Khosrov Bek Sultanov as provisional governor-general of Karabagh and Zangezur. Sultanov was the owner of vast tracts of Karabagh. He was also an ardent pan-Turkist, a friend of the Ittihadists of Constantinople, and a terror to all Armenians. Thomson can hardly have failed to know this; but evidently his upbringing told him that a powerful local landlord – one of 'our traditional friends' – was likely to squash any 'unrest' in the region.

The people of Karabagh resolutely refused to recognise Sultanov's authority. They insisted on the right of self-determination. The British compelled them to stop all political activities in April 1919. At the same time a local Azerbaijani detachment encircled the Armenian quarter of Shushi, demanding the inhabitants to surrender their fortress. Shots were fired, but the Armenians were too well dug in. The British mediated, and the Armenians agreed to surrender to them.

But the methods of Sultanov were not so straightforward as those of his British backers. Like other similar local potentates, he could muster a large number of mounted 'irregulars'. In mid-June this force, about 2,000 strong, attacked, looted and burnt a large Armenian village, Khaibalikend, just outside Shushi. When they had departed, it and the surrounding hamlets were in ruins, and approximately 600 Armenians lay dead.

The Karabagh affair was a grave one for the British. Accusations of direct British complicity in Armenian massacre cannot really be sustained; but the killings were a result of the almost unconscious British tendency to support 'our traditional friends' – the wealthy – and to disregard the wishes of the majority. This had been the basis of over half a century of pro-Turkishness among the British.

Even after widespread criticism, the British refused to remove Sultanov from his post; and the Armenians, sickened by the prospect of further bloodshed, eventually agreed to Azerbaijan's provisional control of Karabagh. Provisional, however, it never was; and Mountainous Karabagh with its large Armenian majority remained Azerbaijani throughout the pre-Soviet and Soviet

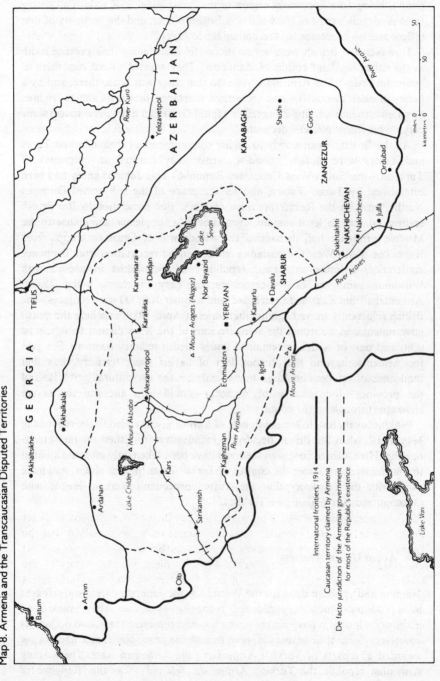

Map 8. Armenia and the Transcaucasian Disputed Territories

GEORGIA

AZERBAIJAN

KARABAGH

ZANGEZUR

NAKHICHEVAN

SHARUR

• Akhaltsikhe

• Akhalkalak

• Ardahan

• Artvin

Batum

• Oltu

Kars

Sarikamish

• Kaghzman

Mount Akbaba

Alexandropol

Karakilisa

Karvansarai

Dilidjan

Lake Childer

River Aroxes

Mount Akababa

Echmiadzin

Igdir

Kamarlu

Mount Ararat

Mount Aragats (Alagoz)

Nor Bayazid

Lake Sevan

YEREVAN

Davalu

River Aroxes

Shakhtakhti

Nakhichevan

Juffa

Ordubad

Shushi

• Gorıs

River Aroxes

River Kura

Yelizavetpol

TIFLIS

Lake Van

International frontiers, 1914

Caucasian territory claimed by Armenia

De facto jurisdiction of the Armenian government
for most of the Republic's existence

miles 0   50

kilometres 0   50

period, being an autonomous region of the Azerbaijani SSR today; all dating from Andranik's trust of the word of a British officer, and the partiality of that officer and his successor to Azerbaijani landowners.[80]

However, the British were not so successful in installing their protégé south in the other highland region of Zangezur. They wanted to put him there to 'maintain order'. The Armenians retorted that there was order there, and by a policy of bluff, demonstrations and armed resistance, they were able to frighten Shuttleworth into quitting Zangezur's capital Goris in a hurry, and successfully defying his fellow-officers' decisions.[81]

As the British began slowly to realise that numbers of their admired Turks and Tatars were in fact Ittihadist agents, they crushed an outgrowth of Turkism – the 'South-West Caucasian Republic'. This dubious entity had been established by Turko–Tatars, and by the grace of the still armed Ottoman Ninth Army, in the former province of Kars. For some months the British seemed content to let it remain, even though a supplementary clause to the Mudros armistice had demanded the withdrawal of Ottoman troops from Kars. The South-West Caucasians even demanded recognition from the peace conference, claiming that their republic was established in accord with Wilsonian principles of self-determination – easy to claim, when 25,000 Armenians from Kars had been killed, and another 100,000 were refugees! The British reluctantly moved against the Turks in April 1919, expelling the quasi-government and awarding the southern part of the Kars district to Armenia. (Olti and part of Ardahan remained under British military control.) The gain for Armenia, beyond the obvious fact of having more territory, was that thousands of refugees could go home, and that the agriculturally rich land of the province – the granary of Armenia – could help alleviate the severe shortages throughout the country.[82]

Nakhichevan, too, to the south-east of Yerevan, was added to the republic in May 1919, when the British decided to relinquish it from their military governorship. Here, too, the decision seems to have been taken only after the attempt to put the territory under the control of Turko–Tatar 'proper chaps' had gone awry with the discovery that the trusted proconsuls were in league with Ottoman and Azerbaijani pan-Turkists.[83]

The 'Act of United Armenia'

Nothing had yet been done for the Western Armenians; they were still refugees in a country which they did not recognise as home. They wanted an authority – indeed a government – which would represent them, and declare its sovereignty over their homeland, even though the peace conference had not yet awarded any parts of Turkish Armenia to the Armenian state. The existing Armenian republic the Turkish Armenians referred to as the 'Republic of

Ararat'; Armenia was only a dusty province without the *yerkir*, the homeland, of Turkish Armenia whose salvation Armenians had been seeking for 40 years.

In consequence of this pressure the government in Yerevan proclaimed, on 28 May 1919, the first anniversary of the Republic, the unification of Western and Eastern Armenia: the 'act of United Armenia'. It was an act of hope only, an attempt to goad the peace-making powers into creating a new reality.

But the result of this symbolic gesture was, instead of uniting Armenia, to divide the Armenians among themselves. Boghos Nubar, head of the National Delegation in Paris, believed that the government in Yerevan was trying to pre-judge the issues that his delegation was painfully trying to push through at the peace conference; he called the proclamation of the Act a 'painful surprise'. Within a matter of days the Populist members of the coalition had with-drawn from the government, even though they had initially approved the proclamation.[84]

Party Differences: the Elections of June 1919

The dispute that the Act of 28 May brought to the surface is fundamental to Armenian political and social attitudes. The conflict – which endures to this day, although time has mellowed its harsher outlines – is an almost instinctive suspicion between the Ramkavars (Populists in Russian Armenia) and the Dashnaks. The Ramkavars, or Constitutional Democrats, were cautious, refor-mist and believed in evolution rather than revolution. They were the party of Armenian big business, but they were also charitable, and founded a number of hospitals and schools. Their opponents have portrayed them as collaborationist yes-men, but this is unfair; having firm roots in Turkish Armenia, they realised that they had to proceed slowly, dealing on the one hand with despotic empires, and on the other with a peasant population which in our arrogance we call 'simple', but which was merely innocent of the corrosion of industrial society, clinging instead to its ancient soil and ancient Church. The tenets of the Ramkavar party never added up to an ideology, and their organisation was correspondingly lax. The Dashnaks, by contrast, were a product of the revolutionary, socialistic ferment in the Russian Caucasus in the declining days of tsardom. They were well organised and active, and were not frightened to use strong-arm methods against fellow Armenians, as well as non-Armenians, when they suspected them of collaboration with the enemy. They laid stress on obedience, holding that members should carry out the dictates of the Bureau, the party's supreme executive body, without question or demur. At the same time, the Bureau drew its authority from the local and general congresses of party members.

In an atmosphere of growing political rancour, elections were held throughout the republic on 21–3 June 1919. The Populists withdrew officially from them; the results distributed the 80 seats in the Parliament as follows:

Dashnaks   72
Social Revolutionaries   4
Tatars   3
Independent Peasants' Union   1[85]

The Dashnaks won what *The Times* described in another context as an 'inartistic majority'.

Any realistic opposition to Dashnaktsutiun had been eliminated; the two groups with alternative policies, the Populists and the Bolsheviks, had declined to take part – the latter on the grounds that the elections were a Dashnak exercise, although their opponents claimed that they boycotted them because they knew they would capture only a fraction of the vote. The net result – whichever side was to blame – was that the politics of Armenia remained largely in the world of secret decisions. Opposition was non-existent, government was entirely Dashnak, and parliamentary questions might not be asked without the approval of the Bureau of Dashnaktsutiun. In a much-quoted passage Hovhannes Kachaznuni later put it thus:

> Armenia was a democratic republic. It had the proper organs of a democratic, parliamentary government: a legislative body composed of the people's representatives and a responsible administration. The parliament was composed of representatives from four existing parties and minorities with the widest true democratic principles. The government received its authority from the legislative body and was responsible to it. This was the form. But the reality was otherwise.
>
> In practice our party [Dashnaktsutiun] tended to subject to itself and to control the legislature and the government. We did not have the courage or ability openly to declare a dictatorship, yet did not wish to remain within parliamentary limits either. Instead we tried to establish in Armenia the Ittihadist system – a party dictatorship disguised as a democracy. An intolerable dualism resulted from it: on the surface, the parliament and the government; behind the scenes, invisible, the party and its organs.
>
> There was no parliament; it was an empty form without content. The problems of state were being discussed and solved behind closed doors, in the rooms of the Dashnak faction, and then declared from the rostrum of the parliament.
>
> In reality, there was not even a parliamentary faction, because the latter was under the very strict supervision of the Dashnak Bureau, and was obliged to carry out its orders. There was not a government either. This too was subject to the Bureau; it was a kind of executive body for the Bureau in the state. This was the Bolshevik system. But what the Bolsheviks are doing openly and consistently, we were attempting to veil under democratic forms.[86]

Kachaznuni's strictures belittle the immense problems posed by the growing menace of Tatar sedition, and the perpetual threat of Armenia's western neighbour. In these circumstances 'open government' was a mirage. The only practical disadvantage of the lack of democratic forms was that it led European democracies to think twice before committing aid to Armenia. It would, however, be wrong to ascribe the setbacks and disasters that Armenia suffered in the succeeding months entirely to the structure of the Dashnak party. The situation in Armenia itself was still too disturbed following the war, and external events were moving too fast and unpredictably for even the most experienced politicians to cope. When Armenia's new prime minister, Alexander Khatisian, introduced his all-Dashnak Cabinet* to the Parliament he spoke of the serious condition of the country, and the need for massive new legislation. The administration had to be thoroughly reformed; feudal and church lands to be nationalised; the Armenian question had to be solved and the refugees from Turkish Armenia repatriated.

Kemalism and Bolshevism

Yet as he spoke events were taking place in Anatolia which would ensure that the Armenian question was not solved. The Allies' delay in completing a Turkish treaty at the peace conference had enabled the Turks to create an organisation capable of preventing the imposition on Turkey of the terms fitting for a defeated empire at the end of a world war. Together Mustafa Kemal and Kiazim Karabekir (commander of the Ottoman Fifteenth Corps, which was 18,000 strong) were preparing to defy any terms that the Allies might impose on Turkey. By July they were strong enough to hold a congress in Erzerum[87] – significantly 'the capital of Turkish Armenia'. For the Armenians the most noteworthy resolution to be passed at that congress was: 'The return of refugees to the eastern vilayets is strictly forbidden without the permission of the representative committee.'[88]

Other resolutions made it clear that the main priority of the Nationalists – as the followers of Kemal and Karabekir became known – was the prevention of the establishment of an Armenia in any part of the six provinces of Turkish Armenia.

Within a few months this new organisation had seized the attention of the traditional Turkish leaders in eastern Anatolia. The burning resentment engendered by the Greek occupation of Smyrna found expression in support

*Prime minister and foreign affairs: A. Khatisian
Minister of the interior and justice: A. Giulkhandanian
Minister of finance: S. Araratian
Minister of labour and public health: A. Sahakian
Minister of education and fine arts: N. Aghbalian
Minister of war: Major-General K. Araratian (non-partisan)

for the Nationalist movement, determined at all costs to reject the imposition of Allied peace terms. Soon the influence of the Nationalists had spread to Constantinople, and swept away the government of Damad Ferid Pasha, which had been obedient to the dictates of the Allies. By October the Nationalists could call the tune in Constantinople: that is, a group of rebels, upon whom the Allies could not impose their terms, was now in control in Turkey.

The effect of this in diplomatic terms was enormous. No longer would the Allies be able to force Turkey to sign a treaty of their bidding. By delaying so long in deciding on a Turkish treaty and by not disarming the Ottoman army entirely at the end of the war, they had ensured that they could not impose a treaty upon it that would do justice to the peoples who were subjects of the defeated Asiatic empire. The Kemalists were 'outlaws' and 'outcasts', upsetting the dilatory, self-interested games that the winning powers were playing in various locations of western Europe, in a manner which was worse than their nineteenth-century counterparts. The Kemalists at least would solve matters in their own way.

The other power outlawed by the Entente was Soviet Russia. It was not long before the two were making overtures to one another. The friendship between Bolshevik internationalism and Turkish nationalism was based only on temporary interest: one has only to look at subsequent events like the murder by the Kemalists of the Turkish Communist leader Mustafa Subhi, and the whole course up to the present day of Russo–Turkish relations, to see that the post-war warmth was only an irregular interlude in the historic enmity between the two states. Yet while it lasted it was strong enough to accomplish, among other things, the destruction of Allied influence in the Caucasus, and the wreck of independent Armenia.

Debate on the Future Status of Armenia: the Harbord Commission

While the new world was taking shape in Turkey and Russia – while the Kemalists were still considered as mere 'brigands' by the powers – the question of a mandate for Armenia was being raised. In May 1919 Britain announced that she intended to terminate her occupation of the Caucasus in August, and at the same time Foreign Secretary Lord Curzon approached the Americans with a view to their taking on the mandate for Armenia. The American ambassador, J. W. Davis, gave him a very accurate assessment of the likelihood of his hope being fulfilled. Davis said it was very unlikely that America would take on a Caucasian mandate. The main reason that he gave was America's unwillingness to be entangled in foreign alliances; and he also pointed out, with prophetic clarity, that philanthropy would not survive expediency.[89]

President Wilson himself despatched a commission in August 1919 to enquire about the possibility of America taking on the Armenian mandate. Headed by Major-General J. G. Harbord, it spent two months travelling through Turkish Armenia and the Armenian republic.[90] The commissioners heard tales of woe from the remaining Armenians in Turkish Armenia, and saw the abject state of wretchedness they were still living in, persecuted by the relentless Turks and near starvation. They also met Mustafa Kemal in Sivas, who impressed them as a realist, a forceful politician, and no fanatic. They crossed into the Armenian republic on 25 September, where the boundless faith of the people and their leaders in America was immediately apparent. Everywhere they went the commissioners were fêted as saviours. The country was still on the edge of starvation, and had to support half a million refugees; Oliver Wardrop, the scholar and diplomat who had been appointed Chief British Commissioner to Transcaucasia in July 1919, described Yerevan thus, after visiting it in October of that year:

> The aspect of the city is pitiful. The streets are ill-kept, and the wind carries clouds of infected dust. Everywhere there are wretched refugees in rags, hungry, diseased, demoralised ... this great mass of suffering ... the appearance of some of the children was very painful to see; they were picking up refuse in the streets and eating it ... Yerevan at present is more depressing than any other place I have seen.[91]

Faced with a resurgence of Turkish aggression and infiltration from both Ottoman lands and Azerbaijan, Armenia looked desperately for a protector.

Harbord's report did not come to any specific conclusion; it merely gave 13 arguments against and 14 in favour of an American mandate. Points in favour were humanitarianism (meaning the ending of the starvation, wretchedness and desolate wreckage which was the lot of most Armenians at the time), and America's technical ability to put things to rights. Against were the traditional unwillingness of the United States to get involved in Old World politics, and the consequent lack of experience of America in administering colonial or mandated people.[92] There was the cost, too: estimated expenditure for five years was put at $757 million.[93]

The Harbord commission, however, exercised no discernible effect on American policy, and despite the labours of its members the Armenians benefited not a whit from it. It reached President Wilson in November 1919, a month after he had had his first serious stroke; it was April 1920 before he submitted it to the Senate, and when in the following month the Senate voted on an American mandate for Armenia, the proposal was rejected. America, dragged half-heartedly and superficially from her isolationism, had now returned to it; in future 'realistic' matters, like the Chester railway concession for Turkey, were to determine policy, rather than any attempts to restore a wrecked nation.

Armeno–Azerbaijani Conflicts

British troops were withdrawn from the Caucasus in late August 1919, and a farcical plan to replace them with Italians came to nothing. The decision to withdraw was taken on two grounds: that Turkey was complying with the armistice, and that British troops were in heavy demand elsewhere.[94] Only the district of Batum remained occupied by Allied forces. The withdrawal led to a sharp increase in hostility between Armenia and Azerbaijan, and to increasingly harsh treatment by the Armenian government of their Tatar minority, and by the Azerbaijani government of the Armenians whom they controlled *de facto* in the disputed territories of Karabagh and Nakhichevan. Already, in the early part of 1919, the Azerbaijani diplomatic representative in Yerevan, Khan Tekinski, had sought to subvert the existence of Armenia, successively attempting to create economic difficulties for Armenia and then, more seriously, planning a revolt of Armenia's Tatar population, and trying to co-ordinate it with the movement of Azerbaijan's forces. The Armenian government, which had been deciphering Tekinski's cables, insisted on his recall.[95]

On 18 July, shortly before the British withdrawal, a Tatar rising in Nakhichevan began. It was commanded by a Turkish colonel, Khalil Bey. Soon the insurgents were in control of Bash Norashen (Norashen on today's maps). The revolt spread north-west, towards Yerevan; within weeks Armenia was compelled to withdraw its authority from Nakhichevan and Sharur as far north as Kamarlu (modern Artashat).[96] At the same time the Turko–Tatars did not limit their actions to military operations; there occurred the usual concomitant of slaughter of the defenceless Armenian village population. T. B. Hohler, of the British embassy, Constantinople, reported privately to a colleague in London on 4 August, 'There seems to be a fine old massacre going on in Nakhichevan.'[97]

Armenia, so recently expanded, was surrounded on almost all sides by a fire of insurrection and massacre. On 20 September Avetis Aharonian recorded that the Armenian government had been forced temporarily to evacuate Kars; that the Tatars were threatening the Ulukhanlu–Echmiadzin section of the railway, very close to Yerevan itself, and that they had taken Davalu and Kulp (south and east of Yerevan). In these operations, they were led by Turkish officers.[98] The very existence of the Republic of Armenia was threatened.

The conflict erupted further in Karabagh. Although Azerbaijan held this territory more securely than the other disputed areas, its Armenian populace suffered the full fury of 'our traditional friend', the landlord Dr Sultanov, who brought fire and death to his Armenian tenants.

The only possible mediator was the representative of the peace conference, Colonel Haskell. Haskell had strong influence with the Azerbaijanis for dubious reasons which will become apparent later. He initially persuaded them to recognise Zangezur and Nakhichevan as a neutral zone under American authority, while holding on to Karabagh. But the violence continued; fierce battles were fought in all areas in mid-November. Haskell's deputy, Colonel Rhea, managed to get Armenia and Azerbaijan to sign an agreement on 23 November.[99] Under it they agreed to end hostilities and settle their conflict by arbitration, but it had little effect, for in mid-December Tatars from Ordubad, in the southernmost tip of Nakhichevan, fell upon the nearby town of Lower

Akulis (whose population was 80 per cent Armenian), and sacked the town, killing as many Armenians as they could. Some Armenians were able to escape to the stronghold of Upper Akulis.[100] This was destroyed, too. The Armenian government took heavy reprisals; according to Fat'h Ali Khan Khoisky, they destroyed about 40 Tatar villages in Zangezur.[101] The earlier policy of the Armenian government of conciliating the Muslims was discarded in favour of one of suppression, which in turn only hardened Muslims into non-recognition of the Yerevan government, and of acting more vigorously as agents for Turkey and Azerbaijan.

Armenia in Early 1920

Rather surprisingly, Simon Vratsian says that the year 1920 started well:[102] there was peace in the country and along its borders and work for the people in rebuilding the nation. The country was (he said) unrecognisable from its condition of one year earlier. But the forces threatening Vratsian's vision of Armenia were strengthening themselves in all ways. They were able to operate in the vacuum created by the Allies' inability to come to grips with the Armenian question – the future of Turkish Armenia. It was over a year now since the end of the war, and still the Allies had decided nothing about the future of Armenia. Chiefly responsible was President Wilson, and his delays were now compounded with the problems of an unco-operative Congress and his own serious illness. Britain's resolve, too, was weaker, with the growth of agitation among Indian Muslims and their supporters, who held that any diminution of the Turkish empire was an offence against Islam. Other things that boded ill were the crumbling of Denikin's Volunteer Army, which Armenia had cautiously hoped might be of assistance (it collapsed altogether in March 1920) and the strengthening *entente* between the Bolsheviks and the Turkish Nationalists.

The Bolshevik-Milli (Turkish Nationalist) alliance was rooted in the common interests of both parties. It was not an ideological pact, although in the propaganda of both parties it often appeared to be so. The Turkish Nationalists were, like most nationalists, more concerned with the extent of the land they governed than about the nature of the government. Under the terms of the 'National Pact' of February 1920 they demanded all of Turkish Armenia, and Kars, Ardahan and Batum as well. They did not demand Surmalu, on the northern slopes of Mount Ararat, an important point in view of later negotiations. The Bolsheviks for their part detested nationalism, and believed that it would soon disappear under the impact of workers' revolution. Nevertheless the two were drawn together by hatred of the Allies, and a determination to stamp out the power of the Entente. Hence the opposition of both Bolsheviks and Milli to the Transcaucasian republics, which they saw as puppets of Britain and France.

Another factor, too, drew them together. This was the attempt by the

Bolsheviks to win over Muslim opinion (by pointing out the vast exploitation of the Muslim peoples by the 'Christian' West) with a view to shaking Britain's rule in India. The sheer *numbers* of the Muslims made them attractive to the Bolsheviks – as they had been for complementary reasons to English imperialists half a century earlier. With blandishments from Nationalist Turkey and Bolshevik Russia, it is hardly surprising that Azerbaijan was unable to tell the difference between the two when a *coup* was staged in Baku in April 1920.

Thus the picture for Armenia in early 1920 was not good. She had clung blindly to the Allies, but had received nothing tangible in return, except relief supplies. As a result of her devotion to the Allies she could expect only hostility from the new Turkey and Russia, which were growing stronger every day. (Moreover, the new Turkey, as personified by Kiazim Karabekir, commander of the eastern front, seemed as keen to make the extermination of Armenians as axiomatic to Turkish policy as any of the older Turkeys.) And, most serious of all, those very Allies to whom Armenia looked for salvation were appearing as irresolute, devious, self-interested and quarrelsome as their forerunners of a generation back. Already Italy, like a grand lady scorned and derided at the banquet of the Allies, was arming the Turkish Nationalists, out of little more than pure spite. France had already sent an envoy to Ankara; her position in Cilicia (see below, pp. 292–303) was precariously weak, and after the Kemalist assault on Marash (February 1920) it was little more than one long retreat. Britain was keeping her ear to the ground for signs of discontent among Indian Muslims, and was far less disposed to listen to Armenian claims than a year earlier. And finally America was paralysed by Wilson's personal and political difficulties.

Allied Conferences in London and San Remo

It was in these circumstances that Britain and France convened the first London Conference, with the aim of working out a treaty with Turkey (December 1919–March 1920).[103] Plans more realistic for the future size of Armenia prevailed now than those put forward in Paris in February 1919. The idea of a Greater Armenia from the Black Sea to the Mediterranean had been scrapped, even if largely because it conflicted with French territorial aspirations for a 'mandate' area embracing Cilicia and stretching north-eastwards as far as Kharput and Diyarbekir. Both Britain and France realised that any areas of Turkish Armenia that would become an Armenian state would now encompass parts of the provinces of Bitlis, Van, Erzerum and (to enable Armenia to have a coastline) Trebizond; this was the recommendation of an Allied Commission in its report of March 1920.

But what to do with Turkish Armenia once its size had been decided? A mandate was essential; in contrast to Allied propaganda and pretensions in the Arab world, where blatant colonialism was half hidden under the unconvincing fig-leaf of 'bringing the peoples up to a level of civilisation', Armenia, ruined by massacres and heavy warfare during the world war, and now starving, really needed the assistance of a stronger power. Yet each power in turn said apologetically that it could not take the mandate for Armenia. At the London Conference the powers agreed to ask the League of Nations to accept the mandate.

The League considered the matter on 9–11 April. In its report it pointed out that it was not a state, and had no army and no finances. It could not accept and exercise a mandate; only give a right to supervise one. A power had to be found.[104]

Still hoping that America would, somehow, accept the mandate, the Supreme Council of the League (Britain, France, Italy and Japan) met in San Remo (18–26 April) to try to bring their deliberations about the former Turkish empire to a conclusion. There is a pathetic triviality about the proceedings, as far as they related to Armenia, occurring as they did on the very eve of the Bolshevik *coup* in Azerbaijan, which tightened further the hold of the anti-Entente forces in the Caucasus. As if they were playing an elaborate and formal game of croquet, the world leaders spent nearly all the brief time they allotted themselves to discuss Armenia scoring off one another over the matter of whether or not the city of Erzerum should be included in the proposed Armenia. Like players in the game making careful strokes merely to send their opponents flying from the hoops, so our modern Atlases marshalled their arguments about Erzerum – Lloyd George and Signor Nitti against its inclusion in Armenia, Lord Curzon and M. Berthelot in favour.[105] Since none of them intended actually to do anything on the ground to help this Armenia come into existence the exercise was of tedious aridity – without even a suggestion of the excitement afforded by a real game of croquet.

The upshot of the deliberations at San Remo was that the leaders decided once more to appeal to President Wilson to accept the mandate, or, failing that, to fix boundaries of the state.[106] But when the president proposed the acceptance of the mandate to Congress on 24 May, the Senate, after four days' discussion, voted by 52 to 23 to decline to take it on.[107] So the president was left to draw the map of an Armenia which seemed unlikely to come into existence at all; his stroke through the next hoop. Meanwhile on 11 May Britain and France handed to Turkish representatives from the puny puppet government in Constantinople the text of the treaty with which they intended to wind up the affairs of Turkey and solve the Eastern Question, the treaty to be known as the treaty of Sèvres, perhaps the most elegant and pointless of all the shots in the game.

Recognition of Armenia: Further Clashes with Azerbaijan

On 3 January 1920 Oliver Wardrop, British Chief Commissioner in Transcaucasia, cabled London: 'It would be prudent to consider possibility of complete collapse of Denikin at an early date. This would immediately be followed by vigorous Bolshevik attack on Transcaucasia.'[108] He had been urging recognition of the Transcaucasian republics since his arrival in Tiflis four months earlier, and now the threatening situation reinforced his appeal.

Within three weeks the republics received *de facto* recognition. *De jure* recognition would follow when the peace treaty with Turkey was signed. Armenia was recognised on 19 January; Yerevan was swept with a tide of joy. Yet the Allied move had nothing to do with the intrinsic importance or value of Transcaucasia and the struggle of the peoples who lived there. It was an attempt to keep Bolshevism out of the Caucasus – or rather, to create the conditions under which Bolshevism could be withstood – and to weaken the Soviet–Kemalist alliance.

There is a disastrous significance in the grounds for this diplomatic recognition. During the world war, and in the period immediately after it, Armenia was, according to the statements of representatives of the Entente powers, something valid *in itself*; freedom and a secure future for Armenia were apparently one of the axioms of a post-war settlement.[109] Now Armenia was a mere pawn in the struggle to contain Bolshevism, and the interest of the Allies in her was merely a function of their own global manoeuvrings. When they had ceased to be interested in Transcaucasia, they would drop her like a stone.

Judging from its policies, the Armenian government would seem to have been largely unaware of the grim diplomatic outlook. Throughout January and February Armenia was embroiled in her struggle with Azerbaijan, carrying on a guerrilla war in the disputed and cross-populated areas. Ranald McDonell, formerly British consul in Baku and now desk-bound at the Foreign Office, held that the Dashnaks themselves were to blame; and notwithstanding the anti-Dashnak attitude typical of British officials of the time, it is hard not to blame the militant, activist members of the ruling party at the time for the lack of any conciliatory policies.[110] Lord Curzon addressed a letter to Avetis Aharonian, briefly in London, 'impressing on his people the necessity of reconciliation rather than revenge'.[111] But the fighting continued, increasing rather than decreasing in violence.[112]

Crisis in Azerbaijan

In the early months of 1920 Armenia's eastern neighbour, Azerbaijan, was racked by a series of internal government crises. These centred around the attitude that Azerbaijan should take towards the victorious Bolsheviks, now just the other side of the Caucasus.[113] Since the establishment of the three Transcaucasian republics Azerbaijan had been the least anti-Bolshevik: as one of the most politically sophisticated Muslim nations of the time, she was very aware of her common detestation with the Bolsheviks of the exploiting 'Christian' nations of the West which had done so much to impoverish Muslim peoples. In recent months the alliance between Turkish Nationalists and Bolsheviks had strengthened pro-Bolshevik sentiment in Azerbaijan, with the presence there of Khalil Bey and Enver's relative Nuri, former Ittihadists who now, like many others, were working all out for Mustafa Kemal and the Nationalist movement.

Throughout January and February 1920 Chicherin, Soviet commissar for foreign affairs, was conducting a 'dialogue' with the administration of Nesib Bek Usubbekov. As the Red Army virtually came into view across the mountains, the government in Baku became paralysed with uncertainty and fear, and resigned in March. Formation of a new government was put in the hands of the weak pro-Bolshevik Mahmed Hasan Hajinski; but he was unable to assemble a Cabinet. The Red Army massed on the northern frontier, while almost the whole of the Azerbaijani army was tied up in Karabagh. As the government was still politically paralysed and incapable, the Baku Bolsheviks and the Military Revolutionary Council of the Eleventh Red Army made their own arrangements: an uprising would be staged in Baku, which would give legitimacy to the entry of Soviet troops.

Soviet Azerbaijan

And so, at midday on 27 April, the local Communist bodies in Baku handed an ultimatum to the president of the Azerbaijani Parliament, demanding that power be handed over to the Communists. The government (such as it was) was given 12 hours in which to reply.[114]

Hours before midnight Soviet troops were pouring across the frontier. By 11.00 p.m. that same night Baku was in the hands of the local Communists. Next day it was a Soviet city.[115] Only one man was killed in the entire operation.[116]

The Sovietisation of Azerbaijan was a triumph above all for Mustafa Kemal. Russian arms and supplies were now physically very close. The only obstacle remaining between the two was Zangezur, disputed territory at the time in the hands of the Armenians.

Armenia was now face to face with Soviet power; and it was in this position that the final act of her independence was played. Throughout the next five months Soviet opposition to Armenia was to be territorial, political and logistical. The territorial aspect was to be the least important, although viewed from strongly nationalist Yerevan it often appeared the most important. The relentless Soviet Azerbaijani demands for Karabagh and Zangezur were part of the logistical battle to secure a link between Soviet and Kemalist forces, and of the political fight to squeeze Armenia as hard as possible while she remained pro-Entente and anti-Bolshevik. Ultimately, the conflict was one which existed purely in an international dimension, since the Soviet desire to give weaponry to Kemalist Turkey was not through any love of Turkish nationalism, but because Kemal and his colleagues were dedicated to smashing the power of Britain and France from Thrace to Erzerum.

The new Soviet Azerbaijani regime instantly applied territorial pressure against Armenia: Yerevan received an ultimatum to quit Karabagh and Zangezur, and to stop taking severe measures against the Tatars within Armenia, 'otherwise the Revolutionary Committee of the Soviet Socialist Republic of Azerbaijan will consider itself in a state of war with the republic of Armenia'.[117] Armenia was given three days to make up its mind.

Bolshevism in Armenia: May Day Celebrations

As if in defiance of this threat, the Armenian government resolved to celebrate May Day in grand style, with marches, parades and demonstrations, to show that it would not be intimidated by Bolshevik threats, and that the Armenian people were behind their government. In Yerevan a demonstration was organised in which different factions took part; besides pictures of Dashnak founding fathers Kristapor Mikayelian, Stephen Zorian (Rostom) and Simon Zavarian there were posters of Lenin and Shahumian.[118] There was some pushing and shoving, but it was mostly good-humoured.

Before the October revolution there were almost no Bolsheviks in Armenia; the country was overwhelmingly agricultural, with almost the only industry at the railway centre of Alexandropol. In late 1918 a number of Armenian Bolsheviks who were not native to Armenia – most were from Georgia and Azerbaijan – fled to Armenia, to escape persecution in their own countries; they were allowed in, on condition that they desisted from political activity. But engaging in political activity is a necessary condition of being a Communist; and by the end of the following year they were spreading propaganda among the Armenian armed forces, telling them not to fight the insurgent Tatars in Buyuk Vedi and elsewhere. Arrests followed. In January 1920, at the party's secret conference, two opposing strategies emerged: one, proposed by Sargis Kasian, was that the party was not ready yet to attempt to establish a Soviet regime in Armenia; with only 500 members it lacked the strength, organisation and the ability to defend itself militarily against an invasion from Georgia; and the wretched condition of the country, with thousands still dying from starvation and exposure, meant that an armed Communist uprising was not, for the moment, relevant. The opposing policy, put forward by the young hothead Avis Nurijanian, was for the immediate overthrow of the government and the establishment of Soviet order, and this strategy appears to have been adopted.[119]

Now, on May Day, three days after the Bolsheviks had taken Baku, their comrades in Armenia were full of confidence. There was also another current of feeling prevalent among many of the ordinary people – a current which was to broaden and swell in the coming months. This was a yearning to be rejoined with Russia, and an almost instinctive belief that only this way would the starvation and suffering end – only this way would the condition of Armenia change; the silent winter deaths, and the chronic diseases of summer. It was as though they guessed that the European diplomats, who in a year and a half had only delivered to them a few crumbs, might now desert them completely, and instead they looked to their old protector, Russia.[120]

Uprising in Alexandropol

In contrast to the festive co-operation in Yerevan, the Bolsheviks in Alexandropol took advantage of the relaxed atmosphere to stage an uprising. Amid the celebrations local Communists hoisted the Soviet flag, and, from an armoured train, *General Vardan*, proclaimed a Soviet government.[121] From this train, under the command of Captain Sargis Musayelian, the insurgents sent a stream of telegrams, proclaiming their 'state of tense war with the Dashnak anti-revolutionary government', begging Baku for provisions, and so forth. When news of the Alexandropol uprising reached Yerevan, the minister of war ordered Musayelian to the Kamarlu front; he refused, and instead proclaimed a Bolshevik Military Revolutionary Committee,* which declared itself in command of the country. The committee captured Alexandropol station, gaining the loyalty of some army units.

Next, Musayelian telegraphed Yerevan, requesting that the government should hand over full powers to him. Telegrams were also despatched to Sarikamish, Kars and Karakilisa, claiming that the Revolutionary Committee was in control.[122] The telegrams found a measure of response in the armed forces, and also among the non-Armenian populations, such as the Tatars (understandably, in view both of the Kemalist and the Bolshevik propaganda to which they had been subjected, and the uncompromising way in which the Armenian government dealt with their disloyalty) and Russian minorities such as the Molokans.† On 9 May a military revolutionary committee was set up in Kars, demanding recognition of the Soviet government in Alexandropol. Kars stayed in rebel hands for two days. In Sarikamish some of the soldiers mutinied, and sent fraternal greetings to Turkish soldiers. The revolt spread to Kaghizman, too. Near Nor Bayazid the situation was more serious. At Basar-Gechar Hamazasp's volunteer regiment rebelled, and a local schoolmaster, one Sarukhanian, took command of the rebel troops. In an inflamed speech he bid his listeners overthrow the government. The troops themselves arrested General Silikian and all the officers; then moved on to Nor Bayazid itself, and captured the city with little fighting on 17 May.[123]

---

*President and military commissar: Sargis Musayelian
Commissar for foreign affairs: Avis Nurijanian
Commissar for the interior: Artashes Melkonian
†Russian dissenters who had been settled in Transcaucasia during tsarist times.

After a moment's hesitation, the Armenian government took severe steps to crush the rebellions. At a special session of Parliament the resignation of Alexander Khatisian's government was accepted; and then Parliament itself was declared closed for one month. The entire Bureau of the Dashnak party entered the government;*[124] government was henceforward synonymous with party dictatorship. A state of emergency was declared. Every member of Dashnaktsutiun was ordered to 'put himself completely at the disposal of the party'.[125] The army was mobilised, and a special division created, under the command of General Sebouh, to recapture Alexandropol. First, though, Prime Minister Hamo Ohandjanian telegraphed Musayelian, ordering him to end the rebellion, adding that the guilty would be amnestied. In reply, the Military Revolutionary Committee sent a flat refusal. Thereupon the government decided to move against the rebels.[126] The headquarters of the revolt was still the armoured train, moving uncertainly in the northern part of the Alexandropol–Yerevan railway, its occupants, despite their tough talk, not venturing outside its armed exterior. On 13 May it was between Ani and Aghin stations.[127] There it had an encounter with government troops in which the rebels were considerably worsted. The armoured train sped off, and as it left its crew attempted to blow up bridges. The rebels, realising they had not won the support they had hoped for, tried to salvage the remnants of their revolt in Alexandropol itself, but without success. They finally resolved upon surrender; the government's terms were that the armoured train be surrendered in good condition by 6.00 a.m. on 14 May. They escaped by night: some fled to Akbaba, while others hid in Alexandropol. Government forces entered the town without bloodshed on the 14th; Musayelian and Melkonian were arrested, but Nurijanian escaped, to return six months later and wreak a terrible revenge not only on leading Dashnaks but upon Armenia itself.[128]

The Old and New Order

April and May 1920 were the two months in which the new order began to appear, and the old to disintegrate. The Sovietisation of Azerbaijan was hardly noticed in that embodiment of the old, America, and yet its impact on Armenia was greater than any number of petitions to Congress, or the utterances of the bellicose and chauvinistic organisation, the American Committee for the

---

*The 'Bureau government':
    Prime minister and foreign minister: Hamazasp (Hamo) Ohandjanian
    War minister and minister of the interior: Ruben Ter-Minasian
    Minister of finance and justice: Abraham Giulkhandanian
    Minister of agriculture and labour: Simon Vratsian
    Minister of communications: Arshak Djamalian
    Minister of education and arts: Gevorg Ghazarian
    Minister of public care and repatriation: Sargis Araratian

Independence of Armenia (ACIA). At the same time, the true mettle of certain of the Americans actually there, on the ground, in Armenia was proved.

The Americans in Armenia are remembered above all for their generosity in sending relief. Individuals and organisations poured thousands of dollars into funds for the starving Armenians. Men like Barton and Green worked untiringly for the distribution of relief supplies.[129] The charity of individuals had been formalised into Allied policy when in July 1919 Colonel William H. Haskell had been appointed Allied High Commissioner in Armenia, a man who seemed the embodiment of disinterested American justice and concern. Yet Haskell was a crook, who during his time in the Caucasus was systematically selling to the Azerbaijani government the food supplies given by charities in the West to Armenia. (Thereby Azerbaijan was able to continue her campaign against Armenia in Karabagh and Zangezur.) On 5 May 1920, with the Caucasus shaken by the uncertainties of the Bolshevik *coup* in Azerbaijan and the uprising in Armenia, Haskell received notice that an investigative commission, together with auditors, was on its way. Quick as a flash he and his staff fled from Tiflis, giving away stores right and left. His excuse was his fear of the growth of Bolshevism. He gave orders that records were to be destroyed. Similar orders were given to his staff in Yerevan. All this is related in a memorandum by Rev. H. W. Harcourt, who had been sent out by the Lord Mayor's Fund, the main British relief charity.[130] Hinting, too, at the reasons for Haskell's sudden departure, but too polite to disclose them, is Sir Harry Luke, in his witty autobiography *Cities and Men*. Luke noted that 'Haskell occupied one of the more imposing private residences of Tiflis':

> The four Allied and Associated flags surmounted his desk and the door of his palace; his official stationery, of somewhat unorthodox heraldry, was similarly emblazoned; an achievement the size of a hatchment, composed of the colours of the four powers, filled almost completely the panels of his car.[131]

Haskell, in fear of a full-scale investigation (Dr Frederick MacCallum had already visited Tiflis, with auditors), quit without giving any notice of the fact to the Allied missions.[132] Luke adds that with all his flags it looked as though the Allies were themselves leaving. A shiver of panic ran through the pro-Entente peoples of the Caucasus. Another leaf had fallen off the withering bough of the old order.

The Levon Shant Mission: Negotiations with the Bolsheviks

Already the Armenian government had decided that it had to come to terms with the new order. Much as it looked to the Allies, and to Europe, it was not blind to what was happening around it: it saw that the Allies had delivered nothing but promises and uncertain amounts of food, even though it continued to trust those promises. Armenia had to have some sort of dialogue with Russia's new masters, for practical reasons, not least because of the shortages in Armenia, of food and (since the Sovietisation of Azerbaijan) *mazout*, the fuel on which the trains ran, obtained after kerosene had been extracted from petroleum.[133]

Hence Armenia realised that, whatever the Allies might think, she must negotiate with the Soviet government. On 30 April 1920 a three-man delegation left Yerevan for Moscow; it consisted of Levon Shant (an author and playwright whose works were known in Russia), Hambardzum Terterian and Levon Zarafian. The delegation was authorised to sign a treaty with Soviet Russia along the following lines:[134]

(i)   Soviet Russia will recognise the independence of Armenia, including Karabagh;
(ii)   Russia will accept at least in principle the notion of the annexation of Turkish Armenian provinces to Armenia;
(iii) Russia will not interfere in the internal policy of Armenia, either directly or indirectly;
(iv)   Soviet Russia will permit the return to Armenia of Armenians stranded in the North Caucasus and Russia;
(v)   Armenian workers would receive some compensation for their hardships during the 'imperialistic' war.

It was 20 May before the delegation reached Moscow. At their first meeting with Chicherin, the Soviet commissar for foreign affairs spoke of quite another matter: the vital need of the Bolsheviks to secure their alliance with the Nationalist Turks, who were resolutely opposed to Britain and France. At the moment (Chicherin continued) Turkey was prepared to attack the Allies, but was frightened that Armenia would strike her from the rear. Hence the Soviet government desired to reconcile Armenia to the Turks, and make her abandon the Allies. This would be the principle which would animate the proposed friendship treaty with Yerevan.[135]

This was a modification so radical that the Shant delegation felt it could not accept it without demur. They suspected that the Soviet moves were part of a Turkish ploy to make Armenia rid herself of the Allies and lose what she stood to gain from the Allies' treaty with Turkey (the treaty of Sèvres). They also felt that the Soviet government was trying to force the Allies to recognise it by using the Turkish threat. According to Terterian's account, the reply that they gave to Chicherin – a prophecy almost too accurate to be true – went as follows: 'We know the Turks best. They will use your supplies to attack first the Armenians, then the Greeks. Then they will abandon Russia and come to an agreement with the Allies.' But Chicherin was not to be outdone. 'We are giving aid to the Turks because this will lead to the Sovietisation of Turkey,' he replied. 'And of Armenia?' asked the Armenians. 'No,' replied Chicherin, 'since we shall then be seen as an oppressor of small nationalities.' Then the Armenians raised another point. 'What of the National Pact' (by which Kemalist Turkey claimed not only Turkish Armenia but Kars and Ardahan as well); 'the Allies have promised us much of Turkish Armenia.' Chicherin: 'Look at the past record of the Allies. Besides, to claim Erzerum for Armenia is unsupportable.' 'There are many monuments of Armenian culture there.' 'These belong to the period of Tigranes the Great. Today there are no Armenians there.' 'That's the kind of argument that bourgeois nationalists use: they accept accomplished facts, and thereby justify mass murder and deportation.' An uneasy truce was reached, with both sides accepting the axiom that the soil belongs to the worker. Chicherin also asked for a set of population statistics for the six provinces of Turkish Armenia:. he would delimit the Turkish–Armenian frontier. Clearly the Soviet government believed that it could persuade the Turkish Nationalists to give up part of Turkish Armenia.[136]

A Turkish Nationalist delegation, headed by Bekir Sami Bey, was in Moscow at the same time. Terterian and Zarafian were in favour of making contact with them, with the possible idea of drawing up a treaty directly between the two; but Shant demurred, on the grounds that Yerevan had not authorised them to do so, and that he felt unable to negotiate with mass-murderers and war criminals.[137] Whatever Shant's scruples, his decision lost an opportunity.

In mid-June the Shant delegation had another meeting with Chicherin. They declared their readiness to accept the Soviet proposal of mediation, a very significant reversal. In reply the commissar said that he would secure certain territories for Armenia, and also an outlet to the Black Sea. As regards the disputed territories, he declared that Zangezur and Nakhichevan would be assigned to Armenia, while Karabagh would continue to be disputed, until its final status was determined by a referendum. Soviet Russia would also make large gifts to Armenia to build her shattered economy.

Then, delay. Even though all seemed settled and final, there was no meeting to discuss final details leading to the signing. It became clear that this was due to the sabotaging activities of the Armenian Bolsheviks, frustrated and bitter after the failure of the May uprising in Alexandropol, and the subsequent crack-down on Bolsheviks in Armenia. (On 15 June the Armenian authorities executed 17 leaders of the revolt.[138]) Those who could had fled to Baku, where they sent exaggerated and distorted accounts of what had happened to Moscow. Chicherin was trying to solve the Armeno–Turkish dispute along lines most favourable to the Soviet state, but *they* sought only the Sovietisation of Armenia, and were determined to make this Moscow's official policy.[139]

At the end of June, the Shant delegation was presented with a new proposal on the disputed territories: Nakhichevan to Armenia, Karabagh to Azerbaijan, and the status of Zangezur to be decided by the Soviet emissary who was to be despatched to the spot, B. V. Legrand. (His name is sometimes spelt 'Legran'.)

Levon Shant himself was opposed to signing a treaty along those lines; he felt quite unable to sign away Karabagh. So the delegation cabled Yerevan for guidance. It was a month later before they received an answer – by which time Chicherin had declared that the negotiations in Moscow had ended, and would be continued at a later date in Yerevan between Legrand (acting with plenipotentiary powers) and the Armenian government.[140]

Armeno/Bolshevik Clashes and the Agreement of 10 August

As the Bolsheviks delayed the negotiations, so their military squeeze on Armenia began. On 5 July a division of the Eleventh Red Army invaded Zangezur, via Karabagh, and reached Goris. The Armenians, commanded by General Dro, counter-attacked, and re-occupied all of Zangezur. The Bolsheviks received reinforcements, and seized Goris again; and also attacked from Kazakh in the north-east. By early August Armenia saw no end to the conflict, and sued for peace. On 10 August the two sides signed an agreement, intended to be a preliminary to a final peace settlement.[141] Armenia agreed to an occupation, stipulated as 'temporary' by the Bolsheviks, of all of Karabagh and Zangezur, and of Nakhichevan south of Shakhtakhti.[142] Ironically, this was far more than Chicherin had demanded from the Shant delegation in Moscow, and to which the Armenian government had sent its firmly worded negative telegram. The month-long war had nevertheless also brought clear gains to the Armenian government, since it had been able to re-establish its authority over Zangibasar, Buyuk Vedi and Sharur as far as the Shakhtakhti railway station (south and south-east of Yerevan), as well as Surmalu, regions to the west almost as far as Olti, and the Karakunli district north of Lake Sevan.[143]

The British protested vigorously against the agreement. Commander Harry Luke, Chief Commissioner, expressed himself strongly against it, since early in July the Armenian government had received a consignment of British weapons.* He described the agreement as 'almost an act of revolt against Great Britain' – unusually exaggerated language for Luke, for in truth the Armenian government had hardly any other option at the time.

---

*25,000 Ross rifles, 400 light machine guns, 40,000 uniforms, 500 telescopes (W. L. Woodward and R. Butler (eds.), *Documents on British Foreign Policy*, 1st series (London, 1947–63), vol. XII. p. 629). They arrived at the Georgian port of Poti; the Georgians took 27½ per cent of the consignment as payment for permitting it to cross their territory. Prime Minister Ohandjanian said that he feared that the consignment had arrived six months too late. Moreover, according to another memorandum by Revd. H. W. Harcourt, the Canadian Ross rifle

is heavy, difficult to manipulate, and the mechanism is of a complicated type, easily thrown out of order – and no straps for carrying them were sent out with those that came to Armenia: it has also an almost useless bayonet which, on all the examples examined at Erevan, did not fit properly, but wobbled about. It is scarcely to be expected that a weapon that proved useless to trained British troops could be of much service to the ignorant peasants of Armenia, yet

The Treaty of Sèvres

By coincidence, 10 August was also the day upon which the treaty of Sèvres was signed. This was the peace treaty with Turkey that the great powers had been labouring, but more often not labouring, to produce ever since the end of the war. This treaty has been widely condemned as imperialist, as the imposition of the dictates of the Western powers for their own political and economic ends, and there is certainly some truth in that. But it was not nearly so imperialist, so greedy for other people's territory, as the conditions which the Kemalists demanded and ultimately obtained. Let us remember again a central fact: the Ottoman empire was itself an *empire*, a system of government of one ethno–linguistic group over a number of others. The treaty of Sèvres provided for what we describe today as *decolonisation* – with the difference that many of the territories liberated from Turkish rule were taken under the wing, either overtly or covertly, of other powers. (Parallels for this can be found today, too.) Certainly there was nothing imperialist in the six articles of the treaty (88–93) that related directly to Armenia. In them, Turkey recognised Armenia as a free and independent state (88); the signatories agreed to let the president of the United States determine the boundary between the two (which would pass through the provinces of Erzerum, Trebizond, Van and Bitlis), and to prescribe an outlet for Armenia to the sea (89). Turkey renounced any claim to the ceded land; and the powers who drew up the treaty also made it clear that Armenia would have to assume financial obligations in proportion to the former Turkish territory which was awarded to her. (Since, in the treaty, the Western powers proposed to cripple the new Turkey financially, it is curious that for all their expressions of sympathy for 'starving Armenia', they proposed to transfer some of these financial burdens on to Armenia too.) Articles 91 to 93 referred to the establishment of a boundary commission, to the determination of the Caucasian frontiers (by the states themselves, or failing that, by the Western powers), and to the protection of non-Armenian citizens within Armenia.[145]

The fault with the Armenian clauses of the treaty of Sèvres was not that they were imperialist, it was that they were more than a year out of date. They embody the wistful idealism of the old order – albeit underpinned by the Western money-grubbing that even the current of liberal idealism that had

---

they, called up in September, had in October to face the Turks with the weapons in their hands. In the rain and snow of the exposed positions in the region of Kars these rifles rapidly became jammed, and with an unworkable weapon in their hands the soldiers lost all confidence. It is not too much to say that the Ross rifle had much to do with the degeneration of the Armenian army in three weeks from what appeared to British and French military observers a stout and well-disciplined force to the disorganised rabble which gave up one position after another with very little fighting. It is noticeable that the demoralisation did not take place to any large degree in the artillery, where the men had good guns and knew how to handle them (FO 371/6265.46, p. 5).

coursed through so wide a span of public and official opinion after the first world war had been unable to sweep away. A glance at the financial clauses of the treaty will show that the West had, in over 70 years of direct financial transactions with the Ottoman empire, lost none of its desire to squeeze the last piastre out of Turkey. According to the Sèvres treaty, the Turkish finance minister was to be wholly subject to a financial commission composed of representatives of Britain, France and Italy. No budget could be presented without the approval of this commission. This was capitalistic imperialism of the crudest and most blatant sort. Little wonder that the treaty was denounced in both Moscow and Ankara. The shame was that the eminently reasonable Armenian clauses should have appeared amidst all the farrago of greed that the treaty represented.

The treaty of Sèvres was never implemented. It would have required another war to impose it now, over a year after Mustafa Kemal had held his congress at Erzerum; and none of the Allies had any intention of committing any more men against Turkey, at least in Asia. (Indeed, just one month earlier, on 7 July, the last Allied troops had left Batum.) It remains a mystery how any of the signatories expected the treaty to take shape on the ground; it seems most likely that, in the face of all the evidence, they still clung to the myth that the Turks were incompetent idlers, incapable of organising themselves for a nationalist end. Even in mid-1920 many people who should have known better still dismissed Kemal and his followers as mere 'brigands'.

Cilicia

It is now necessary to break the narrative of events surrounding the Republic of Armenia, and, by way of interlude (like the intermezzo in Henze's *The Bassarids*) to travel to a parallel situation, in this case 600 miles south-westwards, to Cilicia.

Ottoman Cilicia – that is, the *sanjaks* of Marash, Kozan (Sis), Jebel Bereket and Adana – was a region of mixed and turbulent populations. Most of the population figures are contrived;[146] but it is fairly clear that the Armenians (both urban and peasant) were a large minority in a region where no one religious or ethnic group constituted a clear majority, as a result of their continuous habitation of the land since medieval times, when they had reconstituted their homeland there at the time of the Crusades.

Cilicia was the scene of fierce rivalry in the period just after the first world war. The Armenians, while they still confidently entertained extensive designs, wanted it to be part of the new, sea-to-sea Armenian state. The French felt it should be theirs, in accordance with the Sykes–Picot agreement (1916) and the St Jean de Maurienne agreement (1917). The British found themselves in occupation of it at the end of 1918, and showed some reluctance to hand it over to France, since they had done most of the fighting in the Levant (67,000

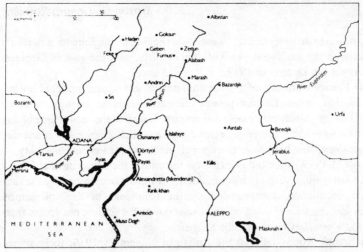

Map 9. Cilic

troops, as against 7,000).[147] And finally, it became the target for the first deadly attacks of the Nationalist Turks.

To take account of the initial conflicting jealousies and aspirations, a bizarre system was constructed. France was to control the civilian administration of Cilicia, while (from February to November 1919) Britain provided the forces for military occupation. In both, spheres of activity were ill-defined, and the source of confusion and difficulty. Moreover, the civilian administration was hampered by working through the existing Ottoman Turkish system. Functionaries could only be appointed or dismissed from Constantinople; everything was done in conformity with Ottoman law.[148]

Nevertheless by mid-January 1919 a measure of agreement had been reached; Colonel Edouard Brémond was appointed by General Allenby to be Chief Administrator, OETA North – that is, Cilicia.[149]

In Cilicia, France had two political options; that they were mutually incompatible meant that, when one failed, the other could be adopted. The first was to occupy the country directly, in the hope of turning it into a colony. This was the policy adopted at first. It entailed squashing any signs of resurgent Turkish nationalism, and using the Armenians to do the imperialist dirty work for her. The Armenians, naïvely trusting her as a great civilising power, willingly assumed the role designed for them. Any humanity that France showed towards Armenians – such as repatriating 60,000[150] survivors of the deportations from Cilicia (an estimated 200,000 had been murdered) – was purely incidental to her main designs.

France's other option was to work with Turkey. She held 61 per cent of the Ottoman Public Debt, the tobacco monopoly (*régie des tabacs*), as well as important concessions for Turkish railway construction, mining, ports and so forth. With this set against her hankering to supplant Germany as a great economic power, it would appear to be in France's interest to work with Turkey, should direct occupation fail. (It might even be more profitable.) It comes as no surprise to learn that France was the first of the Entente powers to open talks with the embryonic Turkish Nationalists, with the visit of Georges Picot to Angora in December 1919.

Despite France's attitude of blatant commercial adventure, it should not be overlooked that as an Entente power she had a right to occupy parts of Ottoman Turkey, which was a defeated empire. It was to the misfortune of the Armenians – who had suffered so extensively from that empire – that she did not choose to exercise her power more widely and with greater responsibility.

For most of 1919, while the British were in control, the occupation of Cilicia proceeded fairly quietly, apart from initial disturbances occasioned by the fact of foreign occupation, compounded by the behaviour of the still armed Armenian Legion, who showed an enthusiasm more for settling old scores than for creating a new, harmonious Cilicia.

When French troops relieved the British in November 1919, their arrival coincided with the first active stirrings of the Kemalist movement. It was very soon apparent that the task of controlling Cilicia was beyond them. Moreover, there was the odd case of indiscipline and corruption. A Syrian lady put it thus (and the same was true at this time for both Syria and Cilicia): *'Les anglais ont envoyés les fils de leurs "Lords", mais les français ont envoyés leurs valets.'*[151] Such was the stuff of the *mission civilisatrice*.

The most critical places for the French were the outlying towns which spanned the unclear border between them and the Kemalists: Urfa and Marash in the east, and in the west the towns on the Konya–Adana road, by the Cilician Gates, notably Bozanti. Marash showed the situation most starkly: initially, when the French took over, there were 300 Armenians serving with the French as Légion d'Orient, 30 Algerian cavalry and 80 French soldiers, all under French officers. This handful was later increased to about 3,000, the additions being mostly Armenians and French colonial troops.[152] Commanding them all was General Quérette, a Gilbertian figure whose grandiloquence was only matched by his incompetence.

The Turks tested the temper of the French in late 1919: a few rifle shots were fired in the town on one occasion (and no action was taken); and leading Turks made a great fuss over the raising of the French flag over the citadel of Marash.[153] Then leading Turkish notables, confident but not over-confident of their strength, invited their Armenian counterparts to see if they could plan the future of Marash together. Meeting in the Ulu Djami on Friday, 16 January 1920, the Turks put this proposal to the Armenians: join us, fight with us against the French, and we will live together as partners. The Armenian response was 'indefinite',[154] and on the evidence of Turkish treachery over the last 40 years it had to be so; however, a second meeting was arranged for 20 January. But it never took place. The chief Muslim notable, Dayyi Zade, called it off. No understanding between the two was possible, he said.

Meanwhile, commerce in the city had come to a standstill, with the shops of both communities closed. Large numbers of armed Turks were entering the city from outside. Then, in the situation of extreme tension, firing broke out on 21 January between Turks and French. A full-scale urban battle soon developed, with Turks firing indiscriminately at French and Armenians, and the French firing on the fortified houses that the Turks had turned into military posts, and setting fire to the Turkish quarters of the city.[155] General Quérette seemed to have little real idea of whom – or what – his forces were fighting; he made no attempt to stem the flow of armed Turks entering Marash from the north.

The battle continued relentlessly and brutally, the French bombarding the Turkish parts of the city, and the Turks aiming volleys of rifle fire from their fortified houses. Once battle had been joined, the Turks threw all scruples to the wind, and killed with that unrestrained ferocity that is characteristic of Turkish warfare. Dr C. F. H. Crathern, a YMCA secretary who was in Marash during the battle, reported harrowing stories: of children taken from their mothers' arms and ripped up with knives, of young and old women with their flesh savagely torn by dum-dum bullets, of the betrayal of women and children, who, having given themselves up under promise of protection, were slaughtered with hatchets and knives.[156]

French reinforcements were sighted by Crathern on 8 February in the valley to the south of Marash, and they broke through to the besieged city later that day; this, together with the fact that the Turks were visibly weakening, brought relief and hope to the Armenians.[157] But bad communications* and feeble leadership from Quérette led to a ghastly reversal of fate, like the peripeteia of a Greek tragedy.

The same evening that the reinforcements were seen, Quérette received an order from the French divisional commander in Adana, General Dufieux, to evacuate Marash if the situation was not re-established in the city within 24 hours.[158] The orders were apparently garbled; but Dufieux was nevertheless prepared to sacrifice Marash, since French forces had come under pressure in Urfa. On the 9th the battle was still continuing and General Quérette obeyed the command to the letter. Crathern wrote in his diary: 'General Quérette informed us today that he has received orders to evacuate the city at midnight on the 9th. This news caused alarm through all the compounds. ... Women and children are crazed with fear.'[159] Quérette, however, was able to delay the evacuation by 24 hours.

On the following day the Turks believed themselves beaten. The Turkish leader, Dr Mustafa, got in touch with the Americans, hoping that they would act as mediators between him and the French.[160] But he was unaware that the decision had been taken, that the French would withdraw that night.

The Armenians too were in the dark, although they felt that the afternoon of the 10th was their hour of dazzling triumph. The Turks were evacuating the

---

*'The French have no wireless, no aeroplanes, no telegraph, no armoured cars, and to make the situation worse, neither food nor ammunition for an extended siege.' – Crathern, diary entry for 25 January.

town; the attacks had ceased; the sufferings of the past 20 days were justified by this victory. Congratulations and smiles.

Then the French withdrawal began. Most troops left between 6.00 and 9.00 p.m.; General Quérette and his staff at 10.30.[161]

The Armenians were gripped by panic as they realised what was happening. Barely comprehending the terrible reversal, as many as could gathered together a few belongings and followed the retreating French.

As they were leaving, transformed from victors to destitute refugees, the winter stretched out an icy hand to them: a blizzard raged round the mountains and gorges as they passed. Behind, the city of Marash blazed, lighting up the midnight snow, as they trudged onward in yet another familiar frightful Armenian exodus. Islahiye was 75 miles to the south; three days' march. Three thousand refugees managed to straggle after the troops, but in the weather conditions – which grew worse the further they marched – about a thousand of these perished.

A second column fared worse. Leaving a few hours after the first refugee convoy, unguarded by soldiers, about 2,000 Armenians tried to get out of Marash, but most were shot or hacked to pieces before they could leave the city. Only about 200 escaped; of these only 20 reached Islahiye.[162]

In Marash itself a truce was arranged by the Americans: the Armenians were to hand over their weapons, then they would be spared. Peace of a sort returned to Marash on 12 February, although many of the 10,000 Armenians who remained died from starvation during the punitive curfews ('white massacre') that the Kemalists imposed.

The battle of Marash was a catastrophic, pointless disaster for the Armenians, the French and the Allies. Lord Curzon commented thus on 13 March 1920:

> As long as the British were in occupation of Cilicia and Syria no trouble had occurred. ... In deference, however, to the insistent pressure of the French government, we had in November last evacuated both Cilicia and Syria.[163]

What had happened? In Cilicia there had occurred the lamentable events in Marash, by which had been placed in jeopardy not only the position of the French in Cilicia, but the entire fortunes of the Allies in the Middle East.

'Un frémissement d'orgueil galvanisa le Kémalisme encore hésitant,' comments Brémond.[164] Marash was the beginning of the end for the French in Cilicia; thereafter they beat a steady retreat until they finally quit altogether in October 1921. Yet, while the French still considered that Turkish nationalism might be as pliable as the old sultans, their abandonment of Cilicia was less a retreat than a change of balance. Only when Kemal proved to be an implacable nationalist dictator did their imperial ambition have to be satisfied with their control of Syria and Lebanon.

As the French were preparing to quit Marash, so the Kemalist attack on Urfa began (9 February). For almost two months a small French garrison held out against the Kemalists. By 7 April they had eaten their last transport mule. The French commander, Major Hauger, thereupon negotiated terms with the Turkish chief: he would hand the town over to the Turks if the garrison could receive a safe-conduct out of the town. When they were passing through a ravine known as the defile of Feris Pasha, about ten miles out of Urfa, they were attacked and slaughtered almost to a man.[165] It was another sickening piece of Turkish treachery, and it makes one understand why the Armenians were wary of the invitations from the Turks to co-operate with them.

There is one town in Cilicia, now obliterated from the map, where the struggle of the Armenians against a relentless Turkish siege was at its most heroic, and most sublimely tragic. The remote town of Hadjin lay in the northern part of the province of Adana, on the very edge of Cilicia. It was 'perched upon a knoll in the middle of a deep basin, formed by bare rugged mountains, which command it on every side' (Capt. Townshend).[166] Out of a pre-war population of 25,000–30,000, 8,000 were repatriated in 1919 from the deserts and death camps, to rebuild their life in their native city, continuously inhabited for hundreds of years.[167]

Hadjin slowly re-established itself throughout 1919. In early February 1920 the town received news of the events in Marash. Many considered that Hadjin would be attacked next. In March Kemalist irregulars – *chétés* – were sighted. Snow still lay on the ground. A week or so later an old Turkish woman on horseback conveyed a message to the Hadjintzis, to the effect that an organised effort was being made to drive the French from Cilicia; Armenians and other Christians would not be harmed if they remained neutral. To which the Hadjintzis replied that they had no quarrel with the Turkish forces, but merely wished to protect their own homes and loved ones. Besides, there were no French in Hadjin.[168]

The French, for their part, sensing the imminence of an attack upon Hadjin, sent a high-flown, rhetorical message: keep up your courage, in ten days there will not be a single Turk to oppose you! But nothing was seen of the French; an aircraft circled overhead twice in March, the second time dropping a few parcels and a message saying that French reinforcements were coming, who would clear the Turks from Hadjin. The Hadjintzis should prepare a landing strip for the aircraft, which would return next day. Feverishly the population worked to be ready to receive the aircraft. On the following day the aircraft was heard – it approached nearer – it circled above – and it flew away. That was the last the defenders of Hadjin saw of the French.[169]

Women and children were shortly afterwards evacuated from the city, and 300 orphans were taken to the American missionaries' summer compound on the mountainside.[170] From this vantage point the six Americans were to witness almost all the subsequent battle.

Battle began in earnest on 31 March 1920: the Turks advanced over the western mountain range, forcing the Armenians to entrench themselves behind rocks at the foot of the mountains. Then more of them appeared from the south.

The Armenians, for their part, commanded by Sarkis Djebedjian (a man who had fought for two years alongside Andranik) could count on a fighting force about 600 strong, armed with about as many rifles, sent in by mule by the French.[171] They believed that they only had to deal with a band of outlaws, perhaps 300 strong, not against a movement of Turkish national resurgence.

For about a month the Hadjintzis fought in the mountains, but then they were forced back into their town. Then the Turks, who by now completely encircled Hadjin, started shelling; on 4 April, Easter Sunday, they brought up a machine-gun and directed it on to the city. Bombs fell on the city, too. All around the town the Turks were building trenches; more cannon and machine-guns appeared.

But the Hadjintzis fought back fiercely, and gave the Turks no quarter. Although they had been driven back into Hadjin, they were on the offensive by mid-April. The Turks were compelled to quit their entrenchments. For this the American missionaries in their summer compound were blamed; the Turks alleged they were sending secret signals by candle flame.

Djebedjian took great care to strengthen the fortified outposts all the time. Firing was continuous, but the Turks let forth an especially heavy barrage each day just before dawn and just after nightfall.[172]

During May the American missionaries attempted to mediate between the warring parties, but their efforts were in vain since the Turks did not allow them to proceed normally; they were obstructed, and eventually fired on, as they walked the perilous way from their summer compound to the town, squashy with bloated corpses.

By mid-June the battle was raging again. Once or twice the Turks managed to reach the edge of the city, and to hold their position for a few hours, but in each case the Armenians fought back relentlessly and expelled them.

One day in late June the Armenians began a particularly heavy attack, an hour after midnight.[173] The Turks at the time were short of ammunition, and they replied with whatever they had – machine-guns, cannons, bombs, rifle fire. But the Armenians were advancing steadily out of the city. The Turks tried to frighten them back in, but were forced to give way. Everywhere there was the din of battle shrieks, yells, groans; the Turks called on God to favour them, the Armenians cried continually, *'Haratch, haratch!'* ('Forward, forward!') The missionaries in their compound could not tell the position of either side. A huge assault on the front gate, and swarms of armed men poured in shouting – surged over the building. Who were they? If they were Turks, it was the end for them and the 300 orphans. Doors were broken down; more troops poured in.

Dawn began to break, and with a sense of relief as broad as the lightening sky the missionaries realised they were Armenians. The Hadjintzis had broken out of the confines of their town, and captured the valley and a portion of the surrounding mountains.[174]

But despite this incredible action, and the amazing bravery that had made it possible, their days were numbered unless they received reinforcements; they were still surrounded, and their lines were now longer and less protected. They again tried to contact the French – a number of messengers got through – but no help came.

The Armenians took all the orphan children into the city for safety. Battle raged around the compound for the next two days; it became a scene of fallen plaster and blood-spattered walls. The missionaries were frequently forced to take shelter in the cellar, beneath stairs slippery with blood. Bullets rained pitilessly on the building, and a shell whined overhead. On the third day after its capture the Armenians became convinced that the compound was not worth holding. A sense of doom and a barely suppressed panic seized them. Their anguish was palpable, as they rushed in all directions. But the decision had been made, and at dusk they retreated back into the town. On the following day the Turks re-occupied the compound (after a sleepless night for the missionaries); intense firing was resumed almost at once. The American missionaries, for their part, escaped to Kayseri.[175]

Throughout the burning Anatolian summer the Hadjintzis continued their brave defence of their town; but as the sun began to decline, lengthening the shadows, so their strength diminished and so, correspondingly, the power of the Kemalists increased. So, too, their hope for French reinforcements proved wholly illusory. Even in August they had been hoping for the French to appear – or rather for the French to sanction the arrival of Armenian volunteers (who made up part of the French army of occupation), who, even if they could not actively assist them, would at least be able to cover their retreat.

But none came. And finally, in mid-October, with only 480 men left, they decided to abandon the city. This way and that they fled, in twos and threes, south towards Feke and on to Adana. Those who could not escape were butchered. Thus was a town of 30,000 Armenians in 1914 reduced to 8,000 in 1919, and to 480 fleeing exiles by the following year.[176]

The siege of Hadjin astonishes us by the daring and dour determination of its defenders. Yet the bravery of these men – what did it bequeath to their children? Unlike the defenders of Tegea, it handed down no city blossoming in freedom, but a charred ruin full of blackening corpses decaying in the sun, uninhabited to this day; and there are a few elderly men in the Hadjin quarter of Beirut – and until recently one in west London – who, over many cups of coffee, will relate the story of the siege of Hadjin, and the bravery of its heroes. They were a witness that Armenians would not die like sheep, and that the price of expelling them from their ancient native city was very high indeed.

Throughout Hadjin's terrible siege the political and military situation in Cilicia had been changing – for the Armenians, for the worse. Sis and Bozanti were forced to capitulate; Adana, Tarsus and Mersina came under extreme pressure. A cease-fire (for which the French were compelled to go to Ankara) served only to give time to the Kemalists to regroup. In early August, when the French seemed to be almost on their knees, the Armenians (together with the few Assyro–Chaldaeans) declared the region between the Sehun and Jehun rivers self-governing. The French demanded that the official Armenian bodies condemn this action. They refused. On the contrary, endorsing the Sehun–Jehun action, two days later they declared the independence of Cilicia under French mandate. The day following (5 August 1920) Mihran Damadian, veteran of the Sasun uprising and now representative in Adana of the Armenian National Delegation entered the office of the governor of Adana, together with other Armenian functionaries and representatives of all Armenian political parties, and proclaimed himself governor of Cilicia, under French mandate.[177]

It was a protest, rather than a serious attempt to seize power. All Cilician Armenians were appalled by the way French policy was shifting towards the Turks, and failing to introduce any measures to protect the Armenians. The French appeared more and more to be collaborating with their wartime enemies, the murderers of the Armenians. (The soul of the Turk, Armenians surmised, had not been magically laundered by the coming of Mustafa Kemal.) This action was to remind the French of their obligations to the Armenians.

But the independence of Cilicia lasted only about an hour. Colonel Brémond ordered the telephone to be cut, and told Damadian to stop *'cette comédie ridicule'*. Damadian replied that he would have to be compelled to come out. A sharpshooter took up a position opposite the government building, and beside him a cannon was trained on it too. Damadian and his colleagues left. The French henceforth ceased all official relations with him, to the obvious delight of the Turks.[178]

It is fitting to end this account of the French in Cilicia with the siege of Aintab, for it shows clearly the qualities in evidence during the brief sojourn of the French in the region: the unremitting battle between the Kemalist Turks and the Armenians, the bravery and victory of the Armenians in their determination not to be ousted from their native city, and their betrayal by a political decision of the French. It is a paradigm of what the Armenians experienced under the French. Of course there were other sieges; but Aintab is memorable for its vividness, and its achievement.[179]

In late 1919 the Aintabtzi Armenians sensed they were becoming caught in the cross-fire between Kemalist Turks and occupying French, and attempted to set up a conciliation committee with the Turks. At this time they believed the Kemalist propaganda that the Turks wanted merely to rid themselves of the French, and only later did it become clear to them that the Kemalists were just as keen to throw the Armenians out[180] – to 'cleanse' the land of Armenians, in the manner of almost all Turks of the past 40 years.

When the Armenians of Aintab heard of the siege of Marash, the three parties – Hunchak, Dashnak and Ramkavar – formed themselves into a united front (*Azgayin Miutiun*, or national union), and showed that they were on the alert for any Turkish moves – to the displeasure of the Turks, who were themselves on the look-out for a chance to attack the Armenians.

The Turks believed that they had their opportunity on 1 April 1920, when a large part of the French forces left south for Killis. They launched an attack on the Armenians, but quite failed to subdue them.[181] For two weeks the Armenians, without French aid (for the French troops which remained were quartered outside the city), fought off the Turks.[182] French reinforcements arrived on 16 April: during the succeeding months they often fought bravely, but with an alarming inconsistency (thus, in late May they were advising the Armenians to quit, since they were incapable of bringing help themselves, while in November French forces under General Goubeau entered the city, only to be withdrawn soon after.[183]) But the Turks were kept at bay, and the knowledge that for the Armenians there was really no alternative to fighting stiffened their resistance; for if they laid down their arms and evacuated they would all be murdered before they got to Killis, in accordance with the usual manner in which the Turks treated defeated enemies going into exile.

The general truce proclaimed in late May hardened into an armistice.[184] But all three parties – French, Turks and Armenians – knew that it would only be temporary. On 29 July the Turks, believing that they had regrouped their forces sufficiently, broke the armistice with the French. Throughout September the French found themselves under increasing Turkish pressure, and twice asked the Armenians to break their armistice with the Turks, the second time (29 September) adding a veiled threat. The Armenians accordingly did so on 1 October; and the whole of Aintab again raged with battle. With Goubeau's entry into the city it appeared that the Turks had taken on more than they had bargained for, although his sudden withdrawal appeared to give them a chance. However, they were seriously weakened, and on 8 February 1921 they surrendered to the French.[185]

Two weeks later the French and Turks signed a treaty which included, among other things, acceptance of the relevant clauses of the treaty of Sèvres. Armenians were to participate in the government of Aintab. For them it was the vindication of a long struggle, which had ended with the Turks well and truly defeated.*[186]

But the reversal at Aintab was in its way as grim a nemesis as that suffered by the Armenians at Marash. While Aintab was still a scene of dust and smoke, rent by the rattle of rifle fire and the thud of exploding shells, France was planning to negotiate the quickest way out of Cilicia. The Second London Conference (21 February–14 March 1921) had been called to try to amend the treaty of Sèvres so that it would be workable. During it the French prime minister, Aristide Briand, negotiated a separate peace with the Kemalists. The

---

*It is puzzling why the Turks renamed the city *Gazi*antep, signifying victory and success.

French would abandon Cilicia, including Aintab and Killis. And what would they obtain in return? Clause G of the agreement read:

> Franco–Turkish economic collaboration, with a right of priority for the concessions to be granted for the purpose of improvement and economic development in Cilicia (the regions evacuated by French troops) and also in the vilayets of Mamuret el-Aziz, Diyarbekir and Sivas, insofar as such development will not have been undertaken directly by the Ottoman government or by Ottoman nationals with the help of national capital.
>
> A concession to a French group for the mines of Argana-Maden.
>
> Concessions involving monopoly or preference will be exploited by partnerships constituted in accordance with Ottoman law.
>
> The widest possible partnership between Ottoman and French capital.[187]

France had found that direct, military colonialism had failed, and was abandoning the strategy of confrontation for one of economic collaboration. But the overriding aim was the same – to harness Turkey to the French economy. In the face of this the *mission civilisatrice*, friendship going back to the time of the Crusades, even military alliance during the world war was as nothing, and disappeared like civilised values in a crowd of football hooligans. And the cost? Tens of thousands of Armenians again compelled to quit their homes, forced to trudge across the frontiers agreed upon by diplomats, with only so much as they could carry; this time permanently. Seldom can Lord Byron's admonition have been more relevant:

> Trust not for freedom to the Franks;
> They have a king who buys and sells.

The accord signed on 9 March between Briand and Bekir Sami Bey was, however, not ratified by the Turkish assembly at Ankara. It was not extreme enough for them. (A further agreement, signed by Henri Franklin-Bouillon and Yusuf Kemal Bey officially terminated the French occupation of Cilicia six months later.[188]) But the Armenians understood the direction of French policy, and saw that their only option was to quit. The Turks, now masters, gave some of those who thought they might stay a few worthless assurances, but the end result was the same for all of them: harassment, oppression and confiscation, cemented by an icy, inhuman bureaucracy.

In this way, double-crossed by the French, about 50,000 Armenians were forced out of a land which had been theirs for a thousand years, to become refugees, mostly in Lebanon and Syria. There were other factors, too, besides French treachery, which forced them out: above all ruthless Turkish racialism. A measure of blame too must attach to the Armenians themselves, for quite so enthusiastically filling the role assigned to them by French colonial ambitions; however, the French had been expected to come in as protectors and guarantors, occupying Cilicia impartially until the signature of an enforceable treaty, and in such circumstances a pro-French policy was unavoidable for Armenians. Given the history of their subjection to their Turkish imperial rulers, especially during the years 1915–16, a pro-Turkish orientation was impossible for them.

The Armenian Republic in the Autumn of 1920

Cilicia, and especially Marash, was the theatre in which the Kemalists first tested their strength. But the first region where they enforced their terms was the Republic of Armenia, and it is there that we now return.

The outlook for Armenia in early September 1920 was dark. Internally, the government was in control after the May uprisings, and indeed the area of its control had been extended by the war of June–July, even though the government had temporarily abandoned its claim to the disputed territories. But clashes were continuing, and Tatar villages were continuing to proclaim themselves as *shuras*, that is, city-states which were no-go areas for the government. In the alliance of Turkism and Bolshevism, Turkism appeared to be the stronger partner, since in Armenia the intention was not so much revolution as wrecking the country altogether. In Baku, the Communist International called a Congress of Peoples of the East[189] (August–September 1920), which was bitterly hostile to Armenia, not only because Dashnak Armenia was outside the Soviet orbit, but because of the same need felt by the Bolsheviks to support the stance of the Turks in order to maintain their pact. Under the cover of workers' internationalism, a number of cold-blooded Turkists were present at the congress, scheming Hagen-like for the destruction of Armenia. Chief of them was the educated intellectual Dr Behaeddin Shakir, who never rested from plotting and making propaganda for the elimination of Armenia.

Internally, the country was beset by problems, too. Chief of them were the continuing lawlessness of the armed bands of Dashnaktsutiun (the 'Mauserists'), whom the Dashnak government itself was unable to control; and the disastrous economic situation. Firuz Kazemzadeh says, quoting Soviet historian B. A. Borian:

> From September 1918 to January 1920 the state treasury of Armenia had an income of 30 million roubles, while it spent 300 million. The deficit of 270 million was covered by the ever ready printing press, bringing about inevitable inflation. The value of the Armenian rouble decreased with astonishing rapidity. In March 1920 an American dollar was worth 1,000 Armenian roubles; in November it bought 28,000 roubles.[190]

As regards her relations with the outside world, Armenia was appearing isolated and deserted. The British were gone, and any kind of Allied support seemed quite remote. Armenia's leaders clung to the treaty of Sèvres as though it were a magic talisman. No progress had been made in the negotiations with Legrand for a 'treaty of friendship' with Soviet Russia (indeed it was 11 October before Legrand even deigned to visit Yerevan), and the promised Soviet mediation seemed a bodiless fiction; on the other hand, a Turko–Soviet draft treaty was initialled on 24 August. Under article 1 of this treaty the signatories 'declined to recognise any treaty imposed on the other', and Soviet Russia said she would not recognise any agreement not ratified by Kemal's Grand National Assembly in Ankara; and under article 3, 'In order to secure ... unhindered relations between the two countries, the two countries agree to take all necessary measures to ensure the traffic of goods and people, free from all impediments.'[191]

The previous March Lenin had stressed the importance of the Sovietisation of the Caucasus in a wire to Orjonikidze; as a result, a special Caucasian Bureau (*Kavburo*) had been set up, with the aim of installing Soviet regimes in the region.[192] If we recall the links between Armenia's adversary and her alleged mediator, the prospect for any genuine mediation between her and the Kemalists was dim indeed. Nevertheless, there was far from total accord between Soviet Russia and Kemalist Turkey: the draft treaty (initialled on 24 August) was not ratified in Ankara for one important reason, that the Soviet state planned that some of the land of Turkish Armenia should be awarded to Armenia – an idea as heretical now in Ankara as it had been in Constantinople in the days of Abdul Hamid.

Now, as ever, the main threat to Armenia came from the Turks. But within Turkish strategy we must distinguish two strands. One sought to impose a military defeat on Armenia solely for reasons connected with the Nationalist struggle (against the Allies and the puppet sultan's government). A defeat on Armenia would serve two purposes: it would forestall the threat of an Allied attack on Turkey from the east, and it would hasten the flow of Soviet weapons and gold roubles from Azerbaijan. The chief proponent of this course was Mustafa Kemal himself. The other strand was that of the fanatical anti-Armenian extremists, whose pan-Turkism dictated the extermination of Armenians. Chief of these was General Kiazim Karabekir,[193] commander of the eastern front, a man whose desire to eliminate Armenia was only matched by his brilliant instinct for military strategy – no rash Enver-like dreamer he. Thus not only were there divergent aims to the parties of the Turko–Soviet alliance, but even within the Turkish camp there were differences. Each party sought to make maximum use of the others, but as they struggled over Armenia their differences were to be brought into the open.

As early as February 1920 Kemal had himself been meditating on a Caucasian offensive, to reach the Bolsheviks who were on the northern slopes of the Caucasus. Karabekir, in Erzerum, eagerly mobilised and equipped his troops by the spring. Kemal was, however, sceptical of the strength of the Eastern Army, and forbade any troop movements. But Karabekir pressed for the attack to start. In May he made three separate requests to the Grand National Assembly in Ankara for permission to attack Armenia, on the 6th, the 9th and the 30th.[194] (To Karabekir's third request Kemal replied, 'You cannot succeed with a section of $3\frac{1}{2}$ men.'[195]) Acting on his own, Karabekir sent an ultimatum demanding the surrender of Sarakamish within 48 hours, claiming that the forests were needed for construction in Erzerum. The Armenian government refused to accede to the demand, and Karabekir took no action in enforcing his ultimatum.

To a further request from Kiazim Karabekir, Mustafa Kemal gave orders for a partial mobilisation of the Eastern Army on 6 June.[196] But the support of Soviet Russia was essential, and some days later a note (dated 3 June) reached Kemal from Soviet foreign affairs commissar Chicherin, which spelled out the conditions for a Soviet–Kemalist friendship treaty.[197] One of these conditions was that the peoples living in Turkish Armenia (Chicherin's term), Kurdistan, the district of Batum, eastern Thrace and regions inhabited jointly by Turks and Arabs should be given the right to decide their own fate. Refugees living in Soviet Russia and those made homeless against their will were to be accepted back, and allowed to participate in a referendum. So the alert was cancelled, to Karabekir's displeasure.

The Turks were not at all pleased with Chicherin's note of 3 June, and they orchestrated all their most chauvinist arguments against it. Karabekir comments:

In Turkey there has been neither an Armenia nor territory inhabited by Armenians. . . . Those |Armenians| living in Turkey committed murders and massacres, and have escaped to Iran, America, Europe, and some of them to Armenia. How is it possible to call back these murderers and give them the right to vote?[198]

When Chicherin persisted, and put the same proposal on 13 August to the Turkish delegation in Moscow, he was told, 'No Armenian provinces have ever existed in Turkey.'[199]

Chicherin's repetition of these principles shows that he meant them and was not just making propaganda. Nevertheless his theoretical position is hard to square with the actions on the ground of the Bolshevik forces in Transcaucasia: the simultaneous occupation of Karabagh, Nakhichevan and Zangezur, the adoption of a position towards Armenians very similar to that of the pre-Boshevik Musavatist regime, and the use made by the Bolsheviks of notorious Armenocides like Khalil, Enver and Nuri.

But although Chicherin's note cooled the Kemalists' ardour to strike at Armenia, a local dispute was sufficient to inflame relations between Ankara and Yerevan. The district (*okrug*) of Olti was the most westerly part of the province of Kars. In pre-war days its Turko–Tatar population had been over five times greater than all the Armenians there. It was a district claimed by

Armenia, Azerbaijan and (without much conviction) Georgia. Only briefly in 1919 had Armenia been able to establish her authority there; for many months it had been a *shura*, or self-governing Tatar city-state.

In June 1920, as part of the war waged by the Armenian government on all sides in order to impose its rule of law, Armenia occupied part of the district, including the rich coal-mines. The Turkish Nationalists protested, and demanded an Armenian withdrawal, basing their demands on the treaties of Batum and Brest-Litovsk. In return the Armenian government claimed that such demands were invalid, since those two treaties had been signed by the Constantinople government, against which the Nationalists were now in revolt. These exchanges continued until the end of July.[200]

Despite the chill cast on Turko–Soviet relations by Chicherin's note of 3 June, Karabekir still pressed ardently to attack Armenia. At one stage he seemed about to launch an attack without the sanction of the Grand National Assembly, and Ismet (Inönü) was compelled to make him stay his hand. In early September he travelled to Ankara, to persuade Mustafa Kemal in person of the necessity of an attack. Weighing up the possibilities – believing that the Allies would not now intervene, and that the Bolsheviks were preoccupied with the Russo–Polish war, Kemal authorised the attack to start.[201]

Winterreise

The Kemalist offensive began in late September 1920. Already, on 13 September, according to a report of Commander Luke, at least four battalions of Kiazim Karabekir's troops had forced the Armenians out of Olti.[202] On the 24th the Armenians moved, to try to repel the Turks, whereupon the latter considered that they had their pretext for launching the offensive.

The position of the Bolsheviks was equivocal at this juncture. Clearly they wanted to make as much political and military capital as possible out of the Kemalist attack on Armenia – a state with such close links with the Entente. To this end there was simultaneous pressure on Armenia in the Dilidjan region – the northern end of Armenia's frontier with Soviet Azerbaijan, where troop movements were most practicable. There was no full-scale military invasion comparable to the Turkish operation; just the occupation of a few villages, which the Communists claimed were theirs anyway under the terms of the provisional agreement of 10 August (something the Armenian government hotly denied).[203] To speak of a 'concerted Turko–Bolshevik plot to destroy Armenia' is to make a disproportionate claim; but one cannot deny Communist opportunism.

By 28 September the Turks had managed to occupy Karaurgan, the old Russo–Turkish frontier post, as well as Bardiz and Mount Ziyaret: together these three points made up a triangle, which enclosed Sarikamish. That night, the Armenians were compelled to evacuate Sarikamish.[204] On the 29th

Map 10. The Kemalist War, September-November 1920

Kaghizman fell. Captain George F. Gracey, head of the British military mission in Yerevan, sent an 'extremely urgent' cable to Commander Luke in Tiflis, conveying the request of the Armenian government for intervention to stop the Turkish advance.[205] But nothing at all was done in reply; by now, despite the pledges of the past, the emotional, massively cheered speeches (filling the speaker with a wonderfully complacent sense of doing good), Armenia was all alone, as deserted as one of the derelict caravans of deportees in 1915.

By 4 October the Turks were closer to Kars; Lieutenant-Colonel C. B. Stokes, the new Chief British Commissioner for the Caucasus, reported that they held Merdenek on the Olti–Kars road, and Novo Selim on the Sarikamish–Kars road.[206] But the Armenians were putting up a spirited fight, he implied.

By chance, on the same day, Colonel Haskell, the black-marketeer who had filled his pockets by selling to the Azerbaijanis charitable relief supplies intended for Armenia, was in London, where he was received by the Foreign Office. The man in the Eastern Department who received him was a stubborn, chilly Armenophobe, by the name of D'Arcy Godolphin Osborne, almost all of whose minutes on papers relating to the Caucasian situation betray a profound racial hatred of Armenians. Osborne missed no opportunity to belittle them, or to make them seem cowards or charlatans. He reported a self-satisfied Haskell saying of Armenia: 'The country is a desert and the people nothing but professional beggars.'[207]

The only nation at all able to stop the Turkish advance was Soviet Russia: and at this time Russia offered to arrange a Turkish withdrawal. But the terms were severe: Armenia must sever all contact with the Entente.[208] This would entail the irrevocable abandonment of the promises made in the treaty of Sèvres.

Colonel Stokes had a curious notion that the British could halt the Kemalist advance, even though there was scarcely a section of British soldiers in the entire Caucasus at the time. His John Buchan-ish idea was that the British should raise a revolt in the North Caucasus.[209] This would occupy the Bolsheviks, and turn their attentions away from giving guns and money to the Kemalists. If (for a moment) his proposal is taken seriously, it represents an overestimation of the strength of the Turko–Bolshevik accord. In the first place, although the Turks were moving forwards, capturing towns and villages in the Kars province, the Bolsheviks were *not* pressing their advance against Armenia in the region of Dilidjan. And, secondly, Lenin himself wrote on 9 October that he believed that the Kemalists were seeking Baku, a prospect he can scarcely have viewed with joy.[210] So even if an anti-Bolshevik uprising had been staged in the North Caucasus, it is unlikely that it would have changed the granite resolve of Kiazim Karabekir in any way at all.

Legrand's Phony Mediation

On 11 October Legrand, the Bolshevik plenipotentiary, arrived at last in Yerevan, and shortly afterwards made his conditions known. These were:[211]

(i)   Armenia must repudiate the treaty of Sèvres;
(ii)   Armenia must allow the Bolsheviks to use her roads and railways;
(iii)   All Armenian border disputes must be solved through the mediation of Soviet Russia.

The first was categorically rejected, and Armenia made a great display at the time of rejecting the second too, just to see if the Allies would do anything at all for them; when they did nothing, the objection was dropped and the draft Russo–Armenian treaty, initialled a week later, said in essence:

(i)   Soviet Russia recognises the independence and integrity of Armenia. Zangezur will go to Armenia; the fate of Karabagh and Nakhichevan will be settled by arbitration.
(ii)   Russia is to intervene immediately and stop the Armeno–Turkish war. A neutral zone is to be established on the 1914 frontier, and Armenian/Turkish frontier disputes are to be solved by Russia.
(iii)   Free passage through Armenia was to be granted to Communist forces *en route* for Turkey. Thirty per cent of the munitions passing through would be left for Armenia.
(iv)   Armenia accepts the mediation of Russia in solving her territorial disputes.
(v)   Soviet Russia is to give assistance to Armenia to enable her to recover economically.[212]

With this draft under his arm, Legrand left. He said he was going to Moscow, to obtain approval for the treaty, and would be back when that was done. But he dallied for many days in Baku; and by the time he was back in Yerevan, the war had progressed to such a state as to make the treaty meaningless. In the opinion of Alexander Khatisian, Legrand was only playing at negotiations; his real aim was to decrease Armenian watchfulness, so that when Armenia was sufficiently prostrate she would be unable to resist Sovietisation.[213]

Until late October the war continued only inconclusively. In the south, a fierce to-and-fro battle was fought for Igdir. In the north, Armenian forces attempted a counter-attack in the Kars sector on 14 October, but it was a failure.[214] The new recruits brought in for the attack were too raw, and the Armenian army lacked a strategist as able as Kiazim Karabekir. The Armenians were driven back to Haramvartan, north of Benliahmet, on the Sarikamish–Kars road.[215]

On the 18th Ruben Ter Minasian, minister of war, travelled to Tiflis, to try to persuade the Georgians to make common cause with the Armenians against the Turks; but they replied optimistically that their treaty with Soviet Russia protected them against the Turks.

The Fall of Kars

Six days later the Turks began a massive thrust along a front from Kars all the way down to Igdir. The Armenians fought back desperately, and recorded some successes, especially in the Igdir region.[216] Simon Vratsian notes the relief felt in Yerevan when the distant thud of the guns at Igdir ceased. The Armenian air force – three aircraft bought from the French – was in operation for the first time. But around Kars the story was one of failure, tragedy and despair. Continuing from his description of the Igdir successes, Vratsian writes:

> Events followed an altogether different course on the Kars front. . . . Aircraft were in action for the battle of Kars, as well as the armoured train *Azatamart* ('Freedom fighter'). In command of the fortress of Kars was General Pirumian, while commanding the artillery of the fortress was a Bulgarian officer, Col. Babajanov. The commander-in-chief of the Kars garrison was General Silikian, and his staff officer was Col. Vekilian. Parts of both the fortress and the field were organised laxly; the great part of the soldiers had been recently recruited and had not yet been properly integrated. In many sections the relations between officers and men were not very close. Also relations were not good between General Pirumian, General Hovsepian and Governor Ghorghanian; this attitude was reflected on the men who surrounded them. A part of the troops had been hastily armed with Ross rifles, newly received from England, which they were not accustomed

to. The rear was not organised, and anti-state elements – Bolsheviks – were able to promote difficulties. So, on 2 October, seven *versts* distant from Karayal station, near the village of Shahnalor, a train taking soldiers to the front was destroyed; fourteen wagons were smashed, and of the soldiers twelve were killed and forty-three wounded. This was the work of Bolsheviks.

In order to test the military ability of our troops, and with the intention of increasing their fighting spirit, the high command resolved to undertake a general offensive. In the event of success, the intention was to move forward. The assault did not command success. As a result of the enemy's firm resistance our troops retreated almost up to Kars. After that the initiative passed entirely into the hand of the Turks. Squeezing us step by step, on 28 October they occupied the heights of Vezenköy. For the whole of the 28th fierce battles took place; Mazmanian's regiment attempted to re-take Vezenköy. In these battles both sides sustained heavy losses. The leader of the front, General Gnduni, was wounded. On 29 October the army re-grouped. In accordance with a given command, on the morning of 30 October our troops would have gone over to a counter-attack, with the intention of occupying Vezenköy. But the 1st regiment refused to carry out the order, and did not move from its position. In despair and powerless, Col. Mazmanian committed suicide with two shots of his Mauser, in view of everyone. Even this did not influence the disposition of the troops. At that time the Turks launched an assault with great force. A confused flight began. A part of our troops and the armoured train retreated towards Mazraa. The population and the rest of the troops flung themselves down towards the gorge in the direction of the village of Prokhladnaya. Our aircraft flew to Yerevan. Kars fell into the hand of the enemy. They took prisoner Gen. Pirumian, Gen. Araratian, Col. Shaghubadian, Col. Vekilian, Col. Babajanov, Lieut-Col. Ter Arakyalian, thirty-odd officers of various ranks, and nearly 3,000 soldiers, Minister A. Babalian, Garegin Abp. Hovsepiants, provincial sub-governor Chalkhushian, mayor Norhatian and a great number of native citizens. For three days uninterruptedly the Turks looted, raped and killed, and perpetrated every kind of savagery in the city.

Minister A. Babalian, himself a witness of the events, describes with terrifying colours the cruelties done by the Turks. The Armenians were subjected to slaughter, beautiful women were taken into concubinage, able-bodied men were driven away into the interior of Turkey. Additionally, he gives shocking information of the role played by the Bolsheviks. 'On the fifth day of our captivity', he writes, 'four Armenians decorated with red bands visited us, accompanied by a few Turkish officers. They were the Armenian Communists of Kars. They were visiting the hostels and were betraying their enemies to the Turks. They were members of the Revolutionary Committee. The Turkish officers had persuaded them that they were going to hand over Kars to a Bolshevik administration, and in every way they were flattering

the dregs of the Communists. In return these men were making denunciations, and were showing them the sites of ammunition dumps and giving
them essential information about the Armenian troops and regarding the
terrain.'

However, the following extract, from the Baku Armenian-language paper
Komunist (no. 42), described in the following manner the behaviour of the
Turks in Kars:

'On 30 October the vanguard of the Turkish troops entered Kars, not
meeting any resistance at all from the Armenian forces, and occupied Kars.
Until the entry of the Turkish troops the Armenian soldiers were firmly convinced that the troops attacking Kars were Bolsheviks, and for that reason
they offered no resistance to the Turks. The same opinion was shared by the
working people of Kars, who were absolutely convinced that the troops
attacking under the red banner were the revolutionary army of Red Turkey.
But the troops which entered the city spared neither women, children nor the
aged. For five days these bloodthirsty soldiers and the Kurds perpetrated
upon the head of the peaceful population atrocities which were beyond the
imagination of man. Armenians alone they killed. Everyone was looted
indiscriminately.

'They did not even spare the Communists, who presented certificates
proving identification. In Kars alone 6,000 Armenians fell victim to Turkish
brutality.

'Mass arrests of Armenians followed the terrible massacre. They stripped
them from head to foot, and in hundreds they dispatched them to work in
Erzerum and Sarikamish. Those sent were struck down by cold and died
from hunger and suffering.

'At the same time a movement of Turkish immigrants towards the region
of Kars began. Those who saw it related with fear how a crowd of many
thousands of old men, women and children were moved in during that cold
weather to Sarikamish and Kars, to be installed as quickly as possible in
villages and houses of the Armenians who had fled.'[217]

Alexander Khatisian, who was in Yerevan at the time, describes how the
Armenian capital heard the news, and the effect it had there:

On 30 October at nearly 2.00 p.m. I noted an aircraft flying over the city
of Yerevan. Its noise could be clearly heard in the city. The plane landed. No
one could guess that that plane had brought terrible news; in the morning of
30 October the Turks had taken Kars.

At 3.00 p.m. I received an invitation to attend a government meeting.
When I entered the hall there were about twenty people present: the corps of
ministers, the president of parliament, a few members and a few military
men. A deep silence reigned. All were profoundly depressed.

Opening the session the chairman announced that he had received news that Kars had fallen. Details were sketchy, but the officer who had arrived by air announced that he personally had seen Turkish *askers* enter the city from the direction of the station, and that Armenian soldiers and people were fleeing from the city. The pilot had considered it his duty to fly on, in order to save the aircraft and to take the news of the capture of Kars to Yerevan.[218]

Eyewitnesses related on the following day (Khatisian continues) that Kars had fallen almost without a shot being fired. The collapse of the morale of the garrison was total. One detail that Khatisian mentions, which Vratsian omits, is that the killers and looters in the city were 'bandit groups [that is, *bashibozuks*] which the troops had allowed in'. Little had changed, it appeared, in a thousand years of Turkish warfare.

Summing up, Khatisian describes the fall of Kars as 'a catastrophe in all respects', adding that 'from that day the independent days of Armenia were numbered'.[219] The Armenian army had suffered a disastrous reverse; and the state had been reduced to a tiny size, crammed with cold, starving, ragged refugees. Conditions were very similar to those prevailing at the birth of independent Armenia in May 1918, when, too, a Turkish Caucasian offensive was in progress.

Further Turkish Advances

Now, as then, the Armenian leaders realised that they had to make peace with Turkey at any price. But whereas the humiliating peace of Batum (June 1918) was lightened by the prospect of the destruction of the Central powers, and the emergence of – as they thought – a new, just world led by Britain, France and the United States, now there was no hope. For Armenia at this moment the sense of abandonment, despair, desolation, misery and death was complete. All that remained was to salvage what could be saved from utter destruction.

Perhaps, though, there was a choice; alternatively to making peace with Turkey (as in 1918), she might make peace with Soviet Russia, and then obtain, as Georgia believed that *she* had obtained, protection against a Turkish attack. But the negotiations with Legrand had ground to a halt. Besides, the Dashnak leaders of Armenia listened very carefully to the advice of Colonel Stokes in Tiflis, and Lord Curzon a few days later was to endorse Stokes's suggestion that Britain favoured a Turkish orientation.[220]

In the meantime, the Turkish advance continued. By 4 November the Turks had pressed forward 30 miles east of Kars, and the Armenians attempted to halt them at Kizilchakchak; but to no avail. They were only briefly held up by heavy snow west of Alexandropol.[221]

Then on 6 November Yerevan received Kiazim Karabekir's terms for an armistice. These were:

(i)   Armenian forces were to withdraw to positions 15 kilometres east of the Arpa Chai;

(ii) Turkish forces would occupy the fortress and the railway station of Alexandropol (but not the city itself), and Turkish forces would occupy the vicinity of the city for a radius of 10 kilometres;

(iii) The Turks would guarantee order in Alexandropol.[222]

All this was to be accomplished within 24 hours.

The Armenian government accepted these terms, and hoped that negotiations would start at once. But within 24 hours Armenia had received a crushing new ultimatum. Ahmed Mukhtar, Turkey's commissar for foreign affairs, had overruled Karabekir's terms, and made fresh demands, utterly crippling for Armenia. These were, in essence:

(i)   Armenia was to give Turkey a vast quantity of war material;

(ii) Turkey was to be in control of the railway line as far north as Sanahin;

(iii) Armenian forces were to withdraw to a line Surmalu–Araxes station–Mount Kizil Ziarat–Mount Alagöz–Tanagermaz village–Novo Mikhailova–Nurikend–Talvanadagh (that is, roughly along a line from Araxes station to the north end of Lake Sevan).[223]

However defenceless she might be, this near-annihilating ultimatum was unacceptable to Armenia. It was rejected.[224] Instead, on 10 November Yerevan proposed a peace conference, based on Karabekir's initial terms. The Turkish reply came back the same day: no; the war resumes. Hostilities recommenced the following day,[225] and Kiazim Karabekir transferred his headquarters to Alexandropol.

Anticipating – or so they claimed – an Armenian counter-attack on Alexandropol, the Turks launched a fierce attack on 14 November, and forced the Armenians to retreat still further to Hamamlu, east of Alexandropol. South of it they captured Aghin. With the prospect of nothing but further defeat, ruin and cold extinction, the Armenians finally accepted Ahmed Mukhtar's armistice terms on 17 November at 3.00 p.m.[226] At last the guns were silent.

After the Kemalist War: Attitudes and Manoeuvres

At the same time, the Allies made it clear that they would help Armenia in no way whatever. None of them considered themselves bound by promises and verbal undertakings to support Armenia which had been made during the first world war and the post-war period. Armenia was now without food, without warmth, and all but overrun by a ruthless inveterate foe. The desolation and death that the country had been reduced to were reminiscent of the terrible winter of 1918–19. Moreover, this time the abandonment was international too. When Avetis Aharonian came to London in the second week of November, the Foreign Office – in the person of the Armenophobe D. G. Osborne – advised Lord Curzon not to receive him. Curzon assented. Instead, Osborne treated Aharonian to a lecture, in the form of a letter drafted by himself and signed by Curzon, which concluded with the precept: 'What we want to see now |*sic*] is concrete evidence of some constructive and administrative ability at home, instead of a purely external policy based on propaganda and mendicancy.'[227]

In Yerevan Alexander Khatisian was designated leader of the delegation to make peace with Kemalist Turkey. In these extreme circumstances making peace meant manipulating one power – Turkey or Russia – against the other, so that Armenia might gain some small advantage. And so, in these last critical days of independent Armenia, there were in effect two peace efforts continuing, one led by Khatisian, to keep the Turkish army from overrunning what remained of Armenia, and the other (albeit on ice for the moment) attentive to the Bolsheviks, to see if there was any way of reaching agreement with the Communists without actual Sovietisation of the country.

Differing views were held on the nature of the Armenia that should be saved. Some of these were dangerously hypothetical, and only concerned in a cerebral, unrealistic way the saving of the remnant, and had little regard for the real Armenia: the villagers, their homes and their livelihood. One such intellectual concoction had just been dashed to the ground, and that was that Britain and France would 'rescue' Armenia. With that fantasy out of the way – with the realisation that all the statements and declarations from Western Europe about Armenia were as meretricious as Klingsor's magic garden – there was a very belated chance to pursue the path of reality. Yet there were other nebulous theories hanging in the air, based on allegiance to political parties. Since, however, a pro-Communist slant meant that Armenia would be underpinned by the might of the Eleventh Red Army, it represented realism disguised as theory; the only realism left to the country.

The first action of Khatisian, as the leader of the delegation to make peace with Kemalist Turkey, was to travel to Tiflis in order to discuss matters with the representatives of the Allied governments.[228] As expected, none could give him any real help. Stokes told him that it was preferable that Armenia should come to an agreement with Turkey, since a treaty with Soviet Russia would be 'worse'.[229] To the end Britain was using Armenia as an instrument of her own foreign policy; the slaughter of Kars, the flight of refugees, the shivering starvation of the country and all the other inhuman barbarities that a Turkish invasion brought were nothing if the Bolsheviks could be kept a few kilometres further away.

Change of Government

But Armenia did not intend to bare its throat to the Turks for the sake of any foreign power. 'Nothing remains for the Armenians to do but choose the lesser of two evils,' says Vratsian.[230] In these sombre, grief-stricken days, which for the Armenians often seemed like the very end of time, the eyes of all Armenians were (to quote Vratsian again) fastened on the north, seeking salvation from the Russians.[231] In response to this feeling Prime Minister Ohandjanian tendered his resignation; the man who had suppressed the Bolshevik uprising six months earlier was clearly unacceptable to Soviet Russia. The man most widely supported as his successor was Hovhannes Kachaznuni, Armenia's first prime minister. When asked to form a government, he accepted with these words:

> Gentlemen, I know well what is being asked from me. You require a sacrifice to save the shipwrecked vessel and you want me to be the sacrifice. If that is the way to the salvation of the fatherland, and the will of the people, I bow before it.[232]

But Kachaznuni found himself unable to form a government. The other parties – Populists, Social Democrats – refused to collaborate with the Dashnaks. So Kachaznuni himself resigned, and recommended that Simon Vratsian, known for his pro-Russian views, be appointed prime minister. In his own words, Vratsian 'had no choice but to accept' (23 November).[233]

Once prime minister, Vratsian lost no time in re-opening negotiations with Legrand, representative of Soviet Russia. He confidently expected that Russia would mediate between Armenia and Turkey, and that Budu Mdivani, another Bolshevik plenipotentiary in Yerevan, would travel to Alexandropol for that purpose.[234] But – a vital demonstration of how the Kemalists and Bolsheviks were moving further apart politically the closer they came to one another physically – this plan was rejected by both sides. On the one hand, the Turks would not allow Mdivani to be present at Alexandropol, and on the other hand Legrand gave Vratsian these stark terms for Russian aid: Khatisian's peace delegation must be recalled from Alexandropol, the terms of the Armeno–Turkish armistice of 17 November must be rejected, and Soviet forces should be invited into the country. These terms Vratsian turned down, believing in the first place that Soviet forces would be physically unable to stop a renewed attack of the Turks who were poised near the Markara bridge, 40 kilometres from Yerevan, and also that to invite Soviet forces into Armenia would be to end the independence of the country.[235]

President Wilson's Award

Amid these realistic efforts to reach an agreement a strange echo, like the rattle of bones, reached Armenia from the old world of the New World. This was

Map 11. President Wilson's Award, November 1920

President Wilson's award of territory to Armenia, as stipulated under article 89 of the treaty of Sèvres. It was announced on 22 November. Armenia was awarded a huge amount of land – 42,000 square kilometres – from Ottoman Armenia, including a 400-kilometre coastline, from Giresun (Kerasond) to the Georgian frontier. Such towns as Gumush-khana, Erzindjan, Moush and Bitlis were to be included in the new Armenia. Eighteen months earlier such an award would have been possible; now, because none of the powers had any intention at all of enforcing it, it was an antique irrelevance which served only to distract the parties from reaching an agreement with one another based on the existing political and military realities. It was in the main a fair and just award (although the vast coastline was over-generous, meaning that large numbers of Greeks and Laz would be incorporated into the projected Armenian state*) and it made ample recompense for the mass murder of the Armenians five years before. But it was predicated upon the notion that right and justice prevail in the world, not force, cunning and self-interest. As such, it served no purpose.[236]

Khatisian in Alexandropol

Vratsian had tried to negotiate with Legrand, but had been rebuffed. Khatisian, for his part, was just beginning to negotiate – in rather the same way that the cornered mouse negotiates with the cat – with Kiazim Karabekir in Alexandropol. His delegation had gone to Alexandropol with the hopes of an

---

*The Pontic Greeks would have preferred their own state, but would have chosen Armenian sovereignty as a second alternative. As it was, they remained in Turkey, and within a couple of years most of them had been deported and murdered.

Armenia consisting of the republic as it had existed for the past two years, together with Van, Lake Van, Moush and, to given outlet to the Black Sea, the port of Rize. Trebizond and Erzerum would go to Turkey. Kiazim Karabekir, with a finely wrought mixture of realism and hypocritical solicitude, confronted the Armenians with their fate: all members of the League of Nations have abandoned you, Europe has exploited your value and thrown you away, Russia is advancing south to the warm waters she needs and will engulf you. Only one power can protect and help you: Turkey.[237] (Georgia, he continued, was pledged by a secret treaty not to intervene in the Turkish–Armenian conflict.) Karabekir indicated that the Armenian delegation's map of the projected Armenia was too large for a defeated country, and on 30 November he presented his own proposals: Kars and Surmalu would go to Turkey, Nakhichevan and Zangezur would become Azerbaijani protectorates. Armenia would be left with 27,000 square kilometres. She would be permitted to keep an army of only 1,200 troops, armed with 20 machine-guns and 8 cannons. The representatives of the Allies should leave.[238] The only Armenia that Karabekir was permitting was a tiny protectorate, wholly dependent on Turkish goodwill.

The Bolsheviks Act

Karabekir was racing to create 'his' Armenia, to forestall the Bolsheviks from creating theirs, which would put dreams of capturing Baku even further off. Yet as he was negotiating with Khatisian, the Bolsheviks had decided to act. On 27 November Stalin instructed Orjonikidze (in Baku) to begin operations against Armenia.[239] Two days later Legrand informed the government that 'the Central Committee of the Russian Communist party has decided to establish a Soviet regime in Armenia. The Revolutionary Committee (Revkom) has already arrived in Armenia. Any delay is detrimental.'[240] Meanwhile, on that very same day, the 29th, Armenian Bolshevik forces entered the country at Karvansaray (modern Idjevan), followed by the Revkom, who proclaimed that 'by the will of the insurgent toiling people of Armenia it declares Armenia henceforward a Soviet Socialist Republic.'

Late at night on the following day there was a special meeting in Yerevan of the Cabinet, with a number of MPs and all members of the Bureau of Dashnaktsutiun, as well as some army officers. All agreed to accept Legrand's conditions and not to try to oppose the situation as it had developed.[241] Already negotiations on the practicalities for the hand-over of power were taking place, between Dro and Terterian on the one hand and Legrand on the other. But that night, too, the Parliament had another matter to discuss. They had received details of Karabekir's demands given to Khatisian that day. Now, in view of the fact that power was being handed over to the Bolsheviks, should Khatisian sign the treaty with Karabekir? Should not all negotiation with the Turks be left to the Bolsheviks, who were about to become the government, and Khatisian's delegation be recalled from Alexandropol? Thereby the Dashnaks would at least be spared the task of signing the humiliating treaty which Karabekir had prepared. But what would happen if the delegation was recalled from Alexandropol? Members voiced the fears that Vratsian had expressed to Legrand a week earlier – that the Turks would invade and lay waste Yerevan and Echmiadzin before Red forces could arrive. Later the Bolsheviks might be able to compel them to quit; but by then the heartland of Armenia would have been denuded of Armenians. Finally, almost all agreed that the treaty should be signed, and they comforted themselves with the thought that if the Bolsheviks really were so influential with the Turks, they would soon be able to sign another treaty with Turkey, more favourable to Armenia.[242]

The Hand-over of Power

At the same time talks began between Dro, Terterian and Legrand, on the hand-over of power. These were successfully concluded on 2 December, by an eight-point agreement.[*][243] The two parties agreed that the hand-over of power to a Communist-controlled coalition would take place at midnight, 2/3 December. To this end a decree was published by the government, saying that due to external factors it had agreed to surrender the reins of government, and that the entire country was temporarily under the dictatorship of Dro.[244]

Thus the transfer of power was achieved in an orderly and peaceful manner.

Khatisian's Puzzle in Alexandropol

But what of Khatisian's delegation at Alexandropol? Let us recall that Karabekir had made known his terms to Khatisian on 30 November, and these had been telephoned to Yerevan, where they had been discussed deep into the night, with the upshot that the country's leaders agreed to accept them. But Karabekir was impatient, and fearful that the Bolsheviks would gain Armenia before he did, thus destroying his plan for creating a corridor through to Baku.

---

*In essence: (i) Armenia is an independent socialist republic; (ii) power is temporarily vested in a provisional Military Revolutionary Committee; (iii) Soviet Russia recognises as Armenia: the province of Yerevan; part of Kars province (to ensure military control of the railway from Jajur to Araxes stations); the Zangezur district, part of the Kazakh and Tiflis districts; (iv) the army command is not held responsible for the army's actions prior to Sovietisation; (v) members of Dashnaktsutiun and other socialist parties will not be victimised for belonging to their parties; (vi) The Military Revolutionary Committee will consist of five Communists and two left Dashnaks appointed with the approval of the Communist Party; (vii) Soviet Russia will immediately introduce sufficient military forces into Armenia for its defence; (viii) on the signature of this agreement the authority of the Armenian republic ends, and until the arrival of the Revkom power is transferred to a Military Command, headed by Comrade Dro. Comrade Céline (Silin) is appointed Soviet Russian commissar for the Military Command of Armenia.

So at 11.00 a.m. on the morning of 1 December he issued an ultimatum, saying that unless signature was immediate his troops would move on Yerevan.[245]

Khatisian, realising the supreme importance of delay at such a critical moment, objected and asked for permission to communicate the main points of the treaty to Yerevan in order to receive explicit instructions. Karabekir assented in the afternoon, and a message was sent to Yerevan with a request for an urgent reply. Late that night the reply came back:

> The government has resigned; our forces at Dilidjan and Karvansarai met Bolshevik forces without any opposition. With Dro and Terterian from the Dashnaks a coalition government is being formed with the Bolsheviks. We are obliged to accept the Turkish terms. You are fully authorised to sign the treaty.[246]

There is a curious inconsistency in the wording of that reply, which troubled Khatisian. On the one hand it says that the government has resigned, and on the other it authorises him to sign the treaty. When, at 6.00 p.m. on the following day (2 December), Dro telegraphed Khatisian, there was both clarification and a deeper ambivalence. His message ran: 'On behalf of the Revolutionary government I herewith inform you that you are free to sign or not to sign the treaty.'[247]

Khatisian was both confused, and aware of the great responsibility that rested on his shoulders: to make a false move might lead to the Turks overrunning all that remained of Armenia. So he asked Dro a second time: 'Is the government itself in favour of signing or of refusing to sign? We are waiting here for clear and simple instructions.'[248]

Dro replied: 'I have already told you that you may act as you think best [literally, "according to your understanding (*hasgatsoghutiun*)"]. I am speaking in the name of Comrade Céline and myself.'

Thereupon Khatisian called a meeting of all 16 members of the delegation, and asked each for his opinion. They were unanimously in favour of signing the treaty.

At 8.00 that evening the final session of the Alexandropol conference opened. Both sides went through the treaty, clause by clause. The Armenians were able to make a few small changes in their favour (such as increasing the permitted size of the Armenian army from 1,200 men to 1,500); but on matters such as Ani, Nakhichevan and Surmalu the Turks made no concessions at all. Finally, at 2.00 a.m. on 3 December, the treaty of Alexandropol was signed.[249]

The Treaty of Alexandropol

The circumstances of the signature of the Alexandropol treaty present several puzzling features, which have provided the materials for anti-Dashnaks to build elaborate conspiracy theories about Turko–Dashnak collusion. For instance, why were Dro's answers to Khatisian so oracular? And what was the point of a delegation representing a defunct government signing a treaty? But both these points can be answered by the absolute necessity of Khatisian to keep talking, to make the Turks think that they were engaged in a significant activity, in order that they would not take up their arms again.

The treaty consists of 18 clauses,[250] the first of which states that war between Turkey and Armenia is ended. The boundary between the two states is similar to today's Soviet–Turkish border, that is, roughly, along the Araxes river in the south, then north along the Arpa Chai, to Mount Akbaba. Nakhichevan, Shakhtakhti and Sharur were to be disputed land, whose future was to be decided later by a plebiscite* (article 2); likewise too the region between the old 1914 frontier and the new one, if Armenia requested it (article 3).

*It seems incredible that the Turks could mouth terms of political sophistication like 'plebiscite', at the same time as their soldiers and 'irregulars' were perpetrating death and destruction similar to, or even worse than, that in Kars. A Soviet document describes the situation in Kars and Alexandropol as follows:

> Those people who were saved from massacre are condemned to starvation and untold privation, since the districts of Kars and Alexandropol are in total economic ruin. The Turks have taken away all the bread, rice and other foodstuffs from these places. They have left behind not even one single animal, whether cow, horse or sheep – all are herded in droves towards Erzerum. Parallel with this deathly economic breakdown are the relentless massacres which the Turks have perpetrated in these same regions from the very first moment they invaded them. . . . The Armenian population of Alexandropol and of some tens of towns in various regions of Armenia have been put to the sword. (E. K. Sarkissian and R. G. Sahakian, *Vital Issues in Modern Armenian History*, trans. E. B. Chrakian (Watertown, 1965), pp. 54–5; see also FO 371/6266.3428).

Another Soviet document, dated 24 December 1920, describes the situation in Alexandropol thus:

> Hitherto unseen and unheard-of crimes are being perpetrated in the rural districts. . . . All the towns are plundered, there is nothing left behind – no livestock, no bread, no clothes, nor yet fuel. The streets of these towns are filled with dead bodies. This is nothing yet; it all becomes far worse when the soldiers harass their prisoners and punish the people in more horrible ways. Not content with this, they seek more pleasure by subjecting them to a variety of tortures. They force parents to hand over to these executioners their eight-year-old daughters and twenty- to twenty-five-year-old sons. They rape the girls and murder the young men – all this in the presence of parents. This is the way they conducted themselves in all the towns. Young girls and women up to the age of forty are snatched away, no one knows where to, while men up to forty-five years of age are murdered. These towns are depopulated. The situation has no precedent; it is beyond description (Sarkisian and Sahakian, *Vital Issues*, p. 56).

Oliver Baldwin, son of the future British prime minister, socialist, anti-Bolshevik and British agent, records his impressions of Turkish-occupied Alexandropol thus:

> The streets were dirty, the town almost empty of inhabitants. Here and there an aged Armenian tailored for the Turkish soldiery or baked Turkish cakes or cobbled shoes, but the rest of the population were scattered, massacred, or living in caves by the side of Alagöz, waiting for death. The silence of the town was enhanced by the snow in the streets, and our rumbling wheels were the only sounds, except for the soft patter of a Turkish soldier's feet on the pavement (Oliver Baldwin, *Six Prisons and Two Revolutions* (London, 1924), p. 150).

With the sincere desire that conditions and movements violating public order, which are the results of provocation and incitement by the imperialist states, will never again be possible, the Yerevan republic agrees that it is not permitted to form an army except for a lightly armed police force.

Thus begins article 4 with a preamble of stunning hypocrisy, in that it is this article which encapsulates the ruthless imperialism – though the word is too weak – of Kemalist Turkey towards Armenia. For defending the country's borders Armenia was allowed a 'detachment' of 1,500 soldiers equipped with 20 machine-guns and 8 field cannon. Compulsory military service was forbidden. All these matters could be inspected at any time by a Turkish political agent resident in Yerevan (article 5); and, the same article alleged, Turkey would come to Armenia's aid against internal and foreign threats. Refugees might be allowed to return home (6), but only if they returned within a year (7). Turkey will not demand an indemnity (8). 'With the sincerest benevolence' – a benevolence similar to that of the Walrus and the Carpenter towards the Oysters – Turkey would aid the development and preserve the sovereignty of Armenia (9). Armenia declares the treaty of Sèvres null and void, and recalls its ambassadors from Europe and America (10). Muslims in Armenia will elect their own *muftis* directly, and the election of the Grand Mufti of Armenia will be subject to confirmation by Turkey (11). Freedom of transit will be assured; and Turkey will have the right to supervise and inspect goods entering Armenia

---

The same author, travelling west from Sarikamish in mid-March 1921, records the following:

Eventually our train snorted and creaked and we started slowly on the last stage of our journey, rolling through high banks of snow that had been made by the clearing of the track by poor Armenian peasants who stood waist deep in the snow and watched us with hungry eyes, clutching their rags round their shoulders, their teeth chattering with the cold, their shovels held loosely in their yellow hands. . . . The sight of these little gangs of prisoners made one's heart bleed. Here and there a body in the snow; here and there we saw a man drop as he shovelled the snow, whilst his colleagues worked on, making curious whimpering sounds, like starving dogs (ibid., pp. 187, 189–90).

Colonel A. Rawlinson, Mustafa Kemal's prisoner in Erzerum for most of 1920, noted at about this time:

On leaving our old quarters we first saw 'Armenian prisoners'. Those we saw were being used as labourers (slaves would be the proper word), and accustomed as I had become to see starvation, misery, and privations of every description, yet the appearance of these men gave me, even at that time, a shock such as I had never before experienced, and a memory which will remain with me whilst life lasts. It was then midwinter, the snow everywhere lying deep, the force and temperature of the arctic wind being beyond description; yet those miserable spectres were clothed, if the word can be applied to their condition, in the rottenest and filthiest of verminous rags, through which their fleshless bones protruded in many places, so that it seemed *impossible* that humanity could be reduced to such extremities and live. In fact, the duration of their tragic misery depended only upon the individual vitality, which enables some, possibly the least fortunate, to continue to exist longer than others, to whom death brought a speedier relief from their sufferings (A. Rawlinson, *Adventures in the Near East, 1918–1922* (London, 1934 edn), p. 238).

(12). Turkey may undertake temporary military action inside Armenia if she feels herself threatened (13). Armenia declares as null and void anti-Turkish stipulations in treaties with other states (14). Diplomatic and commercial relations will begin on the signature of the treaty (15), as will rail, telegraph and postal communication (16). The Turkish military occupation of part of Armenia will end, and an exchange of prisoners take place, when Armenia has fulfilled all her treaty obligations (17). The treaty will be ratified within one month (18).

The treaty of Alexandropol was crushing; yet, in terms of international diplomacy, it was meaningless. Since it was signed after midnight on 2/3 December, the signature was that of a superseded administration. (Dro's words 'I am speaking in the name of Comrade Céline and myself' cannot alter this fact; they merely show that the Bolshevik, too, was in favour of keeping the Turks happy by negotiating, and signing, or whatever.) Moreover, it was never ratified. Yet the treaty of Alexandropol has a considerable historical significance. It represented the last act of independent Armenia, and the forced closure of the Armenian question, that is, of the attempt by Armenians to enlist foreign diplomatic and military aid to enable them to wrest an autonomous or independent Armenia from the eastern provinces of imperial Turkey. Now independent Armenia itself had signed away its claims not only to pre-1914 Ottoman imperial regions but to pre-1878 as well. It was a grave and sad moment for those who had dreamed of an independent Armenia; all the hopes, the efforts, the terrible sacrifices of the past 40 years had turned to dust beneath the boot of the Turkish soldier. This had happened in the past, certainly, but then there had always been the hope of eventual restitution. Now there was none.

Bolshevik Armenia

But if the hope of independent Armenia comprising Russian and Turkish Armenias was dashed, at least the advent of the Bolsheviks in Yerevan meant that Caucasian Armenia was reverting to her old position as Russia's younger brother. The dreadful shortages would end, the seething uncertainty and political instability that had racked the whole region since 1917 would be over. Few Armenians had any real idea what Communism entailed, and only a very few of that largely non-industrial land had any understanding of its theory; yet most were prepared, in December 1920, to give it a try. Vratsian, who had himself always favoured a Russian orientation, agrees that the change of government was initially welcomed.[251] Leon Surmelian, the author and translator, who was in Nor Bayazid at the time, remarked simply: 'What disturbed me was the attitude of the natives towards this sudden change in regime: they were too glad about it.'[252]

Internal Excesses and External Failures

But Russia did not come bringing bread and peace. Within a few days Armenia, even now in its exhausted and prostrate condition, found itself gripped by the reign of a new terror. The Revkom, consisting of Armenians from Azerbaijan, entered the country on 5 December, and the Cheka – the secret police – was set up on the 6th. What followed has been described thus by Soviet historian B. A. Borian:

The Revkom started a series of indiscriminate and peremptory seizures and confiscations, without regard to class principle and without taking into account the general economic and psychological condition of the peasantry. Devoid of planned or revolutionary character, and executed with unnecessary brutality, these confiscations were wholly unorganised and arbitrary. Unattended by a disciplined machinery, without the preliminary propaganda or enlightenment, and with utter disregard of the country's unusually distressing conditions, the Revkom issued its slogan of seizing and nationalising the food stores of the towns and the grain of the peasantry. With amazing recklessness and unconcern, they seized and nationalised everything – military uniforms, artisans' tools, rice mills (whether publicly or privately owned), all the water mills, barbers' tools, beehives, linens, woollens, household furniture of citizens regardless of their class status. . . . Naturally, this forcible requisitioning was the basic cause of the people's rebellion.[253]

Plots and conspiracies against the state were searched out where there were none; the people were too cold and hungry to bother with such things. When the Communists had moved in there was no opposition to them at all; even the Dashnak party had accepted that only their presence could save the country, and the Parliament had voted in favour of letting them in.

The excesses committed internally by the Revkom, headed by Sargis Kasian, but with the 21-year-old adventurer Avis Nurijanian as its guiding spirit, were only paralleled by its failures externally. Although Soviet Azerbaijan agreed, in a fraternal gesture, to hand over to Soviet Armenia the disputed regions of Mountainous Karabagh, Zangezur and Nakhichevan,[254] of those territories only Zangezur was actually attached. The reason was that when the status of these lands came to be formally laid down, the objections of Kemalist Turkey were taken more seriously than the wishes of the Sovietised Armenians. The new Soviet government of Armenia met with no greater success with respect to Georgia, which had occupied the neutral zone of Lori-Borchalo during the Armeno–Turkish war; now, despite notes from Yerevan, she refused to budge from this land with its clear Armenian majority. Nor would Georgia release large quantities of food stores destined for Armenia, which were held up in Black Sea ports. But the greatest failure was in relation to Turkey itself. The notes that Yerevan sent Ankara requesting immediate withdrawal from Alexandropol were rejected; and indeed it was 22 April 1921 before Soviet troops were able to enter the town amidst ruin and death. Moreover, even though one of the first actions of the new Soviet Armenian regime was to repudiate the treaty of Alexandropol, the representative of Ankara, Ahmed Mukhtar, saw no reason for doing so, and intimated that Turkey still held it to be valid.[255] Indeed the Turks continued to occupy villages after Sovietisation, and murdered Communist Armenian officials with as much enthusiasm as they had ever killed other Armenians (for example, after occupying the village of Kaftali on 13 December they butchered 13 young officials).[256]

The agreement signed on 2 December between Legrand, Dro and Terterian was entirely disregarded. Arrests followed: the first wave included Hamo Ohandjanian and General Hamazasp, later on the president of the Parliament, A. Sahakian, and later still of Hovhannes Kachaznuni and Nikol Aghbalian.[257] The country, whose day-to-day conditions were wretched beyond description, cowered beneath a tyranny of pure intellectual ideology.

There was only one way out: rebellion. The Dashnak party was still strong, and although it had agreed to co-operate on handing over power to the Communists, its outlook was basically hostile to the Communists, if only because they represented a political force which was centrally organised, like itself. A secret Dashnak organisation, the Committee for the Liberation of the Fatherland, was established under the leadership of Simon Vratsian.

Zangezur declared itself independent of the Yerevan government on 25 December.[258] At the same time mass purges of the army were being carried out. But the Cheka felt itself hindered by the presence of the great national figure Dro; consequently he was ordered to Moscow in early January 1921, and left on the 10th. Mass arrests and purges followed. Fifteen hundred Armenian officers were deported to Azerbaijan.[259] In the outlying areas opposition was crystallising into action.

But, as their rule was snapping in Armenia, the Bolsheviks began military operations against Georgia, perhaps fearing that a counter-revolution in Armenia allied with an anti-Bolshevik government in Tiflis would provide the opportunity for Britain and France again to strike at Soviet rule. The immediate result was that Soviet troops were withdrawn from Armenia, which simplified the situation for the Dashnaks.

The February Uprising

Fighting broke out on 12 February. The Communist government replied by issuing a decree (signed by Avis Nurijanian, minister of war, and countersigned by the sadistic, leather-clad Cheka chief Gevorg Atarbekian, known as the 'bloody-jawed') saying that unless the revolt ceased at once, about 100 of the arrested Armenian leaders would be shot in jail.[260] It did not stop, and that night the first 50 were shot in cold blood. The following night, as the sounds of the insurgents' gunfire grew closer to Yerevan, a second group were hacked to death (the Armenian Communist soldiers had refused to fire on them).

The Dashnaks re-established themselves in power in Yerevan on 18 February, after first freeing the remnant of the prisoners who had escaped the Communist slaughter. Yet what could they do – what political options were open to them? The answer must be, almost none at all. The Dashnaks had handed over power to the Communists 11 weeks earlier because they realised that they were impotent. Nothing had changed to make their situation any better; indeed, with the Sovietisation of Georgia proceeding, it was considerably worse. They sent off a flurry of telegrams – to the powers and to the League of Nations, appealing to their 'conscience', and to Lenin and Chicherin, claiming that their action was 'not directed against Russia or Soviet authority'.[261] They also asked Georgia for assistance; but Georgia, in the throes of Sovietisation, was in no position to help.

'The proletarian flag flies over Tiflis!' cabled Orjonikidze to Lenin and Stalin on 25 February;[262] and with the capture of the Georgian capital, the Communists were able to reinforce their forces in the south. The following day Yerevan was shelled, and on 1 March a Soviet attack was repulsed with heavy losses.[263] The same day Vratsian, clutching at burning straws, asked the Turkish political agent in Yerevan to pass on a request for Turkish military aid.[264] Armenia stood by the treaty of Alexandropol, he said. No reply came from Ankara; the Turks were keener on getting good terms from the Russians at the forthcoming Moscow conference than giving aid to the anti-Soviet rebellion in Armenia which would jeopardise their position.*

By 9 March Yerevan was surrounded by Soviet troops; Vratsian implored Moscow to settle the dispute by negotiation rather than by weapons. Moscow did not reply.

The Treaty of Moscow

One week later, as the Dashnaks still held out against an ever-tightening steel ring of Soviet forces, the Russians and Turks concluded their negotiations in Moscow with a treaty: Chicherin and Jellaleddin Korkmasov represented the Soviet state, and Yusuf Kemal, Riza Nur and Ali Fuad Nationalist Turkey.[265] No representative from Armenia or Georgia was there, even though the main subject was relations between the Caucasian states and the new Turkey. It was like a return to the cynical old days of the tsars and sultans, when imperial rulers dispensed the fortunes of their vassals according to their own whims and

---

*Vratsian's request to Turkey has been taken as a *de facto* ratification of the treaty of Alexandropol, and of evidence that the Dashnaks all along were keener to do a deal with the Turks than with the Soviet Russians; but it is perfectly explicable by the need simply to improvise.

interests. The frontier between Turkey and Armenia was (as far as I can make out, from the names of the relevant border villages) exactly the same as for the treaty of Alexandropol; if there were any differences, they were minimal. Kars and Ardahan went to Turkey, and the new frontier was to be from Mount Akbaba south along the Arpa Chai (Akhurian) and then east along the Araxes. Surmalu, with its main town Igdir, never Turkish except intermittently in the eighteenth century, went to Turkey, as did Mount Ararat. The district of Nakhichevan was to be autonomous territory under the protection of Azerbaijan. Other clauses dealt with elegant diplomatic niceties like consular representation and reciprocal treatment of each other's nationals, all of which was redundant, while the Turks' main ambition, as deduced from their actions, was to make as many Armenians as possible die from cold and starvation, after extorting a measure of forced labour from them. However, in the Moscow treaty the Armenians were spared the hypocritical and humiliating 'protection' verbiage – of being protected by only maintaining an army of 1,500 and suchlike, as Alexandropol had laid down. At least the remnant of the Armenians had got the Turks off their backs. Turkey would not be able to intervene in Armenia, as she had been able to under the Alexandropol treaty (articles 5, 9, 12 and 13). The treaty of Moscow would, its final paragraph said, be later ratified at Kars.

Why the Bolsheviks Favoured Non-Bolshevik Turkey

The immense favour shown to Turkey by the treaty of Moscow did not result from the circumstances of the counter-revolution proceeding at the time of its signature. It sprang from the curious view that the forces of the left – specifically of the anti-colonial left – held about the Kemalist movement. Although Kiazim Karabekir could be said, in his unquenchable thirst for territory, to be stepping straight into the imperial boots of Sultan Selim the Grim, the Kemalist movement was hailed – by that periodic blindness and moronic befuddlement to which international leftists are notoriously prone – to be an 'anti-imperialist' struggle. The Congress of the Peoples of the East, held in Baku, reinforced this view. The presence there of Enver and Behaeddin Shakir should have been sufficient to raise suspicions. This congress proved the high regard in which Kemal's defiance of the Allies was held by the forces which might weaken the international hold of British capital. It threw the Bolsheviks and Kemalists deeper into their tactical alliance. B. A. Borian comments, referring to the subsequent treaty of Kars, which kept the borders of the treaty of Moscow:

> The eastern question constituted the cornerstone of the international revolution and the international policy of Soviet countries, in whose opinion Turkey was the organising centre and idealistic leader of the national emancipatory movements of the east; consequently the fate of imperialism in

the east wholly depended upon Turkey's political activity in the east. It was under these conditions that Soviet Armenia was forced to sign a peace treaty with Turkey; by the contingencies of history Turkey was given a free hand in the determination of Soviet Armenia's boundaries. Turkish diplomacy had prepared the draft of the peace treaty, according to which Armenia could either sign or reject the eastern policy of the Soviet fraternal republics.

By rejecting the proposal of the Soviet fraternal republics, Armenia would have had to sever her political and economic relations with them, and wage a war with Turkey, which she could not. At the same time, without the economic and political aid of the neighbouring Soviet republics, Armenia was not in a position to build up a soviet government.

Armenia's choice was predetermined by her historical setting. In signing the treaty to be included with Soviet Georgia and Soviet Azerbaijan, and to enjoy the participation of Russia, Armenia was made the ransom price in the eastern policy of the Soviet, in the interests of world revolution. This was quite a price to pay for the interests of the world's working men, for the Soviet countries and for world revolution. For the adverse economic and political consequences which resulted, the Soviet countries later paid dearly by hastening material aid to ravished Soviet Armenia.[266]

The Bolsheviks Return: Lernahayastan

In Yerevan it was only a matter of days before the collapse of the central part of the anti-Soviet revolt. The Bolsheviks received reinforcements, and pressed tighter and tighter around Yerevan. On 2 April they reached Kanaker, on the city's outskirts; panic seized Yerevan, and thousands fled south towards Zangezur and Iran. The following day Atarbekian telegraphed Moscow that 'the detestable adventure of the Dashnak party was today liquidated'.[267]

Nevertheless, despite the words of the Cheka boss, the revolt continued in the mountains of Zangezur. Zangezur had been independent from 27 December; morale had been boosted by hearing of the February rebellion by radio. Leader of the Dashnak forces there was Garegin Nzhdeh. Extending his authority to Daralagiaz in February, he declared the region independent *Lernahayastan*, mountainous Armenia. So firmly lodged were the Dashnak forces in the mountains that the Bolsheviks decided upon negotiations (see below, p. 352); but these broke down, and a series of military thrusts in July 1921 finally destroyed the quasi-republic of Lernahayastan. Large numbers of fighters and refugees were forced to ford the fast-flowing waters of the Araxes into Iran.[268]

In this way, amidst suffering and privation greater than she had known for any of the two and a half years of her existence, independent Armenia died. A vision of a potential state collapsed. It is possible to speculate endlessly about the reasons for the collapse, but one thing must stand as the major factor: the

Turkish offensive of autumn 1920, and the unbreakable resolve of Kiazim Karabekir to crush Armenia. Without that attack it is perfectly possible that Armenia could have kept her independence. Of course there were other things that aggravated the situation; especially Armenia's geographical remoteness, the lack of a sea coast, the perfidy of Britain and France (who, even if they broke no specific undertaking or treaty, acted in a way contrary to all their declarations on Armenia), the delay in producing the treaty of Sèvres, and in Armenia itself the nature of the Dashnaktsutiun, which so seldom seemed to understand the value of compromise. Also – reflecting the statements of European leaders concerning them – many Armenians held an amazing and misconceived belief and trust in Europe and America, which amounted to a dogmatic refusal to see themselves as Easterners and Asiatics, whose political connections must necessarily be in that part of the world. Yet all these factors were subsidiary to the deadly blow wielded by Karabekir's troops.

Did the Bolsheviks save Armenia? The notion that they did would seem to be a curious proposition, in view of the close political ties between Moscow and Ankara, and the ease with which the treaty of Moscow handed over large tracts of purely Armenian-inhabited land to the Turks. Then, too, when the Bolsheviks eventually arrived in Yerevan, the terror they created cannot fail to have reminded some of a Turkish occupation. But the Bolsheviks did not murder Armenian women and children merely for the sake of exterminating them, as the Turks did. Even a shocking act such as the slaughter of the 75 officers is not in the same category as the utterly relentless, ruthless and indiscriminate actions which accompanied the Turkish capture of a town. It is with this in mind that even Avis Nurijanian's murderous reign of terror must be seen as a saving grace, because it was backed by the might of the Eleventh Red Army, which was the only power capable of halting a Turkish advance. However cynical the Communist seizure of power in Armenia may have been in its design and execution, it resulted in a small area of the globe remaining to Armenia, and not being relegated to the history books, as had been the fate of Cappadocia, Commagene or Caucasian Albania. Moreover, despite the close alliance between the Kemalists and Bolsheviks, there is strong evidence that in the last desperate days before the Sovietisation of Armenia, there was a race between Bolsheviks and Turks for control of the country; hardly the action of two powers acting together to destroy the third situated between them.

Lenin's Letter

After the grim events of the spring of 1921, Lenin took personal charge of events in the Caucasus, and he despatched Alexander Miasnikian to Yerevan as his own representative. Arrogant intellectual youths such as Avis Nurijanian, who believed that they knew the solution to every problem from cold theory alone, were barred from entry into Armenia. To Miasnikian Lenin gave a letter, addressed to local Bolshevik leaders, whose sentiments were healing and conciliatory:

> You will need to practise more moderation and caution, and show more readiness to make concessions to the petty bourgeoisie, the intelligentsia and particularly the peasantry. You must make the swiftest, most intense and all possible economic use of the capitalist west through a policy of concessions and trade . . .
>
> What the republics of the Caucasus can and must do, as distinct from the RSFSR [that is, Russia], is to effect a slower, more cautious and more systematic transition to socialism . . .
>
> You must make immediate efforts to improve the condition of the peasants and start on extensive electrification and irrigation projects. What you need most is irrigation, for more than anything else it will revive the area and regenerate it, bury the past and make the transition to socialism more certain.[269]

The Kars Conference

Finally, there was the conference at Kars, to ratify the Moscow treaty. This conference sealed the border in the form that it has today, and its resultant treaty wound up all the suffering, slaughter, starvation and incessant uncertainty that the region had endured since 1914. It also spelt an end to any Armenian hopes of Turkish Armenia.[270] The conference lasted from 26 September to 13 October 1921.[271] Kiazim Karabekir represented Turkey; the Soviet states of Armenia, Georgia and Azerbaijan were represented respectively by Askanaz Mravian, Shalva Eliava and Bebut Shakhtakhtinsky. But the real spokesman for the Caucasian states was Yakov Ganetzky (or Hanecki), Chicherin's own representative.

On the subject of borders, Ganetzky accepted those laid down in the Moscow treaty, with two small revisions: the first was the ruins of Ani, situated on the west bank of the Arpa Chai, the actual border between Turkey and Soviet Armenia; and the second was the salt mines of Goghb (Kulp), between Igdir and Kaghizman, which he described as an 'inseparable part of Transcaucasia'.

But Karabekir's response was that of an inflexible bureaucrat. He referred to the treaty of Moscow, pointing out that since these changes were new to it, they lay outside the scope of the conference. By way of response, at a later session, Ganetzky read a prepared statement:

> We were hopeful that the Turkish delegation would give us an affirmative answer in regard to Armenia's claim to Ani, which is wholly devoid of any military, economic or geographical significance. At the last moment, as in

the case of Goghb, so too in the case of Ani, the Turkish delegation rejected the claims with the objection that, in ceding Ani which is on the west of the Akhurian river, the treaty of Moscow would be impaired.

The delegation of the Transcaucasian republics record with deep sorrow the rejection of their proposal in regard to Ani, which mean so much to the Armenians from the national, historical and artistic point of view. It should be added that the Transcaucasian peoples will take that rejection with genuine sorrow.[272]

On the two matters of Armenian concern – the frontier with Turkey and the status of Nakhichevan – the Kars and Moscow treaties were the same (and the border itself was the same as that laid down in the treaty of Alexandropol). Soviet historian B. A. Borian said of the Kars treaty, 'A more intolerable and more unfavourable treaty than the treaty of Kars can scarcely be found in all the pages of history,'[273] and while allowing for justifiable exaggeration, it is hard to avoid the conclusion that just as the Allies refused to recompense Armenia for her losses during the first world war, so now the Communists were discriminating against Soviet Armenia (and Georgia, for that matter) in favour of non-Soviet Turkey; and doing so at a time when the international situation was clearly improving for Moscow. But this was only a subsidiary element in the Armenian tragedy of the past six years, which was now at an end. For at every juncture, until this time, as Armenia had looked for a political solution to her problems, or as she had had incomplete solutions imposed on her, the cost in human suffering to her people had increased. The fixing of the border would end that suffering by ending the political uncertainty. It was harsh and unjust, but at least it meant that the inhabitants of the Armenian Soviet Socialist Republic would henceforth be able to live.

Notes

1. Richard G. Hovannisian, *Armenia on the Road to Independence, 1918* (Berkeley and Los Angeles, 1967), p. 63 (henceforward cited as 'Hovannisian, *Independence*').
2. W. E. D. Allen and Paul Muratoff, *Caucasian Battlefields* (Cambridge, 1953), pp. 363, 368, 383, 409.
3. Hovannisian, *Independence*, p. 63.
4. Ibid., pp. 75–80.
5. Allen and Muratoff, *Caucasian Battlefields*, pp. 422–3.
6. Hovannisian, *Independence*, p. 81.
7. Ibid., pp. 85–6.
8. Ibid., pp. 86–90.
9. Ibid., p. 108.
10. Ibid., pp. 109–10.
11. Ibid., p. 119; also G. Korganoff, *La participation des arméniens à la guerre mondiale sur le front du Caucase, 1914–1918* (Paris, 1927), p. 103.
12. Korganoff, *Participation des arméniens*, p. 95.
13. Firuz Kazemzadeh, *The Struggle for Transcaucasia, 1917–1921* (Oxford and New York, 1951), p. 91.

14. Hovannisian, *Independence*, p. 100.
15. Ibid., p. 99.
16. Kazemzadeh, *Struggle for Transcaucasia*, pp. 93–4.
17. Hovannisian, *Independence*, pp. 113–17.
18. Ibid., pp. 134–7.
19. Korganoff, *Participation des arméniens*, p. 113.
20. Kazemzadeh, *Struggle for Transcaucasia*, pp. 95–6.
21. Ibid., p. 97.
22. Ibid., p. 70.
23. Ibid., p. 73.
24. Hovannisian, *Independence*, p. 159.
25. Ibid., pp. 162–9.
26. Ibid., p. 168.
27. Ibid., p. 172.
28. Ibid., pp. 173–5; also Allen and Muratoff, *Caucasian Battlefields*, p. 471.
29. Allen and Muratoff, *Caucasian Battlefields*, p. 472.
30. See Jacques Kayaloff, *The Battle of Sardarabad* (The Hague, 1973), especially Chapter 2.
31. Allen and Muratoff, *Caucasian Battlefields*, pp. 472–6.
32. Hovannisian, *Independence*, pp. 193–4.
33. Ibid., pp. 181, 184; Kazemzadeh, *Struggle for Transcaucasia*, p. 119.
34. Kazemzadeh, *Struggle for Transcaucasia*, pp. 122–3.
35. Ibid., p. 115.
36. Hovannisian, *Independence*, p. 189.
37. Ibid., pp. 190–1.
38. Ibid., p. 191.
39. Simon Vratsian, *Hayastani Hanrapetutiun* (Beirut, 1958), p. 177.
40. Hovannisian, *Independence*, p. 198.
41. Ibid., p. 191.
42. Richard G. Hovannisian, *The Republic of Armenia*, vol. I, *The First Year, 1918–1919* (Berkeley and Los Angeles, 1971), p. 40 (henceforward 'Hovannisian, *Republic*, I').
43. Ibid., pp. 40–2.
44. Ibid., pp. 51–5.
45. Kazemzadeh, *Struggle for Transcaucasia*, p. 128.
46. Ronald Grigor Suny, *The Baku Commune, 1917–1918* (Princeton, 1972), p. 275.
47. Ibid., p. 304.
48. Ibid., p. 305.
49. CAB 23/6.435 (8).
50. Suny, *Baku Commune*, p. 312.
51. Ibid., pp. 326–7; Hovannisian, *Independence*, p. 221.
52. Hovannisian, *Independence*, p. 222.
53. L. C. Dunsterville, *The Adventures of Dunsterforce* (London, 1920), p. 279.
54. Jacques Kayaloff, *The Fall of Baku* (Bergenfield, N.J., 1976), p. 12 (slightly adapted).
55. Suny, *Baku Commune*, p. 338.
56. Ibid., p. 339.
57. Ibid., pp. 342–3.
58. Hovannisian, *Independence*, pp. 238–41.
59. A. J. Toynbee, *The Times History of the War* (London, 1919), vol. XX, pp. 103–4.
60. FO 371/3657.10607.
61. Hovannisian, *Independence*, p. 303.
62. George Antonius, *The Arab Awakening* (London, 1938), p. 435.
63. Hovannisian, *Independence*, p. 251.
64. Ibid., p. 252.
65. Hovannisian, *Republic*, I, p. 277.
66. Great Britain. Foreign Office, *Documents on British Foreign Policy, 1919–1939*, 1st series, eds. W. L. Woodward and Rohan Butler (London, 1947–63), vol. IV, p. 914 (henceforward '*DBFP*').
67. Hovannisian, *Republic*, I, pp. 277–81.

68. Ibid., p. 64.
69. Kazemzadeh, *Struggle for Transcaucasia*, pp. 175–6.
70. Hovannisian, *Republic*, I, pp. 93–113.
71. Ibid., pp. 126–30.
72. *The Times*, 4 January 1919, p. 5.
73. Ibid., 16 January 1919, p. 8.
74. Ibid., 22 January 1919, p. 7.
75. Ibid., 2 May 1919, p. 13.
76. Kazemzadeh, *Struggle for Transcaucasia*, pp. 167–8.
77. Ibid., p. 241.
78. Hovannisian, *Republic*, I, pp. 157–8n.
79. Ibid., pp. 88–9.
80. Ibid., pp. 175–82.
81. Ibid., pp. 192–6.
82. Ibid., pp. 199–227.
83. Ibid., pp. 228–49.
84. Ibid., pp. 459–67.
85. Ibid., pp. 471–5.
86. Hovhannes Kachaznuni, *H. H. Dashnaktsutiunë anelik chuni ailevs* (Vienna, 1923); trans. *The Armenian Revolutionary Federation has Nothing to Do Any More* (New York, 1955), pp. 8–9.
87. Hovannisian, *Republic*, I, pp. 434–7.
88. Michel Paillarès, *Le Kémalisme devant les alliés* (Paris, 1922), p. 57.
89. FO 406/41, p. 162.
90. See James B. Gidney, *A Mandate for Armenia* (Kent, Ohio, 1967), pp. 168–91.
91. FO 406/41, p. 360.
92. Gidney, *Mandate for Armenia*, pp. 187–9.
93. *DBFP*, vol. XIII, p. 60.
94. Graham Nicol, *Uncle George: Field-Marshal Lord Milne of Salonika and Rubislaw* (London, 1976), p. 210.
95. Hovannisian, *Republic*, I, pp. 241–2.
96. FO 608/78.16453, 17750, 17582.
97. *DBFP*, vol. IV, p. 716.
98. Ibid., pp. 778–9.
99. *DBFP*, vol. II, pp. 563, 569–70.
100. FO 371/4933.1570.
101. FO 371/4953.1561.
102. Vratsian, *Hayastani Hanrapetutiun*, p. 356.
103. *DBFP*, vol. VII, pp. 643–9.
104. League of Nations, *Official Journal*, no. 3 (April–May 1920), pp. 85–7.
105. *DBFP*, vol. VIII, pp. 107–22.
106. Ibid., p. 177.
107. Gidney, *Mandate for Armenia*, p. 237.
108. *DBFP*, vol. III, p. 746.
109. FO 371/4352, FO Memo of 21 November 1918, pp. 19–20.
110. FO 371/4932.1097.
111. Ibid.; also *DBFP*, vol. XII, pp. 573–4.
112. *DBFP*, vol. XII, p. 591.
113. Kazemzadeh, *Struggle for Transcaucasia*, pp. 277 ff.
114. Ibid., p. 283.
115. Ibid., p. 284.
116. FO 406/44, p. 8.
117. *DBFP*, vol. XII, p. 602.
118. Vratsian, *Hayastani Hanrapetutiun*, p. 387.
119. Ibid., pp. 378–86.
120. FO 371/6265.48, p. 3.
121. Vratsian, *Hayastani Hanrapetutiun*, pp. 388–9.
122. Ibid., p. 389.

123. Ibid., p. 390.
124. Ibid., p. 390n.
125. FO 371/4942.7619.
126. Ibid.
127. Vratsian, *Hayastani Hanrapetutiun*, p. 396.
128. Ibid., p. 398.
129. James L. Barton, *Story of Near East Relief* (New York, 1930), pp. 120 ff.
130. FO 371/4942.7619.
131. Sir Harry Luke, *Cities and Men* (London, 1953), vol. II, p. 146.
132. *DBFP*, vol. XII, p. 610.
133. Ibid., p. 609n; Luke, *Cities and Men*, p. 110.
134. Hambardzoum Terterian, 'The Levon Chanth Mission to Moscow', I, *Armenian Review*, vol. VIII, no. 2–30 (June 1955), p. 6.
135. Ibid., p. 8.
136. Ibid., pp. 9–10.
137. Ibid., p. 12.
138. Luke, *Cities and Men*, vol. II, p. 154.
139. Terterian, 'Levon Chanth Mission to Moscow', p. 13.
140. Ibid., p. 14.
141. Vratsian, *Hayastani Hanrapetutiun*, p. 457.
142. *DBFP*, vol. XII, pp. 633–4.
143. See map in FO 371/4962.1398, p. 176.
144. FO 406/44, p. 23.
145. Treaty Series, no. 11 (1920), pp. 25–6.
146. Paul du Véou, *La Passion de la Cilicie, 1919–1922* (Paris, 1954), p. 47.
147. Col. É. Brémond, *La Cilicie en 1919–1920* (Paris, 1921), pp. 4–5; du Véou, *Passion de la Cilicie*, p. 59.
148. Brémond, *La Cilicie*, pp. 9–11; du Véou, *Passion de la Cilicie*, pp. 70–2.
149. Brémond, *La Cilicie*, p. 8.
150. Ibid., p. 11.
151. FO 406/43, p. 231.
152. Ibid., p. 240.
153. Brémond, *La Cilicie*, p. 33.
154. FO 406/43, p. 240.
155. Ibid., pp. 242 ff.
156. Ibid., pp. 243, 244.
157. Ibid., p. 247.
158. du Véou, *Passion de la Cilicie*, p. 131.
159. FO 406/43, p. 248.
160. Ibid., p. 248.
161. Ibid.
162. Ibid.
163. Ibid., p. 221.
164. Brémond, *La Cilicie*, p. 41.
165. du Véou, *Passion de la Cilicie*, pp. 180–4; Stanley E. Kerr, *The Lions of Marash* (New York, 1973), pp. 216–18.
166. Capt. A. F. Townsend, *A Military Consul in Turkey* (London, 1910), p. 116.
167. Brémond, *La Cilicie*, p. 46.
168. D. B. Eby, *At the Mercy of Turkish Brigands* (New Carlisle, Ohio, 1922), pp. 100–1.
169. Ibid., p. 106.
170. Ibid., p. 108.
171. Personal interview with Khatchig Metribian, Chiswick, June 1973.
172. Eby, *At the Mercy of Turkish Brigands*, p. 160.
173. Ibid., pp. 206 ff.
174. Ibid., p. 216.
175. Ibid., p. 221.
176. Brémond, *La Cilicie*, p. 46.
177. Ibid., p. 66.

178. Ibid.
179. M. Abadie, *Les quatre sièges d'Aintab* (Paris, 1922); K. A. Sarafian, *A Briefer History of Aintab* (Arlington, 1957).
180. Sarafian, *Briefer History of Aintab*, pp. 151 ff.
181. Ibid., p. 154.
182. Abadie, *Les quatre sièges d'Aintab*, pp. 47–50.
183. Ibid., p. 100.
184. Ibid., pp. 47–50.
185. Ibid., p. 111.
186. *DBFP*, vol. VIII, pp. 809–65.
187. G. F. de Martens, *Nouveau receuil général de traités*, 3ième série (Leipzig, 1925), vol. XIII, pp. 332–4.
188. Turkey no. 2 (1921).
189. See Brian Pearce (trans. and ed.), *Congress of the Peoples of the East* (London, 1977).
190. Kazemzadeh, *Struggle for Transcaucasia*, p. 212.
191. Tevfik Biyiklioglu, *Atatürk Anadoluda (1919–1921)* (Ankara, 1959), vol. I, p. 20.
192. Richard Pipes, *The Formation of the Soviet Union* (Cambridge, Mass., 1954), p. 224.
193. Kazim Karabekir, *Istiklal Harbimiz*, 2nd edn (Istanbul, 1969), pp. 661–846.
194. Ibid., pp. 661, 682, 714–15.
195. Ibid., p. 805.
196. Ibid., p. 727.
197. Ibid., p. 735.
198. Ibid., pp. 736–7.
199. Ali Fuat (Cebesoy), *Moskova Hatiralari* (Istanbul, 1955), p. 70.
200. Alexander Khatisian, *Hayastani Hanrapetutian dsagumn ou zargatsumë*, 2nd edn (Beirut, 1968), pp. 254–60.
201. Karabekir, *Istiklal Harbimiz*, p. 830.
202. FO 371/4960.11896.
203. FO 371/4962.13994, pp. 188–91.
204. Ibid., pp. 181, 182.
205. Ibid., p. 184.
206. FO 406/44, p. 48.
207. FO 371/4960.12174.
208. FO 406/44, p. 49.
209. *DBFP*, vol. XII, p. 637.
210. Quoted in E. K. Sarkissian and R. G. Sahakian, *Vital Issues in Modern Armenian History*, trans. E. B. Chrakian (Watertown, 1965), p. 54.
211. Hambardzoum Terterian, 'The Levon Chanth Mission to Moscow', II, *Armenian Review*, vol. VII, no. 3–31 (Autumn 1955), p. 97.
212. Ibid.; see also Khatisian, *Hayastani Hanrapetutian dsagumn ou zargatsumë*, pp. 261–2.
213 Khatisian, *Hayastani Hanrapetutian dsagumn ou zargatsumë*, p. 263.
214. FO 371/4964.14902, p. 1 of report of 22 October.
215. Ibid., p. 3.
216. *DBFP*, vol. XII, p. 642; FO 371/4964.14902, p. 4 of report of 28 October.
217. Vratsian, *Hayastani Hanrapetutiun*, pp. 479–81.
218. Khatisian, *Hayastani Hanrapetutian dsagumn ou zargatsumë*, pp. 278–9.
219. Ibid., p. 280.
220. FO 371/4964.14759.
221. *DBFP*, vol. XII, p. 643; FO 371/4963.14100.
222. FO 371/4963.14301.
223. Vratsian, *Hayastani Hanrapetutiun*, pp. 482–3; Karabekir, *Istiklal Harbimiz*, pp. 844–5; FO 371/4964.14541.
224. FO 371/4964.14636.
225. FO 371/4963.14293.
226. FO 371/4963.14373; FO 371/4964.14568.
227. FO 371/4963.14033.
228. Khatisian, *Hayastani Hanrapetutian dsagumn ou zargatsumë*, p. 290.
229. *DBFP*, vol. XII, p. 653.

230. Vratsian, *Hayastani Hanrapetutiun*, p. 485.
231. Ibid., p. 490.
232. Ibid., p. 487.
233. Ibid., p. 488.
234. Ibid., p. 495.
235. Ibid., p. 498.
236. United States, *Foreign Relations of the United States, 1920*, vol. III, pp. 790–804.
237. Khatisian, *Hayastani Hanrapetutian dsagumn ou zargatsumë*, p. 307.
238. Ibid., p. 308.
239. Pipes, *The Formation of the Soviet Union*, p. 232.
240. Vratsian, *Hayastani Hanrapetutiun*, p. 500.
241. Ibid., p. 503.
242. Ibid., p. 504.
243. Pipes, *The Formation of the Soviet Union*, pp. 232–3.
244. Oliver Baldwin, *Six Prisons and Two Revolutions* (London, 1924), photograph of document facing p. 32.
245. Khatisian, *Hayastani Hanrapetutian dsagumn ou zargatsumë*, p. 309.
246. Ibid., p. 310.
247. Ibid.
248. Ibid.
249. Ibid., p. 311.
250. Copy of the treaty, translated from the Turkish text by Prof. T. Halasi-Kun, in the hands of the author, courtesy of Jacques Kayaloff.
251. Simon Vratsian, 'How Armenia was Sovietized', IV, *Armenian Review*, vol. I, no. 4 (October 1948), p. 94.
252. Leon Z. Surmelian, *I Ask You, Ladies and Gentlemen* (London, 1946), pp. 164–5.
253. Quoted in Vratsian, *Hayastani Hanrapetutiun*, p. 512; also Simon Vratsian, 'How Armenia was Sovietized', IV, *Armenian Review*, vol. I, no. 4 (October 1948), p. 95.
254. Kazemzadeh, *Struggle for Transcaucasia*, pp. 291–2.
255. Ibid., p. 292.
256. Simon Vratsian, 'How Armenia was Sovietized', V, *Armenian Review*, vol. II, no. 1–5 (February 1949), p. 119.
257. Vratsian, *Hayastani Hanrapetutiun*, p. 511.
258. Ibid., p. 551.
259. Baldwin, *Six Prisons*, pp. 82–3.
260. Ibid., pp. 102–7; on Atarbekian see Oliver Baldwin, *The Questing Beast* (London, 1932), pp. 122–3.
261. Vratsian, *Hayastani Hanrapetutiun*, pp. 529–30; see also FO 371/6266.
262. Pipes, *The Formation of the Soviet Union*, p. 238.
263. Baldwin, *Six Prisons*, p. 130.
264. FO 371/6267.3698; see also 'Survey of the Press', *Caucasian Quarterly* (Berlin), no. 3 (1938), p. 130.
265. Text in J. Degras (ed.), *Soviet Documents on Foreign Policy* (London, 1951), vol. I, pp. 237–42.
266. Quoted in Vratsian, 'How Armenia was Sovietized', V, p. 125.
267. S. R. Harutiunian, *Hai Zhoghovrdi Patmutiun* (Yerevan, 1970), vol. 4, p. 155.
268. Vratsian, *Hayastani Hanrapetutiun*, pp. 546–61.
269. V. I. Lenin, *Collected Works* (in English) (Moscow, 1965), vol. 32, pp. 316–18.
270. Text in Degras, *Soviet Documents*, vol. I, pp. 263–9.
271. See Vratsian, *Hayastani Hanrapetutiun*, pp. 643–8.
272. Vratsian, 'How Armenia was Sovietized', V, p. 123.
273. Quoted in ibid., p. 125.

Epilogue

9 Peace on the Plain of Ararat

Armenia Soviet

Eastern Armenia was now securely behind the Soviet shield, and with this protection she was able to start the immense task of reconstruction. All of Western Armenia, and some of Eastern, was lost, but the border was fixed, and even in these cramped and deprived conditions the nation could at last begin to fulfil, in a radically changed form, the hopes expressed by Noel Buxton as he saw the sun set over Ararat in September 1913.

The status of Soviet Armenia was initially that of an independent Soviet republic (roughly in the sense that Poland or Bulgaria is independent today). She negotiated agreements bilaterally with Soviet Russia, and maintained consular relations with Persia (in Tabriz) and Turkey (in Kars), as well as with other Soviet republics. She had her own stamps and currency. Her semi-independent status came to an end in 1922, when, on 13 December, she was absorbed into the Transcaucasian Soviet Federated Socialist Republic, which in turn became a constituent part of the USSR upon its formation on 30 December 1922.[1] The situation remained thus until the USSR's constitution of 1936, when the Transcaucasian SFSR was dissolved, and Armenia became a union republic of the new Soviet state.*

The New Economic Policy (NEP) was instituted by Lenin in March 1921, and its adoption in Armenia paved the way for rebuilding a country that was economically shattered. The NEP allowed a mixed economy, being tolerant of small-scale private enterprise, while keeping the most important sectors in government hands. In 1925 46 per cent of Armenia's trade was privately owned.[2] The peasants were allowed to run their own affairs; there was no collectivisation yet. But progress in the rural economy was held up by the shortage of land; the problem of the 200,000–300,000 Turkish Armenian refugees remained and put as much strain on Armenia now as during the period of Dashnak rule.

Peace, and the dedication of the new rulers of Soviet Armenia, led to a kind of normality in a surprisingly short time. Even those who one would imagine hostile to Bolshevism noted the achievements of the commissars. Dr Clarence Ussher, the eyewitness of the defence of Van and of the anti-Bolshevik rebellion of February 1921, wrote of the leaders of Armenia on 15 December 1921:

*There is a widespread belief that Stalin planned to deny the status of republic to regions with less than a million inhabitants. Armenia would thereby have been reduced to an autonomous region. Apparently it was only the advocacy of Mikoyan which dissuaded him.

Map 12. Soviet Armenia

I am convinced that under present circumstances it would be a mistake to oust them. . . They are all amateurs. The real Communists in Armenia are very few. They deserve credit for what they have accomplished. [Here Ussher criticises them severely for their taxation policies.] Whatever happens to the country I hope the old partisan government will not again take control. It will be pure adventure if they do.[3]

And the Revd. Harold Buxton noted:

Individually the members of the government at Erivan are serious, intelligent and hard-working men; it was a common sight to see these commissars sitting in cold, fireless rooms with their overcoats on while the available fuel was reserved for heating the larger rooms of their staffs.[4]

Until 1928 Armenia moved towards socialism at a leisurely pace. Merely getting the country on its feet again absorbed almost all the energies of the leadership. At the same time there was no attempt to make the inhabitants of Soviet Armenia conform to the new model of Soviet man. Non-Communist writers and thinkers were tolerated, because the government needed their skills. Such men were usually socialists with a nationalist hue, such as the 'Specifist' David Ananoun.[5] (Dashnaktsutiun was of course a proscribed organisation, and had 'abolished' itself within Armenia at a showy meeting in November 1923, set up by the Communists.[6]) The Church, too, came under no direct attack in the 1920s (although religion *per se* was ridiculed), and the clergy were tolerated. Secularism had in any case become entrenched in Armenia in the years before Sovietisation; the Dashnaks had themselves taken most of the parochial schools out of the control of the Church.[7]

Despite the problems which beset Soviet Armenia, the first decade or so of her existence saw a burst of cultural activity, signalling that the country was prepared to put the past behind it, and build for the future. Communist party First Secretary Alexander Miasnikian was himself a highly cultured man, a poet and essayist who had the capacity to recognise genius in others. Of Armenian writers, he held the poet Yeghishe Charents in the highest esteem. Charents was a wild, romantic figure, who became the unofficial poet laureate of Soviet Armenia in her early years. His poetry was characterised by a passionate vitality; it touched on the past with restraint and with what one might describe as a magnificent burnt-out pathos; but dwelt forcefully and brilliantly on the future which the nation would fashion for itself. His work seemed both to reflect and to create the new mood of Armenia. Others who articulated the mood of the country, its muted yearning and militant hope, were Axel Bakounts, Vahan Totovents, Zabel Yesaian and Gurgen Mahari, writers who transmuted the experience of their countrymen into an indelible identity for the citizens of the new state.[8]

But this period did not last for long. The regimentation of art and poetry that accompanied Stalinism crushed those with talent or genius, just as its political manifestations bowed the people down. Not all of Armenia's 'second revolution' was bad, but for those who ventured an opinion, and for the human spirit, the effect was devastating.

The abandoment of NEP and the adoption of the first five-year plan (1928–32) signalled a fundamental change. In 1928 agriculture was collectivised, initially on a voluntary basis. This met with almost no response from the peasantry, so forced collectivisation was introduced in 1930. Peasants who refused to co-operate were deported; one estimate puts their number at 25,000. So great was the oppositon to the initial government measures that the unbelievable occurred in some mountainous districts: Armenians and Tatars united to resist collectivisation. To the forced measures of late 1930 the Armenian mountaineers responded with an armed rebellion; Zangezur, which had been the seat of the fiercest resistance to the Communists ten years earlier, held out against Stalin's imposition until 1934, when, as in 1921, the rebels were forced to flee into Persia. Nevertheless, collectivisation proceeded apace, and could be said to have succeeded by 1936, by which time four-fifths of peasant households were included in the scheme.[9]

Armenia's industrialisation took place at the same time, laying the foundations for what is one of the most heavily industrialised of the Soviet republics today. Factories were set up in Yerevan and Leninakan (as Alexandropol was renamed in 1924), which were already centres of small-scale industry; and the mining districts of Alaverdi, Artik and Ghapan were expanded. For the first time Armenia developed a proletariat; her new labour force came from the villages, from the unemployed (of whom there were a substantial number in the 1920s), and from the women. Out of the whole population of the country, the percentage figure for industrial and white-collar workers was, in 1935, almost double that of 1926. At the same time houses were being built throughout the land, and public services were established.[10]

In charge of the 'second revolution' in Armenia was Aghasi Khandjian. He had been in Russia, not the Caucasus, since 1921, and had been close to Stalin; in fact one could regard him, from 1928, when he returned south, as Stalin's man in Transcaucasia. He became First Secretary of the Armenian Communist party in May 1930. He developed a genuine popularity with the peasantry, and worked hard to build the new Armenia; but as Soviet Communism became characterised more and more by paranoia and purge, so he too purged the Communists of Armenia. The party became taken up with frightening, labyrinthine quarrels, with ruthless power struggles, and with bitter betrayals. The intrigues even crept up upon Khandjian himself, despite Stalin's support for him; for above Khandjian, in Tiflis, there was Lavrenti Beria, First Secretary of the Transcaucasian regional committee of the Communist party. Beria was jealous at the reception that a speech of his, *On the History of Bolshevik Organisations in Transcaucasia* (a grisly fabrication), had received in Armenia, and sought to destroy anyone who might rival his authority. So despite six years of struggle and purge to assure his place as party leader in Armenia, Khandjian was himself murdered by Beria in July 1936.[11]

Khandjian's murder signalled the start of the great purge, which lasted until 1939. The presence of Beria meant that the terror hit Armenia, and Transcaucasia in general, with particular ferocity. Absurd charges were made against men and women from all sections of the population; tens of thousands were jailed; the prisons became filled beyond capacity, so that all basements of government buildings were commandeered for use as extra jails.[12] The 'Old Bolsheviks' were finally wiped out, as were the men who had pioneered the second revolution. Thousands were liquidated in Armenia. One of the most tragic losses was Charents himself, who died in jail in 1937.

The extent of the purge, and its quality of a vast violent nightmare, may cause one to wonder: was Bolshevik Russia really a better choice for Armenia than Kemalist Turkey? The answer must be that for all their blood-stained horror, the Stalinist purges had none of the entirely genocidal qualities that the Turks manifested towards Armenians, right up to the period of Karabekir's occupation of Alexandropol. Women and children were not killed merely for the sake of eliminating them. If the Turks, rather than Stalin's henchmen, had unleashed their fury on the Armenians, there would have been no Armenians left, and the buildings of Armenians would have been razed as if they had never been. By contrast, the sheer amount of construction (both of factories and homes) that the Communists had undertaken in the decade before the purges assured Armenia of security and ultimate progress.* Once the purges were past, progress could re-start.

The purgers were themselves purged from January 1938 to February 1939. The paranoia of the past years receded, and relative normality returned. Political stability was re-established, and the witch-hunts for 'nationalists' ceased. The novels of Raffi were republished in 1940, and the edition sold out (in considerable disorder) within a few hours. The following year the 135th anniversary of Abovian's birth was celebrated in Yerevan. On the eve of the entry of the USSR into the second world war, it was clear that, within the confines of Stalinist Communism, considerable concessions were being made to Armenia.[13]

Turkey and the Remnant of Turkish Armenians, 1919–39

After the first world war the Ittihadist leaders who had planned and executed the Armenian genocide fled, mostly to Germany. With the presence of an Allied fleet at Constantinople, the Ottoman council of ministers began an investigation into the war crimes. But it was carried out in such a dilatory

---

*This period was, in fact, the first occasion in modern times that any government had actually built anything for Armenians within Armenia.

fashion as to make sure that as little justice as possible was done.[14] Only in April 1919 were any Ittihadists arrested; but the following month the British, impatient with the inertia of Turkish justice, shipped to Malta some suspected war criminals (or 'statesmen and intellectuals', as Professor Niyazi Berkes calls them in his article on Zia Gökalp in the *Encyclopedia of Islam*). The tribunals sat, with increasing ineffectiveness, throughout 1919 and 1920. Only one man of even slight significance – Kemal of Yozgat – was convicted, sentenced and hanged (June 1919). Enver, Talaat and the bleak fanatic Dr Nazim were sentenced to death *in absentia* in July 1919; Behaeddin Shakir in January 1920. All these men had escaped, or were in hiding. No attempt was made to extradite them to Ottoman Turkey. Moreover, after Kiazim Karabekir's assault on Armenia in the late autumn of 1920, some further sentences which had been passed were 'reconsidered' by the military court of appeals, which ultimately, on 9 January 1921, annulled the verdicts and set the criminals free.

So Dashnaktsutiun decided that it would carry out its own executions of the mass-murders of Armenians. A secret Dashnak network, named Nemesis, was set up to track down the convicted war criminals and to execute them. First to go was Talaat himself, 'the soul of the Armenian persecutions'; after weeks of watching and waiting, a young Armenian named Soghomon Tehlirian, almost all of whose family had been exterminated in the genocide, gunned down the former Ottoman minister of the interior in a Berlin street on 15 March 1921.[15] (Tehlirian was arrested, and tried on 2–3 June; among those appearing for the defence were Dr Lepsius and Liman von Sanders. It did not take the jury long to acquit him.) Next to die was Said Halim, former Ottoman foreign minister, assassinated in Rome by Arshavir Shirakian on 6 December 1921.[16] Two quite different but equally murderous individuals were next to be skittled down, again by Shirakian (working with a colleague): Behaeddin Shakir, the cold-blooded 'intellectual' and Paris-trained doctor, and Djemal Azmi, the butcher of Trebizond.[17] Both were assassinated in Berlin on 17 April 1922. Djemal Pasha met his end in Tiflis on 25 July 1922, gunned down in front of the Cheka head-quarters by two Armenians. Enver himself, pursuing some crazy pan-Turkist fantasy, was killed in an ambush while leading Muslim Basmachis against the Red Army in Central Asia two weeks later, on 4 August – a 'martyr to Turkism', in the words of Dr Nazim.[18] There is an unsubstantiated story that the Soviet soldier who fired the shot was an Armenian.[19] Dr Nazim himself, a chilling intellectual like Behaeddin Shakir with a European medical background, and a *dönme* – a member of a Jewish–Muslim syncretist sect, eluded them. (He was hanged for treason in 1926.)

With the establishment of the Nationalist regime of Mustafa Kemal, and the birth of modern Turkey, it would be comfortable to believe that persecution of Armenians had ended, and that the few survivors were permitted to live unmolested: Armenians had been pitilessly exterminated during the genocide of 1915–16; the Turkish Nationalists had crushed the Republic of Armenia, and forced the Sovietisation of the remnant of it; and Turkey had received quite disproportionately favourable terms by the treaties of Moscow and Kars. Mustafa Kemal was known personally to hate fanaticism and to despise religious extremism, and to be devoid of the anti-minority sentiments that had characterised Turkish leaders in the past. Would he use his authority to let the frightened remnants of the Armenians subsist quietly?

Unfortunately this was not to be. The Pontic Greeks (in Trebizond province) were savagely persecuted in the years 1922–4, until the community was virtually wiped out; and as a spin-off of their persecution Armenians were subject to renewed attacks. In May 1922 Major Yowell of Near East Relief reported from Kharput:

> Armenians in this district are in a state of virtual slavery, and are not per-
> mitted to travel even within the country. All property of the Armenians who
> died in the recent deportations has been confiscated by the Turks.
> Armenians have no rights in the courts.[20]

Other relief workers confirmed Yowell's account, despite an attempt to hush the facts up by the United States, which was longing to do business with Kemal's new Turkey.*

Most spectacular (and subject to the most careful cover-up) was the Kemalist conquest of Smyrna (Izmir), on 9 September 1922, which was followed by looting, rape and murder by the Turkish forces, and by their setting fire to the Greek and Armenian quarters. For decades afterwards the myth was fostered that the Greeks and Armenians set fire to their own areas before quitting them – an untruth, recently (and finally) exploded in a book by Marjorie Housepian.[21] In its ferocity and ruthlessness the sack of Smyrna resembled the sack of Baku by the Turkish army almost exactly four years earlier.

While Smyrna was being sacked and burnt by the Kemalists, a fleet of warships belonging to Great Britain, France, Italy and the United States was anchored in the harbour. No attempt was made to intervene (to have expected that would have been an insult to the virtue of the Allies) and only the most reluctant efforts were made to rescue some of the 280,000 refugees who stood, crushed together and terrified, on the quayside. Little attempt was even made to 'protect the national property' of the immobile powers: despite the existence of

---

*Notably by Admiral Mark L. Bristol, United States High Commissioner in Constantinople. He was a great admirer of Turkish rule, especially its harsher aspects. There was also the concession-hunting family of the Chesters (father and sons). Chester senior believed he was on the point of building 2,800 miles of railways in Turkey. In the September 1922 issue of the magazine *Current History* (New York) he had written that

the Armenians in 1915 were moved from the inhospitable regions where they were not welcome and could not actually prosper, to the most delightful and fertile parts of Syria ... where the climate is as benign as in Florida and California whither New York millionaires journey every year for health and recreation. All this was done at great expense of money and effort.

American buildings and stores in Smyrna, the United States landed sailors to protect only one of any importance, the plant of the Standard Oil Company.[22] Armenian refugees from the city (of whom there are a number in London) claim that British sailors turned hosepipes on any refugees swimming towards their vessels and trying to board them.

The episode was the climax of the relationship that had developed between the Ottoman empire and the 'Western' powers since the Crimean war loan. Underneath all was the relentless and basic support for Turkey for commercial reasons, and for strategic reasons when those and other commercial enterprises were endangered. Support for the non-Turks, or for those forces which sought to modify the oppressive government (which a number of dedicated imperialists supported just because it was so merciless) was seldom more than transitory. The assurances that the European powers gave the minorities were propaganda, designed to appease their liberals at home, while they got on with the job of working with the Turks.

After the capture of Smyrna, and the re-occupation of Constantinople (henceforward Istanbul), the Allies were compelled to sign an armistice with the forces of Mustafa Kemal. This they did at Mudanya, on 11 October 1922. Just over two weeks later the Nationalists were invited to a peace conference, which eventually was convened at Lausanne on 21 November 1922.

The negotiations at Lausanne and subsequent peace treaty represent the final collapse of the hopes of the Western Armenians that they would be permitted to have any independent or autonomous existence on former Ottoman territory, either in Turkish Armenia or Cilicia. The Turkish delegation, representing a nation victorious now, only four years after being quite defeated, was headed by Ismet (Inönü). Ismet's diplomacy was a mixture of unbending inflexibility, irrelevant objection and exasperating lecture, which served his own purpose ideally. The Capitulations were abolished, the Greco-Turkish frontier was fixed to his liking, and no homeland was given to the Western Armenians, despite the advocacy of Lord Curzon. Armenians were indeed not mentioned in the subsequent treaty, although the subject came up in an insubstantial way.[23] Ismet indicated that any serious discussion of the Armenian question would lead to the break-up of the conference. American representative Joseph Grew noted, 'There is no subject upon which the Turks are more fixed in obstinacy.'[24]

One argument which Ismet used at Lausanne has been echoed by supporters of the Turks ever since. It is summed up in a simple phrase: Turkey for the Turks. By a magical alchemy the Ottoman empire – with a ruling people and subject peoples, just like any other empire – had become 'Turkey' – an appellation of European origin, signifying to the European mind a normal nation-state with a reasonably homogeneous population, which Turkey, with boundaries as defined by Ismet, was not. No one could object to 'Turkey for the Turks' if Turkey consisted only of the lands indubitably and legitimately Turkish. But not only were there Kurds and Laz in the east; there were also the deserted homes and villages of the hundreds of thousands of Armenians who had been exterminated or driven out. 'Turkey for the Turks' seems just to be the banal statement of a political truism; but really it is a concealed argument for not recognising the crimes of the past, and for denying that the former empire should be decolonised.

Although the treaty of Lausanne did not mention Armenians, seven of its articles (38–44) refer to them.[25] Life and liberty were guaranteed, without distinction of 'birth, nationality, language, race or religion'; free movement was allowed, and all were equal before the law (articles 38 and 39). Article 40 established that Turkish nationals belonging to non-Muslim minorities might 'establish, manage and control at their own expense any charitable, religious and social institutions, and any schools and other establishments for instruction and education'. The minorities might teach their children in their own languages, and the government would provide facilities; but the teaching of Turkish would be obligatory (article 41). The next two clauses stated that the minorities' own customs might be used for regulating their own internal affairs, and that they would not be compelled to do anything which their religion forbade. Article 44 stated that the League of Nations itself guaranteed the foregoing articles, thereby giving them international significance.

If we accept today that the United Nations is the legal successor to the League of Nations – a claim which has been definitely established in the case of South-West Africa (Namibia) – then the UN must be bound to be guardian of articles 38–43 of the Lausanne treaty. They are in fact disregarded by the Turkish government, especially article 40. The harassment and government obstruction which Armenians have faced in their attempts in recent years to keep their schools going is reminiscent of the days of Abdul Hamid. The United Nations could prove that it is guardian of those disregarded pledges, and though there is little chance of the world body doing so, it is worth remembering that it has the power to do so.

The Turkish government refused to discuss Armenian claims for compensation for Armenian material losses during the massacres and deportations. Everything was done to pretend that such events had never really taken place; so naturally claims for compensation were superfluous.

In one place, however, Mustafa Kemal allowed his drive for modernisation to override the traditional Turkish attitude towards Armenians. In 1928 the villagers of Everek Fenese, near Kayseri, petitioned the Turkish leader for the re-opening of their church; and they wrote out their request in the reformed Latinised script, which had only just been introduced. Impressed by the manner in which Armenians demonstrated their support for his modernisation plans, he assented at once.[26]

But in the following year further grim events awaited Turkish Armenians. On 1 January 1929 the Turkish government issued a punitive, discriminatory decree which stated that Armenians might not sell or bequeath their property, which was to go to the state upon their death. Then, in the summer of that year, new deportations of the sad remnant of Armenian peasants and artisans, living on the fringes of the ancient homeland of Turkish Armenia, were set in motion. In a despatch dated Aleppo, 14 November 1929, British consul A. Monck-Mason reported that refugees had been arriving continually for the preceding six months from the regions of Kharput, Diyarbekir and Mardin.[27] In his opinion, 'the settled policy of the Turkish government seems to be to get rid of all Christian elements in the distant Anatolian provinces by all means short of absolute massacre, of which there has been admittedly very little.' Aleppo, he continues, has been the sanctuary for the daily caravans of Armenians. 'Whole families are sick, and nearly all are absolutely destitute.' He quotes an Armenian from Kharput saying: 'In Turkey today we have no means of existence; we are persecuted, suspected, robbed, ill-treated, thrown into prison, judged, and, if we are lucky, deported.'[28] Bombs had been thrown into churches, and the Armenian bishop of Diyarbekir murdered by seven drunken soldiers. Estimates of those expelled in the 1929–30 deportations put the number at 30,000.[29]

After these deportations had died down, leaving Turkish Armenians who still clung to their ancient soil more remote, more frightened and more prepared than ever to 'pass for Turk', Armenians were free from more than the usual discrimination or government hostility for the next few years.

Less than ten years later republican Turkey began agitating for the annexation from Syria of the *sanjak* of Alexandretta, on the Mediterranean coastline. France was the mandatary for Syria, and when she had occupied Syria after the battle of Khan Maysalun, she effected an administrative division of the country, showing a high degree of colonial cynicism. The *sanjak* of Alexandretta enjoyed 'special administrative status' within what the French deigned to call the 'state of Syria' – a sadly truncated entity, deprived of the Djebel Druz and the region of Latakia (the latter known as the 'state of the Alawites').[30] Alexandretta's special status derived from the Franklin-Bouillon agreement of October 1921. Turkish agitation for the *sanjak* began in September 1936, and did not cease until she had annexed it in October 1939.

Within the *sanjak* were about 23,000 Armenians. Most of them were villagers who had lived there since medieval times; 6,000 were refugees from Cilicia, whom the American Near East Relief had settled there. In all, they constituted 11 per cent of the total population of the district. No linguistic or religious group was in the majority in the *sanjak*. The Turks constituted 39 per cent of the population, and were outnumbered by the combined total of the Arabic speakers. Of all those Turks, only about a third actually wanted union with the Turkish republic. Nevertheless Mustafa Kemal's threats of force eventually compelled the French, and the League of Nations, to give way; and in 1938, in an action which recalls Hitler's occupation of the Rhineland two years before, the Turkish leader sent his troops to occupy the *sanjak*. When the Armenians realised that they were faced with Turkish rule, they saw no alter-

native but to quit.* Eight thousand left in the year following the Turkish
military occupation, and in one week in the summer of 1939, there was a mass
exodus of 14,000. All left to face the poverty, refugee camps and harsh struggle
for life that fellow Armenians faced in Lebanon and Syria.† Only 600
Armenians remained to face the Turkish administration in the *sanjak* (renamed
'Hatay' for phoney historical reasons).[31] Although not directly aimed at the
Armenians, the Kemalist annexation of the *sanjak* of Alexandretta had further
wretched consequences for Armenians; nor was this to be the last time, as
events during the second world war will show.

Refugees and Relief

During the period of the Republic of Armenia, there were about 300,000
refugees from Turkish Armenia scratching a living from her dry and stony soil.
By the time that Armenia became Soviet they had been reduced probably to
nearer 200,000, mainly as a result of starvation and exposure. Of all the
refugees, they were probably the luckiest, since they were in *an* Armenia,
whose inhabitants spoke the same language as themselves, and which, during
the industrialisation of the 1930s, could assimilate them. Indeed 40,000
Armenians who were almost all refugees from Turkish Armenia, but had
sought shelter in other countries, went to Soviet Armenia to settle in the period
1922–36.

The situation of the refugees in the Near East was the gravest. In all there
were about 200,000 of these throughout the countries of the Eastern
Mediterranean, distributed approximately as follows:

Greece	45,000
Bulgaria	6,000
Egypt	4,000
Syria and Lebanon	90,000
Constantinople	5,000
Iraq	14,500
Palestine	2,500[32]

Of those, the situation of the refugees in Greece was widely considered to be
the most acute, since Greece was herself saddled with the gigantic problem of

*It also appears that some Armenian leaders actually encouraged their people to leave,
obeying in a rather craven manner the dictates of the French authorities in Damascus, who
sought a counterbalance of Christian, non-Arab peoples in Syria to outweigh the gathering and
insistent forces of Syrian nationalism.

†The people from the villages of Musa Dagh were settled in a camp, which has become a
village, at Ainjar, close to the Lebanese–Syrian border and just off the main road. Their distinctive church is clearly visible from the road. Visitors to the interesting Umayyad ruins at Ainjar
are likely (as I did) to have an Armenian from the *sanjak* of Alexandretta as their courteous and
informative guide.

settling the Anatolian Greeks, who by early 1923 had reached the figure of 1,200,000. The greatest concentration of Armenians was in Syria and (especially) Lebanon, where they constituted in succeeding years a political force of some consequence.

The problems of settling these refugees, and especially of looking after the orphans, seemed at first intractable, especially in Syria and Lebanon, which were themselves undeveloped countries. Nevertheless relief workers laboured with unflagging dedication, and the spirit of the people might have been low, but it was far from burnt out. The American Near East Relief spent almost $100,000,000 on relief (largely, but not all, in Lebanon and Syria); the British Armenian (Lord Mayor's) Fund also contributed; and the Armenian General Benevolent Union (AGBU), which had been founded in 1906, worked tirelessly too. Indeed AGBU was the inheritor of the European and American philanthropic enterprises when these agencies wound down their activities, and remains today a most important Armenian charity and a vital resource for the Armenian people.

International attempts to solve the refugee problem were bedevilled by politics. A scheme to resettle some of the Near Eastern refugees in Soviet Armenia was put forward by the Armenian National Delegation in Paris in August 1923.[33] The idea was to irrigate the Sardarabad desert, and populate it with 50,000 Armenians; it was taken up by the council of the League of Nations, which requested the great Norwegian explorer and philanthropist, Dr Fridtjof Nansen, to investigate the possibilities of the scheme. Dr Nansen had already won renown for his work with post-war refugees. Initially he declined the new assignment, but accepted when offered the co-operation of the International Labour Bureau.[34] Various countries offered aid: France put up 335,000 francs; Greece offered some, despite her own appalling problems. Even Albania, a largely Muslim country, was prepared to give cash for Armenian resettlement. Britain, however, did not offer anything, and when requested to do so (to give a moral lead, over and above any sum involved) in March 1924, the government responded coolly, saying that there was insufficient information to judge whether the scheme was workable. In the meantime H. H. Asquith and Stanley Baldwin, then out of government, had sent a joint memorandum to Prime Minister Ramsay MacDonald proposing that 'a substantial contribution should be made to the scheme'.[35] Dr Nansen travelled to Armenia in the summer of 1925, and found the scheme to be technically and financially sound. About £1,000,000 was required – not a great sum, if divided among a number of countries. Thereby they would discharge themselves of having failed the Armenians so often in the past. It would be a small, but notable recompense. A Foreign Office draft memorandum put it thus:

> The withholding of so small a sum would be interpreted abroad, where our own needs and difficulties are imperfectly appreciated, as a cynical

gesture, dispensing other countries from financial sacrifice. It would be regarded, and not least by the Armenians themselves, as a deliberate repudiation of our pledges as well as a disavowal of the humanitarian claims of a small and bitterly afflicted nation on a large and prosperous one.[36]

But despite the cogent pleading of Nansen at the League of Nations, Britain refused the small sum. The reason was political: control of Armenia rested with Moscow. Winston Churchill was chancellor of the exchequer in Baldwin's Conservative administration, which took office in November 1924, and he saw such a grant as tantamount to giving aid to Soviet Russia. Baldwin's advocacy of support for the scheme, of only a few months earlier, evaporated like so many other expressions of support for Armenians. Financial assistance to the refugees was blocked. It was not, however, the end of the matter. Another commission travelled to Yerevan, to check the soundness of the scheme, and came to the same conclusion as the earlier one. This time, the Norwegian philanthropist asked, in November 1926, for a repayable loan, to circumvent the political objection of aiding Soviet Russia. During 1927, five countries agreed to contribute to the new scheme: Germany, Greece, Norway, Romania and Switzerland.[38] What of Britain? After an inordinate delay, the Foreign Office delivered its judgement on 28 January 1928: even though as little as £100,000 was requested, His Majesty's government would not contribute to the later scheme. In justification, it was claimed that Britain had spent £1,180,000 on Armenian relief (in Iraq) since 1918. In a parliamentary question on 21 February 1928, the indefatigable Noel Buxton asked the government spokesman on foreign affairs 'if he can now state whether HMG had decided to comply with the request of the council of the League of Nations to assist with a grant the settlement of Armenian refugees in Yerevan': the reply was, wrapped round in the usual quasi-Ottoman verbiage, no.[39]

Nansen's own hopes were raised again later in 1928, when Armenians themselves contributed £100,000; but nothing further was actually received, apart from £50,000 from Germany; so a year later he announced that the entire scheme was to be abandoned for lack of support.[40] In future, Armenians carried on their charitable activities directly with the Soviet government, from which they got actual results, and avoided the high-principled but stone-fisted men who talked at the assembly of the League of Nations.

It was a depressingly appropriate way for Britain to bow out of her engagements with Armenians. All the way back to the Berlin congress her record is a shabby one, to use no stronger word. It is hard to avoid the conclusion that Armenians would have been more fortunate if Britain had never had anything at all to do with them.

Internal Armenian Politics

The mutual hostility between Dashnaktsutiun and Bolshevism should not be considered absolute. At the time of Armenia's Sovietisation there is evidence of a measure of goodwill from the Dashnaks towards the Bolsheviks, which was rapidly dispersed by the actions of the Revkom in entering Armenia, and was finally dissipated by the revolt of February 1921. The Bolsheviks for their part did not seek simply to crush Dashnaktsutiun. Even after Red forces had recaptured Yerevan they were prepared to negotiate a Dashnak surrender in Zangezur, rather than simply resort to a military solution.

Negotiations to this end began at Kaladjik, in Zangezur, on 12 May 1921: A. Karinian and V. Melnikov represented the Soviet side.[41] But less than a month after the start of the negotiations, on 10 June, the Dashnaks signed an agreement in Paris with the other ousted regimes of Transcaucasia and the North Caucasus, in which all four declared that they would unite in political and economic fields. (How much easier it was to unite in exile, than when the governments actually controlled tracts of land!) They planned to sign a military defence treaty, and to establish a united foreign policy. The four republics would work together in settling the Turko-Armenian frontier (which they clearly envisaged as including some pre-1914 Ottoman territory); they also demanded the withdrawal of the Red Army from the four Caucasian republics.[42]

This agreement was the first example of the shadow politics which were to give Dashnaktsutiun a sense of purposeful activity in the succeeding decades, but whose benefit to the Armenian people was questionable. On this occasion the agreement might possibly have given heart to the rebels in Zangezur, for on 15 June they attacked Soviet forces in Daralagiaz. On 19 June party chief Alexander Miasnikían proposed to the Dashnaks that they lay down their arms, but they refused, so the Red Army launched an all-out campaign against them, retaking Daralagiaz on 26 June, and conquering the rest of Zangezur village by village until Meghri was captured on 13 July, an event which signalled the end of Dashnak rule in Armenia.[43]

At the very same time that the Dashnaks were forming an anti-Bolshevik alliance in Paris, and refusing to co-operate with the Bolsheviks on the ground in Armenia, they were carrying on talks for an accommodation with the Bolsheviks. The initiative for these talks, held in the Latvian capital of Riga from 8 to 14 July 1921, came from the Dashnaks themselves. It is hard to see them as doing other than playing a double game. The Bolshevik side was represented by A. I. Ioffe, Vahan Ter-Vahanian and Sahak Ter-Gabrielian, and Dashnaks were Arshak Jamalian, Vahan Navasardian and Vahan Papazian (Koms). An agreement was reached under which the Armenian Bolsheviks would do all in their power to secure the return of Armenia's lost lands, while the Dashnaks would adopt a stance friendly to Soviet power. The agreement was initialled, but not signed; the Bolshevik side heard of the Paris agreement, and broke off relations with the Dashnaks.[44]

At the same time, in this strange period of alliances and counter-alliances, of secret and suspicious – and entirely profitless – discussions and pacts, another anti-Bolshevik agreement was made. Although similar to that agreed in Paris by the ousted Caucasian governments, it was different in that it planned to use Kemalist Turkey as the agent for overthrowing the Bolsheviks in the Caucasus. It was established in Tabriz in mid-July 1921, with the title of Prometheus (or Prométhée; it is spelt 'Promete' in Armenian). Khosrov bek Sultanov was the Azerbaijani representative. Dashnaks say that they did not take part; however, non-Dashnaks say that they did, and that Simon Vratsian was their representative. Non-Dashnaks also hold that the treaty of Alexandropol was to be the basis of the pact (and that the Dashnak government had signed the Alexandropol treaty anticipating such a pact). It is further claimed by opponents of the Dashnaks, and indeed by one senior member of the party who formed an opposition splinter group and was later expelled from Dashnaktsutiun, that the Prometheus orientation was of great importance in Dashnak political councils throughout the 1920s.[45]

But one thing shows that by 1927 the Dashnaks sought no further contacts with Turkey, if they had ever had them. This was their participation in the steps which led to the Kurdish revolt of Ihsan Nuri and others in the summer of 1930. The Kurds had already been in revolt in Turkey in 1925, when Sheikh Said raised a revolt which eventually encompassed a broad stretch of land from Lake Van westwards to Kharput and Siverek. The character of the 1925 Kurdish revolt was religious, but the large measure of success that it commanded showed that there were extensive political forces operating, since observers of the Kurds have habitually noted that their desires and aspirations lie much more with this world than the next.

After Sheikh Said's revolt, Kurdish anti-Turkish activities took on an overtly political complexion. A Kurdish nationalist political organisation, called the Khoybun, was founded in 1927. At its inaugural meeting, held at Bhamdoun, Lebanon, leading Dashnaktsakan Vahan Papazian was present, and it is clear that in succeeding years the Dashnaks built up the political structure of the Khoybun, eventually enabling it to stage an armed revolt in 1930, in the region stretching from Mount Ararat to the north-east extremity of Lake Van.[46] If there ever had been a 'Prometheus orientation', it was now dead. The revolt lasted for two months, before the fate of the rebels was sealed by an agreement between the Turkish and Iranian governments.

Thereafter the Dashnaks appear to have turned their attention away from Turkey, and to have focused again on Soviet Armenia.* Three years later this change of emphasis was to be made grimly apparent.

In March 1933 the Dashnak party held its general congress in Paris. It did so against a fairly widespread belief among party stalwarts that the Soviet government was using some of the Armenian clergy for political purposes.

---

*There is a noticeable difference in attitude between Dashnaks of Ottoman origin and those born in the tsar's dominions. The former are more aware of the Turkish threat to their people, and consequently more ready to engage in anti-Turkish protests and demonstrations, while a number of Caucasian Dashnaks have been known to take a fiercely anti-Russian (and specifically anti-Bolshevik) stance, provoking charges of pro-Turkishness from their opponents.

Dashnaktsutiun soon after showed that it was pursuing an activist policy among diaspora Armenians. One of the main points at issue was loyalty to the Armenian flag. The red, blue and orange tricolour had been rendered obsolete within Armenia by Sovietisation, which had introduced a new flag replete with Soviet symbols.* Now the Dashnaks sought to kindle loyalty to the former flag, and their insistence led to a number of incidents in Armenian communities.

At the Chicago World Fair, 1 June 1933 had been designated 'Armenian Day'. Guest speaker was Archbishop Ghevond Tourian, recently appointed by Catholicos Khoren I (of Echmiadzin) to be prelate of the Armenians of America. Unknown to the archbishop, the platform had been decorated with the tricolour; when he saw the old flag, he refused to speak until it was removed. Eventually he spoke beneath the Stars and Stripes.

The archbishop was thereafter severely criticised in the Dashnak press. He was physically attacked in August at Westboro, Massachusetts. Then, on Sunday, 24 December 1933, as he was in procession down the aisle of the Armenian church of the Holy Cross on West 187th Street, New York, he was murdered by Dashnak hit men:[47] a shocking act, all the more grievous if one recalls that 15 years earlier Dashnaktsutiun had been the party of government in Armenia, with all the dignity and responsibility that that entailed.

The parties in the diaspora realised that something had to be done to curb the fratricidal tendencies that were manifesting themselves. After the Sovietisation of Armenia, the parties of the diaspora amounted principally to three: the Hunchaks, whose Marxist socialism led them to support Soviet Armenia and her leadership in all major issues; the Dashnaks, unchanged in essential structure since their foundation in 1890, and a member of the Second International since 1907; and the Ramkavars. This last, properly the Ramkavar Azatakan Kusaktsutiun or Democratic Liberal party, was formed in 1921 out of a triple merger – of the Armenakans, of the Verakazmial, or Reformed, Hunchaks, who had seceded from the Hunchaks in 1896, and of the Sahmanadir Ramkavar party, founded in 1908 in Cairo. The two most powerful parties in the diaspora emerged as the Dashnaks and the Ramkavars; the Hunchaks commanded considerably less adherence and funds. Although the new Ramkavar Azatakan party numbered among its members rich merchants of a conservative outlook, like its predecessors it was the party of the Armenian open-minded intelligentsia, of teachers, doctors and lawyers. Ramkavars have always held that Soviet Armenia is the best Armenia that they are likely to get, since it is protected by Russia; and without Russian protection (of whatever political complexion) Armenia would disappear from the map of the world for ever. So, despite their liberal principles, the facts – as they see them – of Armenia's geography and history compel them to support Soviet Armenia.

*Initially there was no specifically partisan identity to the tricolour. However, the current of political events meant that it had become obsolete, being identified with the period of Dashnak rule.

In the summer of 1938 representatives of the Dashnaks and the Ramkavars met in Cairo to see if they could establish some common goals, and to define their different spheres of interest. A measure of agreement was reached. Both parties accepted that Armenia, as it was constituted at that time, was the nucleus of Armenian existence, irrespective of the regime in power. The Dashnaks agreed not to take part in any act leading to the dismemberment of the USSR, upon which the safety of Armenia depended. They also agreed not to provoke any internal disorders or try to overthrow the regime. However, they would continue their relations with anti-Soviet forces, because, should the USSR collapse, it was prudent to be on good terms with any regime that might take its place. They remembered 1917–18. They would also give due respect to Echmiadzin, and not fight over Church administration outside Armenia. Both sides agreed to differ on which day they celebrated Armenia's rebirth – whether on 28 May or 29 November – as well as on the issue of the Armenian flag. By this agreement a dangerous collision was averted.[48]

In the years before the second world war a small Fascist element appeared within Dashnaktsutiun. It is wrong to say that the Dashnak party itself adopted Fascism; and the few pro-Fascist comments that appeared in its press at the time can no more be taken as wholesale endorsement of Fascism than can the favourable remarks of some European leaders on the first year of Fascist rule in Germany. Garegin Nzhdeh, dictator of Lernahayastan until it fell to the Bolsheviks in July 1921, arrived in the United States as a Dashnak field-worker in 1933, and founded a youth movement named the Tseghakrons, or racists (*tsegh* = race; *kron* is a suffix signifying 'devotee of'). The Dashnak party itself would not endorse Nzhdeh's notions, and some time afterwards it expelled him from its ranks.[49] The name of the youth movement he had founded was changed to 'Armenian Youth Federation'. Nevertheless, the flirtation of certain Armenian circles with Fascism was not over.

The Second World War

Armenia was not a theatre of the second world war, although in March and April 1940 Britain and France were seriously studying the possibility of bombing Baku (to which the French attached great importance) – a course of action which would have brought Transcaucasia into the war, with fearful consequences for Armenia: Turkey would have invaded from the west, overrunning Armenia, exterminating her people and wrecking her cities more thoroughly than in 1918 and 1920. Lack of enthusiasm on the part of Britain and the fall of France put paid to that piece of adventurism.[50]

After Hitler's invasion of the Soviet Union (22 June 1941), and with the beginning of what is known in Soviet terminology as the 'great patriotic war', the Armenians contributed extensively to the Soviet armies. The number of Soviet Armenian serving soldiers has been estimated at between 300,000 and

500,000; more than 50 Soviet generals were Armenians, including the renowned General (later Marshal) Baghramian. Three Soviet admirals were also
Armenians, which is all the more surprising when one considers that Armenia
has never had a coastline; they included Admiral Isakov, whose account of the
Soviet war at sea has been translated into English. Over 32,000 Armenian
soldiers were decorated in the war, and over 100 received the award 'Hero of
the Soviet Union'.*[51]

Nor should one overlook the fact that on the other side of the world 20,000
Armenians served in the United States army during the war.

Besides actually fighting, Armenians – those outside their homeland – also
contributed to the establishment of a Soviet tank corps, known as Sasuntzi
Davit (i.e. David of Sasun, the legendary fighter of the eleventh century, whose
activities are recounted in the epic poem which bears his name). This corps was
set up, initially from Echmiadzin, in January 1943. After a world-wide appeal
for funds, the tank corps was in the field in late February 1944. Two months
later Sasuntzi Davit was reported to have advanced 200 kilometres, destroying
the occupying forces of the Axis. The main contributions from Armenians
abroad were: United States, $115,000; Lebanon, £L185,000; Syria,
£Syr276,000; Egypt, £14,000; Iran, $2\frac{1}{2}$ million rials. Armenians in Tehran
were planning to set up a 'Hovhannes Baghramian' tank corps when the war
ended. Altogether it was a remarkable display of patriotic fervour, and of
loyalty to the reality of Armenia both as part of the USSR, and as one of the
components of the anti-Nazi alliance.[52]

Nevertheless, Armenian enthusiasm for the Allied cause in the second world
war was not wholehearted. Armenia's history and geographical position meant
that total support for the Allies could not be assumed automatically. The fact
that some Armenians collaborated with the Germans should not be the cause
of smug moralising. To have antagonised the Nazis would have been suicide.

Members of the Dashnak party living in the occupied areas, including a
number of names famous from the period of the republic, adopted a pro-Nazi
stance. The *whole* Dashnak party did not take this stance; the section of the
party in Cairo affirmed its loyalty to the Allies.[53]

A letter in *The Times* (London) of 19 July 1941 indignantly rebutted the idea
that any of the Armenian people entertained pro-Axis sympathies. It was
written by J. |Zhirair| Missakian, then the only Dashnak party member in
Britain. He wrote of the 'fantastic hints' that Armenians were leaning towards
the Axis – hints which had indeed been fed to *The Times* from its
correspondent in Istanbul, whose despatches echoed official Turkish attempts

---

*Marshal Baghramian's command of the First Baltic Front in Byelorussia and East Prussia
(June–October 1944), which inflicted heavy defeats on the Nazis, is fairly well known. Less
known are the exploits of Major-General Nver Safarian, commander from February 1943 of the
89th (Armenian) Army, liberating the Taman peninsula (on the east side of the straits of Kerch),
gaining for the victors the title of the 'Tamanian' army. The Armenian army was the only one of
the Soviet national armies to enter Berlin in 1945.

to smear Armenians. Missakian also referred to a report in an American magazine which claimed that the Nazis had picked on Dashnaktsutiun to do fifth-column work, promising the party an autonomous state for their co-operation. All this was, he said, devoid of foundation. 'The utterances of German statesmen from Bismarck to Bethmann-Hollweg, and the preachings of a galaxy of militant German philosophers, cannot be described as manifestations of Teutonic affection for our people.'[54] Missakian's claims were bolstered by the action of his brother Shavarsh, who stopped publishing the Dashnak paper *Haratch* in Paris during the occupation.

Nevertheless there remains the incontestable fact that relations between the Nazis and Dashnaks living in the occupied areas were close and active. On 30 December 1941 an Armenian battalion was created by a decision of the Wehrmacht, known as the 'Armenian 812th Battalion'. It was commanded by Dro, and was made up of a small number of committed recruits, and a larger number of Armenians from the prisoners of war taken by the Nazis in their sweep eastwards. Early on the total number was 8,000; this number later grew to 20,000. The 812th Battalion was operational in the Crimea and the North Caucasus.

A year later, on 15 December 1942, an 'Armenian National Council' was granted official recognition by Alfred Rosenberg, the German minister of the occupied areas. The 'Council' 's president was Professor Ardashes Abeghian, its vice-president Abraham Giulkhandanian, and it numbered among its members Nzhdeh and Vahan Papazian. From that date until the end of 1944 it published a weekly journal, *Armenien*, edited by Viken Shant (the son of Levon), who also broadcast on Radio Berlin.[55]

Except for Nzhdeh, no Armenian has ever been a theoretical Fascist. So what was the motive for the collaboration in the occupied areas? It is possible to see it as a purely vengeful desire to retake Armenia from the Bolsheviks. But I do not think that the alliance was motivated by such a crude ambition. There were probably several considerations which led to the decision. In the first place, there is in the untutored mind a tendency to class Armenians and Jews together (offensive to both peoples); and the malevolent paranoia of the Nazis might have manifested itself against Armenians as well as Jews. Hence it was important to prove to the Nazis that the Armenians were 'Aryans'. With the aid of Dr Paul Rohrbach they seem to have achieved this. The Nazis did not persecute Armenians, just for being Armenians, in the occupied lands. In the second place, Dashnaks such as Dro remembered – and the memory had been an overwhelming constituent of their policy in the preceding two decades – the events of 1917–18, when the strength and organisation of their party apparatus was the only guarantee against the final extermination of the children of Haik from the Armenian plateau. With Russia again threatening to break up, it made sense to prepare to enter Yerevan with the forces that might supplant Bolshevism, in order to assure public security before the Turks swept in from the west.

Nevertheless, it is hard to feel much sympathy for the pro-Axis group, since in terms of cosmic evil the Nazis surpassed the Young Turks. But perhaps that is a consideration one may only enjoy with the benefit of hindsight, and to the men there in the occupied areas, the immediate and overwhelming concern was to secure the safety of other Armenians.

Turkey, for her part, maintained a grudging neutrality throughout the war, until it was won, when she joined the winning side. Although under the terms of the Anglo–Franko–Turkish treaty of 19 October 1939 she had pledged to join in a European conflict in which Britain or France were engaged, she chose not to, and, displaying the old Ottoman diplomatic skill, went on to sign an agreement with Germany on 18 June 1941, which, while not contradicting the earlier treaty, was directly opposed to it in spirit, and fulsomely lauded German–Turkish friendship.*[56]

During the second world war, two tendencies appeared in Turkey, which showed how shallow had been her much-lauded changes with regard to her non-Turkish populations. They showed that of her two treaty parties, she was much closer to Nazi Germany than to democratic Britain. The first was the revival of pan-Turkism. This murderous ideology resurfaced in July 1941 under the leadership of professor Zeki Velidi Togan of Istanbul University. Unashamedly racist, in imitation of the Nazis its leaders adopted the trappings of Fascism, down to an imitation-Hitler hairstyle and colourful uniform.[57]

On 5 August 1941 German ambassador Franz von Papen reported to Berlin that Turkish *government* – not just maverick party – circles were showing increasing interest in the fate of their kinsmen, 'particularly the Azerbaijan Turks'. Von Papen continued:

These circles tend to recollect 1918 events: their wish is to annex the above area, especially the rich Baku oil fields. To these ends a committee of experts has been set up, embodying specialists who once officiated in this type of work during Abdul Hamid's time. This committee is to gather all pertinent material and is to enlist, in Turkey from the ranks of recent emigrants, and from immigrants – notably those in the Azerbaijan province of Iran – support for a union of the new Turkey with the Turk-inhabited regions bordering on it in the east, up to the Caspian sea.[58]

One year later, while the Nazi armies were pushing eastwards, Turkish premier Shukri Sarajoglu said (5 August 1942):

We are Turks, we are Turkists, and we shall always remain so. For us Turkism is a matter of blood, and no less of consciousness. Our ambition is

---

*Four days later Germany invaded Russia. There is a curious parallel with the first world war here, since two days after the Turko-German agreement of 2 August 1914, Germany had invaded Belgium.

to see 'the Turk' increase in numbers, and not to assist in his decrease, as in the past.[59]

After Stalingrad these Fascist notions were put back in the filing-cabinet, and the Turkish authorities felt compelled to prosecute the official Fascist party in September 1944, to sanitise the country before she joined the Allies. The second example of the re-emergence of the bullying, anti-minority spirit in Turkey was the affair of the Capital Levy Tax, or *Varlik Vergisi*. A number of Armenians were directly involved, and suffered accordingly.

This tax, masterminded in theory and directed in practice by President Ismet Inönü, was introduced in November 1942. The ostensible intention was to get at war-profiteers. To this end tax returns and other relevant documents were examined by boards (composed only of Muslim Turks), and assessments made for the wealth tax. Once the assessment was made there was no appeal: the amount had to be paid in cash, and the penalty for non-payment was deportation to Ashkale (west of Erzerum), to engage in the harshest manual labour, mostly stone-breaking.[60]

The effect of the law was again to show the persistent unwillingness of the Turkish government to include non-Turks as citizens of the Turkish state, whether of empire or republic. The rule of law simply did not extend to Greeks, Armenians and Jews. The assessments of citizens from the minority communities were astronomical in comparison to those of Muslim Turks in similar financial circumstances. The assumption that only Muslim Turks were honest fellows was at once the most ridiculous and odious aspect of the law. (A memorandum issuing from the British embassy dated 1 December 1942 noted, by contrast, that corruption recalled the days of Abdul Hamid.[61])

Lewis V. Thomas, a staunch friend of Turkey, has pointed out that by this tax the government was effectively reviving the Capitulations, inasmuch as the government's official injustice sent members of the minorities scurrying again to the skirts of foreign powers. He adds, 'Overnight, Atatürk's attempts to incorporate the minorities into Turkey, in so far as those attempts had had some measure of success, were undone... Resentment and discrimination welled up everywhere. Republican Istanbul was lapsing into Ottoman Constantinople.'[62]

By late May 1943 the number unable to pay their exorbitant assessment had reached 500. The old and the sick were not spared. All were herded to the east in cramped and foul conditions. There they were forced to work without a break from 7.00 a.m. to 5.00 p.m., even in the appalling cold of the Anatolian winter. (In addition, many had to spend three hours walking to and from work.) They were denied payment and any food except dry bread, and even this was stopped at one stage, leaving them to exist only on the gifts of relatives. (With the typical Turkish difference between the real and the paper world, the provisions of the published law laid down that the deportees were to be both paid and fed.) They slept 50 to a room, or in filthy cafés, or else shared stables with animals. On at least two occasions a sick deportee was denied medical assistance and subsequently died.[63]

Only after the liberation of Italy did Turkey show any pro-Ally sentiments. She eventually declared war on Germany and Japan on 23 February 1945, not with the intention of doing any fighting, but merely to get a seat at the fledgling United Nations. When the tardy and unwilling Turkish participation in the war was set against the massive sacrifice of Soviet Armenia, there was a feeling, as the war drew to an end, that legitimate Armenian national claims deserved a measure of satisfaction, something that they had been denied after the first world war.

Kars and Ardahan; Repatriation

On 19 March 1945 the USSR denounced the Soviet–Turkish treaty of friendship of 17 September 1925.

Almost as soon as the war in Europe was over (8 May 1945) the Soviet Union re-opened the question of Kars and Ardahan, the region which had constituted the Kars *oblast* from 1878 until the first world war, and which the Kemalists had seized in their assault of September–November 1920. As early as 1939 British diplomats had noted minor indications that the Soviet Union might question the status of the region. Now, after the war, at a meeting with the Turkish ambassador, Soviet Foreign Minister V. M. Molotov confirmed that this territorial issue would have to be solved before a new treaty could be signed. Russia, said the Soviet ambassador in Ankara, wished to 'do something for the Armenian people'.[64]

At about the same time a conclave in Echmiadzin was given Soviet permission to meet in order to elect a new Catholicos. (The seat had been empty since 1938, when the then Catholicos had almost certainly become a victim of the purges.) Catholicos Gevorg VI was elected on 22 June 1945. One of his first actions was to address a letter to Stalin stressing two points: that Armenians keenly awaited the day when Armenian territories now under foreign rule would be joined to Soviet Armenia, and that Armenians abroad in the dispersion were waiting to return to the motherland.[65]

Now it is possible to see this as a cynical Stalinist stratagem: that Stalin merely permitted the election of the Catholicos, then told him what to write in his letter, so as to justify Soviet expansionism. But even if that did in fact happen, it is not a full description of those events; for on this occasion Soviet expansionism coincided with what was, in view of the events of the past seventy years, a legitimate Armenian national aspiration – one which was for Armenians overriding, and which, in the context of their history, was of far greater significance than this or that bit of Soviet pressure.

As soon as the action of Catholicos Gevorg VI became known, a campaign began among world-wide Armenian communities of all political affiliations for the return of Kars and Ardahan. They were in no sense organised or directed by Soviet interests – their own national demands pre-dated the establishment of the Soviet state or even the foundation of the Communist party. They knew that the formula which had been valid before the first world war remained so: that Russian rule, despite its restrictions, was preferable to the hand of the Turk. The demand for Kars and Ardahan was even on this occasion supported by Dashnaktsutiun, whose leaders, convinced that on this occasion the USSR was acting in the fullest interests of the Armenians, were prepared to abandon their anti-Soviet stance and support the demand. (Indeed the Dashnaks went further and demanded the full retrocession to Soviet Armenia of President Wilson's award of November 1920.)

Throughout the summer months of 1945 Armenian organisations delivered a flood of petitions to the Big Three, demanding the annexation of Kars and Ardahan to Soviet Armenia. But some of their agitation was unwittingly counter-productive. On 11 July a letter appeared in the *New York Times* from Leon Surmelian, the author and translator, which contained a sentence which was to be picked up by the British Foreign Office and used as evidence against the Soviet claim: 'The fortress of Kars is strategically indispensable to the Soviet Union.'[66] In the context of Surmelian's entire letter it was clear that he was saying that the fortress was indispensable as a *defensive* fortification – the classic view of military geographers from Beaujour onwards. Yet the British Foreign Office took this one sentence out of its context, and flashed it around as a typical 'Red scare', thereby, as so often in the past, creating an atmosphere antipathetic to Armenian claims.

At the Potsdam Conference (17 July–2 August), which mapped out post-war Europe, Molotov formally raised the question of the USSR obtaining Kars and Ardahan; but Churchill refused to accept any frontier rectification. Truman, for his part, believed that it was a matter for Turkey and the USSR to solve bilaterally.[67]

Turkey was in a flattened and dejected state at this time. Her leaders were convinced that she would lose territory to the USSR. The war of nerves intensified in late 1945, with reports of Soviet troop movements along the Turkish border. On 6 January 1946 the Turkish prime minister, Sarajoglu, made a public response to the demands: 'Not one Armenian lives in those regions.'[68] It is a reply which had been heard many times before in Young Turk and Kemalist circles, quite often issuing from the very people who had contrived to make sure that there were no Armenians living in the districts. Yet on this occasion it was an assertion taken seriously, at least in the Foreign Office by the 1940s equivalents of D'Arcy Godolphin Osborne, Geoffrey L. McDermott and W. S. Edmonds, whose minutes display the immutable legacy of Palmerstonian pro-Turkishness. They and their colleagues saw no Armenian claims.

Perhaps, of all the sophistries which shaped British policy in opposing the Armenian claims to the districts, the Foreign Office's most sweeping misconception was that the treaty of Kars (which had established the border in

1921) was a 'freely negotiated' treaty.[69] Only an arid legalist could possibly accept that view. There was nothing freely negotiated about the Kars treaty, least of all as far as the Armenians were concerned (see above, pp. 329–30). The partiality and inaccuracy of Foreign Office views on Kars and Ardahan were summed up in a speech delivered in the House of Commons by Foreign Secretary Ernest Bevin on 21 February 1946:

> In the case of the two provinces, as I understand it from what I have read, the frontier between Turkey and Russia was fixed, not by conqueror and vanquished, but by defeated Turkey and an unfortunate Russia which had not come too well out of the last war through no fault of her own. Therefore, this cannot be said to be an imposed frontier. There is the point of view of the people living in the provinces, but as far as I can study it, there has been such movement of population that there is no nationality problem at all.[70]

This far from confident passage was the subject of a trenchant memorandum from the great orientalist Professor V. Minorsky, living in retirement in Cambridge, which was passed on to Bevin by the admirably open-minded new Member of Parliament, Tom Driberg.[71] Minorsky noted that 'It appears that massacres give a claim to the heritage of massacred persons.' He added:

> It is an astonishing coincidence that Hitler (evidence produced in Nuremberg) suggested that the extermination of enemy races could be carried out with impunity in view of human forgetfulness: 'Who does now remember the *Armenians*' – were the Führer's *ipsissima verba*.
> Now we have lived to hear in the British parliament that there is 'no nationality problem' in Armenia.

However, both Foreign Office and foreign secretary remained as adamant as Abdul Hamid in not recognising any Armenian claims.

As after the first world war, the critical time when alliances were fluid, and when international borders could be shifted with comparative ease, was coming to an end, and the severe hostile post-war pattern was emerging. In February 1946 Churchill made his famous Iron Curtain speech at Fulton, Missouri. Greece was tense, and about to explode into civil war. The cold war had begun, and Western statesmen showed even less ability than usual to distinguish the legitimate national aspirations of much-wronged people from Soviet expansionism.

In April 1947 President Truman enunciated his famous 'Truman Doctrine', that the United States would go to the aid of any non-Communist country threatened by Soviet pressure. This effectively spelt the end of Armenia's post-war hopes for Kars and Ardahan. In the following month US Secretary of State Dean Acheson received an Armenian delegation, and indicated to them that, from the point of view of the United States, in the current international situation, no change in the status of Kars and Ardahan could be considered.[72]

At the same time as the agitation for the additional territory, there was (as the Catholicos's letter to Stalin indicated) a drive for Armenian 'repatriation'. In fact it was settlement rather than repatriation, since most of those who went to Soviet Armenia were refugees from Western Armenia or Cilicia. From all over the Middle East, from Europe and from the USA, Armenians flocked to Soviet Armenia during 1945–8. An estimated 150,000 settled there in that period. (Of those, several thousands went from Turkey, saying that they had no equal rights and no work, a natural response to the capital levy racket.[73])

Were they, too, part of a Soviet expansionist master plan, a plan to fill Armenia with Armenians so that pressure for wider borders would be more compelling? In a narrow sense, probably, but in the broader Armenian national sense (and the frustration felt by minority exile people, most of whom had been driven from their native homes and had become refugees), they were acting in their national interest, which happened to coincide with Stalin's designs.

Complex problems beset those Armenians who emigrated to Soviet Armenia, although their settlement was eased by an interest-free loan of 30,000 roubles. The process of social and political integration was far from easy. One well known story runs as follows: an Armenian from Iran decided to repatriate to Soviet Armenia, and agreed to inform his family back home about conditions there by the simple scheme of sending a photograph of himself. If he was pictured standing up, all was fine; if sitting down, things were not so good. His family received a photo of him lying on the floor.

Moreover, Stalinist paranoia hovered in the air, occasionally striking – as in 1949, when, on suspicion of 'nationalism', thousands of Armenians were rounded up and deported to the Altai region of the USSR.[74] The relief felt in Armenia on the death of Stalin was palpable; 1953, in that sense, was a key date in the emergence of Soviet Armenia not only as a land of workers and peasants, but of tourists, relatives, and of many contacts with the non-Communist world.

Armenians in the Arab World

Before the first world war a number of Armenians had established themselves in the Arab world. The Armenian community clustered around the patriarchate of Jerusalem had existed from pre-Arab times. The seat of the Armenian Catholics had been established at Bzommar, Mount Lebanon, in 1742. The Armenian family of Nubar had distinguished itself in the government of Egypt in the late nineteenth century. And the first and last governors of independent Mount Lebanon, Daud Pasha (1861–8) and Ohannes Pasha Kuyumjian (1912–15) were both Armenian Catholics. Besides these, there were numerous Armenian trading communities, notably in Egypt, Iraq and northern Syria.

Some months before the conclusion of the first world war Sherif Hussein of Mecca issued an edict requesting the protection and support of those Armenians who had been driven into the desert. It was expressed in magnanimous terms, and quoted the Koran.[75] This mood of Arab hospitality and concerned interest lasted even when the Armenian presence in the Levant was much increased after the French withdrawal from Cilicia. In the words of British Consul E. C. Hole:

When Cilicia was abandoned by the French, a large number of Armenian refugees found their way to Damascus and were on the whole well treated. Municipal ground was given to them for settlement, and a certain amount of public hospitality – possibly voluntary – was shown them by the community.[76]

The size of the community throughout the region meant that it became a political entity; and naturally the Armenians transported their political affiliations with them. In this way the Arab world became the authentic successor to Western (Turkish) Armenia as the repository of Armenian identity, and social and cultural organisation. Beirut succeeded Constantinople as the capital of the Western Armenians. (The only communities to rival those of Syria and Lebanon in this respect are those of Boston or California, but these are, despite their large numbers, too thinly spread and too far from their homeland seriously to contest those of the Levant.)

The European mandatory powers saw the Armenians as a community which they could use to secure their shaky and resented authority. Armenians were offered Lebanese citizenship in August 1924, largely with the intention of bolstering the Christian community against the nationalism which the Muslims manifested. In Syria, the French drafted seasoned Armenian fighters into levies for suppressing the Druze revolt (1925–7).

But Arabs are not Turks, and Armenians soon realised they should work with, rather than against, their new hosts. Consul Hole, in the despatch quoted above, noted that the Armenians were voting for Arab nationalist parties by 1928. It was there that their long-term interests lay, rather than with the transitory commercialised French administration. The more politically sensitive Armenians saw too the parallel between their history and that of the Arabs under the Ottoman Turks, and many more noted that the Arab temperament differed from the Turkish – it was for the most part sunny and warm and tolerant.

Considering that, in the 1920s, the Arab countries were undeveloped, and that land and resources were at a premium, the relatively easy manner in which the Armenians were absorbed is remarkable. The Arabs were really the first people actually to do anything for the Western Armenians since the emergence of the 'Armenian question'; they enabled them to build up their lives after three decades of massacre, war and chronic instability. After the mendacity and deceit of the European nations it was left to the Syrians and Lebanese to provide living space, security and the essentials of life for Armenians.

Lebanon, itself a country of minorities, became the land in which Armenians established themselves in greatest strength. They soon constituted, as they do today, about 6 per cent of the population. They were given their first seat in the confessionally organised Lebanese Parliament in 1934, and their representation there steadily rose until they were allocated five seats in the expanded 99-man chamber in 1960. In 1958 they were granted government ministries. Their record, in Parliament and government, has been beneficent towards their new country, and they have from time to time taken up causes which benefited the country generally without specific reference to their own community.[77]

Nevertheless, it has to be said that the Armenian sections of each Lebanese election have been marked by corruption, which has sometimes become electoral fraud.

Until the recent (and continuing) catastrophe in Lebanon, elections, and the political power gained through them, were a matter more of interest than policy. Each election saw a bewildering series of alliances between groups who were *prima facie* hostile. In this situation Armenian allegiances were a blend, the greater part of which consisted of their own Armenian party loyalties (which often had international ramifications *vis-à-vis* the Soviet Union, or the interests of the great powers in the Middle East), and the lesser part of which was local Lebanese loyalties. In this matter Armenians were not in any way acting unpatriotically towards their land of refuge, since the native Arab Lebanese themselves put a lower priority on Lebanese national affairs, putting their own clans above everything else. Despite Lebanese independence in 1943, Lebanon has never been a unitary, independent state, as the recent and devastating civil war has shown. There has never been a Lebanese nationalism to act as a unifying force against sectarian divisiveness, which has had such tragic results.

From the Lebanese elections of 1943 onwards, the international dimension of the Armenian voting pattern has been clear. In that year, following the *rapprochement* of the Dashnaks with the Soviet Union after the battle of Stalingrad, the Hunchaks and the Dashnaks united against the Ramkavar candidates; but in 1947, after the promulgation of the Truman Doctrine, the Dashnaks stood on their own, as strongly pro-'Western'. The Hunchaks and Ramkavars combined to present an alternative policy, labelled Bolshevik by their opponents. In the bitter days of the cold war, the divisions within the Armenian community were profound. The elections of 1947 set the pattern; only one party received official support, and the other candidates withdrew at 10.30 a.m. The Ramkavar paper *Zartonk* commented bitterly on the outcome.[78]

In the early 1950s the Dashnaks strengthened their ideological commitment to the United States. The party joined the 'Paris Bloc', and its members broadcast to Soviet Armenia from the Munich-based Radio Liberty. Both in the Middle East and the United States they conducted a campaign against their Armenian rivals.

With the split in the Armenian Church of 1956, the Lebanese elections of 1957 were conducted in a state of near hysteria. Battles developed between opposing factions in the Armenian quarters of Beirut. As in 1947, only one party received the backing of the police. No one was surprised by the result.[79]

The same pattern was apparent in the following year, when the first Lebanese civil war took place. Armenians had their own civil strife after the conclusion of the main war: in late November 1958 there was a vicious outbreak of bloodletting, in which over 50 Armenians were killed in the Bourdj Hammoud and Nahr areas of Beirut. National and international tensions had combined to reduce Armenian intra-communal relations to the bullet and the knife.[80]

At about this time the Dashnaks formed close alliances with the Lebanese Maronite paramilitary groupings of the Kataib (Phalangists) of Pierre Gemayel, and the National Liberals (Ahrar) of Camille Chamoun. The Hunchaks for their part affiliated to Kemal Jumblatt's Progressive Socialist Party. It is hard to see if any benefit accrued to the Armenian community as a whole as a result of these moves. Were the Ramkavars, for all their caution and inertia, by not participating in activist politics the repository of Armenian political wisdom?

The Dashnaks remained close to the Americans in their political thinking for much of the 1960s; but with the 1967 Middle Eastern war, which signalled a radically new political map in the area and the end of direct American tactics in Lebanon, they moved to a more middle-ground position. All Armenian groups realised that a new period of crisis and instability was inevitable, and that protection of their own communities should come before the intellectual enticements of international politics.

This attitude was reinforced by the Lebanese civil war of 1976–7, in which Armenians of all factions remained neutral, a move which proved its benefit in the relatively small number of casualties in the war. It was a move which embittered the right-wing Maronite militias (who are said to have counted upon Dashnak support), but which again proved absolutely right when one sees the incapacity of the Maronites to think realistically in political terms for the future of Lebanon.

Besides Lebanon, Armenians are scattered around the Middle East, but nowhere else are they sufficiently numerous to constitute a significant political force. In Syria their presence is strong around Aleppo, and in the clutch of villages along the border with the *sanjak* of Alexandretta. Currently they have one member in the Syrian Parliament, Krikor Eblighatian. In Egypt, the community is proportionately too small to be of any political significance.

Communal politics and political alignments are only one way of looking at the Armenian presence in the Middle East. The part that they play in the professional life of their new countries is another aspect of it, one which is proportionately greater than their numbers. Throughout the region one finds Armenians as doctors, pharmacists, engineers, lecturers and artists (both in painting and music). Their role in keeping commerce, industry and the arts flourishing in the area is considerable.

As regards the central Middle East problem, the Arab–Israeli conflict, most Armenians keep a cautious neutrality, which if anything slightly favours the Arab side – where after all most of them live. They have seldom, if ever, shown any real enthusiasm for Zionism, except for those who confuse in their emotions Turks and Arabs. Several hundreds were forced to flee from Palestine in the war of 1948–9; others lost property and businesses. They were of the wrong race to fit into the Procrustean bed of Zionist ideology, and were more at home in the ordinary, tapestry-like life of the real Middle East. And being themselves an indigenous people made homeless by political Turkism, some have a measure of sympathy for those dispossessed by political Zionism. When they have put forward ideas for a solution of the Middle East conflict, they have nearly always supported the United Nations position as put forward in Security Council Resolutions 242 and 338.

Conflicts in the Armenian Church: the Cilician Catholicosate and Jerusalem

The conflict over the Armenian catholicosate of Cilicia (situated at Antilias, Lebanon) is, despite its ecclesiastical garb and reference to theological precedent, essentially political in nature, or at least in origin.

There have been two catholicoses – the word 'catholicoi' is a spurious classicism – in the Armenian Church since 1441. Until then the seat of the Catholicos had been determined by political and social phenomena; but in 1441, when the supreme patriarch resided at Sis, Cilicia, there was a move among sections of the clergy to reconsecrate Echmiadzin, the site of St Gregory the Illuminator's original vision, as the spiritual centre of the Armenian Church. But the Catholicos declined to move to Echmiadzin; so an assembly proceeded to elect and consecrate a new Catholicos there. In the following centuries there was little conflict between the two, except over minor matters of personal vanity. It became recognised that Echmiadzin had jurisdiction over Greater Armenia, and Sis over Cilicia and the Levant. Echmiadzin was recognised as the primal Armenian see, and the Catholicos who resided there had the title 'Catholicos of All Armenians'; but he had no actual rights to intervene in matters under the jurisdiction of the 'Catholicos of the Great House of Cilicia'.[81]

Until 1956 there were no fundamental disagreements between the two. It should be noted that both catholicoses are elected by a conclave of laymen and priests. (Indeed it is the democratic nature of the Armenian Church which makes it possible for divisions to occur.) Since political affiliations determine such a wide range of communal activities for Armenians, the members of the conclaves naturally voted in accordance with their political beliefs. Thus in 1943, when Garegin Hovsepiants was elected Cilician Catholicos, none of the parties raised any objection to his candidature, since there was at the time a united Armenian front. When Garegin died in 1952 the situation was very different: the cold war had sunk its icy blade into the Armenian community; moves which had been afoot in 1945–6 to re-unite the parts of the Church which had been virtually separate since the murder of Archbishop Ghevond Tourian in 1933 had come to an abrupt end. And one dedicated Dashnak party member was to note at about that time: 'An aggressive Dashnak electorate which could conceivably win the catholicosate of Sis (Antilias) would emasculate the power – political or otherwise – of Echmiadzin.'[82]

The date for the election of the new Catholicos of the Great House of Cilicia was set for 14 February 1956.[83] A fortnight beforehand the Catholicos of All Armenians, Vazgen I, who had been elected in September 1954, announced that he was coming to Lebanon to attend the Cilician election. This was an unprecedented move, and not strictly justified canonically. Pro-'Western' observers simply saw it as Soviet intervention. But this is an over-simplification. It had become clear that the new Cilician Catholicos would most likely be the nominee of Dashnaktsutiun. About two-thirds of the fifty-man Cilician electorate were Dashnak supporters. With such an election at such a time, the Armenian Church, a vital force for her people scattered throughout the world, would be irremediably split, not on doctrinal matters, nor even on matters of jurisdiction (although this would become a problem), but purely as a result of the international hostility generated by the cold war. Vazgen I travelled to Beirut to try to avoid that split.

At the same time it has to be said that a number of diaspora Armenians simply did not want the ultimate authority of their Church to reside inside the Soviet Union, where there was always the possibility – indeed likelihood – of state manipulation. With the Dashnak party's espousal of the Western camp in the cold war, this aspiration could receive satisfaction. Until the second world war the Soviet record towards Echmiadzin had been a bleak one: the catholicosate had been left empty for long periods, and Catholicos Khoren had been murdered during the purges of 1938. It did not take much to shift the adherence of members of Dashnaktsutiun away from the catholicosate of Echmiadzin.

Vazgen I arrived in Lebanon on 12 February 1956. So profound were the issues involved in the election that it was postponed for a week, to 20 February. One of the matters which was uppermost in the minds of those who sought to keep the Church united was the position of the lay delegates from Aleppo. One-fifth of these (who numbered 15 in all – sufficient to tip the balance) had to be re-elected in communal elections every two years, according to the Armenian National Constitution of 1863. No communal elections had been held in Syria since 1953, during the rule of Adib Shishakly, who had been overthrown in a *coup* in 1954.

The Syrian government, whose intervention demonstrated the seriousness of the affair, now indicated that, therefore, the credentials of the Aleppine delegates were invalid; and on 17 February the Syrian foreign minister, Said Ghazzi, travelled to Beirut to confer with the Lebanese prime minister, Rashid Karameh, concerning the election. He suggested its postponement. The position of the delegates from Aleppo remained unchanged.

No compromise could be found, and so, with the matter unresolved, Catholicos Vazgen flew on to Cairo.

The election took place on 20 February; Bishop Zareh Payaslian was legitimately elected by 32 votes out of 36 voting; the other 14 had withdrawn from the election.

Vazgen I, who had been warmly welcomed on his arrival in Cairo by President Nasser, called an assembly of 16 bishops there, which condemned the recent election as 'defective'; but no formula could be found to resolve the difference between the parties. The consecration of the new Catholicos – a ceremony more akin to an enthronement – took place on 2 September. Traditionally three bishops have to be present at this ceremony; but only two were willing to attend, Khoren Paroyan and Ghevond Chebeyan. So a third was delegated by the Syrian Orthodox Church of Antioch (whose theology is very close to that of the Armenians), in the person of Mar Severios Yacoub. Present at the ceremony were leading Lebanese figures.

Attempts to heal the breach between the two sees have, to date, not been successful. The Cilician see adopted a new constitution after 1956, which laid down that if a diocese hitherto under the jurisdiction of Echmiadzin desired to become attached to Antilias, it would be accepted by it. To Echmiadzin this was expansionist interference, at variance with the traditions of the relationships between the two sees. The dioceses which have thereby come under the jurisdiction of Antilias are Greece and the three Iranian dioceses of Tabriz, Tehran and Isfahan, as well as sections of the Church in North America and Kuwait.

The whole affair has the stamp of the cold war upon it, and once again one feels that the fragile barque, the Armenian people and its Church, has had needlessly to suffer indignity and affliction. Whatever views are held on Soviet Communism, no one can physically shift Echmiadzin out of the USSR, and to pretend otherwise is to produce an inevitable split, with its attendant communal weakness. Moreover, it is hardly possible today to sustain the claim that the Armenian priests and bishops loyal to Echmiadzin are agents of Soviet Communism; their supreme pontiff, Vazgen I, is too independent-minded and altogether of too noble a cast of mind to permit such a thing to happen. Most Armenians, although recognising the part politics play in all Armenian affairs, try nevertheless to minimise their part in the Church.

The Middle East correspondent of *The Times* (London) commented:

There seems little doubt that the rank-and-file of Armenians in the Middle

East are opposed to the Dashnak policy of involving the Church in political movements, and there is wide dissatisfaction at the election last year of a new catholicos who was a Dashnak candidate and is alleged to have been 'railroaded' in with the support of the Americans in both Church and government, as well as the Roman Catholic Church and the Lebanese government.[84]

With the election in 1977 of Garegin II as co-adjutor Catholicos to the ailing Khoren I of Antilias, there is hope that a way will be found out of the impasse, since he has undertaken a review of the articles in the Cilician constitution which permit it to expand its jurisdiction. Garegin II is likewise a man of strong and independent mind, with a deep and broad understanding of his people's history and destiny.

The conflict over the patriarchate of Jerusalem is more curious; distressing to Armenians, especially to those who see in, say, Khrimian Hairik the model of an Armenian church and community leader. In the mid-1950s there was a conflict for the patriarchate between Bishop (later Archbishop) Yeghishe Derderian and Archbishop Tiran Nersoyan, which appeared to end with the latter being elected as patriarch of Jerusalem in March 1957.[85]

But on 30 August 1958, as the patriarch was in procession to the Tomb of Mary in Jerusalem to celebrate the Assumption, he was kidnapped by Jordanian soldiers, and at once put on a plane to Beirut, without even his passport or a change of clothing. We can only guess what political and personal motives led to this action.[86]

The Armenian patriarchate of Jerusalem remained vacant until March 1960, when a new election was scheduled to take place, with the elderly, frail Suren Kemhadjian as the only candidate. But again political and personal matters intervened, and the election did not take place. Only on 5 April 1960 did it occur, when the brothers were compelled at the gunpoint of the Jordanian army to elect Archbishop Derderian *locum tenens* of the patriarchate. Two months later he was elected patriarch, and consecrated to the office in August of that year.[87]

The un-ecclesiastical nature of circumstances surrounding the election distressed many Armenians, as did the attempted sale in 1967 of 23 important illuminated Gospel manuscripts from the treasury of the patriarchate, with an estimated value of £300,000–£500,000. Those with a historical perspective may be forgiven for wondering whether manuscripts from the Varak monastery would ever, during Khrimian's time, have appeared in the sale-rooms of Europe.

The Transformation

The greatest cause for pride among Armenians – a pride sorely needed after the cataclysm of death and disaster earlier in the century – has without doubt been the development of Soviet Armenia since 1953, and more especially in the relaxation which followed the Twentieth Party Congress of the CPSU, held in February 1956. One of the earliest indications that the ice of Stalinism was breaking was a speech delivered by Anastas Mikoyan in Yerevan in March 1954, in which he rehabilitated, besides certain nineteenth-century Armenian nationalist writers, the great poet Yeghishe Charents. Mikoyan said, 'The works of Charents, which are outstanding in their great talent, are steeped with revolutionary pathos and Soviet patriotism, and must become the property of the Soviet reader.'[88] Other writers, purged for their nationalism in the 1930s, were rehabilitated too.

Yerevan was substantially rebuilt in 1956, so that it became a well-laid-out city of wide avenues. In the central square the architect consciously copied the motifs of the medieval Armenian stone-masons, so as to stress the continuity of the Armenian cultural heritage. (Some critics, however, hold that the designs and their embellishments are a trifle laborious and academic.) At about the same time the authorities permitted the building of two impressive monuments which related to the pre-Soviet period of Armenia. One was the sombre memorial, on the outskirts of Yerevan, to the victims of the 1915–16 genocide, which, in its stark simplicity, cannot leave the visitor unmoved. The other is a relief-sculpture recalling the battle of Sardarabad (modern Hoktemberian).

Both memorials were a significant concession to the awareness of all Armenians of the critical events in their modern history which have shaped their destiny, but which fall outside the straitjacket of Marxist economic historiography. (And let us remember the large part played by the Dashnaks at the battle of Sardarabad.) Both, too, have contributed to the friendly feeling which Armenians in the dispersion (many of whose families were savagely cut down at that time) feel towards Soviet Armenia.

Within Soviet Armenia there exists perhaps the most thriving, vigorous and open society anywhere in the Communist world. A small country, with a population of just under three million, its economic performance can today compare with that of advanced industrialised nations of similar size. It also has a flourishing cultural and scientific life. In the visual arts, paintings whose inspiration is far from dull political conformity can frequently be seen in the art galleries; and in opera, ballet, drama and cinema there is an exuberance of expression which would surprise those who are conditioned by sterile anti-Sovietism. Armenians are also very proud of possessing, since 1943, their own Academy of Sciences; attached to it is the Biurakan Observatory, which is directed by the internationally renowned astrophysicist Viktor Hambartsumian.

There are, however, a handful of 'dissidents' in Soviet Armenia. They highlight abuses within the country, and there is no doubt that their allegations are of substance. They charge the regime with holding political prisoners, and with harassment of citizens. They also complain that the authorities give precedence to Russian over Armenian as an official language, and give greater support to Russian schools than to Armenian. (Shades of Prince Golitsyn!) But the complaint upon which the Yerevan Helsinki Monitoring Group lays greatest stress is the refusal of the USSR to pursue the legitimate claims of the Armenian people against Turkey. In other words, the heart of Armenian dissidence is the powerful and insistent complaint of Armenians throughout the world against the Turks; only in a secondary manner is it against the Russians.[89]

This impression is borne out by making the comparison, which Armenians have made since 1828, between Turkish and Russian treatment of their people. Of course, today there is but the barest handful of Armenians in Turkish Armenia. So Turkey's problem, inasmuch as it is unencumbered with people, is altogether lighter. But even where a sizeable concentration of Armenians exists, in Istanbul, the harassment and systematic anti-minority measures of the Turkish government make Soviet Armenia appear a free society by comparison. The community of Istanbul is hemmed in by bureaucratic restrictions and constraints. For instance, Armenians in Istanbul have to receive official permission even to put a coat of paint on their schools. If this is given at all, it is given tardily and lethargically, by which time the fabric of the school has deteriorated, presumably to the satisfaction of the authorities who, like their late-Ottoman predecessors, appear to detest ethnic diversity and aim to see even the tiny remnant of Armenians in the former imperial capital turned into Turks.

Within Soviet Armenia the hostility towards Turkey remains, and the sense of grievance and injustice at the hands of the Turks. It is, however, concerned not with the minor details of the community in Istanbul, but with the wider issues. Sometimes this sentiment boils over in a manner which is embarrassing to the Soviet authorities. One such occasion was the gigantic demonstration in Yerevan on 24 April 1965, the fiftieth anniversary of the genocide. This was perhaps the largest genuinely popular demonstration that the USSR has ever seen, and it expressed fury and resentment towards Turkey. Over and over again the participants shouted, 'We want our lands!' Disturbances occurred in the evening, and as a result the First Secretary of the Communist party was replaced. There is little question that the hostility of the people of Soviet Armenia towards Turkey is far greater than any resentment that they feel towards Moscow.

Where there is grievance in Soviet Armenia (and this is another point raised by the Helsinki Monitoring Group), it is not against Moscow's authority *per se* as against the refusal of the authorities to grant Mountainous Karabagh, whose population is 85 per cent Armenian, to Armenia, rather than leaving it with the status that it has today, that of an autonomous region within Soviet Azerbaijan. As recently as October 1977, a leading member of the Armenian Communist party and of the Soviet Writers' Union, Sero Khanzatian, wrote a strongly worded letter to President Brezhnev putting forward the arguments for Karabagh to become Armenian. Really, it is only the Communist authorities' conservative fear of the unknown outcome of altering internal national boundaries which is preventing Karabagh from becoming part of Armenia. (The only argument of any substance for maintaining the *status quo* is that the mountainous region is used as summer pasture for the transhumant Azeri shepherds, but this is not an objection which can be seriously sustained, since there is no reason why Soviet Armenian authorities in Karabagh would not continue to grant them their traditional summer grazing rights.) Armenians also feel that they have had a raw deal over the Nakhichevan enclave, which became an 'autonomous Soviet Socialist Republic' administered as part of Azerbaijan, virtually at the dictation of the Turks in the discussions leading to the treaty of Moscow in 1921. (Turkey's continuing interest in Nakhichevan is signalled by the fact that in the 1930s she altered her frontier with Iran, exchanging small areas of territory, so that she would have a directly contiguous frontier with Nakhichevan, even though it was only a few kilometres wide.) There is not an Armenian majority in Nakhichevan today, or anything like one: but the region was taken from Armenia after the local Azeris had killed off, under the direction of Turkish officers, hundreds of Armenians in the summer of 1919 and the spring of 1920; the region was thereupon assigned to Azerbaijan for little other reason than appeasement of the Turks.

Periodically hopes have been raised among Armenians that the status of Karabagh and Nakhichevan would 'shortly' be altered in their favour, but these hopes have always been disappointed.

Yet despite its internal and external problems, Soviet Armenia contrives to be a flourishing and relatively prosperous society, with a quality of openness to confound those who think of the USSR as a huge prison camp. Without doubt this is largely due to a universal Armenian determination to snatch a human victory out of the catastrophe of the beginning of the century, and to heal the wounds with a tangible success; to see smiles on the faces of the new generation, instead of just hearing of the tortured anguish of the old. It is also due to the fact that Armenians in Soviet Armenia have plentiful contacts with their kinsmen outside Hayots Ashkharh – the land of Armenia. A number of those who immigrated to Armenia in 1946–9 left behind relatives, especially in the Arab countries of the East Mediterranean. Visits from Armenians of the *ëspiurk* (dispersion) are a commonplace, and mean that Armenia is very far from a hermetic Soviet republic. The flow of ideas is two-way, and life-styles in Armenia – at least in Yerevan – show considerable similarity to urban manners in Europe or North America. (Every Armenian male who can get into them wears a pair of blue jeans.)

Since the flow of ideas is two-way, the direction of criticism extends both in and out of Armenia. Soviet Armenians can look at those of the world-wide communities and say, 'We have survived on the soil of Armenia; are you going to sell out your identity, language and culture to the inert capitalist conformism of "the West"?' The criticism of Armenians from the Middle East, Europe and America of Armenia are even more valuable, and have undoubtedly also led to the comparatively free and relaxed society enjoyed in Soviet Armenia, where the grimmer aspects of totalitarianism are for the most part absent. (There seems little doubt that of the critics of Soviet Armenia Dashnaktsutiun is taken seriously – where its criticism is constructive, which for the past ten years or so it has been.) The support of Armenians across the globe is felt to be important in Yerevan, not with the intention of turning every Armenian into a Soviet agent, but merely so that Armenians abroad will take a balanced view of the USSR and of Soviet Armenia in particular. And he would be a cynical and embittered Armenian today who did not feel a measure of pride in the society which has been established in Soviet Armenia.

Ëspiurk

Although the subject of the growth and development of the Armenian communities outside Armenia is one of great interest, it is one which I have deliberately avoided. The central issue for Armenia is the land itself. The world-wide communities have only been discussed where they directly reflected the political problems of the land. Nevertheless, Armenians far from their homeland have an ability to prosper, and to remain Armenian, which adds up to a national characteristic, if such a thing exists.

Whether they have emigrated freely or under duress, a pattern of expatriate activity is noticeable among them. First, they build a church (or two churches), then a school, and then a community centre. They seldom just disappear into the hinterland of their adopted countries, and then only in pursuit of the glamorous false gods of acceptability and stifling middle-class 'respectability'. (The first sign is the abandoment of a robust Armenian name for an anaemic local one.) More often they *celebrate* the fact of being Armenian, whether in poetry, drama, dance, music, or even in making interminable speeches. One cannot fail to be struck by the fact that, although to be born Armenian is not to have the blessings of life automatically bestowed upon one, Armenians themselves treat it as a cause for joy, and something that is in a most profound manner worth preserving.

Only advocates of sterile conformity and heavy-fisted rulers who have disfigured the history of the world would dispute that ethnic diversity is something in itself worth preserving, which enhances the civilisation in which it occurs. But nevertheless in the societies of Europe and America, with their subtle and insidious pressures to conform, it is not easy to remain Armenian, and to bequeath such a legacy to the next generation. Amongst other qualities, it requires a vivid historical imagination to recreate the life in the 'old country', and to perceive its validity; to discover the constant thread of existence amid the fire and wreckage of history. Luckily there is a network of Armenian societies and cultural foundations throughout the world dedicated both to caring for the dispersed sons and daughters of Armenia, and to preserving their heritage. The most important of them are Dashnaktsutiun, a political, social and cultural organisation of immense vitality, and the Armenian General Benevolent Union, with headquarters in New York.

Another quality about the Armenian dispersion is that, given a reasonable opportunity, they make good, and emerge from tin-shack poverty to professional status in a remarkably short time. A study of the 25,000-strong community in Montreal (to take just one example), almost all of whom arrived after the second world war, largely from the Middle East and Greece, would show that very few indeed are without a responsible and significant profession. Even where opportunities are far fewer, such as in a Third World country like Syria, the qualities of industry, thrift and preparedness to learn new techniques, mean that here too a man, even if he only mends kerosene stoves, will not go without the essentials of life, and will be able to provide a start which he did not have for the new generation.

'New generation' (*nor serount*) are the key words in any Armenian community of the dispersion. There is ambivalence towards the young ones: on the one hand there is delight at seeing smiles and laughter, instead of misery and hollow-eyed starvation, and at witnessing achievement and self-reliance after destitution and dependence on charity; but there is also the doubt, that the new generation away from Armenia will not grow up Armenian, or disappear as completely as those Polish Armenians who, having fled there after the fall of Ani and maintained their identity for five centuries, converted to Roman Catholicism in the sixteenth century and vanished from history. Perhaps only in Armenia itself can Armenians be sure of continuing to exist as an identifiable people; but even amid the pressures of Europe and America it is possible for the new generation to remain Armenian, if they retain their language and an understanding of their own history, and if above all they are bold enough to confront the majority – at best indifferent, at worst chauvinistically hostile – with the conviction that to be Armenian is something to be proud of. Survival of any minority depends first and foremost on an attitude of mind; even language and cultural awareness are secondary. Thus the communities have it in their power to keep the new generation Armenian, as long as they are not seduced by the materialist aspects of Western society, which have the power to stifle any vivid and interesting distinctions among citizens; as long as they themselves resolve not to disappear.

Towards Restitution

During the last thousand years – between a half and a third of the period of their residence in their highlands – the suffering and dislocation of the Armenians has only been matched by their persistence in sticking to their land. Much of this dislocation has been part of the ebb and flow of historical events – the rise and collapse of empires, the fury and vanity of power – for which no blame can be apportioned today. But in this century, especially since the first world war, a new type of discourse has developed; ideas have gained currency that not brute force alone, but that the rights of the ordinary people, too, should be taken into account. At the time when these ideas were being enthusiastically formulated, the Armenians were enduring some of their worst onslaughts. It does not take much insight to realise that Armenians have had very little of the justice and rights that have been talked about in our century.

So, what can be done? Very little, it would seem. The Soviet Union has given repeated assurances to Turkey that she has no territorial claims against her. The dream of Kars, Van and Moush becoming Armenian again in the near future would seem to be unrealistic, let alone the whole of 'Wilson Armenia' of the treaty of Sèvres. Naturally these are things that Armenians continue to strive for in the long term: what, after all, is it to be kicked out of your land for 60 years, when you have lived there, in many cases as a majority, for two and half millennia? But even the most ardent nationalist is aware that international considerations mean that no solution is possible in the foreseeable future.

Nevertheless, there are, I believe, two things which could be done without any embarrassment to the respective parties, yet which would constitute a small but significant restitution for the tragic events which the Armenian nation suffered in the early part of this century. In the first place, Turkey should acknowledge what the former regime did to Armenians. At the moment both the Turkish government and Turkish universities, together with their Turkist supporters in other parts of the world, maintain a stony attitude of non-recognition towards the subject, and resort to strange sophistries to explain away uncomfortable facts. It would be good if they could display a little moral courage, and recognise what happened.

In the second place, the frontier between Turkey and the USSR could be shifted slightly but very significantly. The uninhabited medieval city of Ani, at present situated exactly on the Turkish–Soviet border, could be restored to Armenia. The government of Soviet Armenia did hold talks with Turkish officials in 1968 concerning an exchange of Ani for one or two Azeri villages in the region of Mount Akbaba (in the north), but to my knowledge nothing came of the discussions. With a little international help, and an assurance that none of the parties involved would be losing any 'face', there is a chance that they might succeed. Ani is of no political or military significance to Turkey or to the NATO alliance (despite a set of meretricious articles which appeared in British national newspapers in October 1977 – another example of Turkism in action[90]). It is, however, of profound historical significance to Armenians, and its restoration would go a tiny way to making amends for the vast sufferings of their people during the last hundred years.

Notes

1. Mary Kilbourne Matossian, *The Imapct of Soviet Policies in Armenia* (Leiden, 1962), p. 40.

2. Ibid., p. 115.

3. FO 371/7728.624.
4. Harold Buxton, *Transcaucasia* (London, 1926), p. 55.
5. Matossian, *Soviet Policies*, p. 50.
6. Ibid., p. 37.
7. Ibid., pp. 90–5; Buxton, *Transcaucasia*, p. 57.
8. See *Ararat* (New York), vol. XX, no. 1 (Winter 1979), *passim*.
9. Matossian, *Soviet Policies*, pp. 102–8.
10. Ibid., pp. 113–14, 135–6.
11. Ibid., pp. 120–8.
12. Ibid., p. 161.
13. Ibid., p. 164.
14. FO 371/4174.88761.
15. Richard G. Hovannisian, *The Republic of Armenia*, vol. I, *The First Year, 1918–1919* (Berkeley and Los Angeles, 1971), p. 420n; Oliver Baldwin, *The Questing Beast* (London, 1932), pp. 201–4.
16. Arshavir Shiragian, *The Legacy: Memoirs of an Armenian Patriot* (Boston, 1972), pp. 103–17.
17. Ibid., pp. 169–81.
18. Hovannisian, *The Republic of Armenia*, loc. cit.; V. Minorsky, 'Turan', *Encyclopedia of Islam*, 1st edn (Leiden, 1934).
19. Hovannisian, *The Republic of Armenia*, loc. cit.
20. *The Times*, 5 May 1922, p. 10.
21. Marjorie Housepian, *Smyrna 1922: The Destruction of a City* (London, 1972).
22. Ibid., p. 51.
23. Turkey no. 1 (1923), pp. 178–308, especially 199 and 206–12.
24. Joseph C. Grew, *Turbulent Era* (Cambridge, Mass., and London, 1953), vol. I, p. 531.
25. Treaty Series, no. 16 (1923), pp. 28–33.
26. *Massis* (London), vol. I, no. 2 (December 1928), p. 29.
27. FO 371/13827.6419.
28. Ibid.
29. Ibid., enc.
30. A. Hourani, *Syria and Lebanon: A Political Essay* (London, 1946), p. 172.
31. Jean Mécérian, *Le génocide du peuple arménien* (Beirut, 1965), pp. 107–8; Christopher Walker, 'Lessons of Turkey's subtle land-grab', *The Times*, 5 September 1974, p. 14.
32. J. Burtt, *The People of Ararat* (London, 1926), p. 119; Alexander Khatisian, *Hayastani Hanrapetutian dsagumn ou zargatsumë* (Beirut, 1968), pp. 369–70.
33. FO 371/12324.4934.
34. Fridtjof Nansen, *Armenia and the Near East* (London, 1928), p. 5.
35. Text in Burtt, *The People of Ararat*, pp. 172–8.
36. FO 371/12324.4934.
37. Burtt, *The People of Ararat*, p. 163.
38. FO 371/12324.4934.
39. *Hansard*, 5th series, Commons, vol. 213, col. 1423.
40. FO 371/13827.4911.
41. S. R. Harutiunian, *Hai Zhoghovrdi Patmutiun* (Yerevan, 1970), vol. 4, pp. 158–62.
42. Khatisian, *Hayastani Hanrapetutian dsagumn ou zargatsumë*, pp. 345–6.
43. Harutiunian, *Hai Zhoghovrdi Patmutiun*, loc. cit.
44. G. Aharonian, *Meds Yerazi Jamboun vra* (Beirut, 1964), p. 173.
45. See Gabriel Lazian, *Hayastan yev Hai date Hai-yev-Rus haraberutiunneru luisin tak* (Cairo, 1957), p. 328; Aharonian, *Meds Yerazi Jamboun vra*, p. 182; Z. Avalishvili, 'From San Stefano to Batoum (1878–1921)', *Caucasian Quarterly* [issue 2, undated], p. 75, diary entry for 20 March 1921; personal interview with Shahan Natali, Boston, November 1971.
46. Abdul-Rahman Ghassemlou, *Kurdistan and the Kurds* (Prague and London, 1965), pp. 53–5.
47. *The Times*, 27 December 1933, p. 9.
48. Eugene Papazian, *Inknakensagrutiun yev husher* (Cairo, 1960), pp. 55–9.
49. Sarkis Atamian, *The Armenian Community* (New York, 1955), pp. 388–94.
50. Llewellyn Woodward, *British Foreign Policy in the Second World War*, vol. I (London, 1970), pp. 104, 110–12.

51. FO 371/59246.2094; FO 371/48795.
52. *Edjmiatsin*, vol. I no. 1 (January 1944), pp. 4–5; personal information from Zaven M. Messerlian.
53. FO 371/27056.4328.
54. *The Times*, 19 July 1941, p. 5.
55. Personal information from various sources.
56. Woodward, *British Foreign Policy*, vol. I, pp. 25–7.
57. Alexander Henderson, 'The Pan-Turanian Myth in Turkey Today', *Asiatic Review*, vol. XLI, no. 145 (January 1945), pp. 88–92.
58. C. W. Hostler, *Turkism and the Soviets* (New York, 1957), p. 172.
59. FO 371/33376.5472.
60. See Lewis V. Thomas and R. N. Frye, *The United States and Turkey and Iran* (Cambridge, Mass., 1952), pp. 96–7; FO 371/33389, FO 371/37399; FO 371/37404.
61. FO 371/33389.8681.
62. Thomas and Frye, *United States and Turkey and Iran*, p. 97.
63. FO 371/37404.5055.
64. Woodward, *British Foreign Policy*, vol. IV (1975), p. 207.
65. FO 371/59246.1320.
66. FO 371/59247.5532.
67. Woodward, *British Foreign Policy*, vol. IV, p. 209.
68. Quoted in Zaven Messerlian, 'The Question of Kars and Ardahan', *Armenian Studies* (Beirut) (1973), p. 86.
69. FO 371/59246.2299, 3219.
70. *Hansard*, 5th series, Commons, vol. 419, col. 1355.
71. FO 371/59247.4551.
72. Messerlian, 'The Question of Kars and Ardahan', p. 88.
73. Personal communication with Zaven Messerlian, Beirut; also FO 371/59246.17662.
74. Aharonian, *Meds Yerazi Jamboun vra*, p. 273.
75. V. Melkonian, *An Historical Glimpse of the Armenians in Iraq* (Basra, 1957), p. 16.
76. FO 371/13096.5631.
77. See Zaven M. Messerlian, 'Armenian Representation in the Lebanese Parliament' (unpublished MA thesis, American University of Beirut, 1963), *passim*.
78. Quoted in ibid., p. 159.
79. Ibid., pp. 230ff.
80. Ibid., p. 262.
81. Avedis K. Sanjian, *The Armenian Communities in Syria under Ottoman Dominion* (Cambridge, Mass., 1965), pp. 226ff.
82. Atamian, *The Armenian Community*, p. 434.
83. On the crisis see Dickran Kouymdjian, 'The Recent Crisis in the Armenian Church' (unpublished MA thesis, American University of Beirut, 1961).
84. *The Times*, 4 October 1957, p. 9.
85. *Armenian Mirror-Spectator* (Watertown), 30 March 1957.
86. Ibid., 23 April 1960.
87. Ibid., 26 March 1960, 30 April 1960, 25 June 1960.
88. Matossian, *Soviet Policies*, p. 201.
89. *Armenian Mirror-Spectator*, 10 June 1978.
90. *Financial Times*, 11 October 1977; *Daily Telegraph*, 11 October 1977; *The Times*, 13 October 1977; *The Guardian*, 18 October 1977.

10 Confronting Denial

By the late 1970s the main issue confronting the Armenian community worldwide was denial. This denial centred on the subject of what had happened to the Armenians in 1915. Independent eye-witness sources of that date agree to a great extent that the Ottoman Armenians, including women and children, were systematically driven to their deaths by the authorities, in a form of mass ethnic liquidation amounting to what was later connoted by the word 'genocide'. Yet Turkey refused to acknowledge that the Armenians died in this way, and preferred not to talk about the subject, even though the anti-Armenian measures had occurred under a superseded regime. The subject appeared to be largely taboo, and friends of Turkey were expected either not to raise it, or to follow the Turkish viewpoint on the matter—that the Armenians had been in revolt and got what they deserved; it had been an unfortunate chapter, which was now closed, and Armenians and their friends would be advised not to try to reopen it. Foreign academics friendly to Turkey writing about the events of the first world war were apt to ignore matters of internal Ottoman policy, and to disregard the dispatches and reports from German or neutral consuls and relief-workers which focused on the plight of the Armenians and on the attitude of the authorities.

But the Armenian voice became more persistent. This came about because a new generation of Armenians was growing up which was receiving education in American and other universities, and was naturally keen to know about the nation's history, and what had happened to their forebears. The time was one when minority cultures in the US were being asserted, rather than submerged. In this climate, the evidence that Armenians found, with only a minimum of effort, in accounts written by eye-witnesses at the time, or even in national archives (including those in the US), supported the version of events that they had been told about from members of their own families. American Armenians did not see why they should quietly and complicitly accept the versions to which aspects of late Ottoman history had been reduced, which appeared to avoid awkward issues and to ignore difficult documents, so as to keep perceptions of the past in line with current American regional political interests.

At the same time, there occurred a more fundamental radicalization of the Armenian youth in Lebanon and in Paris, a youth which was disillusioned with the inertia and in-fighting among the established Armenian political parties of the diaspora, and was angry at their failure effectively to pursue Armenian political claims on the international stage. They saw other minority groups who had legitimate but unheard political grievances gaining a hearing through the use of force, and they saw a possibility of using the same methods. This led to the phenomenon of Armenian terrorism. This form of terrorism was not aimed at extorting actual political concessions; it was directed at forcing remembrance of the Armenian genocide, and at bringing the issue of Armenia and the losses of 1915 somehow on to the political agenda. It aimed to overcome the worldwide denial about the subject—the bland assumption that the events in Armenia in 1915 had been no more than normal events in a normal war; it seemed to be a way of making the world community remember what it had chosen to forget. Part, too, of the motive force behind the terrorist campaign (which, as with all terrorism, often murdered shockingly inappropriate people, such as the wife of Zeki Kuneralp, whose family had been instrumental in seeking rapprochement between the different nationalities of post-Ottoman Turkey) was sheer crude revenge—the same counter-productive emotion which had stifled true political progress in the 1890s (see above, p. 130).

In the course of nine years, from 1974 to 1983, some 45 Turkish diplomats and state personnel were killed worldwide, in a series of operations executed usually with alarming precision. The deeds were in the main masterminded by two shadowy organizations: ASALA, or the Armenian Secret Army for the Liberation of Armenia (which was Armenian and secret, but could have no pretensions to being an army or to having anything to do with liberation), and the JCAG, or the Justice Commandoes of the Armenian Genocide, which later re-styled itself the New Armenian Resistance. As with any organizations that employ secrecy and terror, they were a prey to internal splits and divisions, and after a particularly gruesome attack in 1983 at Orly Airport, Paris, even the hardened men of the bomb and gun were revolted, leading to a split in the main organization, and to the virtual end of Armenian terrorism.

In passing, it should be noted that one of the claims put about by the terrorists was that they had resorted to violence because Armenians had tried, by peaceful methods, to awaken the consciousness of the world, and these methods had failed. This is much less than the truth. No serious political campaign had ever been launched; no information was available in a coherent and scholarly form about the events which were central to the Armenian experience. The Armenians have only just, in the late 1980s, begun putting together the beginnings of a systematic account of the genocide of 1915–16. Nothing had been written in a mature manner, using proper archive sources, about those events at the time of the terrorist campaign. There was no detailed account of what happened, and why it happened, and who ordered it, and who carried out the orders. It was puzzling why this should be—why the Armenians should be keen to make it clear to the world that they have felt injustice and anger as a result of the mass-extermination of 1915, and yet find it difficult to describe and analyse the events. In a strange way the Armenians themselves appeared to be almost colluding with the denial that they opposed. It is possible that the exposed subjects of the cruel mass-death of their own people, and the centralized unrelenting power of the imperial government which had sought to destroy them, are issues which even recently were too painful to face calmly and methodically. Outrage was easier; so was violence.

A series of minor diplomatic breakthroughs helped the Armenian case throughout the 1980s. The first was of little or no international standing, but gave the Armenians a taste for the use of world fora for exploring the justice of their case. At a meeting in 1984 of the 'Permanent Peoples' Tribunal', the commission established by the Italian senator and jurist Lelio Basso, and with François Rigaux, of the Catholic University of Louvain, as its president, Turkey was found guilty of genocide, according to the terms of the UN Convention of December 1948. The jurists who delivered this verdict were a distinguished and impartial group of international lawyers and human rights' specialists; and the moderation, legal precision, and lack of political rhetoric in the judgement that they produced showed the seriousness with which they took their task.[1]

Another success for the Armenians occurred in Geneva in 1985. On 29 August, the United Nations Sub-Commission on the Prevention of Discrimination and the Protection of Minorities accepted for further study a report on genocide, prepared by Benjamin Whitaker of Great Britain. A footnote to Paragraph 24 of this report said that 'At least 1 million, and possibly well over half the Armenian population, are reliably estimated to have been killed or death-marched.' This seems fairly uncontroversial, and in line with the eye-witness accounts of the time, but the argument and lobbying by Turkish representatives against the wording had been powerful.[2]

The vote, taken in Geneva, was 14 in favour, one against, four abstentions and six absent. Britain, France and the USA were among the countries voting in favour; the USSR was the sole vote against. (It appeared that the USSR was voting against not on the Armenian issue, but on the terminology elsewhere in the document which might be taken to cast a dim light on the USSR's own treatment of minorities in Stalin's time.) The terms of the resolution were not that genocide against the Armenians had taken place; just that the sub-commission would accept the report for future reference. Nevertheless the topic, before the voting, aroused strong emotions. In an interesting form of words, which was used in the compromise formula, the Zambian representative noted that 'the Armenian massacre was not adequately documented'. If that means the notion that the Armenians were victims of genocide in 1915 lacks credibility because no explicit orders have been published, then the response should be that genocide is not necessarily carried out in this way, with written orders. Secrecy and word-of-mouth orders are the usual conveyers of orders for racial mass-death. There is sufficient eye-witness evidence of the events of 1915, especially of the behaviour of officials, to deduce the policies of the authorities. But if the representative meant that the Armenian side, claiming to have been the victim of the crime of genocide, had not prepared a full account of the events, then he was correct.

The third, and most significant, victory for Armenians occurred in Strasbourg, when on 18 June 1987 the European Parliament voted, by 68 votes to 60, with 42 abstentions, to recognise the Armenian Genocide.[3]

Opponents have castigated this resolution as pointless, and dealing with a matter which was outside the competence of the parliament. But it could easily be argued that since genocide is such a serious matter, any parliament of a body that refused to consider it, where it was seriously alleged against a prospective member of that body, was failing in its duty by ignoring such an allegation. Moreover, the resolution demonstrated that the fate of the Armenians mattered, and that they were not the negligible quantity to which Turkish power and international politics had attempted to reduce them. In one of the preambles to the bill, the ministers noted that the Turkish government, by refusing to recognize the genocide of 1915, 'continued to deprive the Armenian people of the right to their own history.' A further clause pointed out that such a recognition of genocide, if it occurred, would 'be viewed as a profoundly humane act of moral rehabilitation towards the Armenians' by the Turks. This is surely the language of the humane Europe that for many people is the one most worth building.

In clause after clause this resolution not only held up an accurate mirror to Armenia's history, but also emphasized some of the best European qualities and virtues. The resolution held that the Armenian question, and the question of minorities in Turkey, 'must be re-situated within the framework of relations between Europe and the Community', and pointed out 'that democracy cannot be solidly implanted in a country unless the latter recognizes and enriches its history with its ethnic and cultural diversity'—a fine assertion of the idea that diversity is an integral part of democracy, and a reminder that it is not a quality much in evidence in Turkey, whose polity is characterized by statist army-based monolithic notions, which are often argued in favour of the country (and paradoxically of Turkish democracy, even though they are the very negation of democracy) by militarists, ex-diplomats and certain academics and journalists who, for whatever reasons, continue to endorse the power of Turkey, and to follow almost uncritically the line of the government in Ankara.

The resolution went on to say that it held that the tragic events in 1915–17 involving the Armenians 'constituted genocide within the meaning of the convention on the prevention and the punishment of the crime of genocide adopted by the UN General Assembly on 9 December 1948'. It also, significantly, recognized that the Turkish Republic cannot be held responsible for those events, and that no claims against Turkey today can be derived from the recognition of genocide in the past.

What the resolution sought was an acknowledgement of the genocide, and the promotion of a political dialogue between Turkey and representatives of the Armenians. A clause followed saying that Turkey's refusal to acknowledge the genocide of Armenians, together with its reluctance to apply standards of international law to its dispute with Greece, along with the maintenance of

Turkish troops on Cyprus, the denial of the existence of a Kurdish question, and the general lack of individual freedom in Turkey, constituted obstacles to Turkey's joining the European Community.

Nine clauses contained the rest of what the Community was seeking from Turkey, on the matter: fair treatment for Armenians within Turkey, and protection of the Armenian historical monuments there. It reminded Turkey of the provisions of the 1923 Treaty of Lausanne concerning minorities. It also pointed out the difficulties experienced by Armenians in Iran and the USSR, and condemned Armenian terrorism, calling for reconciliation between Armenians and Turks.

The resolution perhaps became somewhat too diffuse and ill-focused in its targets in its concluding clauses; but the basic notion which animated it—that the past, when it contains terrible deeds, cannot be forgotten, merely because it is past—surely represents an important part of the idea of post-Hitler Europe; and the concept that minorities are admirable in themselves, and that diversity is to be encouraged, as an expression of something that is among the finest flowers of European history and culture, can be seen as a praiseworthy expression of the spirit of Europe. It was a triumph, and not just for the Armenians, when it was passed.

Turkey's response was a veiled hint at pulling out of NATO—a modern version of the Ottoman tactic that, when all else failed, the sultan would remind the powers of the strategic importance of Turkey, and this would bring them to heel.[4] It was also claimed that the resolution 'encouraged terrorism'. This idea, that pro-Armenian (or pro-Kurdish) resolutions encourage terrorism, is one that needs to be looked at.

All three Armenian diplomatic successes—that of the verdict of the Permanent People's Tribunal, that of the UN sub-commission on the prevention of genocide, and the vote at the Strasbourg parliament—were said by Turkey, with great foreboding, to be encouragements of terrorism. Yet no Armenian terrorism occurred. There was, it is true, a fairly gruesome attack by the Kurdish PKK, doctrinaire marxists with politics of the out-of-sight variety, after the June 1987 vote; but this attack cannot fairly be laid at the door of the one reference to the Kurds, in a resolution which was basically about Armenians. Not a single Armenian attack occurred after any of these three decisions. Indeed, by taking the Armenian question into the arena of political discussion and dialogue, the pressure that had built up by the denial, not only of the genocide, but of the fact that the Armenians even had any serious grievances, has been reduced, and the matter has been given a legal articulation. Armenians are now finding legitimate ways to express their grievances, and this has naturally reduced the demand for illegitimate or terroristic expression. Turkey's claim that pro-Armenian verdicts and resolutions encourage terrorism is no more than a tactic to try to maintain its failing control on the silence and denial which have surrounded substantial discussion of the topic of Armenia.

At the same time, in the United States, a campaign developed to pass a resolution in the House of Representatives declaring April 24th to be a day of remembrance for the victims of genocide. The implication was that the Armenian genocide would thereby be recognised by the US Congress. To many members of Congress, the idea seemed a reasonable and humane one, in line with good American humanitarian traditions. But the opposition was fast and furious, especially from the US administration. Much of the anti-Armenian lobbying was low key in 1985 and 1986, but in 1987 US Secretary of State George Shultz came out with a forthright assertion of the administration's viewpoint.

Shultz's framing of his department's views came about in reply to a letter from Alex Manoogian, the Armenian millionaire philanthropist and benefactor of Detroit, Michigan. Manoogian had said that concern for Turkey's position in NATO 'cannot and should not deter us from seeking the historic truth and exercising our sense of justice about the Armenian genocide, the truth of which has been affirmed by 10 US presidents and fully documented by the US State Department archives including reliable eye-witness accounts . . .'. Shultz's reply was a crude raspberry of political expediency. After referring to 'intercommunal strife' during the first world war, which resulted in 'massive suffering among the mixed populations of the area', phrases which are instantly recognizable as a denial of debate on the policies and intentions behind the events, and a crumbling submissiveness to Turkish power of the past and present, Shultz continued by saying, 'There is no doubt that HJR 132 [the resolution before Congress] would very seriously damage US-Turkish relations. The Resolution is seen in Turkey as an endorsement of Armenian terrorism and a precursor of demands for reparations and eventual territorial dismemberment. So perceived, HJR 132—like its predecessor in 1985 and like the European Parliament's recent resolution—generates anger, resentment and hostility across the political spectrum in Turkey.'[5]

What was extraordinary about Shultz's reply was its lack of an expression of an American perspective. The views of Americans, reflecting the reports of past generations of Americans on the spot at the time, and American standards of truthfulness, objectivity and impartiality, were by their omission entirely subjected to the overriding aim of not offending Turkey, and maintaining denial. The modern Turkish version of the events of 1915 was accepted by the State Department unquestioningly. Turkey's right to feel anger, resentment and hostility was similarly not questioned. The only matter at issue was how the resolution was seen in Turkey. Nowhere was there even a hint that the United States, the leader of the Western alliance, might be able to assess the subject independently, or that the Turkish government version might not be the last word on the events of 1915, and that impartial eye-witnesses might have had something important to say about it. All was subjected to the fundamental principle that Turkey was right, and to the craven notion that it must not be offended by showing it a mirror of its own history. The idea that governments are sometimes less than fully committed to the truth about the past apparently did not occur to Shultz. Moreover, by talking apocalyptically about territorial dismemberment, the administration was raising bogies that were not in the original resolution. Many Armenians would be satisfied with a simple acknowledgement by the Turks of what happened; some want a territorial adjustment (not necessarily a large one); only a few extremists seek 'dismemberment' of Turkey.

In the event, the administration had its way, and the resolution was defeated in the House on 7 August 1987 by 189 votes to 201.

The American administration appears to have accepted fairly uncritically the Turkish arguments that have developed in recent years about the events of 1915, so perhaps it is worth looking at them.[6]

Turkish discussion of 1915 omits all reference to the power, structure and decisions of the Committee of Union and Progress, which was the party in power at the time, or to the Special Organization (*Teshkilat-i Makhsusiye*), the organized brigands who despoiled and killed Armenians. It ignores eye-witness accounts, even if they come from neutral or pro-German sources. It claims, by contrast, that many of the Armenians were in a state of revolt in 1915, that there was a 'limited form of civil war' going on in Anatolia in 1915 (a parallel has been drawn with the situation in Lebanon from 1974 to 1989); and that in particular the Armenians of Van were in a state of revolt which led to the Ottoman government's anti-Armenian measures. Apologists also indicate that many Muslims died as well as Armenians in the world war. They further point out that the Bryce/Toynbee Blue Book (published by the British government as Miscellaneous no. 31 (1916) and published commercially as *The Treatment of Armenians in the Ottoman Empire*), which constituted a major piece of evidence of Ottoman mass ethnic liquidation, was later admitted by Toynbee to have been published as war propaganda.

These claims, propounded in Ankara, and accepted virtually uncritically in Washington, are either fallacious, irrelevant, or ignore the vital matter of intention. There was no revolt in Van; the actions of the citizens of that town were just acts of self-defence against a harsh governor, who was acting with great violence in the town and province of Van. The defence of Van began on 20 April 1915, the day after widespread slaughter of Armenian villagers throughout the province by government forces, and fully two weeks after the start of the deportations of Armenians in Cilicia. The action was thus a reaction to policies being instigated by the authorities, not a self-motivated rebellion.

The claim that there was a 'limited form of civil war' going on in the region, or as the Shultz document has it, 'intercommunal strife', is a curious invention. There is no reference to any 'civil war' in either of the standard military histories of the period, that by Commandant Larcher (*La Guerre turque dans la guerre mondiale*, Paris, 1926), or the magisterial work by W.E.D. Allen and Paul Muratoff, *Caucasian Battlefields*, Cambridge, 1953. No new impartial evidence has been adduced to support this claim; indeed its claimants (who in-

include a number of American academics) appear unfamiliar with the standard texts on the military history of the period. The idea of a small-scale civil war is one that avoids having a hard look at the position of the party, the army and the gendarmerie at the time, as well as at an outgrowth of the party such as the Special Organization. 'Civil war' is an idea which ignores, and thereby negates, the massive state power of the Ottoman empire, and the policies and decisions of the Ministry of the Interior. In Lebanon there has been no powerful central state power; the war has continued between conflicting militias of approximately equal fire-power. The situation was quite different in the Ottoman empire in 1915, where a massive access of state power was arrayed against the Armenian civilian population; the few isolated armed groups of Armenians, who (except briefly in Cilicia) sought to defend themselves only did so when provoked or threatened with death by the government. The most famous of their acts of self-defence, that at Musa Dagh in September 1915, led to the freedom of about 4,000 Armenian villagers, who would otherwise have been murdered on a death-march. To describe such self-defence as an act of civil war, or even as 'terrorism', is a gross abuse of language.

On the matter of Turkish/Kurdish losses in 1915–17, there are two points to make. The first is the comment of Joseph Pomiankowski, Austrian military attaché in the Ottoman capital during the war. In his book *Der Zusammenbruch des ottomanischen Reiches,* (Zurich, 1928), he says: 'The gruesome annihilation of the Armenian nation in Asia Minor by the Young Turk regime was a barbaric act, arousing all human feelings to the highest extent . . . The cost of this war was carried in the first place by the Turkish army operating in Asia Minor . . . hunger caused the loss of hundreds of thousands of Turkish soldiers in Armenia. The Armenian caravans, totally devoid of any cleaning facilities and hygiene, became the carriers of diseases . . . a general epidemic of typhus broke out from which at least a million Muslims died. This was the vengeance of the deported murdered Armenians on their executioners.'[7]

Similarly, in his biography of Atatürk, Lord Kinross makes the following point about the Ottoman campaign in Anatolia during the winter of 1916–17: 'Nor could an army any longer subsist here on the country, for the ironical reason that in the earlier stages of the campaign the Armenians had been massacred or deported *en masse,* leaving the land a virtual desert, without peasants to grow food or artisans to provide service . . . and, following blizzards, whole detachments were found in caves, dead from hunger and cold.'[8]

Both quotations make it clear that, where the Turks and Kurds suffered, they suffered as a result of anti-Armenian decisions taken by the authorities in the Ottoman capital.

The Armenians were massacred intentionally, and the Turko-Kurds died unintentionally at this stage. Armenians cannot be made responsible for Ottoman war losses in Anatolia. Later, with the advance of the Russian army in the north in late 1916 and early 1917, Armenians did carry out revenge killings of Turkish villagers; but the numbers they killed were to be counted in hundreds, or at most thousands, rather than in the hundreds of thousands which were the number of the Armenians whom the Ottoman authorities had intentionally destroyed in 1915 and 1916.

Was the volume entitled *The Treatment of Armenians in the Ottoman Empire*, produced in 1916 by Viscount Bryce and Arnold Toynbee, propaganda or not? Its publication as a British government Blue Book was certainly a propaganda act, designed to discredit the chief ally of Germany. In the same way, accounts of the sufferings of the Belgians had been published early on in the war. But no one has ever subsequently said that the Belgians did not suffer as they were said to have done, merely because their sufferings were made public in this way. Similarly with the Armenians. Although the volume was published as part of a propaganda campaign, the origin of each of the documents was unimpeachable. Nothing was invented, or empty hearsay gossip. All the documents stand up as historical documents today. So far as I know, no effort has ever been made to challenge the origin and trustworthiness of any of the documents individually.

The weakness of the Turkish arguments exemplifies the essential defensiveness of their position; and there appears to be an underlying assumption that most representatives of nations friendly to Turkey will automatically and uncritically accept any arguments that Turkey proposes, in view of the axiomatic notion of old-fashioned Western diplomacy that the process of soothing Turkey (which is not treated as a mature state, able to take criticism) is a prime concern.

In these circumstances, as hard truth has gradually become known about the nature of the events of 1915, the official arguments have slowly started to crumble, although there has been enormous rearguard action by Turkey and its supporters. History has seldom been a helpful handmaid to regimes, especially to statist, dirigiste ones offering a quasi-ideological version of government success.

Up to the present moment, Armenians have not been very successful in projecting an effective challenge to Turkey's denial about 1915. Vested interests, and individual self-censorship, backed by a massive Turkish campaign working through public relations agencies and funded by budgets of millions of dollars, have largely been able to keep the lid pressed down on the objective, impartially recorded facts of 1915. But as more reliable material is published from the archives of the USA, Germany and Austria, even the massed public relations experts of Messrs Hill and Knowlton of Washington DC, and Saatchi and Saatchi of London, both of whom have been taken on to handle Turkey's public relations, will find it difficult to continue to ignore the observed reality of the fate of Armenians in the Ottoman Empire in 1915–16.

Turkey's offer, made in January 1989, to open its state archives, is an interesting one, and one that all who strive to gain a clearer understanding of what happened in the Ottoman Empire in the years when the Armenian Question was a matter of significance will welcome.[9] But some words of caution are in order. One is that, according to some reports, the archives of 1894–1923, the critical years for Ottoman Armenians, are to remain closed. If that is so, the opening of the archives will solve nothing as regards the Armenians. Secondly, the archives are reported to have already been examined by Turkish scholars of strong nationalist sympathies, and it appears that possibly compromising documents have been removed from public view. This operation was apparently done under the auspices of the Turkish army, which provided space in army buildings in Ankara for the purpose. Thirdly, if permission is ever granted for Ottoman archives of the first world war to be examined, the important ones are not so much the state archives, but the party archives of the Committee of Union and Progress, which, although the party of government, had established a para-government, working alongside official government employees, and which was acting as a ginger group imbued with chauvinist extremism.[10] Without the party archives, any account of the behaviour of those in power in the Ottoman empire towards the Armenians is incomplete.

Turkish sensitivity on the Armenian issue is manifestly still very high, and on the surface it is rather difficult to see why this should be. If Turkey were to accept what happened in 1915, and make some sort of statement about it, a much calmer atmosphere would be created, where dialogue was possible, and such an action might even set the matter to rest as a live political issue, as opposed to a mild, unimportant dispute between specialists. It is unlikely that the Republic of Turkey would, through serious and mature discussion of the Armenian question, lose massive areas of Eastern Turkey, although some sort of border rectification is probably desirable. (The region anyway was 'Ottoman' as opposed to 'Turkish'; and some of it, the region of Surmalu, between Mt Ararat and Yerevan, was Persian/Russian and not Ottoman.) What we are confronting here appears to be not so much fear for the safety, viability and integrity of the Turkish state, as the massive pride of Turkey in the achievements of its state and army, even though many of these achievements run rather counter to present-day ideas about democracy and human rights. This is what blocks sensible analysis of Armenia. Until Turkey can find pride in human rights and human diversity, rather than in the conquest of territory by its armies, there will be little chance of movement on the subject of Armenians. Western diplomats and Western journalists, publicists and some scholars who collude with Ankara in promoting the glories of the Turkish army and state without sparing a thought for the fate of the people who lived or live there, are keeping alive the notions of militarism, conquest and suppression of dissidents and ethno-religious minorities, which may have been part of the Ottoman achievement (and the achievement of other empires), but which today are entirely out of fashion as desirable political objectives. In the light of Turkey's intention to join the European Community, it might be beneficial for Turkey and her supporters to place less stress on armies and conquest, and more on human qualities and ethnic and cultural diversity. With such a change of emphasis, a clear, objective and unbiased approach to the Armenian question would be possible, and dialogue would be created.

*   *   *

Nevertheless, the Armenian cause (in the form principally of recognition of what happened to the Armenians) has made some progress. Some serious collections of documents have been published. But there are still large gaps, and the most important of those is the essential need for the Armenians themselves to face the experience of 1915 in detail in a clear and objective manner. But with the Armenian case a live issue now at the UN Sub-Commission on Human Rights, and at the European Parliament (which has recently achieved a higher profile and significance), there is a better hope of the possibility of sound and clear-headed discussion on the historical, legal and moral aspects of the Armenian question.

Notes

1. See Permanent People's Tribunal, *A Crime of Silence* (London and New York, 1985).
2. *Erebouni*, September 1985, p. 7.
3. *Armenian Mirror-Spectator* (Watertown, Mass.), 27 June 1987; *California Courier* (Glendale, Calif.), 25 June 1987. Text in *Armenian Mirror-Spectator*, 18 July 1987, p. 3.
4. *The Guardian*, *The Independent* (London) both of 23 June 1987.
5. *Armenian Mirror-Spectator*, 25 July, 15 August 1987.
6. See for example the full-page advertisements appearing in the *New York Times* and the *Washington Post* of 18 May 1985.
7. Joseph Pomiankowski, *Der Zusammenbruch des ottomanischen Reiches* (Zurich, 1928), p. 165.
8. Lord Kinross, *Atatürk: the Rebirth of a Nation* (London, 1964), p. 100.
9. *Asbarez* (Glendale, Calif.), 7 January 1989.
10. See Count von Wolff-Metternich's dispatch, quoted on p. 235 above; also E. H. Keeling, *Adventures in Turkey and Russia* (London 1924), p. 226.

11   Perestroika and Karabagh

When, in April 1985, the era of glasnost and perestroika came to the USSR, people wondered how, and when, the developments would affect Armenia. Glasnost indeed took time to appear in any form there. Conditions remained static and 'Brezhnevite'. Armenia, like other non-Russian republics of the USSR, had benefited from the looser control that had been exercised by Moscow since the death of Stalin; but this had been accompanied by a tighter control imposed by the local party apparatus. An elaborate system of bribery and corruption had developed, leading to the establishment of a kind of mafia within the republic. With such a system in place, there was not much response to ideas of openness and reconstruction.

Changes, however, appeared inevitable in Armenia after the plenum of the Central Committee of the Communist Party of the Soviet Union, held in June 1987, in which criticism was expressed by M. S. Gorbachev against the operation of the party in Armenia. It was, he said, 'stuck in a rut'. The following month an Armenian regional Communist Party official, Haik Kotanjian, echoed this criticism, adding that positions of power in Armenia could only be obtained after payment, and that there was even a scale of charges operating. He suggested that Karen Demirjian, First Secretary of the Central Committee, should voluntarily transfer to different work. His speech, which was reported in the local party newspaper, *Sovetakan Hayastan,* was not popular; at the meeting he was shouted down. The criticism was repeated in a speech in January 1988, and given wide publicity in *Pravda,* in the issue of 18 January. For the first time the top ranks, or *nomenklatura,* of an entire local party were being criticized.[1]

Political consciousness, however, operates on two tracks in Soviet Armenia. One relates to internal matters: the nature of policy and decision-making within Armenia for the livelihood of its citizens—citizens who, while wishing that corruption did not exist, are not especially surprised by allegations of it. The other element is the cluster of issues which relate to the Armenian question. These include Armenian nationhood, national borders, the Armenian language, national history, and the Armenian cause as an international struggle. National feeling has persisted strongly in Armenia; indeed, where it conflicts with attitudes handed down by Moscow, it appears to override awareness of the security that the country has gained through membership of the USSR. Armenians are conscious of their history, language, script and culture, and are determined to prevent these aspects of their life from vanishing into the kind of amorphous and indistinguishable medley which opponents of the value of national cultural identities (whether politically on the right or the left) propose. Almost all Armenians show a devotion to, or at least a respect for, their Apostolic Church, which besides being the protector of their faith has also been the symbol, indeed the vehicle, of national continuity. Eastern Armenia has for the last 150 years been linked to Russia, but has remained quite distinct.

Armenia's enormous losses at the hands of the Turks in the earlier part of this century have reinforced the popular determination to protect the nation's culture, history, and identity. They see assimilation occurring in the diaspora. Within the USSR, they have seen in this century the Armenians of Nakhichevan (a territory which is administered as part of Azerbaijan, but which is part of the historic land of Armenia, and geographically a continuation of the Ararat valley) dwindle to a small minority. In such circumstances the determination to preserve national identity and traditions becomes understandable. Armenian nationalism is a defensive movement, aimed principally at preserving the existence of the people in its land. It does not seek to oppress other nationalities.

At the same time, few Armenians wanted (or want) independence. In this matter they were different from the citizens of the Baltic states, and they were much less assertive than nationalists within Georgia. Many Armenians understand the risks attached to independence: that Turkey with its massive army would be virtually unstoppable, if it decided to invade and found a pretext to do so, and that, on the evidence of Cyprus, no outside power would ever stop Turkey. (General Evren had boasted in early 1986 that the Turkish army could fight 'even beyond Aghri Dagh [Mount Ararat]', conveying a message which was not lost on Armenians.) Also, on a lower but still important level, Armenia is well integrated economically in the USSR, and would not be able to feed its population if it gained independence within its present boundaries.[2]

One subject emerged as a focal issue for the social and political re-evaluation that was beginning. This was industrial pollution, and the destruction of Armenia's environment. Green issues were aired, in the second half of 1987, in articles written by Zori Balayan, Yerevan correspondent for *Literaturnaya Gazeta*. These subjects, hitherto ignored, gained prominence in Armenia and the rest of the Soviet Union. They were symbolic of the manner in which the people's attention was returning to the land itself.

The problem of pollution related to three main sites.[3] The first was the nuclear reactor situated at Metsamor, 25 kilometres from Yerevan, built in, strange as it may seem, not only one of the few fertile districts of Armenia (the Ararat valley), but also a region liable to earthquakes. This reactor was reported to be, on occasion, discharging raw nuclear waste into the ground. In the period after the Chernobyl disaster, there was a much increased consciousness of the dangers attached to nuclear power plants. Secondly, environmentalists were concerned about the presence of the Nayirit synthetic rubber factory, in the heart of Yerevan itself. This plant (which in mid-1989 was still operational) emitted large quantities of poisonous chloroprenes. Other factories in Yerevan which were environmentally dangerous were a polyvinylacetate plant, and an aluminum factory. None of these or other factories in Yerevan had any safety zone around them, and many were situated in the middle of areas of dense population with schools nearby. The third indicator of a serious ecological situation was the condition of Lake Sevan. In 1965 the famous English tenor Peter Pears, on a working holiday, had written of this lake: 'The Armenians call it their country's heart and love it dearly. Forty miles long and 5–10 miles wide, its waters are sweet to taste and dazzlingly kingfisher-blue and wine-dark violet.'[4] By the 1980s the situation was very different. Hydro-electric plants which used the lake's water had depleted the water level, and industrial effluents, together with the leaching of agricultural fertilizers and pesticides into the lake, had led to the near-extinction of the famous species of trout found in the lake, known as *ishkhan,* or prince.[5] Planning controls were, as with the factories and nuclear installation, ignored.

The first demonstration against the violation of the environment took place in September 1987; about 100 people took part. It was organised by Paruyr Hairikian, a well-known dissident of strong nationalist views, and the protestors marched to the Nayirit factory. In the following month, on 17 October, another demonstration took place on the same theme, not organised by Hairikian; this time 1,000–2,000 people took part. The police tried to prevent it occurring, but made no attempt to stop it once it had started.[6]

On the following day, the political discourse took a new turn. Armenian political consciousness, and awareness of relationship between the people and the land, developed from local regional concerns, to the wider arena of the Armenian question itself. The disputed territories of Nakhichevan, and Mountainous Karabagh (or Nagorno Karabakh, to give it its Russian title) entered the vocabulary of political demands. These territories had long been a cause of grievance to Armenians; Armenia had a claim on both of them, and a strong one in the case of Karabagh. One thousand people were said to have taken part, some of whom carried placards bearing Mr Gorbachev's picture. Nevertheless the police stopped the march and dispersed the demonstrators.[7]

The intellectual backing for this movement was provided mainly by a group of Armenian intellectuals. The one with the highest public profile was Zori Balayan, who had been active on the Green issue and was himself a native of Karabagh. Later Sergei Mikoyan, son of the former foreign minister of the USSR, and editor of the Academy of Sciences' magazine 'Latin America', became a spokesman. Abel Aghanbekyan, Mr Gorbachev's chief economic adviser, also made speeches in favour of the movement. In November 1987, in interviews in both Paris and London, Aghanbekyan indicated that solutions favourable to Armenia on the question of the status of both Nakhichevan and Karabagh were probably on the point of being reached in the USSR at a high level.[8] Whether Aghanbekyan intended to hint that Mr Gorbachev was favourably disposed to a re-drawing of boundaries within Transcaucasia is questionable; certainly, none of Gorbachev's later pronouncements showed sympathy with the idea of changing boundaries.[9] The Soviet President has shown himself committed to an internationalist view of the USSR; that is, that national grievances must be subjected to the general interests of the USSR, and conversely, that only by acting in a way which transcends local national sentiment will the different nationalities find a secure and full place in Soviet society.[10]

But for Armenians, inhabitants of the smallest union republic of the USSR, and members of a nation that had had a brutal experience in the earlier part of this century, the priorities were population, national rights and territory. Armenians are by nature internationalist, but within Transcaucasia they have felt the need to protect and preserve the people on its land. Internationalism in the Caucasus is possible so long as the essentials for the survival of the nation and for the democratic rights of its members are assured.

The basic facts of the history of Karabagh and Nakhichevan indicate why Armenians feel they have had a rough deal over those territories, and are not quite ready to express internationalist sentiments yet. Karabagh had been denied an Armenian administration by the British occupation of 1918, when General W. M. Thomson had halted the entry of Armenian forces into the territory, and installed a violent Tatar landlord, Dr Sultanov, as governor instead. Both regions had been, along with Zangezur, 'disputed territories' between Armenia and Azerbaijan throughout much of the time of the independent republics of 1918–20. The matter appeared to have been solved when, on the eve of Armenia's sovietization in 1920, the leader of neighbouring Soviet Azerbaijan, Nariman Narimanov, declared publicly that 'Mountainous Karabagh, Zangezur and Nakhichevan are considered part of the Soviet Republic of Armenia', an apparent gesture of generosity. Stalin endorsed this decision in the edition of *Pravda* dated 4 December 1920.[11] But the territories were never actually attached.

Nationalist Turkey was moreover very interested in the matter. It went on to cement a deal with the Soviet state so that Nakhichevan gained the protectorate of Azerbaijan, under the terms of the treaty of Moscow, which was signed in March 1921 between the Soviet state and Mustafa Kemal's Nationalist Turkey. The Armenians were not even invited to state their case. The territory was disposed of in the manner of a straightforward regional carve-up, executed by two states allegedly creating a new democratic world order, but in fact acting rather more with the cynicism of the Habsburgs or the Hohenzollerns of half a century earlier. Early Bolshevism could show as much deference to regional power as any other government seeking to influence a neighbour. The treaty of Kars of October 1921 confirmed the status of Nakhichevan as a region under the control of Azerbaijan, and the territory was forbidden to change its status without the consent of Turkey: an interesting (and perhaps unique) example of the Soviet state permitting the interference of a non-Soviet state in its own internal affairs. Neither treaty contained any reference to Mountainous Karabagh.[12]

Within the Soviet Caucasus itself, the status of Karabagh was discussed. In early June 1921, after the whole of Transcaucasia had become Soviet, the Kavburo (or Bureau of Caucasian Affairs) voted by five to two in favour of the union of Mountainous Karabagh to Armenia. But the link between the two territories was never made. Some days later a Plenary Session of the Kavburo, under the influence of Stalin, decided that it should be an autonomous region, but should remain part of Azerbaijan.[13] Karabagh was kept outside Armenia. It was not allowed the adjective 'Armenian', even though other Soviet autonomous regions are designated by the name of the predominant national group that inhabits them. It seemed that the Azerbaijanis, like the Turks, were full of anti-minority Turkist feeling and did not like to be reminded of Karabagh's ethno-linguistic designation 'Armenian'.

Armenians consider that Narimanov's original offer of the preceding December was thereby shown to be a deceit. There is however evidence of fairly intensive consideration of the problem by the Soviet leadership. The nature of the population of Mountainous Karabagh was the most obvious point at issue: in 1920 it was 92 per cent Armenian Christian. On the Azerbaijani side, there was an economic argument: that the region was used as a summer grazing ground by Azeri semi-nomadic shepherds, for whom the lowlands of the Mughan steppe (the extensive plain of Azerbaijan) proved hot, malarial and unendurable in summer. And in the wider political field, the Bolsheviks were still showing deference to Nationalist Turkey, believing that Kemal's new Turkey, by virtue of its anti-imperialist rhetoric, was half way towards becoming a Bolshevik state, and that favour shown to the Turko-Tatar people of the Caucasus would be further encouragement for Kemal. Democratic arguments favoured the union of Karabagh with Armenia; but regional arguments favoured the region's inclusion in Azerbaijan.

Maybe too the 'argument from Late Antiquity' surfaced then, which, since it has surfaced later, needs to be looked at. This is that Soviet Azerbaijan is the successor-state to the medieval Christian realm of Caucasian Albania—a state which existed in the eastern Caucasus, and which is unrelated to European Albania.[14] (The origin of the Caucasian name 'Albania' is unknown.) Of the three nations of the region, two (Georgia and Armenia) have remained Christian to this day, while the lowlanders in the south-easternmost region largely became Shiite Muslims, connected by religion to Iran, but linguistically related to Turkey, and eventually being designated first independent, then Soviet, Azerbaijan.

Ancient geographers, notably Strabo, placed Karabagh in Armenia. Thereafter, in pre-Islamic times, the highland area of Mountainous Karabagh (or the provinces of Uti and Artsakh) constituted a region that has been described as 'rather more Armenianized than truly Armenian'[15]. Caucasian Albanian statehood appears to have been a precarious entity, and the stronger cultural identity of the Armenians was consequently a greater draw to the highlanders of Uti and Artsakh. After the Islamic conquests the mountaineer villagers of the region did not become Islamicized (whereas most of the steppe-dwellers appear to have converted); the Caucasian Albanian language disappeared—an alphabet survives, but no texts—and the people identified with Armenia, in the manner described by the ancient geographers. The Albanian Church had usually been anti-Chalcedonian, and it united with the Armenian Church as early as the eighth century; although the nations themselves did not merge at this stage, the move propelled forward the unity of the peoples.

From the fourteenth century, the region between the Kura and Araxes river became known as Karabagh (*kara* is Turkish for black, and *bagh* Iranian for garden, or vineyard.) Its inhabitants, hitherto in a marchland, became fully Armenian in language, faith and culture. This is the manner in which the people have defined themselves ever since. (Here, as elsewhere, the term *race* is meaningless, not being susceptible to scientific definition, and not being a concept which the people themselves use.) The church leader of the chief monastery there retained the title 'Catholicos of the Albanians', but this was for reasons of historical jurisdiction, rather than actual reality. In the early eighteenth century, the region became the focus for the idea of the liberation of Armenia: the Armenian soldier-adventurers Israel Ori and Joseph Emin saw in its cohesive and armed populus a nucleus for the future liberation of Armenia. (At this date Karabagh was a more important Armenian centre than the khanate of Yerevan, which had been largely depopulated by Shah Abbas in 1605.) Karabagh, with its four Armenian principalities, achieved a wide degree of autonomy, and repelled Turkish armies on several occasions in the 1720s, notably at Ganja (or Gandsak) and Halitsor. In the twentieth century, the inhabitants have at almost every turn since 1918 sought to be part of Armenia, and are not interested in a connection with the predominantly Shiite Muslim, Turki-speaking state based in Baku. Besides the Christian Armenian nature of their past, it is surely their own democratic wish that, in any part of the world which pays homage to principles of the Enlightenment, they should be considered paramount.

Mountainous Karabagh was, in contradiction to the wishes of its people, in 1921 designated part of Soviet Azerbaijan, to which it was joined in 1923. During the 1920s and 1930s there were sporadic campaigns by its inhabitants for its unification to Armenia; the campaigners usually landed up in jail or suffered worse fates.[16] Aghasi Khanjian, Armenian Party Secretary in the early 1930s, and a strong advocate of Karabagh's unification with Armenia, was shot dead by Lavrenti Beria, chief of the secret police, for speaking in favour of this issue.

Stalinism meant that there could be no discussion or expression of grievances with relation to national boundaries. However, a decade after Stalin's death, in 1964, the 'kholkhozniks, workers and toilers of mountainous Karabagh' addressed a petition to Mr Khrushchev. After stating that they had reached the 'point of desperation' because of the 'crushing burden of our living conditions', the petitioners stated that the Azerbaijanis had made economic life virtually impossible in Karabagh (usually by placing control of small-scale ventures in far-off towns in Azerbaijan), and were continuing the insidious process of changing the population of the region in favour of Muslim Azeris.[17]

Three years later another petition was addressed by the people of Karabagh, this time to their compatriots in Armenia, saying that living conditions were virtually impossible. The Azerbaijani government could not even guarantee them the elementary security of leaving their houses to go to work and returning home in the evening. The petition gave a list of acts of violence and oppression done towards the Armenians of Karabagh by the ordinary Azeris in the street, with the connivance of the authorities. The conclusion of this petition was that the rule of law barely existed for Armenians in Karabagh. It ended with the words, 'The Armenians of Karabagh are awaiting salvation from you, people of the motherland.'[18]

In passing, it might be asked, How could this be? How, in the communist internationalist state of the USSR could repressive, chauvinist attitudes hinting of pan-Turkism, with apparent ambitions to change the population in favour of the Turkist element, continue? How could such an ideology, expressed in violence and hostile to the spirit of Lenin's letter, get a firm hold?

Old hatreds linger for a long time, and the spirit of ethnic hatred which the tsar had whipped up in 1905, and which surfaced again in 1919–1920, has persisted in Transcaucasia. Under the surface many old attitudes exist: one must be realistic about this. Soviet Russia has given Transcaucasia the benefit of peace; but the animosities continue to smoulder. Ethno-religious jealousies are perhaps the hardest negative elements to root out of any polity. With the granting by Khrushchev of limited autonomy to the union republics, unreconstructed leaders could manipulate their minorities as they wanted.

Nothing changed after the 1967 petition. Ten years passed, until Sero Khanzatian spoke out against conditions in the region. Khanzatian is a brave Armenian writer, the author of *Mkhitar Sparapet*, a novel set in the eighteenth century, which is much admired by Armenians both in Armenia and in the diaspora; he is also a man with a list of credentials very acceptable to the Soviet regime, and more recently (April 1989) he was elected to the USSR Congress of People's Deputies. His letter, written to Mr Brezhnev, covered much of the same ground, albeit in a rather unfocused manner. Historical, national, regional and economic issues were not examined in detail; but it took as a starting place the wishes of the people of the territory, which was an unexceptionable origin for political discourse, either in the western or Soviet model. Nothing resulted from the publication of his letter, except a flutter in the newspapers of the Armenian diaspora, and an article in the *New York Times*.[19] Karabagh was far from the consciousness of most Armenians, let alone the rest of the world. Diaspora Armenians who were engaged in political issues tended to concentrate all their attention on Turkey, rather than look east or south to other Soviet territories. But in Yerevan the issue of Karabagh was always present. Each year the foreign minister of Armenia, Jon Kirakosian (who died in 1985), used to raise the subject at meetings of the Supreme Soviet, and each year he received the same negative reply.

So it remained until the new attitudes and outlook fostered by Mr Gorbachev filtered down to national consciousness both in Armenia and in the territory of Karabagh itself. The reasoning appears to have gone thus: This is the era of the ending of abuses and injustices in the USSR. The separation from Armenia of Karabagh, and to a lesser extent that of Nakhichevan, was one of the abuses of early Soviet history; it was in part a continuation of the inequitable policies of the British occupation, and part too of a failed Stalinist design to curry favour with Nationalist Turkey, and it has led to the denial of natural rights for the native villagers of Karabagh for the duration of the Soviet state. In Nakhichevan the effect has been a massive reduction of the Armenian population in favour of the Azeri. Karabagh's population has been engineered by the Baku authorities against the indigenous Armenians and their fate might become that of the Armenians of Nakhichevan—expelled from their native homeland, as a result of Baku's social, economic, educational and cultural policy. Therefore it seemed appropriate to air the grievance.

But this reasoning seems to have disconcerted the Soviet leadership; for although there was no doubting Mr Gorbachev's committment to openness and reconstruction, it appeared that, in his committment to a concept of 'Soviet internationalism', he had, as had his predecessors, played down the fierce ethnic tensions, deriving usually from local injustices, that still persist in some of the republics that edge the Soviet Union, especially in the Caucasus. He backed away from radical action on giving the nationalities more realistic and ethnically appropriate borders. Gorbachev's priority at this time was the need to change the party apparatus in Armenia—to make it less corrupt, and more responsive to what the economy and the people needed, in terms of employment and goods and services. His speech at the June 1987 plenum, together with the reporting of Kotanjian's speech in Sovetakan Hayastan in July, and the article in *Pravda* in January 1988, were evidence of the determination to clean up the party. But there was no hint that a new deal was needed for the nationalities as well. Disputes between the nationalities appeared to him a diversion from, not an expression of, perestroika.

It was this very matter of national borders which was the paramount concern of the intellectuals who were in the vanguard of the Armenian movement (Zori Balayan, Sergei Mikoyan, and to some extent Abel Aghanbekyan). To them, change had to come to the status of Karabagh and possibly Nakhichevan. They also sought an uncorrupt leadership; but the unresolved national question entailed a greater amount of oppression and injustice, and it required the more urgent attention. Armenia, the smallest Soviet republic, with a history of actual and potential threats from violent neighbours, could not afford to delay on national questions.

After the demonstrations of October 1987, the situation remained quiet, until February 1988. Political activity resurfaced in Karabagh itself. Here, in sessions of its regional soviets of 11 and 12 February, motions were passed, calling for Karabagh's unity with Armenia. This was a direct and unprecedented challenge to Moscow. Leaflets and posters appeared on the streets of Stepanakert from 11 February, demanding the region's unification with Armenia. Demonstrations continued on a daily basis in Karabagh until 20 February.[20]

News of these demonstrations first reached Yerevan on 15 February, four days after they had occurred (a point which indicates the astonishing lack of contact at this time between Armenia and Karabagh). New marches, concerned with the environment, were planned in Armenia. The first of these took place on 18 February in Abovian, a new town to the north of Yerevan, part of whose population consisted of men and women from Karabagh, a number of whom were unemployed, owing to conditions at home. With the news from Karabagh, the focus of the demonstrations was shifting from the environment to the status of Karabagh. The demonstration in Abovian was the first of the large manifestations: the number of protesters was put at 20,000 on the first day, rising to 50,000 on the 19th.

In Karabagh itself, following the sessions of soviets calling for union with Armenia, something occurred to create a radical change. In another move of great bravery and defiance, the regional soviet of Mountainous Karabagh voted, on 20 February 1988, 'to transfer the Autonomous Region of Mountainous Karabagh from the Azerbaijani SSR to the Armenian SSR, [and] at the same time to intercede with the Supreme Soviet of the USSR to reach a positive resolution regarding the transfer of the region from the Azerbaijani SSR to the Armenian SSR'.[21]

Yerevan knew nothing yet of this decision. A demonstration was held on the subject of Karabagh, drawing fewer participants than the Green issue. A few days later Moscow gave its initial verdict: The Politbureau of the Supreme Soviet, reflecting only bureaucratic perplexity and alarm at the 'unrest' which had occurred in Transcaucasia, and unable to comprehend the sense of the possibility of liberty from Baku's oppression that had emerged in Karabagh, voted that there should be no change in the region's status. Those calling for change were dubbed extremists by Tass news agency.[22]

This official statement came as the news was received in Yerevan of the vote for union in Stepanakert. It was a setback to the demonstrators, but it was also a challenge. Throughout the night of 21–22 February, 50,000 people marched in a rally covering 40 kilometres through Yerevan, ending in Marshal Baghramian street, where the headquarters of the Armenian Supreme Soviet are located. The mood of the demonstrators was depressed, but determined. There was also a measure of anxiety, since an executive member of the Azerbaijani ideological committee, a certain Asadov, had just claimed that 100,000 armed Azeris were ready to enter Karabagh and carry out killings. The Kremlin showed its concern by dispatching on 23 February, two non-voting politbureau members, Dolgikh and Lukianov, to Yerevan; two other Russians left on the following day for Stepanakert, the capital of Karabagh. They were to assess the situation and to appeal for calm.[25] But calm did not return to Yerevan.

On 23 February the subject of Karabagh became a channel for expression of the vast pent-up but denied national pride and hope of the Armenian people. From all corners of Armenia, the people came to demonstrate for their brothers and sisters in Karabagh. They travelled on foot, on horseback, or by car. Every day colossal demonstrations took place, with crowds numbering hundreds of thousands. The people converged on Opera Square, which though not in the very centre of Yerevan holds a space wide enough to contain all who came to express their hopes there. Two points were worth noting about these demonstrations. One was that they were peaceful. There was no violence, nor extreme demands or loutish behaviour, which can characterize demonstrations, especially where nationalist issues are at stake. The second was that demonstrators continued to carry placards of Gorbachev. This indicated that they supported the regime, and believed that the campaign for the restoration of Karabagh to Armenia was in line with the process of perestroika.[24]

For a week the demonstrations continued every day. Normal life in the Armenian SSR came virtually to a standstill, as sometimes as many as 800,000 to a million people converged peacefully on Opera Square in the last week of February 1988. Nothing like it had been seen in Soviet or Armenian history before. Armenians manifested a great and united national pride in expressing their desire for unification with Karabagh. It seemed to them reasonable and moderate. This was the first time that Armenians had showed such unanimity, and expressed it so forcefully, since the battle of Sardarabad of May 1918.

At the height of the demonstrations, on 26 February, two respected figures travelled to Moscow to put the case of the demonstrators to the Central Committee. They were Sylva Kaputikyan, a distinguished poet, and Zori Balayan. They made long and eloquent speeches, covering important points in detail; but it is possible that in these circumstances more powerful advocacy would have been shown by brevity, and a punchy and economical marshalling of the relevant arguments. It seems too that they did not address the viewpoint of 'national internationalism within the USSR' that Gorbachev holds. Gorbachev's response was to urge them to do what they could to keep the situation calm. He said he would study the issue, make an appropriate response to their concern. On the same day Gorbachev made a public appeal for the end of demonstrations. 'I call on you to display civic maturity and restraint . . . The hour for reason and sober decision has arrived.' The demonstrations in Yerevan did indeed begin to subside on 27 February. Moscow promised a decision in a month, and the Armenians agreed to bide their time.[25]

What of Azerbaijan, the republic whose tenure of Karabagh, which made up less than 5 per cent of its total land area, was being challenged? Its response came not in a cogent intellectual argument (for indeed there scarcely was one), nor in the feared form of a direct attack on Karabagh, but in the manner of a violent pogrom against the minority Armenian community in an Azerbaijani city on the Caspian Sea, about 30 kilometers from Baku. Sumgait is a dull new town, built (by Armenians) in 1946–47, with a rough population. Part of the population is made of up ex-convicts. The standard of living is low, and tensions (which have built up around the issue of the allocation of housing) are strong between the different sections of the population. There is one main street, which it is possible to block off without difficulty. The population consisted of 150,000 Azeris, 16,000 Armenians, and some Russians.

The pogrom took the form of an organized assault lasting for three days (27–29 February). Armenians were killed with hatchets and knives, or thrown out of windows. Revolting atrocities were committed, reminiscent of the events of the turn of the century. The official death toll of 32 is very much an underestimate. Probably 200–300 died, as well as a few Azeris. (There were cases of successful Armenian self-defence.) Soviet troops intervened on the 29th and imposed martial law; even then they were under orders not to open fire.[26] Therein lies a mystery.

All Armenians believe that Sumgait was an organized assault on the people; in a sense, it was a warning. The only question of any importance is, Who organized it, and how high up did those orders actually issue from? Several aspects of the pogrom point to its organization. In the first place, telephone lines to the emergency services were cut shortly before the killings started, and after the process had got under way. Secondly a number of paving stones were brought into Sumgait, which were of a type not known in the town, and which were heaped up on street corners and used by the mobs to smash into houses. Also, with the prevalence of surveillance and organization and order throughout the USSR, maintained by the pervasive presence of the KGB, it would have been impossible to arrange a mass-killing spread out over three days without the knowledge and acquiescence of some authorities. Some weeks later T. Muslimzade, First Secretary of the party organization of Sumgait, was expelled from the Central Committee of the CPSU, for 'administrative and political mistakes and shortcomings' that had led to the 'tragic events in Sumgait'.[27] This seemed to be a coded assertion that he had got the boot for organizing the killings.

The Armenian response was not to launch into a counter-attack on the minority Azeri population within Armenia, but to trust the judicial process of the USSR. Trials of those suspected of involvement in the Sumgait pogrom opened in Sumgait in mid May 1988.[28] Demonstrations continued sporadically in Yerevan, but for three months the situation was relatively quiet.

On 23 March the presidium of the Supreme Soviet discussed Karabagh and made its promised statement. It recognized that national rights had been infringed in Karabagh, but (reflecting an unwillingness to embrace change, which seems more a characteristic of Brezhnevism) declared that a change of status was impossible. A programme of economic development was approved instead.[29] In Armenia the people were disappointed, but appeared to take the matter philosophically. They knew that despite the rhetoric of change, real change where it mattered would not occur quickly. But in Karabagh there was anger, and the people declared a general strike.[30] This was a gesture of confrontation.

The situation in Armenia erupted again following what was seen as an excessively lenient sentence given to one of the killers of Sumgait, and with a nationalist upsurge coinciding with the approach of the anniversary of 28 May, the date of the proclamation of the pre-Soviet independence of Armenia in 1918. Demonstrations broke out in Yerevan again, and the authorities in Moscow took the occasion to dismiss, on 21 May, both the First Secretary of the party in Armenia (K. S. Demirjian) and in Azerbaijan (K. Bagirov).[31] Armenia's new chief was Suren Harutyunyan, and the new boss in Baku was Abdul-Rakhman Vezirov. At least Gorbachev had been able to use the unrest to get rid of obstacles to perestroika. But what was the meaning of perestroika, when the whole republic was from time to time at a standstill with the people making impassioned national demands?

The strike in Karabagh persisted; Soviet troops had been dispatched there on 28 March. In neighbouring Azerbaijan, anti-Armenian rioting broke out in early June, and there was at least one fatality. In Yerevan the frustration built up to a demand for a strike, and this took place on 13 June. Two days later, the Armenian Supreme Soviet, responding to the popular movement and in defiance of Moscow, voted to accept the proclamation made on 20 February by the regional soviet of Nagorno Karabakh for unity with Armenia. At once the Armenian people returned to work. The Azerbaijan Supreme Soviet voted equally decisively to reject the move.[32]

It would be wrong to see the events of the three months after the events of February as being only characterized by negative political and military phenomena, strikes, troop movements and angry demonstrations, and so forth. Genuine advances were made within Karabagh at that time. Cultural links, frozen for decades, were re-established between Armenia and Karabagh. Armenian books were taken and sold there—something that the Azerbaijanis had not permitted before. Forty thousand were reportedly sold in one day. Teaching of the Armenian language was allowed in the schools, and Yerevan television and radio was relayed to Mountainous Karabagh.

Also, in those June days, there was a move towards a deepening democratization within Armenia itself. Members of the Armenian Supreme Soviet were being called upon to take note of what the people who had elected them wanted. The first stirrings of true parliamentarianism emerged within the republic.[33] Newspapers and television relays became more in tune with the popular mood, and less with the wishes of the rulers. Historical subjects long considered taboo were openly discussed in the media.

Nevertheless, on one level there was a risk attached to the proceedings. Gorbachev was looking to the Special Party Conference of 25 June. Here his reforms would be discussed. He needed calm in Transcaucasia, to show that perestroika was a benefit and not an incitement to disorder. Would the situation calm down in time, so that the conservatives could be routed? In the end it did so, with Armenia though defiant back at work on the 15th, and Karabagh voting to return to work actually on the 25th. In the unstable situation, Soviet troops were dispatched to Stepanakert, Karabagh's capital, but not to Baku or Kirovabad, where there was actual danger of ethnic clashes.[34]

But the mood in Yerevan soon turned angry again, with the feeling widespread among the demonstrators that the regime was stonewalling, and avoiding seeking a solution to the crisis in Karabagh. Gorbachev, seen as a hero in February, was now almost reviled. A new strike was called again for 3 July, and a round of mass-demonstrations broke out. In an effort to bring the republic to a complete halt, 3,000 demonstrators tried to blockade the airport. This was seen by the authorities as virtually treasonable, and troops from the interior ministry were dispatched to confront them. In the ensuing affray one demonstrator was shot dead. The strike continued in Armenia and Karabagh.[35]

The presidium of the Supreme Soviet was set to discuss Karabagh on 18 July. Perhaps to put pressure on that meeting, the soviet of Mountainous Karabagh decided on another action of defiance, imbued with the spirit of liberty. On 12 July the soviet of people's deputies of Nagorno Karabakh put out a statement saying that it had seceded from the Azerbaijani SSR and would henceforth be known as the Artsakh autonomous region of the Armenian SSR.[36] This declaration was later declared invalid by the Supreme Soviet.

The July session of the Presidium was characterized by impassioned and vigorous and often angry debate. But for all its discussion, one point got strangely lost: the injustice of allocating the territory of one people against their will to that of a neighbouring country with an unfriendly and often hostile record towards members of the national group in the territory. Gorbachev himself took a lively part in the debate, and did not hesitate to upbraid wordy or self-righteous speakers.[37] His standpoint was the familiar one: that Soviet internationalism should take precedence over the rights of this or that national group. However, it could be argued that this approach only perpetuates old injustices. The final resolution pointed out that article 78 of the Soviet constitution lays down that change in the frontiers of a republic can only occur with the consent of all sides, and that since Azerbaijan was unwilling to give up Karabagh, nothing would be done. This appeared to be a convenient device for avoiding change and the risks that accompany it. No republic will, unpressured, voluntarily yield territory.

To the party hierarchy, nationalism is not only distasteful since it puts local issues above general ones which affect the entire USSR. It also has the potential for danger. Nationalism could bring about a violent situation such as that which racked Transcaucasia in 1918–20. There is also danger, they feel, attached to the idea of re-drawing internal USSR boundaries. (However, this fear probably has more to do with an unwillingness to face change, since the number of serious internal disputes is not great.) Another reason might be fear of a further unpredictable and violent Azerbaijani response; and possibly too the Moscow leadership was piqued that the party had virtually lost control in Yerevan since February 1988.[38]

The situation remained tense: although there were few demonstrations in August, they resumed in early September. Although the overwhelming issue was that of Karabagh, the environmental issue also emerged: the people demanded the closure of a chemical plant in the suburb of Abovian, and an enquiry into a gas leak at a textile plant in the Masis region on 24 June, when 45 women workers had to be taken to hospital, some sustaining permanent injuries. The mood of the 'meeting' (the English word was used) of 9 September, at which more than 200,000 took part, was described as one of pessimism and defiance.[39]

Protesters were hardening their demands at this time. The Karabagh Committee, a group of intellectuals recognized by many Armenians as their true leaders since the initial demonstrations in February, put forward a list of demands including the right to open Armenian consulates in countries with large Armenian populations, the creation of an Armenian-speaking army detachment to serve on the home soil, freedom to fly the *yerakuyn*, the pre-Soviet tricolour, and the power of veto over all-union projects built in the republic.[40] Some of this was reasonable, but some (especially the detail about the disposition of the army) seemed adventurist. There was a clash between Armenians and Azeris in Khodjalu, north of Stepanakert, on 18 September.[41] Twenty-five people were injured, a number which comprised both Armenians and Azeris. The day before, unreported by Tass, a group of armed Azeris had ambushed a bus containing Armenian students approaching Stepanakert, destroying the bus and injuring 18 of the students, four of them critically.

Nevertheless there was some easing of the situation in early October, with many people returning to work in Yerevan, although a strike continued in Karabagh, where a curfew was also in force.[42] Armenians received some belated support from an editorial in *Pravda* of 10 October, which for the first time blamed Azerbaijan for the critical situation in Karabagh. Maybe the forced resignation of Yegor K. Ligachev, Gorbachev's deputy, on 30 September, was an element in this reversal.[43] Attention was focussed on the convening of the USSR Supreme Soviet planned for 27 October.[44]

In mid November 1988, a new crisis emerged in Transcaucasia. This was inter-ethnic flight. Baku had a total population of 2 million, 10 per cent of whom were Armenians. The mood of inter-republic and inter-ethnic conflict had put these people in a very dangerous situation. By early November about half of them had fled to Armenia.[45] The situation deteriorated after the first sentence to be handed down to the killers of Sumgait, whose trial had been moved from Azerbaijan to Moscow, and had been progressing there since 18 October.[46] On 18 November Ahmed Ahmedov, who had used a megaphone to shout 'Kill the Armenians' as the mob stormed various apartments in Sumgait, was sentenced to death.[47] He was in no way an organiser of the events, just a low functionary in the process of killing. But the sentence enraged the Azerbaijanis, some of whom had formerly boasted that the events in Sumgait had 'taught the Armenians a good lesson'.[48] In several locations in Azerbaijan they went on the rampage, injuring about 200, and burning 60 Armenian homes to the ground. Many thousands of Armenians were forced to flee to Armenia from this reign of terror. The towns worst affected were Kirovabad, where three Armenians and three Soviet soldiers were reported killed, and in the Nakhichevan enclave, where the inhabitants of Dsnaberd, the last Armenian village left in the 'autonomous republic', were evacuated to safety in Armenia by helicopter. A curfew, and martial law, were imposed on Baku, Yerevan and Kirovabad.[49]

The refugee situation grew to one of great magnitude. Of the 400,000 Armenians in Soviet Azerbaijan, 180,000 fled to Armenia in the following few weeks; and correspondingly, of the 161,000 Azeris in Armenia before the Sumgait killings, 150,000 left for Azerbaijan. Many Armenians left Azerbaijan for other parts of the Soviet Union too, especially Ashkhabad, Tashkent and Dushanbe. (Unofficially there are said to be 60,000 Armenians from Azerbaijan living in Moscow.) Housing was a major problem, but within Armenia they found immediate shelter in public buildings and halls. The Armenian government sent many of them to the northern cities of Leninakan and Kirovakan.[50]

It was here, at 11.41 in the morning of 7 December 1988, that an earthquake struck with terrifying force. Whole districts were devastated, and system-built blocks of flats came crashing down on their inhabitants. Older, pre-Brezhnev buildings showed greater resilience. But the devastation was of terrifying proportions, and the loss of life catastrophic. 50,000 people were conservatively estimated to have perished, but the figure was probably closer to 100,000. A further 500,000 people were rendered homeless. Armenians and many others throughout the world mourned the appalling losses.[51]

The effects of this gigantic disaster were various. In the first and most obvious place, there was a massive sense of loss by the Armenian people, which was given extra emphasis by the enormous man-made losses that Armenia has suffered in the past. It was particularly poignant that the disaster should have occurred in a region which was giving shelter to so many refugees from Azerbaijan. At the same time there was a vast and spontaneous expression of sympathy for the Armenians from governments and even more so from individuals throughout the world. Human generosity can seldom have been greater. Aid came rushing in from other parts of the USSR too. Nevertheless, despite this extensive Soviet assistance, which was given by the military and civilian authorities, viewers often saw on television pictures of Soviet tanks in the main streets of Yerevan, and in the actual earthquake zone, Soviet soldiers 'guarding the ruins' and making no apparent attempts to offer help to the survivors. It was often hard to resist the impression that the relief effort was not occurring in a reconstructing socialist state, but rather in an impassive military dictatorship.

This impression was somewhat reinforced when on 10 December the authorities suddenly and inexplicably arrested half of the Karabagh Committee, the unofficial group who had been steering policy on the future of Karabagh, and jailed the remaining members in early January. Armenians and others laboured on regardless, in efforts to mitigate the tragedy of the earthquake, and to bring help and support to the survivors. Supplies and funds poured into Armenia in a truly astonishing outburst of generosity.

A small move was made apparently in Armenia's favour on the Karabagh issue when, on 13 January 1989, Mountainous Karabagh was given a 'special form of administration' under which it would be ruled directly from Moscow. It remained technically part of Azerbaijan; but Baku had no say in the administration of the territory. In charge was Arkady Volsky, a Russian who had been in the Caucasus working on the Karabagh problem since July 1988.[52] It has since reverted to Azerbaijan.

The earthquake muted, to some extent, the Armenian campaign on the Karabagh issue. But only until life returned to a semblance of normality with the republic. For several months the Armenians felt deeply alienated from the regime in Moscow. They had been stunned by the earthquake; and the manner in which their reasonable, democratic wishes for Karabagh were ignored made them feel that perestroika had passed them by. A new round of demonstrations began on 11 May, with the main theme the freeing of the Karabagh Committee. The twelve members of this committee were in fact released in late May. At last it seemed that Armenia was ceasing to be ruled by a bureaucracy. At the same time concessions were made on other national matters. The *yerakuyn*, the red-blue-orange tricolour of pre-Soviet Armenia, was recognised as the national flag, but not the flag of the republic; and 28 May, the anniversary of the beginning of Armenian independence of 1918, was acknowledged as a national day. Neither of these decisions pleased the non-Dashnak parties of the diaspora very much, the Hunchaks and the Ramgavars; but on this occasion national identity and aspirations seemed to be embodied more in what the Dashnaks had adopted and had continued to use as their emblems— even though the yerakuyn was originally a non-partisan flag of Armenia, and the government which followed the declaration of Armenian independence was a coalition.[53]

The people of Armenia were, in May 1989, feeling a sense of political exhaustion. The struggle over the last 15 months had been vast, and the gains small. One side issue that has yet fully to be explored is that Karabagh, and indeed the earthquake, have also created a rational basis for the discussion of historical and ethnic questions in the region. International attention can focus on Armenia as a geographical and indeed political reality, without the irrelevancies of Turkish anti-historical fantasy. Turkey might try to claim the intellectual high ground of the discussion of Armenians in the Ottoman Empire;

but the events of 1988 and 1989 have shown that areas of Armenia's history lie outside the tentacles of Turkish 'scholarship'. Russian Armenia, of the past and the present, has never been part of either Ottoman empire or Turkish Republic. There is however no doubt that the struggle over Karabagh will continue. Armenia will press ahead, basing its demands on the democratic rights of the majority of the inhabitants, and Azerbaijan will claim the precedent of having held it since 1923. Russia will look on in anxiety, perhaps more concerned at the prospect of offending the Muslim republic than the Christian one. Muslim opinion is something that the Russians have now to pay close attention to (as did the British imperialists of 100 years ago)—a point that the politically unsophisticated Armenians often forget. A sensible and patient campaign for Karabagh carried on by the Armenians might yet win the territory for them. But wild demands, and hot-headed appeals to natural rights (which in the world are seldom natural), will gain little. It is however reasonable to see the struggle in terms of seeking the freedom of a group of mountain-dwelling villagers, the Armenians of Karabagh, from an oppressive and manipulative bureaucracy, which through 70 years of misrule has lost the right to govern Karabagh. Whether this message can get through to the Politbureau in Moscow, and whether there they will have the courage to embrace change (always the hardest concept to face in political life), is doubtful; and the recent reports of the deterioration in Karabagh to serious ethnic violence cannot make anyone optimistic about a reasonable solution to a difficult problem.

Notes

1. *The Guardian,* 19 January 1988.
2. *Erebouni* (London), March 1986.
3. *Asbarez* (Glendale, Calif.), 23 January 1988.
4. [Peter Pears], *Armenian Holiday* (Aldburgh, 1965), p. 27.
5. *Armenian Mirror-Spectator* (Watertown, Mass.), 13 February 1988, p. 8.
6. Gerard Libaridian (ed.), *The Karabagh File* (Cambridge, Mass., 1988), p. 88.
7. Ibid., pp. 88–9.
8. *Armenian Mirror-Spectator,* 5 December 1987.
9. *Armenian Life* (Glendale, Calif.), 4 March, 1 April 1988.
10. *Armenian Mirror-Spectator,* 24 October 1987, 6 February 1988.
11. Libaridian, *Karabagh File,* pp. 34–5.
12. See above, pp. 325–6, 330.
13. Libaridian, *Karabagh File,* p. 36.
14. See *Encyclopedia of Islam,* 1st and 2nd editions, articles 'Arran'.
15. Cyril Toumanoff, *Studies in Christian Caucasian History* (Washington, DC, 1965), pp. 128–9.
16. Libaridian, *Karabagh File,* p. 41.
17. Ibid., pp. 42–6.
18. Ibid., pp. 47–8.
19. Ibid., pp. 49–52.
20. *Armenian Mirror-Spectator,* 5 March 1989; personal interview in Yerevan, May 1989.
21. Libaridian, *Karabagh File,* p. 90.
22. Ibid., pp. 98–9.
23. *Armenian Mirror-Spectator,* 5 March 1988, p. 2; *Asbarez,* 7 May 1988.

24. *The Times*, letter to the editor, 14 March 1988; Libaridian, *Karabagh File*, p. 93.
25. Ibid., p. 94; *Armenian Mirror-Spectator*, 5 March, 19 March 1988.
26. *Asbarez*, 12 March 1988; *California Courier*, 21 July 1988; *Armenian Mirror-Spectator*, 6 August 1988 (article by Z. Balayan), 5 November 1988.
27. *Armenian Mirror-Spectator*, 11 June 1988.
28. Ibid., 21 May 1988.
29. *The Independent* (London), 24 March 1988; *California Courier*, 31 March 1988; text in *Armenian Mirror-Spectator*, 2 April 1988.
30. *The Independent*, 31 March 1988; *Sunday Times* (London), 3 April 1988.
31. *The Independent*, 23 May 1988; *California Courier*, 26 May 1988; *Asbarez*, 28 May 1988; *Armenian Mirror-Spectator*, 18 June 1988.
32. *Armenian Mirror-Spectator*, 2 July 1988; *Asbarez*, 18 June 1988.
33. Ibid., 13 August 1988.
34. Ibid., 18 June, 2 July 1988; *The Times*, 24 June 1988.
35. *Asbarez*, 9 July 1988.
36. Ibid., 16 July 1988.
37. BBC, *Summary of World Broadcasts*, 22 July 1988, SU/0210, pp. B/1-B/17; *California Courier*, 10 November 1988.
38. See article by Jonathan Steele in *The Guardian*, 27 July 1988.
39. *Armenian Mirror-Spectator*, 10, 17 September 1988; *Asbarez*, 3 September 1988.
40. *California Courier*, 15 September 1988.
41. Ibid., 22 September 1988; *Asbarez*, 24 September 1988; *Armenian Mirror-Spectator*, 24 September 1988.
42. *California Courier*, 6 October 1988.
43. *Armenian Mirror-Spectator*, 8, 15 October 1988.
44. *California Courier*, 27 October 1988.
45. Ibid., 17 November 1988.
46. *Armenian Mirror-Spectator*, 29 October 1988.
47. Ibid., 26 November 1988.
48. *California Courier*, 17 November 1988.
49. *Armenian Mirror-Spectator*, 3 December 1988.
50. *Asbarez*, 3, 10 December 1988.
51. *Armenian Mirror-Spectator*, 17 December 1988, 21 January 1989; *California Courier*, 15 December 1988; *Asbarez*, 17 December 1988.
52. *Asbarez*, 21 January 1989.
53. *Asbarez*, 3 June 1989.

Biographical Notes

These entries are intended as a guide to the lives of some of the important Armenian figures of the past 150 years or so, many of whose names appear in the foregoing pages; they do not add up to a comprehensive 'Who's Who' of the modern period of Armenian history. Much the greater part of the information contained in them has been given to me by Zaven Messerlian of Beirut, to whom I repeat my thanks. However, the choice of entries has been mine. With some exceptions, my criterion for including a biography has been that the individual had some direct contact with the land of Armenia, or in shaping her destiny. A long entry does not necessarily mean that the person was correspondingly important.

ABOVIAN, KHACHATUR (Kanaker ?1809 – ? Yerevan 1848) Educated at the Nersesian Academy, Tiflis. Appointed secretary to the Catholicos, Echmiadzin. Acted as guide for the ascent of Ararat by the German scientist F. Parrot in 1829; through Parrot's efforts he obtained a scholarship to Dorpat university (modern Tartu, Estonia), 1830–6. Received hostile reception from clergy and traditionalists on his return home. To Tiflis as a teacher in a state school in 1837. Encountered further hostility. Wrote novel *Verk Hayastani* ('Wounds of Armenia') based on fact, 1840–1; first published Tiflis, 1858. Translated from Homer, Schiller, Goethe, Rousseau and others. Appointed principal of a village school in Yerevan in 1843. Disappeared April 1848.

AGHASI (Karapet Tursargisian) (Zeitun 1871 – 1937) Leading Hunchak; most significant leader of the battle against the Turkish forces in October–November 1895. Wrote a history of Zeitun from its origins to 1895. (French translation by Arshak Chobanian, Paris, 1897.)

AGHBALIAN, NIKOL (Tiflis 1875 – Beirut 1947) Educated Nersesian Academy and Gevorgian Seminary. Became a teacher; contributed to *Murdj* ('Hammer'). Continued education at universities of Moscow, Paris and Lausanne. Leading Dashnak party member. Returned to Transcaucasia in 1905. Headmaster of Armenian school in Tehran 1909–12. Co-editor with Arshak Djamalian of *Horizon* (Tiflis), 1913. Participated in 8th Dashnak party congress, Erzerum, 1914. Member of Armenian National Council 1914–15; also one of the organisers of the Armenian volunteer forces. Member of Armenian Parliament from 1918; minister of education in Khatisian's Cabinet. Established a centre of higher studies at Alexandropol, 31 January 1920.

Arrested by the Bolsheviks; released after February uprising. Fled the return of the Bolsheviks into Persian Azerbaijan. Director of an Armenian school in Alexandria 1923–8. In 1928 founded in Beirut Hamazkayin cultural/ educational organisation, and, with Levon Shant, the Djemaran (academy), Taught *grabar* and history of Armenian literature there until his death.

AHARONIAN, AVETIS (nr Igdir 1866 – Marseilles 1948) Educated at Gevorgian seminary, Echmiadzin. Taught 1886–96, mainly in Igdir. Became active member of Dashnak party. Higher education in Lausanne and Paris, 1898–1901. Returned to Transcaucasia; pursued journalistic and literary labours. Appointed in 1906 to the board of *Droshak* ('Flag'), official journal of Dashnaktsutiun. Headmaster of Nersesian Academy, Tiflis, 1907–9. Arrested and jailed successively in Metekh, Baku, Rostov and Novo Cherkask. Developed lung condition. Bribed his way out of jail in 1911; escaped to Europe via Constantinople. Settled in Switzerland, maintaining links with Caucasian press. Returned to Transcaucasia 1916. One of the organisers of the Armenian National Congress (September 1917), which elected the National Council. President (speaker) of the Parliament of the Republic of Armenia. Delegated to confer with Ittihadist leaders in Constantinople, June 1918. Appointed permanent delegate at the Paris peace conference, 1919. Signed the treaty of Sèvres on behalf of the Republic of Armenia, August 1920. Stayed on during negotiations leading to treaty of Lausanne (July 1923), at which he protested. Settled in Marseilles. Paralysed by a stroke while giving a speech in February 1934; an invalid for the rest of his life.

AKNUNI, E. (Khachatur Malumian) (Meghri, Zangezur *c.* 1865 – Ayash 1915) Dashnak party activist. Contributed to *Mshak* ('Labourer', Tiflis). Spent some time in St Petersburg. Active in Paris in 1904 plotting the overthrow of Sultan Abdul Hamid with the Young Turks. After Armeno–Tatar clashes of 1905 wrote strongly anti-Russian work, translated into French as *Les plaies du Caucase*. Played important role in 1907 in smoothing way to Young Turk revolution; to Constantinople in 1908, where he gave enthusiastic speeches in support of the revolution. Toured Armenian colonies in Europe and America in 1912. Arrested on 24 April 1915 and murdered during genocide.

ALISHAN, Father GHEVOND (Constantinople 1820 – Venice 1901) Baptismal name Keropé. Sent to study at Mkhitarist monastery, San Lazzaro, Venice, in 1832. Ordained Armenian Catholic priest in 1840. To England in 1852; also visited other Western European states. Teacher and later headmaster of the Murad Rapayelian school, Venice. Students included Arpiar Arpiarian. His nationalistic poetry and prose were an inspiration to Kamar Katiba, Dserents, Raffi, Khrimian Hairik, Mikayel Nalbandian and Grigor Ardsruni. Publications include: *Houshikk Haireniats Hayots* (1869), *Sisouan* (1885), *Hayapatum* (1901).

ANDRANIK (Ozanian), General (Shabin Karahisar 1865 – Fresno 1927) Trained as a carpenter. Began revolutionary activity in Sivas province in 1888. Joined the Dashnak party in 1892. Defended Armenian villages in Moush-Sasun district in 1895–6. To Transcaucasia in 1897, to the party headquarters in Tiflis. Returned to Turkish Armenia well armed and with extensive powers. Leader of the guerrilla forces in Sasun from 1899, with 38 villages under his command. After the murder of Serop in 1900, Andranik assassinated his killer, Bshara Khalil *agha*; became leader of Armenians of entire Bitlis and Moush district. Besieged at Arakelots monastery (near Moush) in November 1901, he broke out with his men after donning the uniforms of Turkish officers. Confronted by large Turkish force in spring 1904, he and his men – the elite of the Armenian guerrillas – effected a retreat to Van via Aghtamar. Left Turkish Armenia for Persia. To Transcaucasia; then Vienna. Resigned from the Dashnak party in 1907. Spent some time in Geneva and Egypt; then to Sofia. Soon identified himself with the Macedonian struggle; led a troop of 230 Armenian volunteers in the First Balkan war, 1912. To Transcaucasia on outbreak of first world war; commanded a volunteer troop of 1,000 men, active on the North Persian front, contributing to the Russian victory at Diliman (Shahpur, April 1915). His forces joined with the Armenian legion in expelling the Turks from south of Lake Van; but forced to retreat by a Turkish counter-offensive (July 1915). His unit dissolved by the authorities in early 1916. Commander of the Western Armenian division, in December 1917, whose three brigades constituted part of the Armenian Corps (established January 1918). Forced to evacuate Erzerum, March 1918. Resigned his command and left for Tiflis in same month. Formed new Western Armenian brigade; did not participate in the battle of Sardarabad. Angry with the leaders of the Republic of Armenia for signing the treaty of Batum; recognised the government of Soviet Russia, and declared Nakhichevan to be part of it (July 1918), having gone to Zangezur via Nakhichevan. About to march on Shushi (Karabagh) in December 1918, when a message from the British commander halted him, thereby causing Karabagh to remain outside Armenia to this day. To Echmiadzin via Daralagiaz, March 1919; forced by British pressure to disband his brigade. Left Transcaucasia in April 1919; to Paris and London, trying to persuade Allies to occupy Turkish Armenia. To the USA fund-raising for the Armenian army. To Fresno, California, where he died in 1927; his body shipped abroad for burial in Armenia; refused entry by Communist authorities, so laid to rest in Père Lachaise cemetery, Paris. In 1970 his grave visited by Marshal I. Kh. Baghramian. A bust of him has been erected in Soviet Armenia.

ARAKELIAN, HAMBARDZUM (Shushi 1855 – Yerevan 1918) Member of the committee convened 1912 in Tiflis to discuss Turkish Armenian matters. Contributor to *Mshak* ('Labourer'); editor 1913–18. Leader of the Zhoghovrdakan (Populist) party after its formation in 1917 as eastern equivalent of the Ramkavars. Advocated strongly pro-Russian stance; held that Transcaucasia should always maintain links with Russia. Opposed independence of Armenia; in spring 1918 used to speak at 7–8 meetings per day putting forward his views. Assassinated by Dashnaks during the course of one such speech in May 1918.

ARAM Manukian (Sergei Hovhanessian) (Zeiva, nr Ghapan, Zangezur 1879 – Yerevan 1919) Educated Shushi and Yerevan. Leading Dashnaktsakan. To Baku in 1901 to organise the Armenian workers. In 1903 to Yelizavetpol (Gandja; Gandzak) to set up Armenian self-defence. Travelled on to Kars. To Van in 1904. Taught in Ordu after 1908 Ottoman constitution. Returned to Van in late 1912. In 1915, along with Armenak Yekarian, organised the Van self-defence. Governor of Vaspurakan during Russian occupation. To Tiflis after Russian withdrawal. Sent by the National Council to Yerevan in 1918. 'Dictator of Ararat region' May–July 1918; with others he organised the defences against the invading Turks. Held by Dashnaks to be the founder of the Republic of Armenia. Minister of the interior and of supplies in the government of Kachaznuni. Died 19 January 1919, of typhus.

ARAPO (*c*. 1863–93) *Fedayi* active in Bitlis–Sasun region before Sasun revolt. Sentenced to 15 years' hard labour; escaped from Bitlis jail. Organised villagers against Kurdish *aghas* and Ottoman tax-collectors. Killed in a skirmish in valley of Kyali-sor.

ARGHUTIANTS, HOVSEP Archbishop (Russian: Iosif Arguninskii) (Sanahin 1743–1801) Ordained a celibate priest; initially a brother at Echmiadzin. In 1773 appointed primate of the Armenians of Astrakhan. A friend of Prince Potemkin. In 1779 secured permission from Catherine the Great for the establishment of Nor Nakhichevan (nr Rostov-on-Don) as a settlement for Armenians from the Crimea. In 1780 discussed with Potemkin, Gen. Suvarov and H. Lazarian (of Moscow) the possibility of liberating Armenia; proposed that a future Armenia should be a vassal to Russia paying tribute and participating in Russian wars. Opened a school in Nor Nakhichevan in 1790. Contributed to *Azdarar* of Madras.

ARMEN GARO (Garegin Pasdermadjian) (Erzerum 1873 – Geneva 1924) Educated Sanasarian College, Erzerum, and Nancy (France). Joined Dashnak party 1895. Participated in seizure of Ottoman Bank, Constantinople, 1896. Returned to Europe to pursue scientific training. To Transcaucasia; in command of the Tiflis sector in combating the 1903–5 tsarist measures and Tatar attacks. Returned to Erzerum after Ottoman constitution of 1908; elected a deputy in the Ottoman Parliament. Quitted Ottoman empire on outbreak of war; helped establish Russian–Armenian volunteer units. Became the Republic of Armenia's unofficial ambassador in Washington. A member of the revised delegation at the Paris peace conference April 1919. Took part in organising assassinations of Turkish leaders in 1921–2.

ARPIARIAN, ARPIAR (Samsun 1852 – Cairo 1908) Educated Murad-Rapayelian school, Venice. Founded *Arevelk* ('East') newspaper in 1884, then *Hairenik* (both in Constantinople). Played major role in spreading liberal ideas in the vernacular. Also edited *Masis*, and contributed to *Mshak*. Joined Hunchak party. Arrested in Constantinople 1890 for alleged seditious activities. Left Constantinople for London 1896, where he edited *Mart* ('Battle') monthly 1897–1901. Became leader of the non-Marxist Verakazmial Hunchaks, along with Mihran Damadian, Mkho Shahen and others. Left London for Venice in 1901. To Cairo in 1905, where he edited *Shirak* and contributed to *Lousaper*. Assassinated in Cairo in 1908 by Hunchaks.

ARTSRUNI, GRIGOR (Moscow 1845 – Tiflis 1892) Educated Tiflis, Moscow and St Petersburg 1864, where fellow Armenians awoke national sentiment in him. Contributed to *Meghou Hayastani* ('Armenian Bee') and *Haykakan Ashkharh* ('Armenian World'). Strongly influenced by meeting Mikayel Nalbandian. To Europe in 1865, partly for health reasons and partly to pursue further education. Obtained degree at Heidelberg university in 1870. To Venice to study Armenian with the Mkhitarist Fathers. To Tiflis in 1871, where he founded *Mshak* ('Labourer') (1872), which he edited with intervals until his death. (*Mshak* continued until 1920.) Critical of conservative circles; defended idea of liberating Western Armenia.

ASHTARAKETSI, NERSES see NERSES V

ATABEKIAN, LEVON (Kusabad (Karabagh) 1875–1918) Educated Shushi, then Leipzig and Tübingen universities. Qualified as a doctor at Zurich. Returned to Transcaucasia; active member of Dashnak party, combating anti-Armenian policies of tsar. Left the Dashnaks in 1907 to join the Social Revolutionaries; established Armenian SR organisation. Jailed in 1909; freed in 1912. Member of Transcaucasian Commissariat and of Seim (1918), but did not participate, holding that it was an instrument of the Turks.

ATOM (Harutiun Shahrikian) (Shabin Karahisar 1860 – Ayash 1915) Higher education at the Galata Saray Lycée, Constantinople. Taught in his native town. Moved to Trebizond, where he narrowly escaped the massacre of 1895. Jailed; escaped to Batum and Tiflis. Qualified as lawyer there; worked for Mantashev of Baku. Became prominent leader of Dashnak party. Returned to Constantinople after 1908 constitution. Contributed to *Azatamart* ('Freedom Fighter') and other Dashnak papers. Member of Armenian National Assembly in Constantinople. Author of works on Ottoman empire and reforms. Killed during 1915 genocide.

AVETISIAN, MKRTICH (M. Terlemezian) (Van 1864 – Persian border 1896) Follower of M. Portugalian. Became leader of the Armenakans of Van in 1885. Organised and led the defence of Van (supported by armed men of all three political affiliations) in June 1896. He defended the population against government troops, but was himself killed with others in retreat to Persia.

AVIS see NURIJANIAN, AVIS

AZAT VOSTANIK (Melkon Mir Sakoyan) (d. 1913) Hunchak leader. Early collaborator with Paramaz. Nicknamed by the Turks *sachli fedayi*. One of the organisers of Van resistance, June 1896. Arrested and jailed. Freed on proclamation of Ottoman constitution, 1908. To the Caucasus, and then to Constantinople to study dentistry. Organised defence of Kayseri, April 1909. Joined the Turkish Red Crescent as dentist during Balkan war, 1912. To Van in 1913; assassinated by an Ittihadist.

BABAKHANIAN, ARAKEL see LEO

BABKEN SIUNI (Petros Parian) (Agn (Egin), nr Arabkir 1879 – Constantinople 1896) Educated in Constantinople. Became member of Dashnak party; expelled from school for political activities. Led Ottoman Bank raid (August 1896); killed early on in the siege.

BAGHRAMIAN, Marshal IVAN (Hovhannes) Kh. (Chartakhlu, Azerbaijan, 1897–) Educated Tiflis. Volunteered in 1915 in Russian army. Bolshevik. Fought for Sovietisation of Lori and Georgia (1921). Commander of the First Armenian Cavalry Brigade 1923–31. At the Frunze military academy 1931–4. On outbreak of second world war in Kiev from where he effected a skilful withdrawal (winter 1941). Commanded First Baltic front in Byelorussia and East Prussia (June–October 1944). Promoted to marshal in 1955; deputy defence minister of the USSR under Khrushchev; member of the Central Committee CPSU, 1961. Memoirs published in Moscow in 1971.

BAGHRAMIAN, MOVSES Born Karabagh; settled in Madras. Tutor of Hakob Shahamirian, son of a merchant. Published in 1772 *A New Tract, Entitled Admonishment*, saying that progress was impossible without political freedom.

BEKZADIAN, ALEXANDER (Shushi 1881–1937) Educated Kiev. Social Democrat from 1901, siding with the Bolsheviks. Member of Baku Committee 1904–5. In Europe 1906–14; took part in a Bolshevik conference in Paris in 1911 under the leadership of Lenin. Member of the Bolshevik delegation at the Basle congress, 1912. Returned to the Caucasus in 1915. Engaged in party work after 1917; member of the illegal Transcaucasian district party committee 1919–20. In Moscow at signing of treaty of Moscow, 16 March 1921, but did not sign it. Member of Revkom that declared Armenia Soviet in November 1920. Foreign minister of the Armenian SSR 1920–1.

Transcaucasian minister of trade, then finance. Member of the presidium of the Transcaucasian party committee from late 1930. Soviet ambassador in Norway. Victim of Stalin/Beria purges.

BEZDJIAN, HARUTIUN Amira (1771–1834) Born Constantinople. Educated at the cathedral school. Entered employment of Duzian family (controller of Ottoman state mint) in 1802. Saved his boss's life from the Janissaries. On the death of Hovhannes Duzian, became head of Ottoman mint. Managed to prevail upon the sultan to abandon plan of exiling 3,000 Armenians into interior of Anatolia. Benefactor to Armenian community in Constantinople; founded Surp Prgich (Holy Saviour) hospital at Yedikule in 1832. Secured various rights for Armenians in Jerusalem. Buried in the Armenian cathedral of Constantinople, on orders from the sultan.

BOGHOS NUBAR PASHA (Alexandria 1851 – Paris 1930) Son of Nubar Pasha, three times prime minister of Egypt. (Family originated from Karabagh.) Educated Egypt and France. Engineer and public works civil servant in Egypt: worked on Cairo water supply and irrigation in the Sudan. One of the founders of Heliopolis. In 1906 founded with others the Armenian General Benevolent Union, of which he remained president until 1928. Appointed by the Catholicos in 1912 to be head of an Armenian delegation in Paris to co-ordinate pro-Armenian activities and publicise the Armenian case. To London in September 1916 to be told where he fitted into the Sykes–Picot plan. In 1918 Boghos Nubar helped set up the largely Armenian Légion d'Orient. In 1919 he became president of the Armenian delegation at the Paris peace conference, representing Western Armenians; despite friction with the Republic's delegation, the two achieved a working relationship. Retired from politics in 1921, concentrating on welfare and construction. Boghos Nubar remained in Paris until his death in 1930.

BOYADJIAN, HAMPARTSUM see MURAD

BOYADJIAN, MARDIROS see ZHIRAIR

BZHISHKIAN, HAIK see GAI

CHARENTS, YEGHISHE (Y. Soghomonian) (Kars 1897–1937) Born to a family which had migrated to Kars from Maku. Educated Kars and Tiflis. First poem published 1912. Briefly with Armenian volunteers at the outbreak of the 1914–18 war. To Moscow in 1915; joined Red Army in 1917. Fought at Tsaritsyn (Stalingrad), November 1917. To Yerevan in 1919, as a teacher. His experiences gave his poetry power and directness. Published in 1921 *The Cats and I*. To the Lazarian Institute 1921. Published in 1922 a manifesto to take poetry out of the closets and on to the streets. Published the *Charentsnameh* in

1923; also *Yerkir Nayiri* ('The Land of Nairi'). Met Osip Mandelshtam in 1930; published *Epikakan Lousapats* ('Epical Dawn') in same year, and *Girk Chanaparhi* ('Book of the Road') in 1933. Denounced as a Trotskyite in 1933; more serious denunciations in 1934. To Moscow in 1935; defended Pasternak. Jailed 1936; died in prison following year. Rehabilitated in a speech by Anastas Mikoyan in Yerevan, 11 March 1954. Much translated within the USSR.

CHELLO (Toros Dzarugian) (Gurun 1871–1893) Educated Yozgat, under Zhirayr. Joined Hunchak party; fought as a *fedayi* in Anatolia. Arrested and hanged in 1893.

CHERAZ, MINAS (Khaskugh (Hasköy), Constantinople 1852 – Marseilles 1929) Educated Constantinople. Became editor of *Yerkragound* ('Globe') in 1870. Member of Armenian National Assembly. As secretary-general of the Armenian patriarchate he went to Berlin as part of the Armenian delegation, in 1878. Principal of leading Armenian school in Constantinople, 1886–9. Forced to flee in 1889; passed through Russian Armenia, eventually coming to London, where he founded the monthly *L'Arménie*. After 1898 he continued its publication in Paris. Returned to Constantinople after the 1908 revolution; elected president of the Armenian National Assembly. To Paris again in 1910; to Marseilles in 1918 for health reasons.

CHILINGARIAN, ARTASHES see DARBINIAN, RUBEN

CHOBANIAN, ARSHAG (Constantinople 1872 – Paris 1954) Educated Constantinople. Writer, translator and political figure (Ramkavar). To Paris in 1893 where he met a number of French writers, including Daudet and Zola. Returned to Constantinople in 1894 as editor of *Dsaghik* ('Flower'). Left Constantinople for Paris again at end of 1895, at height of Hamidian terror. Published *Anahid* 1909–11 and 1929–49. With Boghos Nubar in the National Delegation at the Paris peace conference, 1919. Visited Yerevan in 1933. Killed in a car crash in Paris.

DAGHAVARIAN, Dr NAZARET (Sivas 1862 – Ayash 1915) Parents settled in Constantinople, where he was educated. To Paris, to study agricultural methods. Returned 1883; headmaster first of school in Sivas, then Constantinople. Back to Paris in 1887, to study medicine at the Sorbonne. In Constantinople again, was arrested and held for four months in 1896. Chief consultant at Armenian National Hospital, Constantinople, in 1899. Jailed again 1900; released through French intervention. Still persecuted, forced to seek refuge in French hospital. To Marseille; in 1905 to Cairo. One of the founders of the Armenian General Benevolent Union in 1906. Returned to Constantinople after 1908 revolution; deputy for Sivas in Ottoman Parliament.

A founder both of the Ottoman Itilaf party, and the Armenian Sahmanadrakan Ramkavar (Constitutional Democrat) party, 1908. Arrested 24 April 1915; murdered soon after in the genocide.

DAMADIAN, MIHRAN (Constantinople 1863 – Cairo 1945) Born to an Armenian Catholic family. Early education at the school of the Viennese Mkhitarists, Pangalti (Constantinople), and at school of S. Hagop. Then to the Murad Rapayelian school, Venice, graduating in 1880. Returned to Constantinople; became a teacher. Principal of an elementary school in Moush, 1884–8. His first-hand experience of Armenian conditions persuaded him to become a revolutionary in 1886. Returned to Constantinople; joined the Hunchak party. One of the main participants in the Kum Kapu Affray, July 1890. Escaped to Athens, contacted other anti-Ottoman revolutionaries; took part in a demonstration in Athens, July 1891. Returned to Sasun in disguise; organised some Armenians into a guerrilla band. Prepared for British consul at Erzerum a report on Armenian conditions. Arrested in May 1893; taken to Constantinople, where he was amnestied (1894). In Constantinople during the Bab Ali demonstration. Then on orders from the party he fled to Bulgaria. On to Romania; arrested; put aboard a Romanian vessel bound for Constantinople. Saved by the British ship's captain who, mistaking him for a fellow freemason, hid him and dropped him off at Piraeus, Greece. Then to London for the first Hunchak general congress, held in Frithville Gardens, Shepherds Bush (September 1896). To Alexandria, on party work. Resigned from the party after disputes; but in 1908 founded the Sahmanadrakan Ramkavar (Constitutional Democrat) party by uniting the Armenakans with part of the Verakazmial (reformed) Hunchaks. Planned an armed attack on Cilicia in 1913; dissuaded by Catholicos Sahak II of Cilicia. In the USA and Europe (mostly Paris) during the first world war. Associated with the Armenian National Delegation of Boghos Nubar Pasha after the war; its representative in Adana 1919–20. Installed himself in the governor's office and proclaimed himself governor of Cilicia under French mandate, 5 August 1920; forced out the same day. Became leader of the Ramkavar Azatakan party from its foundation in 1921. In Beirut 1929–37; member of AGBU committee; one of the founders of *Zartonk* ('Awakening') newspaper, 1937. Retired to Cairo, where he died a member of the Armenian Apostolic Church.

DARBINIAN, RUBEN (Artashes Chilingarian) (Akhalkalak 1883 – Boston 1968) Parents moved to Ekaterinodar in his childhood. Educated Tiflis and Ekaterinodar. To Moscow university in 1903 to study law; further study in Germany. Member of Dashnak party; in 1906 president of its North Caucasus Central Committee. Forced to flee in 1909; to Constantinople, where he wrote for *Azatamart*. Returned to Tiflis 1914; on to Baku as editor of Dashnak papers. To Moscow with Simon Hakobian in 1918 to try to secure Bolshevik aid against Turks besieging Baku; met with hostility when news of the murder of the 26 commissars reached Moscow. To Yerevan in 1919; minister of justice in early 1920 in Khatisian's government. Editor of Dashnak party organ *Harach*. Tried to flee the approach of the Bolsheviks; apprehended and jailed. Released by the February 1921 Dashnak rebellion; editor of *Azat Hayastan* ('Free Armenia'). Escaped the return of the Bolsheviks by going to Tabriz. Eventually settled in Boston, where he assumed editorship of *Hairenik* (March 1922). Began publication of *Hairenik Amsagir* ('Hairenik Monthly'), recording memoirs of Dashnaks when they held power. Advocated strong anti-Russian stance. Editor from 1948 of Hairenik newspapers, taking a severe attitude towards Ramkavars.

DAVITIAN, YEPREM see YEPREM KHAN

DJAMALIAN, ARSHAK (Yelizavetpol (Gandja) 1882 – Paris 1940) Educated locally and at Echmiadzin seminary. Joined Dashnak party. Took part in Armeno–Tatar conflict; jailed for 7 months for being party to assassination of tsarist gendarme. To Germany for further study. Returned to Transcaucasia 1909; became editor of *Harach* at Tiflis. Member of Dashnak Bureau 1914; organiser of the volunteer groups. Fought in Van region, alongside Anastas Mikoyan. Member of Transcaucasian Seim, 1917; delegate at signing of Erzindjan truce. To Berlin, to see if Germany would act as moderating influence on Turkey. Armenia's ambassador in Tiflis after May 1918. To Yerevan 1919; became Member of Parliament. Minister of communications in 1920. Extended the railway. Signed agreement of 10 August 1920 ending Armeno–Bolshevik hostility in Sharur and Nakhichevan. To Tiflis, Constantinople and USA after Armenia's Sovietisation. Participated in the 1921 Riga talks between Dashnaks and Communists. Represented Dashnaktsutiun at the 1925 (Marseilles) meeting of the Second International. On editorial board of *Droshak* 1925–33. Member of the party's Bureaux until 1933. Helped establish an 'Armeno–Georgian union' in 1936. Travelled on party work in Greece, Egypt and Lebanon. Died in Paris.

DRO (Drastamat Kanayan) (Igdir 1884 – Boston 1956) Educated Yerevan Gymnasium. Attended military school. Joined Dashnak party. Very active in 1903–5; with others assassinated Prince Nakashidze and General Alikhanov; fought the Tatars in Zangezur. Fled to Turkey after proclamation of constitution in 1908. Returned to Transcaucasia in 1914; one of the commanders of the volunteer units. Wounded; decorated by the tsar. In 1917 appointed by the Armenian National Council military commissar of the Ararat region. Defended the Bash Abaran defile during the battle of Sardarabad, May 1918. With Aram organised the dictatorship of Armenia until the government arrived in July 1918. Commander of the front during Armeno–Georgian war, December 1918. In early and mid-1920 commander of the Surmalu front. Minister of war in Vratsian's government, November 1920. With H. Terterian signed agreement on hand-over of power to Bolsheviks. Became dictator of Armenia until arrival of Soviet forces. To Moscow 1921; received amicably by Stalin. Later to Paris; settled in Romania. Co-operated with the Nazis on the Crimean and north Caucasian fronts during the second world war, commanding an Armenian battalion; supporters claim that this was to ensure the survival of Armenians, should the Nazis reach Armenia; opponents claim that he acted out of Nazi sympathies. Arrested at Heidelberg by the Americans at the end of the war; released after one month as an 'old exile'. Settled in Lebanon, making frequent trips to Egypt, Europe and the USA. To America for medical treatment in December 1955; died in Boston 8 March 1956.

DSERENTS (Dr Hovsep Shishmanian) (Constantinople 1822 – Tiflis 1888) Educated San Lazzaro, Venice. Returned to teach at Armenian school in Ortaköy (Constantinople). To Tiflis; travelled in Russian Armenia (1843). To Paris in 1848 to study medicine and to teach at the Samuel Muradian school there. Returned to Constantinople in 1853 as a doctor. Wrote in Armenian journals and participated in Armenian organisations such as the Benevolent Union; said by some to have taken part in the Zeitun revolt of 1862. Keen on improving condition of Armenians by introducing better agricultural methods. Settled in Cyprus in 1875; wrote historical romances.

DUMAN, NIKOL (Kishlak village, Khachen, Karabagh 1867 – Baku 1914) Attended the diocesan school of Shushi until 1887. Worked for two years in Shushi, then spent three years teaching in the North Caucasus. Joined the Dashnak party. To Tabriz in 1891, ostensibly as a teacher but with the real intention of becoming a revolutionary. To Salmas in 1893; led a band of 50 men against Van in 1895, having several dust-ups with Kurds *en route*. Returning (May 1896) there were more skirmishes, notably at the Armenian monastery of Derik, just inside Persia. Arrested; soon released. Planned a punitive expedition against Kurds of the Mazrik tribe, who had served the sultan's ends in the Hamidiye regiments; this plan endorsed by Mikayelian in November 1896, and carried out at Khanasor, 24–5 July 1897. To Baku, where he worked for an oil company. Established a new guerrilla group in Persia in 1904, with the intention of going to Sasun; stopped at the border. At the time of the Armeno–Tatar clashes, he was initially despatched to Baku on party organisation and Armenian self-defence; then assigned to the Yerevan sector. Left Transcaucasia in 1909; successively to Constantinople, Egypt and Bulgaria. Participated in the Copenhagen conference of the Second International in 1910. To Trebizond, Erzerum and Van in late 1911. Banished from Van as a result of representations from the Russian consul. To Persia, where he participated in the Persian constitutional movement, fighting in the defence of Tabriz. Returned to Transcaucasia; contracted tuberculosis in Tiflis; taken from hospital and jailed in Metekh castle in May 1914. Then sent to Baku. Failed in a suicide attempt; died in Baku, September 1914.

EMIN, HOVSEP (Joseph) (Hamadan 1726 – Madras 1809) To Baghdad in 1731; to Isfahan in 1742; to Basra, thence to India. To England in 1751 as a deck-hand aboard the *Walpole*. Lodged at Wapping; endured the discomforts of beer-drinking to gain the respect of the common people. Became a porter at £8 per annum. Chanced to meet Edmund Burke; joined the Duke of Cumberland's regiment. Took part in the expedition against St Malo in 1758. Resolved to travel to Armenia; travelled thither in 1759 via Alexandretta and Aleppo. Returned to London; on to St Petersburg in 1761. In the service of King Heraclius of Georgia in 1763; took part in many plots, counter-plots and pseudo-plots in the Caucasus 1763–8. Travelled to Karabagh and Zangezur. Returned to India in 1768, in an attempt to raise money for a small army. Settled in Madras in 1773 and joined the group of patriotic Armenians there. Again in Persia in 1775; back to India in 1783. Thought by some to have been the co-author of *Vorogait Parats*. His autobiography was published (in English) in London, 1792.

GAFAVIAN, ARSHAK see KERI

GAI (Haik Bzhishkian) (Tabriz 1887–1937) His father a schoolmaster, and member of the Hunchak party. The family moved to Tiflis in 1901. Attended the Nersesian Academy. Took part in revolutionary movement from 1903. One of those who attempted the life of Prince Golitsyn in 1905. Expelled from school; went to Baku to work as a labourer, and to write articles in Social Democratic papers. Exiled in 1912 to Astrakhan; amnestied at outbreak of war; he enrolled in the imperial army, and was sent to a military school in Tiflis. In 1915 he joined the Hunchak VIth volunteer troop; serving on the Turkish front he assumed command when his commander was killed. Decorated. In Moscow during February 1917 revolution. After October revolution participated in the defence of Moscow. In 1918 led forces formed by himself against the White Czechs and White Cossacks. Commanded the 24th Rifle Division; took Simbirsk (Ulyanovsk) for the Reds; his forces given the title 'Samara–Ulyanovsk Iron Division'. In 1919 commanded the First Army of the Eastern Front; later commanded the Southern Front. During the Soviet–Polish war of 1920 he commanded the 3rd Mounted Corps with distinction, reaching the Vistula. In August, covering the retreat of the 4th Army, he was cut off and interned in East Prussia. Highly decorated. To general staff academy in Moscow after the civil war, graduating in 1922, upon which he was appointed commissar for military affairs in Armenia. Organised Armenian Red Army. To Moscow's Frunze military academy 1925–7. Professor and head of military history department at the Zhukovsky air force academy 1933. Killed by NKVD agents 'while resisting arrest' on 11 December 1937. Posthumously rehabilitated.

GAREGIN I, Catholicos (G. Hovsepiants) (Nakhichevan 1867 – Antilias

1952) Attended Gevorgian seminary, Echmiadzin. Ordained deacon in 1890. To Leipzig in 1892 to study theology. Received degree in 1897; returned to Echmiadzin; ordained celibate priest. To Tiflis in 1900, where came into intellectual contact with Hovhannes Tumanian, Shirvanzade, Nikol Aghbalian and others. Headmaster of the Yerevan diocesan school, 1901–4. Dean of Echmiadzin seminary 1905. Counsellor to Catholicos Mateos Izmirlian 1909–11. Travelled in Armenian communities of Russia 1916–17. Consecrated bishop in 1917. Took part in the battle of Sardarabad (1918). In Kars at the time of its fall (November 1920). Member of Armenia's institute of science following Sovietisation; contributed to its journal *Banber* ('Messenger'). Toured Armenian communities in Soviet Russia in 1924 to raise money for the seminary. Elected primate of Armenians of Russia, Crimea and Nor Nakhichevan in 1927. Delegated by the Catholicos to visit Europe and the USA in 1934 to try to heal the wounds which followed the murder of Archbishop Ghevond Tourian in 1933. Primate of the Armenians of North America 1938–43. Elected Catholicos of the Great House of Cilicia (at Antilias, Lebanon) in May 1943. Took up the post in 1945. Leader of a delegation representing Cilician sees at the election of the Catholicos at Echmiadzin (June 1945). Took part in the consecration of Catholicos Gevorg VI; initiated period of co-operation between Echmiadzin and Antilias. Encouraged cultural and intellectual activities at Antilias; author of over 30 books. Died at Antilias.

GAREGIN II, Co-adjutor Catholicos of the Great House of Cilicia (Kessab 1932–) Baptismal name Nshan Sargisian. Educated locally, and at the seminary at Antilias (from 1946). Ordained deacon in 1949. Ordained *vardapet*, taking the name Garegin, in 1952. Appointed dean of the Antilias seminary in 1957. To Oxford university 1957–9; his B.Litt. thesis, 'The Council of Chalcedon and the Armenian Church', was published by SPCK. Director of the Antilias seminary, and editor of its journal, 1959–67. Consecrated bishop in 1964. Appointed chancellor of the Cilician catholicosate 1969–71. Attended seminars in Romania and Moscow (at the Zagorsky monastery), both in 1969; has attended, as observer or participant, theological congresses in Rome (Vatican II), Montreal, Addis Ababa and London. Member of the executive committee, World Council of Churches, 1970–7. Prelate of the New Julfa–Isfahan diocese 1971–3. Prelate of North America (representing Cilician catholicosate based at New York 1974–7. Elected co-adjutor Catholicos of the Great House of Cilicia, 1977.

GEVORG V, Catholicos (G. Sureniantz) (Tiflis 1846 – Echmiadzin 1930) Educated locally and at Echmiadzin seminary. Rose in Church hierarchy, eventually being elected Catholicos in 1911. In co-operation with Russian viceroy Vorontsov-Dashkov established the Armenian National Delegation in Paris, in 1912. Remained in Echmiadzin in the critical days of May 1918, against the advice of the military authorities. Reorganised Armenian ecclesiastical procedures May 1926.

GEVORG VI. Catholicos (G. Cheorekjian) (Nor Nakhichevan 1869 – Echmiadzin 1954) Educated locally and Gevorgian Seminary, Echmiadzin. Taught at Nor Nakhichevan. To Leipzig to study theology and philosophy; he also attended the Conservatoire there. Returned first to Echmiadzin then to Nor Nakhichevan, teaching music, Church history and ethics until 1913. Ordained celibate priest in 1913. To Echmiadzin, in 1916, to assist in relief work. Consecrated bishop in 1917. Worked largely in Georgia during the 1920s. In 1938, upon the death of Catholicos Khoren, he was appointed *locum tenens*. Supported Soviet authorities during the second world war; condemned Dro for working with the Nazis. Encouraged donations to build *Sasuntzi Davit* tank corps. To Moscow in April 1945 to meet Stalin. Elected Catholicos in June. Appealed to world powers for retrocession of Kars and Ardahan. Re-established seminary at Echmiadzin.

GHAZARIAN, ARMENAK see HRAIR

GHUKASIAN. GHUKAS (Kalaran, Yerevan province, 1899 – Kars 1920) Became Marxist while a student. Joined the Bolsheviks in 1917. In 1919 he represented Armenian Bolshevik youth at convention of Spartak youth organisation at Tiflis. Sent to Kars in February 1920 to prepare for May uprising. Killed in battle with the authorities on 14 May.

GIULKHANDANIAN, ABRAHAM (nr Yerevan 1875 – Paris 1946) Educated Echmiadzin seminary. Went on to study law. Joined Dashnak party in 1894. Active in Baku region, especially during Armeno–Tatar conflicts of 1905. Arrested by the authorities, and briefly jailed. Among the organisers of the volunteer units in 1914. Worked with Rostom during 1917–18. Member of Armenian Parliament; minister of information and posts in Khatisian's government; also minister of justice. In Khatisian's delegation that signed the treaty of Alexandropol, December 1920. To Romania after Sovietisation of Armenia; afterwards to Paris. During the second world war he was vice-president of the 'Armenian National Council' in Berlin which came to an agreement with the Nazis. Arrested by the French on the termination of the war. Died 1 January 1946. Author of books on the Caucasus, the Armeno–Tatar conflict, Armenian revolutionary women, etc.

HOVHANNESIAN, SERGEI see ARAM

HOVSEPIANTS, GAREGIN see GAREGIN I

HRAIR (Armenak Ghazarian) (Aharonk, Sasun 1864–1904) Educated S. Karapet school and Moush central school. Became a teacher. Some revolutionary activity in Sasun, 1891–3. Active in 1894 Sasun rebellion. To Transcaucasia, where he joined the Dashnak party. Travelled to Romania on party business. Severely critical of internecine struggles of Armenian armchair revolutionaries; believed in co-operation of all Armenian fighters. Chief Dashnak agent in Moush, Sasun, Bitlis and Akhlat, 1895–1904; the chief spirit of the 1904 Sasun rebellion. 'Hrair' means 'man of fire'. His other revolutionary soubriquets were D'zhokhk ('the hell') and Ourvakan ('the ghost').

ISAHAKIAN, AVETIK (Alexandropol 1875 – Yerevan 1957) Educated locally and at the Gevorgian seminary, Echmiadzin. To Europe (Vienna and Leipzig) in 1893 for further study. Returned home in 1895. On a second visit to Europe (1899) he met Father Alishan in Venice. A lyric poet, also influenced by the bards of earlier centuries. Joined Dashnak party; arrested in 1908 and jailed for six months. His masterpiece, *Abul Ala al-Maari*, was published in 1909. He left for Europe in 1912. Quit the Dashnak party. Returned to Soviet Armenia in 1926; respected there, and called 'the master'. Left again for Paris in 1930, returning permanently to Yerevan in 1936. Participated in the conclave which elected Catholicos Gevorg VI in 1945.

ISAKOV, Admiral IVAN (Hovhannes) (Hadjikend, near Kars, 1894–1968) On the death of his father Stepan Ter-Isahakian the family moved to Tiflis. At naval school during the first world war. Demonstrated for the Bolsheviks at Petrograd; transferred. Sent to the Caspian sea by Lenin in 1920; took part in the civil war. Chief of the naval section of the supreme staff of the Red Army in 1929. Deputy minister of Soviet naval building in 1938. During the second world war took part in naval operations in Baltic and North seas; in 1942 served in the Black Sea; wounded. Appointed a deputy minister of the fleet; retired in 1947, but re-appointed in 1954. Appointed admiral of the Soviet fleet in 1955. Elected corresponding member of the Soviet academy of sciences in 1958.

ISHKHAN (Nikoghayos Poghosian) (Karabagh 1879 – nr Van 1915) Educated Shushi. Joined Dashnak party; active first in Shushi district. One of the leaders of the Khanasor expedition, 24–5 July 1897. From 1905 in Van. Contributed to *Ashkhatank* ('Labour', Van). Treacherously murdered with three companions when investigating (at the behest of the Ottoman governor) a local trouble near Van in mid-April 1915.

IZMIRLIAN, MATEOS (Constantinople 1848 – Echmiadzin 1911) Ordained a celibate priest in 1869. Primate of the Armenians of Egypt 1886–90. Returned to Constantinople in 1890; elected Armenian Patriarch of Constantinople, in 1894; known as the Iron Patriarch; supported the Armenian revolutionary movement. Exiled to Jerusalem by the Ottoman authorities in 1896; returned to Constantinople in 1908 on the proclamation of the constitution; re-elected patriarch (1908–9). In 1908 he was also elected Catholicos of all Armenians at Echmiadzin (as Mateos II) in which post he served from 1909 until his death.

KACHAZNUNI, Ruben HOVHANNES (Akhaltsikhe 1868 – ?Yerevan 1938) His family originated from Erzerum. Attended Russian and German universities, studying architecture and mining engineering. Settled in Baku; joined the Dashnak party. Published a work on poets of eastern Armenia (1902). Visited Erzerum after Ottoman constitution (1908). Criticised establishment of volunteer units (1914). After 1917, he was a member of the Armenian National Council; in November one of nine Dashnaks chosen to represent the party in the new Constituent Assembly, Petrograd. Chief spokesman for Dashnaktsutiun in the Transcaucasian Seim (February–May 1918). A member of the Transcaucasian delegation at the Trebizond conference (March). Minister of welfare in Chkhenkeli's government (Transcaucasian). After Armenia's independence, he was a member of the delegation that signed the treaty of Batum (4 June 1918). Appointed first prime minister of Armenia, arriving in Yerevan on 17 July. Criticised by hard-line Dashnaks for his conciliatory policies. Travelled to Europe and America in April–May 1919 (together with a Populist minister) to obtain funds and aid. Relinquished premiership to Khatisian, August 1919. Approached to take premiership again in November 1920; accepted, but unable to form a government. Arrested after Sovietisation; released by February revolt. Left Armenia for Europe in 1921. Published manifesto at a Dashnak convention, Bucarest, March 1923, entitled *Dashnaktsutiun has Nothing More to Do*, in which he argued that Dashnaktsutiun should terminate its existence as a party and all Armenians should support Soviet Armenia. Repatriated to Soviet Armenia and worked there; killed during Stalin/Beria purges.

KAMAR KATIBA (Rapayel Patkanian) (Nor Nakhichevan 1830–1892) To Moscow in 1840 to study at the Lazarian Institute. To Tiflis in 1850 to assist his father in the publication of the weekly *Airarat*, which he had started. To the university of Dorpat (modern Tartu, Estonia) in 1851, but left the following year owing to shortage of funds. To Moscow; helped organise Armenian literary club (1854) which became known acronymically as Kamar Katiba, later becoming his own pen name. To St Petersburg in 1855; received degree in oriental studies in 1860. Contributed to *Hiusisapayl* ('Northern Light') and *Krounk* ('Crane'). Published his own paper *Hiusis* ('North') 1863–4. Returned to Nor Nakhichevan in 1866; devoted himself to education in Rostov and Bessarabia. In his poetry he advocated that Armenians make a new start, minimising the past. His poems express the exaltation felt by Armenians at the crushing of the Ottoman armies by those of Russia in 1877–8, and bitterly echo the disillusion and gloom felt after the Berlin settlement. He visited Constantinople in 1890.

KAMO (Simon Ter-Petrosian) (Gori 1882 – Tiflis 1922) His father a rich contractor. A mischief-maker as a boy. Learnt less than nothing at school, forgetting what he had known beforehand. Expelled in 1898. Sent to Tiflis to study; coached by Stalin. Nicknamed 'Kamo' from his ignorance of Russian ('kamu' means 'to whom'). Joined the secret Social Democrat organisation of Tiflis in 1902. In February 1903 hurled seditious leaflets from the balcony of the Tiflis Armenian theatre into the orchestra, calmly leaving before the police arrived to search all other members of the audience. Arrested for carrying revolutionary literature in November 1903; spent four months in solitary confinement; contracted malaria; escaped while convalescing (September 1904). Wounded five times during 1905 revolution. To St Petersburg in March 1906, where he met Lenin. Leader of the Caucasian 'expropriators' from 1903, his activities culminating in the raid on the state bank of Tiflis, 13 June 1907, which netted 250,000 roubles for the Bolsheviks. Took the money to St Petersburg disguised as a Georgian nobleman. Fled to Berlin; betrayed by an *agent provocateur* in November 1907, arrested and imprisoned; feigned extreme insanity in order to avoid repatriation. Successfully hoaxed Berlin's leading psychiatrists. After four months of raving in his cell, transferred to an asylum (May 1908). Handed over to the Russians in October 1909; imprisoned in Metekh castle, then moved to Tiflis asylum. Escaped in August 1911, foiling subsequent police search by hiding in the police administration building, Tiflis. To Constantinople, then Paris (where he again met Lenin); returned to Tiflis in late 1912. Arrested after another hold-up (January 1913); sentenced to death March 1913; amnestied, because of the 300th anniversary of the Romanov dynasty. His sentence commuted to 20 years' hard labour. To Kharkov in 1915. Released in March 1917. Sent by Shahumian to Petrograd with correspondence for Lenin, December 1917; returned to Tiflis with Shahumian's appointment as extraordinary commissar. To Astrakhan by boat in 1919. Formed a partisan group which operated near Kursk and Oryol. Arrested by Mensheviks in Tiflis, January 1920; briefly jailed. To Baku in March 1920 to prepare its Sovietisation. To Moscow in May 1920; worked in foreign trade ministry. Returned to Tiflis, working in finance commissariat. Died in a road accident in Tiflis, July 1922. The town formerly known as Nor Bayazid now bears his name.

KANAYAN, DRASTAMAT see DRO

KARAKHAN, LEV (Levon) (Kutaisi province 1889–1937) Social Democrat (Bolshevik) from 1904. Studied law at St Petersburg university 1910–15. Active in trade union movement from 1912. Arrested autumn 1915; exiled to Tomsk. Member of the Petrograd Soviet, and of the Petrograd military-revolutionary committee in 1917. A diplomat after the Bolshevik revolution. Secretary and member of the Soviet delegation at Brest-Litovsk, 1918. Soviet deputy foreign minister in March 1918. Negotiated treaties with China

(September 1920), Persia (December 1920 – January 1921); appointed Soviet ambassador to Poland in August 1921, and to China (1923–6). Again Soviet deputy minister of foreign affairs in 1927. Ambassador to Turkey, 1934–7. Sentenced to death on 16 December 1937 on trumped-up charges of terrorism and espionage. Later rehabilitated.

KARAPETIAN, NSHAN see KHAN-AZAT, RUBEN

KASIAN, SARGIS (S. Ter-Gasparian) (Shushi 1876–1937) Educated in Baku. Higher education in Berlin and Leipzig; became interested in German Social Democrat movement. Initially a member of the Hunchak party; sent with its representative to the Dresden meeting of the German Socialist party, 1903. Joined Bolsheviks in 1905. Exiled to Siberia before the first world war; returned to Tiflis in 1917. Fought the Turkish advance in 1918. Went to Yerevan in July 1919 to tighten party organisation. President of the Revkom which on 29 November 1920 declared Armenia Soviet; minister of agriculture in the first Soviet government. Ousted by the February 1921 rebellion, and not replaced in April. Member of the presidium of the Central Committee of the Transcaucasian Communist party 1927–31. Victim of Stalinist purges; rehabilitated later on.

KAZAZIAN, HAGOP Pasha (Pera, Constantinople 1832–91) Educated locally. Initially a businessman, later entering the Ottoman civil service. Served principally as a banker. Also a member of the Armenian National Assembly, Constantinople. In 1879 appointed head of the sultan's privy purse; when this became a ministry, he became treasury minister. Showed great ability at raising Ottoman loans and easing payment of its debts. Died from a fall from his horse. Given a state funeral.

KELEGIAN, DIRAN (Kayseri 1862 – Ayash 1915) Parents settled in Constantinople when he was six months old. Educated locally; went to Marseilles in 1880 to study business administration. Wrote for Turkish newspapers *Manzumiye Efkiar* and *Saadet* ('Prosperity'), becoming managing editor of the latter. Left for Europe after the massacres of 1894–5; wrote articles for the *Daily Mail, Daily Graphic, Contemporary Review* and *Nineteenth Century*. Returned to Constantinople in 1898; wrote for *Sabah* ('Morning'; Turkish). Left Constantinople again, for Egypt, where he worked on the editorial staff of the *Journal de Caire*, then as editor of *La Bourse égyptienne*. Also worked on the *Egyptian Gazette* and *Yeni Fikir* ('New Idea'; Turkish). Returned to Constantinople after the constitutional revolution of 1908, to become editor of *Sabah*. Also wrote regularly for Armenian papers. Compiled a French–Turkish dictionary. Member of the Sahmanadrakan Ramkavar (Constitutional Democrat) party. Arrested 24 April 1915; murdered during the genocide.

KERI (Arshak Gafavian) (Erzerum – Ruwanduz 1916) Became member of the Dashnak party. Took part in 1904 Sasun rebellion, 1905 Armeno–Tatar conflict, and with Yeprem in Persian constitutional revolution, leading the Caucasian troops after the death of Yeprem. Commander of the 4th volunteer troop in 1914; took part in the battle of Sarikamish (at the Barduz pass). Relieved the besieged Russian and Armenian troops at Ruwanduz in 1916 by a daring and successful attack, in which he was killed. His body was transferred to Tiflis and buried there.

KEVORK CHAVUSH (Moush province c. 1870 – Sulukh 1907) Elementary education at S. Garabed monastery 1876–8. Left school to join Arapo and *fedayis*; Arapo arrested; Kevork assassinated Arapo's betrayer. Became an associate of Murad (H. Boyadjian) and M. Damadian in 1892. Arrested in 1894; sentenced to 15 years in jail. Escaped; joined Dashnak party; served under Serop, Gurgen and Andranik. Participated in 1904 Sasun uprising; a leading *fedayi* until his death.

KHAN-AZAT, RUBEN (Nshan Karapetian) (Yerevan 1862 – Tabriz 1929) Higher education at the University of Montpellier. One of the six founders of the Hunchakian Revolutionary Party at Geneva. To Tiflis in 1890, in an abortive attempt to found another branch of the party. Travelled throughout Ottoman lands and Transcaucasia on party work. To the USA in 1893 on the same mission.

KHANDJIAN, AGHASI (Van 1901 – Tiflis 1936) The son of an Armenakan leader. The family took refuge from the 1915 massacres in the monastery at Echmiadzin. He entered the Echmiadzin seminary, then to Yerevan school. Joined a Marxist youth group in 1918; one of the founders of the Spartak Bolshevik youth organisation in 1919. Arrested twice by the authorities of the republic. To Sverdlov university (Russia) in 1921. Active in Leningrad 1922–8. Sided with Stalin against Zinoviev in 1925. Returned to Armenia in 1928; became First Secretary of the Central Committee of the Armenian CP in 1930. With the confidence of Stalin he purged Armenia of Old Bolsheviks, specifically Sargis Kasian. Crushed the opposition to collectivisation. Worked for retrocession of Karabagh and Nakhichevan to the Armenian SSR. Murdered by Beria in July 1936, due to the latter's suspicion and jealousy. Despite being Stalin's man in Armenia, he was genuinely popular with the peasants. Subsequently he has been rehabilitated.

KHANFERIANTS, ARMENAK see KHUDIAKOV, S. A.

KHAPAYAN, GABRIEL see SAHAK II

KHATISIAN, ALEXANDER (Tiflis 1876 – Paris 1945) His father was controller of the government estates in Tiflis province. Educated in Tiflis state school; then to Moscow university for 3 years to study medicine, and to Kharkov for 2 years. Further study in Germany. Political activities began in 1900. Counsellor to the administration of Tiflis 1902–6; assistant to the mayor of Tiflis 1906–10; mayor of Tiflis 1910 and 1917. President of the Armenian National Council 1915–17; chief organiser of the Armenian volunteers. Joined the Dashnak party in 1917. Member of Transcaucasian delegation at the Trebizond negotiations, March 1918. Minister of finance in Transcaucasian Cabinet. Delegate at the Batum conference, May 1918. Negotiated and signed the treaty of Batum, 4 June 1918. To Constantinople to revise the treaty at the insistence of Germany in the same month. Foreign minister June–November 1918. Minister of welfare briefly in November 1918 after assassination of Khachatur Karjikian; minister of the interior after the death of Aram. Acting prime minister spring 1919, during Kachaznuni's absence. Prime minister of Armenia, August 1919–May 1920. After relinquishing premiership, travelled to Tiflis, Constantinople, Paris, London, Rome and the Balkans soliciting aid for the republic. Chief negotiator at the Alexandropol conference, November–December 1920; signed the treaty of Alexandropol. Settled in Paris after Armenia became Soviet. Wrote *Hayastani Hanrapetutian dsagumn ou zargatsumë* ('The Origin and Development of the Armenian Republic' (1930, rev. edn. 1968)) and *Kaghakapeti më hishataknerë* ('The Memoirs of a Mayor'). During the second world war he worked for an Armenian refugee organisation. Arrested after the liberation of France; set free soon after. But his health had deteriorated. Died 10 March 1945.

KHRIMIAN 'Hairik', MKRTICH (Catholicos Mkrtich I) (Van 1820 – Echmiadzin 1907) Brought up by an uncle, who taught him weaving. Travelled to Echmiadzin in 1841. Married in 1845. Further travels, to Jerusalem, Constantinople and Cilicia (in 1851). After the death of his wife and daughter, ordained a celibate priest in 1854. Began publication of *Ardzvi Vaspurakan* (in Constantinople) in 1855. Returned to the Varak monastery as abbot in 1858; continued printing the journal there. As abbot of the monastery of S. Karapet, Moush, began another journal *Ardzvik Darono* in 1863. Consecrated bishop in 1868. Armenian Patriarch of Constantinople, 1869–73; compelled to resign by the Ottoman government. At the instance of Patriarch Nerses Varzhabedian he travelled to Berlin with Archibishop Khoren Nar Bey, Minas Cheraz and Stepan Papazian in June 1878 to put the Armenian case to the congress; only permitted to submit a written memorandum. After the congress he travelled to Paris and London. Returning to Constantinople, he gave a famous sermon in the cathedral at Scutari comparing the 'iron spoons' of the Balkan peoples to the 'paper spoons' of the Armenians. Exiled to Jerusalem by the government in 1889. Elected Catholicos of all Armenians 17 May 1892; forbidden by the Ottomans to travel to Echmiadzin across Ottoman territory (so compelled to travel Jaffa–Alexandria–Trieste–Vienna–Volochinsk–Odessa–Sevastopol–Batum–Tiflis). Supported Dashnaktsutiun in his encyclical of 1896. Confronted by the tsarist seizure of the property of the Armenian Church, June 1903; reacted with patience. Patient, too, in 1906, when, at an assembly called to clarify *Polozhenye*, he was faced with anti-religious tirades. Clarified relations between the patriarch of Constantinople and the catholicoses in 1907, emphasising the 'primary, universal and apostolic see of Echmiadzin'.

KHUDIAKOV, Air Marshal S. A. (Armenak Khanferiants) (Karabagh 1906–1950) To Baku to study; then worked in Mantashev's oilfield. Joined the Bolsheviks. Organised Red Guards of Baku, April 1918. In Astrakhan during Russian civil war. Saved from drowning by his friend Sergei Khudiakov; when the latter was killed fighting the Whites, Khanferiants assumed his name as a memorial. Admitted to Tiflis Cavalry School 1929. To the Ukraine, and later to Moscow to the air force academy. Served mainly on the western front during the second world war, becoming an air marshal in 1944. Took part in the Yalta conference as a military adviser.

KOCHINIAN, ANTON (Yerevan province 1913–) Joined Communist youth in 1928, and the party in 1938. Graduated as agriculturalist in 1935. Mainly on party work until the second world war. Joined the Central Committee of the Armenian CP in March 1940. Third Secretary of the ACP 1946–52; appointed First Secretary in 1952. In November 1952 became prime minister of the Armenian SSR: also a member of the Supreme Soviet of Armenia and the USSR. Dropped from premiership in 1966, becoming First Secretary of the ACP. Replaced in this post in November 1974.

KOMITAS (Soghomon Soghomonian) (Kutahya 1869 – Paris 1935) Orphaned at the age of 11. Taken by the local prelate to Echmiadzin seminary in 1881. Graduated from the seminary in 1893. Ordained celibate priest. To the Berlin conservatoire in 1896 to study music under Richard Schmidt; also attended the Friedrich Wilhelm university studying philosophy of music. Appointed choirmaster and head of music department at Echmiadzin seminary in 1899; became first non-European member of the International Musical Society. Collected more than 3,000 folk songs – Armenian, Kurdish, Arabic, Turkish and Persian (most subsequently lost). Gave concerts in Paris, Geneva, Berne, Venice, Constantinople, Cairo and Alexandria. Published first ever collection of Kurdish folk songs, 13 in number, Jurgensen, 1904. His song *The Homeless* was praised by Debussy, on hearing it in 1906, when Komitas visited Paris. Met Egon Wellesz in Vienna, who admired his harmony and counterpoint. Left for Constantinople in 1910, where he founded a choir of 300 voices named Kusan ('Minstrel'). Encountered some opposition from conservative religious circles for his use of religious melodies. Arrested 24 April 1915; deported to Chankiri; driven mad by the sight of the slaughter of fellow Armenians; saved from death. Put in an asylum in Constantinople in 1916;

taken to Paris in 1919, where he died in 1935. His body was transferred to Yerevan in 1937.

LEO (Arakel Babakhanian) (Shushi 1860 – Yerevan 1935) Received patchy education, but read very widely; soon writing historical and political articles. Wrote in *Mshak* from 1895; became its editor in 1918. Opposed the policies and activities of Dashnaktsutiun; joined the Populist (Zhoghovrdakan) party on its formation in 1917. An adviser to the Seim delegation in the Trebizond negotiations with the Turks in March 1918. President of the Karabagh Armenian Patriotic Association 1918–20. Welcomed the formation of the Armenian SSR. His *Hayots Patmutiun* ('History of the Armenians') is famous (vol. I, Tiflis, 1917; vols. II–III, Yerevan, 1946–7).

LORIS-MELIKOV, General Count MIKAYEL T. (Tiflis 1825 – Nice 1888) Educated Lazarian Institute, Moscow. Joined a Hussar regiment. To the Caucasus in 1847; gained a distinguished reputation in bringing the region from military to civilian rule. (Fictionalised portrait of him in Tolstoy's *Hadji Murat*.) Commander in Russo–Turkish war of 1877–8; took Ardahan; repulsed by Ahmed Mukhtar at Zivin; defeated Mukhtar at Aladja; stormed Kars and laid siege to Erzerum. Received title of Count. Temporary governor of the Lower Volga in 1879; great success in sustaining morale during an outbreak of plague, so he was transferred to combat nihilism and anarchism in central Russia. Appointed chief of supreme executive commission dealing with revolutionary activity; showed a preference for legal against extra-legal methods. Suggested striking at the root of the problem by introducing economic reforms. Came to the attention of Tsar Alexander II in 1880, who appointed him minister of the interior (with exceptional powers). Proposed scheme of reforms; this was negated by the assassination of the tsar in March 1881. Loris-Melikov resigned under the reactionary policies of Alexander III; lived in exile until his death.

LUKASHIN, SARGIS (S. Sraponian) (1884–1937) Joined the Social Democrats (Bolsheviks). With Vahan Terian discussed Turkish Armenia with Lenin in November 1917. Member of Miasnikian's Cabinet of May 1921; president of the people's economic council and secretary of the Central Committee of the Armenian CP. Dropped from the latter post in February/March 1922, and appointed prime minister of Armenia. Transferred to Tiflis in 1925 to assume a position in the Transcaucasian SFSR. Victim of Stalinist purges; later rehabilitated.

MALKUM Khan, Mirza (New Julfa 1833 – Rome 1908) Educated at the Samuel Muradian school, Paris, 1843–51. Returned to Persia; converted to Shia Islam; entered government service. Selected as instructor in the newly established Tehran Polytechnic in 1852. To Paris in the diplomatic service in

1857. Introduced freemasonry into Persia in 1859; exiled by Shah Nasir od-Din for doing so in 1862. Pardoned; given post in the Constantinople embassy. To Tehran in 1872 as assistant to Grand Vizier Moshir od-Dowlah. Chief of Persian legation in London (later ambassador) 1872–88; visited Berlin at the time of the congress (1878), advising Armenians to take an anti-Russian stance. Lost his position in 1889 as the result of a scandal over selling a cancelled concession for a lottery. Attacked the shah and Persian government from London; edited from 1890 the news-sheet *Qanun*, which was banned in Persia but read by the shah and his ministers. Became recognised as the most important Persian moderniser of the century. Pardoned and reinstated by Shah Mozaffar od-Din in 1898; appointed ambassador to Italy, with title of Nezam od-Dowlah. Remained at this post until his death.

MANUKIAN, ARAM see ARAM

MELIK-HAKOBIAN, HAKOB see RAFFI

MIASNIKIAN, ALEXANDER (Nor Nakhichevan 1886 – near Tiflis 1925) Educated Lazarian Institute, Moscow. Graduated from Moscow university's law faculty in 1911. Member of Social Democrat (Bolshevik) party 1906. Arrested; escaped to Baku; returned to Moscow. Enlisted in the Imperial army 1914; service largely on the western front. Head of the Bolshevik faction on the western front, early February 1917. With Frunze he founded the newspaper *Zvezda* in Minsk. In Minsk during the October Revolution; briefly acting supreme commander-in-chief, western front. In spring 1918 commander, Volga front. Minister of war in Byelorussia, 1919. In Moscow 1919–21, becoming secretary of the Moscow party committee. To Armenia after the suppression of the revolt of February–April 1921, as prime minister; had a fair measure of success in restoring law and order, fighting famine and epidemic, organising small-scale repatriation and rebuilding the country. An enemy of illiteracy. In his premiership the Transcaucasian Confederation was established (11 March 1922) out of the three republics; it later became the Transcaucasian SFSR. Presidium member of the USSR Central Executive Committee 1922. Author of political and literary works, including a volume on literary criticism. Died in a plane crash near Tiflis.

MIKAYELIAN, KRISTAPOR (Akulis, Zangezur 1859 – Mount Vitosh, Bulgaria 1905) Orphaned at the age of 10. From 1870 to 1880 at the state teacher-training institute, Tiflis. Wrote and distributed leaflet protesting at state closure of Armenian schools in 1885. To Moscow in 1885; attended the Piotrovsky agricultural academy. There he met Simon Zavarian and Rostom. Joined the *Narodnaya Volya*. Returned to the Caucasus without completing his studies in 1887; taught in Akulis and Tiflis 1887–90. Founded the Young Armenia society in 1889; this led to the foundation by Mikayelian, Rostom and Zavarian of Dashnaktsutiun in 1890. Mikayelian was exiled to Kishinev in 1891, whence he escaped to Romania. There he edited the party paper *Droshak*. Again in the Caucasus 1892–8. Jailed for 6 months in 1895. Organised the Khanasor expedition, 1897. To Geneva to edit *Droshak* 1898. Instrumental in gaining support of French intellectuals to publish *Pro-Armenia* (from 1900). From 1901 led the *Potorik* ('Storm') movement, which extorted money from rich Armenians to aid the national movement. After the decision of the third Dashnak congress to assassinate Abdul Hamid, he undertook the task, and was killed by his own bomb on Mount Vitosh, Bulgaria, in 1905.

MIKOYAN, ANASTAS (Sanahin 1895 – Moscow 1978) Born to a peasant family. Educated at the Nersesian Academy, Tiflis, and the Gevorgian seminary, Echmiadzin. Engaged in political activity while at school. Joined the Bolshevik party in 1915. Enlisted in Gen. Andranik's Armenian volunteer regiment. To Baku in 1917, where he met Stepan Shahumian. Served on staff of Armenian-language newspaper *Sotsial-Demokrat*: also edited *Izvestia*. With Shahumian in the Baku commune; Bolshevik˙ spokesman when the elder Bosheviks were in gaol. Led the commissars through Baku as the Turks were entering it, 14–15 September 1918. To Nizhny Novgorod (Gorky), 1920; in the same year to Baku, after the Sovietisation of Azerbaijan. In Rostov-on-Don 1922–6, as secretary of the North Caucasus party organisation. Member of the Central Committee of the party from 1923. Commissar for foreign trade, 1926; commissar for supplies, 1930; commissar for food, 1934–8. Minister of foreign trade 1938–49; minister of trade 1953–5. Member of the Politburo of the party's Central Committee from 1935. Survived attempts by Beria to have him purged in the 1930s (and the intense suspicion of Stalin's latter days). Member of state defence committee, 1942. Opposed Malenkov over dismantlement of German industry in 1945; became vice-chairman of the council of ministers, 1946. The first to denounce Stalin in 1956. Visited the US, Mexico and Japan 1959–61. Played a central role in settling the Cuban missile crisis. Attended the funeral of President John F. Kennedy 1963. Chairman of the presidium of the Supreme Soviet, 1964–5; Memoirs published 1970. Retired from all public life in 1974.

MOVSESIAN, AGHEKSANDR see SHIRVANZADE

MRAVIAN, ASKANAZ (Yelizavetpol (Gandsak) 1886–?1937) Educated at the Gevorgian seminary, Echmiadzin, and Yerevan diocesan school. Joined Yelizavetpol Social Democrats (Bolsheviks) in 1905. Sent to Armenia in July 1919 to establish a Communist organisation. Member of the Revkom which took power in Armenia in November 1920. Foreign minister of the Armenian SSR in May 1921. One of the signatories of the treaty of Kars. Minister of education, 1923. Liquidated during the purges; later rehabilitated.

MURAD (Hampartsum Boyadjian) (Hadjin 1867 – Ayash 1915) Educated at his birthplace and at Constantinople, where he studied medicine. Further medical studies at Geneva. Joined the Hunchak party soon after its formation (1887). Active against the Ottoman government in the following year. The chief organiser of the Kum Kapu demonstration, July 1890. Escaped to Athens; thence to Transcaucasia. To Sasun in 1892 to encourage the people to resist the depredations of the Kurds. Again in Transcaucasia for much of 1893, returning to Khnus in the autumn. Leader of the Sasun revolt, 1894, after the arrest of Mihran Damadian. Murad was himself arrested and sentenced to death; foreign pressure commuted the sentence to life imprisonment. In Tripoli (Barbary) gaol for 12 years before escaping to France in 1904. To Egypt where, as a representative of the Hunchaks, he signed a document of reconciliation with Damadian (representing the Verakazmial Hunchaks), 24 November 1907. Thence to the USA. Returned to Constantinople after the Ottoman constitution of 1908; member of both the Armenian National Assembly and the Ottoman Parliament (deputy for Adana). Murdered during the 1915 genocide.

MURAD of SIVAS (Sivas province 1874 – Baku 1918) Born in a village in the province of Sivas. A *fedayi* leader in the 1904 Sasun rebellion; member of the Dashnak party. In Transcaucasia during the 1905 Armeno–Tatar conflict, fighting in Nakhichevan and Zangezur. Joined the Armenian volunteers on the outbreak of the first world war. At Erzindjan at the time of the Erzindjan truce (December 1917); became the actual leader as the Russian command ebbed. Fought the renewed Turkish offensive all the way east to Baku, being killed in the defence of that city on 5 August 1918.

MUSAYELIAN, SARGIS (1882 – Yerevan 1920) In the Russian army in 1914. Joined the Social Democrats (Bolsheviks). In Russia in 1917; transferred to Transcaucasia, first to Yelizavetpol (Gandsak) and then Baku. In Baku during the Commune. Joined the army of the Republic of Armenia in 1919; became head of the *General Vardan* armoured train group, while working underground for the revolution. Led the May 1920 rebellion from his armoured train at Alexandropol; proclaimed a Soviet regime in Armenia, with himself president and military commissar. Arrested on 15 May; shot on 14 August.

NALBANDIAN, MIKAYEL (Nor Nakhichevan 1829 – Kamyshin 1866) Early education until 1846 under the guidance of Kamar Katiba. Appointed secretary of the prelacy of the Armenian diocese of Bessarabia in 1848. In conflict with his employers over the traditional structure of Armenian society, he left for Moscow. Appointed as teacher of Armenian at the Lazarian Institute. His traditionalist opponents secured his dismissal, so he was forced to work as an auditor for the medical faculty of Moscow university. Became a close friend of Stepanos Nazariants; worked on the latter's *Hiusisapayl* (monthly, founded

1858). Became ill in 1859; travelled to Constantinople and certain European cities (including London) to recover. Delegated by the Armenian community of Nor Nakhichevan to travel to Calcutta in 1860 to receive a sum of money willed to the community. Travelled again to Constantinople and in Europe in making preparations for his trip. In London he met Herzen and Bakunin. In Constantinople his radical ideas helped develop plans for the Zeitun uprising of 1862. On returning to Russia in 1862 he was arrested after the police had found an incriminating letter from Herzen on him. Imprisoned in the fortress of Petropavlovskaya 1862–5; transferred to Kamyshin under guard, where he died of tuberculosis, 31 March 1866. His body was transferred (in accordance with his wishes) to Nor Nakhichevan.

NAVASARDIAN, VAHAN (Shushi 1888 – Cairo 1956) A graduate in economics of St Petersburg university. Member of Dashnak party from youth. Briefly taught Russian, politics and economics at the Gevorgian seminary at Echmiadzin. Mayor of Alexandropol. Participated in the Karakilisa section of the battle of Sardarabad. Briefly editor of Dashnak organ *Horizon* (Tiflis) in late 1918. Settled in Yerevan in 1919; became a Member of Parliament. Fought in the Armeno–Kemalist war of September–November 1920. Active in the February 1921 revolt. After the Sovietisation of Armenia he eventually settled in Egypt, where he remained a leading (and hard-line) member of the Dashnak Bureau. Editor of *Housaper*. Took an uncompromising attitude towards non-Dashnak Armenians. Author of *Bolshevizme yev Dashnak-tsutiune* (Cairo, 1949), etc.

NAZARBEKIAN, AVETIS (1866–1936) Published poetry under pen name of Avo Lerentz in 1883. Initially a collaborator with Portugalian, writing in his journal *Armenia*. Broke with him on the issue of revolution, founding the Hunchak party with six fellow students in Geneva in August 1887. Friend of Plekhanov and Vera Zasulich. Edited *Hunchak*. In London 1892–3, as organiser of the party branch there; travelled extensively to Paris, Athens and Geneva. Back in London for the first general congress of the Hunchak party, 18 September 1896, held in Frithville Gardens, Shepherds Bush. Disagreed with Plekhanov, Lenin and Martov on the Armenian situation, the Russians holding that the issues of Russian and Turkish Armenia should be separated. An attempt on Nazarbekian's life by a Verakazmial Hunchak failed in October 1903. Split developed between him and fellow Hunchak Sabah-Gulian, over relations with the Social Democratic movement; the party congress of 1905 (in Paris) sided against Nazarbekian, who had sought virtually to dissolve the party's identity. The same conflict emerged at the 8th party congress, Athens, 1924; he was elected vice-chairman of the party committee, but his views were criticised.

NAZARBEKIAN, General TOVMAS (Foma I. Nazarbekov) (Tiflis 1855 – Tiflis 1931) Born to a wealthy Russianised family. Attended the military academy in Moscow. Participated in the Russo–Turkish war of 1877–8, and in the Russo–Japanese war of 1904–5, in which he was decorated with the Cross and Sabre of St George. Resigned his commission when tsarist policy turned against the Armenians; but returned to the army when Russia abandoned her anti-Armenian stance. Appointed a general on the Caucasian front in 1914; scored great victory over Khalil Pasha at Diliman (not mentioned in Allen and Muratoff, *Caucasian Battlefields*). Occupied Bitlis. Commissioned to lead the Armenian corps, December 1917. Ordered by Chkhenkeli to abandon Kars, 23–4 April 1918. Driven back to Dilidjan during the battle of Sardarabad. Commander-in-chief of Armenian army after the republic's independence; found establishment of discipline impossible, with abolition of death penalty (May 1917). Held that this led to demoralisation which lost Kars. Arrested in January 1921 after the Sovietisation of Armenia, along with 1,200 other officers. Amnestied in May 1921. Settled in Tiflis; lived quietly for the last ten years of his life.

NAZARIANTS, STEPANOS (Tiflis 1812 – Moscow 1879) Educated first at the Nersesian academy, then at the school and university of Dorpat (Tartu, Estonia). Lecturer in oriental studies at Kazan university in 1843. Lecturer in Arabic, Persian and Latin at the Lazarian Institute in 1849. Published a work in classical Armenian in 1851, and in the vernacular in 1853. Edited and published *Hiusisapayl* ('Aurora borealis') 1858–64, advocating progressive ideas and the use of the vernacular, for which he was opposed by clerical circles. (Not interested in Turkish Armenia.) Became headmaster of the Nersesian Academy, Tiflis; returned to the Lazarian Institute.

NERSES V, Catholicos (Nerses Ashtaraketsi) (Ashtarak 1770 – Echmiadzin 1857) Showed a reforming spirit soon after his ordination. Consecrated bishop in 1809; soon recognised as a man of great authority. Appointed prelate of the Armenians of Tiflis in 1814. Established the Nersesian Academy in Tiflis in 1816. Led a contingent of Armenian volunteers against the Persians in July 1827. One of the executive of three men appointed to administer Yerevan and Nakhichevan after their conquest by the Russians. Manoeuvred out of his influential position by Prince Paskievich, who had him appointed primate of the Armenians of Bessarabia (1828–43). Elected Catholicos of all Armenians in 1843. Improved the school, printing press and environment of Echmiadzin (he built Echmiadzin lake). Known by the people as *pashtpan hayreniats* ('defender of the fatherland'). Tried without success to modify *polozhenye*. Came into conflict with Khachatur Abovian and other intellectuals, and towards the end of his life grew somewhat autocratic. Died while writing a letter to the Russian minister of the interior.

NERSES, Patriarch (Varzhabedian) (Khaskugh (Hasköy), Constantinople 1837 – Constantinople 1884) Left school at 15 on the death of his father.

Taught at a local school, 1853; at a school in Adrianople in 1855. Became a celibate priest in 1858; shortly afterwards a *vardapet*. Participated in the drawing up of the Armenian national constitution. Consecrated bishop in 1862 by the Catholicos of Cilicia. Visited Echmiadzin on ecclesiastical business in 1866. Elected Patriarch of Constantinople 3 November 1873 (at the age of 37), despite his wish not to stand as a candidate since he suffered from diabetes. Settled problems of jurisdiction of Aghtamar catholicosate, but not those of the Cilician see. Issued encyclical instructing Ottoman Armenians to support Ottoman war effort on outbreak of Russo–Turkish war, 1877; on hearing of atrocities committed on Armenian villagers, travelled to San Stefano to present requests for security to Grand Duke Michael. Despatched an Armenian delegation to Berlin, which returned unheard. Active in establishment of schools. Asked to resign, on health grounds, but resignation not accepted. Elected Catholicos of all Armenians in May 1884; declined on health grounds. Resigned as patriarch 11 days before his death, 26 October 1884.

NERSESIAN, ARSHAK see SEPOUH

NORADOUNGIAN, GABRIEL (Constantinople 1852 – Paris 1936) Born to a family from Agn (or Eghin). After local schooling, he studied international law in Europe. Returning to Constantinople, he took an active part in the Armenian National Assembly; also served the Porte as legal adviser. Published a *Recueil d'actes internationaux de l'empire Ottoman* (4 vols., Paris, 1897–1903). After the constitutional revolution of 1908 he became minister of public works. Briefly Ottoman foreign minister in 1912 in the 'father-and-son' Cabinet of Ghazi Ahmad Mukhtar; forced to resign on outbreak of Balkan war. During and after the world war in Paris, as a member of the Armenian National Delegation. To the USA in 1921 on an inquiry mission; met President Harding. Returned to Europe to work in Armenian National Delegation attempting with Avetis Aharonian, without success, to influence the treaty of Lausanne. Vice-president, then honorary president, of the Armenian General Benevolent Union then centred in Paris.

NURIJANIAN, AVIS (Vachakan, Karabagh 1896–1937) Orphaned at the age of 3. Educated at local diocesan school and at Shushi. Higher education in economics faculty of Kiev trade institute. To the Caucasian front in 1914. Joined the Dashnak party in 1917, but soon quit it. In defence of the Baku commune, April–August 1918; became secretary of the commune. Joined the Bolsheviks in September 1918; responsible for underground activities. Jailed by Musavatist Azerbaijan for two months in 1919; expelled from the country. Given refuge by Dashnak Armenia; settled in Alexandropol. Secretary, from January 1920, of the illegal Armenkom. A leader of the May uprising; commissar for foreign affairs of the military-revolutionary committee which seized power in Alexandropol. Escaped when the rebellion was crushed. Military commissar when the Revkom, headed by Kasian, entered Armenia in December 1920. Instigated a savage reign of terror which led directly to the uprising of February 1921. Expelled from Armenia when Miasnikian entered Armenia. To Petrograd to study in 1923. On party work in Petrograd, Ryazan and Transcaucasia. A victim of the purges.

NZHDEH, General GAREGIN (G. Ter-Harutunian) (Nakhichevan 1886 – Siberia 1957) Joined the Dashnak party in his teens. Enrolled in a military academy in Sofia (Bulgaria) in 1905, at age of 19; graduated in 1907. Returned to Transcaucasia; imprisoned by tsarist authorities; escaped from jail in 1911 and sought refuge in Bulgaria. Joined Gen. Andranik's brigade fighting in the 1912 Balkan war; served as a second lieutenant. Later given command of a Bulgarian brigade. To Transcaucasia in 1914; joined the Armenian volunteers. For two years adjutant to General Dro. Commander of the 3rd volunteer battalion. Fought with Gen. Nazarbekian at Karakilisa in the battle of Sardarabad, May 1918. One of the organisers of the republic's army after independence. Appointed commander to suppress Tatar rebellion in Goghtan (Nakhichevan), autumn 1919. Commander in Karabagh and Zangezur in 1920. Fought Bolshevik and Tatar forces almost continuously from July 1920 to July 1921; commander-in-chief of Lernahayastan (Zangezur) April–July 1921. Crossed into Persia; thence to Bulgaria. Member of Dashnak Central Committee of Bulgaria. Invited by the US Central Committee to go to America as a field-worker in 1933. Formed Dashnak youth societies into H.H.D. Tseghakronner (= A.R.F. Race-devotees); name soon changed to Armenian Youth Federation of America. Expelled from Dashnak party for extreme views, though Dashnak papers continued to print his articles. To Berlin in 1942; member of the 'Armenian National Council'. With Dro in the Crimea and North Caucasus. To Bulgaria in 1944. Sent to Siberia on capture by the Russians. *Nzhdeh* means 'exile'.

ODIAN, KRIKOR (Constantinople 1834 – Paris 1887) Trained as a lawyer. Rose within the Ottoman civil service. One of the architects of the Armenian national constitution, 1863. Assisted Midhat Pasha in the preparation of the Ottoman constitution, 1876. To London in January 1877 as Ottoman government emissary, seeking to oppose the proposals of the Constantinople conference; proposed instead that the execution of the Ottoman constitution should be a matter of international obligation. After the suspension of the constitution and the fall of Midhat, left for Paris, where he died 9 years later.

OHANDJANIAN, HAMAZASP (HAMO) (Akhalkalak 1873 – Cairo 1947) Elementary schooling locally; sent to Russian school in Tiflis in 1883. Thence to Moscow, to study medicine. Participated in revolutionary activities; sent back to Tiflis as a result. To Lausanne for further medical studies, 1899–1902. Returned to Transcaucasia to practise medicine, mainly in Baku; became a member of the eastern Bureau of Dashnaktsutiun in 1905. Co-ordinated relations with Russian and Georgian revolutionaries during Armeno–Tatar conflict. To Vienna for 4th congress of Dashnaktsutiun, 1907. Caught up in tsarist persecution of Dashnaks; sent to Novocherkask in 1909. Chief defendant at the trial of Dashnaktsutiun, 1912; exiled to Siberia in 1913. Married Rupina, fellow Armenian revolutionary, while in exile. Returned to Transcaucasia in 1915; in Van to give medical assistance in May. Commissar for public welfare in Transcaucasian Commissariat, November 1917; in same month chosen by Dashnaktsutiun to be one of its representatives at Constituent Assembly (Petrograd). Delegated to seek German mediation between Armenia and the Turks, May 1918. To Berlin in June as quasi-ambassador, seeking recognition and protection for Armenia. To Geneva in November. Member of Armenian republic's delegation at Paris peace conference. To Berne to put Armenian case to Second International, February 1919. To Armenia; appointed foreign minister in Khatisian's Cabinet, January 1920. Took over premiership after May 1920 Communist uprising; his administration saw fierce conflicts with the Communists. Resigned after the fall of Kars. Jailed after the Sovietisation of Armenia; released by February rebellion. To Persia after the return of the Communists, thence to Egypt. A leading member of the Dashnak Bureau until his death. Opposed Gen. Dro's activities during the second world war. Known as Mher.

ORMANIAN, Patriarch MAGHAKIA (Constantinople 1841 – Constantinople 1918) Born to an Armenian Catholic family. Sent to Rome in 1851; ordained priest in 1863. Served as Armenian teacher to the *De Propaganda Fide* congregation until 1866, when he returned to Constantinople via San Lazzaro, Venice. To Rome again in 1868 to take a degree; elected a member of the Rome theological academy. Took part in the Vatican Council of 1870. Met Garibaldi in 1875. Converted to the Armenian Apostolic (*Lousavorchakan*) Church in 1879, with 75 others at a ceremony celebrated by Patriarch Nerses Varzhabedian. Appointed primate of the Armenians of Erzerum in 1880; succeeded in reducing local tensions after the Erzerum demonstration of 1882. Consecrated bishop in 1886 at Echmiadzin, where he became professor of theology in 1887. Forced to quit by government pressure in 1888; returned to Constantinople. Dean of the seminary at Armash (near Ismit) from 1890; under him it became a critical academic institution. Elected Armenian patriarch of Constantinople on resignation of Patriarch Mateos Izmirlian in 1896; very unpopular with radical and revolutionary Armenians, who saw him as the sultan's yes-man. Prevailed upon the sultan to release many Armenian prisoners. Tendered his resignation to the palace in 1899, but the sultan would not accept it. Compelled to resign six days after the constitutional revolution of 1908; denounced by Armenian National Assembly in November; physically humiliated; suffered a partial stroke as a result. In 1913 declared innocent of the accusations. To Jerusalem in 1914 on ecclesiastical business; deported to

Damascus in 1917. To Constantinople in May 1918; died there in November. Most famous for his *Azgapatum* ('History of the Nation') (3 vols., Constantinople and Jerusalem, 1913–27).

OZANIAN, ANDRANIK see ANDRANIK

PAPADJANIAN, Marshal HAMAZASP (Chartakhlu, Azerbaijan 1908–77) Admitted to the A. Miasnikian military school, Yerevan, in 1925. Then to the Frunze military academy, Moscow. Commander in the Russo–Finnish war, 1939–40. After German invasion of Russia, he was one of the defenders of Moscow; later crossed the Dneistre river; wounded. Took part in the liberation of Poland, then of Germany (entering Berlin). Promoted to major-general. In 1968 he was appointed marshal of tank forces.

PAPADJANIAN, MIKAYEL (Yerevan 1868 – Tiflis 1929) Grandfather had served in the Russian army. Educated at state gymnasium. Studied law at Rostov, Odessa and St Petersburg, graduating in 1892. Practised as a barrister at Baku. Active against the authorities during the events of 1903–5. Married an oil heiress in 1907. Elected Armenian member of the Fourth State Duma in 1912. Supported P. Miliukov and Kadets. One of the five members of the *Ozakom*, March 1917. Founder member of the Zhoghovrdakan (Populist) party, 1917, the eastern equivalent of the Ramkavars. Participated in the Russian Armenian National Congress, October 1917; he and the other members of the Ozakom were criticised for ineffectiveness. Negotiated at Batum with Vehib Pasha and Khalil Bey, May–June 1918; signed Batum treaty. To Paris in 1918 as a member of the delegation of the Republic of Armenia. To Moscow in 1923 to discuss matters of Armenian immigration. Joined Ramkavar Azatakan party after its foundation; elected to its Central Committee; also member of central executive of AGBU, Paris. In 1929 delegated by his party to discuss with Soviet Armenian government the re-establishment of ties between Eastern and Western Armenians. Died on his way out, in Tiflis.

PAPAZIAN, VAHAN (Koms) (Tabriz 1876 – Beirut 1973) Parents came from Van. Father killed in Salmas when he was 9. To Nor Nakhichevan in 1893. First contact with Armenian revolutionaries – initially Hunchaks – in 1895; met Dashnaks in the same year at Alexandropol, and joined the party. Returned to Nor Nakhichevan in 1896; to Baku in 1897, and on to Moscow university. Not a success, so he returned to Transcaucasia, settling in Alexandropol. Decided to return to studies, so he enrolled at St Petersburg university. There (with Nikol Aghbalian) 1900–2; compelled to flee to Finland when suspected of implication in assassination of wealthy Armenian. Thence to Geneva, until 1903, when he returned to Transcaucasia; on to Van, where he remained until 1908, directing Dashnak revolutionary activity. After the proclamation of the Ottoman constitution in 1908 he was elected deputy for Van. Participated in Tiflis meeting of September 1912 which, in the wake of Armenian disillusion with the Young Turks, decided to reactivate the Armenian question. To Paris in 1913 to confer with Boghos Nubar Pasha. Returned to the Van region in August 1914, to look after the interests of people there. Helped reduce tension in local dispute in February 1915. Fled with Ruben Ter-Minasian to Yerevan to join the Armenian volunteers; his abandonment of the Armenians of Moush and Sasun has been heavily criticised. Chairman of the council of the Western Armenian Congress, May 1917. To Tiflis 1918; to Paris in 1919 to participate in the Armenian delegation at the peace conference. Returned to Yerevan October 1919 to take part in the 9th general congress of Dashnaktsutiun. Returned to France in September 1920 for further peace talks. To Riga in July 1921 with Djamalian and Navasardian for the (fruitless) talks with the Communists. Again with the Delegation of the Republic of Armenia in trying to influence the Lausanne treaty. Assisted establishment of Kurdish Khoybun, 1927. In Berlin during the second world war, as a member of the 'Armenian National Council'. Thereafter in Beirut; member of the Central Committee of Hamazkayin (1947–8); president of the organisation (1951–3). Candidate in Lebanese parliamentary elections of 1951; lost. His brother VRTANES was a well-regarded writer who lived (and died) in Soviet Armenia.

PARAMAZ (Karabagh – Constantinople 1915) Leading Hunchak. Participated in the Van defence, June 1896. Active in Transcaucasia in the conflict of 1903–5, in part playing a conciliatory role. One of the organisers of the attempt on Golitsyn's life. Several times imprisoned by the autocracy. Leading participant in the Constantsa (Köstendje) Hunchak convention, 1915, which demanded the overthrow of the Ottoman empire. Returned to Constantinople; arrested; hanged, after a long trial, in Bayazid Square, June 1915.

PARIAN, PETROS see SIUNI, BABKEN

PASHALIAN, LEVON (Scutari, Constantinople 1869 – Vichy 1943) Attended the Berberian school, Constantinople. Journalist and critic; began writing in 1884. Wrote for *Arevelk*, *Masis* and *Hairenik* (all of Constantinople). Joined the Hunchak party soon after its foundation (1887). Escaped the Hamidian crack-down by fleeing to Paris, August 1890. Returned to Constantinople after 2–3 years; worked with Arpiar Arpiarian on *Hairenik*. Fled with Arpiarian to London after the Bab Ali demonstration (1895); together they founded *Mart* ('Battle') and *Nor Giank* ('New Life'). Abandoned the socialism of Nazarbekian; one of the founders of the non-socialist Verakazmial ('reformed') Hunchaks. In Baku 1901–20 as director of a French oil company; gave up writing, seeming to lose interest in political and literary matters. To Paris in 1920; in 1922 a member of the Armenian delegation seeking to influence the Lausanne treaty. Executive secretary of the Central Council for Armenian Refugees from 1923. Member of the central board of AGBU. To Yerevan in 1924 to investigate viability of League of Nations plan for settling 50,000 Armenian refugees on irrigated Sardarabad desert. Sought relief for victims of 1929–30 deportations. Editor of *Le Foyer*, 1928–34.

PATKANIAN, RAPAYEL see KAMAR KATIBA

POGHOSIAN, NIKOGHAYOS see ISHKHAN

PORTUGALIAN, MKRTICH (Kum Kapu, Constantinople 1848 – Marseilles 1921) Educated in the Ottoman capital; aware from an early age of the conflict between progress and stagnation in the Armenian community. Became a teacher in Tokat in 1867; arrested in 1869 by the Ottoman authorities on the instigation of conservative Armenians for his progressive educational activities. Released; returned to Constantinople. Edited *Asia*; forced to close by opposition. Contributed to Turkish-language *Manzume*; also to *Meghu Hayastani* ('Armenian Bee') of Tiflis. Founded the Araratian Society in 1876, seeking to further Armenian education in the provinces; became director in Van (in the same year), whither he travelled, visiting the villages of the district *en route*. To Tiflis in 1877, to confer with Grigor Artsruni; back to Van, via Constantinople, in 1878. Founded a school open to all; forced to close by factionalism. To Constantinople briefly again in 1881, before founding another school in Van, the Kedronakan Varzharan. Banished by the government in March 1885; the school closed in June. To exile in Marseilles, where through the journal *Armenia* he acted as the guiding spirit of the Armenakan party (the first Armenian political party). His later plans for a united Armenian front were nullified by the emergence of the revolutionary parties.

RAFFI (Hakob Melik-Hakobian) (Bayajuk, near Salmas, Persia 1835 – Tiflis 1888) After elementary education locally, to Tiflis in 1847 for further schooling. Forced to discontinue in 1855. Travelled to Turkish Armenia in 1857 – Moush, Van (where he met Khrimian Hayrik at the Varak monastery). Began writing seriously in 1860; contributed to *Hiusisapayl* ('Northern Lights', Moscow). To Tiflis in 1868; destitute from business failures. Joined the staff of *Mshak* ('Labourer', Tiflis) on invitation from Grigor Artsruni in 1872. To Tabriz to teach in 1874; forced to quit in 1877 when suspected of agitation. Novels included *Jellaledin, Khente* ('The Fool'), *Kaitzer* ('Sparks'), *Davit Bek, Samuel*, all of nationalist significance. Died from lung trouble.

ROSTOM (Stepan Zorian) (Tsghna, 1867 – Tiflis 1919) Educated at Tiflis state school. To the Petrovsk agricultural academy, Moscow, in 1889; expelled after a year for taking part in a demonstration. With Mikayelian and Zavarian founded Dashnaktsutiun in summer 1890. Taught in Tabriz, 1891–2. Worked on the party platform with the other founders in 1892. In Geneva working on *Droshak* ('Flag') 1893–5. To Erzerum in 1895; arrested and expelled to Persia. To Tiflis; thence to the Balkans to work with Macedonian revolutionaries. Back to Transcaucasia in 1902; active against Russian confiscations and in the Armeno–Tatar conflict, 1905. Persuaded the 4th Dashnak congress, Vienna, 1907, to approve his participation in the Persian constitutional movement. Briefly in Stuttgart, and Bulgaria, before returning to the Caucasus, and on to Persia to take an active part in the fight for the Persian constitution. To Varna for the 5th Dashnak congress. On to Constantinople and Erzerum, where he remained as a party worker until 1914. One of the Dashnak leaders who discussed policy in the event of war with the Young Turk leaders at the Erzerum (8th) congress. To Transcaucasia on the outbreak of war; assisted in organisation of volunteer units and of relief for refugees. Warned of the danger of revolution in wartime when the tsar abdicated. One of nine Dashnak representatives chosen as deputies to the All-Russian Constituent Assembly. To Stockholm to present the Armenian case to the Socialist International. In Baku in 1918, fighting the Turkish invasion. On to Persia, then to Tiflis, where he died.

SABAH-GULIAN, STEPAN (Djahri, a village just north of Nakhichevan, 1861 – USA 1928) Attended the Nersesian academy, Tiflis. Appointed director of Nakhichevan schools; met Paramaz, with whom he discussed revolutionary ideas. Briefly in Jerusalem, as a director of the Armenian school. To Paris for further education; graduated from the École libre des sciences politiques with Raymond Poincaré. Became a leader of the Hunchak party. Founded and edited a number of journals, including *Yeritasard Hayastan* ('Armenian Youth', 1903), *Hunchak, Veradsnound* ('Revival'), *Nor Ashakharh*. An attempt on his life by the Verakazmial Hunchaks failed in 1903. After the Ottoman constitution he declared his opposition to the Committee of Union and Progress. Condemned to death (*in absentia*) along with other Hunchaks in 1915. At the time he was in Cairo. Thence he travelled to the USA to recruit for the volunteer units and to obtain assistance for the Armenians in the war. Edited *Yeritasard Hayastan* in New York. Opposed the idea of an American mandate for Armenia, favouring Bolshevik Russia. Disagreed with Nazarbekian on relations between Hunchaks and Social Democrats; showed determination to maintain independence and integrity of Hunchak party.

SAFARIAN, Major-General NVER (Ardjish, Van province, 1907–) Father a victim of the 1915 genocide. Family moved to Echmiadzin in 1915. Orphaned in 1917. To Yerevan to study in the A. Miasnikian military academy in 1923; graduated in 1927. Further military education at the Frunze academy, Moscow. Chief of staff in the western Ukraine when Nazis invaded in 1941; in February 1943 appointed commander of the 89th Armenian division fighting at Novorosiisk and Taman. His forces liberated Taman; known as the

Tamanian army. Also fought at Kerch and Sevastopol. Promoted to general. After the liberation of the Crimea his troops fought in Poland, at Frankfurt-an-der-Oder and Berlin.

SAHAK II, Catholicos of the Great House of Cilicia (Yeghek, village in Kharput province, 1849 – Antilias 1939) Baptismal name Gabriel Khapayan. Taken by his parents to the seminary of the Armenian monastery at Jerusalem in 1867. To Constantinople in 1869; again to Jerusalem in 1872 as teacher, then as editor of the journal of the patriarchate, *Sion* (1874–7). Ordained celibate priest in 1877. In 1879 he undertook a tour of Kharput, Aleppo, Aintab, Erzindjan, Trebizond and Constantinople on the business of the patriarchate. In Transcaucasia 1881–6 raising funds for the patriarchate. Consecrated bishop in 1885 at Echmiadzin. Returned to Jerusalem as chamberlain of the patriarchate in 1886. Appointed representative of the patriarchate to the Cilician catholicosate in 1900. Elected Catholicos of Cilicia at Sis on 12 October 1902; mentioned name of Catholicos Mkrtich (Khrimian) of Echmiadzin during the service of consecration, thereby signifying reconciliation with mother see. Visited Constantinople in 1904, trying (unsuccessfully) to solve problems of jurisdiction of the Cilician catholicosate and Constantinople patriarchate; problem remained unsolved. Protested at the Adana massacre of 1909. Informed Patriarch Zaven of Constantinople of rumours of deportations on 2 March 1915. Strongly protested on 13 June 1915 to Djemal Pasha about the condition of Armenian deportees, and of the Armenian soldiers in labour battalions. On 21 October 1915 compelled on instructions from the ministry of the interior to leave, first for Aleppo then for Jerusalem. In May 1916 ordered by Djemal Pasha to assume, after the abolition of the sees of Sis, Aghtamar, Constantinople and Jerusalem, the new post of Catholicos-patriarch of all Armenians in the Ottoman empire, based at Jerusalem. Reluctantly accepted, thereby hoping to end the government's persecution of Armenians. Exiled by the government to Damascus in November 1917. Returned to Cilicia after the armistice of 1918. Forced to flee again with the rise of the Kemalist movement, quitting Adana in December 1921. After remaining a short while in Aleppo, he settled in Antilias, north of Beirut, in 1931, making it the seat of the catholicosate. Took over responsibility for dioceses of Beirut, Damascus and Latakia in 1929, hitherto the responsibility of the patriarchate of Jerusalem.

SASUNI, KARO (Aharonk, Sasun, 1889 – Beirut 1977) Attended Mkhitarist intermediate school of Moush 1900–6. Joined the secret youth group of the Dashnak party in 1904. Taught in Diyarbekir 1906–9. To the law school of Constantinople in 1909. Sent by the Dashnak Bureau of Constantinople to Moush and Sasun in 1912. Graduated from the Constantinople law school. To Transcaucasia in October 1914, to assist in organisation of the Armenian volunteer units. Sent as an activist to the border region of Pasen (between

Erzerum and Sarikamish). To Moush and Sasun in 1916, as leader and military adviser. To Constantinople and Smyrna in January 1919, where he worked in collaboration with Ramkavar leader Suren Partevian. To the Republic of Armenia in June 1919, where he was elected a deputy in the Parliament; also governor in the Alexandropol region. After the anti-Communist rebellion of 18 February 1921 he acted as minister of the interior in the Committee for the Salvation of the Fatherland. After the return of the Communists he was in Paris for 10 years, before settling finally in Beirut. There he continued as a leader of the Dashnak party, and became a respected elder statesman of the community. Of his published works *Kiurt azgayin sharzhumnere yev Hai-Krtakan haraberutiunere* (*The Kurdish National Movements and Armeno-Kurdish Relations* (1932, rev. edn. 1968)) is especially to be noted. Visited Soviet Armenia in the 1970s.

SEGHPOSIAN, LEVON see SHANT, LEVON

SEPOUH (Arshak Nersesian) (Tomna, village north of Baiburt, 1872 – USA 1940) Showed early aptitude as craftsman. Educated Trebizond. Left for Constantinople in 1889; joined the Hunchak party. On party orders assassinated an Armenian working for the Turks. Took part in the Kum Kapu Affray. To the Crimea; thence to Yalta and Sevastopol. Joined the Dashnak party in 1894. Moved on to Tiflis and Yerevan. Active in the Sasun uprising of 1904; led the Mrrik ('Storm') group helping the peasants against the government. Took part in battles at Tabek, Shenik and Semal; wounded. Thence to Tadvan, Aghtamar Island and Van. Participated in the 1907 Dashnak party congress at Vienna. To Ashkale in 1912; thence to Erzerum, Tiflis and Kharkov. To Tiflis on the outbreak of the first world war; assumed leadership of a force of 500 volunteers which was sent to Salmas, Persia. To Tiflis again in 1915; then to the front once more, to Khoy and Diliman. With the Russian forces in their advance to Erzerum in 1917. In the Baku commune under Shahumian in 1918. To Petrovsk and then to Armenia (via Batum), where he was elected to the Parliament in 1919. Appointed commander of the special division created to crush the Bolshevik uprising of May 1920. After the Sovietisation of Armenia he left for the USA via Constantinople, where he died. His sons joined Nzhdeh's Tseghakrons.

SEROP (S. Vardanian; known as Aghbur Serop) (Sokhort, a village near Akhlat, *c.* 1865 – Moush 1900) In Romania in the 1890s; joined the ranks of the Dashnaks in 1893. A revolutionary guerrilla in the Akhlat region from 1895. (His wife Sosse was also a revolutionary.) Extended his revolutionary activities westward throughout the Moush and Sasun region, establishing a quasi-autonomy in the area. Poisoned by an Armenian traitor in the pay of Kurdish chieftain Bshara Khalil.

SHAHAMIRIAN, HAKOB (b. Madras 1745) The son of the following. A pupil of Movses Baghramian. Published (allegedly) *Vorogait Parats* ('Trap of Glory') in 1773, a manual for the constitution of a future Armenia, which he envisaged as a democracy.

SHAHAMIRIAN, SHAHAMIR Born Madras. Initially a tailor, then a jeweller, whereby he became very rich. With Movses Baghramian and Hovsep Emin turned his attention to Armenia, initiating political discussion. In correspondence with King Erekle (Heraclius) II of Georgia. Shahamirian favoured a republic for Armenia, with strong ties to Russia.

SHAHAN NATALI (Hakob Ter-Hakobian) (Husseinik, near Kharput, 1884–) His father was killed in the massacre of 1895. To S. Hagop orphanage, Constantinople, in 1897; adopted. Educated at the Berberian school. Back in Husseinik as a teacher 1901–4. Joined Dashnak party in 1904. To the USA in 1904; worked in a shoe factory. Returned briefly to Constantinople in 1908 after the constitutional revolution; sceptical about its effectiveness; to USA again in 1909. At Boston university 1910–12, studying literature and philosophy. Homesick, planned to return to Husseinik in 1912; arrested in Greece as an Ottoman citizen. Again to America. Edited *Hairenik* (Boston) 1915–17 and 1919. Chosen as US delegate to 9th general congress of Dashnaktsutiun, Yerevan, autumn 1919. Leader of Nemesis organisation which tracked down and assassinated Turkish war criminals. Became member of the Dashnak Bureau. Travelled widely in Europe. Left the Dashnak party in 1929; formed in 1933 the Western Armenian Liberation Alliance. Back in the USA, he became a member of AGBU, and was for 10 years secretary of the New England chapter. Visited Soviet Armenia in 1960 and 1962. Lives in retirement in Watertown. Author of several books, including *Turkism from Angora to Baku, and the Turkish Orientation* (Athens, 1928) and *From the Treaty of Alexandropol to the Caucasian Rebellions of the 1930s* (Athens, 1933); also of a number of volumes of poetry.

SHAHRIKIAN, HARUTIUN see ATOM

SHAHUMIAN, STEPAN (Tiflis 1878 – desert near Ashkhabad 1918) In the revolutionary movement from 1898. Began a Marxist study group in Lori in 1899. Social Democrat from 1900. To Riga Polytechnic Institute in 1900; expelled for revolutionary activity. Formed (with Hunchaks and Left Dashnaks) the Union of Armenian Social Democrats in 1902. Co-founder of *Proletariat* (Tiflis) in same year. To Germany also in 1902; worked with RSDRP members. Member of the Caucasian joint RSDRP committee on his return in 1904. Founded and edited a number of Bolshevik newspapers; wrote on philosophy, literature and art besides politics and economics. Delegate to the fourth and fifth RSDRP congresses. Active in party work. Took part in preparation of Prague RSDRP congress of 1911; arrested; exiled to Astrakhan. Elected member of the Central Committee of the Social Democrats in his absence. Returned to Baku in spring 1914. Directed oil-workers' strike May–July 1914. Arrested again in 1916 and exiled to Saratov. Released March 1917. Elected chairman of the Baku Soviet *in absentia* 6 March 1917, returned two days later. To Petrograd in June 1917, at all-Russian Congress of Soviets. Appointed extraordinary commissar for Caucasian affairs in December 1917. In Tiflis January–February 1918; attacked Transcaucasian Seim; Commissariat ordered his arrest; he escaped to Baku. In close contact with Dashnaktsutiun March–July 1918. His power strengthened by the 'March Days', which meant the submission of the Musavat party. Leader of the Baku commune after establishment of Soviet rule, 25 April 1918. Despite his awareness that the revolution was unfinished, he brought about an extensive social and economic transformation of the city. Resigned after vote to let the British in, 25 July 1918. Shahumian and the other commissars left Baku openly on 14 August; forced by a storm on to Zhil island. Sighted and arrested the next morning; returned to Baku. Saved from the invading Turks by Mikoyan, who led them to the port. Taken by ship to Krasnovodsk; jailed by anti-Bolshevik committee based at Ashkhabad. Decision taken to kill them on 18 September; all 26 murdered on 20 September.

SHANT, LEVON (L. Seghposian) (Constantinople 1869 – Beirut 1951) Attended Armenian school at Scutari (Uskudar) until 1883; then to the Gevorgian seminary at Echmiadzin until 1891. Returned to Constantinople to teach and write; his first literary work accepted by *Hairenik* of Constantinople in that year. To Germany in 1892 for seven years to study science, child psychology, education, literature and history: Leipzig, Jena and Munich. Returned to settle in Constantinople. Joined the Dashnak party. Worked as a writer and teacher. As an author most renowned for his plays: *Hin Astvadsner* ('Ancient Gods', 1909), *Kaisre* ('The Emperor', 1914), *Inkads Berdi Ishkhanuhin* ('The Princess of the Fallen Castle', 1921), *Oshin Payl* (1929). One of the vice-presidents of the Armenian Parliament during the Republic. Led the Armenian delegation to Moscow in April 1920 to negotiate with the Communists. Left Armenia after its Sovietisation, eventually settling in Beirut. One of the founders of the Hamazkayin cultural association. Principal of the Nshan Palandjian Djemaran (College), Beirut, from 1929 until his death. His works were published in Soviet Armenia in 1968.

SHIRVANZADE (Agheksandr Movsesian) (Shemakha 1858 – Yerevan 1935) Born in Shirvan province, hence his pen-name. His father went bankrupt in his childhood, and the family house was wrecked by an earthquake in 1872, events which strongly influenced him. Educated partly at the Protestant school of Shemakha, and at an independent one. To Baku in 1875, first as a local government official, then in an oil company. There he encountered the

Armenian language and literature. Began writing in 1880, first in Russian, then in Armenian (in *Mshak*). Moved to Tiflis, where his writings included the plays *Namus* ('Honour', 1885) and *Kaos* ('Chaos', 1896–7). Briefly assistant editor of *Ardzagang* ('Echo'). Worked in city administration of Tiflis 1889–92; sacked for writing during office hours. Joined the Hunchak party; toured some Russian cities as a political educator. Jailed for three months in 1895. Left the party; exiled to Odessa for political offences nevertheless in 1898 on orders of the tsar. On his return he left to settle in Paris (August 1905). Back to the Caucasus in 1910. To the USA in 1918. Again to Paris in 1922, then to Soviet Armenia, where he died. His complete works published in Yerevan 1930–4.

SHISHMANIAN, HOVSEP see DSERENTS

SHMAVONIAN, HARUTIUN (Shiraz 1750 – Madras 1824) Ordained a *kahana* (married priest). Appointed to the diocese of Madras. Established a printing press in 1789. Influenced by the publication of an English newspaper, published the first Armenian paper, *Azdarar* ('Monitor'), 16 October 1794. Financial difficulties forced it to close in February 1796.

SIAMANTO (Atom Yardjanian) (Agn (Egin) 1878 – Ayash 1915) To Constantinople in 1892, to study at the Berberian school. Joined the Dashnak party. In Europe 1896–1908; wrote for *Droshak* in Geneva, and studied literature for 3 years at the Sorbonne. Returned briefly to Constantinople after the constitution of 1908; on to the USA as a party worker and editor of *Hairenik* daily (Boston). Wrote his first book there. Returned to Constantinople in 1910. Wrote heavily symbolist poetry, and also more direct and stirring lyrics celebrating the activites of Armenian *fedayis*. Arrested on 24 April 1915; murdered in the course of the genocide.

SMBAT (S. Baroyan) (Moush 1882 – Yerevan 1955) Early engagement in guerrilla activity against Turks. Became a Dashnak *fedayi*, joined the Vardanantz group when aged 15. Served under Andranik at Arakelotz Vank and in the 1904 Sasun rebellion. Then to Persia with Andranik and Kaidsak Arakel; fought at Urmia and Khoy. In Transcaucasia during the 1905 Armeno-Tatar wars; fought under Nikol Duman at Yerevan and Kamarlu (modern Artashat). Returned to Moush after the constitutional revolution of 1908. A member of Andranik's troops in 1914; took part in the battle of Diliman (Shahpur), April 1915. Wounded; transferred to Tiflis. His wife was killed by the Turks. To Moush and Sasun in 1916, with Andranik and Dro, and Russian support, to save the survivors of the massacres. Returned to Igdir and Yerevan. During the republic served under Ruben Ter-Minasian, fighting Tatar insurgency around Kars and Mount Akbaba. Imprisoned after Armenia's Sovietisation; released by February rebellion. Continued to fight in Zangezur after the Bolsheviks had retaken Yerevan. Escaped to Tabriz.

Remarried. Simon Vratsian arranged for him to go first to the USA and then to France (Marseilles). Repatriated to Soviet Armenia in 1947. Died in Yerevan; buried at Echmiadzin.

SOGHOMONIAN, SOGHOMON see KOMITAS

SOGHOMONIAN, YEGHISHE see CHARENTS

SRAPONIAN, SARGIS see LUKASHIN, SARGIS

TEHLIRIAN, SOGHOMON (Kemakh 1896 – San Francisco 1960) Attended the Armenian Protestant school of Erzindjan, then the Yeznikian and Kedronakan schools. To Serbia in 1913 whither his father had emigrated to escape the Turks. Joined the Dashnak party. Fought in the volunteer army of Sepouh, 1914–17, enlisting without his parents' knowledge. Lost his mother and all relatives in the genocide. To Constantinople in 1919, seeking out Turks who had executed the Armenian genocide; also looked for Armenian collaborators. To the USA in 1920, on orders from the party; thence to Geneva and Berlin, where he assassinated Talaat on 15 March 1921. Acquitted by the Berlin court on 3 June. Settled in Belgium, where he remained until 1945; then emigrated to San Francisco, where he died.

TEKEYAN, VAHAN (Constantinople 1878 – Cairo 1945) Attended the Nersesian, Berberian and Kedronakan schools in Constantinople. Did not complete his studies. To Britain in 1896, thence to France, Germany and Egypt on business; began contributing to Armenian journals. Founded literary magazines *Shirak* (1905) and *Nor Zhamanakner* (1907). One of the founders of the Sahmandrakan Ramkavar (constitutional democrat) party, Egypt, 1908. Returned to Constantinople after Ottoman constitutional revolution of 1908. To Echmiadzin in 1910, representing the Armenians of Egypt at the election of the Catholicos (Gevorg V, in 1911). Delegated by the Armenian National Assembly of Constantinople in 1914 to go to Jerusalem to inspect the patriarchate's accounts. Thence to Egypt. An attack by a political opponent in 1916 caused a permanent injury to an eye. Delegated by Egyptian Armenians to go to Cyprus in 1916 to liaise with the French, who were training the Légion d'Orient. To the Paris peace conference in 1919, as part of the delegation headed by Boghos Nubar Pasha. Delegated to Yerevan in September 1919 to negotiate co-operative agreement between the Armenian National Delegation and the delegation of the Republic of Armenia; the negotiations failed. In Constantinople in late 1920, editing *Zhoghovurdi Dzayn* ('People's Voice'). Founder member of the Ramkavar Azatakan (Democratic Liberal) party, Constantinople, 1922; forced to quit when the Kemalists took over. Successively to Bulgaria, Greece, Egypt and Syria, organising relief for orphans. Settled in Egypt as editor of the Ramkavar Azatakan daily *Arev*;

briefly in Beirut in 1937 as editor of its equivalent, *Zartonk*. Appointed dean of the education faculty of the Melkonian Institute, Nicosia, in 1934. Published six volumes of poetry between 1901 and 1945. Died in Cairo. The Tekeyan Cultural Associations, established throughout the world by the Ramkavars, are so named in his memory.

TEMIRDJIAN, KAREN (Yerevan 1932–) Higher education at the Karl Marx Polytechnical Institute, Yerevan. Joined the Communist party in 1955. In Leningrad on scientific work 1954–8. Then to Yerevan, holding senior position in an electro-technical factory; later as secretary of the same factory's party committee. Chief engineer and director after graduation from the party college in 1961. Second secretary of the Yerevan city committee of the Armenian Communist party, 1966–72. Appointed First Secretary of the Central Committee of the ACP on 28 November 1974, replacing Anton Kochinian.

TER-GABRIELIAN, SAHAK (Shushi 1886 – 1937) To Baku to work as a carpenter in 1900. Joined the Social Democrats in 1902; sided with the Bolshevisks after the 1904 split. Elected to the Baku Soviet in 1917; participated in the All-Russian Conference of Soviets in Petrograd in March 1917. Returning to Baku he was appointed commissar for oil, and president of the extraordinary commission suppressing counter-revolutionary activity. To Moscow after the fall of the Baku commune; worked for the food supply of the Red Army. To Armenia in 1920, working with the Soviet delegation negotiating with the Dashnak government. Representative of Soviet Armenia in Moscow in 1920. With Ioffe negotiated (fruitlessly) with the Dashnaks in Riga, July 1921. Transcaucasian SSR's representative to Russia, 1922–8. Chairman, Armenian council of people's commissars and deputy premier of the Transcaucasian SFSR 1928–35. To France and Germany in 1931 to set up Armenian repatriation scheme. Victim of Stalinist purges, later rehabilitated.

TER-GASPARIAN, SARGIS see KASIAN, SARGIS

TER-GRIGORIAN, VAHAN see TERIAN, VAHAN

TER-HAKOBIAN, HAKOB see SHAHAN NATALI

TER-HARUTUNIAN, GAREGIN see NZHDEH, GAREGIN

TER-MINASIAN, RUBEN (Akhalkalak 1882 – Paris 1950) Born to parents who had migrated from Erzerum. Higher education at Gevorgian seminary, Echmiadzin and Lazarian Institute, Moscow. Returned to the Caucasus in 1903; joined the Dashnak party; became a *fedayi* in Turkish Armenia. Active as a fighter until the proclamation of the Ottoman constitution in 1908. Did not trust the constitution, so he moved to Geneva to pursue scientific studies; these he completed in 1913. Returned to Turkish Armenia to be general director of all Armenian schools in Moush region. Prepared Armenians for self-defence after Turkey entered the first world war. Resisted the Ottoman troops for several months in 1915, breaking through a circle of them. To Transcaucasia in 1916; became a member of the National Council in 1917. An adviser to the Seim delegation in the Trebizond negotiations with the Turks in March 1918. Opposed declaring the independence of Armenia in May 1918. Against putting forward extravagant territorial demands at the peace conference. War minister and minister of the interior in the Bureau government, headed by Ohandjanian, May–November 1920, a post which gave him full scope to implement his militant, punitive and non-compromising policies: very severe in his suppression of the Tatars. In Zangezur after the Sovietisation of Armenia; thence to Persia and to Europe. Published his memoirs in seven volumes. Cautious, even suspicious, by nature. In Palestine during part of the second world war. Died in Paris, 29 November 1950.

TER-PETROSIAN, SIMON see KAMO

TERIAN, VAHAN (V. Ter-Grigorian) (Kantsa, nr Akhalkalak, 1885 – Orenburg 1920) To Moscow to study at the Lazarian seminary until 1906. To Moscow university; studied history and languages. Joined the Bolshevik party. Wrote poetry, initially symbolist (*Day-dreams of Anticipation*, 1908, *Verse*, 1912); later optimistically revolutionary. Also translated from Oscar Wilde, Baudelaire and Shota Rustaveli. Further study at the oriental faculty, Petrograd university, 1913–17. In Moscow at the time of the October revolution; discussed the Armenian situation with Lenin in November 1917, requesting that Russian troops should remain in Turkish Armenia. Made initial draft of Bolshevik declaration 'About Turkish Armenia', adopted 11 January 1918. Appointed deputy commissar of the Armenian Affairs commissariat in January 1918. With Trotsky as part of the Bolshevik delegation at the Brest-Litovsk peace talks. Died from tuberculosis. Collected works published in 1923.

TERLEMEZIAN, MKRTICH see AVETISIAN, MKRTICH

TORKOM, 'General' A one-time Dashnak *khmbapet* (*fedayi* leader), he declared the independence of Armenia in Erzerum in early 1918 in a desperate attempt to stabilise the situation after the Russian withdrawal from Turkish Armenia. In Smyrna 1921–2, helping the Greeks. During the Spanish civil war he created and led a small Armenian volunteer force, formed from Armenians living in Greece, which fought on Franco's side.

TUMANIAN, HOVHANNES (Dsegh, Lori 1869 – Moscow 1923) Attended the Nersesian Academy, Tiflis, but did not complete the course of studies.

Thus, largely self-taught, he emerged as a poet of great directness, simplicity and lyricism, with a universal appeal. The unofficial poet laureate of Armenia. Also wrote stories and folk-tales. Most famous poems include *Krounk* ('The Crane'), 1896; *Hayots Lerneroum* ('In the Armenian Mountains'), 1902; the long poem *Sasuntsi Davit* ('David of Sasun'), 1902; *Hayots Vishtë* ('Armenian Grief'), 1903; *Hogehangist* ('Rest in Peace'), 1915, etc. Stories include *Kach Nazar* ('Nazar the Brave'), 1908. Tumanian was elected a member of the permanent bureau set up in Tiflis, November 1912, to seek a solution to the problem of Turkish Armenia. Sponsored several charitable societies in Tiflis in 1917–18, also the Union of Eastern peoples, which sought to unite the small nationalities of the Middle East. Advocated strongly pro-Russian stance throughout; profoundly distrusted Europe, seeing it as a manifestation of little more than greed and rapacity. Presided over meeting in Tiflis, June 1919, condemning the British for their activities in Karabagh. After the revolt of February 1921, he was sent by Orjonikidze to Yerevan on 20 March, to try to persuade the Dashnaks to surrender. They refused. Appointed president of HOK (Armenian Assistance Committee) in September 1921; briefly in Constantinople on relief work late 1921; returned a sick man. To Moscow for medical treatment in late 1922, where he died. Buried in Tiflis. His birthplace now bears his name.

TUTUNDJIAN, KHOSROV (Van 1894 –) Born to an Armenakan family. To Constantinople in 1907 for further education, at Armenian schools. To Lausanne university in 1913 to study law. Graduated in 1919 with doctorate in law and social sciences. To Yerevan, where he served in the ministries of the interior and justice. After the Bolshevik uprising of May 1920 he was appointed attorney-general for the Yerevan extraordinary court. Lectured in law, July 1920. During the Kemalist war he served as a volunteer in the division of Colonel Sepouh. Went into hiding in Yerevan after the Sovietisation of Armenia; helped organise the rebellion of 18 February 1921. Member of anti-Bolshevik extraordinary commission. Wounded in skirmishes with Bolsheviks. Fled to Persia when the Bolsheviks crushed the uprising. To Lebanon in 1924, on the invitation of the Dashnak Central Committee of Beirut. Published, with Arshak Hovhannisian, *Punik* ('Phoenix'), then *Nor Punik*. President of the community's civil council, 1934–41. Elected MP in Lebanese Parliament in 1937 as leader of Dashnak party's Lebanese committee. In this capacity he quarrelled with the party Bureau, led by Ruben Ter-Minasian and Vahan Navasardian. Suspended from the party in 1944, expelled altogether in 1953. Became editor of *Azdarar* daily (1953–5), which claimed to represent the true Dashnaks, criticising the Bureau. Published in 1959 *Buroyakan Snankutiunë yev Irav Dashnaktsutian Ughin Arabakan Ashkharhi Verchin Depkerun Luisin Tak* ('The Bankruptcy of the Bureau and the Path of True Dashnakism in the Light of Recent Events in the Arab World'). Although anti-Communist, he sees Russia as the necessary ally of Armenia. Continues to write in *Nayiri*, the Hunchak *Ararat*, and other Armenian periodicals. Visited Soviet Armenia in 1977 and 1978.

VARANDIAN, MIKAYEL (Varanda, Karabagh 1872 – 1934) Educated at the diocesan school of Shushi, then in Europe (especially in Geneva, and at various German universities). Joined the Dashnak party; settled in Geneva; became a member of the party's western bureau, and a member of the editorial board of the party newspaper, *Droshak*. Represented the socialist wing of the party; cultivated links with European socialist leaders, including Albert Thomas and Arthur Henderson. Represented Dashnaktsutiun at the Copenhagen conference of the Second International, 1910. Put forward the Armenian case in the conflict with Georgia at a meeting of the Second International, Paris, May 1919. During the period of the republic he was Armenian ambassador in Rome. A party theoretician, his chief work is *Hai Heghapokhakan Dashnaktsutian Patmutiunë* ('History of the ARF' (vol. I, Paris, 1932, vol. II, Cairo, 1950)).

VARDAN (Sargis Mehrapian) (Karabagh – Yerevan 1943) Received some military training in youth. A close collaborator of Kristapor Mikayelian and Simon Zavarian, he early joined the Dashnak party. With Hovsep Arghutian led the Khanasor attack of 1897. In command of the Karabagh defence during the 1905 Armeno-Tatar conflict. Commander of the Araratian volunteer units formed in 1915; these troops reached Van on 19 May.

VARDANIAN, SEROP see SEROP

VARTKES (Hovhannes Serangilian) (Erzerum 1871 – nr Diyarbekir 1915) Educated in his native town. Took part in the demonstration there of June 1890; arrested, but pardoned. To Constantinople, where he became headmaster of the Armenian school at Gedik Pasha. Joined the Dashnak party in 1892. Took part in the Ottoman Bank incident (1896). To Marseilles, Geneva, Bulgaria and the Caucasus. Secretly to Van in 1899; betrayed in 1903, arrested, tried and sentenced to death; his sentence commuted to life imprisonment after the intervention of French friends. Set free after the Ottoman constitutional revolution of 1908; went to Constantinople. Elected to the Armenian national assembly, and to the Ottoman Parliament, as deputy for Erzerum. Despite parliamentary immunity, arrested 24 April 1915, and murdered by the Turkish authorities on the road to Diyarbekir.

VARUZHAN, DANIEL (D. Chibukkyarian) (Sivas province 1884 – Ayash 1915) Born in the *vilayet* of Sivas. Sent to Constantinople to study in 1896, and to Venice for further study at the Mkhitarist monastery at San Lazzaro in 1902. Thence he went to the university of Ghent. Returned to Constantinople after the declaration of the constitution in 1908; headmaster of Armenian schools of Sivas and Tokat 1909–12. Again in Constantinople as principal of the Armenian Catholic Lousavorchian school. A distinguished poet, his poems include *The Shepherd, The Heart of the Nation* and *Pagan Songs*. Arrested on 24 April 1915 and murdered in the course of the genocide. A monument has been erected to his memory in Ghent.

VARZHABEDIAN, NERSES see NERSES

VAZGEN I, Catholicos (Bucarest 1907–) Baptismal name Garabed Baldjian Educated at the Armenian school and the Bucarest German *lycée*. Studied education and philosophy. To Leipzig university to take a doctorate in theology. Teacher and secretary of the Armenian school of Bucarest on his return, until 1942. Wrote books on *The Armenians of Musa Dagh in Franz Werfel's Novel* (1940), *Khrimian Hayrik as Teacher* (1944), *Our Mass* and *About our Fatherland* (both 1945). Ordained a celibate priest in Greece in 1943, with the name Vazgen. Elected deputy prelate and then prelate of the Armenians of Romania. Took part in the conclave that elected Catholicos Gevorg VI at Echmiadzin in 1945. Consecrated bishop in 1951; appointed prelate of Bulgaria as well as Romania. Elected a member of the supreme spiritual council of Echmiadzin in 1954. In the same year published a book, *Hayreni Arevin Tak* ('Beneath the Native Sun'). Elected by the conclave at Echmiadzin the 130th supreme patriarch and Catholicos of all Armenians in September 1955. Soon faced two crises: the election of a new Catholicos of the Great House of Cilicia, February 1956, and the disputes within the congregation of St James, Jerusalem. The first entailed a split within the Church which persists (although with less bitterness) to this day. Since his becoming Catholicos the Armenian Church has joined the World Council of Churches. He took part in the conference of Eastern Churches, Addis Ababa, 1965; many other extensive travels. A number of improvements and renewals have taken place during his catholicosate at Echmiadzin.

VRAMIAN (Onnik Derdzakian) (Constantinople 1871 – Van 1915) Early education at the Surenian school, Constantinople; then to Echmiadzin to study at the Gevorgian seminary. Joined the Dashnak party. Returned to Constantinople, where he worked at the Russian post office, at the same time transporting bombs for Dashnak comrades. Forced to seek refuge at the Russian embassy at the time of the Ottoman Bank incident (1896). Escaped to Geneva via Bulgaria, where he helped edit *Droshak*. To the USA in 1899, where he became editor of *Hairenik* (Boston). To Transcaucasia in 1907; to Van and then Constantinople after the Ottoman constitution (1908); contributed to *Azatamart*. Elected deputy for Van in the second Ottoman parliamentary elections. A liaison with Young Turk leaders at the Erzerum congress of Dashnaktsutiun, July 1914. Imprisoned by Djevdet Bey, governor of Van, in April 1915, after being invited to see him, and murdered in jail.

VRATSIAN, SIMON (Simavon Gruzian) (Great Sala, nr Nor Nakhichevan, 1882 – Beirut 1969) Attended local Russian and Armenian schools, then the prelacy school of Nor Nakhichevan. Joined the Dashnak party in 1898, mistakenly believing – by going through the wrong door – that he was joining the Hunchaks. At the Gevorgian seminary, Echmiadzin, 1900–6. Returned to Nor Nakhichevan as a Dashnak party worker. Took part in the 4th general congress of Dashnaktsutiun, Vienna, 1907, supporting the party's adoption of socialism. To St Petersburg in 1908 to study law and education. To Moscow, where a collection of literary pieces, *Psak* ('Crown') was published in 1910. To Constantinople in the same year, taking refuge from the anti-Dashnak measures of the tsarist authorities. On to Erzerum, where he edited *Harach* and taught at the Sanasarian academy. To the USA in 1911; edited *Hairenik* (Boston). To Erzerum for the 8th general congress of Dashnaktsutiun, July 1914; elected to the party's Bureau. Discussed policy with the Young Turk leaders. Briefly jailed as a Russian spy, August 1914. Escaped to Transcaucasia, where he became an organiser of the Armenian volunteer units. Often visited the front. After the disbandment of the units in late 1915, he served as a common soldier in Tiflis. Appointed editor of *Horizon* (Tiflis) after the March 1917 revolution. Attended the Moscow state conference, July 1917. A leading figure at the Armenian National Congress, September 1917, he was elected a member of the National Council. In southern Russia throughout the summer of 1918, gaining support of the volunteer army, obtaining as a result 3,000,000 cartridges, some machine-guns, and grain. Returning to Transcaucasia in October 1918, he was instrumental in gaining Populist support for the government coalition. Asked by H. Kachaznuni to accompany him on his tour of Europe and America in the spring of 1919, he was refused a visa by the British authorities in Tiflis, on the grounds of his being a radical socialist. Edited *Harach* (Yerevan) on his return. Elected to the Parliament; helped organise the 9th general congress of Dashnaktsutiun, Yerevan, autumn 1919. Re-elected to the party Bureau. Accepted ministry of labour, agriculture and state property in Khatisian's Cabinet. Held the same ministry in the Bureau government of H. Ohandjanian; additional responsibilities for information and propaganda. After the resignation of the Bureau government, and the failure of Kachaznuni to form a coalition, Vratsian accepted post of prime minister, 24 November 1920. Agreed on hand-over of power to Bolsheviks, 2 December; his government also agreed to the signing of the treaty of Alexandropol. In hiding a few weeks after Sovietisation. President of the Committee for the Salvation of the Fatherland after the 18 February 1921 rebellion. Appealed to Europe for assistance against the Bolsheviks; finally to Kemalist Turkey too. To Tabriz in July 1921. On to Tehran, Bombay, Alexandria and Constantinople. In Vienna, Geneva and Paris, 1923–5. Edited *Droshak* (Paris, monthly) 1927–33. Wrote *Hayastani Hanrapetutiun* (Paris, 1928, rev. edn, Beirut, 1958). To South America in 1936; back to Paris, then to North America in 1939. In 1945 he presented a petition to the UN General Assembly at San Francisco demanding the retrocession of provinces held by Turkey to Armenia. In 1951, on the death of Levon Shant, he was appointed principal of the *Djemaran* (the Nshan Palandjian College), Beirut. Expressed a wish to visit Soviet Armenia at the end of his life, but circumstances prevented it. Died in May 1969.

YARDJANIAN, ATOM see SIAMANTO

YEKARIAN, ARMENAK (Van 1869 – Cairo 1926) Influenced in his youth by Khrimian, Portugalian and Avetisian. Failed in an attack on local Kurds after the murder of two Armenian youths; forced to flee to Transcaucasia (1887). Member of the Armenakan party (after 1908 Sahmanadrakan Ramkavar). Returning, he was jailed after a revolutionary scheme he had made was discovered in its early stages. Released through foreign pressure; crossed into Persia. Returned to Van in 1896. Military commander in the successful defence of Van, April–May 1915. Appointed commander of the Armenian forces when the Russians occupied Van in May 1915. To Cilicia on party business in 1920, then to Constantinople. To Alexandria in 1922.

YEPREM KHAN (Y. Davitian) (Yelizavetpol (Gantsak) 1871 – Hamadan 1912) Took part in the Gugunian expedition, September 1890; arrested by Russian authorities, sent to Sakhalin island, Siberia, in 1892. Escaped after three or four years; made his way to the Caucasus, and, since he was a fugitive, on to Persia. Settled in Tabriz. Joined the Dashnak party. Studied military tactics. After the party's decision to participate in the Persian constitutional movement, he became a leader of the constitutional forces; in 1908, after the shah's counter-revolution, his small army of Armenians, Georgians and Persians took the province of Gilan (including Qazvin) for the constitutionalists. Marched on Tehran in 1909 (at the same time as the Bakhtiaris were advancing on it from Isfahan), which he captured in June after bombing the shah's palace. Appointed chief of police, Tehran. When in 1911, the shah, banished to Russia, succeeded in mustering an army and marching on Persia, Yeprem and his army compelled him to flee. Killed by a stray bullet, Hamadan, May 1912. Succeeded by Keri.

YERZINKIAN, ARAMAYIS (Haghpat, Lori, 1878–?1937) Educated at the Nersesian academy, Tiflis, and Geneva university. Joined the Russian Social Democrats in 1901, siding with the Mensheviks after the split; played a part in spreading social democracy among Armenians. Assisted in publication of *Proletariat* (Tiflis). Participated in Armenian National Congress, October 1917. Minister of labour in Transcaucasian Cabinet, 26 April 1918. Political stance moved to the Bolsheviks in 1919–20. Minister of agriculture of the Armenian SSR in Miasnikian's Cabinet, 1921. Held the same post in the Transcaucasian SFSR 1930–1. Subsequently first deputy premier of the

Armenian SSR's council of ministers, and president of the Yerevan city Soviet's executive committee. Played an important role in the rebuilding of Yerevan, building the first hydro-electric power stations, organising Armenian settlement in the Armenian SSR from abroad and setting up new towns. As an Old Bolshevik a prime victim of the Stalin/Beria purges; rehabilitated after Stalin's death.

ZAROBIAN, HAKOB (Yakov) (Artvin 1908–) Family moved to Russia during the first world war. Worked in Kharkov 1925–41, initially as a factory worker. Joined the Communist party in 1932. Party committee secretary of the main Kharkov factory in 1939. Committee secretary in Kharkov itself to October 1941. In Kubyansk, Lazovaya and Stalingrad during the second world war. To Omsk on party work in 1942. To Armenia in 1949 as head of the department of the Central Committee of the Communist party. Secretary of the Yerevan city committee of the Armenian Communist party in July 1950. Deputy minister of security, Armenian SSR, in April 1952. First deputy premier of Armenia, June 1953 – July 1958. First secretary of the Armenian Communist party 1958–66. Partly as a result of the huge demonstrations in Yerevan in April 1965, on the occasion of the 50th anniversary of the Armenian genocide, he was dismissed in February 1966 from his post and returned to factory administration.

ZAVARIAN, SIMON (Igahat, Lori, 1866 – Constantinople 1913) Secondary education in Tiflis; then to Moscow, to the Petrovsk agricultural academy. Joined the *Narodnaya Volya*. Returned to Tiflis in 1889; with Mikayelian and Rostom founded Dashnaktsutiun in summer 1890. (With Mikayelian he represented the socialist wing of the party.) To Trebizond as a headmaster also in 1890; arrested and banished from the Ottoman empire. Briefly in Bessarabia. Returned to Tiflis; assisted in preparation of the party platform, 1892. Remained in Tiflis until 1902; executive officer of the party's eastern Bureau. To Geneva in 1902 as member of the editorial board of *Droshak*. To Cilicia and Lebanon in 1905; founded a union of students in Beirut. Then to Egypt. In Tiflis again 1905–8. To Moush after the Ottoman constitutional revolution, as inspector-general of all Armenian schools. To Constantinople in 1911 to teach in the Yessayan school; also wrote in the party paper, *Azatamart*. Died from a heart attack; his body was returned to Tiflis for burial.

ZAVEN, Patriarch of Constantinople (Mosul 1868 – Baghdad 1947) Baptismal name Mikayel Ter-Yeghiayan. Studied at the Miatsial Engerutiants (United Fellowship) school, Sghert (Siirt), 1881–4, then at the Armenian school, Baghdad. To the theological seminary, Armash. Ordained a celibate priest by Archbishop Ormanian in 1895, taking the name Zaven. Received the title of *vardapet* after writing a thesis on Catholicos John of Otsun. Preacher at

S. Stepanos church, Khaskugh (Hasköy), Constantinople; prelate of the Armenians of Erzerum, 1898–1906; *locum tenens* of the prelacy of the Armenians of Van 1908–9; prelate of the Diyarbekir Armenians 1909–13. Consecrated bishop in 1910. Elected Armenian patriarch of Constantinople, September 1913. Protested in vain to the grand vizier and the Sublime Porte about the arrests of 24 April 1915 and the consequent genocide. The Young Turks exiled him to Baghdad in 1916, and abolished his see. Returned to Constantinople in 1918, but left again before the arrival of the Kemalists. To Bulgaria, Egypt and then Baghdad (in 1924). To Cyprus as an executor of the Melkonian brothers' will, by which AGBU set up the Melkonian Institute. Again in Baghdad, 1927, until his death. His body was transferred to Jerusalem for burial.

ZAVRIEV, Dr HAKOB Born to a rich family. Educated in a Russian environment; did not know Armenian. Graduated from the army medical academy, St Petersburg. Became chief administrator of the Baku working men's hospital. Joined the Dashnak party. Forsook his hospital work and took up arms when he heard of Nikol Duman's planned guerrilla attack on Sasun. (The expedition did not reach Sasun.) Sent as a doctor by the Russian government to establish a hospital at Moush; but the Turks objected, and he was expelled. Returned to Moush after the Ottoman constitution, as chief consultant at the hospital he had founded. The viceroy of the Caucasus consulted him over the formation of the Armenian volunteer units, 1914. Zavriev had discussions with Sazonov after the outbreak of the war, which led to assurances on an autonomous Armenia; departed to Paris to convey their substance to the French government. After the February revolution, his requests led the Provisional government to formulate its plan for Turkish Armenia, May 1917. He was at the same time appointed civilian assistant to the general commissar for Western Armenia. Tried to persuade the Provisional government to strengthen the Ottoman front after the Turks recaptured Moush. Chosen in November 1917 as a Dashnak representative in the Constituent Assembly. To Transcaucasia shortly after the October revolution. Returned to Petrograd in early 1918 to seek an agreement between Dashnaktsutiun and the Soviet government. Jailed after the murder of the 26 commissars, September 1918; released in March 1919. Allowed to leave Moscow in early 1920. Returned to work in a hospital; died in a typhoid epidemic.

ZHIRAIR (Mardiros Boyadjian) (Hadjin 1856 – 1894) Educated at Constantinople; returned to Hadjin to teach. Joined the Hunchak party; embarked on party organisation and revolutionary activity. In Erzindjan and Yozgat 1890–3 as a *fedayi*; hunted by gendarmes and *zaptiyes*. Besieged with his comrades at Chomak Dagh by 1,500 soldiers in March 1894; surrendered when his ammunition was exhausted. Sentenced to death and hanged on 24 March.

ZOHRAB, KRIKOR (Constantinople 1860 – nr Diyarbekir 1915) Educated at the Shahnazarian school and the Galata Saray Lycée. Qualified as a lawyer. (Also held engineering qualifications, but did not practise.) Co-edited *Masis* 1892–3. Fled to Paris in 1895; also in Egypt. Returned to Constantinople after the proclamation of the constitution, 1908. Became a member of the Armenian National Assembly, and deputy for Constantinople in the Ottoman Parliament. Author of a large number of literary works: novels include *A Vanished Generation, Mute Sorrows* and *Life as it is* (the last has been translated into French). Published in Paris, under the pseudonym of Marcel Léart, *La question arménienne à la lumière des documents* (1913). Protested strongly to Talaat (with whom, he had believed, he had cultivated a close friendship) at the arrests of 24 April 1915 and subsequent killings; he himself was arrested on 3 June and murdered *en route* to Diyarbekir.

ZORIAN, STEPAN see ROSTOM

Select Bibliography

The bibliography is extensive. This list does not pretend to be more than an introduction. Readers needing a more thorough survey of the field are advised to glance at the bibliographies in H. F. B. Lynch's work (1901) and in the two volumes by Professor Hovannisian (1967 and 1971), as well as at Dr A. Salmaslian's *Bibliographie de l'Arménie* (Yerevan, 1946, revised 1969).

Abadie, M. *Les quatre sièges d'Aintab* (Paris, 1922)

Abbott, G. F. *Turkey in Transition* (London, 1909)

Aghassi, *Zeitoun, depuis les origines jusqu'à l'insurrection de 1895* (Paris, 1897)

Aharonian, G. *Meds Yerazi Jamboun vra* (Beirut, 1964)

—— (ed.), *Hushamatian Meds Yegherni, 1915–1965* (Beirut, 1965)

Ahmad, Feroz. *The Young Turks* (Oxford, 1969)

Ahmed Emin. *Turkey in the World War* (New Haven, 1930)

Aknuni, E. *Les plaies du Caucase* (Geneva, 1905)

Allen, W. E. D. and Muratoff, Paul. *Caucasian Battlefields* (Cambridge, 1953)

Anderson, M. S. *The Eastern Question 1774–1923* (London, 1966)

Andonian, A. *Documents officiels concernant les massacres arméniens* (Paris, 1920)

Atamian, Sarkis. *The Armenian Community* (New York, 1955)

Baddeley, J. F. *The Russian Conquest of the Caucasus* (London, 1908)

Baghdjian, Kevork (Vaskène Aykouni). 'Le problème arménien' (unpublished doctoral thesis, University of Montpellier, 1969)

Baldwin, Oliver. *Six Prisons and Two Revolutions* (London, 1924)

——, *The Questing Beast* (London, 1932)

Barton, James L. *Story of Near East Relief, 1915–1930* (New York, 1930)

Bechhofer-[Roberts], C. E. *In Denikin's Russia and the Caucasus, 1919–1920* (London, 1921)

Bedirian, Levon, 'The Republic of Armenia' (unpublished MA thesis, American University of Beirut, 1963)

Blaisdell, D. C. *European Financial Control in the Ottoman Empire* (New York, 1929)

Blunt, Wilfrid Scawen. 'Turkish Misgovernment', *Nineteenth Century*, no. 40 (November 1896)

——, *My Diaries* (New York, 1932)

Borian, B. A. *Armeniia, mezhdunarodnaia diplomatiia i SSSR* (2 vols., Moscow and Leningrad, 1928–9)

Brémond, E. *La Cilicie en 1919–1920* (Paris, 1921)

Bryce, James. *Transcaucasia and Ararat.* 4th edn (London, 1896)

Buchan, John (ed.). 'Baltic and Caucasian States', *The Nations of Today* (London, 1923)

Burtt, Joseph. *The People of Ararat* (London, 1926)

Buxton, Harold. *Trans-Caucasia* (London, 1926)

Buxton, Noel and Harold. *Travels and Politics in Armenia* (London, 1914)

Carswell, John. *New Julfa: The Armenian Churches and Other Buildings* (Oxford, 1968)

Carzou, Jean-Marie. *Un génocide exemplaire* (Paris, 1975)

Cebesoy, Ali Fuat. *Moskova hatiralari* (Istanbul, 1955)

Curzon, Robert. *Armenia: a Year at Erzeroom* . . . (London, 1854)

Davison, Roderic H. 'The Armenian Crisis, 1912–1914', *American Historical Review*, vol. LIII, no. 3 (April 1948)

Degras, Jane (ed.). *Soviet Documents on Foreign Policy*, vol. I, *1917–1924* (London, 1951)

Der Khatchadourian, Ardashes. 'The Republic of Armenia and the West during the Years 1918–1921' (unpublished MA thesis, American University of Beirut, 1965)

——, see under Ter-Khachaturian

Dunsterville, L. C. *The Adventures of Dunsterforce* (London, 1920)

Eliot, Sir Charles |Odysseus|. *Turkey-in-Europe* (London, 1900 and reprints)

Emin, see under Ahmed Emin

Encyclopedia of Islam (Leiden, continuing), especially articles (in 1st edn) 'Turan' and (in 2nd edn) 'Anadolu', 'Arminiyya'

Fischer, Louis. *The Soviets in World Affairs, 1917–1929*, 2nd edn (2 vols., Princeton, 1951)

Feis, Herbert. *Europe: the World's Banker* (New Haven, 1930)

Ghassemlou, Abdul Rahman. *Kurdistan and the Kurds* (London and Prague, 1965)

Gidney, James B. *A Mandate for Armenia* (Kent, Ohio, 1967)

Graves, Sir Robert. *Storm Centres of the Near East: Personal Memories 1879–1929* (London, 1933)

Great Britain, Foreign Office. *The Treatment of Armenians in the Ottoman Empire*, Miscellaneous, no. 31 (1916)

——, *British Documents on the Origins of the War, 1898–1914*, ed. G. P. Gooch and Harold Temperley (11 vols., London, 1926–38)

——, *Documents on British Foreign Policy 1919–1939*, first series, ed. W. L. Woodward, Rohan Butler, J. P. T. Bury *et al.* (London, 1947–   )

Great Britain. Parliamentary Papers, 1854–1923

Gregorian, Vartan. 'The Impact of Russia on the Armenians and Armenia' in Wayne S. Vucinich (ed.), *Russia and Asia* (Stanford, 1972)

Grew, Joseph C. *Turbulent Era* (Cambridge, Mass., and London, 1953)

Hartill, L. R. *Men are Like That* (London, 1928)

Hartunian, A. H. *Neither to Laugh nor to Weep* (Boston, 1968)

Harutiunian, S. R. *Hai Zhoghovrdi Patmutiun* (4 vols., Yerevan, 1970)
Haxthausen, A., trans. J. E. Taylor, *Transcaucasia* (London, 1854)
Henry, J. D. *Baku: an Eventful History* (London, 1905)
Herbert, Aubrey. *Ben Kendim* (London, 1924)
Hertslet, Sir Edward. *The Map of Europe by Treaty* (London, vol. II, 1875, and vol. IV, 1891)
Heyd, Uriel. *Foundations of Turkish Nationalism* (London, 1950)
Hostler, C. W. *Turkism and the Soviets* (London, 1957)
Hourani, A. *Minorities in the Arab World* (London, 1947)
——, *Syria and Lebanon* (London, 1946)
Housepian, Marjorie. *Smyrna 1922: The Destruction of a City* (London, 1972)
Hovannisian, Richard G. *Armenia on the Road to Independence, 1918* (Berkeley and Los Angeles, 1967)
——, *The Republic of Armenia*, vol. I, *The First Year, 1918–1919* (Berkeley and Los Angeles, 1971)
——, 'Russian Armenia: a Century of Tsarist Rule', *Jahrbücher für Geschichte Osteuropas* (Wiesbaden, March 1971)
——, 'The Armenian Question in the Ottoman Empire', *Armenian Studies* (Beirut, 1973)
Hozier, Capt. H. M. *The Russo-Turkish War* (5 vols., London, ?1878)
Hurewitz, J. C. *Diplomacy in the Near and Middle East* (2 vols., Princeton, 1956)
Jonquière, A. de la. *Histoire de l'empire ottoman* (Paris, 1881)
Kachaznuni, H. *H. H. Dashnaktstiunë anelik chuni ailevs* (Vienna, 1923); Eng. trans. by M. A. Callender, *The Armenian Revolutionary Federation (Dashnagtzoutiun) Has Nothing to do Any More* (New York, 1955)
Karabekir, Kâzim. *Istiklâl Harbimiz* (Istanbul, 1st edn, prosecuted, 1960, 2nd edn, 1969)
Kayaloff, Jacques. *The Battle of Sardarabad* (The Hague and Paris, 1973)
——, *The Fall of Baku* (Bergenfield, N.J., 1976)
Kazemzadeh, Firuz. *The Struggle for Transcaucasia, 1917–1921* (New York and Oxford, 1951)
Kedourie, Elie. *The Chatham House Version and Other Essays* (London, 1970)
Kemal, Mustafa (Atatürk). *A Speech . . .* (Leipzig, 1927, Istanbul, 1963)
Kerr, Stanley E. *The Lions of Marash* (Albany, N.Y., 1973)
Khatisian, Alexander. *Hayastani Hanrapetutian dsagumn ou zargatsumë* (1st edn, Athens 1930, 2nd edn, Beirut, 1968)
Kinneir, J. M. *A Geographical Memoir of the Persian Empire* (London, 1813)
Kinross, Lord (J. P. D. Balfour). *Atatürk: the Rebirth of a Nation* (London, 1964)
——, *The Ottoman Centuries* (London, 1977)
Korganoff, Général G. *La participation des arméniens à la guerre mondiale sur le front du Caucase, 1914–1918* (Paris, 1927)

Krikorian, Mesrob K. *Armenians in the Service of the Ottoman Empire, 1860-1908* (London, 1978)

Lang, David Marshall. *A Modern History of Georgia* (London, 1962)

——, *Armenia: Cradle of Civilization* (London, 1970)

Larcher, M. *La guerre turque dans la guerre mondiale* (Paris, 1926)

Lehmann-Haupt, C. F. *Armenien Einst und Jetzt* (3 vols., Berlin and Leipzig, 1910-31)

Leo [Babakhanian, Arakel]. *Haiots patmutiun* (vol. I, Tiflis, 1917, vols. II and III, Yerevan, 1946 and 1947)

Lepsius, Johannes. *Bericht über die Lage des armenischen Volkes in der Türkei* (Potsdam, 1916) (French trans.: *Le rapport secret sur les massacres d'Armènie* (Paris, 1918))

—— (ed.), *Deutschland und Armenien, 1914-1918: Sammlung diplomatischer Aktenstücke* (Potsdam, 1919)

——, *Der Todesgang des Armenischen Volkes*, 4th edn (Potsdam, 1930)

Lewis, Bernard. *The Emergence of Modern Turkey*, 2nd edn (London, 1968)

Luke, Sir Harry. *Cities and Men: an Autobiography*, vol. II (London, 1953)

Lynch, H. F. B. *Armenia: Travels and Studies* (2 vols. London, 1901, reprinted Beirut, 1965)

McCoan, J. C. *Our New Protectorate: Turkey-in-Asia* (London, 1879)

MacDonell, Ranald. '. . . *And Nothing Long*' (London, 1938)

Mandelstam, Andre. *Le sort de l'empire ottoman* (Paris, 1917)

——, *La Société des Nations et les puissances devant le problème arménien* (Paris, 1926)

Marx, Karl. *The Eastern Question* (London, 1897)

Matossian, Mary Kilbourne. *The Impact of Soviet Policies in Armenia* (Leiden, 1962)

Mears, Eliot Grinnell. *Modern Turkey: a Politico-Economic Interpretation 1908-1923* (New York, 1924)

Mécérian, Jean. *Le génocide du peuple arménien* (Beirut, 1965)

Messerlian, Zaven M. 'Armenian Representation in the Lebanese Parliament' (unpublished MA thesis, American University of Beirut, 1963)

——, 'The Question of Kars and Ardahan', *Armenian Studies* (1973)

Miller, David Hunter. *My Diary at the Conference of Paris* (22 vols., New York, 1924-6)

Minorsky, V. 'Turan', *Encyclopedia of Islam*, 1st edn (Leiden, 1934)

Monteith, W. *Kars and Erzeroum: With the Campaigns of Prince Paskievitch in 1828-1829* . . . (London, 1856)

Morgenthau, Henry. *Secrets of the Bosphorus: Constantinople 1913-1916* (London, 1919)

Nalbandian, Louise. *The Armenian Revolutionary Movement: the Development of Armenian Political Parties through the Nineteenth Century* (Berkeley and Los Angeles, 1963)

Navasardian, Vahan. *Bolshevizmë yev Dashnaktsutiunë* (Cairo, 1949)

Nersisian, M. G. (ed.). *Genotsid armian v Osmanskoi imperii* (Yerevan, 1965)

Nogales, Rafael de. *Four Years Beneath the Crescent*, trans. Muna Lee (London, 1926)

Norman, C. B. *Armenia and the Campaign of 1877–1878* (London, 1878)

Ormanian, Małakia, *Azgapatum* (3 vols., Constantinople and Jerusalem, 1913–27)

——, *The Church of Armenia*, trans. G. Marcar Gregory (London, 1955)

Paillarès, Michel, *Le Kèmalisme devant les alliès* (Paris, 1922)

Papazian, E. *Inknakensagrutiun yev husher* (Cairo, 1960)

Papazian, K. S. *Patriotism Perverted* (Boston, 1934)

Parsamian, V. A. *Hai Zhoghovrdi Patmutiun* (3 vols., Yerevan, 1967)

Pastermadjian, H. *Histoire de l'Arménie* (Paris, 1st edn, 1949, 2nd edn, 1964)

Pears, Sir Edwin. *Turkey and its People* (London, 1911)

——, *Forty Years in Constantinople* (London, 1916)

——, *Life of Abdul Hamid* (London, 1917)

Pipes, Richard. *The Formation of the Soviet Union* (Cambridge, Mass., 1st edn, 1954, revised edn, 1964)

Poidebard, A. 'Rôle militaire des Arméniens sur le front due Caucase après la défection de l'armée russe (décembre 1917–novembre 1918)', *Revue des études arméniennes*, vol. I, no. 2 (1920)

——, 'Le Transcaucases et la République d'Arménie dans les textes diplomatiques du Traité de Brest-Litovsk au Traité de Kars, 1918–1921', *Revue des études arméniennes*, vol. III (1923) and vol. IV, no. 1 (1924)

Pomiankowski, Joseph. *Der Zusammenbruch des Ottomanischen Reiches* (Leipzig, 1928)

Price, M. Philips. *War & Revolution in Asiↄ Russia* (London, 1917)

Rawlinson, A. *Adventures in the Near East, 1918–1922* (London, 1st edn, 1923, revised edn, 1924)

Rustow, Dankwart A. 'The Army and the Founding of the Turkish Republic', *World Politics*, vol. XI (July 1959)

Sachar, Howard M. *The Emergence of the Middle East: 1914–1924* (London, 1969)

Sanders, Liman von. *Five Years in Turkey* (Annapolis, 1927)

Sandwith, Humphry. *A Narrative of the Siege of Kars…* (London, 1856)

Sanjian, Avedis K. *The Armenian Communities in Syria under Ottoman Dominion* (Cambridge, Mass., 1965)

Sarkisian, E. K. and Sahaќian, R. G. *Vital Issues in Modern Armenian History* (Watertown, Mass., 1965)

Sarkissian, A. O. *History of the Armenian Question to 1885* (Urbana, Ill., 1938)

Schuyler, Eugene. *Peter the Great* (2 vols., London, 1884)

Senior, Nassau. *A Journal Kept in Turkey and Greece…* (London, 1859)

Seton-Watson, R. W. *Disraeli, Gladstone and the Eastern Question* (London, 1935)

Shahan. *Tiurkism Angoraen Baku yev trkakan orientatsion* (Athens, 1928)
——, *Aleksandrapoli Dashnakren 1930-i Korkasean apstambutiunnerin* (2 vols., Marseille, 1934)
Shiragian, Arshavir. *The Legacy: Memoirs of an Armenian Patriot* (Boston, 1976)
Shub, David. 'Kamo: the Legendary Old Bolshevik of the Caucasus', *The Russian Review*, vol. XIX, no. 3 (July 1960)
Spry, William J. J. *Life on the Bosphorus* (London, 1895)
Suny, Ronald Grigor. *The Baku Commune, 1917–1918* (Princeton, 1972)
Surmelian, Leon Z. *I Ask You, Ladies and Gentlemen* (London, 1946)
Sykes, Sir Percy. *History of Persia* (2 vols., London, 1915)
Ter-Khachaturian, Artashes. 'Hntkahayots Npastë Hai Mshakoytin', *Spiurk* (Beirut), 31 December 1961
Ternon, Yves. *Les Arméniens: histoire d'un génocide* (Paris, 1977)
Toriguian, Shavarsh. *The Armenian Question and International Law* (Beirut, 1973)
Toumanoff, Cyril. 'Armenia and Georgia', *Cambridge Medieval History*, vol. IV, part 1 (1966)
——, *Studies in Christian Caucasian History* (Washington, D.C., 1965)
[Toynbee, A. J.], 'The Extermination of the Armenians', Chapter CXXXIII of *The Times History of the War*, vol. VIII (London, 1916)
[——] (ed.), *The Treatment of Armenians in the Ottoman Empire* (London, 1916) (= Miscellaneous, no. 31 (1916)); reprinted with decoding appendix (Beirut, 1972)
——, *Turkey: a Past and a Future* (London, 1917)
Ubicini, A. *Lettres sur la Turquie* (Paris, 1854; Eng. trans. (by Lady Easthope) London, 1856)
Ussher, Clarence D. *An American Physician in Turkey* (Boston, 1917)
Vambéry, Arminius. *Life and Adventures* (London, 1884)
——, *The Story of my Struggles* (London, 1904)
Varandian, Mikayel. *H. H. Dashnaktsutian patmutiun* (2 vols., Paris and Cairo, 1932–50)
Véou, Paul du. *La passion de la Cilicie* (Paris, 1937)
Villari, Luigi. *Fire and Sword in the Caucasus* (London, 1906)
Vratsian, Simon. *Hayastani Hanrapetutiun* (1st edn Paris, 1928, 2nd edn Beirut, 1958)
——, 'How Armenia was Sovietized', 5 articles, *Armenian Review* (1948–9)
Voskerichian, M. *Zeitun Alpom* (Beirut, 1960)
Washburn, George. *Fifty Years in Constantinople and Recollections of Robert College* (Boston, 1911)
Wolf, Lucien. *The Russian Conspiracy* (London, 1877)
Woods, H. Charles. *The Danger Zone of Europe* (London, 1911)
Yalman, see under Ahmed Emin
Young, George. *Constantinople* (London, 1926)

Zarevand. *United and Independent Turania*, trans. V. N. Dadrian (Leiden, 1966)

Zenkovsky, Serge A. *Pan-Turkism and Islam in Russia* (Cambridge, Mass., 1960)

Index

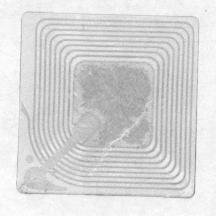